Studies in Judaism

JEWISH EDUCATION WORLDWIDE

Cross–Cultural Perspectives

Edited by

Harold S. Himmelfarb

and

Sergio DellaPergola

WITHDRAWN

UNIVERSITY
PRESS OF
AMERICA

Lanham • New York • London

Copyright © 1989 by

The Institute of Contemporary Jewry

University Press of America,® Inc.

4720 Boston Way
Lanham, MD 20706

3 Henrietta Street
London WC2E 8LU England

Printed in the United States of America

British Cataloging in Publication Information Available

Library of Congress Cataloging-in-Publication Data

Jewish education worldwide : cross–cultural perspectives / edited by
Harold S. Himmelfarb, Sergio DellaPergola.
p.   cm.
Includes bibliographies and index.
1. Jewish religious education—History—20th century.   2. Jewish religious
education—Cross–cultural studies.   I. Himmelfarb, Harold S.
II. Della Pergola, Sergio, 1942–   .
BM103.J394   1989   296.6'8'09048—dc20   89–33646 CIP

ISBN 0–8191–7483–1 (alk. paper)

All University Press of America books are produced on acid-free paper.
The paper used in this publication meets the minimum requirements of American
National Standard for Information Sciences—Permanence of Paper for Printed Library
Materials, ANSI Z39.48–1984.   ∞

The Hebrew University of Jerusalem
The Institute of Contemporary Jewry
Division of Jewish Demography and Statistics
Project for Jewish Educational Statistics

Director of Division: Sergio DellaPergola
Past Director: Uziel O. Schmelz
Founding Director: Roberto Bachi

Mount Scopus, Jerusalem 91905, Israel.
Telephone: (972) 02–882470

The publication of this volume was funded by

The Joint Program for Jewish Education of
the State of Israel – Ministry of Education and Culture,
The Jewish Agency for Israel
and the World Zionist Organization

Table of Contents

Introduction

Contemporary Jewish education has become an area of international concern and cooperation. This volume is intended to provide a needed cross-cultural perspective on Jewish education in order to advance this cooperative effort through serious and systematic analysis.

For the first half of the twentieth century the vast majority of world Jewry – mostly European in residence or origin – were beset by severe problems of social and economic adaptation and survival. Migration to new lands, occupational retraining, defense against antisemitism, and the establishment of new Jewish organizations and institutions – were all tasks undertaken while the world was suffering two wars and a great economic depression. At the peak of upheaval, the Jewish people suffered the greatest loss of its long anguished history – the *Shoah* which destroyed over a third of world Jewry and over 80% of East European Jewry. Soon after, the world witnessed the reestablishment of political nationhood in the land of Israel – a dream for over two thousand years brought to reality. Human survival, economic reconstruction and social integration became absorbing goals for individual Jews and their communal bodies.

As we approach the last decade of the 20th century, we find a Jewish people that in most parts of the world is no longer on the move, and that has reached high levels of educational, occupational, and economic attainment. Its sophisticated communal agencies are well organized and coordinated, and professionally managed. Yet, amidst socioeconomic achievement and communal stabilization, it seems that there is a high level of individual assimilation and a loss of Jewish identification. Intermarriage has increased and religious practice has declined. Participation in Jewish voluntary organizations has also declined among the younger generations. Many believe that there is a growing worldwide crisis of Jewish identity.

In such an environment, then, it is not surprising that Jewish education, long the step-child in the budgeting priorities of Jewish communities, has become the object of renewed interest and increased support. It is recognized that Jewish schools, despite their many problems, are major transmitters of identity. Indeed, the resolution of the 'identity crisis' may well depend on the improvement of Jewish education.

Moreover, creation and development of the State of Israel has internationalized Jewish education in a manner that was not possible previously. The World Zionist Organization, through its education departments, has become a central clearinghouse for the curricular, personnel, and even financial problems of Jewish education in many countries. Nearly 40 million dollars are spent annually by the World Zionist Organization and the Jewish Agency for Israel on Jewish education in the Diaspora. Far greater amounts are spent globally in Jewish education by other international, national and local Jewish organizations. In this age of research and evaluation, such large expenditures need to be informed by current and accurate scientific data.

A comprehensive understanding of Jewish education today necessitates collection of quantitative data on Diaspora Jewish populations and on their Jewish educational systems. The founding of the Division of Jewish Demography and Statistics at The Hebrew University of Jerusalem's Institute of Contemporary Jewry was an attempt to satisfy the need for general Jewish population research, but until recently a comparable center for data on Jewish educational systems was lacking.

In the late 1970s, careful examination showed that the existing statistical information on Jewish education in the Diaspora was partial in scope and character, scattered, and not always accurate. Moreover, the diversity of Jewish educational systems, both within and between countries, made comparisons difficult, and the development of an overall portrait of the status of Jewish education very problematic. Therefore, the Project for Jewish Educational Statistics was established in 1980 to fill the need for uniform worldwide information on Jewish education. The aim of the Project was to establish a data bank and to serve as a center of statistical research for national and international Jewish educational bodies, the academic community, the broad community of Jewish educators, and all other interested persons.

The Project operates under the sponsorship of the Joint Program for Jewish Education, a cooperative venture of the Ministry of Education and Culture of the State of Israel, the Jewish Agency for Israel and the World Zionist Organization. It is conducted by the Division of Jewish Demography and Statistics of the Institute of Contemporary Jewry at The Hebrew University of Jerusalem, in cooperation with the University's Melton Center for Jewish Education in the Diaspora at the School of Education, and in conjunction with major Jewish educational institutions worldwide.

Since its inception in 1980, the Project for Jewish Educational Statistics has attempted to fulfill its mandate.

1. Existing statistical data were collected and analyzed for broad trends in enrollment, by type and level of school (Himmelfarb and DellaPergola, 1982).

2. Jewish population surveys from four different countries (the United States, France, Italy and South Africa) were analyzed for current enrollment trends, amount of Jewish schooling attained by adults, and the factors influencing differences between countries (DellaPergola and Genuth, 1983).

3. For the first time, during school years 1981/82 and 1982/83 Jewish edu-

cational statistics were collected worldwide, through a synchronized effort and with a uniform questionnaire. Data were collected from over 3,500 Jewish schools in 40 countries, including information about student enrollment, teachers, school characteristics, hours of Jewish and secular studies and ideological orientation. The main results of this Jewish school international census were published for each of the main countries and regions in the Diaspora (Genuth, DellaPergola and Dubb, 1985), and in greater detail for the United States (Dubb and DellaPergola, 1986) and Canada (Dubb, 1987).

4. A more in-depth survey of teachers in Jewish schools was carried out as part of a series of special surveys on particular educational issues. Data were gathered in 1983/84 in six of the largest Western Diaspora communities: the United States, France, the United Kingdom, Canada, Argentina and South Africa. Several thousand teachers, of both Jewish and secular studies, were surveyed about their general and Jewish education, professional training and experience, teaching activities and work conditions. Special attention was given to the teachers of Jewish studies.

5. During the school year 1986/87 – five years after the first census – the Project launched a second census of Jewish schools in the Diaspora. Data collection is expected to be completed by the end of 1988. Then, it will be possible for the first time to provide a systematic assessment of trends in the size and structure of Jewish education in the Diaspora.

Although the Project was designed to provide quantitative information about Jewish education, all statistics must of course be interpreted with a knowledge of the historical background and social context from which they were drawn. For some countries such analyses already existed, but for others there was hardly any information. The comprehensiveness of existing materials varied widely from place to place, and the comparability of information between countries was sketchy at best. Therefore, it was decided to commission articles about Jewish education in the major countries and the regions of Jewish residence around the world, resulting in this publication.

About this Volume

This volume consists of nine parts including 26 articles and comments about Jewish education in North and Latin America, South Africa and Australia, Western and Eastern Europe, the Muslim countries and Israel. Some of the chapters are devoted to the international scope of Jewish educational activities.

In order to get essays that would be both fairly comprehensive and comparable from place to place, a standard outline was composed (see Appendix) and all of the authors of the major single country or regional chapters were asked to address themselves to the topics mentioned in the outline. Of course, East European and Muslim countries, on the one hand, and Israel, on the other hand, present different phenomena for which the outline was not quite appropriate.

We did not want just descriptive essays, but also critical analyses that would cover the existing material for future researchers, and would offer policy recommendations for community leaders, planners and educators. Therefore, wherever possible we commissioned academic experts on the subject with no institutional ties that might strongly affect their objectivity or critical tendencies. Where it was not possible to get academic specialists on Jewish education, we invited contributions by educators who were knowledgeable about a particular educational system. In some cases, like the United States and Latin American countries, we thought that comments were needed by persons representing different institutional and ideological perspectives. Therefore, we invited several experienced practitioners to add their comments to the chapters on the respective countries that had been prepared by academic researchers.

Overall, we feel that even when a particular chapter does not cover one or more of the topics that had been proposed in our original outline, the main issues of Jewish education in each country or region have been identified by the different authors – each with his own peculiar disciplinary focus and topical emphasis. Moreover, some sense of the context and problems of Jewish education in a given country can be obtained by jointly reading all the chapters which refer to the same geographical region. Indeed, within regions one often finds similar historical and social factors affecting the Jewish educational systems of different countries.

Most of the articles in this book were commissioned in mid-1981; however, some of them were not finished until late 1986. Consequently there is a significant gap between the recency of data presented in the articles that were finished earlier and those completed later. Nevertheless, we are quite certain that in most cases the general outline and basic trends of the systems have not changed much, and we are grateful to those who completed their work promptly. Clearly, the volume's major contribution is not intended to be in the recency of the data presented, which, as already mentioned, are covered by other publications of the Project for Jewish Educational Statistics. Rather, the intention here is to provide the reader with a comprehensive picture of Jewish education in the recent past and at present through analysis of the comparative social contexts in which such education occurs.

The book opens with two essays that are general in perspective rather than specific to a particular country. The first chapter by Harold Himmelfarb was written after most of the others in this volume were completed. It attempts to formulate some general ideas and propositions about Jewish educational systems and their development. No attempt is made to summarize the book, but rather to highlight the similarities and differences of the Jewish educational systems in the various countries discussed. In the second chapter, Sergio DellaPergola and Uziel Schmelz discuss the effects of various demographic trends on Jewish education around the world. In particular, they discuss how fluctuations in the birth rate have effected the size of the school-age population and the enrollment in Jewish schools.

The remainder of the book, except for the last part, is organized by geographic region. Three major parts of the book deal, respectively, with North America (the United States and Canada), Latin America, and Western Europe. South Africa and Australia were placed together because they resemble each other in many respects due to both having been part of the British Commonwealth, and both having school systems which are structurally quite similar to Great Britain's. In fact, readers interested in the comparative aspect of this volume might want to read about Great Britain, South Africa and Australia together. The Muslim countries, the East European countries and Israel were placed at the end of the volume because each has Jewish community contexts and educational structures distinctively different from the other countries of the world.

The last part of the book includes two essays of international scope. Ernest Stock's chapter reviews the major international organizations that are active in Jewish education, and advances some suggestions for improving their work. Finally, an overview is presented of the types of quantitative data necessary to keep abreast of the status of Jewish education around the world.

Appended to this volume are two reference documents: the working outline of the chapters that the authors were asked to use as a guide, and a subject index. We hope these will help the reader to better understand the book and aid in the comparative analyses that we hope will be engendered by it.

Perspective

This volume has a decidedly social science perspective. Although the outline also included other areas, most authors concentrated on the historical and societal issues of schooling in the educational systems that they analyzed. For example, while one will find substantial information in the essays about the general educational systems in particular countries and the place of Jewish schools within them, very few specifics will be found concerning curricular issues. Since there inevitably had to be a disciplinary focus or bias to this volume this is what we preferred.

The comparative study of Jewish education was heretofore almost nonexistent. We believe that concentration on the social context of schooling (broadly defined) is the focus necessary for cross-cultural understanding. Particular reforms and innovations in curriculum, teaching methods, or other aspects of schooling need to stem from a thorough understanding of the social context in which these reforms are to be implemented. Hopefully this volume will significantly advance our understanding in that regard.

We view this volume as an initial step in the development of a research-based cross-cultural analysis of Jewish education today. The essays reflect the great differences between countries in the research available on Jewish education. Clearly, the quality and quantity of our current knowledge is uneven, and certain topical or regional aspects have not received any attention. We hope that these essays will stimulate scholars to further research on Jewish education and will help them focus on those areas most in need of investigation. Similarly, we hope that the analyses provided here will stimulate discussion of Jewish educational issues and their policy implications among Jewish educators, researchers, professionals, and community leaders.

Acknowledgements

A large and complex undertaking such as this collection of essays involves the support of many people and institutions to whom we are most grateful. In particular, the volume was made possible through the financial support of the Joint Program for Jewish Education. Haim Zohar, past Secretary General of the World Zionist Organization Executive, and Director General of the Pincus Fund for Jewish Education, and Daniel Tropper, formerly special assistant to Israel's Minister of Education and Culture, and currently Director of Gesher, co-chaired the Joint Program at the inception of this undertaking and took personal interest in its development and success. Zvi Inbar, currently Director of the Joint Program has continued that support through completion of this volume.

Among those at the Hebrew University who have followed and promoted our effort, a grateful acknowledgement is extended to Seymour Fox, of the School of Education; Roberto Bachi, Professor Emeritus of Demography and Statistics; Haim Avni and Mordechai Altshuler, both former Chairmen of the Institute of Contemporary Jewry, and the current Chairman, Yisrael Gutman; Michael Rosenak, and Barry Chazan, both former Directors of the Samuel Mendel Melton Center for Jewish Education in the Diaspora, and its current Director, Allan Hoffman; Uziel O. Schmelz, former Head of the Division of Jewish Demography and Statistics at the Institute of Contemporary Jewry, and Allie A. Dubb, former Director of the Project for Jewish Educational Statistics.

Several staff members of the Project for Jewish Educational Statistics at the Institute of Contemporary Jewery of the Hebrew University of Jerusalem were involved in editorial and technical tasks related to the preparation of this volume. We wish especially to thank Geulah Solomon for editing significant portions of the book, and Rina Klein, Judith Shaviv and Judy Maltz for editorial assistance. The final, thorough round of editing, including compilation of the index and seeing the volume through preparation of the final copy, was undertaken by Judith Even and Moshe Goodman.[1] Arin Poller patiently typed several drafts of the whole manuscript. To them we extend our sincere gratitude and appreciation.

Since we hope that this book will help improve the state of Jewish education worldwide, we dedicate it to our children who are among the two and a half million Jewish children in the Diaspora and in Israel who are the potential beneficiaries of this effort.

HSH   *SDP*

Jerusalem, 1988

Note

1. All Hebrew words whose transliteration appears in Webster's *Ninth Collegiate Dictionary* have been spelled accordingly and have not been italicized. The *Encyclopaedia Judaica* and/or common usage have been our guides to the spelling of all other Hebrew words, which do appear in italics.

References

Himmelfarb, H.S. and DellaPergola, S. (1982). *Enrollment in Jewish Schools in the Diaspora, Late 1970s*, Institute of Contemporary Jewry, The Hebrew University, Jerusalem (Project for Jewish Educational Statistics, Report No. 1). 97 pp.

DellaPergola, S. and Genuth, N. (1983). *Jewish Education Attained in Diaspora Communities, Data for 1970s*, Institute of Contemporary Jewry, The Hebrew University, Jerusalem (Project for Jewish Educational Statistics, Report No. 2). 74 pp.

Genuth, N., DellaPergola, S. and Dubb, A.A. (1985). *First Census of Jewish Schools, 1981/82–1982/83; International Summary*, Institute of Contemporary Jewry, The Hebrew University, Jerusalem (Project for Jewish Educational Statistics, Report No. 3). 138 pp.

Dubb, A.A. and DellaPergola, S. (1986). *First Census of Jewish Schools, 1981/82–1982/83; United States of America*, Institute of Contemporary Jewry, The Hebrew University, Jerusalem (Project for Jewish Educational Statistics, Report No. 4). 102 pp.

Dubb, A.A. (1987). *First Census of Jewish Schools, 1981/82–1982/83; Canada*, Institute of Contemporary Jewry, The Hebrew University, Jerusalem (Project for Jewish Educational Statistics, Report No. 5). 70 pp.

Part One

Global Perspectives

The two chapters in the first part of this book analyze Jewish education from a global and cross-cultural perspective. They attempt to identify general societal factors which affect Jewish education in contemporary times.

In the first chapter, Harold Himmelfarb, Professor of Sociology at Ohio State University, Columbus, Ohio, presents an overview of major themes and trends which emerge from the other chapters in this volume. He deals with historical developments, trends within the social and Jewish communal contexts in which Jewish educational systems operate, patterns of structural arrangements for Jewish education, and major Jewish educational issues worldwide. This is not a summary of the book, but rather an attempt to integrate, synthesize and highlight trends that are of relevance for the understanding of Jewish education generally, beyond the idiosyncrasies of local systems. Therefore, the emphasis is on common features and universal problems and issues across systems. This cross-cultural analysis is a useful beginning toward the development of a comparative sociology of Jewish education.

In chapter 2, Sergio DellaPergola and Uziel Schmelz, respectively Director and Past Director of the Division of Jewish Demography and Statistics at the Institute of Contemporary Jewry, The Hebrew University of Jerusalem, analyze how demographic factors such as fertility and migration patterns have affected Jewish school enrollment differently around the world. Demographic trends have been important in shaping the size and structure of the Jewish school-age population in the Diaspora. The new estimates of the number of Jewish children presented here have been used to calculate recent enrollment rates and to project future enrollment trends. The authors stress the distinction between the proportion of Jewish children who are currently enrolled in a Jewish school, and the proportion who will ever receive a Jewish education. They have utilized selected findings from the 1981/82–1982/83 First Census of Jewish Schools in the Diaspora.

1

A Cross-Cultural View of Jewish Education

Harold S. Himmelfarb

All societies must transfer their cultural heritage – norms, values and skills – to the next generation. In small, preindustrial communities, or folk societies, this is often accomplished by allowing the young to observe, imitate and assist adults in their activities. In this manner children learn language, values, world views and cultural skills. Under these circumstances all adults are teachers, and special settings and times for learning are not necessary. What children are expected to learn is considered 'relevant' for themselves and their society because it is tied directly to daily life. Under such circumstances, the problem of 'learner motivation' is not severe. With modernization, culture has become more complex and diverse. Social change has become rapid and the transmission of culture has become more problematic. Therefore, modern societies have relegated considerable responsibility for cultural transmission to specialists – teachers, and to specialized institutions – schools (Parelius and Parelius, 1978).

The transmission of culture, teaching the young what we already know, and teaching them to love and revere the established and traditional institutions of society, can be called cultural reproduction. It is the critical obligation of the older generation and the central task of all educational agencies.

However, educational agencies in modern societies are often required to play a role in changing culture. This role can be called cultural production. Higher education, for example, fulfills this role through research. But even primary and secondary schools are expected to diffuse new information, attitudes, values, and ways of viewing the world. Education has been used to teach new values and new habits, particularly during periods of rapid change. Thus, in periods of industrialization and modernization, the schools have been used to foster new ideas and norms which facilitate economic stability. In periods of new political arrangements, such as post-revolution or post-independence, schools have been used to spread the new ideologies and norms which legitimate and stabilize the new political system (Parelius and Parelius, 1978).

The transmission of culture is more easily accomplished by schools than is social change, because it is reinforced by other socializing agents in society. In this sense, the school becomes the institution delegated by the family and community to transmit the cultural heritage that they themselves would transmit in a less complex environment. Thus, what is taught in school is meaningful to the child because it is meaningful to his family, friends and neighbors, and is familiar to the child's experiences. Cultural reproduction becomes more problematic for those who come from cultural sub-groups (e.g., ethnic, social and socioeconomic groups) whose experiences differ substantially from the dominant culture transmitted in school. The problem becomes even greater when students from these sub-groups see very few adult role models in their communities who have become more advantaged in social or economic ways by learning what is taught in school.

Schools attempting to produce culture, and thereby change society, have a much more difficult task than those trying to transmit a cultural heritage to sub-groups who are foreign to it. In the latter, the dominant societal culture reinforces what is being taught in school. In the former, it is the dominant culture that has to be changed. It is no wonder that schools do a better job at cultural reproduction than at cultural production, and have generally been conservative forces in society rather than agents of change. If, however, the diffusion of new cultural elements receives support from community leaders, and the elements are popularly acceptable, schools can be effective in promoting change.

Central to the problems of Jewish education in the contemporary world is the recognition and articulation of its cultural reproductive and productive tasks. It would seem that the teaching of a two thousand year old tradition would be primarily a task of cultural reproduction. However, the circumstances of modernity have caused such sweeping changes in Jewish communities throughout the world that Jews have become detached from their traditional cultural heritage. Thus, the successful inculcation of Jewish tradition in most Jewish children in most Jewish communities, including Israel, is more a task of cultural production than reproduction. Jewish education is faced with the problem of instilling cultural values and norms that are on the one hand ancient in origin, and on the other hand sufficiently different from the cultural experiences of most Jews to be considered new and to require substantial social change. Educators must be able to distinguish between those aspects of the Jewish culture which are widely practiced and accepted as legitimate traditions to be transferred to the next generation and those which require a change in normative values and behavior. Each requires different educational strategies. The success of the school in both cultural production and cultural reproduction is dependent on support and reinforcement from family and community.

Historical Perspectives

Four major trends and events have affected the Jewish people within the last two centuries. All of them, of course, significantly influenced the goals, structure and content of Jewish education, as well as the social composition of Jewish schools.

The Enlightenment and Emancipation

Much has been written about the impact of the Enlightenment and Emancipation periods in Europe and its consequences for Jews and Judaism. There are no exact dates for these periods because they developed over a period of time and at various speeds in different countries. Nevertheless, it is clear that these movements reached their apex during the 19th century.

The *Haskalah* (Enlightenment) was a cultural movement that encouraged Jews to adopt national and scientific modes of thinking and the cultural perspectives, wisdom, and behavior of the modern Western world. Emancipation gave Jews the legal and political status to fulfill the cultural imperatives of Enlightenment. As legal barriers to property ownership, residence, occupational attainment, and education facilities were removed and full or nearly-full rights of citizenship were extended to them, Jews seized every opportunity to advance into the larger societal environment and to break away from the isolation and restrictiveness of traditional Jewish communities. The development of nation-states during this period, which demanded their own allegiance, helped to further undermine the legal authority, autonomy, and legitimacy of the Jewish community and its rabbis, courts, and communal leaders (Katz, 1971). "The state, after all, now regarded the emancipated Jew as an individual, not as a member of a particular national community;...it allowed Jewish affiliation to become optional, while demanding that Jewish identity be religious or at most cultural in content rather than political" (Elazar and Cohen, 1985, p. 212).

Since Emancipation required Jews to relinquish their communal identity and since it was accompanied "by a cultural and economic mobility hitherto unprecedented in either its scope or pace...a thorough re-examination of the nature of the Jewishness of Jews" (Elazar and Cohen, 1985, p. 211) was required. The great dilemma of modern Jewish identity developed: how does one fully integrate into modern society, politically, economically and socially, while at the same time maintaining a distinctive religious or ethnic identity?

This is certainly a dilemma for Diaspora Jews who live as minorities in predominantly Gentile societies, but it is also a dilemma for Jews living in Israel who have adopted to some extent the secular, cosmopolitan, and universalistic values of modern societies.

In one sense, this dilemma can be viewed as a zero-sum game. The more one integrates into modern society, the less distinctively Jewish one becomes (Liebman, 1973). In actuality, it is not played as a zero-sum game, because there are many dimensions to Jewish identity, and changes in one do not necessarily cause changes in the other, although they often do. In terms of one's total Jewishness (if there is such a thing), it can be argued that assimilation in any one sphere reduces Jewish identity. There are about six responses to this dilemma.

Complete Assimilation

A person can resolve such a dilemma by making a clear choice. At one extreme he can choose to completely assimilate into the majority society and withdraw from any activities or involvements that would perpetuate Jewish identity. Many Jews have attempted this alternative, often to find that the host society is not as receptive to Jews in actuality as in theory. Thus, this potential resolution of the dilemma is often not available, as in Nazi Germany or today in the Soviet Union.

Complete Segregation

The alternative at the other end of the integration-identity continuum is complete segregation. This, of course, is not really possible, except for a few individuals who spend almost all of their time in so-called ultra-Orthodox yeshivoth (Talmudic seminaries) of a very select type, cut off from mass media communications and isolated from social contact with non-Jews who are not part of the yeshiva community. Almost anyone else, regardless of piety, must interact somewhat with the modern world for legal and economic reasons. Yet, there are groups of Hasidim who have developed their own residential communities, with their own religious, educational, and even economic infrastructures, who achieve a relatively high degree of segregation.

Zionism can be viewed as an isolationist response to assimilation into the non-Jewish world. The tension between assimilation and Jewish identity is substantially lessened in a society where Jews are the majority because political, economic, and social integration into the modern world does not require the abandonment of Jewish distinctiveness. On the other hand, integration might require the abandonment, or at least the temporary neglect, of certain ritual observances which could hinder the social interaction necessary for advancement in political or economic spheres. In this sense, even aliyah does not completely solve the assimilation-identity dilemma.

Denial

A third response to the dilemma is to deny that there is one. Jews continue to identify as Jews as they see fit and argue that these modes of identification are completely compatible with the norms and values of the societies into which they seek integration. In other words, it is not a zero-sum game, but one can be distinctively Jewish and still be a fully integrated citizen of the modern world and some non-Jewish society. This response has reached its highest level of articulation and persuasion with regard to American Jewry's justification for its loyalties to the State of Israel. While denial does not effectively resolve the dilemma, it has often helped to effectively lessen the tension caused by it.

Compartmentalization

A response that has been attributed primarily to so-called modern-Orthodox Jews, but in fact is engaged in to some extent by all Jews, is compartmentalization. It is a compromise to complete segregation. Here one seeks integration into the political and economic spheres, but maintains relative isolation in the social and personal spheres of life. One dresses, works and fulfills the obligations of citizenship like everyone else in society, but at home and with friends one maintains a distinctively Jewish life-style. This system of compartmentalization has been quite effective in allowing many Jews to keep a balance between integration and assimilation. It is reinforced educationally by the day school system, which maintains a fairly sharp dichotomy between secular and religious studies and does very little in the way of integrating the two in comparison to Catholic schools, for example. The criticism of compartmentalization is that it never confronts the dilemma on an ideological level. It effects certain religious compromises, which are usually denied, and it effects a certain amount of isolation which hinders full integration into the larger society.

Religious Change

Another resolution of the dilemma is to change those aspects of the Jewish religion or identification which most hinder integration. This response is common. In fact, it is so common that it is often viewed as the only viable response. For example, Zvi Adar (1977, p. 24) writes:

> Contemporary life in the Jewish world confronts the Jew and his society with two tasks: (1) to integrate and find his place in modern society and culture, and (2) to reshape the nature of Jewish life inside the new framework. The second task has proved much more difficult and complicated.

This response has encouraged Jewish movements of all sorts, some of which attempt to alter the nature of religious practice (e.g., Reform Judaism), and others which attempt to define Jewishness in primarily cultural rather than religious terms (e.g., Yiddishist movements). Cultural changes should be more adaptable to the vicissitudes of modernity because they are not cloaked in sanctity as are religious norms. Those who take Jewish tradition seriously make great efforts to distinguish between cultural customs (*minhag*) and absolute religious laws (halacha). The former are often viewed as less binding than the latter. In fact, to some extent the distinction between 'modern' and 'right-wing' Orthodoxy has much to do with the amount of Jewish tradition that is viewed as *minhag* and the amount viewed as halacha. The way the scale tips on this matter also has much to do with the extent to which integration into modern society is viewed as necessary and desirable.

Societal Change

A final response to the dilemma is to change society to accommodate Jewish identity. The great number of Jews who joined the socialist and communist movements in Eastern Europe and elsewhere at the turn of the century sought to make their societies more equitable to all groups, and thus better the lot of oppressed minorities such as Jews. Similarly, in the United States Jews have been great proponents of separation of Church and State because many believe that government entanglement in religious matters is ultimately not beneficial to Jewish identity. American Jews have also been among the main advocates of cultural pluralism, asserting that the ultimate American goal is not the blending of cultural differences into some new American and primarily white Anglo-Saxon Protestant style (melting-pot theory), but rather the maintenance of separate cultural group identities within a framework of shared values. Cultural pluralism in a country where Jews constitute less than 3% of the population has obvious advantages.

Many of the great Jewish movements which arose as responses to the integration-identity dilemma fostered specific educational programs in the Diaspora and Israel to foster their ideologies. Nevertheless, most Jews respond in more than one of the six ways outlined. Even ideological groups which usually respond in one way will turn to other responses if a particular issue warrants it. This flexibility and ideological pliability allowed a degree of Jewish identity among those who might otherwise have abandoned it altogether. Educationally, however, it has created severe problems. Educators have been reluctant to face the Jewish identity dilemma squarely, or to discuss the different responses to it. This has left students with serious questions about the nature of Jewish identity and its importance. Adult views and practices seem ambivalent, inconsistent, and not subject to any rationale. In actuality, realistic responses to the dilemma will necessarily be multifaceted.

Nevertheless, educators must develop programs that reflect the existence of these options and articulate rationales for choosing one over another. We must face the fact that in many modern societies, the option of complete assimilation as an alternative is both viable and attractive to increasing proportions of youth.

Jewish Migration

The second historical trend to have a major impact on world Jewry today has been migration. The great migration of East European Jews during the four decades around the turn of the century altered the geographic distribution of world Jewry. About 3 million Jews left Eastern Europe (primarily Russia and Lithuania), and about 80% of them went to the United States. About 7% went to West European countries (primarily Germany, Britain, France, and the Netherlands), about 3% went to *Eretz Israel* (Palestine), and the others to Canada, Australia, Argentina, and South Africa (Gartner, 1984). In many of these countries, the Jewish populations grew by exponential rates from the early years of these migrations until World War II. Elazar and Cohen (1985) report that between 1900 and 1939 the Jewish population in the United States increased from 1 million to nearly 5 million, in *Eretz Israel* from 50,000 to 450,000, in England from 200,000 to 340,000, in France from 115,000 to 320,000, in Argentina from 30,000 to 275,000, in Canada from 16,000 to 155,000, in Brazil from 2,000 to 52,000, and in South Africa from 25,000 to almost 91,000. Most of these countries experienced a further influx of Jewish immigrants from Europe after World War II and from Asian and African countries after the establishment of the State of Israel.

The relevance of these migration patterns from a historical perspective is two-fold: First, all of today's large Jewish communities experienced their major population expansion during this century. Migration, while strengthening communities with new human resources, also initially taxes their institutional resources and capacities. Efforts are usually first directed toward health, shelter, and occupational needs, relegating education, particularly religious education to a secondary place. Thus, in a very real sense, Jewish educational systems around the world are still quite young, and only within the last two to three decades have most communities attained sufficient stability and economic well-being to focus attention and resources upon their improvement.

Second, the educational systems that developed in most of the large Jewish communities of the world reflected priorities of education and identity then prevalent in Eastern Europe. Although perhaps the structure of institutions was based on European and German models, the curricular and ideological orientations of the schools reflected mainly the East European Jewish

culture. Many of the studies in this volume point to the greater traditionalism that developed in those places which received the largest immigrations of
Jews from Eastern Europe. Clearly, their responses to the Jewish identity
dilemma were much less prone to either 'complete assimilation' or 'religious
change' than their West European counterparts. The development of day
schools throughout the Diaspora has been influenced by them, even though
the model originated in Germany (Adar, 1977).

A final migration pattern of which we must take note has been the migration of Asian and African Jews from their homelands after the establishment
of the State of Israel and during the last three decades. More than one million
Jews, primarily from Morocco, Algeria, Iraq, Tunisia, and Iran emigrated to
Israel, the United States, France, and other parts of the Diaspora. The severe
loss of population greatly affected the remaining Jews in those communities
and has made it more difficult for them to maintain proper educational institutions, and to find local Jews to instruct and administer schools. The large
emigration from these countries along with the worsening of political and
economic conditions has created severe crises in the cultural reproduction of
Jewish life there.

The Asian-African, commonly if improperly referred to as Sephardic,
migration has also affected the receiving countries. Both Israel and France, in
particular, have had great problems in increasing the capacity of their educational institutions to serve the needs of the new immigrants, and in reorient-
ing their traditional European (Ashkenazic) Jewish studies curricula to
include the Sephardic culture. The adjustments to these newer migrations are
still in process.

The Holocaust

The third important historical event to affect contemporary Jewish life
was the destruction of two thirds of European Jewry and over one third of
world Jewry by the Nazis during World War II. In addition to the enormous
human and material devastation, there was vast cultural destruction. The
greatest institutions of Jewish learning were destroyed, and entire communities with their cultural institutions were obliterated - lost forever.

The European communities directly affected by the war have had a tremendous job of rebuilding and picking up the pieces, so-to-speak, as docu-
mented in the studies in this volume. The countries which received war refugees were further taxed by the general problems of migration, which
sometimes took precedence over religious educational needs.

It is difficult to assess the effect of such a tremendous loss to Jewish education specifically. It is clear that some of the greatest Jewish educational
institutions were destroyed and many of the great leaders and teachers of the

Jewish world perished. In addition, there has been a significant shift in the locus of Jewish life in the world. Jewish population concentration has shifted from Europe to North America, and Jewish spiritual leadership has shifted from Europe to Israel. In both the United States and Israel Jewish learning has been rejuvenated, and both countries have created great centers of Jewish scholarship and culture. Schiff (1983) points out that in the United States alone there are about fifty academies of advanced Talmudic study, with a total enrollment of over 10,000 students. He remarks: "It seems safe to say that the student enrollment in America in post-secondary yeshivoth, *mesivtoth* and *kollelim* compares favorably with the number who were enrolled in the great yeshivoth of Eastern Europe in their heyday" (p. 6). How this compares in quality to what was, or to what might have been, is difficult (if not impossible) to estimate.

The State of Israel

The fourth historical phenomenon which has affected all of world Jewry is the return of Jewish sovereignty in the land of Israel after over two thousand years. The establishment of Israel as a place of refuge for oppressed Jews, and as spiritual homeland for all Jews, has had an impressive impact on Jews throughout the world. Coming so close upon the heels of the Holocaust, Israel achieved tremendous military, economic, and cultural successes and gave Jews throughout the world a renewed sense of pride, a greater sense of unity, and a central component of Jewish identity. Moreover, in a very tangible sense, Israel has played an instrumental role in revitalizing Jewish culture through language, art, music and literature; also, Israel has provided educational material, personnel, and finances to Jewish schools throughout the world. The establishment of the State of Israel has allowed us to focus on the needs of Jewish education in a manner that was impossible before, and to consider solutions to problems that would have been inconceivable without it.

The Societal Context of Jewish Schooling

Schools must be understood within the context of the societies in which they are located. The permissiveness or restrictiveness of government policies regarding religious and ethnic minorities in general, and Jews in particular, can affect the desire or need of Jews to establish their own schools. Availability of free non-denominational schools, and the normativeness of private schooling, also affect the extent to which Jews will seek to establish their own school system. Of course, the climate of Jewish-Gentile interaction, the receptivity of one group toward the other, will affect the desire to intermingle in many spheres of life including education.

The Religious Context

Stephen Sharot (1976), in his excellent comparison of the factors which affected Jewish identity in previous eras and different countries, argues that:

> Jewish acculturation was much greater in those societies where the dominant religion was syncretic than in those societies where the dominant religion was insular...syncretic religions were more disposed to pluralism and insular religions were more disposed to monopolism. The greater the tendency of the dominant group to coerce the Jews into accepting the majority religion, the more the Jews emphasized their religio-cultural distinctiveness. The greater the tendency of the dominant group to accept the existence of Judaism, the more likely the Jews would acculturate to the majority or core culture....Where Jews were separated, they were less likely to adopt a non-Jewish religio-culture. Where Jews were not so separated and social contacts with non-Jews were more frequent and intimate, acculturation was far more likely. The extent to which Jews were separated within a society was often related to the dominant group's disposition to monopolism or pluralism. A total monopolistic policy, if successful, would have resulted in the disappearance of the Jews, but successful monopolism was very rare. Even when Jews were forced to convert to Christianity, they often remained unassimilated, and this drove the dominant group to segregate them still further (pp. 34–35).

The above quotation is taken from Sharot's discussion of pre-modern times, but he makes a similar statement with regard to the Church's effect on Jews in the pre-industrial period. Because the Church tried to protect its monopolistic position, it contributed to the segregation of Jews. This had the consequence of protecting the distinctively Jewish religious culture from incursions by the wider Christian society. Such separation lasted in most of Europe until the second half of the eighteenth century, and in Eastern Europe until the 20th. Sharot (1976, pp. 176–177) explains:

> As Jews entered gentile society, their religion lost its dominant position in explaining and interpreting the world....The effects on the Jews of the interrelated changes of the economy, political structure, and belief systems of the wider society came at a relatively late stage, but it was

just because of this lag that, when the absorption of the Jews into 'the modern world' did occur, it was an extremely rapid process. In a few decades the separation of the Jews in western and central Europe was broken down, transforming their culture and way of life....For the Jews, the secularising effects of urbanisation and the loss of community were accentuated by problems of identity. Most wished to remain Jewish but they also wished to be accepted into the dominant society, and this appeared possible only if Judaism was restricted to the home and the synagogue and took forms which would meet the demands of Occidental culture.

Sharot argues, with regard to Communist Eastern Europe, that the secular monopolism of Communist authorities has been much more inclusive than the religious monopolism of the medieval Catholic Church. At first, he points out, the anti-religious campaigns against Jews in Russia were not successful, but after industrialization, urbanization, and other changes associated with the Russian revolution had weakened Jewish religious commitment and the insularity and solidarity of Jewish communities, the suppression of Judaism has been extensive and relatively effective.

Today, in most Jewish communities of the world, there is less pressure upon Jews to conform to the majority religion. Overt antisemitism and discrimination have been generally on the decline since World War II; therefore, there is very little to reinforce Jewish distinctiveness within the larger society, allowing acculturation and assimilation to proceed relatively unhindered. However, receptivity to Jews has also permitted a new openness about Jewish identity. This is manifested, for example, in public support for Israel. Sharot claims that the differences in patterns of religious observance and synagogue affiliation between countries are related to the different forms that secularization has taken in those countries. For example, in the Communist bloc, the lack of Jewish religious institutions, religious functionaries, and educational institutions has made even minimal religious observance rare. In France, the secularization involved an ideological rejection of institutional religion and, therefore, synagogue affiliation and ritual observance has been very low, except among the recent immigrants from Muslim countries. In England and the United States, ideological secularization was not important; therefore both countries have relatively high rates of synagogue affiliation and complete non-observance is much rarer than in France. However, in England, as in most European countries, secularization has meant a decline of institutional religion. In America, religious institutions have grown because they adopt secular functions. Thus, synagogues have become community centers, and often their communal functions have become more important than the religious ones.

The Educational Context

In addition to the religious context of the larger society and its acceptance of Jews, the educational context of the general society has had an impact on Jewish schooling. In Western societies, the availability of public elementary schools for the population generally coincided with the period of mass immigration of Jews from Eastern Europe. In fact, along with the political, economic, and religious opportunities that attracted East European Jews to the United States and England was the greater availability of education for their children. Very few countries tried to eliminate religion from the educational system as fully as the United States. In most countries to which Jews immigrated, government support for denominational schools, which were the earliest schools established in all countries, was the norm. Everywhere governments have attempted to use the educational system as a way of investing in the future productivity of the society. By making schools more accessible to greater numbers, a more educated public would hopefully result in a more productive labor force. In countries where economic conditions prohibited the rapid development of free government-sponsored public schools, states were typically inclined to support already existing denominational schools. In some countries, government-run schools were developed alongside of government-supported denominational schools.

Throughout the world, there has been a move in recent decades to increase educational opportunities for all classes of citizens. Therefore, at least at the elementary school level, and to some extent at the secondary school level, there has been increased consciousness of class differences within existing educational facilities. To equalize educational opportunities, some governments have sought to increase support of government sponsored schools and decrease support of denominationally sponsored schools. Other governments have increased the support given to denominationally sponsored schools, so as to have more control over the educational process by setting standards for teacher hiring and curricular instruction. Thus, increased support for denominational education has brought increasing government control and involvement. In countries with new political regimes, such as Muslim and South American countries, schools have been recognized as important institutions for legitimating the new political systems. Here too, along with government support for denominational schools has come increasing control over the institutions and their educational processes.

A low level of government involvement is found in the setting of minimal standards for teacher hiring and instruction. At moderate levels of government involvement, there is control over student access to educational facilities. Restrictions are often imposed upon students from attending schools of their choice outside their neighborhoods, and a mixture of students from various religious backgrounds are required to attend the same school. At the maximum level of involvement, there have been cases, e.g. Iran, where the government actually takes over a Jewish school, and changes both its name and its curricular direction. This is a form of educational nationalization which does not reimburse the Jewish community or other denominational bodies for the substantial investment in the schools they have developed.

One of the interesting reactions to these movements for increasing educational quality, or standardizing educational experiences throughout educational systems, has been the development of all-day Jewish schools. In countries as far away and as different from each other as the United States, France, and Argentina, over the last several decades there has been a substantial increase in the proportion of Jewish children who attend Jewish day schools. The authors of the chapters on these countries in this volume all point to the deteriorating conditions of the public schools as a major determinant of this growth. Jews in most countries today have reached fairly high levels of economic standing, and to protect this status, they now view private schooling as a more viable option than they did when economic integration into the society was their goal. This welcome development of increased enrollment in Jewish day schools has however also had a negative consequence: the emphasis on Jewish studies within the schools has decreased. Many Jewish pupils left the public school systems when less privileged children began to attend because they felt that the standards were lowered. Similarly, some felt that the enrollment of previously uninvolved Jews lowered the standards of Jewish study and observance within the day schools. Whereas these students previously would not have attended any Jewish school at all because of the particularistic emphasis and concentration on Jewish subject matter, they now demanded that aspects of the curriculum which they had tried to avoid altogether receive less time and emphasis. This gave rise to new, less religiously-oriented day schools, as the liberal movements suddenly discovered an interest among their constituencies; but it also brought about a reaction by the more observant Jews who established a growing number of new more Orthodox ('right-wing') day schools. This diversity would ordinarily have been welcome as a healthy development, but it occurred at the same time that the school-age population was declining. Thus, it raised serious questions about the long-term viability of so many schools, and particularly schools which for many years filled a critical middle-of-the-road function and were now losing students to the 'right' and 'left'.

Of course, government support for Jewish schools, while important to the development of those schools, is not the only factor affecting the decision to attend all-day schools or supplementary schools. Great Britain and Canada present an interesting comparison. In Great Britain, there is some government support for the majority of Jewish day schools, while in Canada less than half of the day schools receive substantial government support, these being primarily those in Quebec province, including Montreal. Great Britain, whose Jewish school-age population is larger than Canada's, has a higher percentage of Jewish children who are currently enrolled in Jewish schools (55% and 49%, respectively). Yet, the percentage enrolled in day schools out of all pupils receiving any Jewish education is greater in Canada than in Great Britain (63% and 51%, respectively) (Genuth, DellaPergola and Dubb, 1985).

The authors of the chapters on Great Britain and Canada in this volume have discussed the differences in the natures of these two Jewish communities and their considerations regarding day school and supplementary types of Jewish education. It is clear that the general societal contexts in which Jewish communities find themselves dictate Jewish educational growth and development. However, it is clear that the nature of the Jewish community itself, its immigrant background, ideological propensities, and socioeconomic characteristics also affect its systems.

The Jewish Communal Context of Jewish Schooling

Generation

An important characteristic of the Diaspora today is that in all the sizeable Jewish communities most of the Jews are native-born, and there are no longer large influxes of immigrants from other countries. Moreover, the effects of the tremendous religious and cultural nourishment received by these communities from the immigration of the religious East European Jews in the early 1900s and which continued to some extent until after World War II, will come to an end with the passing of that generation in the next 10–15 years. Despite the apparent growth of the Orthodox minority throughout the world, and especially right-wing Orthodox groups, they will probably not be numerous enough to replace the older generation (Himmelfarb and Loar, 1984). Among Diaspora communities, only the secularized French Jewish community has witnessed a rebirth of religiosity due to the immigration in the past few decades of Jews from North Africa. However, their very rapid integration into French society raises questions about their ability to maintain the traditionalism of their countries of origin. There is likely to be a further decline in religiosity and traditionalism throughout the Diaspora, despite what appears to be a renaissance of Hebraic and Israeli culture. The Jew of the 1980s, in almost all parts of the world, is highly secularized, acculturated and has achieved a high level of socioeconomic mobility and integration into the society in which he lives. Israel has become the principal factor of Jewish identity and the main unifying element among all Jews.

Antisemitism

Perhaps with the exception of the Communist and Muslim countries, antisemitism is less compelling in either hindering or promoting Jewish solidarity, cohesiveness and identity than it was in previous generations. Howard Sachar (1985) states that there is no Western nation today that, at the official governmental level, will allow overt acts of antisemitism. There is also evidence that popular latent attitudes of antisemitism have declined since World War II, at least in the United States (Yankelovich, Skelly, and White, 1981). However, it is a mere forty years since the end of World War II, and it is difficult to know how long tolerance will prevail in a world that has historically persecuted Jews at every opportunity. Indeed, in recent years there has been an unprecedented number of antisemitic reports from the Western mass media, particularly in its coverage of Israeli affairs and an unprecedented (since World War II) number of terrorist attacks on Jewish institutions, particularly in Western Europe. Nevertheless it is probably fair to say that the general climate prevailing in most Diaspora countries does not promote Jewish self-consciousness because of its unacceptance or intolerance of Jews.

Family Patterns

Several societal trends have brought about important changes in family life which also affect the context in which Jewish education takes place.

Professionalization of Women

With the increasing educational mobility of the Jewish community, there has been a concomitant professionalization of Jews. This has extended also to Jewish women and has coincided with greater occupational opportunities for women in general, thanks to the feminist movement of the 1960s and structural and legal changes which occurred as a consequence. Both advantages and disadvantages were created for the context of Jewish education. On the one hand, working women have made dual income families more normative, thereby increasing the overall ability of families to pay for private education, but also creating the need for more hours of childcare during the day. This need has become evident in the worldwide expansion of pre-school enrollment in Jewish institutions. Jewish day schools, with their longer school day, probably also benefitted. On the other hand, professional parents seek greater quality education for their children, which has increased the demands placed upon Jewish schools, particularly with regard to the general studies provided. For those who send their children to supplementary schools, the increased economic ability of parents has also created greater demands for additional cultural education which competes with religious schooling, such as music, dance, art, and sports lessons. Finally, working women have less time for voluntary charitable activities which were always important for the maintenance of educational institutions, either through direct volunteer efforts, or through indirect efforts to raise community funds that were then distributed to the schools (Johnson, 1976).

Marriage and Fertility

Along with the tendency toward more years of education, there has been concomitant postponement of marriage and childbearing. In most countries for which we have data, Jews tend to marry later and have fewer children than the population at large (Schmelz, 1981; DellaPergola, 1983; Schmelz and DellaPergola, 1983). Data from the United States and Canada indicate that between 1970 and 1980 there was a very substantial increase in the proportion of Jews remaining single throughout their early adult years, nor do we yet know whether, in fact, most of these people will ever marry. If they do, they will probably have fewer children than those who married earlier, although there is some debate about that (Goldscheider and Zuckerman, 1984). Fertility rates of the Jews are low throughout the world. Israel is the only country whose Jewish population is growing due to natural increase and, according to DellaPergola and Schmelz (this volume), the fertility rate in other countries is below the level which allows for generational replacement. When attrition due to intermarriage and general assimilation are taken into account, Schmelz and DellaPergola estimate that the lower fertility rate of Jews will by the year 2000 result in a school-age population in the Diaspora that is less than two thirds or even less than half of its size in 1965. Obviously, such a dramatic decline in the number of Jewish children will affect Jewish school systems and will necessitate a severe contraction of professional personnel and facilities unless a substantial increase in the rate of enrollment in Jewish schools occurs. As the Jewish populations in the various Diaspora countries begin to decline, their ability to maintain educational and other Jewish institutions will probably decline as well.

Intermarriage

One important indicator of Jewish acceptance in society at large has been a world-wide increase in Jewish mixed marriages (DellaPergola, 1976). Since World War II, the number of marriages of Jews to non-Jews has risen significantly, and in recent years has reached somewhere between 25 and 50% of newly wed Jews in Jewish communities throughout the world. This is affecting the size of the Jewish population. On the average, fewer children are born to intermarried couples, and among those born, fewer than half identify themselves as Jews. Moreover, intermarriage raises additional challenges for promoting Jewish identity, particularly in light of considerable research evidence indicating an interaction between the Jewishness of family background and Jewish schooling (Cohen 1974; Himmelfarb, 1974).

Divorce

Along with the other changes in family life already mentioned, there has been a substantial increase in divorce and the number of single-parent families (especially in the United States). Studies show that single parent families are less likely to be associated with Jewish institutions or to enroll their children in Jewish schools.

In sum, the changes in the generational, educational, occupational, social and familial characteristics of Jews are determining the decisions of Jewish educators and planners throughout the world. These changes effect which, and how many, students are taught, and will effect their interest and motivation to learn.

The Structure of Jewish Education

Transplantation of European Education

It has often been claimed that Jews transplanted the educational systems to which they had been accustomed in Europe into their new communities. Essentially this is true, particularly when one considers the diversity of ideological and curricular approaches that developed in single communities. However, it must be noted that there are only a limited variety of structural arrangements that Jewish schooling can assume. Most of them were already in use in Europe in the 19th century, and were attempted at the turn of the century in the countries that received large waves of immigration.

Given the necessity of providing secular education for Jewish children (a requirement not taken for granted until the mid–19th century in many countries, and even much later in others), then the essential question is where to include Jewish education. Broadly, there are three options:
- teach Jewish studies in the same school with secular studies by establishing all-day schools under Jewish sponsorship;
- teach Jewish studies in supplementary schools outside secular school hours;
- teach Jewish studies during 'released time' from secular schools.

Each of these options also appeared in a variety of mutations, especially supplementary education where choices were made between a private tutor in the home (*Melamed*), a private-enterprise school, usually in the tutor's home (Heder), a communally or congregationally sponsored school meeting several times a week (Talmud Torah), or a school meeting only once a week (Sunday school). Sunday School became the dominant choice of the Reform movement in the United States, probably modeled on the prevalent form of Protestant religious education there (Gartner, 1969).

Moreover, within a given structure there was considerable diversity regarding curricula and orientation, based on differing views of Jewish identity. For example, the Englightenment in Eastern Europe led to three major educational responses which were structured as all-day schools: Yiddish-Socialist education, Zionist-Hebrew cultural education, and religious (Orthodox) education. These three ideological orientations later appeared also in countries outside Eastern Europe (Adar, 1977). In the United States, they were taught in supplementary schools, but in South and Central America, they appeared mainly in all-day schools. Yiddish-Socialist education, as a formal option to religious education, was stronger in the United States than the Zionist-Hebrew cultural orientation. Yet, it began to decline in the 1930s and has now almost disappeared. Jewish education in the United States has developed mainly along religious lines (e.g. Reform, Conservative and Orthodox) with variations in the degree of Hebrew language and Israeli culture taught. Jewish nationalist identity as an alternative rather than as a supplement to Jewish religious identity has never been a strong factor in the United States.

Generally, where public non-denominational education was not available for new immigrants in Diaspora communities, such as in the very early settlement of Jews in the United States and England, Jews established their own day schools. Where or when non-denominational public schools were made available, Jews chose to attend those schools and establish supplementary schools for Jewish education. It is interesting that everywhere they went the East European immigrants established supplementary forms of Jewish education, heders and Talmudei Torah. This seems to be testimony to their great zeal for acceptance and integration into the wider society, but it became a major obstacle as proponents of day schools became more vocal and began to demand greater community support for their schools. The day school movement, which gained momentum primarily after World War II, struggled everywhere (except in Muslim countries) with the existing Jewish establishment because they were viewed as rejecting the invitation of host nations to full citizenship and participation.

Growth of Day Schools

The aftermath of World War II created conditions that were conducive to the development of day schools. First, the Holocaust called into question integrationist and assimilationist ideologies. Second, it created a need for heightened Jewish awareness and solidarity, and education was viewed as a means to this end. Third, there was new immigration before, during and after the war to various Diaspora countries. These immigrants included Orthodox rabbinical leaders with the stature and following to build intensive Jewish educational institutions. Fourth, in the following decades, immigrants from North Africa and the Middle East made their way to various Diaspora communities, primarily France, and they were more tradition-oriented than were the Jews already living in the countries to which they immigrated, thus adding to a more receptive atmosphere within the Jewish community for day schools. Fifth, the relative prosperity attained by Jews in most of the Diaspora, outside of Europe (until the 1960s) and the Muslim countries, enabled them to establish and support full-time Jewish education.

Finally, and this is a remarkable phenomenon in its pervasiveness, the declining conditions of the public school system made private schooling a more attractive alternative. This was true in countries as disparate as the United States, France and Argentina, where Jewish all-day schools gained popularity. The movements in these countries to expand and equalize educational opportunities for all classes of citizens have brought about a perceived deterioration in the standards and quality of the public education available.

The great growth of day schools in recent decades should not be viewed necessarily as an achievement of the organized Jewish community, but rather more as a product of the tireless efforts of a few devoted individuals in each community, as several authors in this volume have noted. The Jewish communities in Asia and North Africa are the exception to this rule, since international Jewish educational organizations, such as the Alliance Israélite Universelle, have played critical roles in establishing, staffing and maintaining Jewish day schools there.

The term 'day school' implies much more homogeneity and intensity of Jewish studies than is actually true in most cases. In North America, day schools spend around 15 to 20 hours a week on Jewish studies, while in South Africa, Australia, and most of the Latin American and West European countries, only 7 to 10 hours a week are spent on these studies. There are some schools, e.g., ORT schools, where the amount of time spent on Jewish studies is only 2 or 3 hours a week, the equivalent of Sunday schools. There are other day schools whose Jewishness is only specious. For example, there are day schools in Turkey whose directors are appointed by the government and are not Jewish, and the more extreme case of the 'Jewish' boys' school and 'Jewish' girls' school in New Delhi, each with over a thousand students of whom less than five were Jews.

By the early 1980s, nearly 40% of all Diaspora Jewish school enrollment was in day schools. This was more than a 25% increase in about 15 years. Outside of the United States the percentage is nearly 69% (Dubb, 1984). This is a truly significant accomplishment in such a short time and a remarkable reversal from previous generations.

'Part-time' Jewish schooling has also advanced. In most regions of the world, part-time Jewish schooling averages 3–4 hours of Jewish studies per week, particularly when Sunday schools and released time programs are included with weekday afternoon school statistics. However, in Argentina supplementary schools include a full afternoon of study – an average of 14–16 hours a week – more than the typical day school in most Diaspora communities outside of North America. Thus, despite common belief, we see that a supplementary school can sometimes give more hours of Jewish studies than a day school. Efforts must be made to increase and improve the Jewish studies content of all types of Jewish schools. While it is hoped that the expansion of day schools indicates progress in this direction, other indicators to monitor quality and quantity must also be used.

The phenomenon of Talmudei Torah, which remain dominant in the United States and very pervasive throughout Europe and Australia, is perhaps even more remarkable than the growth of the day school movement. Historians have seen the large proportion of enrollment to supplementary schools as an indicator of the minimal Jewish identification extant among Diaspora Jews. Instead, it must be noted that such a part-time school system is probably unique among religious and ethnic groups throughout the world. Other groups have established day schools and Sunday schools, but none of them have established an extensive system of supplementary schools which meet several times a week for several hours a day. These schools are testimony to the seriousness with which Jews both integrate into the dominant society in their respective country, and simultaneously try to preserve their Jewish identities. Unfortunately, the educational strategy adopted to achieve the latter goal is not as efficient as the strategy adopted for the former.

Jewish Schooling for Girls

Formal Jewish education for females has been one of the big changes of the 20th century. In Eastern Europe, very few girls were sent to religious schools. Indeed, they were more likely to receive secular/vocational training, and any Jewish schooling that existed for them was very basic and elementary. As the conditions of Jewish life changed, young girls could no longer receive sufficient training from the home or community alone and the tendency grew to send them to Jewish schools. However, in most countries girls are still less likely to attend Jewish schools for as many years as boys, and in the United States are less likely to attend intensive forms of Jewish schooling (DellaPergola and Genuth, 1983). They are often excluded from Talmudic study and other subjects. These gender differences are not as pronounced among liberal (Reform) Jews. Yeshivoth have never admitted women for study, and non-Orthodox denominations have only recently begun to admit them for rabbinical training. Sanua (1964) states that girls enjoy their Jewish studies more than boys and are more observant of Jewish practices. Since Jewish school teachers are mostly females it is imperative that women get the best Jewish education possible. The fact that so many Jewish females get a formal Jewish education today is a great accomplishment, but considerable efforts must yet be made before gender equity is achieved.

Informal Jewish Education

When Jews lived in relatively isolated or insulated Jewish communities, Jewish identification was not a problem. Therefore, Jewish schools could concentrate on the single goal of transmitting knowledge. However, as Jews began to disperse and integrate into the wider society, Jewish identification became a major concern and Jewish socialization gained priority over Jewish education. That is, the production of knowledgeable Jews became secondary to the production of identifying Jews. Today this is a major difference between Jewish education in Israel and in the Diaspora. In Israel, the major goal is to add knowledge to an identification that already exists from the experience of everyday life. In the Diaspora, there is a need to create the experience to which knowledge can be related.

Schools are better at transmitting knowledge than they are at transmitting experience. The Jewish world has been particularly innovative in creating other educational media for transmitting Jewish experience, the most prominent being youth movements, summer camps, study tours of Israel and recreational centers.

Many youth movements in Western countries began as outgrowths of youth movements in Europe. Most were Zionistic in orientation, with different groups reflecting the ideologies of the supporting movements. Some groups, however, reflected other ideologies prevalent at the time, e.g., Yiddish-culture groups, socialist, communist, etc. Others were simply attempts to create Jewish alternatives to non-Jewish youth groups, such as the Jewish scouts. In communities which are unabashedly Zionist in orientation, e.g., Latin American countries, South Africa, the great majority of those movements remain Zionist. Where Jewish identity is viewed in more religious terms, alternatives to Zionist youth movements have developed. For example, in the United States today, some of the largest youth movements are affiliated with the denominational bodies of the Reform, Conservative, and Orthodox movements. In addition, the *Chabad* and the right-wing Orthodox, *Agudat Yisrael* have also developed a network of youth groups throughout the country.

One cannot discount the indigenous groups that have developed in most countries which are not ideologically aligned, but were established to provide

Jewish fellowships and culture in an informal educational environment. The American-based B'nai B'rith Youth Organization is perhaps the largest of this kind in the world. Although there are also various forms of Jewish college student groups, they do not enroll a significant portion of the Jewish students.

It is difficult to assess the quantitative importance of Jewish youth groups. There are no reliable estimates of how many persons are affected by these groups, nor has their impact been systematically investigated. A recent study of the Jewish population in Greater Paris found a positive relationship between past activity in Jewish youth movements and current levels of adult Jewishness (Bensimon and DellaPergola, 1984). Himmelfarb (1974) found that Jewish adults in Chicago who had participated in Jewish organizations during their college years were more likely to be Jewishly involved as adults on all of the nine measures of Jewish identification used in the study. This was true even after parental religiosity and other self-selection factors were taken into account. College-age participation was most strongly correlated with adult Jewish organizational involvement and Jewish intellectual and artistic cultural involvements.

Most youth organizations attempt to reinforce their programs with intensive Jewish living experiences in summer camps. Camps, of course, are not sponsored only by youth organizations, but also by Jewish community centers, synagogues, schools and private entrepreneurs. Some observers (e.g., Ackerman, 1969) claim that camps are much more effective than schools in promoting Jewish identification. However, the little research that has been done in this area indicates that their effectiveness is dependent on reinforcement by Jewish schooling or other experiences during the year (Himmelfarb, 1985).

Organized study-tours of Israel are a recent innovation in informal Jewish education. Since much of Diaspora Jewish identification today is related to the State of Israel, studying and touring the country should increase Jewish identification. The many different programs offered for students vary in length of time, content and setting (e.g., universities, yeshivoth, teachers' institutions, kibbutzim, etc.). In fact, some youth movements are now providing their summer camp programs for older high school students in Israel. Research evidence indicates that these programs have a positive effect on their participants, particularly on their knowledge of Hebrew and identification with the State of Israel. Religiosity is not necessarily increased. Like any summer camp experience, the impact of study-tours seems to be dependent on reinforcement from subsequent educational programs.

Jewish recreational centers provide an opportunity for Jews to socialize with other Jews. In Latin American countries, Jewish sport clubs are very prominent and, though less exclusive, fill a role somewhat similar to private Jewish country clubs in the United States. Jewish community centers in the

United States provide Jewish cultural programming as well as recreational facilities, and have been attempting to increase the quantity and quality of such programs in recent years. This broader model of cultural and recreational centers is being adopted and developed in Europe today.

Several implications can be drawn regarding informal Jewish education:

1. Informal Jewish education is a more demographically limited form of Jewish socialization than Jewish schools since it reaches a significantly smaller proportion of the eligible population. This is probably due to its voluntary nature. While attendance at Jewish schools is also voluntary, and this is one of the major constraints of Jewish education in the Diaspora, there are social pressures from family and friends which impel parents to send their children to Jewish schools at least for bar/bat mitzvah preparation. These social pressures do not exist with regard to youth group participation, summer camping, or trips to Israel. Indeed, the last two are viewed as luxuries, and youth groups are viewed as a service, which one may or may not want. Thus, because of the high degree of self-selection into these activities, most of those who are strongly affected by the programs have already been affected by previous experiences at home and in school. For example, Geula Solomon (this volume) points out that in Australia, the day schools have become primary recruiting grounds for Zionist youth groups.

2. Participation in youth groups seems to be dependent on the extent of ideological tension, conflict, and fervor in society usually created by severe social crises, e.g., war in Israel, or antisemitism at home. Fortunately, for most Jews, except perhaps those in the Soviet Union and in Muslim countries, current events have not yet reached crisis proportion.

3. The influence of summer camps and trips to Israel is intensive while it lasts, but is generally short-lived. That is why a number of studies point to the necessity of continuing with post-camp or post-Israel activities to reinforce what has been learned there. Schools, in contrast, reinforce themselves by meeting over longer periods of time, but usually do not provide a total living experience. Among the three major informal educational activities considered here, only youth groups have the potential for self-reinforcement over a long period of time, but because of their voluntary nature, participants are a very select few.

4. When taken by themselves, informal Jewish educational programs have a low impact on Jewish identity both because of the necessity for follow-up reinforcing activities, and the limited self-selected participation. Himmelfarb (1974, 1985) has found, as have other researchers, that youth groups, camps, and trips to Israel must be viewed as useful supplements to year-round Jewish educational programs, but not as surrogates for schools. They can not substitute for a good formal education, but rather can reinforce and enrich such education.

5. Most existing programs deal primarily with the elementary and high school age groups. However, research suggests that more time and effort ought to be directed toward the college-age population. In the college years, adult identification patterns are established, and these guide the choice of a spouse who will either facilitate or inhibit Jewish religio-ethnic involvement. This age group will determine the identification patterns of future generations of Jewish youth, and therefore, young adult and college student programming ought to be intensified. Since Jews, wherever allowed, are highly socially mobile, they attend colleges and universities in higher proportions than the rest of the population. In fact, it is estimated that about 80% of American Jews attend college at some time – a higher percentage than ever attend Jewish schools. Certainly, college campuses create potential pools of Jews for recruitment to various forms of Jewish education.

Adult Education

Most communities offer a variety of adult education programs in synagogues, social-philanthropic organizations, federations, community centers, schools, etc. These programs assume a great variety of formats such as occasional lectures, discussion groups, certificate or degree granting courses, or performances and exhibits by Jewish artists. In addition, some larger communities have Jewish radio and television programs. Self-improvement courses have proliferated in recent years; they may be little more than traditional texts translated and annotated, or correspondence courses for home study, or they might be as technologically sophisticated as cassette home libraries or 'Dial-a-Shiur' (dial-a-lesson), a daily telephone subscription service. Whatever the format, there has undoubtedly been a great burgeoning of adult educational initiatives in the last decade. Many of the programs are new and their effectiveness in other than marketing terms cannot be assessed. Nevertheless, the fact that there is a market for translated texts and the various other educational services shows that both the interest and the need exist.

At least two formal adult programs ought to be mentioned as important developments. First, there has been a regeneration of *yeshivoth gedoloth* (post-secondary Talmudic and rabbinic academies) since World War II (Helmreich, 1982). Some of these are transplanted European yeshivot that were destroyed. However, most of them, especially the smaller ones, developed indigenously and cater to selected segments of Orthodox Jews, sometimes followers of a particular *Rav* or Rebbe. Israel and the United States have been the major countries where this expansion has taken place, but yeshivoth have also been established in Europe, Australia, Argentina, and South Africa. While such institutions primarily cater to the Orthodox, a significant number have been especially established to serve students from non-

Orthodox backgrounds – including *Ba'alei Teshuva* ('Returnees to the faith', i.e. newly observant Jews) (Kovacs, 1977; Aviad, 1983).

The growth of *yeshivoth gedoloth* is significant for two reasons: first, they are the training ground for future rabbis and teachers (primarily day school teachers) in the communities. They produce *talmidei chachamim* (Talmud scholars), the traditional scholarly elite that was depleted by the Holocaust. Second, the yeshivoth have had a significant impact on the communities in which they are located, and even beyond. They are the primary source of the renewed Orthodox influence since World War II and have headed the movement to the right within the Orthodox community that has been a world-wide phenomenon. They have encouraged the growth of day schools, and these have in turn provided students for the yeshivoth. The yeshivoth have high standards of Jewish learning and observance and have thereby strengthened traditionalism within the public Jewish organizational establishment.

A second wide-spread phenomenon of the last decade and a half has been a proliferation of Jewish studies programs on university campuses throughout Israel and the Diaspora. In the United States in particular, there has been a tremendous growth of such programs in well over 300 colleges and universities. New faculty positions have continued to open, even at a time when students generally sought more vocationally oriented studies such as business or engineering. The amount of research publications and scholarly activity that have been generated by this development is probably unprecedented in Jewish history (Davis, 1975; Davis, 1986).

The place of university-based Jewish studies in the Jewish educational system is controversial. Unlike other Jewish educational programs, the primary goal is not to enhance Jewish identity, but rather to critically examine Jewish civilization. Yet, it is unlikely that students who, in college, study Hebrew language and literature, Jewish history, philosophy and sociology, at a high intellectual level, will not be enriched by the experience and find their Jewish identities reinforced in some manner. Of the thousands of students who take courses in these areas, very few actually major in Jewish studies or a related area. Yet, there is evidence that many of those who do major eventually decide to receive graduate training toward some Jewish professional career, e.g. federation work, social work, community center work, the rabbinate, etc.. Many others choose careers outside the Jewish community, but become active lay leaders of Jewish voluntary organizations. Thus, these Jewish Studies programs have become an indirect training ground for future professionals and leaders of the Jewish community. The production of a knowledgeable cadre of leaders is critically important, particularly as Jews now move into a generation devoid of persons with rich Jewish backgrounds.

The Jewish population outside of Israel is rapidly aging, the largest segment now being between 25 and 40 years old. Thus, the need for adult education programs becomes obvious. However, the education of adults is not likely to have a long-range impact on the Jewish community unless it can be passed on. Therefore, adult education should not concentrate on adults per se, but on that age group that can have an impact on their children. It is 'parent education' that is the critical mandate of adult educators who are concerned about the future of Jewish life. Research has shown, however, that it is very difficult to get parents involved in adult education for any sustained period of time (Rose, 1974; Goldmeier, 1975). After all, people in this age group are in the midst of career-building and child-rearing, and being so busy, they value their leisure time. Therefore, more must be done using new technologies: video-tape courses, special television programs, adult games, computer programs, and other techniques for the individual pursuit of knowledge. The social structures which reinforce self-study must also be developed (Heilman, 1983), e.g. discussion groups, retreats, etc. The *Dor Hemshech* (Generation of Continuity) programs developed by the World Zionist Organization and established in Latin American communities, might be an appropriate model for adaptation elsewhere to fill the need for social reinforcement in adult education.

Major Issues in Diaspora Jewish Education Today

Among the many problems of Jewish education that have already been mentioned, two problems are universal:
– obtaining qualified teachers; and
– maintaining student enrollment at the secondary school level.

Teachers

One has only to browse through this volume to see that securing qualified teachers has always been a problem in the Diaspora and it is a serious one today. Where there is no secondary Jewish education, the problem may be due to the lack of persons with sufficient Jewish education and training. However, even in countries with developed Jewish high school systems, the problem persists. In fact, Jewish teacher training institutes in most countries are having difficulty recruiting enough students to maintain themselves. In the United States, most have had to become general colleges of Jewish studies in order to survive. They offer higher level Jewish education to a broad age-range of adults, and have relegated teacher training and certification to a secondary role. Stanley Abramovitch (this volume) reports that four institutions for teacher training in England, Switzerland, Belgium, and Italy together produce a total of only 12 to 18 graduates a year.

The problem persists for reasons that have been enumerated by several authors in this volume. Many of these reasons are universal to the teaching profession, whether or not in a Jewish school. First, teaching is poorly remunerated as compared to other white-collar professions. Second, it is primarily a female occupation with very few men because of its low pay, and because working with children is considered women's work. There is always a larger proportion of male teachers at the secondary level, where teaching is subject oriented, than at the kindergarten and primary levels, where it is child oriented. Third, the above two factors combine to reduce the social status of teaching. Nevertheless, because it is intellectual, teaching still ranks near the top third of occupations in prestige within industrial countries. Fourth, as a profession it tends to be mobility-blocked (Lortie, 1975). There are few gradations of status to which a teacher can advance. Thus, while one typically obtains a higher salary by teaching for more years, seniority does not usually bestow more status, privilege or responsibility. The chief avenue for mobility is to move into school administration, which is very different work, and has been overwhelmingly dominated by men.

Another reason that teaching has been more attractive to women than to men is that women often view their salaries as supplementary rather than primary family income. In addition, teaching offers women a work schedule that coincides with their children's school and vacations. It has also been an occupation that is relatively easy to leave and re-enter without much loss of promotion, or obsolescence of skills. Teachers find it relatively easy to interrupt their careers for child-bearing or rearing purposes. Teaching personnel is on the average young and has a high turnover rate, a fact which gives most students relatively inexperienced teachers.

These universal problems of the teaching profession are often exacerbated in Jewish schools when salaries, fringe benefits, and job security are even lower than in the public school system (as in the United States); and the ambivalence of Jewish identity among the students often reduces their motivation to concentrate on Jewish studies. However, salary parity with competing schools, while important, will not solve the problem of recruitment. In fact, where appropriate parity has been achieved for day school teachers (e.g., Australia, South Africa, and several provinces in Canada), the problem of recruiting qualified teachers still persists. The relatively high socioeconomic status of Jews in most Diaspora countries leads an even smaller percentage of them into teaching than from the population at large. Moreover, in some countries, such as the United States, expanded opportunities for women in other professions during the last decade and a half have caused a severe drop in the number and academic qualifications of those entering the field of education. Young Jewish women, who tend to be more advanced academically than non-Jewish women, are probably even less likely to seek careers in teaching as other opportunities become increasingly available.

All of these problems are much more severe with regard to supplementary schools which suffer greatly from the part-time, and thus secondary nature of supplementary Jewish education. There is no full-time commitment on the part of anyone in the system (parent, student, or teacher), except, perhaps, a full-salaried administrator. Most of the teachers in supplementary schools work on a temporary basis, e.g. while their children are small, or while they or their spouses attend university. Both the part-time and temporary nature of the work makes it difficult to demand much prior or in-service training. Thus, the required teacher qualifications are compromised and minimized considerably.

Clearly, Israel has become the major source for providing qualified Jewish school personnel for the Diaspora. By formally sending *shlihim* (emissaries) to be administrators and teachers in the schools and by offering various teacher training courses and seminars, Israel is attempting quite valiantly to alleviate this major problem of Jewish education. In addition, many communities have benefitted from Israelis who are there temporarily for one reason or another, primarily for post-graduate training, who find it economically worthwhile to teach part-time in a Jewish school. Many critics have voiced concern about the inability of all Israeli teachers to relate to Diaspora children (Chanover, 1967; Levine, 1978), because of differences in cultural background. The practice of using non-*shaliah* Israeli teachers has been even more severely criticized. They are untrained pedagogically, and are often untraditional in religious practice, thus creating both cultural and ideological problems. Nevertheless, many schools have found these teachers to be the best available alternative because of their knowledge of Hebrew language and their familiarity with Jewish history and holiday customs.

Even with Israeli backup, it is unrealistic to assume that the personnel problem of Jewish schools in the Diaspora will be easily solved. Since conditions prevail that make teaching relatively unattractive, it is unlikely that Jewish schools which hire local residents will be able to demand much prior training. Thus, more efforts must be made to further in-service training. It is not practical to expect large numbers of teachers from any country to attend seminars in Israel for a significant period of time. It is also not clear whether Israeli institutions or personnel could handle the entire burden. Therefore, in-service training must be brought to those who do not go abroad. With the low cost availability of videotape production, training films can be created by the very best teachers, professors, and specialists in the world and distributed internationally in appropriate languages.

It is somewhat surprising that the United States with its great Jewish studies and educational expertise has not been called upon for help with this personnel problem. It is not inconceivable that the idea of *shlihut* (a teaching mission) to a foreign country would attract some knowledgeable young American Jewish couples to Jewish education in a way that day schools in New

York City or Omaha, Nebraska, for example, cannot. They might also be able to adapt to the cultural differences in some of the countries faster than Israelis.

Beyond this patchwork approach, Jewish schools need to take a lead in changing some of the structural characteristics of teaching as an occupation, which make it unattractive. In the United States today, many states are adopting teacher staffing systems in public schools that create a few more gradations of title, privilege, and responsibility (e.g., the master teacher, who trains and supervises others), and systems of merit bonuses for good teaching. Jewish schools, particularly where unattached to the pay scale of the larger educational system in the community, should be able to initiate such a reward system to make teaching more attractive. For supplementary schools, more multi-function positions could be created to develop the equivalent of full-time jobs (e.g., hiring one person to fill the tasks of an afternoon school teacher, a youth group leader, and a Jewish center Judaica specialist).

For all teachers, but especially for those who teach full-time in a day school, there is a need for summer employment opportunities. The relatively low pay of teaching would be substantially enhanced if it included another two months of salary. Teachers normally are paid an adequate salary for nine months, but must live on it for twelve months! This makes it necessary for many of them to seek summer employment. Such employment is often found in menial, low-status jobs, like factory labor, or seasonal work like gardening or roofing. If summer employment in Jewish educational, religious, or communal service were offered to Jewish school teachers, more persons might be attracted to the occupation.

High School Drop-outs

Nearly everywhere in the Diaspora, most Jewish education is on the elementary level. There is a very high drop-out rate from Jewish schools in the early teen years after bar/bat mitzvah, or after finishing primary school. The most recent data indicate that day school enrollment was almost 31% lower at the secondary than at the primary level. An even more dramatic decrease of 70% was evident after bar/bat mitzvah in the supplementary schools (Genuth, DellaPergola and Dubb, 1985). Of course, this type of comparison across school levels at the same time is not a very accurate estimate of the drop-out rate because of differences in the actual size of birth-cohorts, and the non-availability of secondary level Jewish education in some places. Nevertheless, differences are so large that a substantial portion must be due to dropping out. Anyone familiar with Jewish education in the Diaspora knows that this drop-out problem is extensive; it may not have been readily apparent how universal it is.

A possible exception seems to be France, where enrollment at the secondary school level is higher than at the primary level (see Auron and Lazare, this volume; Himmelfarb and DellaPergola, 1982). This peculiar situation is partly due to the age composition of the North African immigrants of the 1950s and 1960s. Indeed, the overall percentage of school-age children enrolled in Jewish schools in France (22%–26%) is substantially lower than other Diaspora countries (DellaPergola and Schmelz, this volume). However, special efforts were actually made in France to strengthen Jewish day schools at the post-primary level.

Given the earlier description of problems within the teaching profession, one might be tempted to say: "No wonder the drop-out rate is so high!" Yet, I suspect that it is not due to poor teaching, but rather to the fact that Jewish schooling plays such a secondary role in students' lives; many see it as a necessity for training and they drop out as soon as that training is over, or when more rigorous secondary level education begins to encroach upon their spare time.

Actually, there is some evidence from early studies in the United States (Dushkin, 1918; Edidin, 1929) that the drop-outs are not simply a consequence of bar mitzvah, but they present a problem throughout the school years which only reaches its peak around bar mitzvah age. Edidin (1929), for example, found that the proportion of students who dropped out of Jewish schools in Chicago was as great at ages 9 and 10 as at ages 12 and 13 (32% and 31%, respectively). In fact, another 22% had left the schools at even earlier ages. Rubel's article on Argentina (this volume) shows a similar trend. Only 77% of the students enrolled in the third grade in 1978 were in the 7th grade five years later. Only 68% of the 7th grade enrollment was enrolled in the first year of high school the following year and only about two-thirds of them will finish in a Jewish high school. In all, about 35% of those who were in Jewish schools in Argentina in the third grade were still enrolled during the last year of high school. Indeed, this low figure is probably considerably higher than in the United States and many other countries because in Argentina the figures deal almost exclusively with day school students. Dubb's estimates indicate that day school students are more than twice as likely as supplementary school students to continue to the secondary level. Thus, as the proportion of students in Jewish day schools increases, and as more Jewish high schools become available, we might expect an increase in the rate to secondary level Jewish education.

Children who drop out of Jewish schools after bar/bat mitzvah tend to come from homes that are not very Jewishly involved. For them, bar/bat mitzvah is both the chief reason for Hebrew school attendance and the appropriate point of termination (Jacoby, 1970; Selig, 1972). It is the normativeness of bar/bat mitzvah termination that needs to be changed. Schools, synagogues, and communal institutions must take it upon themselves to encourage Jewish school continuation at the secondary level in personal encounters and in structural ways.

On the personal level, rabbis, teachers and principals must assume the tasks encouraging at least a few students each year, who would not otherwise do so, to continue their Jewish studies. On the structural level, graduation, confirmation, and other forms of completion should be postponed for a year or more where possible. Moreover, each appropriate Jewish institution, e.g., school, synagogue, or cultural organization, should offer first year high school scholarships to students who would otherwise not attend. The number of scholarships awarded by a single institution could possibly be matched by a community-wide fund. A similar plan should be adopted to encourage a few supplementary school pupils to transfer to day schools, and those attending high schools to progress to post-high school programs. In these ways, the Jewish religious, educational, and organizational establishment could convey the message that extensive – rather than just elementary – Jewish education is the approved norm. It would undoubtedly take many years and, perhaps, a small miracle, to change the existing norm; but, in fact, substantial changes in the intensification of Jewish education have taken place worldwide in only the last three decades, and this too was beyond expectations.

The old Talmudic saying regarding Torah learning: "*Mitoch shelo l'shma ba l'shma*" (Learning not for its own sake will eventually lead to learning for its own sake) can be applied to high school level Jewish education. In a sense, it gives us license to find other enticements to Jewish schools besides the Jewish education offered. One recurrent theme of the studies in this volume is the importance of high standards of secular education for encouraging enrollment in Jewish schools particularly at the high school level. In those countries where parents believe that Jewish high schools compare favorably with available alternatives in regard to the secular education offered and the preparation given for college entrance exams, there is a greater continuation rate in the Jewish high school. Thus, the creation of top quality Jewish high schools ought to be given priority in communal planning. Perhaps regionally based residential prep schools could be established, offering a snob appeal that seems to be important to some groups of parents (e.g., Kelman, 1979). This would require considerable planning and investment on the part of the community.

Until now, the establishment of high schools in many places has resulted from efforts in the opposite direction. That is, small groups of parents who wanted a particular type of Jewish education for their children, usually Orthodox or ultra-Orthodox, would join together with some benefactors and establish a small school. These parents stressed a more intensive Jewish education for their children, sometimes at the expense of a good secular background. The suggestion here is that high schools be established whose main appeal would be their superior secular programs, and the Jewish studies program would be only secondary, or as some might perceive it, a necessary evil. The social problems which exist even in good suburban secular high schools today, e.g., sex, drugs, etc., might make such Jewish high schools more attractive.

International Jewish Educational Organizations

A new area of focus in the social sciences today views the world, particularly its economy, as a 'World System' (Wallerstein, 1974; 1980). The argument is that true social systems are self-contained or self-sufficient, having at least the potential for self-sufficiency, even if this is not actually practiced. The interdependence of nations today, indeed for the last 500 years, according to Wallerstein (1974), with regard to their economic functions, has created a world economic system with ramifications to the political, social, and other levels, which some scholars view as systems in their own right (Boulding, 1985).

Considering the interdependence of Jewish educational systems around the world today, particularly with regard to financial, personnel, and educational resources, it might be helpful to view Diaspora Jewish education as a type of 'World System'. Ernest Stock's article (this volume) points to the valiant efforts being made by numerous organizations to improve the quality of Jewish education in Diaspora countries. The work of the World Zionist Organization and the American Joint Distribution Committee is the most comprehensive, and the work of universities in Israel, particularly the Melton Center for Jewish Education in the Diaspora at the Hebrew University of Jerusalem, is the newest and most innovative. Yet, there are many other organizations internationally involved with Jewish education whose tasks are not well-defined, divided, or coordinated. Although these organizations seem to have reached a modus operandi that allows them all to continue with their important work and achieve significant results, Stock believes that there is considerably more room for joint effort, elimination of duplication, and general overall coordination. Groups and the individuals involved with them may be more ready to forge a coordinated body at this time than they were previously, and perhaps the lessons of previous attempts can be instructive for any new effort.

On the other hand, there are some obvious advantages to the recipients of the services of these organizations if they can apply to have their needs met at more than one address. Wallerstein (1974, p. 347) writes that the world system is "made up of the conflicting forces which hold it together by tension, and tear it apart as each group seeks eternally to remold it to its advantage." On the other hand, he points out that "prior to the modern era, world economics were highly unstable structures which tended either to be converted into empires or to disintegrate" (p. 348). Clearly, it is the realistic fear of 'imperialism' that prevents more centralized coordination of functions by Jewish educational organizations. Whether the mechanisms can be developed to reduce such tendencies is debatable. In any case, the matter deserves serious discussion, and should be placed on the agenda of Jewish education.

Research

The lack of research in the area of Jewish education around the world is astonishing. Even fairly centralized systems collect data only on enrollment and budgets. Without greater investment in basic and applied research on educational processes and problems it will be difficult to improve educational efforts. Policies should not be made in the absence of accurate information and on the basis of conjecture and personal influence. Incentives need to be created for local researchers to conduct studies which are pertinent to local systems. This could be done through an international research fund, or by making other forms of international aid contingent upon the development of local research, with valid self-evaluation included in budgets of newly funded projects.

Soviet Jewry

Much of the discussion in this overview and in the other comparative chapters of this volume have for the most part excluded consideration of Eastern European (Communist-bloc) countries, especially the Soviet Union. Jewish communities exist in such different restrictive conditions in those countries that they must be considered separately. In the Soviet Union, there is virtually no formal Jewish education. Nevertheless, the magnitude of the problem, in world terms, demands that it not be ignored. Around 12% of the Jewish school-age children of the Diaspora live in the Soviet Union. Even if only a third of them were interested in learning about their Jewish heritage, we would be talking about nearly 50,000 children – more than the number of Jewish school-age children in Australia, Brazil, South Africa, or Argentina, and close to the number in Canada (Himmelfarb and DellaPergola, 1982).

Leon Shapiro (1984) writes about an increase in Jewish cultural activities in the Soviet Union in the early 1980s – Yiddish publications, Yiddish being taught at one of the universities, Yiddish dramatical theater and music, art exhibits on Jewish themes, and occasional organized seminars dealing with Jewish subjects. In 1982, he reports, there were some 60 groups studying Hebrew. Yet, in mid–1985, press reports tell of stepped up harassment, arrests, and violence against Hebrew teachers there; and as is well known,

Jewish emigration has been cut down to a trickle for the past several years. On the other hand, at this writing, there are also press reports of Soviet initiated negotiations to restore diplomatic relations with Israel.

Given the malevolent capriciousness of Soviet policy, it seems as if there is little that world Jewry can plan to do to ameliorate the situation. Nevertheless, it is important that whatever is possible should be done. Publicity concerning the plight of Soviet Jews must become louder. Demands for their right to emigrate must increase, and educational materials must be made available to the few who dare to study and teach about their Jewish heritage. We do not know when the perspective of Soviet officials might change and they will deem it in their own best political interests to allow Jews more freedom of religion and emigration. However, through continuous cultural nourishment from outside, world Jewry can help assure that when those days come, there will be a core of Soviet Jews ready to lead and teach their brethren. Then, hopefully, the 'Jews of Silence' can be included once again in our discussion of Jewish education around the world.

Summary and Conclusions

It is the thesis of this essay, indeed this volume, that Jewish education policies must stem from a thorough understanding of the social context in which Jewish educational systems find themselves. This includes the larger society and its educational system, and the educational needs and resources of the local Jewish community. Nevertheless, some dominant social and educational trends that have been pervasive in Jewish communities worldwide can be noted.

Since the enlightenment and emanicipation, Diaspora Jews have sought various solutions to the dilemma of maintaining a separate Jewish identity while seeking full integration into the larger society. The years of Jewish emigration from Western and Eastern Europe witnessed large-scale attempts by Jews and by the institutions they founded, to first facilitate social integration, and only subsequently the maintenance of Jewish identity. In those societies where general education was nondenominational and allowed Jewish participation, Jews eagerly attended school with other children. They sought to solve their Jewish identity problems with supplementary schooling.

Where Jews were allowed to participate, and often even where that participation encountered major obstacles, they achieved quite rapid educational, occupational and economic integration and mobility. A reversal in priorities in regard to the social integration-Jewish identity dilemma has been caused by socioeconomic mobility, increased distance from the shtetl and from the ghetto generation of immigrant Jews, heightened Jewish identity and the altered structure of Jewish life resulting from the Holocaust and the establishment of the State of Israel, as well as from the post-World War II decline in antisemitism. Unfortunately, that reversal is occurring slowly and is severely hampered by the diminished richness of Jewish cultural life in general, and in particular, by dramatic changes in Jewish family life, e.g., decreased fertility and increased divorce, intermarriage, and female employment. Indeed, it has been suggested that the cultural heritage, norms and values, which are taught in Jewish education are so new to students' realities that the task might be considered one of cultural production rather than cultural reproduction. Therefore, the success of such education requires the cultivation of family and community reinforcement.

Despite the problems of the cultural milieu in which Jewish education must operate it is important to recognize that it has had some major accomplishments. Jewish schooling for females has become almost as universal as for males; the growth of the day school movement has resulted in a large percentage (in some countries, the majority) of Jewish children participating in full-time Jewish education, and the expansion of post-high school Jewish studies in yeshivoth and universities has been truly phenomenal. Some programs of informal or experiential Jewish education have proven efficacious in promoting Jewish identification, but the number of Jewish children who participate in these programs is much more limited than in formal schooling. The same can be said for adult and parent education programs – an immediate need as a large segment of the Jewish population is now in its child-rearing years.

Although the problems of Jewish education are numerous and complex, several of them seem especially important when viewed from a global perspective:

1. There is a great need to improve Jewish-subject teaching. Innovative ways of recruiting and maintaining qualified teachers must be found. These include material and social incentives such as: the creation of multi-task full-time positions, higher salaries, improved fringe benefits, (insurance, retirement, sabbaticals, etc.), job security, more opportunities for job mobility, and greater social recognition. In-service training must be encouraged, particularly at the local level where more teachers can participate. Opportunities for visiting-teacher positions (*shlihut*) can be encouraged on a world-wide basis, and must not be limited to Israeli teachers.

2. Continuation rates to secondary Jewish schools are very low. Jewish education in the Diaspora is mostly on the elementary level. Jewish educational programs should be restructured, and great efforts at all levels are needed to continue studies after bar/bat mitzvah age. Individual institutions and communal agencies should establish scholarship funds to promote post-bar and bat mitzvah school enrollment. The development of Jewish high schools (perhaps on a regional basis) with outstanding secular studies programs can also be an enrollment incentive. In addition, the channeling of

adolescents into informal Jewish education programs (e.g., youth groups, camps, Israel trips) might be helpful in providing some high school level Jewish educational experiences.

3. Jewish education in the Soviet Union must be placed high on the list of priorities. The magnitude of the problem in terms of the number of Jewish children and the almost complete lack of Jewish educational opportunities, has great significance for the Jewish people as a whole. World-wide efforts to encourage the Soviet government to open its doors to Jewish emigration need to continue, but equally vigorous efforts must be made to encourage the Soviet government to allow those citizens who remain in the USSR to receive religious and ethnic education.

4. The establishment of the State of Israel has created a center for world Judaism. The technological changes in travel and communication have created more opportunities for international cooperation and exchange. We live in a world of interdependence and this has affected the organizational and fund-raising activities of Jewish communities. Thus, despite differences in local needs, we can identify problems of universal concern, and perhaps solutions that have the potential for fairly universal application. Therefore, it is time for greater coordination among those organizations involved in international Jewish educational activities.

5. Finally, there is a universal need for scientific research on Jewish education. If we are to improve Jewish education, policies must be based on accurate information. School systems must be encouraged to experiment with new ideas to further Jewish education, but they must also scientifically document and evaluate what they have done so that others can benefit from these innovations.

> Not logic alone, but logic supplemented by the social
> sciences becomes the instrument of advance.
>
> (Benjamin N. Cardozo, *Growth of the Law*, 1924)

Acknowledgements

The author wishes to gratefully acknowledge funds received for travel and student assistance from the Melton Center for Jewish Studies at The Ohio State University in support of the research for this article. He also wishes to express his gratitude to Sabine Himmelfarb for editorial comments on this manuscript.

References

Ackerman, W.I. (1969). "Jewish Education for What?" *American Jewish Year Book*, Vol. 70. pp. 3–36.

Adar, Z. (1977). *Jewish Education in Israel and in the United States.* Hamakor Press, Jerusalem.

Aviad, J. (1983). *Return to Judaism: Religious Renewal in Israel.* University of Chicago Press, Chicago.

Bensimon, D. and DellaPergola, S. (1984). *La population juive de France: socio-démographie et identité.* Institute of Contemporary Jewry, The Hebrew University, Jerusalem and Centre National de la Recherche Scientifique, Paris. (Jewish Population Studies, no. 17). 436 pp.

Boulding, K.E. (1985). *The World as a Total System.* Sage, Beverly Hills.

Chanover, H. (1967). "Israelis Teaching in American Jewish Schools: Findings of an Exploratory Survey" in: Janowsky, O.F. (ed.). *The Education of American Teachers.* Beacon Press, Boston.

Cohen, S.M. (1974). "The Impact of Jewish Education on Religious Identification and Practice". *Jewish Social Studies*, Vol. 36, no. 3/4. pp. 316–326.

Davis, M. (1975). "Jewish Studies in Universities: Alternate Approaches in Different Parts of the World." *Forum*, Vol. 23, Spring. pp. 83–96.

Davis, M. (1986). "On University Teaching of Contemporary Jewish Civilization". *Judaism*, Vol. 35, no. 2. pp. 170–182.

DellaPergola, S. (1976). "Demographic Perspectives of Mixed Marriage". *Encyclopaedia Judaica Yearbook, 1976.* Keter, Jerusalem.

DellaPergola, S. (1983). "Contemporary Jewish Fertility: An Overview" in: Schmelz, U.O., Glikson, P. and DellaPergola, S. (eds.). *Papers in Jewish Demography 1981.* Institute of Contemporary Jewry, The Hebrew University, Jerusalem. (Jewish Population Studies , No. 16). pp. 215–238.

DellaPergola, S. and Genuth, N. (1983). *Jewish Education Attained in Diaspora Communities: Data for 1970s.* Institute of Contemporary Jewry, The Hebrew University , Jerusalem. (Project for Jewish Educational Statistics, Research Report No. 2). 74 pp.

Dubb, A. (1984). "First International Census of Jewish Schools in the Diaspora". Paper presented at the International Research Conference on Jewish Education. The Hebrew University, Jerusalem.

Dushkin, A.M. (1918). *Jewish Education in New York City.* Department of Research, Bureau of Jewish Education, New York.

Edidin, B.M. (1929). "Elimination in Chicago Schools". *Jewish Education*, Vol. 1. pp. 118–120.

Elazar, D.J. and Cohen, S.A. (1985). *The Jewish Polity: Jewish Political Organization from Biblical Times to the Present.* Indiana University Press, Bloomington.

Gartner, L.P. (1969). *Jewish Education in the United States: A Documentary History.* Teacher's College Press, New York.

Gartner, L.P. (1984). *The Great Jewish Migration 1881–1914: Myths and Realities.* Kaplan Center Papers, University of Cape Town.

Genuth, N., DellaPergola, S. and Dubb, A.A. (1985). *First Census of Jewish Schools in the Diaspora 1981/2–1982/3: International Summary.* Institute of Contemporary Jewry, The Hebrew University, Jerusalem. (Project for Jewish Educational Statistics, Research Report No. 3). 138 pp.

Goldmeier, H. (1975). *An Evaluation of the Parent Education Program of the United Synagogue of Three Sites in New England.* Unpublished Ph.D. dissertation, Harvard University, Cambridge.

Goldscheider, C. and Zuckerman, A.S. (1984). *The Transformation of the Jews.* University of Chicago Press, Chicago.

Heilman, C. (1983). *The People of the Book: Drama, Fellowship, and Religion.* University of Press, Chicago.

Helmreich, W. (1982). *The World of the Yeshiva: An Intimate Portrait of Orthodox Jewry.* Free Press, New York.

Himmelfarb, H.S. (1974). *The Impact of Religious Schooling: The Effects of Jewish Education Upon Adult Religious Involvement.* Unpublished Ph.D. dissertation, University of Chicago.

Himmelfarb, H.S. (1985). "The Effects of Informal Jewish Education on Jewish Identification". Paper presented at the Ninth World Congress of Jewish Studies, Jerusalem.

Himmelfarb, H.S. and DellaPergola, S. (1982). *Enrollment in Jewish Schools in the Diaspora, Late 1970s.* Institute of Contemporary Jewry, The Hebrew University, Jerusalem. (Project for Jewish Educational Statistics, Research Report No. 1). 97 pp.

Himmelfarb, H.S. and Loar, R.M. (1984). "National Trends in Jewish Ethnicity". *Journal for the Scientific Study of Religion,* Vol. 23, no. 2. pp. 140–154.

Jacoby, E. (1970). *Continuation and Dropout in Conservative Congregational Schools.* Bureau of Jewish Education, Los Angeles.

Johnson, G.E. (1976). "The Impact of Family Formation Patterns on Jewish Community Involvement". *Analysis,* no. 60. Institute for Jewish Policy Planning and Research, Washington, D.C.

Katz, J. (1971). *Tradition and Crisis: Jewish Society at the End of the Middle Ages.* Schocken, New York.

Kelman, S.L. (1979). "Parent Motivations for Enrolling a Child in a Non-Orthodox Jewish Day School". *Jewish Education,* Vol. 47, no. 1. pp. 44–48.

Kovacs, M.L. (1977). *The Dynamics of Commitment: The Process of Resocialization of Ba'alei Teshuva, Jewish Students in Pursuit of their Jewish Identity, at the Rabbinical College of America.* Unpublished Ph.D. dissertation, Union Graduate School-Midwest.

Levine, A.M. (1978). *Influence of Different Cultural Backgrounds on Teacher-Pupil Interaction and Teacher Attitudes of Israeli and American Teachers in Jewish Education*. Unpublished Ph.D. dissertation, University of Southern California, Los Angeles.

Liebman, C.S. (1973). *The Ambivalent American Jew: Politics, Religion, and Family in American Jewish Life*. The Jewish Publication Society of America, Philadelphia.

Lortie, D.C. (1975). *School Teacher: A Sociological Study*. University of Chicago Press, Chicago.

Parelius, A.P. and Parelius, R.J. (1978). *The Sociology of Education*. Prentice-Hill, Englewood Cliffs, N.J.

Rose, I.B. (1974). *A Clientele Analysis of Participants in Synagogue Adult Jewish Education*. Unpublished Ed.D. dissertation, Columbia University, New York.

Sachar, H.M. (1985). *Diaspora*. Harper and Row, New York.

Sanua, V.D. (1964). "The Relationship Between Jewish Education and Jewish Identification". *Jewish Education*, Vol. 35. pp. 37–50.

Schmelz, U.O. (1981). "Jewish Survival: The Demographic Factors". *American Jewish Year Book*, Vol. 81. pp. 61–120.

Schmelz, U.O. and DellaPergola, S. (1983). "The Demographic Consequences of U.S. Jewish Population Trends". *American Jewish Year Book*, Vol. 83. pp. 141–187.

Schiff, A.I. (1983). "On the Status of All-Day Jewish Education". *Jewish Education*, Vol. 51. pp. 2–7.

Selig, S. (1972). *Profiling Withdrawals from a Jewish Supplementary School*. Unpublished Ed.D. dissertation, Wayne State University, Detroit.

Shapiro, L. (1984). "Soviet Union". *American Jewish Year Book*,Vol. 84. pp. 212–223.

Sharot, S. (1976). *Judaism: A Sociology*. Holmes and Meier, New York.

Wallerstein, I. (1974). *The Modern World-System I: Capitalist Agriculture and the Origins of the European World Economy in the Sixteenth Century*. Academic Press, New York.

Wallerstein, I. (1980). *The Modern World-System II: Mercantilism and the Consolidation of the European and World-Economy, 1600–1750*. Academic Press, New York.

Yankelovich, Skelly and White, Inc. (1981). *Anti-Semitism in the United States*. American Jewish Committee, New York.

2

Demography and Jewish Education in the Diaspora: Trends in Jewish School-Age Population and School Enrollment

Sergio DellaPergola and Uziel O. Schmelz

Jews constitute only a small minority of the total population in all countries besides Israel. The future size of these Jewish populations depends on the overall balance of natural increase and migrations on the one hand, and on the ability to retain group identity on the other. Identity affects the demographic dynamics of a minority in that it is the cohesive power of the group, and thus a causative factor in passages between it and the majority or other minority groups.

At present, Diaspora Jewry faces demographic erosion (Bachi, 1982). The total Jewish Diaspora population is decreasing, though trends are modified by the specific conditions in each country. Low fertility rates and increased aging have combined to reduce natural growth of the Diaspora population, and have actually created a natural deficit with deaths outnumbering births. Since aliyah has reached low levels in the early 1980s, and *yeridah* is numerically insignificant relative to the total Diaspora population, the net balance between those who come to Israel and those who leave is of little consequence to Jewish population size in the Diaspora. Losses due to assimilation have a more significant effect.

Assimilation among Diaspora Jews reflects socio-cultural change - especially secularization – among the majority population of a country, as well as identificational changes within the Jewish minority. Demographic losses due to assimilation are the terminal stage in the process of weakening Jewish identity at the periphery of the Jewish community. Recent socio-demographic studies support the common impression that an identity crisis is affecting significant segments of Diaspora Jewry. Cases of secession are generally more widespread than conversions to Judaism, whether formal or informal.

Jewish education is perceived by many as an important means of strengthening Jewish identity in the longer run. Jewish educational institutions, together with other agents, especially the Jewish family, are expected to impart Jewish knowledge and values to children. Awareness of the importance of these values may later affect the behavior of Jewish adults in such matters as religious observance, the ties to the Jewish community, the choice of a marital partner from within or without the Jewish group, the religion of the offspring, and whether or not the latter will be given a Jewish education.

Jewish education is an investment whose dividends become payable only when the child that was thus educated reaches adulthood and his/her decision-making processes become part of the input to the equation of Jewish population changes.

The Demographic Background of Jewish School Enrollment

Educational systems generally – and Jewish education in the Diaspora in particular – do not operate in a societal vacuum. Rather, they are intended to fulfill certain basic socialization needs of society on the whole or, as in the case of Jewish schools, of a specific ethno-religious group. The study of educational systems, then, besides merely describing the various facets of the educational function, should be able to relate these systems to other relevant characteristics of the populations and societies concerned.

In the field of educational research, important information is provided by data on enrollment. Growth, stability, or decline in the numbers of school-going children may reflect significant changes within the educational system, or within the broader society. This is particularly true of Jewish school enrollment in the Diaspora, which can be viewed not only as an indicator of trends in schooling but also more generally, of group vitality.

Over the last few decades, Jewish school enrollment in many Diaspora communities has undergone significant changes, both upward and downward. Perhaps the most impressive example is that provided by the United States, where Jewish enrollment in day and supplementary schools was estimated at 231,000 in 1945/46, 488,000 in 1955/56, 589,000 in 1961/62, 554,000 in 1966/67, 457,000 in 1970/71, 392,000 in 1974/75, 357,000 in 1978/79, and 372,000 in 1981/82–1982/83 (Pollak and Lang, 1979; Dubb and DellaPergola, 1986). Quantitative shifts like these have often been interpreted at their face value, as symptoms of the changing power of attraction of the Jewish educational system in the country concerned.

To be properly interpreted, however, enrollment data should be examined together with information on the size and age structure of the school-age population. Variations in school-enrollment in a certain country or locality over the years, or between different countries and localities, at the same time, actually depend on corresponding variations in the school-age population – and thus on a number of different demographic factors, such as changes in the birth rate, and international or internal migrations. Generally, only limited and unsystematic attention has been given to the underlying demographic factors which shape the Jewish school-age population, modifying its size and structure.

The instability of the number of Jewish children hampers serious management and planning of Jewish education. Certainly, those deciding on the building of schools or the recruitment and training of teachers should be informed of the long- and short-range demographic trends among their respective Jewish population.

Effects of Migration

In certain Western countries – most notably France during the 1950s and early 1960s – immigration, substantially expanded the demographic base of Jewish education. Other countries which absorbed some inflow of Jewish migrants include the United States, Canada, Australia, Brazil and a few other smaller communities in Western Europe (such as Italy, Germany, and Spain) and Latin America (such as Venezuela). On the other hand, the international migration balance was strongly negative for the Jewish communities of the Muslim countries, Eastern Europe (when Jewish emigration was permitted), and several countries in Latin America, such as Argentina, Uruguay and Chile. Anglo-Jewry, too, lost through emigration more than it gained through immigration. In these countries, migrations tended to cause a shrinking of the Jewish school-age population.

On the local level, where most management and planning of Jewish education takes place, instability in the size of the school-age population is also caused by the substantial extent of Jewish residential mobility, both within and between cities and metropolitan areas – in the latter case, particularly the movement to suburbia and between its various segments. Nor is the effect of this mobility uniform at the places of departure and destination. If a family leaves a particular city or neighborhood, this generally causes immediate withdrawal of the children from the schools there. On the other hand, social integration of the family in its new neighborhood may be slow, thus delaying the enrollment of children in Jewish educational frameworks. This is true especially in the United States where most Jewish education is supplementary and, therefore, optional.

The consequences of residential mobility should also be examined at the institutional level. A growing Jewish population tends to stimulate the need for new schools in neighborhoods that previously may have had none; declining neighborhoods may experience consolidation of old denominational schools into interdenominational ones. Enrollment in existing schools may be affected by differences in accessibility from recently developed outlying areas. Mobility may therefore generate a variety of consequences for both enrollment levels and institutional set-up in a Jewish educational system.

Effects of Changing Fertility Levels

More complex and perhaps even less clearly understood in the Jewish community has been the effect of changing fertility levels and birth rates on the actual number of Jewish children. Rapid changes are occurring in the number of Jewish children of kindergarten or school age in the Diaspora. While the basic trend is one of decline in numbers, temporary increases do occur. At any given period, fluctuations in both directions unevenly influence the different age groups among school children. The situation is therefore both complex and unstable.

Under the present conditions of low mortality, the number of children currently of a given age depends mainly on the initial size of the appropriate birth cohort, that is, on the number of children born in a certain year who have now reached the age under consideration. The number of Jewish children of given age depends more particularly on the number of 'effectively Jewish' born, that is, excluding those children born to a Jewish parent who are themselves not Jewish – mainly the offspring of mixed marriages.

The number of 'effectively Jewish' births is determined by three factors:
- the size of the Jewish population in recent decades. Jewish population size has been influenced not only by the small natural increase in most Diaspora communities,[1] but also by the Holocaust and by major migrations, particularly immigration to Israel;
- the relative frequency of women of childbearing age within the Jewish population, which is subject to modifications due to changes in the age composition of the Jewish population;
- the 'effectively Jewish' fertility, which is in turn affected by the marriage rates within the Jewish population and by the frequency of mixed marriages.

The major trends in Jewish fertility in the Diaspora over the last decades can be summarized as follows (DellaPergola, 1980; DellaPergola, 1983; Schmelz, 1981a). The economic and political crises of the 1930s were followed by the outbreak of World War II. The prevailing conditions caused a great decrease in the fertility of the general population and an even greater decline among Jews. Soon after the conclusion of the war, a temporary increase of both fertility and birth rates (the 'baby boom') occurred in developed countries; in the United States it continued until the end of the 1950s. The Jews participated in the increased fertility and birth rate; however, they did so at lower levels and for a shorter time than the general populations in their countries of residence. During the first stage of the 'baby boom', relatively large numbers of women were in the main ages of reproduction, having themselves been born prior to the decline of the birth rate in the 1930s.

Subsequent to the 'baby boom', fertility declined sharply among the populations in developed countries. In the United States, this decline began in the early 1960s and lasted into the 1970s. As a result, fertility dropped below replacement level – i.e., the level necessary to ensure long-term maintenance of population size, based on natural increase alone and regardless of international migrations. Taking into account very low death rates, the average number of children per woman required to achieve inter-generational replacement is approximately 2.1.[2] Among Diaspora Jews, fertility dropped to especially low levels. By the second half of the 1960s, the number of Jewish births was declining year by year throughout the whole Diaspora. Fertility levels continued to decline until the later 1970s, probably stabilizing in recent years at very low levels.

Until nearly the end of the 1960s, the reduction of fertility was reinforced by a low number of women in the reproductive ages, since these women belonged to the small birth cohorts of the 1930s and early 1940s. At the end of the 1960s, the large birth cohorts of the 'baby boom' (around 1950) started entering their reproductive ages. An upward 'echo' effect could thus be expected in the Jewish birth rate, gradually gaining momentum and reaching its peak toward the end of the 1970s and the beginning of the 1980s. But the actual impact of these shifts in the Jewish age structure seems to have been quite limited, due to the more recent developments in Jewish marriage patterns. These involve less frequent and later marriages, increased rates of divorce, and higher proportions of mixed marriages. Mixed marriage in turn has been proven a factor of erosion in the Jewish birth rate for two complementary reasons: the overall lower fertility of mixed couples as compared to that of homogamous Jewish couples; and the predominant pattern of raising less than one half of the children of mixed couples as Jews[3] (Schmelz and DellaPergola, 1983; Bensimon and DellaPergola, 1984).

The trends now briefly sketched do not only apply to Jews in the Diaspora, but derive from the broader demographic transformation of Western societies. Peculiar to Jews, though, have been fertility rates lower than those observed in the total populations of the respective countries and an often more rapid, sharper response to the determinants of upward or downward twists in the general course of fertility levels. Hence, variations in the size of consecutive age groups, and changes in the overall school-age population in successive years, may have been relatively greater for the Jewish than for the general population of the same countries or localities.

Changing Size of Jewish School-Age Population

This process is reflected in Table 1, which presents estimates and projections regarding the widespread changes that occurred or can be expected to occur in the numbers of Jewish school-age children over the period 1965–2000.

TABLE 1. NUMBER OF DIASPORA JEWISH CHILDREN AGED 3 TO 17 –
ESTIMATES AND PROJECTIONS, 1965–2000[a]

Year	Total 3–17	3–5	6–11	12–17
Absolute Numbers				
1965	2,048,000	360,000	872,000	816,000
1975	1,524,000	231,000	533,000	760,000
1985	1,228,000	251,000	502,000	475,000
2000 Projections				
Medium	1,079,000	173,000	405,000	501,000
Low	950,000	145,000	353,000	452,000
High	1,317,000	235,000	509,000	573,000
Indices (1965 = 100)				
1965	100	100	100	100
1975	74	64	61	93
1985	59	69	57	58
2000 Projections				
Medium	52	48	46	61
Low	46	40	40	55
High	64	65	58	70
Indices (prior date = 100)				
1975 (1965 = 100)	74	64	61	93
1985 (1975 = 100)	81	109	94	62
2000 Projections (1985 = 100)				
Medium	88	69	81	105
Low	77	58	70	95
High	107	94	101	121

(a) Except Eastern Europe. For method and assumptions, see: Schmelz (1981b, 1983a, 1984).

The table applies to all Diaspora communities with the exception of Eastern Europe where, for all intents and purposes, formal Jewish education does not exist. 1965 was chosen as base year because by then the mass migrations of Jews, characteristic of the post-Holocaust period and the founding of the State of Israel, had been completed. The exception is the emigration of a quarter of a million Jews from the USSR during the 1970s. However, neither the USSR nor Israel, to which most of the mass emigrants came, are included in the table. Furthermore, in 1965 the number of Jewish children between the ages of 3 and 17 was at a high level, since that year was still close to the end of the extended 'baby boom' among the large Jewish population of the United States.

Clearly, the data for all Diaspora communities are only rough estimates due to quantitative and qualitative flaws in the available demographic documentation. Furthermore, it is evident that demographic projections are not prophecies, but quantitative predictions of the future development which a specific population may undergo given certain assumptions. As a precautionary measure and also in order to give the reader an idea of the reasonable scope of variation, projections are presented in Table 1 in three versions: high, medium, and low. The projections presented here for the school-age population in the whole of the Diaspora (with the exception of Eastern Europe) constitute a partial summary of regional projections prepared for all age groups of the Jewish populations in nine separate geographical regions.[4]

The number of Jewish school-age children (3–17) has fallen from the high levels around 1965, and there are no indications that the figures will return to this level or to anything near it in the future, even according to the high projection. This trend is very clearly seen in the middle section of Table 1, where all indices from 1975 onwards are lower than the base of 100 for 1965, and in the majority of cases much lower.

Despite the basic trend of decline in the school-age population, limited temporary increases in the number of Jewish children may occur. These are reflected by some indices over 100 in the bottom part of Table 1. The reasons for such temporary increases are as follows:
– the 1980s 'echo effect' of the 1950s 'baby boom' as explained above;
– a significant future increase in the fertility levels of the Jewish population, as assumed in the high projection.

At any rate, the total number of Jewish children in the Diaspora between the ages of 3 and 17 is much lower in the 1980s than it was in the 1960s or even in the 1970s.

However, it must be noted that the total number of 3 to 17 year olds is comprised of 15 separate birth cohorts and that considerable changes can take place in the Jewish birth rate over a 15 year period. In Table 1, the totals for the age aggregate 3 to 17 have been divided into ages 3 to 5, 6 to 11, and 12 to 17. Different patterns of change appear for each of these age groups relative to its size in 1965 or in the other years presented in the table. Such differences result from the fact that each age group is occupied by different birth cohorts at any given time.[5] For example:

-   from 1965 to 1975 there was no considerable drop in the number of 12–17 year olds, because even at the later date this age group still included the birth cohorts of the postwar 'baby boom'. In contrast, the 3–11 year olds reflected the sharp drop in the birth rate subsequent to the 'baby boom';
-   from 1975 to 1985, the sharp drop in the birth rate reaches its broadest representation among the older school-going children (those 12–17 years old), whereas some rise may have occurred among the young age group of 3–5 year olds, due to the 'echo effect' of the 'baby boom';
-   from 1985 to the year 2000 a further decrease in the birth rate can be expected to reduce the number of the 3–11 year olds, except for the 6–11 year olds according to the high projection. However, the number of 12–17 year olds will increase – slightly according to the medium projection and markedly according to the high projection – since some of the relatively large birth cohorts of the 'echo effect' will still be included in this age group at the end of this century.

Therefore, even within the 3 to 17 age aggregate certain sub-groups may increase, while others may decrease concurrently.

Future Perspectives

It is worth noting again that the projections for year 2000 point to alternative levels of the school age population according to the assumptions that underlie each version of the projection – high, medium, or low. Currently, at least two main schools of thought exist among demographers with regard to the expected fertility levels of the general populations of developed countries in the near future. The one contends that low fertility will continue to be a permanent factor in these countries, in consequence of socio-economic and socio-cultural factors that have weakened the position of the family in Western societies (Westoff, 1978). The other school of thought maintains that the favorable labor-market position of smaller cohorts of young adults – a consequence of the low birth rates of the late 1960s and 1970s – could entail a rise in wages, thus stimulating family formation and triggering a greater demand for children (Easterlin, 1978).

In any case, the number of women in the major reproductive ages will be reduced toward the end of the century, since by then most of these will belong to the small birth cohorts born between the 'baby boom' and its 'echo effect' as mentioned above. A reduction in the number of potential mothers must necessarily cause a relative decline in the birth rate for any given level of fertility.

In light of empirical observations made over the past several generations, we may expect that fertility among Diaspora Jewry will continue to be lower than that of the general populations of their countries of residence. This is the result of the fact that Jews have tended to display both a socio-demographic stratification – in terms of educational attainment, and female labor force participation – and a set of attitudes and behaviors, especially with regard to family planning, which are generally consonant with low fertility. Moreover, continuation of high rates of mixed marriage in Diaspora communities may be expected to cause some losses in intergenerational replacement of the Jews, since the 'effectively Jewish' birth rate is lower than that for all Jewish women.[6]

The Jewish School-Age Population in 1982

The total size of the Diaspora Jewish school-age population (3–17) is detailed in Table 2 with regard to each of the major regions and countries.[7] In 1982, the total Diaspora school-age population was estimated to range between 1,349,000 and 1,465,000. Without Eastern Europe and other countries not covered by our enrollment data the total Jewish school-age population ranged between 1,216,000 and 1,318,000. About 65% of all Diaspora Jewish children lived in the United States.

The presentation of estimates of Jewish school-age population in the form of ranges reflects a margin of uncertainty which, however, does not affect the basic orders of magnitude of the age-group considered. In Table 2 we allowed for a margin of error of plus/minus 5% around the most reliable estimate of Jewish school-age population in each country or region. With regard to the United States, estimates for the total country (Schmelz and DellaPergola, 1983) and for the Greater New York area (Ritterband and Cohen, 1984) were used to compute the figures for the rest of the country.

It should be noted that the school-age group constitutes a variable proportion of the total Jewish population in different countries. This variation contradicts the conventional assumption put forward in the past by some analysts of Jewish education in the Diaspora that the school-age population constitutes 20% of the total Jewish population (World Zionist Organization, 1971). Even if this assumption may have been true at a certain time in the past for specific Jewish populations in the Diaspora, it is no longer supported by the contemporary experience, apart from sporadic exceptions.

The percentages of school-age children among the total Jewish populations are presented in Table 2 as ranges of approximately one percentage point plus/minus our best estimate. Taking together the countries covered by the census of Jewish schools, the 3 to 17 age group constituted between 15% and 17% of the total Jewish population in the early 1980s. These percentages are quite low – compared to the corresponding non-Jewish populations – and reflect the continuation of low Jewish birth rates and a marked process of aging throughout the Diaspora. Yet, the picture is not identical everywhere, as a consequence

TABLE 2.   TOTAL JEWISH POPULATION AND JEWISH CHILDREN AGED
3 TO 17, BY COUNTRY - ESTIMATED RANGES, 1982

Country	Total Jewish Population[a]	Jewish Children Aged 3 to 17	
		Number[b]	% of Total Jewish Population
Total Diaspora	9,614,000	1,349,000–1,465,000	14.0–16.0
Total Diaspora, without Eastern Europe and other countries not incl. in the census	7,817,000	1,216,000–1,318,000	15.0–17.0
United States	5,705,000	880,000– 950,000	5.0–17.0
thereof:			
New York	1,671,000	270,000– 290,000	16.0–18.0
Other	4,034,000	610,000– 660,000	15.0–17.0
Canada	308,000	53,000– 57,000	16.5–18.5
France	530,000	78,000– 86,000	14.5–16.5
United Kingdom[c]	352,000	52,000– 57,000	14.5–16.5
Other Western Europe[d]	194,000	28,000– 31,000	14.0–16.0
Argentina	233,000	32,000– 35,000	14.0–16.0
Brazil	100,000	20,000– 22,000	20.0–22.0
Other Latin America[e]	132,000	21,000– 23,000	15.5–17.5
South Africa[f]	120,000	22,000– 24,000	18.0–20.0
Australia[g]	79,000	14,000– 16,000	18.0–20.0
Muslim Countries[h]	64,000	16,000– 17,000	25.0–27.0

(a)   Adjusted from: Schmelz and DellaPergola (1984).
(b)   Estimates and projections of Jewish school-age population prepared by Division of Jewish Demography and Statistics, Institute of Contemporary Jewry, The Hebrew University of Jerusalem.
(c)   Includes Ireland.
(d)   Austria, Belgium, Denmark, Finland, West Germany, Gibraltar, Greece, Italy, The Netherlands, Norway, Spain, Sweden, Switzerland.
(e)   Bolivia, Chile, Columbia, Costa Rica, Ecuador, Mexico, Panama, Paraguay, Peru, Uruguay, Venezuela.
(f)   Includes Zimbabwe.
(g)   Includes New Zealand.
(h)   Iran, Morocco, Tunisia.

of the regional variations in migration patterns and of some differentials in the timing and rhythm of recent fertility reductions. Available data and estimates point to higher proportions of Jewish children in the small communities extant in the Muslim countries; percentages somewhat above the total Diaspora average appear in Brazil, South Africa and Australia. The lowest proportions of Jewish children in the regions studied here have been estimated for the Western European countries and Argentina; they are even lower in Eastern Europe.

Major Patterns of Jewish School Enrollment

The balance of this paper discusses trends and characteristics of Jewish school enrollment in the Diaspora, based on the First Census of Jewish Schools carried out in 1981/82–1982/83. The Census is the most important – and complex – research task accomplished since the establishment of the Project for Jewish Educational Statistics in the Diaspora at the Institute of Contemporary Jewry of The Hebrew University of Jerusalem. The project functions on behalf of the Joint Program for Jewish Education of the Israel Ministry of Education and Culture, the Jewish Agency, and the World Zionist Organization.

The census of Jewish schools in the Diaspora covered about 3,550 educational institutions – day schools and supplementary schools – in 40 countries, with about 550,000 pupils and 40,000–45,000 teachers (Genuth, DellaPergola and Dubb, 1985). Table 3 shows the distribution of pupils between the two main types of formal Jewish education: day schools (including yeshivoth as well as independent kindergartens), where both general and Jewish subjects are taught; and supplementary schools - hadarim, Talmudei Torah, Sunday and afternoon schools – for Jewish studies, as a complement to the general studies taught in other educational institutions. We divided the Diaspora into 11 geographical regions, each consisting of one or more countries. The United States was divided into two regions: Greater New York and the rest of the country.

The number of pupils in the various regions differs widely, and so does the distribution of these pupils between the two types of schools. Mention should be made of the dominance of the United States in the Diaspora as a whole: it accounts for almost half of all day school pupils, and for 85% of all supplementary school pupils. The United States is the only country where the vast majority of the pupils receiving a Jewish education attend supplementary schools. In all the other countries surveyed, most of the pupils in Jewish schools are in day schools; this majority fluctuates between 51% in Britain and 98% in the Latin American countries other than Argentina. Actually, in the Greater New York area most of the pupils in the Jewish education system do attend day schools, so that the exceptional region is the rest of the United States (i.e. without New York). But since this region accounts for about 50% of all pupils in Jewish schools in the Diaspora, it has tremendous influence in

TABLE 3.   PUPILS IN JEWISH SCHOOLS IN THE DIASPORA, BY TYPE OF
SCHOOL AND COUNTRY – 1981/82–1982/83

Country[a]	Total	Day Schools[b]	Supplementary Schools
	Absolute Numbers		
Total Diaspora[c]	544,595	231,828	312,767
United States	372,417	104,752	267,665
thereof: New York	99,515	53,737	45,778
Other	272,902	51,015	221,887
Canada	26,627	16,679	9,948
France	20,664	12,638	8,026
United Kingdom	30,248	15,346	14,902
Other Western Europe	11,276	8,040	3,236
Argentina	21,371	17,997[d]	3,374
Brazil	10,705	10,449	256
Other Latin America	16,881	16,551	330
South Africa[e]	15,658	13,398	2,260
Australia	9,789	7,268	2,521
Muslim Countries[f]	8,959	8,710	249
	Percentages		
Total Diaspora[c]	100	43	57
United States	100	28	72
thereof: New York	100	54	46
Other	100	19	81
Canada	100	63	37
France	100	61	39
United Kingdom	100	51	49
Other Western Europe	100	71	29
Argentina	100	84[d]	16
Brazil	100	98	2
Other Latin America	100	98	2
South Africa[e]	100	86	14
Australia	100	74	26
Muslim Countries[f]	100	97	3

(a)   See notes (c)-(h) to Table 2.
(b)   Including kindergartens not attached to a day or supplementary school.
(c)   Without Eastern Europe and other countries not included in the census. Including about 7,200
non-Jewish pupils, thereof approximately 900 in the United States.
(d)   Including schools offering both day and supplementary programs.
(e)   Including non-Jewish pupils in Jewish nursery schools.
(f)   Underestimated, especially for supplementary schools.
Source: First Census of Jewish Schools, 1981/82–1982/83.

determining the overall statistics of Jewish schools and of their pupils in the Diaspora.

Types of Enrollment Rates

Before we turn to the recent evidence on Jewish school enrollment rates, as revealed by the 1981/82–1982/83 Census of Jewish schools, a basic conceptual distinction should be mentioned. There exist two different and complementary approaches to measuring the relative frequency of Jewish education. The first consists of the current enrollment rates observed during a given school year, i.e. the number of pupils enrolled in a given year divided by the total number of school-age children at that time. The other approach relates to the cumulative exposure to Jewish education experienced during the lifetime of a certain individual or group of individuals. It indicates the proportion of a given child population that ever receives any education in a Jewish school. Obviously, the latter measure refers to a larger number of individuals and a higher percentage of the relevant population, since it includes:
– those who are currently receiving some Jewish education;
– those who received a Jewish education in the past but are no longer enrolled at the time of observation; and
– those who, at the time of observation, have not yet received any Jewish education but will receive some at a later age.

Since the data to be reported here are based on a survey of Jewish education in the Diaspora during a particular school year, the enrollment rates discussed below belong to the more limited, current type. Nevertheless, as we shall see, some inferences can be made, based on the same data, concerning the proportion of contemporary Jewish children who have received or will ever receive some Jewish education.

Current Jewish School Enrollment Rates

Current Jewish school enrollment rates can be computed by dividing the data on the number of Jewish pupils presented in Table 3 by the estimates of Jewish school-age population presented in Table 2. The percent ranges in Table 4 reflect the ranges of the estimated Jewish school-age populations in the various countries. Around 1982, about 36–40% of all Jewish children in the Diaspora aged 3 to 17 studied in a Jewish school. If we exclude Eastern Europe and other countries in which the census was not carried out, the enrollment rate rises to 40–44%.

Regional variations in the percentage of Jewish children currently enrolled in Jewish schools are significant. The highest enrollment rates were computed

for the aggregate of smaller Jewish communities in Latin America (69–73%).
These were followed by South Africa, Australia and Argentina (62–66%), the
United Kingdom (53–57%), Canada and Brazil (47–51%), the United States
(39–43%), the Muslim Countries (38–42%),[8] and the smaller Jewish communities in Western Europe (36–40%). Of the major communities, France, with an
enrollment of 22–26%, had the lowest proportion of Jewish children currently
receiving a Jewish education.

TABLE 4.   CURRENT ENROLLMENT RATES IN JEWISH SCHOOLS[a] PER 100
JEWISH CHILDREN AGED 3 TO 17, BY TYPE OF SCHOOL AND
COUNTRY – ESTIMATED RANGES, 1981/82–1982/83

Country[b]	Total	Day Schools[c]	Supplementary Schools
Total Diaspora	36–40	15–17	21–23
Total Diaspora, without Eastern Europe and other countries not incl. in the census	40–44	17–19	23–25
United States thereof:	39–43	11–13	28–30
New York	34–38	18–20	16–18
Other	41–45	7– 9	34–36
Canada	47–51	30–32	17–19
France	22–26	14–16	8–10
United Kingdom	53–57	27–29	26–28
Other Western Europe	36–40	26–28	10–12
Argentina	62–66	53–55[d]	9–11
Brazil	47–51	46–50	1
Other Latin America	69–73	68–72	1
South Africa[e]	62–66	52–54	10–12
Australia	62–66	47–49	15–17
Muslim Countries[f]	38–42	37–39	1– 3

(a)   Estimates of Jewish school-age population prepared by Division of Jewish Demography and
Statistics, Institute of Contemporary Jewry, The Hebrew University of Jerusalem.
(b)   See notes (c)–(h) to Table 2.
(c)   Including kindergartens not attached to a day or supplementary school.
(d)   Including schools offering both day and supplementary programs.
(e)   Including non-Jewish pupils in Jewish nursery schools.
(f)   Underestimated, especially for supplementary schools.

Source: First Census of Jewish Schools, 1981/82–1982/83.

The significant difference in Jewish school enrollment between the New York area (34–38%) and the rest of the United States (41–45%) is worth noting. The lower New York rate is consistent with the expectation that high Jewish population densities in some neighborhoods make the composition of many public schools distinctly Jewish. This may render the need for separate Jewish schooling less felt in the New York area than elsewhere in the United States.

If enrollment rates are considered separately for the two major types of Jewish education – day schools and supplementary schools – very different regional patterns emerge. In the Southern Hemisphere (most of Latin America, South Africa, Australia) between two-thirds and one-half of the Jewish school-age population currently attend Jewish day schools. This proportion declines to between one-third and one-fourth in Canada, the United Kingdom and the smaller communities of Western Europe; and further down to between one-sixth to one-eighth in France and in the United States. The United States day school enrollment rate is an average of quite different figures for the New York area (18–20%) and the rest of the country (7–9%). On the whole, 17–19% of all Jewish children in the Diaspora aged 3 to 17 were enrolled in Jewish day schools (excluding Eastern Europe) around 1982.

The total enrollment rate for supplementary Jewish education in the Diaspora (excluding Eastern Europe) was estimated at 23–25% of the relevant age group. The highest regional enrollment rate appears in the United States outside the New York area (34–36%). This corresponds to twice the rate in New York (16–18%). The total supplementary school enrollment rate for the United

TABLE 5.   ENROLLMENT OF JEWISH CHILDREN AGED 3 TO 17 IN JEWISH SCHOOLS IN THE UNITED STATES – 1961/62 TO 1981/82–1982/83

Year	Absolute Numbers		Indices (1966=100)		Enrollment Rates
	Jewish Children	Pupils	Jewish Children	Pupils	per 100 Jewish Children
1961/62		559,000			
1966/67	1,539,000	554,000	100	100	36
1970/71	1,383,000	457,000	90	82	33
1974/75	1,165,000	392,000	76	71	34
1978/79	962,000	357,000	62	64	37
1981/82–					
1982/83	880,000	372,000	57	67	42

Sources: Pupils until 1978/79 – Pollak and Lang (1979); Himmelfarb and DellaPergola (1982).
Pupils 1981/82–1982/83 – First Census of Jewish Schools.
Jewish children – authors' estimates.

FIGURE 1.   RATES OF ENROLLMENT IN JEWISH SCHOOLS PER 100 JEWISH CHILDREN
AT EACH AGE, BY TYPE OF SCHOOL AND COUNTRY – 1981/82–1982/83

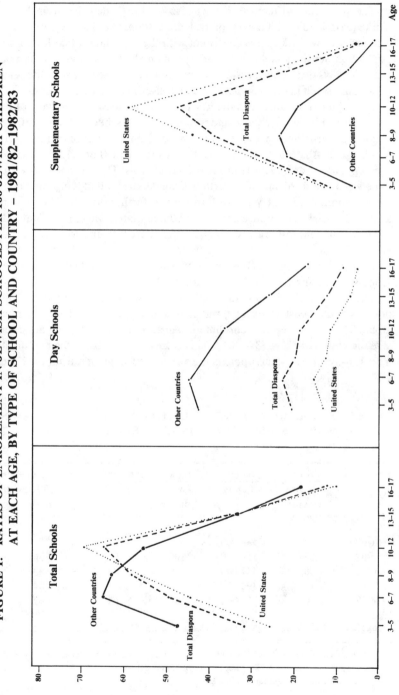

States (28–30%) is the highest in the Diaspora, closely followed by that in the United Kingdom (26–28%). Elsewhere, supplementary enrollment rates reach 15–20% in Canada and Australia; around 10% in South Africa, Argentina, France and the smaller communities in Western Europe; and extremely low percentages in Brazil, the smaller Latin American communities, and the Muslim countries (in the latter region the data are obviously incomplete).

As shown in Table 4, the United States has the lowest enrollment rate in Jewish day schools of all the areas studied, along with the highest rate in supplementary schools. Several censuses of Jewish education have been carried out in the United States since the early 1960s through 1982/83. They indicate an overall decline of 200,000 pupils. However, there is insufficient information regarding the comprehensiveness of the various educational censuses; the latest, which showed a small increase in the number of pupils, was carried out using different, improved methods (Dubb and DellaPergola, 1986).

The sharp decline in the number of Jewish pupils receiving Jewish education is not open to debate. But, according to our estimates, as derived from the various censuses, the enrollment rates in the United States for Jewish school-age children between the ages of 3 and 17 have not fallen. Not only have the rates not declined, but they have in fact recently shown an apparent increase.[9] The solution to this paradox of decrease in the number of pupils as opposed to stability or even a small increase of the enrollment rates is found in Table 5. Indeed, according to our estimates, the total number of Jewish children has dropped even somewhat more than the number of pupils in Jewish schools (compare especially the middle columns in Table 5, presenting the indices). The drastic drop in the number of Jewish children conforms to the demographic trends discussed above (see Table 1). Any smaller decrease in the number of Jewish pupils may have depended on each or both of two different types of factors:

– an improved coverage of Jewish schools in the most recent school census;
– a greater propensity of parents to give their children a Jewish education, especially in Jewish day schools.

Age Profiles of Current Enrollment Rates

Further variation in Jewish school enrollment rates is shown in Table 6 and Figure 1, according to detailed age-groups within the school-age population, by type of school and by major areas. For the sake of simplicity, the Diaspora has been divided into only two areas – the United States and all other countries (except Eastern Europe) – despite the geographical dispersion and lack of uniformity in the latter. The enrollment rates for the entire Diaspora are in the nature of weighted averages of the rates for the United States separately, and the remaining countries together. The overall rate is closer to those of the

United States because two-thirds of all Jewish children in the Diaspora are concentrated there.

The census of Jewish education did not specify pupils' ages but rather their grades; however, the information on distribution by grades can be closely translated into the distribution of pupils by ages.[10] Data on grades was not available from some institutions and, as is usual in such cases, it was assumed that these pupils were distributed like the others in the census. The denomina-

TABLE 6. JEWISH PUPILS IN JEWISH SCHOOLS, BY GRADE/AGE, TYPE OF SCHOOL AND COUNTRY – 1981/82–1982/83

Grade/Age	Total Diaspora			United States			Other Countries		
	Total	Schools		Total	Schools		Total	Schools	
		Day	Suppl.		Day	Suppl.		Day	Suppl.

Absolute Numbers (thousands)ᵃ

Grade/Age	Total	Day	Suppl.	Total	Day	Suppl.	Total	Day	Suppl.
Total	536.1	223.8	312.3	371.5	104.1	267.4	164.6	119.7	44.9
Kindergarten	85.1	54.7	30.4	52.0	26.1	25.9	33.1	28.6	4.5
Grades 1–12	451.0	169.1	281.9	319.5	78.0	241.5	131.5	91.1	40.4
Grades 1–2	84.6	38.7	45.9	55.1	18.9	36.2	29.5	19.8	9.7
Grades 3–4	98.3	34.3	64.0	69.5	16.2	53.3	28.8	18.1	10.7
Grades 5–7	154.9	46.3	108.6	116.9	21.2	95.7	38.0	25.1	12.9
Grades 8–10	87.1	33.1	54.0	62.3	14.3	48.0	24.8	18.8	6.0
Grades 11–12	26.1	16.7	9.4	15.7	7.4	8.3	10.4	9.3	1.1

Enrollment Rates per 100 Jewish Children at Each Age (estimated ranges)

Grade/Age	Total	Day	Suppl.	Total	Day	Suppl.	Total	Day	Suppl.
Total	40–44	17–19	23–25	39–43	11–13	28–30	45–49	33–35	12–14
Ages 3–5	31–35	20–22	11–13	25–29	13–15	12–14	46–50	41–43	5– 7
Ages 6–17	43–47	16–18	27–29	42–46	10–12	32–34	44–48	31–33	13–15
Ages 6–7	48–52	22–24	26–28	43–47	15–17	28–30	63–67	43–45	20–22
Ages 8–9	56–60	19–21	37–39	54–58	12–14	42–44	61–65	39–41	22–24
Ages 10–12	63–67	18–20	45–47	67–71	11–13	56–58	53–57	35–37	18–20
Ages 13–15	33–37	12–14	21–23	33–37	7– 9	26–28	32–36	25–27	7– 9
Ages 16–17	12–16	8–10	4– 6	10–14	5– 7	5– 7	18–22	17–19	1– 3

(a)   Pupils with unknown grade were distributed proportionately.

Source: First Census of Jewish Schools, 1981/81–1982/83.

tors for computation of the enrollment rates were our demographic estimates of the number of children in the Jewish population, according to their ages. Age-specific current enrollment rates were computed for six age-groups: 3–5, 6–7, 8–9, 10–12, 13–15, and 16–17. Apart from total rates, separate profiles were constructed for day and supplementary schools. We turn to these strikingly different profiles first.

Day school enrollment rates start at a comparatively high plateau at preschool age, reach an early relative maximum at age 6–7 (corresponding to first-second grade of elementary school), and subsequently decline quite steadily until the upper grades in high school. This general trend is similar in the United States and the rest of the Diaspora, but United States day school enrollment rates are much lower. The highest enrollment rates recorded correspond to 43–45% of Jewish children aged 6–7 outside the United States, and to 15–17% in the United States. On the other hand, in the passage to higher grade levels, the pace of decline in enrollment rates is sharper outside the United States.

The declining profile of Jewish day-school enrollment per 100 children at each age-group can be interpreted essentially as the consequence of a continuous pupil drop-out from lower to higher grades. This is more accurately described as a continuously negative balance between the numbers of pupils leaving and the number joining Jewish day-schools after a certain grade level. The turning point in enrollment rates seems to correspond well with the passage from elementary to secondary school. It must also be assumed that the lower enrollment in high school classes is due not only to differences in demand for the various levels of Jewish education, but also to differences in supply – the establishment and maintenance of a high school is more difficult and costly than organization of an elementary school.

A further determinant of the age profile of Jewish day-school enrollment rates may be the progressive strengthening of the day-school movement in the Diaspora. That is, the higher enrollment rates for preschool and early elementary school ages could reflect an expanding base for Jewish day schools, relative to the total Jewish school-age population. Such expansion would logically start from the lower grades, only gradually reaching the higher educational levels. Such an explanation – though speculative – is supported by partial data reported in previous research (Himmelfarb and DellaPergola, 1982; DellaPergola, Genuth, 1983), and by some impressionistic observations in a variety of Jewish communities.

If we now examine the age profile of enrollment rates in Jewish supplementary education, we find a major peak at age 10–12, obviously related to pre-bar/bat mitzvah training. This peak is peculiar to the United States, where about 56–58% of the 10–12 age group were receiving supplementary Jewish education in 1981/82–1982/83. The pattern is somewhat different for the aggregate of other Diaspora communities, where the peak is reached at age 8–9 (22–24% of the age group). Thereafter, enrollment rates rapidly decline and even fall below those for day schools in both the major geographical regions considered here.

The overall enrollment rates for both day and supplementary Jewish schools in the Diaspora outside the United States begin falling with the younger age groups in elementary school. This drop reflects the common course of rates of enrollment in both day and supplementary education, since enrollment tends to decline with the increase in age. By contrast, the overall enrollment rates in the United States and their effect on the entire Diaspora mainly reflect the typical pattern of enrollment in US Jewish supplementary schools: that is, a rise in rates until bar/bat mitzvah age, and a sharp decline beyond this age.

Outside the United States, the number of Jewish children of the 3–5 age group attending Jewish kindergartens is high in relation to the total number of children. Half of the pupils in Jewish kindergartens in the United States receive supplementary education, while in the rest of the Diaspora, most of the attendance is in Jewish full-time kindergartens.

Rates of Lifetime Attainment (Ever-enrolled) in Jewish Schools

Census data like those reported in this study do not constitute, in principle, an adequate basis for attempting to assess what proportion of the Jewish school-age population ever receives some Jewish education (i.e., the cumulative enrollment rate). Nevertheless, the age-specific current enrollment rates reported in the preceding section render possible some educated speculation on this topic. Given the considerable public interest in obtaining cumulative rates of Jewish schooling and in comparing them with current rates, it seems worthwhile to present here at least a very rough and tentative estimate.

It is sufficient for this purpose to consider that the highest age-specific enrollment rates shown in Table 6 and Figure 1 constitute – for the age groups respectively concerned – a measure of lifetime exposure to Jewish education. Indeed, about 16% of the 6–7 age group in the United States, and about 44% elsewhere in the Diaspora as of 1981/82–1982/83 started their schooling in a Jewish day school. Even if the subsequent enrollment rates of these Jewish children decline, the percentage values just mentioned constitute a minimum estimate of the proportion of that age cohort that will ever receive some Jewish day school education; the actual proportion will possibly be higher. If one further assumes that the behavior of the immediately preceding and following age cohorts was or will be roughly similar, this finding can be extended to the entire Jewish school-age population of the early 1980s as an approximate measure of its cumulative enrollment rate. The result is, of course, no more than a tentative hypothesis awaiting validation or rejection through further data collection a few years from now. A similar approach may be applied for estimating the enrollment rates in Jewish supplementary education.

For the sake of simplicity, we shall further assume that no passage of pupils occurs between day and supplementary schools and vice-versa. This is obviously not true, since there is some known overlap of lifetime attendance in the two types of Jewish education. The over-estimate tolerated here may compensate for the fact that the enrollment peaks observed in the educational censuses miss a certain proportion of the pupils ever exposed to Jewish schooling: the 'early drop-outs' – i.e. pupils leaving Jewish education for good before the age-specific enrollment peaks discussed above – and the 'late-bloomers' – who attend for the first time after those peak ages. We shall assume that errors due to these over-estimates and under-estimates counter-balance each other.

If one accepts these assumptions, a measure of lifetime Jewish school attendance is provided by the sum of the highest age-specific current enrollment rates separately obtained for Jewish day and supplementary schools (see Table 6). In the United States, by adding the maximum for day schools (15–17%) to that for supplementary schools (56–58%) one obtains a total of 71–75% of children aged 3 to 17 who ever received any Jewish education in the early 1980s. The corresponding estimate for the rest of the Diaspora is 65–69%, obtained by adding the maximum age-specific enrollment rates of 43–45% for day schools to 22–24% for supplementary schools. For the entire Diaspora (excluding Eastern Europe and other countries not covered by our census) an estimated 67–71% of the Jewish school-age population may ever receive some Jewish education (22–24% in day schools and 45–47% through supplementary education).

These percentages are higher than the current enrollment rates already seen in Tables 4, 5 and 6 for the total 3–17 age group. The differences are evident from the percentage ranges reported in Table 7. It thus appears that lifetime Jewish school attainment rates may be one and a half times or more above the current enrollment rates (DellaPergola and Genuth, 1983). Therefore, while at a given point in time, 1981/82–1982/83, less than one half of the Jewish school age population was enrolled in the Jewish educational system, a substantial majority of Jewish children do receive some Jewish education at some stage.

With regard to the United States, both current and cumulative enrollment rates obtained through our census of Jewish schools are very close to those computed from the 1970/71 National Jewish Population Study.[11] According to NJPS, 44% of all Jewish children aged 6 to 17 in 1970/71 were enrolled in Jewish education (excluding private lessons), thereof 8% in day schools, and 36% in supplementary schools. Relative to that same age group the total current enrollment rate had not changed by 1981/82–1982/83 (44%), but day schools had gained some percentage points at the expense of the supplementary schools, the rates being 11% and 33%, respectively. With regard to the per-

TABLE 7. PERCENT OF JEWISH CHILDREN AGED 3 TO 17 CURRENTLY
ENROLLED IN JEWISH SCHOOLS AND EVER RECEIVING SOME
JEWISH EDUCATION, BY TYPE OF SCHOOL AND COUNTRY –
1981/82–1982/83

Country	Percent Currently Enrolled in Jewish Education			Percent Ever Receiving Some Jewish Education		
	Total	Day Schools	Supplementary Schools	Total	Day Schools	Supplementary Schools
Total Diaspora[a]	40–44	17–19	23–25	67–71	22–24	45–47
United States	39–43	11–13	28–30	71–75	15–17	56–58
Other countries	43–47	32–34	11–13	65–69	43–45	22–24

(a) Without Eastern Europe and other countries not included in the census.

Source: First Census of Jewish Schools, 1981/82–1982/83.

centage of children ever receiving some Jewish education, in 1970/71 this was
estimated to be 73%, thereof 13% in day schools and 60% in supplementary
schools. According to the 1981/82–1982/83 educational census, the total
attainment was still 73% as in 1970/71, but day schools had gained somewhat
(up to 16%), and supplementary schools had lost the same percentage point difference (down to 57%).

The two types of enrollment rates – current and 'ever' – thus lead to different conclusions about the frequency of Jewish schooling in the Diaspora. The
apparent discrepancy between the levels of current enrollment and cumulative
attainment can be reconciled by the drop-out from the Jewish educational system as the bridging element. A majority of Jewish children ever do attend a
Jewish school, but for many of them the contact with Jewish education is very
short-lived, to the point that serious questions can be raised regarding the
meaningfulness of such contact.

Conclusions

This chapter reviewed selected quantitative aspects of Diaspora Jewish
education in the context of an assesment of basic changes in demographic patterns that have a bearing on the availability of children as pupils in Jewish
schools. The overall decline in fertility during the last few decades accounts
for the reduction in the size of the Jewish school-age population. Similar
though apparently somewhat more moderate changes have occurred in the

numbers of pupils attending Jewish schools. The major trends and differentials in Jewish school enrollment in the early 1980s were presented based on the results of the first Census of Jewish Schools in the Diaspora. The Jewish school enrollment rates that have been computed, even those that appear relatively high, do not reflect the content or quantity of the education given or its long-range 'effectiveness' as an influential factor for the Jewishness of the pupils as adults. The effectiveness of returns from investments in Jewish schooling needs to be evaluated in conjunction with data on the types of curricula adopted by different schools, intensity of the programs, duration of exposure to Jewish education, teacher training and experience, and other aspects of the contents and organization of the Jewish school system.

At any rate, the material presented in this chapter illustrates the basic importance of demographic data for understanding the state of, and the trends in, Jewish educational enrollment. The frequent and rapid changes in the number of Jewish children and their impact on enrollment population require further periodic demographic and statistical study and evaluation.

Notes

1. This does not apply to Asia and North Africa, but these areas have been virtually emptied of Jews.

2. The birth rate and natural increase are influenced by the age composition of the population. If the population is relatively young, it may continue growing although the fertility rate per se is insufficient to ensure growth. In aging populations, which are fast becoming dominant among Diaspora Jewry, the occurrence of a natural deficit will be speeded up – due to deaths outnumbering births (Schmelz, 1984).

3. Since half of the marital partners in mixed marriages are Jews, unless half of their children are raised as Jews, the size of the Jewish population will be thereby affected.

4. For explanations of the projections, basic data, underlying assumptions, and methods, see: Schmelz (1981b and 1984). Compare also to: Schmelz (1983a and 1983b). Minor changes have been made in the versions printed here as compared to those previously published.

5. The relationships between birth years and age groups are as follows:

Year	Total ages 3–17	Ages 3–5	Ages 6–11	Ages 12–17
1965	1948–1962	1960–1962	1954–1959	1948–1953
1975	1958–1972	1970–1972	1964–1969	1958–1963
1985	1968–1982	1980–1982	1974–1979	1968–1973
2000	1983–1997	1995–1997	1989–1994	1983–1988

6.   For a review of Jewish demographic trends in the United States, and of the recent debate concerning them, see: Schmelz and DellaPergola (1986).

7.   Data, estimates and projections; were prepared by the Division of Jewish Demography and Statistics, The Institute of Contemporary Jewry, The Hebrew University of Jerusalem. See: Schmelz (1981b), Schmelz and DellaPergola (1984).

8.   Underestimate; the data for supplementary schools in Muslim countries are grossly incomplete.

9.   It should be stressed that enrollment rates are based on very rough estimates of the numbers of Jewish children in the United States derived from the incomplete documentation available for the demography of the Jews in that country.

10.   The translation of grades into ages was done as follows: pupils in grade 1 were classified as 6 year olds, grade 2 as 7 year olds, etc. The assumption was that the average age of pupils in every grade approaches the 'official' age. Special difficulties were encountered in working out classifications according to ages for supplementary school pupils because of the increased possibility of disparities between pupils' ages and grades, lack of clarity with regard to the definition of grades in supplementary schools, and the frequent occurrence of joint classes (i.e., small classes that contain pupils from several grades). Partial assistance in dealing with this problem was obtained from the fact that the census questionnaire contained questions about the age limits of the pupils in the institution and its main levels, if such existed. The computation of the rates did not include grade 13 or non-Jewish pupils, even though these are included in the absolute figures of Table 3.

11.   The following estimates are derived from our own processing of the NJPS data files; see: DellaPergola and Genuth (1983). The figures of pupils in Jewish schools derived from NJPS – which was a comprehensive representative survey of the Jewish population in the United States - are greater than those obtained by the census of Jewish education for the same year (1970/71), as reported by Pollak and Lang (1979).

References

Bachi, R. (1982). "Diaspora Population: Past Growth and Present Decline". *The Jerusalem Quarterly*, No. 22. pp. 3–16.

Bensimon, D. and DellaPergola, S. (1984). *La population juive de France: socio-démographie et identité*. Institute of Contemporary Jewry, The Hebrew University, Jerusalem and Centre National de la Recherche Scientifique, Paris. (Jewish Population Studies, no. 17). 436 pp.

DellaPergola, S. (1980). "Patterns of American Jewish Fertility". *Demography*, Vol. 17, no. 3. pp. 261–273.

DellaPergola, S. (1983). "Contemporary Jewish Fertility: An Overview". in: Schmelz, U.O., Glikson, P. and DellaPergola, S. (eds.). *Papers in Jewish Demography 1981*. Institute of Contemporary Jewry, The Hebrew University, Jerusalem. (Jewish Population Studies, no. 16). pp. 215–238.

DellaPergola, S. and Genuth, N. (1983). *Jewish Education Attained in Diaspora Communities: Data for 1970s*. Institute of Contemporary Jewry, The Hebrew University, Jerusalem. (Project for Jewish Educational Statistics, Research Report No. 2). 74 pp.

Dubb, A.A. and DellaPergola, S. (1986). *First Census of Jewish Schools in the Diaspora 1981/2-1982/3: United States of America*. Institute of Contemporary Jewry, The Hebrew University, Jerusalem, and Jewish Education Service of North America (JESNA), New York. (Project for Jewish Educational Statistics, Research Report No. 4). 102 pp.

Easterlin, R.A. (1978). "What Will 1984 Be Like? Socioeconomic Implications of Recent Twists in Age Structure". *Demography*, Vol. 15, no. 4. pp. 397–434.

Genuth, N., DellaPergola, S., and Dubb, A.A. (1985). *First Census of Jewish Schools in the Diaspora 1981/2-1982/3: International Summary*. Institute of Contemporary Jewry, The Hebrew University, Jerusalem. (Project for Jewish Educational Statistics, Research Report No. 3). 138 pp.

Goldscheider, C. (1986). *Jewish Community and Change: Emerging Patterns in America*. Indiana University Press, Bloomington.

Himmelfarb, H.S. and DellaPergola, S. (1982). *Enrollment in Jewish Schools in the Diaspora: Late 1970s*. Institute of Contemporary Jewry, The Hebrew University, Jerusalem. (Project for Jewish Educational Statistics, Research Report No. 1). 97 pp.

Pollak, G. and Lang, C. (1979). *Jewish School Census 1978/79*. American Association for Jewish Education, New York. 42 pp.

Ritterband, P. and Cohen, S. (1984). "The Social Characteristics of the New York Area Jewish Community, 1981". *American Jewish Year Book*, Vol. 84. pp. 128–162.

Schmelz, U.O. (1981a). "Jewish Survival: The Demographic Factors". *American Jewish Year Book*, Vol. 81. pp. 61–117.

Schmelz, U.O. (1981b). *World Jewish Population: Regional Estimates and Projections*. Institute of Contemporary Jewry, The Hebrew University, Jerusalem. (Jewish Population Studies, no. 13). 72 pp.

Schmelz, U.O. (1983a). "Evolution and Projection of World Jewish Population", in: Schmelz, U.O., Glikson, P., Gould, S.J. (eds.). *Studies in Jewish Demography: Survey for 1972-1980*. Institute of Contemporary Jewry, The Hebrew University, Jerusalem and Institute of Jewish Affairs, London. (Jewish Population Studies, no. 14). pp. 1–18.

Schmelz, U.O. (1983b). "World Jewish Population Trends: Projections and Implications", in: Schmelz, U.O., Glikson, P. and DellaPergola, S. (eds.). *Papers in Jewish Demography 1981*. Institute of Contemporary Jewry, The Hebrew University, Jerusalem. (Jewish Population Studies, no. 16). pp. 15–32.

Schmelz, U.O. (1984). *Aging of World Jewry*. Institute of Contemporary Jewry, The Hebrew University and JDC – Brookdale Institute of Gerontology and Adult Human Development, Jerusalem. (Jewish Population Studies, no. 15). 290 pp.

Schmelz, U.O. and DellaPergola, S. (1983). "The Demographic Consequences of U.S. Jewish Population Trends". *American Jewish Year Book*, Vol. 83. pp. 141–187.

Schmelz, U.O. and DellaPergola, S. (1984). "World Jewish Population, 1982". *American Jewish Year Book*, Vol. 84. pp. 247–258.

Schmelz, U.O. and DellaPergola, S. (1986). *Some Basic Trends in the Demography of U.S. Jews: A Reassessment.* Paper presented at Conference on New Perspectives in American Jewish Sociology: Findings and Implications, American Jewish Committee, New York.

Westoff, C.F. (1978). "Some Speculations on the Future of Marriage and Fertility". *Family Planning Perspectives*, Vol. 10. pp. 79–83.

World Zionist Organization (1971). *Jewish Education in the Diaspora.* World Zionist Organization, Press and Public Relations Office, Jerusalem. 94 pp.

Part Two
North America

Nearly half of world Jewry or about two-thirds of Diaspora Jewry live in North America, primarily in the United States. Therefore, it is necessary to understand Jewish education there if one wants to begin to grasp the world-wide situation.

Jewish education in the United States is in a sense one of the more well-established and stable systems in the Diaspora. It has been less effected by war, changing political regimes and Jewish migration since the first quarter of this century than any other Jewish educational system. Nevertheless, in the United States, as elsewhere, there has been a substantial growth in day school enrollment, which has now spread from only Orthodox-sponsored to Conservative and Reform denominations. Yet, the proportion of Jewish children in day schools is the lowest in the Western world, and Jewish education in the United States continues to rely primarily on supplementary schools. In part, this is an outgrowth of the strong separation of church and state in that country, which allows for minimal government support of private schools, but has made the public schools mostly free of religious influences, and, therefore, relatively hospitable environments for Jewish children. The United States Jewish school system is also quite unique in the extent to which it is organized around religious denominations and the prominence given to non-Orthodox bodies. In his analysis here, Walter Ackerman, Professor of Education at Ben Gurion University in Beer Sheva, raises important questions about the effectiveness of the system in – despite its size and stable nature - producing knowledgeable and identifying Jews. Throughout, he points out various aspects in need of change and innovation.

Given the prominence of the United States in the world Jewish education system, and Ackerman's detached academic perspective, we invited comments from three educators who are actively working with the schools, but have different institutional perspectives, and as individuals have different ideological orientations. The first is by Shimon Frost, past Executive Director of the Jewish Education Service of North America (JESNA), the non-denominational educational umbrella organization in North America. The second is by Alvin Schiff, Director of the Board of Jewish Education of New York City, the largest single Jewish education system in the Diaspora. The third comment is by Michael Zeldin, Associate Professor of Education in the Rhea Hirsch School of Education, Hebrew Union College-Jewish Institute of Religion, Los Angeles.

Chapter 4 in this part deals with Canada. Jerome Kutnick, Assistant Professor of History and Jewish Thought at Gratz College, Philadelphia, points out in his essay that the Canadian Jewish educational system is influenced to some extent by the United States, both through organizational connections and through cultural influences. Yet, Canada has its own unique Jewish educational structure and issues. There are considerable differences between provinces with regard to Jewish population size, immigration background and government support of Jewish schools. The chapter discusses the opportunities and problems presented by these differences.

3

Strangers to the Tradition: Idea and Constraint in American Jewish Education

Walter I. Ackerman

The first Jewish school in the United States of which we know was founded in New York City in 1731, seventy-seven years after the arrival of the first group of 24 Jews in the Dutch colony of New Amsterdam, and one year after the Portuguese Jewish congregation, Shearith Israel, had completed construction of the first synagogue building in that city. The minutes of the congregation noted that:

> On the 21st of Nissan, the 7th day of Pesach, the day of completing the first year of the opening of the synagogue, there was made *codez* (consecrated) the Yeshibat called *Minchat Arab*...for the use of this congregation Shearith Israel and as a *Beth Midrash* for the pupils... (Dushkin, 1918, p. 449).

The same source remarked that the cantor of the congregation "obliges himself to keep a public school in due form for teaching the Hebrew language..."; subsequent attempts to engage a teacher for the school specify that he be "Capable to teach our children...Hebrew" and that "English and Spanish he ought to know; but he will not suit unless he understands Hebrew and English at least"; several years later, the *Parnassim* (trustees) of the congregation engaged a teacher to "...teach the Hebrew language, and to translate the same into English, also to teach English, Reading, Writing and Cyphering." (Dushkin, 1918, p. 450).

It is reasonable to assume that even before the founding of *Yeshibat Minchat Arab* some form of Jewish tuition, probably private instruction offered either by a paid tutor or the child's father took place in New York and other places of Jewish settlement in colonial America. The significance of the action of Congregation Shearith Israel is that its commitment to the maintaining of a school – which incidentally still exists today – was the harbinger of the network of Jewish educational institutions which is an integral part of contemporary American Jewish life. It initiated two and a half centuries of uninterrupted educational activity. This is an impressive record by any standard, and even more so considering that we are speaking of educational programs developed and maintained voluntarily by a small minority group without the impetus of the sanctions of compulsory educational legislation or the benefit of government financial aid.

The growth and development of Jewish schooling in the United States has been conditioned by the sometimes jarring interaction of a congeries of factors: the Jewish tradition of learning, patterns of education and behavior which successive waves of Jewish immigrants brought with them from their countries of origin, American law and mores and, above all, the processes of acculturation and assimilation that mark the Jewish experience in America.

When the trustees of Congregation Shearith Israel opened their school they were conforming to the accepted practice of their time: almost without exception, schools of that period were sponsored and maintained by religious institutions and agencies. Toward the middle of the 19th century, Jewish day schools, under either private, congregational or communal auspices, drew from the influx of German Jews, parallelling the rise of the academy in the host society. The first Jewish Sunday School, founded in Philadelphia in 1838, followed upon the spread of this type of school, first in England and then among American Protestants. The Talmud Torah, a mid-week afternoon school which in time was to become the prototypical setting of Jewish education in this country, was an adaptation to conditions in the United States of the Jewish communal school of Eastern Europe.

Not only did the structure of education result from the merger of past experience of newly arrived immigrants with the demands of life in the new country. The search for a teacher who was capable of teaching Hebrew and "English, Reading, Writing and Cyphering" reflects a melding of the secular and religious, which had long been a characteristic of Spanish Jewry; moreover, the maintenance of that tradition was clearly thought critical to successful adaptation to life in New York. German Jews brought with them knowledge of the educational practices introduced by David Friedlander and the adherents of Reform Judaism who followed him (Eliav, 1960). Their sense of America only strengthened their view that traditional Jewish education was no longer a relevant paradigm and that religious studies must be subordinated to secular learning. The adoption of a catechismal mode of teaching and learning in the schools they founded in the United States was an import from Germany, and it was intended to transmit the essentials of Judaism in a manner and style compatible with full participation in the society of which they were now a part (Petuchowski, 1964; Lynn, 1973). The Talmud Torah, in its earliest stages – particularly after the swell of immigration from Eastern Europe – and in its later transformation into the congregational school, embraced the ideas of the *heder metukan* as well as its explicit purpose of moving beyond the boundaries of subject matter set by traditional Jewish schools.

Jewish education in America was established without any constraints rooted in civil law. During the colonial period and the early days of the Republic, as indicated above, religious agencies were the prominent sponsors of educational institutions, and to this day they remain an important factor among the various supporters of independent schools. The constitutional guarantees of freedom of assembly, religion and speech make it possible for anyone so inclined to conduct educational activities. The advent of the public school and free, compulsory education – as a process which spread unevenly across the continent, led some quarters to press for legislation which would deny parents the right of free choice of school for their children. In a 1925 landmark decision, the Supreme Court, responding to an appeal brought before it by Catholic parochial schools joined for the purpose by a private, non-sectarian school, declared unconstitutional an Oregon statute which required all children in that state under the age of 15 to attend a public school. The incisive language of the Court reminded zealous supporters of the public school that:

> The fundamental theory of liberty upon which all governments in the Union repose excludes any general power of the state to standardize its children by forcing them to accept instruction from public teachers only. The child is not the mere creature of the state; those who nurture him and direct his destiny have the right, coupled with the high duty, to recognize and prepare him for additional obligations (King, 1965, p. 58).

A later decision by the Supreme Court forbids any form of religious instruction in public school buildings and heralds public schools as the "symbol of our secular unity...the symbol of our democracy, the most pervasive means for promoting our common destiny."[1] Implicit in the Court's decision, of course, is a corollary principle: the separation of Church and State which removes religion from the public schools, guarantees the freedom of religion and the right of governmental financial aid. Independent schools, religious or secular, are thus a legitimate form of schooling and occupy a unique place in the history of American education. However, even today – a time of clamorous dissatisfaction with public education – they do not begin to rival the overwhelming dominance of the public school.[2]

The freedom provided by the latitude of the law is the legal basis for the Jewish day school network which dots the country today; the primacy of the mid-week afternoon school and the Sunday school, however, bespeaks the Jewish commitment to the norms of America in general, and to the public school in particular. If, as one historian has observed, "The moral and social significance of the public school in American democratic thought has probably surpassed that enjoyed by state schools in any Western society" (Gartner, 1976, p. 157), the loyalty of the Jews to that institution and their perception of it as the avenue which leads to success and status is perhaps altogether unparalleled. Unlike Catholics (Ravitch, 1974, pp. 3–76), Jews never challenged the genteel Protestantism of the public schools. Nor did they protest the crude, and often vulgar, programs of Americanization which were calculated to make immigrants "realize that in forsaking the land of their birth, they were also forsaking the customs and traditions of that land; and they must be made to realize an obligation, in adopting a new country to adopt the language and customs of that country" (Richman, 1905, p. 119 as in Tyack, 1974, pp. 50–54). Moreover, in contrast to other religious and ethnic minority groups in the United States, Jews have never looked to public schools for the transmission of their culture. There is no parallel, for instance, in the history of American Jews with that of German immigrants, who, in their desire to maintain the traditions and customs of their homeland, insisted that German be the language of instruction in the public schools their children attended (Troen, 1975, Ch. 3). Neither the introduction of Hebrew language instruction in secondary schools, 'released time' instruction permitted by law, nor the more recent inclusion of the study of the Holocaust in curricula all over the country, challenge the deeply held conviction of most Jews that instruction in Judaism is the concern of the Jewish community and that the interests of Jews and all other Americans are best served by holding fast to the line which separates between Church and State. The men who laid the theoretical foundations of American Jewish education eschewed the model of the parochial school because "it segregates children along lines of creed" thereby contradicting the dictates of democracy, which require that children "during the formative years of childhood, associate with their neighbors with whom they are destined to live together as American citizens..." (Berkson, 1920, p. 42). The overwhelming majority of American Jews clearly subscribe to the notion that Jewish schools must not interfere "with America's cherished plan of a system of common schools for all the children of all the people" (Dushkin, 1918, p. 138; Ackerman, 1975).

The majority of American Jews today are several generations removed from their immigrant origins and in their education, occupations and income have risen significantly above the socioeconomic status of their forebears. The National Jewish Population Study, conducted in 1970–71, paints the following profile: the heads of "Jewish households were divided roughly into 23% foreign born, 58% first generation born in the U.S. and 19% second or earlier generation U.S. born"; among the "heads of households 54 years of age or younger," that is, those most likely to have children of school age, "the proportion of foreign born was 12% or less", the total Jewish population was approaching the point where 80% would have some college education as a minimum and more than 60% would have acquired a first degree, with a substantial proportion going on to post-graduate work. Occupational distribution was heavily skewed toward the professional and managerial categories. In 1969, some 43% of the Jews in America reported annual incomes of $16,000 or over (Massarik and Chenkin, 1973).[3] Today, fifteen years later, we can safely say that Jewish schools in America cater to third generation Americans, children of highly educated parents whose training, occupations and income place them well above the national average. These data are a key to the understanding of Jewish education in its American context.

Ever since the time of the first Jewish settlement in the U.S., the Jewish passion for learning has been transferred from its original (religious) focus to secular learning. As do American Jews today, the early Jewish settlers who were concerned about the Jewish education of their children by and large chose settings which nevertheless did not interfere with the general education or other activities considered more critical to their personal development and future career opportunities. There may be some exaggeration in the observation of a 19th century visitor who thought "...that men of great learning will never arise among the Jews of America" (Benjamin, 1936, p. 83); it is, however, undeniably true that the traditional ideals of *Torah l'shma* (learning for its own sake) and *lamdanut* (Jewish erudition) never did, and still do not, figure prominently in the value system of American Jews. A study of 230 participants in leadership programs sponsored by local Jewish Federations together with the National Council of Jewish Federations and the United Jewish Appeal – ostensibly a strongly identified group – discloses that less than 50% of those questioned thought that a knowledge of the fundamentals of Judaism was essential to the making of a good Jew and only 22% considered being "well versed in Jewish history and culture" necessary (Woocher, 1981, p. 297). This attitude evidently distinguishes between the educated Jew and the identified Jew as expressed by Borowitz (1961, p. 149). "What the child should know about Judaism is not so important as that he should want to be a Jew", and to "want to be a Jew" does not necessarily require more than a rudimentary knowledge of Judaism.

Notwithstanding the continued growth of day schools, the interplay between Jews, Judaism and life in America has resulted in a system of Jewish education which consists mainly of supplementary schooling conducted in mid-week afternoon schools, meeting for four-six hours a week, and one-day-a-week Sunday or Sabbath schools, offering two-three hours of weekly instruction. This educational enterprise represents the voluntary effort of autonomous institutions, mutually bound more by common aspirations than by formal structure. Since the end of World War II the virtual demise of secular Hebrew nationalist and Yiddish schools has made Jewish education almost entirely a function of the synagogue. The vast majority of Jewish schools – close to 90% in the early 1970s (Hochberg, 1972) – are sponsored, maintained and controlled by individual congregations. Even in the case of schools under communal auspices, the support and active participation of local synagogues is essential to their functioning. The perception and practice of Jewish education as religious education stems both from Jewish tradition and from minority group identification compatible with American mores and norms.

American Jews join synagogues and send their children to Jewish schools because they genuinely want to identify themselves and their children as Jews. They are able to do so, however, because neither synagogue membership nor school attendance dictate behavior that conflicts with what they perceive as the American way of life. While parents often speak of the school as the guarantor of Judaism, they are rarely prepared to accept the implications of this position. They shy away from the recognition of Judaism as a code of behavior central to self-definition. The discrepancy between the desire for Jewish identification as such and the unwillingness to accept Judaism as a formative factor has led one perceptive observer to describe involvement in Jewish education as an exercise in self-deception. More than a year of close study of an afternoon congregational school led to the conclusion that

> ...the goals, the values, and the emotions of...parents seemed tied to a system that appeared little different than that of the non-Jews residing about them. Although these Jews did identify with a Jewish people, history, culture and religion, they did not, in their own suburban American lives, live according to any Jewish way of life. It wasn't that these Jews didn't want to be living a Jewish way of life, but rather they seemed to find the demands of modern life uncompromising. The Jewish way, as they understood it for their own lives, could not serve as a standard of living that suited the modern circumstances of life in America...They have been unable to interpret their Jewish heritage so that it makes sense in their American life... (Schoem, 1978, p. 32).

It is axiomatic that schools function within parameters set by the community which supports them. Close harmony between the values of school and society creates the context of mutual support, necessary for the transmission of culture across generations. If there is a gap between the two, the aspirations of the school are generally subverted by the more powerful impact of the society. Jewish schools are no exception to this rule, and there can be no constructive understanding of the issues confronting Jewish education without acknowledging the disparity betweeen its aims and the leanings of the population it serves.

Goals

While statements of aims and objectives in Jewish education generally lack philosophical rigor, thereby confounding attempts to develop logically consistent programs of instruction (Chazan, 1978, pp. 42–56), their intent is quite clear – to inculcate pupils with the desire and ability to conduct their lives in keeping with Jewish tradition. The various components of that tradition – God, Torah and Israel – are broadly interpreted and their valence, whether separately or in concert, differentially measured and assessed. The same words placed in the context of statements of goals, prepared by different ideological groups, mean very different things.[4]

In recent years there has been a perceptible shift, in some quarters at least, in the focus of Jewish educational purpose. An earlier emphasis, which stressed the centrality of the collective and considered the "fostering of Jewish group life" (Chipkin, 1936, p. 31; Ackerman, 1977) the major goals of the school, has been modified by new attention to the individual and his Jewish identity. This change from public to private concern and its curricular consequences are easily traced. It is rooted in the writings of the radical school reformers; the influence of Piaget's psychology and the theories of Erik Erikson in teacher-training programs and graduate schools of education; the teachings of the 'human-potential movement'; and, as some observers have noted, the narcissism which pervades contemporary American culture. The distressing fact that few Jewish schools in this country have succeeded in imparting any real Jewish knowledge to their students, or in developing even the minimum of intellectual competence required of the literate Jew, has undoubtedly also contributed to the assignation of greater importance to what a person is than to what he knows.

When group survival – and the complementary idea that self-fulfillment is realized only through group membership and a willingness to subordinate personal concerns to the interests of the group – is a dominant motif in educational goals, it determines much of the curriculum. The well being of the group, both present and future, depends upon shared experiences and knowledge as well as a collective commitment to the values of its common tradition. A subject is placed in the curriculum according to its power to move children toward loyalty and identification with the group and not because of any intrinsic quality it may possess. Hebrew as a language and literature, for example, gained high priority, perhaps more than any other subject, since it was thought capable of tying children "with bonds of love and reverence to their people and its land" and of awakening in them "the desire to dedicate themselves to the service of their people and to contribute to the national rebirth" (Ginzberg, 1947, p. 33).

Identity formation as an educational goal brings with it a somewhat different conception of the relationship between the individual and the group.

While one's definition of "who he is and what he is over time and across situations" (Kelman, n.d., p. 3) is conditioned by his cultural, ethnic and religious heritage – that is, the accumulated historical experience of the group into which he was born – it does not follow that one automatically will incorporate the values of that group. Indeed, there is evidence which suggests that the development of personal identity demands some repudiation of one's background (Erikson and Erikson, 1981, p. 254). An authentic personal identity is reflective rather than reflexive; its commitment to group attitudes, norms and behaviors is conditional and not absolute (Kelman, n.d., pp. 26–27).

Identity is complicated, and not easily translated into school practice. A spate of recent books reflects both the current interest in problems of identity formation and the manner in which a profound social science concept can be reduced to triviality or even perverted. The point of the games and exercises in these books, in themselves valuable teaching aids, is to cultivate personal feeling and to encourage students to articulate their attitudes and beliefs. However, the process itself has become the subject matter rather than the knowledge and skills in language, literature and history which are the essential components in formation of an authentic identity (Resnick, 1981, p. 6).

Structure

American Jews who are concerned about Jewish education today cannot complain of a lack of opportunity. From nursery school through Ph.D. programs and beyond, one can attend institutions sponsored and maintained by Jews for the purpose of teaching Judaism. Only the commitment to learning, first by the family and then by the student himself, sets the boundaries to Jewish studies. Jewish education in America is available in varied structures and hues: Sunday Schools which provide a bare minimum of Jewish tuition exist alongside Hasidic yeshivoth hardly tolerant of secular studies; these yeshivoth introduce children to Torah at the age of four, and three years later, allot as much as eight hours a day to Talmud (Schiff, 1966, p. 89); *yeshivoth gedoloth*, similar in form and spirit to their East European predecessors, are available as college level programs of Jewish studies conforming to the standards of the modern academy. The basic school unit, whatever its type, is surrounded by a network of ancillary settings which extend the range of educational activity well beyond the limits of formal schooling.

There are three types of elementary and secondary Jewish schools in the United States: the day school, which combines general and Jewish studies, although there is considerable variation in the time alloted to the latter; the afternoon school, which meets two or three times a week, including a session on Sunday or the Sabbath, for four to six hours; and the one-day-a-week school, Sunday or Sabbath, which requires two to three hours of weekly attendance. The average number of pupil hours per school year was estimated at 248 in the late 1970s, an increase of 35% since 1966–67, largely attributable to a rise in day school enrollment.

The day school is most often associated with the Orthodox movement, the one-day-a-week school with the Reform, and the weekday afternoon school with both the Conservative and Orthodox movements. But these lines are neither hard nor fast: one-day-a-week schools may be found in both Orthodox and Conservative congregations, and more and more Reform communities are offering midweek afternoon school programs. Furthermore, spurred by the example of their Orthodox colleagues, Conservative and Reform rabbis and educators in growing numbers have committed themselves to the development of day schools.

As indicated earlier, almost 90% of Jewish schools are autonomous units maintained voluntarily by individual congregations which, through their boards, have authority over the schools, generally through appointed school committees. Non-congregational schools, a distinct minority, have their own school boards which are responsible for every aspect of the school's activities.

Recent years have witnessed a noticeable trend toward consolidation and merger of these small congregational schools – even those of different religious orientations – and the formation of communal schools under community auspices. Once more common at the high school level, the movement has by now reached the elementary school as well. The creation of intercongregational community-wide schools is not the result of a change in the position that the synagogue is the most appropriate context for Jewish education; rather, it is a pragmatic solution to problems of finance and personnel that strain the resources of all but the largest congregations (Pollak and Efron, 1976).

The idea of community control derives from several sources: the example of the communal Talmud Torah of Eastern Europe, the model of the American public school system and finally, the ideas of Mordecai M. Kaplan. The concepts of peoplehood and community, so integral a part of Kaplan's philsophy of Judaism, lead quite naturally to communal authority in education. Kaplan and his followers, who include among them the architects of modern American Jewish education (Ackerman, 1975; Ackerman, 1981), were convinced that no one agency, congregational or otherwise, should be the basic unit of Jewish life, but rather that the "entire aggregate of congregations, social service agencies, Zionist organizations, defense and fraternal bodies and educational institutions should be integrated into an organic or indivisible community" (Kaplan, 1948, p. 114). From here, it is but a short step to the conclusion that education – "the transmission of the social and spiritual heritage of the Jewish people" in order to create "a bond of unity and brotherhood" – is a primary communal responsibility. The community, working through a central office of education, is thus called upon "to create schools, to supervise them, to train teachers, to establish curricula, and conduct all other educational activities" which are the hallmark of "a well organized civic community" (Kaplan, 1970, p. 171). This is, of course, a blueprint for the Jewish common school, modelled on the pattern of the American public school. Rising above sectarian differences, at least in theory, this institution provides children of diverse backgrounds and outlooks with common experiences, and fashions those shared beliefs and behaviors which bind them together and distinguish them as Jews.

The predilections of American Jews led in other directions than those so rationally charted by Kaplan. His idea of a community was unequal to the task of winning primary allegiance away from the synagogue which was nearer at hand, both physically and symbolically, and more in keeping with American patterns of voluntary religious association. Moreover, the fact that the synagogue is the location of the bar mitzvah, a focal point of Jewish education, strengthened its position in the contest for the control of schooling.

The principle of local community responsibility for Jewish education is commonplace today. Nevertheless, local Bureaus of Jewish Education are merely service agencies which perform functions beyond the ability of the individual school – in-service training for teachers, supervision, central audio-visual and pedagogical libraries, testing programs, placement of teachers, publications, subsidies and a wide variety of other educational activities. The national educational commissions of the major synagogue organizations, as well as the Jewish Education Service of North America (JESNA), the new designation of the reorganized American Association for Jewish Education (AAJE), operate in much the same way – they define broad educational policy for their constituencies, design curricula, attempt to set standards, conduct regional and national conferences, and sponsor extensive publication programs. Meaningful control and direct influence are possible only when a bureau or a national agency contributes directly to the funding of a project or program. Otherwise, their effectiveness depends, in no small measure, upon goodwill and a delicate pattern of personal and institutional relationships.

This loose federation of schools, communal agencies and national commissions clearly safeguards the independence of the individual school. Whatever the advantages of this Jewish counterpart of the American passion for 'local control' in education, the price is extraordinarily high. The absence of definitive boundaries to partisan initiative works against publicly recognized standards and responsibility, and encourages wasteful duplication, school units too small to be educationally viable, and underutilization of limited resources. It also prevents rational, long range, community-wide planning for Jewish education.

The school is surrounded by a variety of informal educational activities. The latter sometimes cooperate with the school, sometimes compete with it, most often ignore it. For those who are interested, youth groups are easily within reach. Zionist youth groups of all ideologies - the distinctions between which are comprehensible only to the initiated - can be found in every metropolitan center; they are generally independent of the schools and are rarely in contact with them. The largest youth organizations are those sponsored by the national synagogue organizations. These are part of the same congregational framework as the schools, and contribute to the creation of a setting which affords innumerable possibilities for the integration of formal and informal programs.

Camping as an educational tool has been a significant development since the end of World War II. Hebrew speaking camps such as Massad, Yavneh, the Ramah camps sponsored by the Jewish Theological Seminary and the network of camps connected with the Union of American Hebrew Congregations - all of which reach their campers through the schools - have had a profound influence on thousands of youngsters who, long after their days in camp, carry the stamp of an intensive educational experience. The expansion of educational camping probably ranks alongside the growth of the day school as a major achievement of American Jewish education in the last 25 years.

The success of summer camping programs has led many schools to utilize camp settings during the school year. Weekend retreats and camping programs, conducted during public school mid-year vacations sponsored by individual schools or organized for groups of schools by a bureau, are by now a common and important part of the curriculum. In many places monthly weekends in camp combined with guided work at home have replaced the Sunday school. We do not know whether this form of schooling is more effective than the conventional pattern, but there can be no doubt that a formal school setting cannot duplicate the special resonance of a shared experience of study, prayer and play in a camp environment.

College age students can study in *yeshivoth gedoloth*, colleges of Jewish studies or Jewish studies programs at regular universities. The former are essentially private institutions built around a respected rabbinical authority who sets the style of learning and who personally attracts the necessary support. The *yeshivoth gedoloth* draw their students from lower schools, which provide the background required for advanced Talmud study, but they have recently been joined by a proliferation of yeshivoth geared to young people with little or no previous preparation. Other than those maintained by the major rabbinical schools, colleges of Jewish studies are community institutions funded primarily by Federation allocations. Students attend schools of this sort - originally conceived as teacher training centers and the capstone of a local system, simultaneously with a regular university. Several of these schools have developed co-operative arrangements with neighboring institutions of higher learning and enjoy the advantages of cross-registration, cross-listing of courses and transfer of credit.

University-based programs of Jewish studies, another major development in American Jewish life, are less easily defined as Jewish education (Adar, 1970, pp. 11–13). Although many such programs owe their existence to Jewish initiative, which often includes initial and continued funding, once introduced into the university, they are subject to its rules and regulations. Moreover, it is doubtful that university instructors of Jewish studies view themselves as 'Jewish educators' or that their goals are similar to those of Jewish institutions. Students who participate in these programs, however, undoubtedly do so because they are interested in deepening their knowledge of Judaism (Band, 1966).

Adult education is also widely available, especially in the major urban centers which contain the overwhelming majority of America's Jews. Congregations, acting alone or in cooperation with others serving the same geographical area, Bureaus of Jewish Education, adult education departments of the national synagogue organizations, Zionist organizations, and fraternal and defense agencies – the entire panoply of organized Jewish life – produce a wide array of material and sponsor programs in every imaginable setting. A particularly interesting development in the area of adult activity is the spread of *havuroth*, in a certain sense the revival of a traditional Jewish institution. There are currently some 500 such groups all over the country, either within congregations or as independent entities without any broader affiliation (Bubis, Wasserman and Lert, 1981, p. 12). The *havura*, a relatively informal grouping which often serves as a surrogate for the traditional extended family, is evidently a response to its members' need for "intimate personal association, autonomy/ participation, ties to the Jewish tradition and transcendence – the opportunity for a significant spiritual experience" (Bubis, et al. 1981, p. 14; Reisman, 1977). This wide range of adult learning opportunities, here described only sketchily, rarely has any connection, administrative or other, with the school system.

A list of the various institutions and agencies involved in formal and informal Jewish education and an attempt to trace the skein of their interaction with one another can mention only a few of the many and varied factors which contribute to the education of the growing child. Historians of education and others point to the importance of many other elements - the family, neighborhood, media, peer groups, voluntary organizations, social service agencies, to name but a few – which are at least as significant as the school, if not more so, in the forming of the individual and his loyalties. To examine the Jewish school in America is to discover, among other things, its detachment and lack of contact with the many factors shaping its character and mediating its effectiveness.

Enrollment

The voluntary nature of Jewish education lends particular importance to the enrollment statistics in Jewish schools. The number and ages of children enrolled, the number of years of attendance and other relevant data are an index not only of the school's ability to attract and hold pupils, but also of its effectiveness. While enrollment in non-governmental schools is often affected by events and circumstances beyond their control, patterns of recruitment and retention still remain important indications for their assessment as educational institutions.

Immediately after World War II, Jewish school enrollment began to rise steadily, reached a peak in the mid–1960s and has been declining since. Between 1946 and 1956, the number of children attending Jewish schools of all kinds more than doubled – from 231,028 to 488,432. In the 1957–58 school year, registers counted 553,600 pupils (Dushkin and Engelman, 1959, pp. 39–40) and in 1966–67, the figure stood at 554,468. Data for 1970–71) show a decline of 17.5% over the four year period to 457,196 (Hochberg, 1972, p. 199); by 1974–75 there were 391,825 pupils enrolled, and a later tally counted only 344,251 (American Association for Jewish Education, 1976; 1979). The pattern is unmistakably clear: Jewish school enrollment suffered a decline of close to 40% in the period from 1960 to the end of the 1970s. The most recent data available show that the downward trend has stopped, and some numerical recovery has actually occurred (Dubb and DellaPergola, 1986).

Year	Pupils
1945–46	231,028
1955–56	488,432
1957–58	553,600
1960–61	588,955
1966–67	554,468
1970–71	457,196
1974–75	391,825
1978–79	357,107
1981/2–1982/3	372,417

Not less important than the absolute number of children enrolled in Jewish schools is the percentage of all Jewish children of school age which they represent. A series of school surveys conducted during the 1950s and 1960s revealed that close to 80% of all Jewish children in the United States received some form of Jewish education during their elementary school years. These findings were corroborated by the 1970/71 National Jewish Population Study. The percentage of children actually enrolled in Jewish schools at any given time, however, is considerably lower – in 1957–58 it was estimated at 40–45% of all Jewish children of school age (Dushkin and Engelman, 1959, p. 44); the enrollment rate estimated from the 1981/82–1982/83 census of Jewish schools was quite the same: 39–43% (Dubb and DellaPergola, 1986). It is further worth noting that comparable figures for the period immediately prior to World War II suggested that only 25–30% of school age children then attended Jewish schools.

There are various explanations for the numerical drop in enrollment - a decline in the Jewish birthrate, population shifts which have taken families with school age children away from areas served by existing Jewish schools, the increasing rate of intermarriage and dwindling parental interest (see also the chapter by DellaPergola and Schmelz in this volume). One study (Pollak, 1978a) that addresses these problems, although conducted in a medium sized community not really representative of American Jewry, provides some possible answers. During the five year period between 1966/67 and 1970/71 Jewish school enrollment in Buffalo, New York declined at a mean annual rate of 5.4%. This figure reflects a significant demographic change among Buffalo's Jews: a lower birthrate among younger families and a growing percentage of adults beyond childbearing age. The combination of these two factors caused a decrease in school registration and indicated a continuation of the downward trend. In 1975, the year of the study, there were 1,708 children between the ages of 4–17 enrolled in Jewish schools - 61% of the Jewish school age population. The highest rate of attendance was among children aged 6–13; more than 80% of the youngsters in this age bracket were in Jewish schools. Those parents who did not send their children to a Jewish school gave as their primary reason either lack of interest or the fact that none of the Jewish schools in the city offered the sort of Jewish education they considered appropriate. Neither the cost nor the quality of schooling appear to have been major factors in their decision.

When the enrollment statistics are analyzed by sex, it becomes apparent that there has been a decided increase in the percentage of girls who attend Jewish schools. The mid–1950s study, *Jewish Education in the United States*, reported that boys and girls were enrolled in equal numbers in one-day-a-week schools, that almost twice as many boys as girls were in day schools, and that boys outnumbered girls by a ratio of close to three to one in afternoon schools (Dushkin and Engelman, 1959). The NJPS reported that "While differences in Jewish education exposure between boys and girls to age nine are small, they become important at age ten and beyond...Among women age 20 and older, typically somewhere above 60% have some exposure to Jewish education, while for men the corresponding figure generally exceeds 80%." Equally important, however, is the observation that among female adolescents and post-adolescents there is a marked increase, approaching 75% in the percentage of girls who attend a Jewish school. The study remarks that "we may predict that an increasingly high proportion of young Jewish women, exceeding the comparable proportion of their parents' generation, will ultimately receive the benefit of some Jewish primary or secondary school experience." This generally optimistic appraisal must, unfortunately, be tempered by the fact that there has been a decline in the number of children of intermarried couples who are reported as Jewish and the conclusion that "if the birthrate remains low and if the rate of intermarriage continues to rise, or holds at high levels...school enrollment," among both boys and girls, "may be expected to decline...." (Massarik, 1978).

Data regarding affiliation in the Jewish community provide yet another perspective of school enrollment. A little more than a decade ago, some 59% of the Jewish heads of households in the United States were 'affiliated', that is, they identified with a Jewish ideology and held membership either in a congregation or Jewish organization or both (Massarik, 1978, pp. 262, 270). Approximately 50% of Jews then in their thirties were affiliated, and among older Jews the percentage hovered around 60%. There is a close correlation, if not a total overlap, between Jews who are affiliated and those who send their children to a Jewish school.

When we examine enrollment by sponsorship and type of school, the following pattern emerges for the late 1970s: some 35% of the students attended schools under Reform auspices; approximately 27% were in schools affiliated with the Conservative movement; and about another 27% were enrolled in Orthodox-sponsored schools; the remaining 11% were in communal or independent schools. One-day-a-week schools accounted for 25% of total enrollment (a sharp drop from an earlier level of 42%); afternoon schools enrolled 49% of the student population (a rate which has remained quite stable for more than a quarter of a century), and day schools accounted for 26% of all registrations (an increase of close to 30% relative to the figure ten-years earlier) (American Association for Jewish Education, 1976; 1979).

Most Jewish education today, as in the past, takes place at the elementary level. Despite a reported rise in high school enrollment – that is, programs for youngsters above age thirteen which meet at least once a week – the majority of pupils in Jewish schools drop-out upon completion of the elementary level. Even the most generous estimate of high school registration is only around 15% (Hochberg and Lang, 1974, p. 237), and a high drop-out rate remains one of the most intractable problems confronting Jewish educators. A whole complex of factors outside the school itself conspires to thwart even the most carefully designed and executed programs. If, as some recent studies suggest, supplementary schooling can be effective if students stay in school long enough, good high school programs are a first order priority for Jewish education.

One positive factor on the Jewish educational scene today is the trend toward more intensive schooling. In Orthodox circles, one-day-a-week schools have all but disappeared; a similar tendency is evident in the Conservative movement; and the number of midweek afternoon schools in Reform congregations is on the increase. As indicated above, the average number of pupil hours per school year in Jewish schools has risen from 182 to 248, an increase of 35% since 1966–67. However, it is the growth of the Jewish day school movement which is surely a distinguishing characteristic of American Jewish life in our generation. In 1944, there were 39 day schools in the United States, most of them in New York City; today, there are more than 550. Of these, 86% are under Orthodox auspices; 8% are Conservative; 5% designate themselves as Communal or Independent; and 1% identify with the Reform movement. Over the 15 years from 1962 to 1977, day school enrollment jumped from 60,000 to 92,000 pupils (Schiff, 1977). Approximately one out of every four children receiving Jewish education at the elementary level is in a day school.

The day school is a signal achievement of Orthodox Jewry, whose steadfast adherence to the religious imperative of *Talmud Torah* (learning of Torah) influenced both Conservative and Reform Jews. In many instances day school supporters established schools despite indifference and even opposition from official quarters. They were frequently accused of parochialism, ghetto thinking and the worst sin of all – un-American behavior. Their persistence, coupled with the manifest failures of the one-day-a-week and afternoon schools, accounts in no small measure for the turnabout in the position of Jewish federations, which were once centers of determined resistance to day schools. In 1971, Max Fischer, then president of the Council of Jewish Federations and Welfare Funds, urged communal leaders "to re-examine their obligations to the day schools...for the day school holds one of the very best answers to further Jewish continuity and has earned our most careful consideration of what could be done to help."

The day school can probably be seen as a combination of the traditional yeshiva and the modern secular school. There was a time, not so long ago, when the mere mention of a yeshiva was enough to irritate those who thought it "...an anachronism for which the United States had neither the time nor the place...A legitimate use can be found for every dollar that the Jews of the United States can spare and there is none to waste for transplanting in American soil an institution of the medieval ghetto" (Klaperman, 1969, p. 137). The process of recognition and acceptance of the day school as a legitimate form of Jewish education in America is strikingly illustrated by the change in the attitude of one of America's most prominent and influential Jewish educators. Writing in 1918, the late Alexander Dushkin, then one of the dedicated young men attracted by Samson Benderly to the newly founded Bureau of Jewish Education in New York City, expressed his reservations about day schools by stating that Jews "must develop schools which will preserve Jewish life in this country without interfering with America's cherished plan of a system of common schools for all the children of all the people" (Dushkin, 1918, pp. 21, 137–138).

This statement was addressed to a community of recently arrived immigrants whose uncertain place in American life was bounded by grinding poverty and the travail of adjustment. Fifty years later, at the close of a long and distinguished career, Dushkin would declare:

> ...There has grown up a third generation of American Jewry whose parents are American born and who...feel themselves at peace as citizens of the American democracy...the Jewish community is now larger, better organized, more influential, actually and potentially than it was fifty years ago...In the years ahead it will be increasingly obligatory for Jewish educators to promote the establishment of day schools as the intensive core of the American Jewish school system...to include 25% of our children.... (Dushkin, 1967, pp. 44, 48).

The striking rise in day school enrollment is evidence of a telling change in the image Jews have of themselves and of their relationship to American society.

There has been much discussion about the motives which cause parents to send their children to day schools. In the case of religiously and otherwise committed families the reasons are obvious. There is also no question that the heightened sensitivity to ethnic identification which has characterized American society in recent years has been a contributing factor. Dissatisfaction with supplementary Jewish schools, busing and the alternative school movements, which legitimized withdrawal from the public school, should also be noted. A recent investigation of parental attitudes toward the day school based on a small sample was conducted in a large midwestern city, a setting which is perhaps more instructive than the traditional centers of Jewish population (Adams, Frankel and Newbauer, 1972–73, p. 28). Responses to a questionnaire indicate that "the most important considerations for the parents in sending their children to this school seem to be the study of the modern Israeli state, the acquiring of a sense of belonging and pride in being Jewish, participation in the religious aspects of Judaism, and the small number of students per teacher." Another study (Kelman, 1978), conducted in Los Angeles in 1977, discloses that while parents who send their children to a non-Orthodox day school are further motivated by specifically Jewish concerns, the primary reason behind the decision is the desire for general education of a high quality.

Any reckoning of the number of people involved in some form of formally structured Jewish learning must include students on college campuses. Over 300 different institutions of higher learning in the United States now offer one or more undergraduate courses in Jewish studies; at least 40 universities offer a major in the area and 27 sponsor graduate programs (Maslow, 1974).

Some estimates suggest that in the 1973–74 academic year as many as 50,000 undergraduates took courses in Jewish studies. That same year the National Foundation for Jewish Culture received grant applications from 125 doctoral candidates in the various disciplines of Jewish studies (Silver, 1978, pp. 212–213). Before World War II less than a dozen scholars taught Judaic Studies on a full time basis in American universities; perhaps an equal number taught Hebrew, mostly in divinity schools. Today the Association for Jewish Studies, the professional organization of university instructors engaged in teaching and research in Jewish studies, counts close to 1,000 members. Nearly 250 have full time appointments and another 400 teach on a part time basis. The majority are American born and trained. Little is known about the students enrolled in these programs – previous attendance at a Jewish school, religious orientation, career plans and the like. One conclusion, however, is permissible: more college students than ever before are now involved in Jewish studies.

The reasons for the growth and expansion of Jewish studies are varied. The general broadening of undergraduate curricula beyond the traditional parameters of the liberal arts – one of the major characteristics of American colleges and universities in the years immediately following World War II – is certainly a factor. Prodding by students and faculty, demands of blacks and other groups for ethnic studies, pressure from local Jewish communities all helped move institutions of higher learning to recognize Judaica as a legitimate area of study for inclusion among their course offerings. Student interest attests to the coming of age of a generation of young American Jews, sure of their place in American society, who looked to their university years as an opportunity for "exploring themselves and their roots as well as their world" (Silver, 1978, pp. 212–213). Faculty support, always decisive, often came from unexpected sources. At one university, a Jewish studies program "emerged out of a Jew in the English department whose interest was radical literature, one Jew in anthropology whose interest was in the shtetl, and a Jew in history who was a specialist in labor organizations" (ibid.).

Curriculum

Two parallel strands are discernable in programs of curriculum development of recent years: heightened attention to the affective component in learning now occupies a prominent place alongside the approach which places a premium on cognitive development and the acquisition of intellectual skills. A new generation of Jewish educators has shifted the focus of Jewish schooling from the traditional pre-determined subject matter to an active concern for the self-expressed needs and interests of the student. These young educators, many of whom have been trained in America's best graduate schools of education, are committed to "...uncovering the thoughts and feelings of the kids themselves, not on a specific issue but rather in a free wheeling open-ended way. This should allow the kids to bring in their own experiences with very little intervention on the part of the teacher...." (Jacobson, 1970, pp. 45–46).

On the high school level this approach involves a high degree of student involvement in all phases of planning and execution, a heightened emphasis on the affective attention to inter-personal relationships, a readiness to move beyond the framework of prescribed forms and structures, and an acceptance of the legitimacy of a wide variety of views and patterns of personal expression. The acknowledgement of the centrality of mitzvoth in Judaism is accompanied by a view of religion as a continued search for self-realization rather than a closed system of preordained imperatives. Religious practice, as a consequence, becomes a highly personal matter, with the final determinant of the student's religious behavior being his own feelings. The legitimacy of Jewish nationalism finds expression in a commitment to the State of Israel and a recognition of its crucial role in the Jewish future. At the same time, the American Jewish community is also accorded a place of primacy. This conception of learning affords place to traditional modes and methods of study but finds them lacking when isolated from broader and more encompassing experiences. The task of the educator then is not simply to direct a school or to inculcate a point of view, but rather to create an environment in which the student is free to experiment in a variety of settings and with an assortment of materials, in an encouraged attempt to define a style of Jewishness which suits his own needs and tastes.

At the elementary level this manner of dealing with the child has led to experimentation with the 'open school' and, to a lesser extent, to the establishment of 'free' or 'alternative' Jewish schools. The 'open school' seeks to create a better environment for learning; the 'alternative school', usually found in university centers and conducted by students, constitutes a protest of sorts against what is thought to be the lack of Jewish 'authenticity' in the organized Jewish community and its schools (American Association for Jewish Education, 1972; Koller, 1971–72).

Much of what has been discussed here has found expression at the annual conferences sponsored since 1976 by the Coalition for Alternatives in Jewish Education (CAJE), a loosely knit group of young educators which is an offshoot of the North American Jewish Students Network. These conferences, held on college campuses around the country and attracting over 1,000 participants, are a pot-pourri of educational method and technique, conducted by imaginative teachers and administrators who prefer their own instructional and curricular material to that prepared by national agencies. The workshops and other activities at a CAJE conference concentrate on the 'doing' of Jewish education and, in their emphasis on the affective, challenge the position of dominance accorded the cognitive domain.

Attention to the affective along with concern for the involvement of students in the development of programs is by no means limited to CAJE. For almost a decade the Rhea Hirsch School of Education of the Hebrew Union College-Jewish Institute of Religion in Los Angeles has conducted a project in 'confluent education'. This project is an adaptation, in the setting of the Jewish school, of work done at the Esalen Institute and the University of California at Santa Barbara. As described by one of its major theoreticians, confluent education calls for the "integration or flowing together of the affective and cognitive elements in individual and group learning..." (Brown, 1971, pp. 10–11). Teachers who participated in the training program reported that they had gained a great deal. Unfortunately, there has been no published report of a systematic empirical investigation evaluating the impact of confluent education on children in Jewish schools.

On a larger scale we may point to the curriculum development program announced several years ago by the Commission on Jewish Education of the Union of American Hebrew Congregations (Spiro, 1971). The conceptual framework of the undertaking rests on the assumption that "...educators must be receptive to the problems and needs of the students and attempt to create a synthesis between ...traditional values and present concerns. The focal points of the curriculum are both what the learner wants to learn and what he ought to learn". Student input was achieved through a "national survey...conducted to determine the interests, concerns and problems of students on all age levels...". Whatever the ultimate form or effectiveness of the curriculum, there is no question that that approach represents a fundamental commitment to responding to student interests.

A study of religious education in the reform movement published in 1977 states that "...it is impossible to identify anything that resembles a uniform curriculum for the Reform movement" (Gertman, 1977, p. 34). Several explanations suggest themselves: the curriculum currently suggested for Reform religious schools was first published more than 25 years ago and has been revised only slightly since then; or perhaps, the diversity of opinion and outlook which characterizes Reform Judaism in the United States militates against uniformity in curriculum. Yet, there appears to be agreement among Reform educators regarding the subject matter areas of the curriculum. Whatever the content of specific courses on the fifth grade level, history, the holidays, Israel and the life cycle are extensively taught. Current Jewish issues and history are wide-spread in the seventh grade; theology, sex ethics, Israel and the Holocaust figure prominently in upper level programs. Curricular concern for students' personal needs is reflected in the observation that "students begin to have sexual experiences at a much earlier age"; hence, what "Judaism has...to say about sex ethics should be said at a time when teenagers are beginning to explore their sexual feelings rather than at a time when their ideas about sex ethics are already formed" (Gertman, 1977, p. 38).

Orthodox day schools, whose curricular options are relatively clear-cut, have also explored the significance of the experiential. There is a familiar ring to the observation of a leading day school spokesman that "too many of our schools are satisfied with formal education conducted in and around the classroom. If our goal of commitment is to be a realistic one we must look for opportunities for students to act out the values and life style we are teaching ...students will 'learn' more about the plight of Soviet Jewry in two hours devoted to neighborhood campaigning for signatures on a petition...than in two weeks of classes on Soviet-Jewish problems..." (Lookstein, 1972, pp. 113-114). A similar motif is evident in the Moral Sensitivity Training Program prepared by *Torah U'Mesorah*, the National Society for Hebrew Day Schools. This program provides a variety of instructional materials, including specially prepared texts, model lessons in print and on tape, and teaching guides for schools interested "in expanding the moral sensitivity and understanding of their pupils" (*Torah U'Mesorah*, 1975-76). This program, building on the knowledge and skills which distinguish the day school pupil from his peers in other settings, addresses itself particularly to the growing number of youngsters from non-observant homes enrolled in Orthodox day schools.

The Curriculum Guide for Afternoon Religious Schools, recently published by the National Commission on Torah Education, is more conventional. Based on a questionnaire survey which elicited responses from over 200 Orthodox educators, the Guide is intended for afternoon schools which offer six hours of instruction per week over a five-year period. Suggested courses of study generally include Hebrew, Torah, Jewish social studies, *mitzvoth ma'asioth* (practical commandments) and synagogue/prayer. Perhaps the most interesting of the Guide's recommendations is the suggestion that the traditional chronological approach to Jewish history which attempts to cover thousands of years in an hour a week over a period of five years be eschewed in favor of a concentration on contemporary Jewish affairs – Israel and Jewish-Arab relations, the Holocaust, Soviet Jewry, the North American Jewish community, and the world-wide Sephardic community (Baum, 1979).

Day school educators have long been interested in defining a relationship between Jewish and general (secular) studies. While some schools, primarily Hasidic and other Orthodox yeshivoth, maintain a strict line of separation between the two, many others, Orthodox as well as Conservative, Reform and communal, seek to create some measure of correlation between the two. Proponents of integration stress the idea that attendance at a day school does not mean being cut off from the mainstream of American life; they want to achieve a measure of parity between Jewish and general studies and avoid the "split personalities within the compartmentalized minds" which result from teaching that the Torah cannot be questioned or criticized while instruction of general studies encourages independent judgement and the challenging of authority; and they prefer uniting the two traditions, the Jewish and the American, to which the child is heir. A symposium directed at this question reveals a wide range of meanings attached to the concept of 'integration' and even greater diversity of practice (Integration in Day School Programs, 1978).

The curricula developed by the Melton Research Center and the United Synagogue Commission on Jewish Education stand apart from the trend described above. While certainly not unmindful of the affective aspects of learning, the materials produced by these two agencies of the Conservative movement emphasize subject matter and the development of cognitive skills. The curriculum of the Melton Research Center is "...designed to teach information, skills and competencies" and is based on the assumption that "Jewish education must embody the thinking and the wisdom found in Jewish texts – Bible, the prayerbook, Talmud, Midrash and historical documents - and that it (is) desirable to have the students confront those texts directly and extract from them the themes which are basic to Jewish life and religion" (Morris, 1979, p. 6). Along with a strict definition of subject matter, provided by members of the faculty of the Jewish Theological Seminary, the Melton material mandates a very specific method. The new Curriculum for the Afternoon Jewish School, published by the United Synagogue Commission on Jewish Education, is another example of a subject-centered program of study (United Synagogue Commission on Jewish Education, 1978). Though different in structure from the Melton program and more flexible in method, it too rests on the assumption that knowledge is central to the life of the Jew and that what a Jewish child should know is best determined by scholars and educators. Both of these programs reflect a renewed commitment to formal schooling, and a belief in the potential efficacy of the supplementary afternoon school. Whatever the power of other settings, the new curricula of the Conservative movement, like that currently under development in the Reform movement, assume that the great majority of children will receive their Jewish education in the afternoon school. Moreover, they reflect a heightened sense of ideology, and stress the religious rather than the nationalist dimension of Jewishness.

The stated goals of the United Synagogue curriculum are noteworthy from yet another point of view. When they proclaim that "...the whole point of studying in the religious school is to learn what makes the Jew different...and to make a decision as to why you should be different" (United Synagogue Commission on Jewish Education, 1978, p. 505), they reveal a shift in the definition of Jewishness and Americanism and the relationship between the two. An earlier generation of Jewish educators stressed the similarities between Judaism and the norms of American democracy. This posture is easily understood when we remember that the perception was mainly shaped by the immigrant experience. A curriculum which consciously teaches the importance of difference is clearly addressing itself to a changed America and to another sort of Jew.

The specific contents of current curricula, whatever their thrust, are by and large drawn from the time-honored subjects of Jewish study. The individual school, working by itself or guided by outlines prepared by national agencies, chooses the material of instruction and the mode of treatment. Both the time available to the school and its ideological orientation determine the curriculum space allotted any particular subject. As a rule, the more intensive the school the greater the concentration on traditional texts or on material drawn from that source. Only day schools are able to introduce students to the Talmud and cognate Rabbinic literature. There is probably no Jewish school in the country which does not teach Bible and history in some form. Hebrew remains a problematic area for afternoon supplementary schools unless they are willing to devote most of their time to language instruction. The new curriculum of the United Synagogue, mindful of the low level of achievement which characterizes most of its affiliated congregational schools, advises that unless there is a commitment to a concentration in Hebrew, language instruction should be restricted to a basic phonics program geared to preparing the pupil to follow the synagogue service.

The core subjects of Bible, history, and Hebrew are surrounded by a wide array of courses, reflecting particular educational outlooks. In recent years Jewish religious thought has been emphasized. As in the case of other subjects, the more intensive and traditional the school – and the two generally go hand in hand – the greater the reliance on classical texts. Mention should also be made of the near-universal inclusion of Israel and the Holocaust in the curricula of Jewish schools. These two topics, more than any others, pose problems for Jewish educators; when treated as 'subjects' they are threatened by the heavy hand of trivialization; when viewed as the central events of modern Jewish existence, they call into question many of the assumptions which guide Jewish schools in the United States.

The manner in which American Jewish schools deal with the Holocaust is worthy of special note. The growing sense of security which characterized a generation of American Jews born to affluence and seemingly limitless opportunity lent support to the view that 'America is different' and complicated the search for an approach to a theme whose details are witness to the fragility of Jewish existence. It was not until well into the 1950s that Jewish educators began to grapple with the educational problems posed by the Holocaust. This delayed reaction is wholly understandable given the enormity of the events themselves and the time required for comprehension of their meaning, the absence of scholarly research in the years immediately following the war, and not the least, the deterring influence of the fact that most children in Jewish schools were of elementary school age. The central issue, of course, was and still is the purpose of teaching the Holocaust.

While some Jewish educators might question the wisdom of dealing with the subject at all at such young ages, most shy away from such a suggestion even as they remain uncertain in their approach. Proposals such as "The *Shoah* should become part of our tradition...a day of rememberance in the calender" (Pilch, 1964, p. 164); the teaching of the Holocaust should "...evoke sentiment for the 'world that is no more'" and provide "the link that the American Jewish child needs in order to identify with that which we wish him to identify with in his own heritage;" ..."the facts of Jewish history may perhaps succeed in inspiring strength,...security and a sense of inner purpose" (Frank, 1964, p. 178); and "the teaching of the historical facts of intergroup conflict and of persecution and discrimination (should include) some elementary information on the findings of the social sciences (on) the psychological structure of prejudiced people and the social and political structures under which prejudice and group hostility manifest themselves" (ibid., p. 174) – all these seem to suffer from a prosaism which denies the cataclysmic nature of the actual events. Moreover, adult needs are rarely translated into educational experiences which are meaningful to children.

A far more powerfully generative approach is to be found in the position of those who would teach the *Shoah* as a subset of an all-embracing theory of Jewish life and experience. It is difficult to cavil with those who hold that

> To teach the *Shoah* in isolation...will not suffice. Instead, the *Shoah* must be treated within the framework of our essential theological concepts, the nature of Jewish existence, and a critical approach to Western civilization...only after the student is exposed to the major issues in Jewish history and thought, can he be ready to grasp some of the awesome and mystical implications of the *Shoah* (Ury, 1964, p. 169).

Without such a context, the tragedy which befell the Jews of Europe is inevitably reduced to an indifferent recitation of meaningless facts and figures. Within such a context, the telling acquires purpose" ...neither to sadden, nor frighten, nor embitter the young, but to strengthen them with mature understanding..." (Schulweis, 1964, p. 187).

The gradual inclusion of the Holocaust as an accepted subject in the Jewish school has not quieted debate. Educators continue to look for new ways to insure that children will come to know and feel the events which changed the physiognomy of their people. Techniques of simulation, role-playing and group dynamics have been employed to create empathy, shock, and even fear. In some instances, that which is specifically Jewish in the Holocaust has been blurred in favor of a more generalized approach in which the *Shoah*, American involvement in Vietnam, and discrimination against blacks and other minority groups are all presented as equally relevant examples of man's endemic propensity for evil. Those who would argue that the child should be exposed to the full brunt of the Jewish catastrophe in Europe are firm in their conviction that the

> ...study of the Holocaust must not be wrapped in the gauze of abstrac-
> tions. If the child is not to be pampered, he cannot be spared learning...
> that Jews are especially vulnerable to the worst excesses of history. He
> cannot be spared reading about the agony of the boy who dies slowly on
> the gallows in Elie Wiesel's *Night*. He cannot be spared the photographs
> in albums on the Holocaust; the frightened little boy who has his hands
> up in the air...the pious-looking, elderly Jew whose beard is being
> snipped off by an amused German lout. Though such photographs are
> hardly things of beauty and joy forever...they can be an occasion for
> underscoring the truth that to be human is to be open to the suffering
> of others; that to be human is to look on the other as a brother and not
> as a stranger...a hard light needs to be kept on the atrocities and suffer-
> ing (Schulweis, 1976).

The patent intractability of this view is countered by those who maintain that a 'hard line' is neither good history nor good education. "To see only man's *yetzer hara*, or view history's evil acts alone, is to distort both men and history, both our past and more significantly our future." The idea that a relentless recounting of Jewish suffering will somehow result in a heightened identification with Jews and Judaism is a vain and unfounded hope; the denial of the human capacity for compassion as exemplified by the selfless acts of those many Gentiles who risked their lives to save countless numbers of Jews produces an imbalance which enthrones death over life. "The whole-sale condemnation of the non-Jewish world blurs all real distinction, blots out the memory of saintliness, records only the acts of infamy and reduces us all to a paralyzing despair" (ibid.).

Despite the wide variety of material currently available for the teaching of the Holocaust, it is difficult to measure its effectiveness. The absence of data based on carefully controlled research restricts evaluation to information gar-nered from impressionistic inference. While the testimony of pupil reaction derived from such sources is slanted in the direction of indifference and igno-rance of basic facts, it also discloses instances of profound empathy and iden-tification. Unfortunately, we know too little to be able to account sensibly for either type of reaction. Reliable conclusions which may serve as the legiti-mate ground for future curriculum development will require a more rigorous and detailed analysis of the teaching and learning of the Holocaust than has been the case to date (Roskies, 1975).

The gloom of the Holocaust was pierced by the establishment of the State of Israel. The wave of enthusiasm which swept American Jewry in 1948 left an indelible imprint on Jewish education. The birth of the new state infused Jews with pride and purpose reflected in increased school enrollments, a renewed interest in the study of Hebrew, a rash of instructional materials, and in countless other ways.

Over the years Israel as subject matter has permeated the overwhelming majority of Jewish schools in the United States. A study conducted shortly after the Six-Day War in 1967 noted that modern Israel was treated as a distinct and definable topic in more than half of the 700 responding schools in the sample. In schools where the study of Israel was not an independent element, various aspects of life in that country were integrated into the curriculum through work in Bible, history, Hebrew language instruction, current events, customs and holidays. In short, there is hardly an area of curriculum which is without some degree of attention to, and emphasis on, Israel. In addition to formal instruction, the relationship to the Jewish state is expressed through special events such as the celebration of Israel's Independence Day, bulletin board materials, exhibits and art objects from Israel in the school building, visits by Israelis to the school, music and dance, penpals, and numerous other activities (Schiff, 1968; Chazan, 1979).

The school, however, is only one locus of Israel-centered activity. The deep concern of American Jews for the welfare of Israel serves to reinforce the work of the school and very often draws youngsters of school age into the circle of community-wide activity. In addition, and perhaps most important, are the educational programs in Israel developed by American Jewish educators working together with, and sometimes prodded by, agencies and institutions overseas. Over the years, thousands of youngsters have spent varying amounts of time in Israel in an almost endless variety of educational settings. Many of these young people have benefitted from scholarship programs established in their communities. Indeed, in a great many Jewish circles, a trip to Israel during the high school or college years has come to be considered an integral part of the Jewish educational experience. This position is mirrored in a statement issued in the aftermath of the Six-Day War by the American Association for Jewish Education, the umbrella organization for Jewish education in the United States: "It should...become part of the responsibility of the organized Jewish community to help American Jewish young people enrolled in our high school programs to have at least one summer of personal experience in Israel." (American Association for Jewish Education, 1969).

The idea of a learning experience in Israel rests on the same assumption that guides all programs in international education – without a living contact with a land and its people, one's knowledge of a country is incomplete. The use of Israel as an educational resource and the large investments of effort and money involved in sending students there are geared to more than getting to know the country, as important as that may be. Jewish schools in America look to programs in Israel as a means of strengthening the Jewish identification of their students; as an experience which affirms and strengthens the bond with the Jewish people; as an opportunity to create some sort of relationship with the Jewish state; and as a source of motivation for continued study and activity at home. Israeli educators and agencies see these various programs as the first stage of a process they hope will culminate in aliyah.

The manner in which Israel is treated, in formal and informal settings both here and abroad, has undergone noticeable change over the years. In the period immediately following the establishment of the state, the dominant tendency was to picture a utopia inhabited by fearless pioneers concerned only with the future of their people. The passage of time, the constant flow of information from Israel, the adaptation of methodological conceptions developed in the public schools and, above all, a deep commitment to Jewish life in America all worked together to force instruction to move closer to the reality of life in the Jewish state. A striving for cogent analysis and balanced criticism replaced the romanticism of an earlier time.

The degree of interest in Israel is in no small measure influenced by events there. Periods of crisis evoke heightened activity and are the occasion for new expressions of loyalty and support. The Six-Day War, for instance, led to the publication of a statement of objectives for the teaching about Israel which urged schools "to present to the student...the very real options which Israel offers to him as a Jew and as a loyal citizen of the land in which he resides. The needs of Israel and the needs of the Jewish people in America require that we explore the critical question of how the individual Jew can best fulfill himself – whether by the enrichment of his Jewish life in America and/or by aliyah to Israel" (American Association for Jewish Education, 1969). The full implications of that declaration can be comprehended only in the context of the events of June 1967.

However, neither the recognition of aliyah as a legitimate goal nor the wide range of activities which focus on Israel has substantially affected the basic orientation of Jewish education in America. Despite the valence of Zionism and its offshoots in the curriculum, Jewish schools are still concerned primarily with educating their pupils to live as Jews in the United States. Israel is, therefore, most often perceived and used as a means of strengthening Jewish life in America – a posture, incidentally, which permits something less than the fullest utilization of the possibilities for education.

The lack of relevant data prevents us from estimating the effectiveness of the various programs cited above – that is, the achievement of their stated goals. We do not know how many schools actually use the curricula prepared by national education commissions; nor do we really know what happens once a curriculum is adopted by a school and introduced into the classroom.

We do know, however, that there is no shortage of curricula and instructional materials: local agencies and individuals rival national agencies in the production of courses of study and learning units; textbook publishers, a more potent influence in curriculum development than generally acknowledged, have attained a level of sophistication which often compares favorably with that of the general field; teachers' centers, a phenomenon of the last decade, encourage teacher initiative and autonomy and provide guidance in the preparation of materials needed for a particular class; a cottage industry of sorts, reflected in the advertisements which dot the pages of educational journals, produces a wide array of classroom aids. It seems safe to state that teachers in Jewish schools today enjoy a choice of materials beyond anything available in the past.

A brief study of the programs and materials we have mentioned is required to discern the pervasive influence of American educational thought and practice on Jewish schools. An examination of a recent issue of *The Pedagogic Reporter*, a quarterly which regularly reports on trends and developments in Jewish education, reveals the extent to which innovations in American education – both those which have been proven effective and those which are little more than passing fads – have been adapted for use in the Jewish school (*The Pedagogic Reporter*, 1976). The fact is that the Jewish school in the United States has modelled itself after the public school in almost every respect – organizational patterns, administrative techniques, means of pupil control and discipline, and methods of instruction.

The 'Americanization' of the Jewish school is surely understandable and perhaps unavoidable. Jewish schools all over the world definitely carry the mark of their host societies, and schools in one country are different from those in another precisely because of the varying contours of local educational environments. One can, however, question the desirability of a process which denatures the distinctive attributes of a culture to the point where specific ethnic and religious components are barely perceptible in the ambience of the school. What a child learns in school derives as much from his total experience in that setting as from the content of instruction. The structure of the school, the methods of instruction it employs, the sanctions it invokes, and the relationships it fosters all denote a particular view of man and the world and are vital to the internalization of the values which the school holds. When Jewish schools adopt the models and manners of American schools, they all too often neglect the relationship between method and principle and deny the practical implications of the tradition they teach. There is much to consider in the observation that

> We have not looked at our own tradition for the kinds of directions we can find for developing our own responses to the need for self-direction and the striving to integrate the roles of emotion and intellect to which

the open and affective education movements have been the responses in the general field...The best thought of general education is certainly necessary...but it is not sufficient without the Jewish core (Lukinsky, 1974, p. 11).

Current curricula exhibit another characteristic, in some ways related to the emphasis on the affective and the interest in identity formation already noted. In its classical formation, Jewish education is a religious imperative. Traditional Judaism required no justification for the education of children other than that contained in the divine command: "Take to heart these words with which I charge you this day. Impress them upon your children." (Deut. 6:67). The study of the sacred texts is a form of worship and the acquisition of knowledge the key to human perfectibility. The vicissitudes of Jewish life and the secularization of modern culture have contributed noteworthy permutations of the original concept. Zionist thought viewed education as the means of fostering national pride and will. The Jewish socialist movement through its network of Yiddish schools stressed the importance of education in the development of class consciousness and an egalitarian society. Jewish education in pre-World War II America, heavily influenced by the work of Kurt Lewin and the mental hygiene movement, was regarded as a means of avoiding social marginality and an important line of defense in the struggle against antisemitism. These latter varieties of Jewish educational ideals offered the individual transcendence through identification with an overarching social purpose. The authority of the divinely ordained principles serves Orthodox Jewish educators to this day. Their colleagues in other quarters, subject as they are to the demands of modernism, enjoy no such sanction, and the materials they produce celebrate a privatism somewhat punctured by appeals to group survival.

Personnel

Whatever the achievements of Jewish education in the United States, it has not succeeded in providing the Jewish teacher with a status commensurate with the importance of his task. There is still much truth to the bitter comment, made many decades ago after repeated failures to guarantee a living wage for teachers, which notes that "Among the guilty must be counted all those organizations, Zionist and others, and their members who speak so eloquently of a renaissance of our national spirit and culture, but who are no where to be found when it comes to doing something tangible about education, the key to national rebirth" (Whitman, 1918, p. 6). The rhetoric of public forums still proclaims the pivotal role of education in the maintenance of Jewish life; words, however, continue to run far ahead of deeds and we are witness to the virtual demise of the profession of Jewish training.

By the late 1970s, there were approximately 3,500 Jewish studies teachers employed in day schools and some 5,500 in weekday afternoon schools. Of this number, less than one-third may be considered full-time teachers, if full-time teaching in day schools is set at 20 hours per week and in afternoon schools at 12 hours per week. We have no exact figures on the number of teachers working in one-day-a-week schools, although it is safe to assume that declining enrollment and school considerations have reduced this number considerably below the 9,559 reported 20 years earlier in the National Study of Jewish Education (Pollak, 1978b). Except in day schools, there are almost no full-time teaching positions available in Jewish education today. During the 1978–79 school year only 15% of 116 teachers appointed to Conservative afternoon schools in the Chicago area were in full-time positions. In the entire Greater Boston area there were only 12 full-time positions available in afternoon schools. The situation was much the same in Cleveland.

Current salary schedules deter all but the most dedicated and compound the difficult problem of developing a corps of teachers committed to Jewish education. A study conducted in the 1975–76 school year by the American Association for Jewish Education found that "teacher salaries in Jewish day and supplementary schools are too low to afford a head of family a decent, comfortable standard of living as the sole wage earner." The analysis of the data gathered from 382 schools in 31 metropolitan areas showed that the median maximum salary of a full-time day school teacher was $13,433 per year, while that of a full-time teacher in a supplementary school was $9,400. The salary for day school teachers was 13.2% below what public school teachers earned. This situation has made it impossible to maintain rigorous standards of certification and professional requirements which are the hallmarks of professionalism.

There has been no dearth of sensible suggestions for improving the economic situation of teachers: employment by the community rather than by individual schools of limited resources; consolidation of schools to increase teaching loads; training teachers to work in both formal and informal settings; and establishing clearly-defined promotion procedures leading to administrative posts.

Teachers in Jewish schools are a varied group: yeshiva graduates who have opted for teaching careers in day schools; graduates of Jewish teacher-training institutions; Israelis in this country either permanently or temporarily; college students, with or without training and background, whose teaching in a Jewish school is just a stop along the way to another profession; and those who arrive at a Jewish school through no recognizable route of Jewish learning or training.

Yeshiva graduates are the backbone of the Orthodox day school system. Israeli teachers, both in day and afternoon schools, pose particular problems, as they are separated from their students by deep cultural differences. While the conscientious teacher from Israel may succeed in bridging the gap, his very residence in the United States seriously compromises a curriculum in which Israel is an important element. The penalties of an excess of imports are as severe in education as in economics.

The diversity of background, training and experience which characterizes teachers in Jewish schools today points to a troubling disparity between their attitudes and beliefs and the stated objectives of the school. Any assessment of school effectiveness must weigh the influence of teachers whose personal life style, frequently seen by pupils, differs significantly from the values they teach. Jewish schools attempt to lead their pupils to a Jewish way of life, but more than one will find a disquieting reflection of itself in the congregational school whose "...teaching staff...was a diverse group within Jewish terms. It included some who were anti-religious, some who were very observant, and a great majority who...were...very confused about their Jewishness..." (Schoem, 1980, p. 39).

No other institution involved in Jewish education has undergone as much change in the last decade as the Hebrew teachers college – even the name is no longer appropriate. Once the pinnacles of non-rabbinic Jewish learning in this country, these schools are now hard put to maintain their undergraduate programs. Enrollment at the undergraduate level, which requires simultaneous attendance at two institutions of higher learning, is considerably below the peak of 1,812 reported in the mid–1960s (Ackerman, 1967). The reasons for the decline are many: an unwillingness to carry the load of two schools; the growth of Jewish studies programs on college campuses, viewed by many as equivalent to Hebrew teachers college programs; the decrease in the number of lower-level schools which provide the knowledge and skills required for admission; skyrocketing college tuition fees which force many people to work during the time formerly available for study in these schools. The decline of undergraduate programs has meant a narrowing of opportunities for comprehensive Jewish socialization of young people. Hebrew teachers colleges, also known as colleges of Jewish studies, were more than schools. Attendance at one of these institutions circumscribed the life of the student; it determined his friends, limited his time for non-Jewish activities, and set the boundaries of possible interests.[5]

Several Jewish teacher training schools have developed imaginative new programs. Spertus College in Chicago supplies Jewish studies programs to several colleges in the area. Hebrew College in Boston is developing a program to attract students who do not meet formal admission requirements but are prepared to do make-up work. At the same time, the College has invested heavily in adult education. The various units of Yeshiva University offer a wide variety of pre-professional and professional programs. The Teachers Institute of the Jewish Theological Seminary and its West Coast School, the University of Judaism, as well as the Rhea Hirsch School of Education of the

Hebrew Union College-Jewish Institute of Religion in Los Angeles, have successfully launched Master's degree programs for college graduates interested in careers in Jewish education. It is doubtful, however, whether these students will long remain classroom teachers; those who do remain in Jewish education have clearly set their sights on administrative posts.

In contrast to the situation in teaching is that in administration. There are currently some 1,300–1,400 administrative positions in Jewish schools, Bureaus of Jewish Education, and national agencies (Pollak, 1978b). Reform congregations employ 245 full-time principals; the remaining 775 Reform schools employ part-time educators, rabbis who perform other duties, or lay administrators. A number of Reform congregations have charged educators with total responsibility for the congregational educational program, formal and informal, from pre-school through adult education. Conservative congregations employ 350 full-time principals, and day school principalships are almost always full-time positions. There is no question that administrators in Jewish schools are as well qualified as their counterparts in public education. The problem is the lack of qualified personnel to meet the demand; each placement season resembles a game of musical chairs. Salary schedules range from $15,000 per year for principals to as much as $50,000 for directors of central agencies. These salaries, which compare favorably with those paid in similar occupations, have not succeeded in attracting the number of people needed to staff positions currently available.

Finances

Adequate financial resources are required for schools to initiate and maintain quality programs. The recruitment and retention of teachers, curriculum development, and the production of instructional materials – even for the less intensive afternoon and one-day-a-week schools – require large investments of money. Although around 1980 the total expenditure for Jewish education in the United States was estimated to be $280,000,000, almost three times the amount expended ten years earlier, it is clear that traditional patterns of funding are inadequate, given the demands of expanding programs in a context of variable levels of inflation.

An analysis of pupil costs by type of school indicates national averages ranging from $2,300 per year (around 1980) in day high schools to $500 in three-days-a-week supplementary schools. Elementary day school expenditures amount to $1,500, communal elementary school expenditures to $750, and communal high school expenditures to $550. Costs for one-day-a-week school pupils are not known.

Varied patterns of record-keeping, coupled with a frequent lack of relevant information, make it difficult to ascertain the exact amounts contributed by synagogues to the maintenance of their schools. One estimate places the allocation of Reform congregations to educational programs at an average of about 15 to 20% of the total institutional budget. The more intensive the program, of course, the larger will be the share of congregational expenditures. It is reasonable to assume, however, that in a period of decreasing membership and increasing operational costs, there will be no significant rise in direct subventions to schools from congregational budgets.

The data on tuition fees for three-day-a-week schools indicate that there is little relationship between charges to parents and the actual costs of maintaining a child in school. Over the 20 years between 1951–52 to 1969–70, tuition fees rose from $50 a year for members and $65 a year for non-members to $85 and $150, respectively (Hochberg, 1972, p. 221). A more recent survey of some 30 Conservative congregational schools shows that tuition fees in 1975–76 averaged $115 (United Synagogue of America, 1975–76). Tuition schedules are also affected by the fear that an increase in fees will result in a decrease in enrollment and perhaps synagogue membership.

Day school tuition is an entirely different matter; here, there is a real possibility that ever higher fees will move intensive Jewish education beyond the reach of many families. Whereas in the 1973–74 school year, day school tuition outside New York City was about $1,000, by 1978–79 fees were around $1,500. At the same time in the New York City area, tuition was $2,000 (United Synagogue Commission on Jewish Education, 1979).[6] Tuition is a major source of day school income, but it does not cover the cost of operations, and schools are increasingly forced to look for outside sources of funding.

Since the end of World War II there has been a steady increase in the amount and proportion of federation funds allocated to Jewish education. In 1947, the sums earmarked for Jewish education represented 8.9% of the total funds budgeted for local needs (Dushkin and Engelman, 1959, p. 148); by 1970 this figure had risen to 13.3% (Hochberg, 1972, p. 209); in 1977, allocations to Jewish education totalled 23.3% of all local disbursements (Council of Jewish Federations and Welfare Funds, 1978). In dollars, federation allocations for the period cited (1947–77) rose from $2,215,911 to $27,492,216. A breakdown of the figures reveals the following pattern of disbursements, expressed as percentages of total allocations to Jewish education in 1977 (Ibid., p. 5):

Total	100.0	
Allocations and subsidies to schools	59.8	
Day schools		44.0
Congregational schools		2.3
Other schools		13.5
Jewish institutions of higher learning	8.5	
Services and programs of central agencies	30.8	
All other	0.9	

As encouraging as the trends reported here may sound, total federation allocations in 1977 represented 10% of the costs of Jewish education – an increase of only 3% over 1947. While day schools have been the major beneficiaries of federation financing, the sums allocated in recent years cover only about 13% of their budgets. Thus, parents who want intensive Jewish education for their children must, by and large, pay for it themselves.

The relatively minuscule allocation of federation funds to congregational schools, an anomalous transfer of the principle of separation of Church and State to Jewish communal life, is today under review. Whereas previously neither federations nor synagogues sought to force the issue, declining enrollment and rising costs pose menacing threats to this type of school. Some communities have designed formulas which make afternoon schools eligible for subsidies (Pollak, 1981; Schwartz 1981). The practice, however, is not yet common and it is difficult to identify a consistent pattern.

The never-ending search for additional funds has led some day school supporters to look to the government. They argue that government support falls in the category of aid to children, that it is fully permissible under the equal protection and free exercise clauses of the Constitution, and that the funds made available would be used only for the secular studies component of the day school curriculum. To date, court decisions have approved the use of public tax funds by Jewish day schools only when applied to textbook loans, transportation as a public safety measure, school lunch programs, and certain therapeutic programs. The eligibility of Jewish day schools and other religious elementary and secondary schools for participation in tax-supported school tuition voucher plans remains a moot constitutional issue (Skeoff, 1975).

There is a clear need to rethink the issue of responsibility in the funding of Jewish education. Congregations should review their fiscal procedures to determine what obligations they can sensibly carry. If tuition is primarily the responsibility of the parent, steps must be taken to relate fees realistically to the costs of instruction in a synagogue setting. The readiness of Jewish parents to shoulder the burden of a high tax rate in support of quality public education must find its counterpart in Jewish education, even if this means a decrease in enrollment. Tuition increases alone, however, cannot solve all the financial problems of day schools, and their supporters must discover new funds (Hershberg, n.d.; Schiff, 1973). The stance of federations must similarly be subjected to a searching review.

Effectiveness

The information available on the effectiveness of Jewish education is divided. Considerable data seem to indicate that schools have very little effect either in terms of cognitive outcomes or in terms of attitude and personality change; other studies argue just as persuasively that schools do make a difference in matters such as political information, 'modern' attitudes and behavior, religious behavior and attitudes, and general information.

The conventional wisdom of the Jewish community is that Jewish education, especially in its supplementary form, has little impact on students. Indeed there are those who argue that Jewish schools not only fail to achieve their goals, but actually have a negative effect on children in that they confirm the impression that Judaism is irrelevant to their lives.

We have no reliable empirical evidence concerning the effectiveness of Jewish schooling when the criteria are the acquisition of knowledge or the development of skills. Published curricula materials sometimes tell us what schools intend to teach, but we know little about what is actually taught, and even less about what children actually learn. We are similarly ignorant regarding the efficiency of the Jewish school – the relationship between what is learned and the investments involved. While critics are quick to charge that Jewish schools provide their pupils with very little knowledge, it is not clear that they achieve less, all factors considered, than other kinds of schools, public and private. Both the critics and the defenders of Jewish education are all too often unmindful of the fact that the object of their concern is a child between the ages of seven and twelve. Even under the best of circumstances we can hardly expect such a young child to acquire anything more than a rudimentary knowledge of Judaism. The postulated ineffectiveness of the Jewish school may very well be the ineluctable consequence of the constraints within which it is forced to function.

Some recent studies, marked by a methodological sophistication all too rare in research on Jewish education, report findings which seem to indicate that Jewish schooling does make a difference. One investigator studied adults between the ages of 30 and 45 who had been exposed to Jewish education of varying intensity to determine "what, if any, residual effect Jewish secondary school education in Philadelphia had on the Jewish life style of its graduates" (Ribner, 1978). The findings of the study indicate that those respondents who had had an intensive Jewish secondary school education were more involved in Jewish affairs than those with a more limited Jewish background. Members of the 'intensive' group rate parents and Jewish schooling as the two most important influences on their Jewish identity.

Two other studies suggest that under certain conditions Jewish schooling has an effect which is independent of familial background and other socializing influences (Bock, 1976; Himmelfarb, 1977). According to Geoffrey Bock, better-schooled Jews are more Jewishly identified. He found that, all other things being equal, there was a positive relationship between a child's time spent in Jewish classrooms and his religiosity as an adult, involvement in informal Jewish social networks, knowledge of Jewish culture, and support for Israel. When identification is defined as public Jewishness – attendance at synagogue services, participation in secular synagogue affairs, support for Israel, and attitudes about American public issues – schooling is often as important a factor as home background. However, approximately 1,000 hours of instruction are necessary before Jewish schooling begins to affect Jewish identification significantly. The relationship between Jewish identification and schooling appears to reach its peak at about 4,000 hours of attendance in a Jewish school.

Harold Himmelfarb attempted to determine the relationship, if any, between adult religious involvement and the intensity and extensity of Jewish education. He reported that Jewish schooling does not have any statistically significant impact on adult religiosity until there are approximately 3,000 hours of attendance. The discrepancy between the two studies regarding the minimum number of hours of instruction required for Jewish schooling to have any effect may be a function of the criteria measured. Both identification and religiosity are complex constructs and the various elements of which they are composed may each require different minimums of instructional hours to have any impact. Himmelfarb also found that there is a steady increase in adult religiosity as attendance moves from 3,000 to 4,000 hours; however, beyond 4,000 hours increased schooling does not result in increased religiosity unless reinforced by other factors, particularly the spouse. If such reinforcement occurs there is another significant increase in religiosity when schooling approaches approximately 10,000 hours. Instruction beyond that point does not appear to have any significant impact on religiosity as defined in this study. These two studies suggest that current curricular changes, no matter how refined and sophisticated, will have little long-range impact on students if they do not inspire attendance at a Jewish school well beyond the elementary level.

Bock's and Himmelfarb's threshold figures place the statistics of Jewish school enrollment in painful perspective. More than 75% of the children who receive a Jewish education attend schools which meet for 2–6 hours a week; the full program of these schools extends over 4–7 years; the overwhelming majority of these children do not continue their studies beyond bar/bat mitzvah or Confirmation, and a large percentage do not get even that far. Even those youngsters who complete the first level of the most intensive kind of supplementary education fell short of the minimum number of hours judged essential for a long-range impact.

The foregoing supports the long-standing contention of Jewish educators that children do not stay in Jewish schools long enough to permit anything positive to happen. The data suggest that it makes little difference what the schools do, and how they do it, if the children leave before a certain point.

An interesting perspective from which to view the impact of Jewish education is gained from the findings of a study designed to gauge the effectiveness of Catholic parochial schools. A relationship between adult religious behavior and Catholic schooling was found only among those students who came from religiously observant families; a datum which leads to the conclusion that "...without the predisposition created by a religious family the school was not likely to accomplish very much." Catholic religious education, independent of familial influence, produces "the effect its supporters seek for it only when it is comprehensive (from first grade to college degree)" (Greeley and Rossi, 1966, pp. 87, 88, 223).

The time, effort, and money which provide young people the opportunity to spend some time in Israel also raises questions of impact and influence. Evidence shows that a sojourn in the Jewish state heightens pride in one's Jewishness, strengthens the sense of kinship with fellow Jews, helps in the definition of one's Jewishness and stimulates a desire to become more involved in Jewish affairs and a readiness to consider the possibility of aliyah (Herman, 1970; Ronen, 1966). Programs whose purpose, among other things, is the development of specific skills, i.e. Hebrew language fluency, usually achieve positive results (Shefatyah, 1974). These findings are not unexpected and can be explained without reference to complicated theories. Unfortunately, we do not know whether the immediate enthusiasm inspired by the experience generates any significant long-term change in attitudes and behavior.

Information about the long range effect of a camping experience is largely impressionistic and hardly the basis for objective evaluation. A survey of graduates of Brandeis Camp Institute, a summer program for college students, reveals that "Alumni take an active interest in Jewish activities, have a strong commitment to Jewish activities; have a strong commitment to Jewish history and tradition and are motivated to provide their children with the tools for leading Jewish lives" (Levine, 1972). The majority of the respondents, already well into adulthood, felt that the camp experience "had exerted a measurable and positive experience on their lives." The study did not attempt to investigate the relationship, if any, between reaction to the month's stay at camp and familial background and/or previous Jewish educational experience.

Jewish educators, like their counterparts all over the world, bemoan the absence of parental interest in the work of their schools; and like their colleagues everywhere they tend to get anxious when parents get too involved. The assumption that cooperation between home and school positively influences children's behavior and attitudes in school led one Reform congregation to initiate a parent involvement program. The results were disconcerting: parental participation in the program "had no effect on their childrens' attitude toward religious education" (Knoff and Smith, 1980). One possible explanation for the failure of the program to generate change in the children may be the nature of the 'parent involvement' activities: they were all short-term and required no significant change in the religious behavior or attitudes of the participants. The parents did much the same as their children; what happened in school had little bearing on what they did at home.

Research: A Caveat

Throughout this paper we have made repeated reference to the results of research. As a result, the reader unacquainted with the workings of Jewish education in the United States may conclude that a wealth of data is available, but the opposite is true. Most writing on Jewish education is hortatory and informed opinion at best. A high percentage of the studies which supply empirical evidence are doctoral dissertations whose importance should not obscure the fact that the choice of topic and strategy of investigation are tailored to the needs of the student. Independent investigators whose experience and sense of the field lead to significant questions are thwarted by the lack of funds. Bureaus of Jewish education and other central agencies have rarely sponsored research beyond the gathering of statistical information.

We know very little about the attitudes of teachers in Jewish schools; no one has studied the results achieved by the different Hebrew language programs currently available; there is no information which tells us whether different curricula affect motivation and attitude while a child is in school; no one has examined the consequences for Jewish education of the changing role of women in America; we know next to nothing about the long-range effect of camping and other forms of informal education or whether a combination of formal and informal educational experiences offsets the negative influence of Jewishly disinterested homes; only a bare beginning exists in the exploration of the climate of the Jewish school; no one has studied decision making processes in Jewish education or the way in which policy questions are identified and translated into programs of practice – the list is endless.

Research does not produce solutions to vexing problems, but without the data base, which only research can supply, proposals for improving the quality of Jewish education fall somewhere between educated guessing and an inexcusable waste of time, effort and money.

Conclusion

Jewish education in the United States is still largely supplementary schooling which engages children of elementary school age. These children are primarily second and third generation Americans. This is a fact of considerable consequence for schools charged with the task of developing the Jewish identity of their students. The enrollment of 372,000 pupils in all kinds of

Jewish schools around 1982 reflects a decline of about one third from the peak of approximately 550,000 reported in the middle of the 1960s. This downturn, largely a function of an aging Jewish population and a lower birth-rate among young couples, has not been accompanied by a parallel decrease in the percentage of children of school age attending Jewish schools. The continued growth of day schools, the decline in the number of one-day-a-week schools, the small but encouraging rise in secondary school programs, and the spread of university-level Jewish studies programs suggest that an increasing number of young people are investing more time over a longer period in Jewish education. That gain, however, is still not large enough to offset the fact that the vast majority of children who enter a Jewish school terminate their studies long before they can be expected to have attained any recognizable or long-lasting skills and competencies. The rate of continuation, surely one of the most critical measures of a school's influence, remains disturbingly low.

Recent research findings lend empirical support to what Jewish educators have long known: as long as Jewish education remains mainly elementary education, restricted to 2–5 hours a week of instruction, there is little reason to believe, or even hope, that it can have any long-term impact. The perennial problems of Jewish education – personnel, curriculum, and finances – are in no small measure a function of its limited range. While the schools themselves contribute to drop-out rates, their efforts at self-improvement through the introduction of new curricula and more sophisticated methods and materials are inadequate for the reversal of long-standing attitudes and practices among parents and children alike. The extension of the reach of Jewish schooling into adolescence and beyond must assume the place of first priority for all those concerned about the future of Jewish life in America.

Recognition of the importance of secondary Jewish schooling, if it is to have any meaning, must bring with it economic and other conditions which will attract able and talented Jewish youth to careers in Jewish teaching. It should also give rise to systematic planning, adequately financed research to help us understand the complexities of Jewish schooling, sophisticated teaching strategies and curriculum development, and working arrangements with all those agencies which impinge upon the lives of those who grow up in the American Jewish community. Without such concerted effort, the Jewish school cannot possibly function as the "treasure house of our people's soul."

Notes

1. "McCullum vs. Board of Education 303 U.S. 203 (1948)", as quoted in Butts, 1950, pp. 203–205.

2. In 1978, 39.5 million elementary and secondary school pupils were enrolled in public schools as compared to 4.7 million in independent schools (U.S. Department of Commerce, Bureau of the Census, 1979, p. 139).

3. For the total U.S. population, the median school grade completed was 12.4; 30% had attended school through one year of college or more, while first degrees or higher were achieved by 16% in 1969, some 22% of American families reported annual incomes of $15,000 and above (U.S. Department of Commerce, Bureau of the Census, 1979, pp. 145, 750).

4. Compare, for instance, the use and meaning of the words Torah and mitzvoth in the following statements: "Jewish education...will enable children, youth and adults to become...Jews who bear witness to the *brith* (the covenant between God and the Jewish people) by embracing Torah through the study and observance of mitzvoth (commandments) as interpreted in the light of historic development and contemporary liberal thought" (UAHC-CCAR, n.d.); and "To engender in our students a love, reverence and appreciation of the Torah, halacha, and teachings which have enabled Judaism to survive...(and) to stimulate our students to learn by doing – fulfillment of the Torah and its mitzvoth..." (Baum, 1979, p. 2).

5. Some sense of the spirit of these institutions may be gathered from the following: "The Seminary College was theoretically committed to what Jewish tradition calls *Torah l'shma*, learning for its own sake, but in actual fact its purposes were very far from being disinterestedly academic. The literal meaning of *Torah l'shma* may be 'learning for its own sake,' but the true, the theological meaning of the idea is 'studying the revealed word of God for the sake of heaven.' The Seminary College did not, I think, consider that it was teaching the revealed word of God for the sake of heaven; it did, however, consider that it was teaching the heritage of the Jewish people as a way of ensuring the survival of that people (my father knew what he was doing when he sent me there). This is not to imply that there was anything covert or devious going on; on the contrary, most professors of the Seminary simply and frankly took it for granted that their business was to deepen the Jewish commitment of their students by making them more fully aware of the glories of the Jewish heritage. There were not training minds or sensibilities; they were training Jews!" (Podhoretz, 1967, pp. 43–44).

6. Although the United Synagogue Commission study deals only with Conservative schools, fees in Orthodox and Reform day schools were comparable.

References

Ackerman, W.I. (1967). "A Profile of the Hebrew Teachers College" in: Janowsky, O. (ed.). *The Education of American Jewish Teachers*. Beacon Press, Boston.

Ackerman, W.I. (1975). "The Americanization of Jewish Education". *Judaism*, Vol. 24, no. 7. pp. 416–435.

Ackerman, W.I. (1977). "Some Uses of Justification". *AJS Review*, Vol. 2. pp. 1–44.

Ackerman, W.I. (1981). "On the Making of Jews". *Judaism*, Vol. 30, no. 1. pp. 87–95.

Adams, L., Frankel, J. and Newbauer, N. (1972–73). "Parental Attitudes Toward the Jewish All-Day School". *Jewish Education*, Vol. 42, no. 1. pp. 26–30.

Adar, Z. (1970). *Hachinuch Ha'Yehudi B'Yisrael U'b'Artzot Ha'Brit*. Guma, Tel Aviv. (Hebrew).

American Association for Jewish Education (1969). *Israel and the Jewish School in America: A Statement of Objectives*. The Commission on Teaching About Israel in America, New York.

American Association for Jewish Education (1972). *Opening the School and Individualizing Instruction*. National Curriculum Institute of the American Association for Jewish Education, New York.

American Association for Jewish Education (1976; 1979). *Trends in Jewish School Enrollment*. New York.

Band, A.J. (1966). "Jewish Studies in American Liberal Arts Colleges and Universities". *American Jewish Year Book*, Vol. 67. pp. 3–30.

Baum, E., ed. (1979). *Curriculum Guide for Afternoon Religious Schools*. National Commission on Torah Education, New York.

Benjamin, I. (1936). *Three Years in America*, Vol. 1. Jewish Publication Society, Philadelphia.

Berkson, I.B. (1920). *Theories of Americanization*. Teachers College, Columbia University, New York.

Bock, G.E. (1976). *The Jewish Schooling of American Jews: A Study of Non-Cognitive Educational Effects*. Unpublished doctoral dissertation, Harvard University, Cambridge.

Borowitz, E.B. (1961). "Problems Facing Jewish Educational Philosophy in the Sixties". *American Jewish Year Book*, Vol. 62. pp. 145–153.

Brown, G.I. (1971). *Human Teaching for Human Learning*. Viking, New York.

Bubis, G.B., Wasserman, H. and Lert, A. (1981). *Synagogue Havurot: A Comparative Study*. Center for Jewish Community Studies and Hebrew Union College-Jewish Institute of Religion, Jerusalem.

Butts, F.R. (1950). *The American Tradition in Religion and Education*. Beacon Press, Boston.

Chazan, B. (1978). *The Language of Jewish Education*. Hartmore House, New York and Bridgeport, Conn.

Chazan, B. (1979). "Israel in American Jewish Schools Revisited". *Jewish Education*, Vol. 47, no. 2. pp. 7–17.

Chipkin, I.S. (1936). "Twenty-Five Years of Jewish Education in the United States". *American Jewish Year Book*, Vol. 38. pp. 27–116.

Council of Jewish Federations and Welfare Funds (1978). *Federation Allocations to Jewish Education*. New York.

Cutter, W. and Dauber, J. (n.d.). *Confluent Education in the Jewish School*. Rhea Hirsch School of Education, Hebrew Union College-Jewish Institute of Religion, Los Angeles.

Dubb, A.A. and DellaPergola, S. (1986). *First Census of Jewish Schools in the Diaspora 1981/2–1982/3: United States of America*. Institute of Contemporary Jewry, The Hebrew University, Jerusalem and Jewish Education Service of North America (JESNA), New York. (Project for Jewish Educational Statistics, Research Report No. 4). 102 pp.

Dushkin, A.M. (1918). *Jewish Education in New York City*. Bureau of Jewish Education, New York.

Dushkin, A.M. (1967). "Fifty Years of American Jewish Education – Retrospect and Prospects". *Jewish Education*, Vol. 37, no. 1/2. pp. 44–57.

Dushkin, A.M. and Engelman, U.Z. (1959). *Jewish Education in the United States*. American Association for Jewish Education, New York.

Eliav, M. (1960). *Hachinuch Hayehudi B'Germania B'yemi Hahaskalah v'ha' emanzipazia*. Jewish Agency, Jerusalem. (Hebrew).

Erikson, E.H. and Erikson, J.M. (1981). "On Generativity and Identity". *Harvard Educational Review*, Vol. 51, no. 2.

Franck, I. (1964). "Teaching the Tragic Events of Jewish History". *Jewish Education*, Vol. 34, no. 3. pp. 173–180.

Gartner, L.P. (1976). "Temples of Liberty Unpolluted: American Jews and Public Schools, 1840–1875" in: Korn, B.W. (ed.). *Bicentennial Festschrift for Jacob Rader Marcus*. American Jewish Historical Society, Waltham, Mass. and Ktav, New York.

Gertman, S.L. (1977). *And You Shall Teach Them Diligently: A Study of the Current State of Religious Education in the Reform Movement*. National Association of Temple Educators, New York.

Ginzberg, A. (1947). "Emet me'Eretz Yisrael". *Kol Kitvei Ahad Ha'am*. Dvir, Tel Aviv. (Hebrew).

Greeley, A.M. and Rossi, P.H. (1966). *The Education of Catholic Americans*. Aldine, Chicago.

Herman, S. (1970). *American Students in Israel*. Cornell University Press, Ithaca.

Hershberg, D. (n.d.). *Re: Financing the Solomon Schechter Day School*. Solomon Schechter Day School Association of the United Synagogue of America.

Himmelfarb, H.S. (1977). "The Non-Linear Impact of Jewish Schooling: Comparing Different Types and Amounts of Jewish Education". *Sociology of Education*, Vol. 50, no. 2. pp. 114–129.

Hochberg, H. (1972). "Trends and Developments in Jewish Education". *American Jewish Year Book*, Vol. 73. pp. 194–235.

Hochberg, H. and Lang, G. (1974). "The Jewish High School in 1972–73: Status and Trends". *American Jewish Year Book*, Vol. 75. pp. 235–276.

"Integration in Day School Programs" (1978). *Jewish Education*, Vol. 46, no. 4. pp. 4–41.

Jacobson, B. (1970). *Report of Work Conference on Current Concerns in Jewish Education*. American Jewish Committee and American Association for Jewish Education, New York.

Kaplan, M.M. (1948). *The Future of the American Jew*. Macmillan, New York.

Kaplan, M.M. (1970). *The Religion of Ethical Nationhood*. Macmillan, New York.

Kelman, H.C. (n.d.) "The Place of Jewish Identity in the Development of Personal Identity". *Issues in Jewish Identity and Jewish Education*. American Jewish Committee, New York.

Kelman, S.L. (1978). *Motivation and Goals: Why Parents Send Their Children to Non-Orthodox Day Schools*. Unpublished doctoral dissertation, University of Southern California.

King, E.J. (1965). *Schools, Society and Progress in the USA*. Pergamon Press, London.

Klaperman, G. (1969). *The Story of Yeshiva University*. Macmillan, New York.

Knoff, H.M. and Smith, C.R. (1980). "The Relationship of Student Attitudes Toward Religious Education and a Parent Involvement Program at a Jewish Supplementary School". *Jewish Education*, Vol. 48, no. 1. pp. 27–34.

Koller, C. (1971–72). "A Time for Joy: The Open Classroom and the Jewish School". *Response*, no. 12. pp. 43–50.

Levine, G.N. (1972). "An Adventure in Curing Alienation: Alumni Reflections on the BCI". *Jewish Education*, Vol. 41, no. 4. pp. 10–18.

Lookstein, H. (1972). "The Jewish Day School: A Symposium". *Tradition*, Vol. 13, no. 1.

Lukinsky, J. (1974). "The Education Program at the Jewish Theological Seminary – Basic Distinctive Assumptions". *Jewish Education*, Vol. 43, no.3. pp. 11–13.

Lynn, R.W. (1973). "Civil Catachetics in Mid-Victorian America: Some Notes about American Civil Religion, Past and Present". *Religious Education*, Vol. 68, no. 1. pp. 5–27.

Maslow, W. (1974). *The Structure and Functioning of the American Jewish Community*. American Jewish Congress, New York.

Massarik, F. (1978). "Affiliation and Non-Affiliation in the United States Jewish Community". *American Jewish Year Book*, Vol. 78. pp. 262–274.

Massarik, F. and Chenkin, A. (1973). "United States National Jewish Population Study: A First Report". *American Jewish Year Book*, Vol. 74. pp. 264–307.

Morris, E. (1979). "The Melton Approach: Accent on the Teacher". *United Synagogue Review*, Winter.

"1974–1975 Program Roundup" (1976). *The Pedagogic Reporter*, Vol. 27, no. 2. pp. 3–33.

Petuchowski, J. (1964). "Manuals and Catechisms of the Jewish Religion in the Early Period of the Emancipation" in: Altman, A. (ed.). *Studies in Nineteenth Century Jewish Intellectual History*. Harvard University Press, Cambridge, Mass. pp. 47–64.

Pilch, J. (1964). "The 'Shoah' and the Jewish School". *Jewish Education*, Vol. 34, no. 3. pp. 162–165.

Podhoretz, N. (1967). *Making It*. Random House, New York.

Pollak, G. (1978a). "The Buffalo School Population Study". *Jewish Education*, Vol. 46, no. 2. pp. 16–22.

Pollak, G. (1978b). "Employment Realities and Career Opportunities in Jewish Education". Paper presented at Hebrew College, Boston, Mass.

Pollak, G. (1981). "On Subsidies to Congregational Schools". *Jewish Education*, Vol. 49, no. 1. pp. 16–18.

Pollak, G. and Efron, B. (1976). "Current Trends in Jewish Communal Education". *The Pedagogic Reporter*, Vol. 27, no. 3. pp. 2–9.

Ravitch, D. (1974). *The Great School Wars*. Basic Books, New York.

Reisman, B. (1977). *The Chavurah: A Contemporary Jewish Experience*. Union of American Hebrew Congregations, New York.

Resnick, D. (1981). "Jewish Identity is not a Subject Matter". *Melton Research Center Newsletter*, No. 12.

Ribner, S. (1978). "The Effects of Intensive Jewish Education on Adult Jewish Life Styles". *Jewish Education*, Vol. 46, no. 1. pp. 6–12.

Richman, J. (1905). "The Immigrant Child". *NEA Addresses and Proceedings*, 44th Annual Meeting, Ashbury Park, N.J.

Ronen, D. (1966). "The Effects of a Summer in Israel on American Jewish Youth". *In the Dispersion*, no. 5/6. pp. 210–280.

Roskies, D.K. (1975). *Teaching the Holocaust to Children: A Review and Bibliography*. Ktav, New York.

Schiff, A.I. (1966). *The Jewish Day School in America*. Board of Jewish Education Press, New York.

Schiff, A.I. (1968). "Israel in American Jewish Schools". *Jewish Education*, Vol. 30, no. 4. pp. 6–24.

Schiff, A.I. (1973). "Funding Jewish Education – Whose Responsibility?" *Jewish Education*, Vol. 42, no. 3. pp. 6–12.

Schiff, A.I. (1977). "Jewish Day Schools in America: 1962–1977". *The Pedagogic Reporter*, Vol. 29, no. 1. pp. 2–7.

Schoen, D. (1978). "Cultural Dilemmas and Self-Deception in an Ethnic Minority School". Paper presented at 77th Annual Meeting, American Anthropological Association.

Schoen, D. (1980). "Inside the Classroom: Reflections of a Troubled People". *Jewish Education*, Vol. 48, no. 1. pp. 35–41.

Schulweis, H. (1963). "The Bias Against Man". *Jewish Education*, Vol. 34, no. 1. pp. 6–14.

Schulweis, H. (1976). "The Holocaust Dybbuk". *Moment*, February. (See also subsequent correspondence in *Moment*, May-June 1976).

Schwartz, E.S. (1981). "Bureau Synagogue Relationships Through Funding". *Jewish Education*, Vol. 49, no. 1.

Shefatyah, D. (1974). *Hashpa'at Ha'bikur B'Yisrael al Hesaigim Limudiim V'al Shinuim B'Amadot*. Jewish Agency, Department for Education and Culture in the Diaspora, Jerusalem.

Silver, D.J. (1978). "Higher Jewish Learning" in: Martin, B. (ed.). *Movements and Issues in American Judaism*. Greenwood Press, Westport, Conn.

Skeoff, B. (1975). *Tax Funds for Jewish Education: Presentation and Analysis of Various Jewish Views 1947–1974*. Unpublished doctoral dissertation, Washington University.

Spiro, J. (1971). "Toward a Conceptual Framework for Reform Jewish Education". *Compass*, no. 13.

Torah U'Mesorah (1975–76). *Publications Catalogue*. New York.

Troen, S.K. (1975). *The Public and the Schools: Shaping the St. Louis System, 1838–1920*. University of Missouri Press, Columbia, Mo.

Tyack, D. (1974). *The One Best System: A History of American Urban Education*. Harvard University Press, Cambridge.

UAHC-CCAR (n.d.). *Goals of Reform Jewish Education.* UAHC-CCAR Commission on Jewish Education, New York.

United Synagogue Commission on Jewish Education (1978). *A Curriculum for the Afternoon Jewish School.* New York.

United Synagogue Commission on Jewish Education (1979). *Tuition Compilation Survey: Solomon Schechter Day Schools.* New York.

United Synagogue of America (1975–76). *Survey on Synagogue Finances, Seaboard Region.*

Ury, Z.F. (1964). "The Shoah and the Jewish School". *Jewish Education,* Vol. 34, no. 3. pp. 168–172.

U.S. Department of Commerce, Bureau of the Census (1979). *Statistical Abstract of the United States.* Washington, D.C.

Whitman, K. (1918). "Agudat Ha'Morim Ha'Ivriim B'New York". *Luach Achie'ever.*

Woocher, J.S. (1981). "'Survivalism' as Community Ideology: An Empirical Assessment". *Journal of Jewish Communal Service,* Vol. 57, no. 4.

Jewish Education
in the United States:
Three Comments

Shimon Frost

Conventional wisdom and learned aphorisms from classical literature provide us with conflicting signals concerning change and human progress. Ecclesiastes' observation that "that which hath been is that which shall be and there is nothing new under the sun" (*Eccl. 1,9*) is counterbalanced by the Talmudic assertion "that there can be no academy without some *hidush*" (innovation) (*Hagigah 3,6*).

Reading Professor Ackerman's essay, "Strangers to the Tradition: Idea and Constraint in American Jewish Education" I found myself caught in a tension between complete agreement with his assessment of Jewish educational realities in America on the one hand, and the claims of other perceptions and perspectives, whether derived from varying interpretations of the same phenomena or from a different vantage point in time. (Ackerman's essay was completed in 1981 and most of the references date back to the 1960s and 1970s).

My comments will address issues raised by Ackerman and will be presented under two rubrics: different interpretations of the same phenomena and some *hidushim* based on more recent phenomena.

The title of the essay clearly expresses the author's commitment to the Jewish tradition of learning – a lifelong pursuit of *Torah l'shma* which is absent in most American Jewish schools. It must be pointed out, however, that the second half of the title, "Idea and Constraint," is valid only from the sociological point of view. There is constraint (defined as "repression of natural feelings and impulses") if one accepts the overriding power of social factors. Happily, the more coercive aspects of constraint, political rather than sociological, are not part of Jewish realities in America, and those segments of Jewish society that are willing to free themselves from the shackles of social pressure can pursue the idea of Jewish education to its logical conclusion, that is to say, to fully embrace the tradition of Jewish learning.

Ackerman begins with an accurate analysis of the genesis of the different types of Jewish schools in America, tracing their beginnings to their European-Jewish or American-general antecedents (the early Jewish day school paralleled the academy in the larger society, the Jewish Sunday school was modelled after its Protestant counterpart and the Talmud Torah/ Congregational school was adapted from an earlier East European version). In this analysis, however, Ackerman does not go far enough. If his logic is pursued, one can explain most of the realities of present day Jewish education, particularly in the non-day school sectors, by the de-schooling and de-intellectualizing tendencies in American society, and by the inexorable effects of mass acculturation, typical to children of second and third generation Americans. Arthur Hertzberg's studies of French Jewry (Hertzberg, 1968), notably on the communities of Alsace-Lorraine, offer both elements of contrast and similarity to the evolution of a post-emancipation Jewish community in any setting. Viewed from this perspective, the Americanization of Jewish education explains the present moment in Jewish education. There is no tradition of *Torah l'shma* because American society, in general, is plagued by anti-intellectual, utilitarian tendencies, as witnessed by the current nadir in the study of the humanities in the United States. The cultural dissonance between the typical suburban Jewish home and the Jewish school has, *mutatis mutandis*, its counterpart in the relationship between school and home for many segments in American society. To the extent that we accept Ackerman's definition of education as "the transmission of a culture across generations," one would have to conclude that neither the Jewish school nor the American school itself is adequate for this task, given the present climate of opinion in America.

As is the case in general education where only a small percentage of high schools offer programs of rigorous studies, a limited number of Jewish schools, overwhelmingly day schools, have opted for the tradition of learning. The other 'non-learning for learning's sake' approach expresses itself in general education in the ever changing fads of 'education for life adjustment,' 'self-actualization' or 'career education,' and in Jewish education in the current vogue of identity formation. One must agree with Ackerman that where primacy is given to the development of personal identity, the values of the group recede to lesser significance. Absence of a social-political ideology in education is as American as apple pie; few Jewish educators would, therefore, have the courage to make their schools *engagé* (committed), in Sartrian terms, by adhering to an overriding ideology ("self fulfillment realized only through group membership").

A few additional issues raised by Ackerman can benefit from a somewhat different interpretation. Egon Mayer's more recent studies on children of intermarried couples are somewhat more optimistic than the findings about children of intermarriage by Fred Massarik (Mayer, 1983), quoted by Ackerman. In like manner, the crisis in Jewish teaching personnel cannot, and should not, be treated in isolation from the current crisis in teaching in America in general (decline in status, poor salaries, lack of job satisfaction, only the least academically able go into teaching, etc.). A significant omission, however, in Ackerman's analysis of the American Jewish educational scene is his silence about the acceptance of Jewish education as the prime instrument for Jewish survival at the highest level of Jewish communal leadership (e.g., statements by Martin E. Citrin, past President, Council of Jewish Federations).

While the level of funding, or even the degree of personal commmitment of Jewish communal leaders does not always match the enthusiasm of verbal assertions, the climate of opinion in the councils of communal decision-making is now supportive of the Jewish educational endeavor.

So much for different interpretations of otherwise very accurately described phenomena. Now a few recent developments:

1. Ackerman is correct in asserting that "meaningful control and direct influence [on schools] are possible only when a bureau or national agency contributes directly to the funding of a project or program". However, there has been some movement precisely in this direction. The Miami model, according to which all federation allocations to schools must be validated by the bureau, is a good example. Other communities, too, have introduced some modalities of the stick-and-carrot variety. With the current vogue for accountability in general education, we may see significant changes in the direction of some influence, if not control, by bureaus on their affiliated schools.

2. New social conditions (two-career families, single parent families) have made it necessary for Jewish schools to cooperate more closely with other Jewish institutions, notably the Jewish Community Centers (for afternoon activities, child care programs, etc.) and the Jewish Family Service (for counselling and guidance, etc.).

3. Increasingly, intergenerational programs are becoming a part of the Jewish educational scene. To mention but a few – *havurot* retreats for the entire family, coordinated programs for parents and children (United Synagogue's PEP program, etc.), and the highly successful Home Start Program developed by the Baltimore Bureau of Jewish Education.

4. The day school is still growing, contrary to all projections, and now embraces close to 30% of the Jewish children (about 100,000 students) receiving a Jewish education.

5. In the curricular dialectic between "what the learner wants to learn and what he should learn," we are witnessing a return to a middle-of-the-road balance, particularly on the high school level. The smorgasboard approach of

disparate electives is being replaced by a more judicious balance of require-ments in sequence and content, with adequate provisions for electives and individual choice.

6. There is significant stabilization of the teaching of the Holocaust. The flood of Holocaust courses, which must have peaked in 1978 around the time of NBC's airing of its series *Holocaust*, seems to have receded. A recent mini-study (Nadel and Frost, 1981) found only two principals, out of a total of 34 respondents, favoring the teaching of the Holocaust in elementary grades, and only four accepted techniques of dramatization and role-playing as suit-able. Generally, the Holocaust is taught in grades 8 through 11, as a mini-course, or in connection with history or Jewish thought. All schools, however, reported *Yom Hashoah* (Holocaust Day) observances.

7. Israel and Zionism are taught in some fashion in all but the most right-wing Orthodox institutions. The problem is now one of methodology, under-lying ideology, and suitable material.

8. Funding of congregational schools, through outright subsidies or special grants for projects, is increasing. Recently, in response to requests by federa-tions, JESNA (Jewish Education Service of North America) published a set of guidelines to assist communities considering programs for support of syna-gogue affiliated schools (JESNA, 1983a).

The agenda of unfinished business in Jewish education is long, onerous and challenging. If I were to list three items which, by their seriousness, con-tain the essence of our educational ills I would, without hesitation, point to:

– the need to lengthen the Jewish child's stay in the Jewish school, in line with the findings of Harold Himmelfarb and Geoffrey Bock;
– the need to restore educational credibility to the supplementary school;
– the need to address our personnel crisis in Jewish education.

All three require imagination, funds, perseverance, and faith, and have no easy solutions. Yet, each of these needs can be 'tackled' if the requirements of "imagination, funds, perseverance and faith" are taken seriously.

The Himmelfarb and Bock studies posit a minimum requirement of 3,000–4,000 hours of exposure to Jewish education for it to have a meaning-ful impact. This minimum is easily met by day school students. Orthodox day schools offer a Judaic/Hebraic program of 15 hours weekly which, in a 40 week school year, totals 600 classroom hours. Grades 1 through 6 alone accommodate 3,600 hours of Jewish schooling. The equivalent figures for the Solomon Schechter network of schools (Conservative) are 12 hours of Judaic/Hebraic study weekly which yields, for a school year of 40 weeks, a total of 480 hours yearly. The magic figures of Himmelfarb and Bock therefore, are attainable.

Not so in the supplementary school. Operating generally on a maximum of 6 hours per week, and usually on a curtailed school year of 36 weeks, the annual yield in classroom hours is no more than 218 per year. For a typical elementary supplementary school, with a five-year program, the students would accumulate only 1,080 hours of instruction.

Supplementary high schools generally offer four hours a week. A four year high school program would thus yield only 576 hours annually which, even added to the elementary years total, still falls short of the required minimum needed for 'impact'.

With imagination and perseverance, this difference can be made up substantially by *shabbatonim* and retreats in the course of the school year and by structuring educational camping experiences and trips to Israel for the vacation period. It is now estimated that national high school enrollment in supplementary schools is 35,000. Teen camping and Israel trips are, likewise, on the increase.

The supplementary school has surfaced as an issue of concern to the community at large and it would be fair to say that this concern is due not only to increased pressures for community funding. Calls for realistic goals, learning accountability, curricular overhaul, etc., in the supplementary school domain are heard throughout the land. This has been translated into a heightened consciousness of the needs of the supplementary school. Thus, *Jewish Education* devoted a full issue (Winter 1982) to the supplementary school; in 1983, JESNA ran a series of regional conferences on the "Viability of the Congregational School" and devoted its Board Institute to this issue (JESNA, 1983b).

It is difficult and too early to assess whether this incipient rise of concern about the supplementary school has developed practical and successful models of learning-oriented, goal-directed supplementary schools. Yet, the heightened consciousness about the need for revitalizing this schooling instrumentality, coupled with the rising interest in mergers of smaller institutions (if not outright communalization of supplementary schools in smaller communities), bode well for those who view the restoration of educational credit in the supplementary schools as a prime necessity.

Far more difficult is the crisis in Jewish school personnel, particularly Jewish teaching personnel. Supply is short, salaries are low, status is nonexistent. With the exception of the day school which still, by and large, employs the elite of the teaching corps in terms of credentials and teaching skills, most of the classes in our supplementary school system are staffed by non-professionals (or paraprofessionals) with varying degrees of underqualification.

Smaller isolated communities have awakened to this crisis sooner than the larger concentrations of Jewish population. Thus, in Omaha, Nebraska, the community instituted a communal hiring system. Hebrew teachers are engaged by the community and, under proper arrangement with front line institutions, are assigned to serve in several schools, day and supplementary.

The result is that the community attracts teachers who are offered a living salary, fringe benefits, and some status as communal employees. A similar plan for a pilot program in communal hiring of Jewish teaching personnel is currently awaiting approval in a larger eastern community. These are hardly world shattering developments, not even significant beginnings unless this trend mushrooms. The major breakthrough, a serious country-wide resolve to upgrade and professionalize Jewish teaching is, at this writing, a combination of dream and hope.

We have, however, a heightened awareness of this crisis. Upper echelon Jewish education officialdom, heretofore unpardonably neglectful about the concerns of teachers, have at long last awakened to the need for action. Thus Miami, via its bureau, offers a wide array of fringe benefits to licensed full-time Hebrew teachers; Baltimore introduced incentive grants for professional growth; New York, through the Fund for Jewish Education, allocates a considerable amount of money for several programs falling under the rubric of educators welfare (health insurance, life insurance, etc.)

To repeat: the unfinished business in Jewish education is long, onerous and challenging. Only a combination of imagination, funds, perseverance and faith will provide the beginning for serious renewal.

References

Hertzberg, A. (1968). *The French Enlightenment and the Jews.* Columbia University Press, New York.

JESNA (1983a). *Guidelines on Communal Support for Congregational Schools.* JESNA, New York.

JESNA (1983b). "Revitalizing Supplementary Education". *Proceedings of the JESNA Board.* JESNA, New York.

Mayer, E. (1983). *Children of Intermarriage.* American Jewish Committee, New York.

Nadel, M. and Frost, S. (1981). "Teaching the Holocaust in the Jewish School". *Jewish Education*, Vol. 49, no. 1.

Alvin I. Schiff

Any attempt to provide within the pages of a single essay an all-embracing analysis of the multi-faceted nature of a complex social-cultural-religious communal enterprise developed over a period of 250 years is fraught with the dangers of oversight on the one hand, and over-emphasis on the other. Nevertheless, Walter Ackerman has succeeded in presenting a comprehensive, insightful and objective treatment of a difficult subject.

The comments that follow provide some thoughts from a fellow sojourner whose background and experience in some ways parallel Ackerman's, and in others, differ. These remarks will serve as a footnote to Ackerman's fine presentation.

*　　*　　*

From the very beginning, American Jewish education was confronted with the impossible task of relating the Jewish school to the development of American Judaism and to the larger American setting – transmitting and vouchsafing Jewish life while the Jewish community was adjusting to the open society. The enormity of the task was confounded by two realities:

– the shift of interest and passion of the acculturating Jews from Jewish learning to secular learning (witness the Jewish talent on university campuses and the success of Jews in the professions); and

– the voluntary nature of fiscal support for Jewish education.

These two realities combined to deprive Jewish education of the necessary resources to insure its full effectiveness. Neither the human nor financial resources necessary for maximum effectiveness were available to Jewish schooling.

Despite this condition, several valiant efforts were made over the years to provide effective Jewish schooling. The yeshivoth and day schools are prime examples of swimming against the tide. As Walter Ackerman correctly points out in his essay, the indefatigable efforts of a small group of committed Orthodox leaders against the strong opposition of most segments of the community actually changed the face of Jewish education in North America.

This phenomenon deserves wider treatment in a comprehensive essay. Moreover, some of the statistics relating to the day school movement need updating. In 1984 some 130,000 students were enrolled in yeshivoth and day schools in North America. The per capita costs ranged from $1,200 to $6,500 and the tuition fees – while generally not reflecting the full cost of instruction – varied accordingly (JESNA, 1984). The average cost per pupil for elementary school is about $3,000. For yeshiva high schools, it is approximately $4,200.

Some 4,000 Jewish studies teachers and 4,500 general studies teachers are employed in Jewish day schools.[1] Their annual salaries range from $8,000 to

$30,000, averaging $16,000 (Schiff, 1982). Most of the Jewish studies personnel have instructional loads in excess of twenty hours a week. The average day school is adminstered by three kinds of personnel – Jewish studies principals, general studies principals and fiscal-plant administrators. Their annual wages generally compare very favorably with their public and private school counterparts, ranging from $15,000 to $75,000 per year, depending upon size of school, location, administrative duties, hours of employment and length of service (Board of Jewish Education of Greater New York, 1984a).

The annual cost of Jewish day school education is about $400 million, of which Federation support accounts for 7% (Council of Jewish Federations. 1984).[2] Interestingly, financial support from government sources in New York State (where two thirds of the yeshiva day school enrollment is found) in the form of lunch subsidies, surplus food, free bus transportation, per pupil textbook allotments and special grants made via Federal Chapter I and II programs (formerly Title I and Title IV programs) add up to more than $25 million per year,[3] equalling and even surpassing the total allocations to Jewish day schools provided by Federations throughout North America. Government support is essentially the result of the efforts of the Board of Jewish Education of Greater New York and the *Agudat Israel* of America, in collaboration with Catholic and independent organizations in New York State.

The phenomenon of the *kollelim* and *yeshivoth gedoloth*, in which thousands of teenagers and young men spend as many as 60 hours a week engrossed in Talmud studies, deserves more recognition and discussion. This is paralleled by the growth of *Beth Jacob* and other Orthodox girls' post-secondary seminars and teacher training schools.

Ackerman correctly notes that "the men who laid the theoretical foundations of American Jewish education eschewed the model of the parochial school". It must be added that, with rare exceptions, they changed their views later in life. In fact, Isaac Berkson, one of the vehement opponents of the Jewish day school idea, suggested in the late 1960s that the day school is the rightful heir of the communal Talmud Torah (Schiff, 1966).

There are about 2,400 Jewish schools in the United States, of which 25% are day schools and yeshivoth, which account for about one-third of the total Jewish school enrollment. The decline of supplementary school enrollment in the United States began in 1962. In New York, it commenced three years later. Thanks to the steady increase of Jewish day school pupil population which began in the early 1940s, by 1978 day school enrollment in New York exceeded supplementary school enrollment. By 1984, Jewish day school enrollment comprised 60% of the total pupils in Greater New York Jewish schools.

*   *   *

Family support and complete association with the goals of the schools which their children attend is an earmark of the sectarian and Hasidic yeshivoth and many modern Orthodox day schools.

In discussing the problem of continuation after elementary school, the difference in drop-out rate between supplementary school and day school must be demonstrated. From information available in Greater New York, about 90% of all yeshiva and day school graduates enroll in Jewish day high schools (Board of Jewish Education of Greater New York, 1984b).

Of the total New York day school enrollment 23% are secondary school students. Continuation outside of New York is substantially less prevalent because of the lack of high school facilities in many smaller and middle-sized communities. This lack is due in large measure to the low level of commitment by parents to Jewish all-day high school education.

It is true "that most Jewish schools in this country have not succeeded in imparting any kind of real Jewish knowledge to their students" and that ways must be found to develop "the minimum of intellectual competence required of the literate Jew." Ackerman correctly stresses the need for Judaic literacy. However, needed here is greater recognition of the importance of the affective domain, of the Jewish life 'processes' in and out of school. This is necessary to provide motivation for learning and to compensate for the lack of Jewish experience in the home.

Examples of summer camping as an effective educational tool in this mode should include yeshiva and day school camps, particularly Camp *Morasha*, sponsored by the Max Stern Community Services Division of Yeshiva University.

* * *

While no definitive study has been made of the ineffectiveness of the supplementary school, one of the reasons – to use the words of David Seeley, former executive of the New York State Public School Association, in commenting on the ineffectiveness of public education –, is "undeliverable merchandise." The children don't want to learn what the parents do not consider important.

While, as Ackerman states, "American Jews join synagogues and send their children to Jewish schools because they are genuinely desirous of identifying themselves as Jews and want their children to remain Jews," synagogue membership does not guarantee or obligate Jewish commitment or religious observance.

The essentiality of the role of the family must be highlighted in any attempt to improve Jewish supplementary schooling. The influence of parents and peers is adequately demonstrated in the educational research literature. This basic ingredient of effective Jewish schools merits greater emphasis.

* * *

Several studies show why Jewish parents do not send their children to Jewish schools.

In 1979, the Fund for Jewish Education in Greater New York sponsored a study to determine the factors involved in non-affiliation of Jewish parents and non-enrollment of Jewish pupils (Federation of Jewish Philanthropies, 1979). The findings of this study corroborate several informal surveys made previously by the Board of Jewish Education of Greater New York and can be classified into the following categories:

1. Alienation from religion. Families do not join synagogues. Congregational affiliation is not part of their lifestyle. Some parents simply "dislike the temple" or "dislike the rabbi." Many young adults "are proud of our Jewishness, but not of the Jewish religion." They do not see religion playing a role in their modern lifestyle. They feel comfortable associating themselves with other Jews and Israel, but not actively. Most parents have no quarrel with the quality of Jewish education, about which they admit they know very little. However, they do not appreciate what they think is the religious content of Jewish education.

2. Autonomy of children. Parental permissiveness with children is an important dimension of home life. When parents involve their children in the decision of whether or not to enroll in a Jewish school, the results are usually negative since the children's friends, Jewish and non-Jewish, do not go to a Jewish school. Also, the parents do not appreciate the "loss of free time after public school hours." Some parents themselves had negative personal experiences in Jewish education, and because of their unfavorable childhood memories, do not force their children to go to a Jewish school.

3. Assimilation and materialism. Parents feel that Jewish education is too expensive. Jewish education for their children is not important enough for them to part with their hard-earned money. By their own admission, most parents are materialistic. Paying for Jewish schooling leaves less money for social, recreational and family activities. They resent paying synagogue membership dues, since they do not believe strongly in synagogue affiliation. Were the synagogue fees nominal or nonexistent, some of them might join. Parents are not aware of the availability of financial aid or scholarships, if such help is needed. Furthermore, some parents may feel it demeaning to appear before a scholarship committee which is often made up of their peers.

A 1978 study by the American Association for Jewish Education on non-enrollment in Buffalo indicates the major reasons for parents not to enroll their children (Pollak, 1978):

- they were not interested in giving their children a Jewish education;
- none of the known schools provides the desired type of Jewish education;
- the cost of Jewish education is too high;
- the quality of Jewish schooling is not satisfactory;
- attendance at two schools would be too burdensome.

In 1980, under a grant made to the Lubavitch Youth Organization by the Fund for Jewish Education, a telephone survey was made of 400 Brooklyn families not enrolling their children in Jewish schools (Lubavitch Youth Organization, 1982). The reasons for non-enrollment revealed by this survey are: financial inability, transportation difficulties, "fear of conflict at home", "fear of segregation from peers" and single-parent families. The latter factor was found to be the most significant.

The significance of the role of intermarriage in non-enrollment is demonstrated by the findings of surveys made by the Board of Jewish Education of Greater New York in 1978 and 1979 (Schiff, 1979). These studies show that only three percent of the suburban supplementary school population were children of intermarrieds, whereas the level of intermarriage was estimated to be over 20% during the period 1958–1970, when the parents of these children were married.

The reasons for non-enrollment suggest the need for development of special outreach programs to unaffiliated families, to single parent families, to Jewish high school students in public schools and to the children of intermarried couples. Special efforts must be made to recruit children into early childhood education programs and to develop alternatives to synagogue-based supplementary school programs. Synagogues currently distinguish between formal and informal educational activities. Integrating these two kinds of programs would be helpful in encouraging continuation. Similarly, synagogues, community centers and YMHA's have to pool their efforts and staff resources in reaching and teaching teenagers. Finally, ways must be found to help make Jewish education available to parents who cannot afford the escalating school and synagogue fees.

* * *

Some of the cogent points Ackerman makes that need to be stressed over and over again are:
- the need to upgrade the professional and economic status of teaching personnel;
- the need to attract talented administrative and supervisory personnel to Jewish education;
- the centrality and importance of Israel and Israel-centered activity to the Jewish education process;

- the need to remedy the lack of "reliable empirical evidence concerning the effectiveness of Jewish schooling when the criteria are the acquisition of knowledge or the development of skills";
- the need to improve the lack of understanding regarding "the relationship between what is learned and the investments involved";
- the need to understand the relationship of funding to "meaningful control and direct influence" in Jewish education;
- the need for long-range, cooperative community-wide planning to eliminate some of the partisanship polarizing the Jewish community.

Notes

1. Pupil enrollment estimates for 1983–84 obtained from the Jewish Education Service of North America (JESNA), New York, and the Office of Research, Board of Jewish Education of Greater New York, Inc.

2. Figure for annual cost of day school education obtained by multiplying number of students by average cost.

3. Based on information from the Departments of School Food Services and Government Relations, Board of Jewish Education of Greater New York.

References

Board of Jewish Education of Greater New York (1984a). "Average Teacher Salaries in 1981–82 and 1982–83." *Report on Education Research.*

Board of Jewish Education of Greater New York (1984b). *Jewish School Enrollment in Greater New York: 1983–84.* New York.

Council of Jewish Federations (1984). "Federation Allocations to Jewish Education, 1979–83". *CJF Reports.* New York.

Federation of Jewish Philanthropies (1979). *An Exploratory Study of Attitudes Toward Formal Jewish Education.* Perspectives Resources, Inc., Hartsdale, New York.

JESNA (1984). "Budgeting and Financing in Jewish Day Schools". *Research and Information Bulletin*, No. 57.

Lubavitch Youth Organization (1982). Unpublished survey sent to the Fund for Jewish Education.

Pollak, G. (1978). "The Buffalo School Population Study". *Jewish Education*, Vol. 46, no. 2. pp. 16–22.

Schiff, A.I. (1966). *The Jewish Day School in America.* Board of Jewish Education Press, New York.

Schiff, A.I. (1979). "On Intermarriage and Jewish Education". *Jewish Education*, Vol. 47, no. 2.

Schiff, A.I. (1982). *Jewish School Demography in Greater New York, 1982–83: An Analysis*. Board of Jewish Education of Greater New York.

Michael Zeldin

Walter Ackerman's description of the development of American Jewish education and its current status is both comprehensive and insightful in its analysis of contemporary sociological and educational realities. It will not be my purpose here to disagree with his portrayal nor to refute any of the particulars of the situations he depicts. Rather, I will seek to identify some of the critical trends currently in their nascent stage which might influence the future course of Jewish education in the United States.

The major theme in the development of Jewish education in the United States is, as Ackerman points out, the full acceptance by American Jews of the public schools. From the 1870s through the middle of the twentieth century, the supplementary pattern of Jewish education was hardly challenged, but following World War II, the emergence of full-time Jewish educational settings marked a break from the American Jewish tradition. While the Orthodox pioneered in these efforts, by the early 1970s every sub-group within the Jewish community had some form of Jewish day school throughout America.

What is remarkable about the development of Jewish day schools over the past decade is their geometric rate of growth. Every year in communities all over America new day schools open their doors. Accompanying the rapid growth of Jewish day schools is the decline in enrollment of Jews in the public schools. Though no systematic empirical data are available to indicate the rate of attendance of Jews in public schools, it seems clear that Jewish attendance in public schools is declining, especially in large metropolitan areas.

It is equally clear that many Jews are disturbed by what they see as a decline in the quality of public education in America. Whether or not the schools are actually as mediocre as the spate of national studies on education conducted in the early 1980s seems to imply,[1] the important fact is that Jewish (and other) parents perceive the quality of educational experiences offered by the nation's public schools to be poor (Syme, 1983). For the Jewish community which has, as Ackerman notes, looked to the public school "as the avenue which leads to success and status" and to "personal development and career opportunities," this new perception represents a dramatic departure from the past. In the 1970s and 1980s, Jews have begun to "shop at the private school market"[2] as never before in American history in order to enhance their oppportunities for future educational and occupational advancement. The public school, in the eyes of many though by no means all Jewish parents, is no longer the universal avenue to success; the private school is now seen as the road to continued upward mobility for Jewish children. Even those parents whose Jewish identification is marginal often select a Jewish day school for their children because it offers the best general education available (Kelman, 1978).

But as Jewish children leave the public schools, many of them select private schools other than Jewish day schools, so that in certain geographic areas, the private schools have a significant percentage of Jewish students. Since these schools are not forbidden from introducing religious instruction, it may be possible to include Jewish religious instruction (as an elective) within some of the programs. If the perception that the public schools do not and cannot offer quality educational experiences continues and expands, we can expect to see further growth in the private sector of American education, with a resultant growth both in Jewish day schools and in the number of Jewish children attending other private schools.

It is clear, however, that regardless of future growth in Jewish day schools, the majority of Jewish children will continue to receive their Jewish education in a supplementary setting. One of the most startling features of supplementary Jewish education in the last decades is the large number of educational options that have become available to parents to choose from. There was a time not too long ago when each synagogue offered only a single program of schooling for all students. The stereotypical view was that Reform congregations offered Sunday schools, Conservative ones provided afternoon Hebrew schools, and the Orthodox developed day schools. These sharp distinctions among the movements have become blurred in more ways than one. It is clear to most observers that Reform congregations have provided afternoon Hebrew schools and even a few day schools, that Conservative synagogues often have Sunday schools and occasionally day schools and that some Orthodox synagogues have educational programs other than day schools.

What has been less apparent is that even within a single institution the options are often numerous. School programs are offered at different times of day on different days of the week; they are designed for fast learners and slow learners, for children with handicaps and learning disabilities and for children with special psychological needs resulting from divorce or death in the family. Synagogues frequently offer educational options that move beyond the confines of the school. It is thus not uncommon for schools to incorporate informal programs as options within the school, usually in the form of one or several weekend retreats away from the city, to supplement formal classroom learning. Trips to Israel and summer camp experiences may also be part of the synagogue's educational offerings, yet these are rarely coordinated in any formal way with the year-round educational program. At the high school and junior high school level, schools often substitute student electives for a fixed series of courses. The rash of new materials from 'cottage industry publishers,' especially 'Alternatives in Religious Education', often becomes the basis for an elective curriculum that explores topics of concern to teenagers from a Jewish perspective. It may be that the difficulty of maintaining smaller schools lies precisely in their inability to guarantee that a variety of educational programs are available from which children and parents can choose.

A second aspect of the proliferation of educational options has developed in response to demographic and other sociological demands. As the American population migrates from the midwest and northeast to the Sun Belt, new community profiles are emerging. In some communities, the overwhelming majority of the population is beyond the child-bearing and even the child-rearing age. The 'empty nesters' and 'senior adults' who populate these communities are demanding educational services from the synagogue and from the Jewish community as never before. These communities may have few children to populate the religious school but may have a vast reservoir of adults who are eager to participate in Jewish educational activities.

Other communities may be witnessing a 'baby boomlet' as the post-war baby boom generation begins to have children of its own. While this generation is having children at a lower rate than previous generations (giving rise to fears of reductions in the Jewish population in the future), nonetheless, this highly educated generation is producing a substantial number of children. Enrollment in kindergartens in many communities is double today than what it was ten years ago, indicating a possible growth in religious schools in the decade to come. Not only does this spurt in population suggest a trend toward increased religious school enrollment in these communities, but it also opens entirely new educational possibilities. Jewish programs for pre- and post-natal care, for infants and toddlers with their parents, for young parents, for nursery school children, etc., are provided as options in many communities. Young parents are flocking to hands-on, how-to classes in celebrating the Jewish holidays. These young parents, third and fourth generation Americans, realizing that they have lost touch with their 'roots' are searching for concrete ways to regain a connection with their heritage, and communities are providing them with educational options to meet their needs. Synagogues are also involved in a variety of programs of family education which seek to provide parents with classes whose Jewish content parallels the subject matter their children are studying, or which provide opportunities for children and their parents to study together.

A third factor leading to the expansion of the network of educational options available within synagogues results from the concern about the high rate of intermarriage. The Reform movement's pioneering efforts in outreach to non-Jews, to encourage them to "choose Judaism" (Kukoff, 1981) and encourage mixed married couples to participate in synagogue life and raise their children as Jews, has led to the development of programs aimed at this newly-recognized population. Courses for converts have long been offered in communities throughout the country; but for the first time, programs which blend group counselling with Jewish education are being offered for people who have already converted and for couples in which the non-Jewish member has decided not to convert. Since it is unlikely that the rate of intermarriage will decrease in the near future, the need for educational programs for adults who are intermarried and for their children will become more urgent if we are not to lose these people to Judaism.

The expanding list of educational opportunities offered by synagogues has created the need for a new type of synagogue professional. No longer can the functions of the synagogue school principal be limited to the administration of the religious school. The synagogue's educational director must be an educational leader who is sensitive to the needs and possibilities of the community. The educator must be able to maintain the existing programs of the synagogue, to administer and direct them and to work towards their continual improvement. But he or she must also be able to develop a vision of what Jewish education can be within the synagogue without being restrained by the limitations of the past.

Graduate professional programs in Jewish education seek to train young educators to fill precisely this role. Concurrent with the professionalization that results from high-level graduate training, there is a renewed interest in Jewish educational research, defined broadly as the theoretical and empirical inquiry into the nature of the Jewish educational enterprise. While still in its infancy, this movement promises to deepen our understanding of the nature of Jewish education and ultimately to lead to improved policy-making and practice. Together, the professionalization of the practioner and the development of a broadly-defined research enterprise promise to contribute to higher quality educational experiences for those children and adults who choose to participate in the broad array of Jewish educational oppportunities that are and will be available in the American Jewish community.

Notes

1. See, for example, the report of President Reagan's blue ribbon panel on excellence in education, "A Nation at Risk."

2. In a speech before the UAHC-CCAR Commission on Jewish Education in November, 1981 ("Reform Day Schools – Why We Changed Our Minds"), Rabbi Samuel E. Karff explained: "The public schools in the Temple neighborhood are quite viable, but parents who seek a higher level of educational excellence in classrooms of limited size are opting increasingly for a private primary school education for their children. There is little if anything we can do to influence those choices. We envisage that the majority of children whom we enroll in our Day School would have been headed for some other private primary school program."

References

Kelman, S.L. (1978). *Motivation and Goals: Why Parents Send Their Children to Non-Orthodox Day Schools.* Unpublished doctoral dissertation, University of Southern California, Los Angeles.

Kukoff, L. (1978). *Choosing Judaism.* Union of American Hebrew Congregations, New York.

Syme, D.B. (1983). "Reform Judaism and Day Schools: The Great Historical Dilemma". *Religious Education*, Vol. 78, no. 2. pp. 153–181.

4

Jewish Education in Canada

Jerome Kutnick

Canadian Jewry has established an impressive array of institutions and organizations to educate its youth. Jewish education receives substantial financial assistance from the government and local federations, and the community has given it broad support. Nevertheless Jewish education is contentious for Canadian Jewry because it deals with issues that expose the ambivalent nature of Canadian Jewry's relationship to Judaism and Jewish culture in a post-traditional society. This chapter will examine the structure and accomplishments of Jewish education in Canada in the context of these issues.

The Societal Context of Jewish Education

The American Influence

Canadian Jewry maintains close ties with the American Jewish community. Jewish education reflects this special relationship and is heavily influenced by developments in both America and Canada. Although Canada's Jews have their own institutions and organizations, including educational ones, they have nonetheless, with some element of truth, been perceived as part of a greater North American Jewish community. This situation is not unique to Canadian Jewish education alone but has its parallel in the broader Canadian society. Indeed, in an effort to contain American influence, the Canadian government has adopted policies designed to promote Canadian uniqueness. The Canadian Jewish community, despite similar desires to maintain its own distinctiveness, places importance on its close relationship with American Jewry. While Canada is somewhat apprehensive of its neighbor to the South, Canadian Jewry is also concerned with the assimilating forces of the non-Jewish society within which it dwells. For the Jews in Canada, the mere proximity of an older Jewish community twenty times its size and with whom it feels a strong sense of kinship, serves as a bulkwark against assimilation and acts as an instrument for survival.

Jewish education in Canada is therefore partially integrated into the American Jewish educational structure. Many of its leaders were either born in the United States, studied there or received prior educational-administrative experience there. Canada's Jewish educational institutions, schools, professional organizations, and even central communal agencies, affiliate with American-based umbrella organizations. Indeed cognizant of this close relationship, the New York based roof organization of American Jewish educational agencies, the former American Association for Jewish Education (AAJE) in 1981 changed its name to the Jewish Education Service of North America (JESNA).

Compared with America, the resources made available to Jewish education in Canada are more substantial and the conditions appear more favorable. However Canadian Jewish education is confronted with the same dilemma as its counterpart in the United States. The Jews in Canada seek to integrate into general society while concurrently maintaining their Jewishness. In many post-emancipation communities, it is the perceived task of Jewish education to help achieve the particularly 'Jewish' component of these dual, and in certain ways, contradictory objectives. Jewish education in Canada may resemble that of other communities not because its institutions affiliate with non-Canadian ones or because its leadership derives its training and experience in America but rather because the values and attitudes of the Jews in all the Diaspora - including Canada – may in fact be quite similar.

Internal Political and Cultural Factors

Canada was settled by two European nations, the French and the English; the cultures of both have taken root in Canada. Although the French comprise only about 20% of the population, they have maintained their status as one of the founding nations. Their numerical preponderance in the second most populous province (they comprise over 80% of the population in Quebec), along with the decentralized nature of the Canadian Confederation, in which much power is entrusted to the provinces, has helped forge a society in which neither the English nor the French culture can completely dominate. The influence of a non-homogeneous culture on Canadian national identity has led to a more tolerant attitude towards ethnic and religious diversity. Such a conception of society, often referred to as the 'Canadian Mosaic', has helped create an environment more conducive to ethnic religious education.

Religious Schools and the States

Some religious schools in Canada receive government financial support; others do not. Although Canada does not have a legally established Church, neither does it maintain a tradition of separation of Church and State. The founding document of the Canadian Confederation, the British North American Act (BNA), unlike the United States Constitution, does not sharply limit the Government's relations with religious bodies.

In 1867 when the BNA was enacted and education was regarded as a function of the Church, there were less than two thousand Jews in Canada. The BNA did not relate to the educational needs of the Jewish population nor did it discuss the possibility of providing non-denominational education. It maintained that education was an area reserved to the provinces and made it incumbent upon each province to guarantee access to the existing Catholic and Protestant schools.

The religious school clause of the BNA led to provincial funding of Catholic and Protestant schools. In some places these allocations for schooling were later expanded to include Jewish schools.

Since the early 1900s Jews have negotiated with provincial governments concerning the eligibility of Jewish schools for government funding. These negotiations proved contentious within the Jewish community. The possibility of establishing a government-funded Jewish school board, similar to the Protestant and Catholic ones, raised the thorny issue of Jewish identity and of the Jews' perception of themselves as Jews and as Canadians.

Presently four of the five provinces in which there are Jewish day schools provide government funds, although in three of these the issue is currently being re-examined. In Ontario, the one province where Jewish day schools do not receive provincial funding, the Toronto Board of Jewish Education, the central educational agency of the largest Ontario Jewish community, has been negotiating for such assistance.

Recency of Canadian Jewish History

The recency of Jewish immigration to Canada also affects Jewish education. Although the beginning of Jewish settlement in Canada can be traced back to the British occupation in the mid-eighteenth century, as an organized community Canadian Jewry has its origins in a much later East-European immigration which began in the 1880s and gained momentum in the 1900s.

Most Canadian Jews are second or third generation Canadians. The school-age population consists mainly of the children or grandchildren of immigrants. These children, even those from non-observant homes, are likely to retain memories of some members of their family observing holidays or Jewish traditions, and may even have a sense of living according to halacha (religious law). The potential clientele of the Jewish schools is composed of children who, even if they do not practice Jewish tradition themselves, are not entirely disconnected from it.

In addition, those immigrants who came to Canada after World War II greatly augmented the Orthodox element of the community. These Jews, who regard Jewish education as a religious imperative, established a number of yeshivoth and Orthodox day schools.

Demographic and Geographic Background

The vast size of Canada and the distribution of its Jewish population are important factors in determining the type and variety of Jewish institutions servicing a community. The decennial Canadian census provides a considerable amount of data on the Jews in Canada.[1]

According to the 1981 census there were 296,000 Jews by religion. Another 16,000 people reported no religious preference and a Jewish ethnic origin – either as their only choice or as one in a multi-choice answer on ethnicity – bringing the total to 312,000. More than 74% of the Jewish population live in the two largest metropolitan areas of Canada. The 129,000 Jews who live in metropolitan Toronto form the largest Jewish community in Canada followed by Montreal with 103,000 Jews. The next two largest Jewish communities, Winnipeg, with 16,000, and Vancouver, with 15,000, are each only 15% the size of the Montreal community. Six other cities, Ottawa, Calgary, Edmonton, Hamilton, London and Windsor have Jewish populations greater than 2,000.

Although these ten communities include more than 90% of Canadian Jewry, most Jewish communities are quite small. Given the vast size of Canada many of the people living in these places feel they are quite isolated from the other Canadian Jewish communities.

The type of Jewish education available to Jews is to a great extent dependent upon the size of the community in which they live. The two largest communities are able to provide a broad spectrum of Jewish schools with different ideological and religious orientations. At times it may seem that the educational structures are over-organized. In contrast, some small Jewish communities find it difficult to maintain even one small afternoon school.

The Structure of Jewish Education

Jewish education consists of an array of educational institutions and organizations among which are schools, professional associations, educational resource centers, central education agencies, school committees, etc. The larger the community, the more diversified are its educational institutions and the more complex is the structure of the educational system. The major component of this system, regardless of size, is the school. It is there that learning takes place and the goals of Jewish education are achieved. All other Jewish educational institutions are in a sense auxiliary, and their function is to assist in providing education rather than providing it themselves.

National Organizations

Canadian Jewry's two major national organizations, the Canadian Jewish Congress (CJC) and Canadian Zionist Federation (CZF) serve the educational structure mainly by creating national forums where educational issues can be discussed and projects can be coordinated. In the past, the CJC and CZF were more directly involved with specific educational institutions; the CJC, for instance, maintained teacher training institutes in both Montreal and Toronto, while the CZF ran a Hebrew-speaking camp in Quebec.

Currently the CZF supports two national councils of profesionnal educators and lay leaders, the National Pedagogic Council and National Educational Council. These councils, which meet four times a year alternately in Montreal and Toronto conduct an annual National Bible Contest and arrange summer Jewish studies courses for Canadian Jewish school teachers at two Israeli universities.

The CJC and CZF jointly convene the National Jewish Education Conference which meets once every three years either in Montreal or Toronto. The Conference does not seek to decide upon a policy for the whole country, but rather strives to enrich the overall quality of Jewish education, and facilitate its provision by the local communities. It does this by providing a forum in which scholars can address Canadian Jewish educators and where administrators, laymen and teachers from different sections of the country can meet and discuss mutual concerns.

The 1983 Montreal conference heard major addresses by Nathan Rotenstreich of the Hebrew University of Jerusalem, on 'Judaism and Modernity', and by Shimon Frost of JESNA on 'New Educational Structures for the American Jewish Community'. The Conference divided into subcommittees where topics such as funding, teacher training and the teaching of Zionism and Israel were discussed.

Schools

The Jewish community generally categorizes schools as either 'supplementary' or 'day'. Supplementary schools hold sessions either in the afternoon or on weekends. They provide Jewish education to pupils who receive their general education in non-Jewish institutions. The Jewish supplementary school does not replace or compete with the non-Jewish public or private school. Rather it seeks to 'supplement' – as its name implies - the Jewish child's general education with a Jewish one. At one time in Canada, as is still the case in the United States, these schools were commonly referred to as 'afternoon' or 'Sunday' schools, depending on the day and time in which sessions were held.

Although there are no hard and fast rules, in the United States such schools are usually congregational. The afternoon school is more often affiliated with the Conservative movement and the Sunday school with the Reform, but there is much overlap and the Orthodox maintain such schools as well.

Canadian synagogues are affiliated either with the Orthodox, Conservative and Reform movements. But in Canada, where there are few Reform synagogues and where the Conservative movement is much less of a presence, the schools are less defined by denominations. Whether a supplementary school meets once or several times a week is more dependent on other factors, such as school budget and the school's perception of how much it can demand of its students. In small communities, meeting once or several times a week is sometimes due to the availability of people to staff the school.

The Day School

The day school assumes a much greater role in Canada than it does in the United States. Here children are taught both Jewish and general studies. The day school is the only educational institution the child attends, and therefore it holds sessions throughout the day.

Both the day and supplementary schools have their roots in the immigrant experience. The East-European Jews who came to Canada at the end of the nineteenth and beginning of the twentieth century provided Jewish schooling for their children in the fashion to which they were accustomed in Europe. Parents sent their son to heder (a one-room classroom) where he was taught by a *Melamed* (teacher or tutor). In Europe this system helped attain nearly universal Jewish literacy for males and few parents felt a need to supplement their child's education by sending him to a non-Jewish school. Indeed the Jews resisted attempts to enroll their children in government schools. In Canada, however, while nearly all Jewish children attended public school, only some of them went to heder and then only after public school hours. The heder of the immigrant community has not survived, but the decision on the part of Jewish immigrants to give priority to general studies continues to influence Jewish education.

The Talmud Torah also had its origins in Eastern Europe where it was a charitable institution intended to provide schooling for the poor. The decision to accept all the children of the Jewish community and charge tuition only of those who could afford it changed the Talmud Torah's image and made enrollment in the school more acceptable. In Canada, where philanthropy and voluntarism became important avenues of Jewish association and identification, the Talmud Torah took on the characteristics of a communal enterprise. Many of these schools evolved into day schools and in time they became the major Jewish educational institutions in the country. The largest Jewish schools and school systems of the eight major Jewish communities (the United Talmud Torahs of Montreal, Associated Hebrew Day Schools in Toronto, the Winnipeg Hebrew School – Talmud Torah, Ottawa Talmud Torah and Hillel Academy Day School, the Vancouver Talmud Torah, the Calgary Hebrew School, the Hebrew Academy in Hamilton, and Edmonton Talmud Torah) all trace their origins to the small local Talmudei Torah of the immigrant community.

These schools are communal in the sense that they see their constituency as the entire Jewish community. However, with one exception in Winnipeg, these schools are not formally under the auspices of the organized Jewish community; indeed, two of them, in Calgary and Edmonton, are affiliated with the local government's board of education. The other five are organized as independent schools and have their own school boards to which they are responsible.

In a 1982 survey conducted by JESNA, Canadian Jewish schools were asked to report their affiliations as Orthodox, Conservative, Reform or other. Six of the eight Talmud Torah day schools responded; two checked off 'Orthodox' and four did not answer the question. Of the four, the principal of one was the rabbi of the community's only Orthodox synagogue. The principal of another school had just accepted a new position as headmaster of a yeshiva day school in the United States. A third school principal described his school's philosophy as having "three major thrusts: traditional Judaism... nationalism...(and) a curriculum designed to teach Hebrew as a living language". The fourth school was somewhat of an exception. Whereas it did not issue a formal statement concerning its orientation, its own recruitment literature refers to 'Hebrew education' rather than 'religious' or 'Jewish' education. Thus, while none of the eight day schools which evolved from communal Talmudei Torah designated themselves as either Conservative or Reform, four either declared themselves Orthodox and/or had principals who served as heads of Orthodox institutions.

A school with a different kind of orientation, the secular Yiddish school also has its roots in the immigrant community. This school was a product of the second wave of immigration (1903–1914) which saw the arrival in Canada of Jews who had been influenced by revolutionary politics and Jewish national and cultural ideologies. Like the Talmud Torah, these schools recognized the supplementary nature of Jewish education in Canada and started out conducting their classes in the afternoon, after public school hours. These schools have modified their non-religious stance and teach Hebrew as well as Yiddish. They no longer teach a secular and radical curriculum. Nor do they expect to halt the attrition of Yiddish. In general, these schools define themselves as 'cultural' and 'nationalist' rather than 'Orthodox', 'Conservative' or 'Reform'. Five of these schools have become day schools, and of these, two made the transition as early as the 1920s. In the four communities where they are located, Toronto, Montreal, Winnipeg and Calgary, they have provided an alternative to the Talmud Torah day school.

According to the principal of one of these schools, "though this institution is a non-synagogue oriented school, it does familiarize its students with the Siddur...and religious practices are taught." The recruitment pamphlet of a second former secular Yiddish school describes the school's goal "to effect a positive attitude...and degree of intimacy with Jewish...holidays, customs, ceremonies and traditions".

Since these schools seek to serve all segments of the community they cannot afford to vary too much from what they perceive to be the norms in Jewish education. Just as the Talmud Torah schools which define their orientation as Orthodox feel pressure to accommodate pupils who come from a non-observant background, so these former secular schools find themselves under subtle pressures to demonstrate their loyalty to Jewish tradition and appreciation of Jewish ritual observance.

There is a third type of day school with a very different approach to the community's norms. These schools, yeshivoth and some Orthodox day schools, are located in the five largest Jewish communities in Canada. They do not seek to minimize religious differences between them and other groups, and they limit enrollment to children of Orthodox families. Their curriculum emphasizes the practical application of Jewish studies to the daily observance of halacha.

There are other day schools as well, especially in Toronto and Montreal. In Calgary, where the Talmud Torah described its educational program as 'Hebraic' rather than 'religious', a new Orthodox day school was recently established. This school belongs to an organization of Orthodox day schools, *Torah U'Mesorah*, and only employs Jewish studies teachers who observe halacha, but its student body consists mainly of non-Orthodox children. Perhaps, where the orientation of the school is concerned, the distinction should not be made as to whether the school affiliates with the Orthodox, Conservative or Reform movement, but rather whether the school seeks to serve the whole Jewish community or only that segment which shares its religio-ideological position.

Those schools which regard themselves as Orthodox but accept non-Orthodox pupils face the sensitive problem of the conflict between family and school. The child may resent the school for fostering beliefs and religious obligations which his parents do not accept. Conversely, the school may cause the child to reject his parents' approach to Judaism, thereby creating conflict in the home. The potential for discontinuity between home and school may be especially high in communities that have only one day school to serve the entire community. Indeed, three such communities have a history of strife over precisely this issue. In one of them the local federation intervened and negotiated a change in the school committee representation to allow greater parental input. As Charles Liebman has noted, Jews define "Judaism as a religion but fill...(it) with ethnic or communal content." The policy of accepting non-Orthodox children to Orthodox schools is not merely a means to increase registration but may relate to a religious desire to serve the community.

Given the general propensity of Canadian Jews to regard themselves as both a religious and ethnic group,[2] the issue that distinguishes between schools' orientations may no longer be the secular or religious approach of the curricula, but rather the actual observance or non-observance of religious practices in the school. Yet it is possible that we have too easily dismissed the ideological differences between schools which may be more than just vestiges of the past. A suggestion by the executive director of one of the central Jewish educational agencies that a high school which was once a radical Yiddish secular school merge with a Talmud Torah high school was immediately dismissed by both parties, at least partially because of ideological differences. On the other hand, a merger did take place between two such elementary day schools in Winnipeg. But this merger, which was economically advantageous to both schools as well as to the community as a whole, took nearly a decade to effect.

The Supplementary School

Supplementary schools do not assume the major responsibility for educating the Jewish child. Unlike the day school which must meet government regulations concerning at least the general studies aspect of the curriculum, the supplementary school is under no compulsion to heed any standards but its own self-imposed ones. Most supplementary schools in Canada are congregational. Final authority for the conduct of these schools rests with the congregation which usually acts through an appointed school committee. Enrollment is not restricted but some schools charge higher tuition to children of non-members. In small communities (those with a Jewish population of less than 1,000), the congregation is often the only Jewish institution and thus the congregational school constitutes a communal school as well.

Canada also has ten supplementary Yiddish schools in its communities. These schools were founded in a much earlier period when the community was mainly Yiddish-speaking,[3] and when the Jewish labor movement was a much stronger force in the community. Just as the Yiddish day schools dropped their radical stance, these schools stress culture and history, and teach Hebrew as well as Yiddish. They often suffer low enrollments and are perceived by their opponents to be teaching a curriculum that is no longer relevant. Even their supporters do not really expect them to succeed in keeping Yiddish alive but rather contend that the school's curriculum instills an understanding and a certain reverence for Yiddish and the society which spoke it.

In Canada with its vast land mass and sparse population many small Jewish communities are quite isolated from each other and must rely on their own resources for Jewish education. Whether they even have a school is often dependent upon the voluntary services of community members. The schools in these communities often constitute the only ongoing Jewish activity in the region. They serve as a focal point socially as well as educationally for the Jewish child.

Day vs. Supplementary Schools

In communities that have both supplementary and day schools, the question often arises as to how the organized community should deal with these two different structures. On one hand there is the opinion that all forms of Jewish education should be supported and, since the decision concerning type of Jewish education remains a parental one, the community should stay neutral and offer its support to all the schools. But many Jewish educators are critical of the quality of education which they believe the supplementary school is capable of offering and feel it is their responsibility to promote a better alternative. Moreover, the greater financial expense involved in maintaining day schools has led community leaders to mobilize the community on behalf of the day school, sometimes to the detriment of the supplementary school.

The competition between day schools and supplementary schools has other ramifications as well. Just as the choice of school in which to enroll one's child may be seen as a sign of ideological or religious orientation, so the decision as to whether one's child should attend a day school or a supplementary school has been perceived as a statement of the value one places on Jewish education. In some circles it is taken as a measure of one's commitment to Judaism.

The pro-supplementary school approach is perhaps more concerned with that part of the school age population that does not attend any Jewish school.

It emphasizes the role these schools can play in increasing the number of children who receive at least some Jewish education.

The three central Jewish education agencies in Canada all respond differently to this issue. One agency has hardly any contact with the supplementary schools and does not even have records of their enrollment figures. A second relates to the supplementary schools as it does to day schools and the third agency has just issued a report of what it contends is the tendency to treat the supplementary schools as 'step-children' of the community. In one of the large communities which is able to offer many options, the ambiguous attitude toward supplementary education has led to a plethora of new programs designed to interest Jewish students. Among these are Jewish clubs that meet once a week either in private homes, in public high schools after classes, or as lunch-hour activity programs in a non-Jewish elementary school in a Jewish neighborhood. Critics of these programs, however, have expressed concern with what these programs hope to accomplish and with the quality of the education they provide.

Enrollment Patterns[4]

There are at least 134 Jewish schools in Canada, of which 50 are day schools and 84 are suppplementary. Only the three largest communities have Jewish day high schools, but all ten cities with a Jewish population of 2,000 or more have at least one day school, and some type of Jewish school is found in each of the seventeen largest communities in which 98% of Canada's Jews live. In addition there are schools in some of the very small communities as well. No community with less than 500 Jews maintains more than one supplementary school.

Toronto

There are 46 Jewish schools in the Toronto metropolitan area with a combined pupil enrollment of just over 13,200 pupils. 14 of these schools are day schools and 32 are supplementary. Some 7,200 pupils (55% of all Jewish school enrollment) attend the day schools. Five of the day schools accept students from all segments of the community. One limits its enrollment to children of families who are members of a synagogue and eight receive only children from Orthodox households.

Enrollment drops dramatically for high school. Less than 10% of elementary day school students continue in the day high school. Nearly 600 students attend four day high schools. Of these, more than half are enrolled in a communal school which is responsible directly to the Toronto Board of Jewish Education. The other four schools have restrictive enrollment policies and are maintained as independent Orthodox institutions.

The 32 supplementary schools include 20 schools affiliated or directly responsible to Orthodox, Conservative and Reform congregations, two schools which were once considered Yiddish-secular institutions and now define themselves as cultural and national schools, and ten other schools which are not formally affiliated. Approximately 6,000 pupils are enrolled in Toronto Jewish supplementary schools.

Montreal

The Montreal Jewish school directory listed 35 schools, 24 day and 11 supplementary schools with a combined enrollment of 8,800 pupils in 1983. About 80% of the pupils were in day schools. Of these, 5,200 (or 59% of all Jewish school enrollment) attended elementary day schools. Despite a wide variety of high schools reflecting a broad spectrum of orientations and approaches, substantially fewer students attended Jewish day high schools – about 2,000 in 1983.

Between 1978 and 1983 student enrollment steadily increased in the day high school from about 1,500 to 2,000. This change reflects both a greater number of children graduating the elementary day school – the feeder institution of day high schools – and a greater percentage of elementary school graduates choosing to attend Jewish day high schools (from 87 to 93% in six years).

A recent study of day school space requirements commissioned by the Montreal federation projected a continuing increase in local day high school enrollment despite a levelling off of elementary school graduates. It listed a number of reasons for this phenomenon – "a basic desire for Jewish education...dissatisfaction with the quality of public education...'return to the roots' during hard times...and a sense of belonging to a well-defined community..." – but warned that high school enrollment would probably peak during the next decade. The commission recommended that no new schools be established but that present institutions consider expanding their facilities. One high school is erecting a new building and a second one is adding an annex.

Nine of the eleven supplementary schools listed in the directory are congregational schools, one is a Yiddish school and one is affiliated with the Lubavitch movement. In 1981, 1,600 children were enrolled in these schools.

The enrollment patterns and participation rates of the two largest Canadian Jewish communities vary considerably. A smaller percentage of school-age children attend Jewish schools in Montreal than in Toronto but a greater percentage of these are enrolled in day schools – at both elementary and high school levels. This dissimilarity is at least partially a function of the different internal and external factors affecting the two communties.

The Toronto Board of Jewish Education, unlike the Jewish Education Council of Montreal, has long supported Jewish supplementary schools. The

Board allocates federation subsidies to the schools, regulates the licensing of their teachers and, to some extent, attempts to assure minimal curricular objectives. Whether the Toronto central educational agency's greater involvement in supplementary schools has made supplementary education more acceptable to the community or, vice-versa, whether a larger supplementary school enrollment has led the Board to devote more attention to this aspect of Jewish education is difficult to determine.

Until recently most national Jewish organizations maintained their central offices in Montreal. This situation, as Daniel Elazar has noted concerning New York, tends to make the local Jewish community more ideological and leads to a concentration of the cultural leadership. Today Montreal's pre-eminence is being challenged as some national Jewish organizations have moved and others are considering transferring their headquarters to Toronto. Nevertheless, the past concentration of the national cultural leadership may have been responsible for the founding of a broad and ideologically diverse network of Jewish day schools which still characterizes the city's Jewish educational structure.

In addition, certain political and cultural factors within the province of Quebec – the salience of the language question, the nationalist aspirations of many French-speaking residents as well as a tendency to send one's children to private rather than public school which is more normative and widespread in Quebec than in Ontario – may also account for the larger day school enrollment in Montreal.

Economic factors should also be considered. Although Ontario has not provided Toronto schools with large per-child grants, the schools, through communal support and by other means have been able to fix tuition fees at rates that are comparable to those in Montreal. Likewise both communities offer tuition assistance to children of needy families. Nonetheless Toronto spends less money per enrolled child ($2,885 Canadian) than Montreal ($3,186) on day school education. The effect of this $301 differential on the quality of education and on enrollment patterns is argueable but does not appear to be very significant.

Winnipeg and Vancouver

The educational structure and enrollment patterns of the two largest of Canada's medium-sized communities are also dissimilar.

In Winnipeg three elementary day schools and one day high school amalgamated into a day school system. This system is run by the Winnipeg Board of Jewish Education and is open to all Jewish children of the city. Furthermore, the Winnipeg public school system has a Hebrew language heritage program whose curriculum parallels the Jewish day school's in many ways. Winnipeg also has an independent Orthodox day school whose enrollment is limited to children of observant families. Four supplementary schools also serve the Winnipeg community. These, like the independent Orthodox day school, do not receive federation funds and are neither part of nor affiliated with the Winnipeg Board of Jewish Education.

Vancouver has two day schools, one communal with traditional orientation which receives a community subsidy and accepts all segments of the Jewish school-age population and an Orthodox one, which is affiliated with the Lubavitch movement and receives no communal funds. Vancouver also has six supplementary schools.

The Vancouver community has more Jewish children of school-age than does Winnipeg, but more children and a greater percentage of school-age children attend Jewish schools in Winnipeg than in Vancouver. The different enrollment pattern is especially pronounced in the day schools. Indeed, more children and a greater percentage of the school-age population attended day schools in Winnipeg in 1981 than attended day and supplementary schools combined in Vancouver.

The wide differences in enrollment and educational structure suggests that the number of pupils and types of schools in a given place depends not only on the size of the community. Nor do economic factors offer sufficient explanation: Winnipeg day schools receive provincial grants of $480 per pupil and Vancouver nearly twice that amount ($912).

Winnipeg Jewry regards itself as unique and considers itself a very Jewishly committed community (indeed, a Winnipeg Jewish community leader boasted to this writer that Winnipeg has the greatest per-capita aliyah rate in North America). The large number of day schools in Winnipeg, the functioning of a day high school and the largest per-child federation grant to Jewish education in North America all point to the important role Jewish education occupies in the concerns and priorities of this community.

By contrast, Vancouver has a more recently developed community. Many of its members moved to this city from other parts of Canada rather than directly from the more traditional society of Eastern Europe as did the Jews in Winnipeg. It is possible that such factors at least partially account for differences in enrollment and apparent committment to Jewish education in the two communities.

Other Medium and Small Size Communities

Both Ottawa and Calgary maintain more than one day school apiece, and four other communities each have one day school. The eight medium size communities are served by 19 supplementary schools, most of which are affiliated with congregations.

Although the participation rates vary widely from community to community, the overall rate is similar to the situation in Montreal and Toronto. Yet, very few of the Jewish high school age population are receiving a Jewish education.

Many of the smaller communities lack the economic and human resources to establish a Jewish school. Nevertheless, at least 21 of them provide their children with some sort of formal Jewish education on a regular basis. According to reports sent to JESNA and the Canadian Jewish Congress, 876 pupils attended 23 schools in small communities in 1981–82. There is a dire need for qualified Jewish studies teachers in these communities, but many factors mitigate against the community meeting these needs.

A typical Jewish school in such a community consists of a small number of children divided into one or two classes which meet a few hours a week. Such a school is unable to offer full-time employment to Jewish teachers. Some communities seek individuals who can serve as Rabbi and cantor, as well as Jewish studies teacher. Very few people meet all these qualifications, and in many cases those that do are reluctant to go to small communities that are distant from the main Jewish centers.

On the other hand, the very smallness of such communities necessitates the participation of a large proportion of the Jewish population, and in some places, all or nearly all Jewish children attend the community school. These schools are often the only places where Jewish children can meet on a regular basis, and they serve a social as well as an educational function. Communities view the school not only as a means of teaching their children Hebrew or making them more knowledgeable about Judaism, but also as a mechanism to buttress their Jewishness and act as a bulwark against assimilation.

The size of the small community is a major factor determining the amount and extent of Jewish education a community can provide. Jewish schools in the small communities are all supplementary.[5] The seven 'largest' small communities, those with Jewish populations between 500 and 2,000 (in order by size): Kitchener, Halifax, Saint-Catherines, Kingston, Regina, Victoria and Saskatoon), all maintain Sunday or afternoon schools which meet in a communal building, usually a synagogue. In contrast, some of the smaller communities, such as the twenty-five families in Prince Edward Island, the ten families in Bridgewater, Nova Scotia, or the nine families which comprise the Antigonish Jewish community, meet on a monthly or bi-monthly basis in private homes. The Jewish educational program for these communities often consists of study groups led on a voluntary basis by an adult member of the community. In several of these communities, parents as well as children participate in the sessions, and the teachers or discussion leaders are frequently self-taught.

The existence of any Jewish educational format in many of these communities is due solely to the motivation and concern of their members. The success or failure of that program is often dependent upon the willingness and capability of one or two members of the community. Here, too, as in the case of the larger and medium size communities, the Jewish educational structure in the end is dependent upon the values and concerns of the community itself.

Financing Jewish Education

Jewish education is a multimillion dollar enterprise and is thus one of the more expensive endeavors of the organized Canadian Jewish community, too expensive to be borne by one source alone. Canadian Jewish educational institutions receive their revenue from four major sources – government, federation, tuition and private fundraising. These sources not only enable the community to educate its children, but also influence the type and nature of Jewish education the community can provide.

The two largest communities, Toronto and Montreal, together with Winnipeg and Ottawa, spend $51 million (Canadian) or $194 per person on Jewish education. The largest part of that sum, $43 million, goes for day school education. In these communities, 15,300 children attend day schools, the average cost being $2,800 per pupil.

These four communities depend upon all the major sources of financing to meet the costs of Jewish education. The amount of money each of these sources raises varies considerably and is to a large extent a function of different provincial government support schemes for private education. Montreal day schools receive $2,198 per high school and $1,538 per elementary school pupil from the Quebec government, compared to $480 per pupil in Winnipeg and no provincial grants per pupil in Toronto and Ottawa.

Jewish federation allocations appear to be inversely proportional to government grants in at least three of these four communities. Jewish education in Montreal received 53% of its $24.1 million budget from government (federal and provincial), and only 4% from the local federation, compared to a mere 2% of the combined $24.3 million Toronto and Ottawa budgets from government and 21% from federations. The ratio of government-federation support differed for Winnipeg where government provided 10% and federation 40% of the community's educational budget. As mentioned before, the Winnipeg federation allocation (more than one-million dollars) constitutes the largest per-child communal allocation to Jewish education in North America.

The percentage raised by day school tuition was less in Montreal (38%) than in the other three communities (an average of 58%), probably a result of the much larger per-child provincial grant enjoyed by Montreal.

Government Support

One issue affecting Jewish education today over which the community has only limited control is that of government support for the Jewish schools. Paradoxically the fact that a provincial government is financing Jewish education is a mixed blessing. In general those schools which have attained government support have been able to both raise teachers' salaries as well as lower pupils' tuition. However, in some provinces the prerequisites for government support could be met only by changing the curriculum and restructuring the school. These changes were not acceptable to all members of the community, and sometimes the consequences involved the community in issues not directly related to education which they had assiduously tried to avoid.

Quebec

In 1982 the Quebec government granted $11 million to the Jewish day schools. This sum constituted 46% of the money spent on all forms of Jewish education in Quebec and was indeed greater than the Montreal federation's combined expenditures on local needs for that year.

However, in order to receive these grants, the Jewish schools were forced to comply with two basic conditions. The first required an increase in the number of hours of French instruction per week to fourteen. The second prevented Jewish schools from accepting all Jewish children who wished to attend.

In 1976, in order to ensure the predominance of French language and culture in Quebec, the government had enacted new language legislation, Bill 101, limiting immigrants' access to schools in which the language of instruction and the student body were not French. Jewish schools were soon compelled to exclude from their rolls any Jewish child whose parents had not studied in an English language school in Quebec before 1977. Under Bill 101 Jewish families moving to Montreal from Toronto or from the United States could not send their children to most Jewish day schools. This injustice placed the community in the difficult position of having to refuse to allow parents to send their children to the Jewish school of their choice; it also made it difficult for the Jewish community to attract new members. While the community was united in its opposition to the new government conditions, it was divided over how it should respond. Suggestions varied from objection and rejection to mild protest and quiet accommodation. Editorial opinion in the general English and Jewish press accused the government of sacrificing the educational well-being of pupils to party ideology. The organized Jewish community, however, was less vociferous. It sought to deal with the problem through established channels.

The Association of Jewish Day Schools (AJDS), an organization composed of representatives of Jewish day schools and responsible directly to them, had been established earlier to represent the schools before the government on educational matters. At first, the AJDS, which operates by unanimous consent, found it difficult to agree upon a proper response. However, when one of its member schools, faced with the probability that two of its pupils would be declared ineligible, decided to retain these children even if it meant rejecting provincial assistance, the matter came to a head. Not only did other members of the AJDS worry that such action might endanger government assistance to their schools and to Jewish day school education in general, but certain federation leaders let it be known that schools rejecting government assistance would not receive extra funding from the federation. In the end the government's interpretation of the status of the two children permitted them to remain in their school, but other children facing a similar situation are now excluded. Today the once recalcitrant school receives federation funding and is a member of the AJDS which still operates by unanimous consent and the government continues to fund the Jewish day schools.

Government support for Jewish education has meant not only the exclusion of some children from the Jewish school of their choice, but has led to rifts within the community over difficult questions concerning politics (e.g., the right to dissent, what tactics to use, how to protest effectively), or language and culture (e.g., English instruction versus Jewish studies in Hebrew and Yiddish).

Bill 40, legislation on educational reform which the provincial government recently introduced raises both new opportunities for Jewish education as well as new concerns for Quebec Jewry. Bill 40 would restructure the present denominational school system (Catholic and Protestant boards) and replace it with a structure that would permit each school to decide on its orientation. Theoretically, it would be possible under such a bill for the parents of children in a school that had once been part of the Protestant board, but whose pupils were mainly Jewish, to vote that their school would be a Jewish school. Such a school, according to Bill 40, would be both a government school and a Jewish one. The potential effects of the bill on Jewish education in Quebec are far reaching. Religious and moral education would be mandatory subjects, but parents could form a committee that would decide on the school's approach in accordance with their orientation. There would no longer be questions of how much the government would assist Jewish education for in a sense providing Jewish education would no longer depend on voluntarism and philanthropy but would, if the parents so willed it, become a government responsibility.

However, the bill also raises difficult questions concerning a Jew's right not to seek a Jewish education. Heretofore, Jewish education in Quebec was voluntary. Jewish leaders may have occasionally pressured, perhaps even cajoled other Jews into sending their children to Jewish schools, but there was no question that the amount and type of Jewish education one gave one's children was a private matter. Moreover there were always some Jews, until recently perhaps the majority, who wished to educate their children in local non-Jewish schools where their children could be exempted from religious education. Under the new bill, however, such exemptions would no longer be granted, as the religious and moral education taught in the school supposedly reflects the orientation of the children's parents.

Bill 40 also threatens to end the Protestant School Board, a Board that was regarded as a bastion of the English language. This too, troubles the Jews. Bill 40 raises difficult questions for the community. Should the Jews regard it as a blessing, an opportunity to make Jewish day school education in Quebec nearly universal, or as a threat to the equilibrium the Jews have tried to achieve between being Jewish as well as a member of the general society? Once more Jewish education has become a contentious issue for the community.

Other Provinces

In other provinces Jews are grappling with different problems in their dealings with the provincial government. In Alberta, Jewish day schools in Calgary and Edmonton negotiated a contract whereby their schools joined the Calgary and Edmonton public school system. They became alternative schools that any resident in Calgary or Edmonton could attend; as a result, a small number of non-Jews do attend these schools. Parents still have to pay tuition for certain aspects of the school that differ from the others, such as salaries during Jewish holidays, expenses concerning specifically Jewish studies, etc. But all other aspects are covered by the government. In Calgary, the Jewish Day Talmud Torah had to redefine itself as a Hebrew cultural rather than religious school, but the Board recognized that religion was part of the curriculum.

Then, in November 1983, a newly elected Calgary school board which was ideologically opposed to religious schools voted not to renew its contract with the Jewish school. In June 1984, two Jewish day schools lost their public school status. The future status of these schools is quite uncertain. No one yet knows how much the tuition will be raised or how many children will leave because of that hike. What services will be reduced? Nor is it clear what will happen to the teachers (including those who teach Jewish studies) who have tenure and have accrued seniority within the public school system. At the time of this writing the public school board in Edmonton has raised no such problems and the contract between them and the Edmonton Talmud Torah remains valid.

In Manitoba, the Winnipeg Board of Education opened a special Hebrew language heritage program in two of its schools that provides Hebrew language and culture, where culture has been defined to include a religious dimension, and the curriculum includes teaching of siddur, celebration of holidays, etc. Parents now have the option of sending their children to a public school, where Hebrew and Jewish studies are taught, and paying no tuition or sending them to a Jewish day school and paying several thousand dollars. The resultant loss to the Jewish schools may have caused the Yiddishist Peretz school to merge with the religiously oriented Talmud Torah. The Peretz School building now has a kosher kitchen and its male students must cover their heads during Jewish studies classes in Hebrew but not in Yiddish.

The Manitoba government's new policy to promote Jewish education not only helped affect a merger between two schools with long histories of ideological disagreement but also encouraged the Board of Jewish Education to try to negotiate a new agreement whereby its day schools would become part of the Winnipeg School system. The Jewish community in Winnipeg was divided over these negotiations. The community experienced a 20% decrease in population over ten years, and Federation leaders worried that their campaign (which provided about one-million dollars to Jewish education, or $1,000 per child) might no longer be able to suppport their day schools. They hoped to solve their fiscal problem by means of an agreement with the School Board. On the other hand, two very divergent groups opposed the negotiations. The more assimilated segment of the Jewish community which supported a public school system joined forces with Orthodox members of the communty who feared that government funding would lead to non-Jewish tampering with Jewish education.

In British Columbia, the Vancouver Talmud Torah receives grants made available to independent private schools which meet the general requirements concerning secular studies. The government grant enables the school to reduce the average tuition cost of each pupil by nearly $1,000.

Ontario, the only province whose government does not fund Jewish day schools is the home of half the Jews in Canada. The seemingly skyrocketing cost of Jewish education has led to both increase in tuition and to greater federation allocations. The Toronto federation allocates four-million dollars, five times the allocation of the Montreal federation for almost the same number of day school pupils. Ontario day schools are experiencing the high cost of the absence of government support.

Federation Funding of Jewish Education

In Canada as in the United States, the Jewish community is organized on a federal basis. In both countries local federations serve central fundraising and coordinating functions in all but the smallest of Jewish communities. It is through these federations that most Canadian Jewish day schools and some supplementary schools receive their communal funding.

In the past, Canadian and American federations related quite differently to the Jewish educational needs of their communities. In the early years of their development most Canadian but few federations in the United States allocated funds to Jewish educational institutions. Since the 1960s, as American federations assumed greater financial responsibilities for Jewish education, these differences have begun to diminish. However, Canadian communities still tend to allocate more federation funds to education than do their counterparts in the United States.[6]

The disparity between the percentage allocations of United States and Canadian federations for Jewish education reflects certain historical differences between the two North American Jewish communities. The federation movement in America traces its origin to American German-Jewish immigrants of the mid-nineteenth century and their children who founded and were the mainstays of federations in the early 20th century. These Jews looked askance at Jewish day school education, and believed that it would impede their Jewish children's integration into American society. Canadian federations, however, were founded by East-European Jews who came from a milieu in which Jewish separatism from general society was widely accepted. These Jews also sought to integrate into the general society, but were less fearful of the separatist influence of Jewish day schools.

Greater communal support of Canadian day schools may also be due to the pressure parents of day school pupils have been able to exert on their local federations. Since, in some Canadian communities, the parents of day school children constitute a large segment of the community from which the federation seeks to raise its funds, the parent body is sometimes able to influence federation allocations. In Montreal, for instance, the federation did not provide financial assistance until the mid-1970s when day school parents threatened withdrawal of support.

A well organized or large enough parent-body may also influence the arrangements between the United Israel Appeal (UIA) and local federation over the division of communal funds for local and overseas needs. In 1981 when the hardships of the recession made it necessary for many more Montreal parents to seek tuition scholarships for their children's day school education, the local federation demanded and received an additional $400,000 of its annual campaign receipts for local needs. In 1983, the Winnipeg federation negotiated a non-interest bearing loan from the UIA that would allow the federation to liquidate its local indebtedness most of which was due to expenditure on Jewish education.

Although federation policies towards education may differ from community to community, on certain issues there is no disagreement. All eleven federations (Toronto, Montreal, Winnipeg, Vancouver, Ottawa, Hamilton, Calgary, Edmonton, London, Windsor and Halifax) help finance Jewish education. All federations, as a pre-condition for financial support require that schools submit their annual budgets and enrollment data, and that the financial needs of parents requesting reductions in tuition be verified.

Although the constitutions of some federations provide them with a mandate to "enhance Jewish education...in all its aspects" federations for the most part have hesitated from intervening in non-economic matters and have steered clear of ideological controversy. Nonetheless federation funding of Jewish education has forced the commmunity to relate to its own educational needs and to give thought to the relative value it places on Jewish education.

Communal Support in Non-Federated Communities

In communities that are too small to maintain federations the situation is somewhat different. In some of the smaller congregational communities, the funding of Jewish education is a communal responsibility. Not all Jewish residents are necessarily members of the community in the area, and membership in the congregational community is a voluntary matter as it is in the federation. But once people join the organized community, they and their families are entitled to all the community's services, including Jewish education.

Tuition Fees

Tuition comprises the parents' major financial obligation towards the day school. The determination of tuition fees and the actual amount charged is often a function of government policy, as the size of the government grant helps determine how much the schools must raise in tuition. But government's influence on school tuition policy, although substantial, is usually indirect. Generally, in Quebec and Alberta, where government grants are largest, school tuition rates are lowest.

Federations are more concerned than governments with how much schools charge their parental body. Even in Quebec where the law limits tuition fees to 50% of government per-pupil grants, the government has not become involved in this matter since, theoretically at least, tuition pays for the school's religious education, an aspect of the curricula not covered by the law. In Winnipeg where the day schools are communally operated, tuition fees are determined by the Winnipeg Board of Jewish Education, an agency funded almost completely by the federation. In Toronto and Hamilton where schools are autonomous institutions, the federation has insisted that schools receiving its funding set tuition fees at least per pupil cost. In these communities, federation allocation to education is based mainly on the amount needed to cover tuition-fee reductions which, in turn, are granted according to established communal guidelines. Montreal, where each school follows its own criteria for determining tuition fees, is somewhat of an exception. The Montreal federation finds itself called upon to help parents pay tuition fees over which it has little control. This situation had led to the formation of a day school funding committee composed of representatives from both the schools and the federation. The committee has discussed the establishment of standardized criteria and has considered the idea of unified fees for different day schools.

In Alberta and Quebec where government grants have substantially reduced the amount of money needed from other sources, many schools have set tuition at higher than the actual cost per pupil after the government grant, yet seemingly low enough not to dissuade parents from enrolling their children. The fact that these fees were higher than cost has enabled the schools to make up most of the difference between the fee reductions offered to low income families and actual costs. The policy in some schools of charging more than per-pupil cost has led to complaints that high tuition rates unfairly force some parents to subsidize others. These parents contend that the responsibility of providing Jewish education for the less affluent should be borne by the community, and not by other day school parents.

In Calgary, Alberta, a new relationship between the schools and the board of education was expected to lead to substantially higher tuition fees. Because of reduced government support, actual per-pupil costs were expected to increase substantially. Higher tuition fees, however, were not expected to adequately meet the increased per-pupil costs.

Although people may disagree over how fee reductions should be financed, there is a general consensus that day school education should be available to all children of the community regardless of their parents' ability to pay tuition. But here too the community may be faced with a dilemma, especially when it has to decide between assisting needy parents or supporting other worthwhile causes.

When the 1981-82 recession led to a much greater demand for fee reductions, some school committees found themselves in the difficult position of having to act in a 'financially responsible manner' in terms of their schools' budget, and sometimes refused to admit children whose parents were unable to pay. Some of these schools confronted their federations, which because of the recession were also strapped for funds. Some federations, as already noted, negotiated with the United Israel Appeal extra funds for tuition fee reductions. Jewish educational needs and the tuition policies of the schools found themselves in conflict with financial support for Israel.

Little is known of the actual effects of tuition rates on day school enrollment. It is generally assumed that by charging tuition, even if fee reductions are available, schools deter some of the less affluent of the community from enrolling their children in day schools. But other factors are also important. On the one hand, people who may not hesitate to take out a loan for a car or pay thousands of dollars annually for day-care or perhaps much more for a university education might be reluctant to pay or borrow similar amounts for Jewish day school education. On the other hand, studies of the American Jewish community have noted the importance of investing in the associational process, to develop "formal or lasting Jewish attachments" (Elazar, 1976). In Canada where the community is also organized on a federal basis and where philanthropy serves as a major source of communal revenue, the situation is probably the same. There too, enrolling one's child in a Jewish day school is one way of establishing "formal or lasting Jewish attachments".

Tuition policy deals with much more than with the dollars and cents issues of who is to pay how much for Jewish education. This policy affects the very availability of Jewish education. It also reflects the manner in which the community is organized – the relationship of financial expenditure to communal participation – as well as the priority Canadian Jews place on their children's Jewish education and the schools' and community's assessment of that priority and the commitment it implies.

Private Fundraising

In an earlier period when government grants, federation allocations and tuition fees provided a smaller share of school budgets, day schools were much more dependent upon private fundraising. Yiddish and national-cultural schools relied on fraternal and labor-Zionist organizations for support, and Talmud Torah schools sought out wealthy lay leaders to join their school boards. Today, the membership of the organizations supporting Yiddish and national-cultural schools has greatly declined and is no longer able to provide much economic assistance. Likewise, the lay-boards of the Talmud Torah schools, which are composed mainly of parents, also lack the resources for major fundraising projects.

These developments hold implications regarding the type of education the school will provide. Indeed, greater parental representation on the board may help rectify the problem of discontinuity between home and school. In the realm of funding, however, it presents difficult problems. Such problems may be especially acute when schools decide to embark upon capital expansion which involves expenditures not usually funded by governments and federations.

Staffing Jewish Schools

Teachers

Teachers in Jewish schools in Canada are often categorized according to the type of school in which they are employed. This division reflects the different conditions and needs of day and supplementary schools. However, many teachers teach in both types of schools and there is much overlap between the two categories.

Supplementary School Teachers

In all but one community there are no formal binding rules regarding qualifications for teaching Jewish subjects in supplementary schools, and the schools are free to determine their own criteria for hiring teachers. Only in Toronto, where federation funded schools are required to engage certified teachers, has the organized community attempted to regulate the qualifications of its supplementary school teachers.

There are few institutions in Canada where one can train to become a supplementary school teacher. Again, Toronto is an exception. One Toronto synagogue maintains its own teacher training program for the teen-age graduates of its supplementary school, and the Toronto Jewish Teachers' Seminary conducts a summer institute to train teachers for the supplementary schools. In addition, some students majoring in Jewish education at York University in Toronto and McGill University in Montreal teach part-time in supplementary schools while preparing to become day school teachers.

Many supplementary school teachers gained their expertise in Jewish education from sources other than Jewish teacher training programs. The teaching staff of supplementary schools often includes university students who are majoring or have taken courses in Jewish studies, ordained rabbis or their wives, immigrants whose knowledge of Hebrew and Jewish studies is derived from their education in their country of origin (usually Israel, or Poland before World War II) or Canadian Jews who have lived in Israel and acquired a knowledge of Hebrew.

The limited number of hours in which the supplementary school holds sessions makes full-time employment difficult to attain. In order to work full-time one must somehow find teaching positions in schools which hold sessions at different times. Some teachers teach at more than one supplementary school, while others teach in a day school in the morning and a supplementary school in the afternoon. When supplementary schools, which hold classes in the afternoon after public school sessions are concluded, were first established, one of the pioneers of these institutions, Samson Benderly, hoped to make them "so interesting and so stimulating as to get response even of tired children." But even experienced and qualified teachers find it difficult to "interest" and "stimulate...tired" children when they themselves arrive already fatigued from teaching in the day school. The supplementary school, however, is dependent upon such teachers. Indeed, many principals of these schools prefer teachers who work full-time in Jewish education and regard teaching as their career, to others who perhaps relate to supplementary Jewish education as a means of complementing their spouses' income with a few hours of afternoon or weekend teaching.

Most supplementary schools pay their teachers an hourly rate. The central agencies of the two largest communities have issued guidelines on these rates, which, however, are not binding. These wage-rates are not easily comparable as the Montreal scale is based on weekly hours while the Toronto one is concerned with annual hourly income. Nonetheless they may give an idea of how much the supplementary school teacher can earn in the large communities in Canada.

According to the Montreal scale, a beginning teacher with a B.A. with or without certification, should receive $11 (Canadian) an hour. The same teacher, with five years experience, should receive $17 an hour. Since full-time employment at a supplementary school which meets two hours a day for five days a week provides 10 hours of instruction, a full-time beginning teacher, and a teacher with five years experience would earn $110 and $170 a week respectively, or $4,400 and $6,800 for a 40 week school year.

The Toronto wage-guideline which does not differentiate between the hourly wages earned by teachers in supplementary and day schools recommends higher rates than does its counterpart in Montreal. In both cases a beginning teacher with a B.A. and teacher's certificate would earn $653 per hour per school year. A teacher with the same academic qualifications and five years teachers' experience would earn $889 per hour per school year. Ten hours of weekly instruction, according to this suggested scale would provide $6,532 and $8,888 annually, respectively.

Since Statistics Canada (the Canadian Central Bureau of Statistics) defined the poverty level of a family in a large city for the year 1981 as $19,751 ($17,183 U.S.) such teachers are barely eking out a living, and supplementary school teaching can hardly be considered a viable profession.

The woeful lack of academic and professional standards for supplementary school teachers and the poor remuneration offered them cause serious problems for a community seeking to attract qualified supplementary school teachers.

Day School Teachers

Most day schools pay higher salaries and offer greater opportunity for full employment than do supplementary schools. They also maintain more rigorous standards concerning the academic and pedagogic training of the teachers they hire.

In four of the five provinces in which day schools are located and which are provided with government funding, Jewish studies day school teachers must meet government certification requirements. When the Manitoba provincial government began providing per-child grants to the day schools in Winnipeg, it required that non-certified teachers already employed in the Jewish schools begin studying towards a Bachelor of Education degree at a minimum rate of six credits per year.

In Alberta, where Jewish day schools are part of the local public school system, the local school board rather than the Jewish school hires the teachers and determines whether they have the proper credentials. Here too, special arrangements have had to be made concerning both the teachers who were working in the day school before it joined the public school system and the Israeli *shlihim*. Since the *shlihim* teach in Canada for only a limited time, the Alberta government classified them as exchange teachers and provided them with a special waiver allowing them to teach up to two years without certification.

The impact of provincial government requirements on the quality of Jewish studies teachers and their teaching is difficult to assess. One assumes that even without government regulations, day schools would seek to hire the more qualified Jewish studies teachers available. Nevertheless, provincial regulations compelling Jewish studies teachers to attain an undergraduate university degree in education may have a salutary effect on the Jewish studies teaching profession.

The effect of provincial regulations is also a function of government enforcement and interpretation. Whereas the Quebec government has been more concerned over the certification of general studies teachers than of Jewish studies teachers in Montreal day schools, the Vancouver Talmud Torah in British Columbia has been given a wide latitude over the interpretation of the Jewish studies teachers' qualifications. The Province of Ontario requires that the general studies teachers in the day schools hold an Ontario Ministry of Education Certification, but has not set conditions concerning Jewish studies teachers. Instead, each of the five communities which maintain day schools is free to determine its own standards. The Toronto Jewish federation has insisted that the schools it subsidizes hire only teachers who are certified and whose certification is recognized by the Toronto Jewish Board of License and Review.

In general, day school teaching salaries are commensurate, or nearly so, with those of the public sector. This holds true not only for Alberta where as already noted, the Jewish day schools are part of the public school system and Montreal where the Jewish teachers' union negotiated an agreement attaining parity with the salary scale of the Protestant School Board but in other places as well. In Winnipeg, Vancouver and Ottawa day school salaries are slightly below those of the largest public school boards but are equal to those paid by some of the boards in the suburbs. In Toronto where no linkage exists, the Board of Jewish Education has drawn up a wage-scale guideline for the various day schools and it has been able to assert some influence on wage-scale agreement.

Salaries in Canadian Jewish day schools, which are comparable to local public-school salaries are generally higher than those paid by most Jewish day schools in the United States. But public school teachers in Canada as in the United States usually receive smaller remuneration than that received by other professionals with similar years of academic training. The feminization of the teaching profession in both Jewish and non-Jewish schools in both countries is at least partially due to such economic factors.

Recruitment and Training of Jewish Studies Teachers

In many day schools the Jewish studies teaching staff consists primarily of teachers educated outside of Canada, mainly in Israel. A study of Montreal Jewish studies teachers in the early 1970s found that less than 25% of these teachers were born or educated in Canada, while about 75% came from Europe and Israel. A study of Jewish studies teachers in Toronto, also conducted in the early 1970s, found that only 29 of the 168 day school Jewish studies teachers responding to the survey were born in either Canada or the United States. Moreover, according to these surveys the Jewish teacher training institutions at that time (1970s) seemed unable to affect the compositions of the teaching staff in even the schools of these two communities themselves. The *Midrasha L'Morim* in Toronto and the United Teachers Seminary in Montreal consisted mainly of Israeli Jewish women, and only the orthodox *Beth Jacob* Seminary for Girls of Montreal was able to attract Canadian-educated Jewish teachers. The same surveys claimed that "children would have a more positive attitude toward their Jewish studies if Canadian young men and women could be induced to serve as teachers and as educational models", and recommended that "the *Beth Jacob* Seminary be granted a subsidy (by the Federation)" and that new "Jewish teacher training programs be university based." These recommendations led to the development of Jewish education programs at McGill (Montreal) and York (Toronto) universities. Recently the University of Manitoba announced the formation of a third Canadian university program in Jewish education.

The decision to create Jewish educational programs in non-Jewish institutions was in certain respects quite radical. Traditionally Canadian Jews have viewed Jewish education as a means of strengthening and reinforcing their Jewishness. Jewish educational institutions may differ in their understanding of Judaism and their concept of the Jewish people, but they generally agree on the broad purpose of Jewish education, i.e. that it should contribute to the continued existence of the Jewish people and Judaism. Such a goal would cause the Jewish community to develop its own institutions to train Jewish studies teachers rather than depend upon non-Jewish sources.

In Canada with its ethnic diversity and conscious awareness of language and cultural differences, the goals of Jewish education appear less threatened by the general society and more capable of achievement in non-Jewish institutions than in, for instance, the United States, Perhaps for that reason, the three largest Jewish communities in Canada felt secure enough to negotiate the establishment of Jewish teacher training programs in local non-Jewish academic institutions.

The success and failings of these programs help shed light on Canadian Jewry's attitudes toward Jewish education. The university's and the organized community's approach to Jewish education are juxtaposed. Jewish education in the Jewish schools serves a communal function; it is supposed to help maintain Judaism and the Jewish people by inculcating a behavior code, a set of values or a sense of commitment. It is the function of a university education, however, to question accepted values and challenge commitments. A university education does not seek to reinforce what is known but rather teaches the known in order to develop the capacity to discover the unknown. Indeed, when one considers the divergent functions of a university and a Jewish school, the Jewish community's reliance on university trained teachers to imbue its children with a loyalty to Judaism and the Jewish people is difficult to comprehend.

The apparent success of the program at least in terms of alumni placement (43 of the 46 graduates of the McGill program have been employed in the field of Jewish education) suggests that the orientation of a university trained program has not created the problems anticipated. Perhaps it reflects the community's acceptance of the university approach toward the study of Judaism as well as of general studies and its desire to integrate general knowledge with Jewish knowledge – one of the declared goals of day school education.

On the other hand, although over 15,000 pupils are enrolled in Jewish day schools in the three communities which have university based Jewish education programs and about 580 students graduate from the Jewish day high schools each year, very few of these go on to major in Jewish education. Of the 46 students who completed the McGill program, only three had graduated from the Jewish day high school.

The McGill, York and University of Manitoba programs have not graduated enough students to meet the recruitment needs of the Jewish schools and have not greatly affected the composition of the Jewish studies teaching staff which is still mainly non-Canadian. Indeed, only in the *Beth Jacob* and perhaps the one-day a week schools, where the language of instruction is English, are most of the Jewish studies teachers Canadian-born or educated. Indeed, Jewish schools in Canada – like those in the United States – have had to rely on Israeli immigrants and on the employment of Israeli *shihim* to teach their classes. This dependence on Israeli *shihim*, whom the educational director of one of the largest Canadian day schools often describes as the 'backbone' of his school, reflects the community's inability to meet its own educational needs. If, as the Montreal and Toronto surveys contend, Canadian youth find it difficult to model themselves after foreign educated teachers, then the practice of hiring mainly Israeli Jewish studies teachers is self-defeating. While Jewish day schools provide competent instruction in Hebrew and in Jewish studies largely because of their Israeli teachers, the origins and educational background of these teachers subtly signal to their students that only someone born or educated in Israel can master Hebrew and Jewish studies. This may be among the factors that deter Canadian students from starting a career in Jewish studies and Jewish education – along with other factors, such as the perceived lower-middle class status of teaching and pursuit of more highly paid careers.

The professional standards and certification requirements of the Jewish studies day school teachers, full-time employment opportunities, and salary scale commensurate with the public sector's, constitute impressive achievements for Canadian Jewry's education system, especially when compared with the situation prevailing in the United States. In addition, the community's role in developing university Jewish education programs testify to its concern for Jewish education and demonstrate its determination to seek out new solutions.

However, the continued reliance on *shihim* as teachers and the lack of success in persuading graduates of the system to pursue careers in Jewish education, are difficult problems with which Canadian Jewish education must still contend.

Curriculum Development and Research

Canadian Jewry's close ties with the American Jewish community are aptly illustrated in the area of curriculum development. Canadian educational institutions are affiliated with American-based umbrella organizations which develop curricula for schools in both Canada and the United States. The Reform movement's Joint Commission on Jewish Education; the Melton Resource Center and the United Synagogue Commission on Jewish Education, under Conservative movement auspices; *Torah Umesorah* Publications which serve Orthodox schools, as well as the Central Organization for Jewish Education of the Lubavitch Hassidic movement, all publish curricula employed in Canadian schools.

A major exception, the Canadian developed *Tel-Sela* curriculum, merely confirms the strong linkage between North American Jewish institutions in matters of curriculum. The impetus for *Tel-Sela* (a spiral bound Hebrew language curriculum package for grades 2–6, produced by the Jewish Education Council of Montreal and funded by the Canadian government) stemmed from the perceived curricula needs of Jewish day schools in Quebec. Nevertheless, both the government's and the Jewish community's decision to support the project was at least partially based on the program's marketability in the United States.

Few studies on Canadian Jewish education have been published in the academic educational press and Jewish education in Canada suffers from a dearth of serious research. Indeed, a 1983 computerized search through ERIC (Educational Resources Information Center) disclosed only four publications on Canadian Jewish Education in the more than 250 academic and professional journals indexed in that system.

Despite the great efforts expended to provide Jewish education in Canada, difficulties in defining educational goals have hindered the capacity to assess achievements and what has been learned. Educational goals are but derivatives of educational philosophies. Canadian Jewish educational institutions, and perhaps Canadian Jewry, need to clearly articulate their philosophies of Jewish education. While the community has learned to handle problems of how to provide Jewish education, it must begin to ask itself why it deems education to be important.

The urgent desire for improvements promotes a search for quick, sometimes hastily conceived, solutions. Research has been designed and reports have been written in order to meet immediate needs of the educational structure, e.g., the report of *Space Needs of Jewish Day Schools* commissioned by the Montreal Jewish community in order to decide whether to build a new school. Along with such research, studies should also be conducted on the less action-directed aspects of Jewish education. The community, however, does not yet seem to recognize the importance of such studies.

Likewise, the central Jewish educational agencies of Montreal and Winnipeg have employed the 1981 Canadian census data in order to project Jewish school enrollment. But, by the time of this writing, such data for all of Canada have not been utilized.

People interested in improving Jewish education must be patient enough to first examine the underlying issues and foundations upon which the current state of education rests. Canadian Jewry might develop instruments to promote and enhance this type of Jewish educational research. Perhaps a national data gathering and central depository for data and studies on Jewish education could be established. Just as in the 1970s communities sought the help of universities to train Jewish studies teachers, so now they might also turn to the universities for help in developing and promoting research on Jewish education.

Conclusion

Canadian Jewish education like other aspects of Canadian Jewish life is affected by developments in the older, much larger Jewish community in the United States. In general, Canadian Jewish institutions are more influenced by their American counterparts than the opposite. However, Canadian Jewry's success in establishing a viable educational structure along with the difficulties it encounters in maintaining that structure has important implications for the United States' as well as its own Jewish community.

The development in Canada of a wide array of Jewish educational institutions and a variety of educational options testify to the importance of Jewish education for Canadian Jewry. Moreover, the day school with its greater demands on the community, parents, and pupils, occupies a central place in Jewish education in Canada. But while the establishment of this educational system is largely due to the support and concern of the well-organized Canadian Jewish community, the difficulties confronting it also reflect the problems of the community it serves.

Our examination of Canadian Jewry's handling of ostensibly financial matters (government grants, federation allocations, tuition fees and scholarship assistance) has revealed disputes over communal and parental responsibility for Jewish education and controversies concerning the type and extent of Jewish education the community should help provide. Likewise, the community's difficulty in persuading young Canadian Jews to enter the Jewish teaching profession – despite day-school salaries commensurate with those in the public schools – and notwithstanding academic Jewish education programs the problems besetting Jewish education in Canada are more complex than mere fulfillment of the financial and personnel needs of the educational system.

Canadian Jewry, like other Diaspora communities in the post-traditional era, seeks to integrate into general society while maintaining its Jewishness. The difficulties and ambiguity involved in pursuing these divergent and sometimes conflicting objectives as well as in educating one's children towards achieving them cannot help but affect Canadian Jewish education. Thus, the success of the impressive Jewish educational structure in Canada is tempered by the basic conflict within Canadian Jewry over its relationship to the organized Jewish community, to local and national government, and to the non-Jewish society.

Acknowledgements

Much of the research for this study is based on information provided by individuals and institutions who requested that they not be identified. However, I would like to single out a few of the many North American educators whose insights contributed substantially to this study: Rabbi Meyer Krentzman, Betty Niktin, George Pollak, Baruch Rand, Bernard Shoub, Richard Wagner and Rabbi Irwin Witty. We would also like to thank Harold M. Waller, the project director of the Studies on Canadian Jewish Communities for making those studies available to our research prior to their publication.

Notes

1. Since the Canadian census asks residents of Canada to state their religion and ethnicity, the category 'Jews by ethnicity' includes some Canadians who regard themselves as Jews by ethnicity, but Christians by religion. The organized Jewish community does not relate to these people as Jews.

2. This is implied, for instance, in the community's request for census data that do not include as Jews people who profess another religion.

3. In 1931, when there were 156,000 Jews in Canada, 149,000 Canadians declared Yiddish their mother tongue.

4. Enrollment figures for the years 1981–82 are based on data provided by the Department of Research and Educational Information of the Jewish Education Service of North America (JESNA). 1983 enrollment figures were made available to this study by the Jewish central educational agencies in Montreal, Toronto and Winnipeg, the Jewish Educational Resource Centre in Vancouver, and individual schools in other communities.

5. There has been some talk of building a residential Jewish day school in the Maritime provinces, where about 1,000 Jewish school-age children live. The concept of a residential day school for outlying areas was broached at the 1983 Canadian National Education Conference but it was not considered viable. Most discussants felt that few parents would send their children to such a school since most Jews with sufficient commitment and concern for their children's Jewish education choose to reside in larger communities.

6. In a recent Council of Jewish Federations study of allocations to Jewish education, the local budgets of 101 federations (including five Canadian), were examined: 43.9 of 169.1 million United States dollars (26%) of local allocations went to Jewish education, compared to 6.8 of 15.8 million (44%) for the five Canadian federations. In 1982 the 16 large cities surveyed allocated 33.4 of 129.3 million (26%) of their local budget to Jewish education, compared to Toronto which allocated 4.6 of 6.1 million dollars (75%) of its local budget for Jewish education. The

only federation providing more money for Jewish education than Toronto was New York City which spent 6.8 of 38.6 million dollars (18%) of federation funds for local Jewish education. The highest percentage allocation in the United States was in Philadelphia where 2.5 of 5.7 million dollars (44%) of the budget went to Jewish education. Likewise, among intermediate size federations which together allocated 6.5 of 25.3 million dollars (26%), Winnipeg allocated both the largest amount, 1 million, and the largest percentage (64%) for Jewish education (Council of Jewish Federations, 1983).

Bibliographical Note

There have been very few attempts to examine Jewish education in Canada on a country-wide basis. Two exceptions are: David Norman Zweig, *Jewish Education in Canada*, unpublished MA thesis, McGill University, Montreal (1949) and Yaakov Glickman, "Jewish Education in Canada: Success or Failure?", in: Weinfeld, M., Shaffir, W. and Cotler, I., eds., *The Canadian Jewish Mosaic*, Wiley, Toronto (1981). Written thirty-nine years ago, Zweig's thesis describes the educational institutions of a primarily immigrant community. Glickman's study is more interpretive than descriptive. It culls the recent literature on Jewish education in various Canadian communities.

The Center for Jewish Community Studies has undertaken a number of studies on organized Jewish communities in Canada. While these studies are not primarily concerned with Jewish education, they examine and describe how educational institutions are integrated into the organized community.

In addition, much of the data (enrollment figures, teacher salary scales, school budgets, minutes of school committee meetings) employed in this chapter are based on current files of various educational institutions. While we have not been able to quote from these files directly, they have provided much of the empirical evidence for our findings.

B.G. Sack, *History of the Jews in Canada* , Harvest House, Montreal (1965); Stuart E. Rosenberg, *The Jewish Community in Canada* 2 vols., McClelland and Stewart, Toronto (1970); and more recently M. Weinfeld, W. Shaffir, and I. Cotler, eds., *The Canadian Jewish Mosaic* (1981) help place Canadian Jewish education in historical perspective. These works are particularly helpful in explaining both the differences and similarities between the Canadian and American Jewish experience. See also: Daniel J. Elazar, *Community and Polity; The Organizational Dynamics of American Jewry*, Jewish Publication Society, Philadelphia (1976).

John Porter, "Ethnic Pluralism in Canadian Perspective", in: Nathan Glazer and Daniel Moynihan, eds. *Ethnicity, Theory and Experience*, Harvard University Press, Cambridge (1975); Cornaelius Joenus, "Mutilated Multi-culturalism", J. Donald Wilson, "Religion and Education, The Other Side of Pluralism", and Robert J. MacDonald, "Language Education and Society in Quebec", in: J. Donald Wilson, ed., *Canadian Education in the 80's* (1983), help explain the current Canadian context for many of the issues confronting Jewish education.

The impact of political developments on the Jews in Quebec and their implications for Jewish education is discussed by Daniel J. Elazar, "The Jews of Quebec and the Canadian Crisis," *Jerusalem Letter* (May, 1978), Morton Weinfield, "La Question Juive au Quebec", *Midstream*, Vol. 23 (October, 1977) and Ruth Wisse and Irwin Cotler, "Quebec Jews Caught in the Middle", *Commentary*, Vol. 64 (1977). *Education and Culture*, a journal published by the Toronto Board of Jewish Education, provides a forum for discussion on current educational issues in Toronto.

Jewish Education in Greater Montreal, A Survey of Jewish Education and Recommendations for its Enhancement in the Jewish Community, Montreal (1972) and *A Study on Jewish Education*, Prepared by the Study Committee on Jewish Education, United Jewish Welfare Fund, Toronto (1975) summarize the results of Montreal and Toronto study commissions in the early seventies. These reports have been supplemented by more recent, less comprehensive studies concerning certain specific educational policy issues. *Space Needs of the Day School*, Montreal (1982) and the *Study Committee on the Jewish Educational Council of Greater Montreal* (1983) are two examples of more recent studies undertaken to find answers for specific communal policy questions.

Jewish Education in Hamilton (June 1976) and *Winnipeg Report, Jewish Education in Winnipeg* (March 1981), two studies conducted by the present Jewish Education Service of North America (JESNA) describe in detail some of the problems peculiar to middle-size communities.

The various reports of the Center for Jewish Community Studies place Jewish educational institutions within the framework of the middle-size organized communities. Among those communities examined are: *Calgary, Alberta*, by Harvey Rich; *Hamilton, Ontario*, by Louis Greenspan; *London, Ontario*, by Allen M. Cohen; *Ottawa*, by Zacharia Key; *Vancouver, British Columbia*, by Edna Oberman; *Windsor, Ontario* by Stephen Mandell; and *Winnipeg, Manitoba*, by Anna Gorer. These studies related to Jewish education from a communal standpoint. Baruch Rand, "Jewish Education under Communal Auspices," *Jewish Education*, Vol. 50 (Summer, 1982) describes the formation of the Winnipeg Board of Jewish Education. Michael Morgan, "Religious Pluralism in the Hebrew Day School," *Jewish Education*, Vol. 49 (Fall, 1981) based on the experiences of the Hebrew Day School in Edmonton discusses the problem of ideological orientation of day schools in middle size communities.

For evaluation of the financing of Jewish education we relied on: Council of Jewish Federations, *Federation Allocations to Jewish Education: A Five Year Analysis of Federation Support to the Field of Jewish Education*, New York (1983).

Tape recordings of proceedings of subcommittee on small communities at the National Canadian Jewish Education Conference (November 1983) provided data on Jewish education in small communities. In addition, personal interviews with some of the residents of those communities, data from JESNA and reports from the Canadian Jewish Congress section in small communities were also helpful.

Part Three
Latin America

Latin American Jewry consists of comparatively recently developed communities. They grew as a consequence of immigration from Europe since the end of the 19th century and throughout the post World War II period. Recent decades have witnessed political turmoil in these countries as well as considerable emigration from them to Israel and other places. Argentina has been particularly susceptible in this regard, while some of the smaller communities, like Venezuela, have benefitted from Argentinian emigration. Latin American Jewish communities are distinctive in their strong communal ties and Zionist orientation. There has been a great emphasis in their educational system on Jewish culture rather than religion, with Hebrew and Yiddish language playing a central role. The Latin American countries are also distinctive in the overwhelming reliance on day schools as the primary form of Jewish education. How this came about is described in the following chapters.

Chapter 5 is on Argentina. The largest Jewish community in Latin America is heavily concentrated in the Buenos Aires area. Ya'acov Rubel, who is in charge of the Instituto de Investigaciones Sociales of the Asociacion Mutual Israelita Argentina (AMIA) in Buenos Aires, describes the growth of Jewish education and the social and communal factors that have played a part in creating the system that exists today.

The Jewish population of Brazil is concentrated in two communities, Sao Paulo and Rio de Janeiro. In chapter 6 David Schers, a political scientist at Tel Aviv University and educational consultant with the organization of major Jewish community centers in Argentina, analyzes Jewish education in Rio based on extensive original research completed there in the late 1970s. He attempts to reach some general conclusions for the whole of Brazil.

In chapter 7, Efraim Zadoff, who has been in charge of the Latin American desk at the *Dor Hemshech* Department of the World Zionist Organization, describes the status of Jewish education trends and issues in the smaller Latin American Jewish communities. In his analysis one detects many of the same issues and concerns throughout Latin America, and also some similarities with North America and Western Europe.

This part closes with two comments, both written by persons with many years of experience with these educational systems. Haim Barylko is Head of the Buenos Aires Jewish community's Board of Education; Moshe Nes-El is Educational Consultant for Latin American countries at the World Zionist Organization.

5

Jewish Education in Argentina

Ya'acov Rubel

It is difficult to present a complete picture of Jewish education in Argentina. Those involved in the field of Jewish education can testify to the discrepancy between the importance ascribed to Jewish education by communal and educational leaders, and the lack of systematic thinking with regard to its purpose, content, goals and achievements. Moreover, information-seeking has been treated with reserve, and a critical approach to any aspect of education is generally interpreted as an expression of hostility.

> When education was a result, a product of Judaism, there was no room for difficulties or reservations. Today, Judaism must develop from education, there is a pressing need for a philosophical world view, an attitudinal framework, in the sense of 'Know from whence you have come and where you are going' (Barylko, 1975, p. 192).

Such a difficult task requires profound discussion of goals and sufficient means to attain them. An efficient educational policy must be based on comprehensive knowledge of the situation (Aguerrondo de Rigal, 1970). One problem is that educational leaders have not always adopted a critical approach to the process of education, and little research has been done in Argentina on Jewish education.

Any systematic approach to education faces a series of problems and obstacles such as:

- the lack of an organized statistical foundation to provide the researcher with accurately substantiated information;
- the lack of studies and surveys of a satisfactory scientific standard and quality;
- the lack of worthwhile educational thought to enable analysis of the content and concepts of Jewish education; and

- the lack of a central archive covering the Jewish educational experience in Argentina (e.g. documents, curricula, journals, lesson plans, memoirs).

Despite all these reservations, this chapter attempts to outline Jewish education in Argentina in the early 1980s, to indicate the major lines of development of the system in the past generation and to illustrate the current major problems. A series of assumptions and conclusions is presented to serve as a basis for further investigation, discussion and research.

Major Trends Since the 1930s

Jewish education in Argentina has made major strides since the 1930s. Various local events of that decade deeply influenced the Jewish educational scene and dictated its development during the 1940s and 1950s.

Among the internal and external forces which interacted to bring about the above-mentioned changes, the following may be cited:

- the 1934 decision of the Buenos Aires *Hevrah Kadisha* to found an education committee which increasingly assumed responsibility for coordinating efforts to provide Jewish education in the capital and its suburbs;[1]
- the consolidation of groups of teachers trained in Eastern Europe who were dissatisfied with the existing educational institutions in the capital and its environs;
- the decision of the Jewish Colonization Association (JCA) to stop all participation in the funding of schools, from 1933 on (Avni, 1972, p. 88). This decision was a severe blow to the Jewish agricultural schools in the agricultural settlements and in Argentina's interior in general, causing them to adjust their educational system to the new situation;[2] and
- the publication in 1938 by the government's education authorities of special regulations for 'foreign' private schools, which determined their status and organization.

These factors determined a series of changes in the internal organization of the Jewish schools and also in educational policy which ultimately brought about the modernization of the Jewish educational system.

Figures for 1935 published in the journal *Dertziung*[3] provide a gauge of the poor scope, content and quality of Jewish education in those years. The 38 institutions attached to the education committee of the *Hevrah Kadisha* encompassed a total of 1,709 children. Of these, 1,648 children were of primary school age and 61 children were of kindergarten age.[4]

The system mainly comprised Talmudei Torah, whose classes were for the most part conducted in unsuitable buildings. The educational enterprise of those years was characterized by a small number of students spread out in dozens of institutions, budgetary difficulties, lack of public support and the absence of a professional attitude towards education. Generally, the same teacher dealt simultaneously with children of different ages and levels of achievement. In most schools, the highest level was fifth grade, though this differed from the present grading system – the fifth year being the final year of formal Jewish education for the small group of pupils who reached this level. All records from this period indicate the lack of importance ascribed to Jewish education by the community at large, and by the parents in particular.

In addition to the Talmudei Torah of the *Hevrah Kadisha*, schools which reflected the ideologies of Eastern Europe, especially Poland, were also developed during the late 1920s and the 1930s. The various socialist movements – Young Zionists, Leftists, Bundists and members of the Ikuf [5] – in particular, undertook educational activities and were responsible for innovative suggestions in the field of education. Probably about 500 nursery and elementary school pupils were included in these educational activities;[6] however, since at the time these movements were not affiliated with the Education Committee of the *Hevrah Kadisha*, they were not included in the statistics cited.

The Sephardic and Oriental Talmudei Torah were also conducted independently, although they maintained a connection with, and received support from, the *Cursos Religiosos* (religious courses) which were founded in the beginning of this century on the initiative of Rabbi Halfon.[7]

With regard to the provinces, data for 1939 show a total of 1,707 pupils, mostly in elementary schools. Of these, 816 were in schools scattered throughout the Jewish agricultural colonies in the province of Entre Rios,

TABLE 1. JEWISH SCHOOLS IN ARGENTINA – 1942–1943

School Level	Buenos Aires and Suburbs, 1942		Sephardic and Oriental Schools		Interior Argentina, 1943		Total
	No. of Institutions	No. of Pupils	No. of Institutions	No. of Pupils	No. of Institutions	No. of Pupils	No. of Pupils
Total	61	3,289	7	1,134	67	2,828	6,251
Kindergarten	10	410	n.a.	n.a.	8	136	546
Elementary School	50	2,823	7	1,134	59	1,692	5,649
High School (Teachers' Seminary)	1	56	–	–	–	–	56

582 in the province of Santa Fe, 216 in the province of Buenos Aires, and 193 in the rest of the country (Cursos Religiosos..., 1940, p. 15).

Thus, during and after the 1930s, there were two distinct agencies which served as umbrella organizations for Jewish education, each of which continued to function separately until 1957:

– the Congregacion Israelita supported the Central Education Committee which supervised the Jewish education system in the interior and several Sephardic Talmudei Torah in the capital;

– the *Hevrah Kadisha* of Buenos Aires founded an Education Committee whose function was to centralize the educational activities of most of the institutions in the Greater Buenos Aires area.

Table 1 summarizes the existing information for 1942, and indicates the following facts:

– over 90% of all pupils were in elementary schools;

– a comparison between the number of schools and pupils suggests that most schools were small;

– relatively few children were enrolled at the kindergarten level; Heder or Talmudei Torah-type nurseries were not yet an integral part of the educational system;

– the only institution at the secondary level was the Teachers' Seminary, founded in 1940 to supply Jewish teachers when Jewish immigration was interrupted at the start of World War II. This institution was to assume an important role in Jewish teacher-training in Argentina (Mendelzon, 1953);

– Sephardic and Oriental schools were still separated from the main Ashkenazic network due to a lack of contact between these sections of the community, a fact which only began to change in the early 1970s;

– about 30% of the total Jewish school enrollment was in provincial localities, where the percentage of Jewish children attending these schools appears to have been larger than in the capital.

The Sholem Aleichem School, founded by the ZWISHO (the Leftist Zionist Workers' Zentrale Weltlich-Idishe Shul Organizatsie), played a special role in the modernization of Jewish education in Argentina. The school pioneered such measures as the construction of a special building in 1942, the development of a detailed curriculum in 1943 (Finkelstein, 1943), the publication of workbooks and an educational journal, and the organization of a summer camp.[8] These activities created a precedent for similar initiatives by other schools and gradually brought about changes in the nature of Jewish education.

The establishment of the State of Israel was a highly significant factor in reinforcing the Jewish educational system. In 1949, the *Hevrah Kadisha* officially changed its name to the Ashkenazic Community of Buenos Aires. The Zionist parties which since the 1930s had been active in Jewish public affairs,

TABLE 2. JEWISH SCHOOLS AFFILIATED WITH THE CENTRAL
EDUCATION COMMITTEE – GREATER BUENOS AIRES,
1949–1965[a]

School Level	No. of Institutions	No. of Pupils	% of Pupils
1949			
Total	81	7,643	100.0
Kindergarten	27	1,884	24.7
Elementary School	53	5,409	70.7
High School	1	350	4.6
1953			
Total	95	9,081	100.0
Kindergarten	37	2,648	29.1
Elementary School	53	5,580	61.6
High School	5	853	9.3
1959			
Total	121	12,153	100.0
Kindergarten	51	4,190	34.5
Elementary School	59	6,838	56.4
High School	11	1,125	9.1
1965			
Total	119	14,591	100.0
Kindergarten	56	5,092	34.8
Elementary School	52	8,415	57.8
High School	11	1,084	7.4

(a) All statistics are based on official data of the Central Education Committee. These statistics need
to be treated with caution since (i) the figures may be inflated; (ii) criteria for registration and
interpretation of data are not uniform; and (iii) while the system functioned as a supplementary
one, the number of pupils who finished elementary school was always small if compared with the
total number of pupils at that level.

were stimulated to greater activity, and Jewish leadership became more interested in Jewish education.[9]

The 1950s were characterized by five major trends:
- the increased construction of new buildings and the enlargement of existing structures, in response to significantly augmented financial support by the community;
- significant growth in the number of kindergartens, which were increasingly perceived as the gateway to the Jewish school;
- a constant increase in the number of children in the elementary schools;
- the establishment of secondary schools as a natural continuation of the elementary schools, which had expanded over the years; and
- the development of the supplementary school network into graded institutions where a teacher presided over each class.

Until 1965, most of the Jewish education in Argentina was imparted by supplementary schools, which taught an intensive curriculum a few hours every day of the week. Despite the fact that various proposals for Jewish all-day schools were presented, neither the parents nor the communal workers felt a need to develop this type of school.[10] Moreover, the ideology of the Jewish community tended toward support of the public school rather than private schools which were perceived as elitist, on the one hand, or as under the aegis of the Catholic Church, on the other.[11]

The hours of instruction provided by the Jewish supplementary schools were dictated by the public school schedule, which was usually half-day. Accordingly, Jewish supplementary schools conducted afternoon classes for those children who attended public schools in the mornings, and morning classes for those who were in public schools in the afternoons.

The structural organization of public school education thereby facilitated the establishment of orderly and coordinated Jewish education outside public school hours, most of which followed one common model[12] – daily lessons on the basis of fifteen hours per week, at both the elementary and high school levels. The official bodies connected with Jewish education apparently felt no need to consider any alternatives.

Tables 2 and 3 show the quantitative increase in the Jewish educational system in the years 1946–1965. There has always been a greater concentration of pupils at the kindergarten and elementary levels, but secondary education has expanded rapidly, and enrollments grew also at the kindergarten level. The enrollment even at the elementary level increased by some 50% during these years.

Analysis of the data indicates that most pupils who studied in supplementary schools left after the first few years. For example, the total number of pupils in all seventh grades in Buenos Aires totalled only 160 in the year 1960.

It should be noted that the data in Tables 2 and 3 do not include schools supported by the Sephardic and Oriental communities. There is indirect evidence that these also expanded rapidly.

TABLE 3. JEWISH SCHOOLS AFFILIATED WITH THE UMBRELLA ORGANIZATION – INTERIOR ARGENTINA, 1949–1965[a]

School Level	No. of Institutions	No. of Pupils	% of Pupils
1946			
Total	73	2,195[b]	100.0[b]
Kindergarten	11	238	10.6
Elementary School	61	1,957	89.4
High School	1	n.a.	–
1957			
Total	95	3,573	100.0
Kindergarten	26	709	19.0
Elementary School	66	2,746	76.9
High School	3	118	3.3
1962			
Total	99	4,159	100.0
Kindergarten	28	696	16.7
Elementary School	63	3,106	74.7
High School	8	357	8.6
1965			
Total	85	4,091	100.0
Kindergarten	28	765	18.7
Elementary School	49	2,847	69.6
High School	8	479	11.7

(a) See note (a) to Table 2.
(b) Not including high school pupils.

Development of Jewish Day School
During the 1960s

As early as 1964, the chairman of the Education Committee expressed positive views about the day schools then in operation in Buenos Aires.[13] Despite his enthusiastic remarks, there is no evidence of any follow-up by the Education Committee. But his comments contain, implicitly and explicitly, all the factors brought up in the public debate on day schools which began in 1965 and which became especially intense in 1967.

The Chairman's statements coincided significantly with the first conference on private education in Argentina which was taking place in Buenos Aires, with hundreds of delegates, both religious and secular, from all over the country (Primera Convencion..., 1964). The Jewish community apparently did not avail itself of the opportunity to send observers. Obviously, at that time the community and its educational leadership were not yet ready either spiritually, ideologically, or practically to see themselves as part of the private education sector. This lack of involvement in the general private education sector on the part of the Jewish education system has persisted, whether one refers to the systematic study of the legal basis of private education or to the establishment of inter-institutional relationships for information exchange, or simply mutual acquaintance.

In 1965, there were four day schools in the Buenos Aires area. By 1966, the number had risen to nine; the five new schools were actually five supplementary schools which had opened elementary school classes under the new system.[14]

The development of day schools may be summarized as follows: until 1966, day schools were founded by individual groups which organized for this purpose, or by communal workers who decided to expand the existing supplementary structure in order to attract more pupils. There are insufficient data to determine why particular supplementary schools converted to day schools. Further research might reveal that the motives varied in each case.[15] However, it was the 1967 government decision to increase the number of schools teaching a long school day which was the main deciding factor in bringing about far-reaching changes in the Jewish educational system of Buenos Aires.

It is unlikely that anyone then confronting the problem remembered Dr. Baruch Ben Yehudah's far-sighted statement at the Educational Congress of 1960:

> Argentina may reach the conclusion that schools should conduct classes seven hours a day. In this case...the problem will be more complicated. A completely new method will have to be found. I cannot describe this new system at the moment, by which we must convince ourselves that only by the establishment of a worldwide network of Jewish schools

based on the same principles do we have a chance of saving the Jewish people (Va'ad Hakhinukh Hamerkazi, 1960, p. 21).

In 1966, the National Education Council (Consejo Nacional de Educacion), which had jurisdiction over all public elementary schools, did indeed decide to institute a long school day (jornada completa) (Consejo Nacional de Educacion, 1969) in a small number of schools on an experimental basis, with the intention of gradually broadening the experiment. When it became known at the end of 1966 that an additional 83 schools in various areas of the city were to adopt the long school day, the decision and policymakers in Jewish education were alarmed. Their uneasiness regarding changes in the public schools was further increased by the appointment of the chairman of the National Education Council who was committed to structural reform, to the post of Minister of Education in the Argentinian Government. The chairman of the Jewish Education Committee commented on this appointment:

> There is room for concern that the direction of government's education policy will not only continue but will be intensified. This requires that we turn to new types of education, which will be able, by means of proper planning, to ensure the survival of our schools under difficult conditions. The new methods require a restructuring of our schools, which will have to turn into Jewish day schools. The longstanding debate among education workers regarding the necessity for day schools has been completely eliminated in light of the new conditions which have left the Jewish day school as the only solution to a difficult situation (Reykhenberg, 1967).

The importance of this commitment to develop Jewish day schools cannot be over-emphasized. It was indicative of the attitude of communal leaders to the subject of education. Despite future difficulties they would experience as a result of this decision and the financial burden it involved for the community and parents, the communal leaders preferred to move toward an intensive mode of Jewish education rather than to weaker structures, such as afternoon schools meeting twice weekly, or one hour only on Sundays.

By 1968, there were 24 day schools operating. All the large supplementary schools affiliated with the Jewish Education Committee had become day schools, and half of the elementary school-age children were already day school pupils.

Since the declared policy of the community was to allow every child who so desired to attend a day school, scholarship provisions were made for needy pupils.

A staff of clerks and social workers was employed to examine application forms and report on the financial position of applicants.

There had been no long-range planning for the training of principals and teachers, no long-term financial backing and no defined goals for the Jewish day schools. Nevertheless, they not only continued to operate, but by 1970, they encompassed a large proportion of the Jewish elementary school population – a total of 75% of all pupils.

The Jewish Educational System in Greater Buenos Aires During the 1970s

In analyzing the structure, organization and development of the Jewish educational system in Greater Buenos Aires at the beginning of the 1970s (see Table 4), the following facts must be taken into account:
–   most of the schools functioning in 1970 were a continuation – through changes, mergers, or adaption – of the schools which existed in the 1930s and 1940s;
–   the few new institutions were initiated by social and institutional groups which had joined the educational enterprise since the 1960s;
–   most elementary schools included a kindergarten, usually in the same building;
–   almost all the large elementary schools established high schools during the 1950s and 1960s;

TABLE 4. PUPILS IN JEWISH SCHOOLS, BY EDUCATIONAL LEVEL – GREATER BUENOS AIRES, 1970

School Level	Capital City	Suburbs	Total Greater Buenos Aires	
	No. of Pupils	No. of Pupils	No. of Pupils	% of Pupils
Total	13,909	2,439	17,348	100.0
Kindergarten	4,216	968	5,204	29.9
Elementary School	7,633	1,213	9,846	56.8
High School[a]	1,553	238	1,791	10.4
Yeshiva	147	–	147	0.8
Institutions of Higher Learning[b]	360	–	360	2.1

(a) Does not include figures for the ORT school.
(b) Includes data for the *Midrasha Haivrit,Beth Midrash* for Kindergarten Teachers and the Religious Academy.

- the overwhelming majority of pupils studied in schools associated with the Buenos Aires Ashkenazi community's Central Education Committee;
- in 1970 some of the Sephardic schools asked to be associated with the Central Education Committee in order to receive advice, materials and teachers, if necessary;
- twelve institutions (totaling about 800 pupils) in the Buenos Aires area were not associated with this umbrella organization.[16]

Despite peak enrollments, education personnel were disturbed by certain trends which emerged during 1970. This was a year of change and consolidation for the Jewish school system in the Greater Buenos Aires area particularly. The schools in the interior were not affected by these factors although many Jewish schools in the interior continued to function under adverse conditions.

Among the developments in 1970 which affected the school system in Buenos Aires were:

- the first signs of economic instability and runaway inflation that were to characterize Argentina in the following years;
- scandals involving Jewish financing cooperatives which forced many to limit their activities and even close. This affected many schools for whom these financial agencies provided grants and fixed subsidies, which financed current expenses including teachers' salaries. This support had become increasingly important as many schools changed into day schools during the last years of the 1960s, necessitating greater investments and larger budgets than those required by supplementary schools;[17]
- the *Kehilla's* financial difficulties increased. Its revenues, which derived mainly from fees paid for the provision of burial services, did not cover its yearly expenses. The weakening of the cooperatives also influenced the finances of the *Kehilla*, since it was they who provided loans and credit from time to time which enabled the *Kehilla* to maintain its liquidity and to carry its ever increasing burden of debt and financial obligations;
- the sizeable increase in the accumulated deficits of most schools; and
- delays in the payment of teachers' salaries, in some cases for three to four months.

The atmosphere of depression and uncertainty about the future was heightened by the rumor that 300 teachers were to be dismissed at the end of the 1970 school year.[18] A large decrease in the number of pupils who had begun their studies that year aggravated the situation even further.

It was natural to conclude that the major, and perhaps only, reason for the decline was economic. this was the official explanation presented in the report of the chairman of the Education Committee, which appeared in the press and was reprinted in various newspaper articles (Shapira, 1971; *La Luz*, 1971). However, the survey, on which the chairman's report was based, did not provide unequivocal evidence that economic factors were the major cause of declining enrollment. Furthermore, economic factors do not explain differences in enrollment decline and dropout rates between day schools and supplementary schools. If they were crucial, a significant drop might have been expected in enrollment in elementary day schools too, but there was no such drop. The Education Committee's statistics show that the decline, both in percentage and absolute terms, was greatest in supplementary elementary schools.

This serves to illustrate, on the one hand, the failure of those concerned with Jewish education to thoroughly analyze a specific problem, and, on the other hand, the lack of a systematic approach to in-depth educational analysis. This impression is reinforced by a study of the attitudes of mothers whose children did not attend Jewish schools, carried out in Buenos Aires in 1972 at the initiative of the local office of the American Jewish Committee. This study showed that the reasons for non-attendance at Jewish schools were not necessarily economic, but were more closely tied to psychological and ideological aspects of the family unit (Epelbaum de Weinstein and Grinspun de Luterstein, 1973).

Nevertheless, the organized Jewish community, its institutions, leaders and communal workers were indeed pressured unrelentingly by the difficult economic situation which affected most schools throughout 1970. Even the 'Education Fund', which was hastily announced in October of that year, did not provide the expected aid until the end of the year. It appeared that the fear expressed in the editorial statement of the Yiddish newspaper was about to be fulfilled. "Should this emergency measure fail to succeed for any reason, the Jewish educational system will be in terrible danger, of which it is frightening even to speak." (*Di Idishe Tsaytung*, 1970).

Under the circumstances, the *Kehilla* decided to approach public bodies in Israel for financial assistance. Negotiations were successful, and a loan was obtained which enabled the *Kehilla* to distribute large sums of money, and to fulfill its obligations to the schools. However, this did not solve the basic problems facing the system. The financial exigencies inhibited clear analysis of current educational problems and prevented exploration of alternative means of overcoming economic difficulties.

At the end of 1971 the communal leaders, who served as the patrons of the Education Committee, reached two decisions: all supplementary high schools were to be merged into one institution and lower tuition fees were to be charged in all kindergartens and elementary schools affiliated with the Education Committee.

The decision to unify supplementary high schools was reached by the communal organizations without prior discussion and without consulting the parties involved. The financial, organizational, or educational benefits of the proposal were never analyzed and it was strongly opposed by the institutions affected, who viewed it as both hasty and arbitrary.

The issue provoked debate in the Jewish press, the ideas expressed often reflecting the writer's political affiliation or proximity to the communal leadership. However, some articles did attempt to analyze the issue itself (Lerner, 1971). Due to the pressure exerted by various groups, including local Jewish political party institutions, the communal leaders were forced to withdraw from their original proposal. In the end, only three of the original group of eight institutions merged with the Teacher's Seminary affiliated with the *Kehilla*.

Moreover, since – as already mentioned – the substantial decline in the number of pupils who registered for school in 1970 was attributed directly by all parties to the economic situation – namely high tuition fees – it was thought that lowering and standardizing tuition fees for all pupils would halt the trend and perhaps even reverse it. Accordingly, the *Kehilla* announced that it would withdraw its subsidies from any school charging more than the standard rates. This new policy was accompanied by extensive advertising in the Jewish and general press.

Despite these measures, enrollment declined further in the Greater Buenos Aires area in 1973. Neither the reduction of tuition fees, which involved increased subsidies by the *Kehilla*, nor the merger of several high schools with the Teachers' Seminary was sufficient to overcome the adverse financial situation of the Jewish educational system. This led the *Kehilla* to approach the Joint Distribution Committee for assistance which, when approved, enabled the system in Buenos Aires to continue operating. The incumbent communal functionaries continued to give top priority to the economic crisis. They attempted to revive the 'Education Fund', with the aim of mobilizing support from the entire Jewish community, not merely from parents of school children. An organizational meeting of the Fund was held and executives were elected. Unlike the short-lived 1970 effort, this time the 'Education Fund' functioned for several years, although it never achieved the economic importance hoped for by its initiators.

Some attempts were made to explain the problems of the educational system – other than just economic – and to analyze its fundamental difficulties. However, since the economic factor continued to be perceived as the one which prevented parents from registering their children, the *Kehilla* decided to increase its subsidies for the coming year. In addition, the *Kehilla* announced that in the future, any child wishing to study in a Jewish school would be accepted, and his parents would be able to set tuition fees according to their means.

Despite the large sums spent on publicity, the number of pupils failed to increase. However, communal and educational leaders were able to point out

TABLE 5.   PUPILS IN JEWISH SCHOOLS, BY AFFILIATION WITH THE
CENTRAL EDUCATION COMMITTEE – ARGENTINA, 1975

School Level	Greater Buenos Aires			Interior			Total
	Total	Affiliated	Not Affiliated	Total	Affiliated	Not Affiliated	
Total	16,444	15,571	873	3,599	3,567	32	20,043
Kindergarten	4,514	4,321	193	870	850	20	5,384
Elementary School	8,816	8,262	554	2,088	2,076	12	10,904
High School	6,301	2,209	92	641	641	–	2,942
Yeshiva	341	307	34	–	–	–	341
Institutions of Higher Learning	472	472	–	–	–	–	472

that the decline in numbers over the past few years had been halted.

In 1973, a crisis of a different nature affected the school system when teacher-school board relations worsened considerably. These problems had actually begun several years earlier. Teachers declared strikes demanding higher pay – a practical necessity under the existing inflationary conditions. The struggle between the educational personnel - teachers, principals and inspectors – and the Education Committee staff reached a peak when the *Kehilla* approved an agreement between the Jewish Agency's Department of Education in the Diaspora and ORT to establish an institute for educational technology in Buenos Aires. The institute was to be located in the ORT building, its purpose being to develop curricula, educational aids, teacher in-service courses and other educational services. Several teachers from Israel were to be sent to Argentina for this project. Those who objected to this plan felt that the new institute would be assuming the functions of the Central Education Committee. Their objections arose from relevant analyses, disagreement on principles, individual attitudes and institutional competition.

1975 was another particularly difficult year for Argentina, both economically and politically. As a result of the mid-year economic upheaval and the ensuing concern for the educational system, the State of Israel once again came to the aid of the Buenos Aires *Kehilla*. The Education Committee initiated systematic data collection related to all components of the system. Table 5 provides details of the situation in 1975. A comparison with 1970 indicates a reduction in absolute numbers, but the numbers also demonstrate stability relative to the decline that occurred prior to the 1971/72 school year.

Table 5 also enables us to establish the relative weight of each educational level (which has been quite stable over recent years). It indicates that the elementary school stage is the backbone of the Jewish school system, accounting for over 50% of total enrollment. More than 25% of pupils attend kindergarten, while a little more than 15% attend high schools and yeshivoth, which serve pupils from 13–17 years of age. The institutions of higher learning are essentially teacher-training institutes. In comparison to the other educational levels, the number of tertiary institutes is small, but their importance in ensuring the supply of local teaching and administrative personnel should not be underestimated.

The activities of the Education Committee in recent years have included the development of a resource center, the appointment of a new director, and the publication of curricula, workbooks, and new textbooks. There has been relative stability in the number of pupils over the past few years, and there have been no significant changes since 1975.

Structure of the Contemporary Jewish Educational System

Three important structural facts emerge from an analysis of the more recent years (up to 1982):
- the overall number of pupils remained stable despite the socioeconomic conditions in Argentina which might have affected the financial options of parents;
- those schools supported by Sephardic and Oriental communities have been gradually merging with the Central Education Committee; and
- the number of institutions of higher learning has grown.

This contemporary analysis includes only those institutions, on all levels, which are organically connected to the Central Education Committee. An estimated 1,000 pupils study in other institutions, for which data collection is difficult. Statistics for the interior are not included due to the incomplete nature of the information collected by the Education Committee. However, spot checks indicate that in the interior as well, no significant changes have taken place in recent years.

Kindergartens

For most Jewish children, the kindergarten serves as the gateway to the Jewish school system. This explains the emphasis placed by all concerned on the development of this educational level, and the efforts made to convince young couples to enroll their children. In other words, most first graders have already attended kindergarten. Data on kindergartens during 1978–82 are presented in Table 6.

TABLE 6. PUPILS IN JEWISH KINDERGARTENS AFFILIATED WITH THE CENTRAL EDUCATION COMMITTEE – GREATER BUENOS AIRES, 1978–1982[a]

Year	Age				
	2	3	4	5	Total
1978	*735*	*1,396*	1,352	1,310	4,793
1979	680	1,374	1,377	1,383	4,814
1980	711	1,304	1,407	*1,394*	*4,816*
1981	711	1,282	*1,410*	1,327	4,730
1982	620	1,191	1,397	1,368	4,576

(a) The peak enrollment for each age level in the five year period appears in italics.

Some 5% fewer children were registered in kindergartens in 1982 than in 1978. It is apparent from Table 6 that there were no dramatic changes during this five year period. Comparison between institutions indicates that some have continued expanding while others have lost pupils. Without more detailed information, neither the small fluctuations in school population nor the increase or decline in registration can be explained for any specific year.

Elementary Schools

Eighty percent of the Jewish pupils at the elementary school level attend day schools which, as we have shown, developed from 1967 on. Despite economic difficulties and prolonged instability of the country, the percentage of day school pupils has not decreased. Parents seem to be prepared to make the effort to send their children to a Jewish school.

In order to understand enrollment trends and retention rates, Tables 6 and 7 need to be analyzed diagonally, i.e. by following age cohorts through progressive grades of the school. In the late 1960s and during the 1970s, fewer pupils entered first grade, but the percentage of those finishing elementary school gradually increased until an average of 900 pupils each year were completing grade 7.

TABLE 7.   PUPILS IN JEWISH ELEMENTARY SCHOOLS AFFILIATED WITH
THE CENTRAL EDUCATION COMMITTEE – GREATER BUENOS
AIRES, 1978–1982[a]

Year	Grade								
	1	2	3	4	5	6	7	Preparatory	Total
1978	1,375	1,206	1,081	1,039	1,062	*1,030*	903	18	7,714
1979	1,336	1,251	1,149	987	969	981	*963*	*93*	7,729
1980	1,305	1,206	1,195	1,079	958	909	891	64	7,607
1981	*1,397*	1,228	1,178	*1,134*	1,031	917	844	63	7,792
1982	1,314	*1,318*	*1,229*	1,112	*1,083*	975	831	88	*7,950*

(a) The peak enrollment for each grade level in the five year period appears in italics.

Tables 6 and 7 point to trends in the late 1970s and early 1980s. Initial enrollment in elementary schools has tended to decline, as has the number of pupils completing the Jewish elementary day school. However, there has been no increase in the drop-out rate which occurs in the transition from grade to grade – 5% to 7% in the lower grades, and 7% to 10% in the upper grades. Thus, only 60% to 70% of pupils entering first grade finish seventh grade. Moreover, there is substantial continuity in enrollment of those completing kindergarten and those entering first grade. This supports the contention that the decision to send a child to a Jewish day school is made early.

A significant proportion of school children are concentrated in a small number of institutions. In recent years nine or ten institutions in Buenos Aires have accommodated approximately half the school children of this age. It is worth noting that in all elementary school grades, the number of boys and girls is equal.

High Schools

Unlike kindergartens and elementary schools, which are similar to one another in regard to hours of instruction, organization, and curriculum, the high schools are less uniform in structure and curriculum. While some schools give 16 to 20 hours per week of Jewish studies, others provide only six to eight hours per week.

The high schools were also effected by the recent tendency to establish day schools, and about 70% of total high school enrollment is in day schools; the remaining 30% of pupils are in supplementary high schools.

This process is largely the result of the tremendous growth of the ORT School, which during the 1970s became the largest Jewish high school in

TABLE 8. PUPILS IN JEWISH HIGH SCHOOLS AFFILIATED WITH THE
CENTRAL EDUCATION COMMITTEE – GREATER BUENOS
AIRES, 1978–1982[a]

Year	Class						
	1st	2nd	3rd	4th	5th	6th[b]	Total
1978	*635*	512	471	373	359	51	2,401
1979	565	522	417	406	339	77	2,326
1980	595	492	487	348	414	87	2,423
1981	576	*557*	435	*458*	342	*88*	2,456
1982	567	555	*500*	416	*417*	86	*2,541*

(a) The peak enrollment for each class-level in the five-year period appears in italics.
(b) ORT school only.

Argentina. Certain elements in the Jewish middle class have been attracted to
high level technical and technological studies, thereby changing the nature of
the ORT school over the past decade. The population of the ORT School
consists both of graduates of Jewish elementary schools and of adolescents
having their first (albeit limited) contact with Jewish studies.

Table 8 summarizes recent enrollment trends at the high school level and,
in conjunction with Table 7, shows that about two-thirds of the pupils who
complete Jewish elementary schools enroll in Jewish high schools. Of these,
some two-thirds remain in the system until the completion of secondary education.

Yeshivoth

A large proportion of yeshiva students are adolescents of high school age,
who normally would have been included in the statistics for the high school

TABLE 9. PUPILS IN YESHIVOTH AFFILIATED WITH THE CENTRAL
EDUCATION COMMITTEE – GREATER BUENOS AIRES,
1978–1982

Year	Pupils
1978	263
1979	204
1980	276
1981	212
1982	287

level. This would have provided a more correct estimate of the numerical relationships between the various educational levels, including the drop-out rate between levels. However, because of their unique organization and because not all the pertinent data were available, the yeshivoth have been dealt with separately (Table 9). Since the 1970s, there has been a great increase in both the number of yeshivoth and their pupils. The data presented do not reflect the situation in its entirety.

Overview

The stability of the absolute figures over the period reviewed here for each level is also reflected in the relation between them (Table 10). In order to facilitate comparison, figures for a number of schools under the aegis of the Sephardic and Oriental communities were not included, since systematically comparable data were not available. If these schools are taken into account, approximately 1,000 pupils must be added to the total figure.

When some 4,000 pupils of all ages studying in schools in the interior are also taken into account, then approximately 20,000 to 21,000 children and youth between the ages of three and 18 currently receive Jewish education in nearly 100 educational institutions developed through the years by the Jewish community in Argentina. 80% of these pupils are of pre-bar mitzvah age which is when they conclude elementary school. Of the remaining 20%, 17% attend high schools and 3% institutes of higher learning. Approximately 80% of all pupils attend schools in Greater Buenos Aires, and the rest in the inte-

TABLE 10. PUPILS IN JEWISH SCHOOLS AFFILIATED WITH THE CENTRAL EDUCATION COMMITTEE – GREATER BUENOS AIRES, 1978–1982

School	1978		1979		1980		1981		1982	
Level	N	%	N	%	N	%	N	%	N	%
Total	15,171	100.0	15,073	100.0	15,122	100.0	15,190	100.0	15,354	100.0
Kinder-garten	4,793	31.6	4,814	31.9	4,816	31.5	4,730	31.1	4,576	29.8
Elementary School	7,714	50.8	7,729	51.3	7,607	50.3	7,792	51.3	7,950	51.8
High School and Yeshiva	2,664	17.6	2,530	16.8	2,699	17.8	2,668	17.6	2,828	18.4

rior. The largest cities and most important Jewish communities after Buenos Aires are Rosario and Cordoba.

The percentage of all Jewish children and adolescents receiving formal Jewish education can only be determined by a detailed analysis of the demographic structure of Argentinian Jewry.

Institutes of Higher Learning

The current picture of Jewish education in Argentina is completed by data relating to institutes of higher learning. Due to their specialized function, only a small percentage of high school graduates are attracted to Jewish institutions of higher education (Table 11). Moreover, with the exception of the

TABLE 11. INSTITUTIONS OF HIGHER JEWISH LEARNING – ARGENTINA, 1982

Name of Institution	Communal Organization, Religious or Ideological Sponsor or Associated Israeli Organization	Goals	Number of Pupils, 1982
Total			349
Shazar College for Education and Judaism	Ashkenazi *Kehilla* of Buenos Aires under the supervision of Tel Aviv University	Teacher training for elementary and high schools	96
Beit Midrash Agnon for Kindergarten Teachers	Ashkenazic *Kehilla* of Buenos Aires	Teacher training for kindergartens	172
Midrasha for Religious Teachers	Ashkenazic *Kehilla* of Buenos Aires	Teacher training	40
Abarbanel Institute	Rabbinical Seminary of *Kehillat Beit-El* (Conservative Movement)	Teacher training; Judaic studies without a teaching license	37
The *Midrasha Datit*	*Agudat Yisrael*	Teacher training	7
Bnei Zion	*Kehillat Yesod Hadat*	Teacher training	7

Abarbanel Institute, there are almost no men attending these institutions which are all seminaries for the training of kindergarten or school teachers. The increase in the number of institutes in recent years is due to the greater educational activity of the Orthodox and Conservative movements and their school organizations.

Personnel

Since 1940, when the first teachers' seminary was founded, Argentinian Jewry has succeeded in creating adequate frameworks to ensure the supply of local teachers for the school system. These teachers have gradually replaced the older teachers of Eastern European origin.

At present, the great majority of teachers are native Argentinians. The number of Israeli *shlihim* is very small compared to other Jewish communities, and most of the *shlihim* fill administrative and educational positions in religious high schools and in the institutes of higher learning. Apart from the Shazar College, there are no *shlihim* in non-religious schools.

At the same time, there is a high turnover among teachers. In recent years, the average age of teachers has risen, though it is significant that most educational personnel have seniority of 10 years or less. The situation in high schools and teachers' seminaries, where the percentage of male teachers is higher, is more stable.

The significant growth of religious education since the early 1970s is also seen in the increased number of religious teachers' seminaries.

Kindergarten Teachers

The 1970 census of Jewish education showed that kindergarten teachers as a group had the highest percentage of untrained personnel. Careful study of the changes undergone by seminaries and courses for the training of kindergarten teachers suggests that the Education Committee and/or other forces tended to view kindergarten as less important than other levels. For many years, no clear criteria were set for entering a training institute or even working in the kindergartens themselves.

However, a substantial change in training methods and in the standard of kindergarten teachers in the seminaries occurred when these became institutes of higher learning (1968), and were recognized by the private education authorities (1970). The kindergarten teachers' seminary expanded more rapidly than any of the other teacher training institutes and, within a decade, changed the image of kindergarten teachers in the Jewish school system. Furthermore, although kindergarten qualification allows a teacher to work in either private or public kindergartens, the great majority of those who complete the training program now work in Jewish kindergartens.

Elementary and High School Teachers

In a discussion held in Jerusalem at the Study Circle on Diaspora Jewry conducted under the auspices of the President of Israel, Alexander Dushkin maintained that:

> Our primary topic must be the problem of teachers in the Diaspora. We see this as the focal point of the entire problem. Educational difficulties begin and end with the teachers. Teacher-child, teacher-parent, and teacher-public relationships, the nature and improvement of teaching, of curricula, and of achievements – all these problems lead to the teacher. Whatever its philosophy, a school is, of course, only as effective as its personnel. As in all other areas of the Jewish civil service, there is a shortage of qualified personnel in Jewish education...The situation is most desperate on the classroom level: the idea of a professional Jewish teacher is either a thing of the past or a hope for the future (Dushkin, 1967/68).

The problem of preparing teachers for Jewish schools in Argentina must be placed in the broader context of worldwide Jewish teacher training. Only a small number of young people, mostly women, choose Jewish education as a profession. There is a high turnover of personnel, since most teachers work for only a few years. Although greater stability has been achieved in recent years, most teachers work for three to five years and then resign. As these years are spent in acquiring teaching experience, it follows that many pupils receive their education from inexperienced teachers. This undoubtedly affects the quality of teaching in the classroom, and is likely to be reflected in the level of academic achievements.

In 1970, 89% of teaching posts were held by women. In this respect, Jewish education conforms to the feminization of education all over the world. In the cities in the interior, the proportion of male teachers is slightly higher (14.5%). Most males involved in Jewish education in the Greater Buenos Aires area hold administrative posts. Here too, the number of men has fallen compared to previous years, and recent data on male enrollments in teachers' seminaries and training programs indicate that a further drop in the percentage of men will occur in the future.

On the other hand, the significant difference between the number of teachers studying at the university and those who have already finished demonstrates that a large proportion of university graduates leave the field of education. While this is understandable with regard to those whose studies are not related to education, there is room to question this phenomenon with regard to those who have studied subjects related to their work, particularly education majors.

No broad study has been undertaken to determine the reasons for leaving the teaching profession. Such a study might reveal that a not insignificant number of teachers go on aliyah. Also, a substantial group of teachers work in informal Jewish educational settings, such as sports clubs and communal centers.

Great differences exist in the training received by Hebrew teachers. Of the teachers in the interior, 90% have no formal training for the profession, and their knowledge and practical experience are limited to the high school level. This fact must effect the level of teaching and the nature of educational achievements. Even in Greater Buenos Aires, approximately one-third of all teachers are not certified. However, the largest group, some 42%, graduated from the *Midrasha Haivrit.*

The number of teachers who have studied Jewish subjects at the university level is small, most being teachers sent from Israel by the Education Department of the Jewish Agency. Only a small fraction of teachers of secular subjects obtained a significant level of Jewish education. This obviously affects the possibility of integrating Jewish and general studies, as the teachers of general subjects are unable to incorporate Jewish knowledge and culture into their teaching, even where appropriate, as in history.

Furthermore, there is a large gap in the formal education level of Hebrew teachers and general teachers. General teachers must fulfill certain requirements in order to qualify for their posts. Accordingly, more than 80% of them have completed their studies at either the National Teacher Training Institute or at the university itself. By contrast, only a very small number of Hebrew teachers are university graduates. However, about a quarter of these teachers are presently attending university, where most are studying humanities and social sciences. Taking into account the drop-out rate among elementary school teachers, it can be assumed that some of these teachers will leave the field of Jewish education on graduation. This will hinder any attempt to create a permanent Jewish professional teaching cadre in Argentina, which must embody a high level of general education, on the one hand, and more intensive Jewish education, on the other.

This is true for all educational personnel in high schools, from policymakers to inspectors, principals and teachers. The problem of bringing about substantial change in the status of the teacher and in the Jewish educational system as a whole has been summarized thus by Walter Ackerman:

> If there is to be any hope of developing a cadre of capable and concerned people who will find their life's work in Jewish schools, nothing less is required than a modern day counterpart of the Eastern European

maskil, whose passion for the Hebrew language, unbounded commitment to the Zionist ideal, and deep faith in the moving power of education informed his entire being and transformed his work as teacher into an inspired vocation.

It follows that, notwithstanding costs, there is a need to provide intensive and multi-faceted in-service courses as a matter of policy.

Conclusions

It seems that creating a local Jewish intellectual cadre is the crucial factor in influencing the Jewish educational system and, through it, the entire Jewish community in Argentina.

The definitions of such an elite have been given by different academics. Ernst A. Simon has presented the concept of intellectuals as a 'serving elite'; Haim Avni refers to the need for a 'fighting elite'. In the unique context of the Jewish community in Argentina, these definitions complement each other. Only a 'fighting elite' can achieve the conditions necessary to enable it to 'serve' the Jewish community.

However, even if such an elite were to develop, its prospects would be limited if the organized Jewish community and its leadership did not take into account how the educational process in its current sociological, political and psychological dimensions influence Jewish education.

Doubtless the Jewish educational system in Argentina has attained impressive achievements in quantitative terms since the 1930s. However, if the criterion for analysis and assessment is the ability of the system to help pupils meet the challenges of the 21st century, our prognosis will be sceptical and uncertain.

Notes

1. The process by which the *Hevrah Kadisha* developed into a *Kehilla* has still not been studied in depth. The interested reader can find information about this unique institution in Shusheim (1953). For the background of the founding of the Education Committee and its activities during its first years, see Mayrn-Lazar (1948, pp. 157–178).

2. For further information about the state of Jewish education in the interior during those years, and especially in the agricultural colonies, see: Yagupski (1940); Mayrn-Lazar (1948, pp. 101–108).

3. Detailed statistics giving a specific picture of the nature of most Jewish educational institutions of that period are found in *Dertziung,* May-June 1935, pp. 10–11.

4. These figures do not include all schools then in operation.

5. 'Ikuf' stands for Idisher Kultur Farband. Founded in the 1920s, 'Ikuf' served as an umbrella organization for social, cultural, and educational institutions with pro-Soviet leftist leanings. Subsequent to the Prague trials (1952), the Argentinian group broke its ties with 'Ikuf' and its schools.

6. For a general description of the development of the school system during the 1930s and 1940s, see Mayrn-Lazer (1948, pp. 123–154).

7. Statistics for these schools for the 1940s can be found in Mayrn-Lazar (1948, pp. 181–197).

8. A comprehensive survey of the activities of this network by the leader of the Sholem Aleichem schools was published in *Yarbukh 5714* (1953, pp. 191–222), under the title: "20 Yor ZWISHO – Sholem Aleichem Shulen."

9. A comprehensive study of the role of the various ideological and political streams of Jewish life in Argentina has yet to be written. A general picture of the activities of the various Zionist groups, especially after the founding of the State of Israel is to be found in Fisher (1963).

10. See the advertisement published in 1950 in the periodical *Mundo Israelita*.

11. This point requires an extended explanation, which is beyond the scope of this study. A brief discussion is presented here. The ideological background for the development of private schools in Argentina, especially of Catholic schools, is found in debates which took place a hundred years ago regarding the nature of the school system. The debate over legislation for free compulsory equal education turned into an argument between liberal forces and conservative Catholic forces. The intent of the liberal legislation was to guarantee homogeneous public school education for children of all religious backgrounds, as part of an overall attempt to attract European immigrants. In fact, this policy made Argentina attractive to Jews, and was the basis of Jewish immigration to Argentina. The immigrants, and the first and second-generation Argentinian born Jews received their education in the public school system from the elementary to the university level, which was also tuition-free. In contrast, the Catholic Church invested effort in creating its own independent institutions. The process of formation of private schools was strengthened by the 1959 governmental decision to subsidize the salaries of private school teachers. The Jewish community supported non-sectarian public education, until the need for day schools was felt.

12. The only exception was the German-Jewish community, which developed a framework similar to the American Sunday school. Such schools, however, never attracted a substantial number of pupils and were not considered important by the Jewish leadership. No statistical data on their enrollment is available.

13. "There are matters which are considered taboo (or) about which prejudice exists... The data indicate that the few existing day schools are developing well pedagogically and quantitatively. There are almost no drop-outs. The opposite is true. The number of pupils has been rising yearly, both in the capital and the interior. Obviously, there is room for improvement, and there are difficulties to overcome. Yid-

dish is not studied in the day schools. In addition, some schools stress secular studies to the detriment of Hebrew studies. But the fact that the child does not have to attend two separate schools is a great advantage. Some day schools have even started high school divisions" (Hanik, 1963–64, p. 7).

14. I have in my possession an internal Education Committee report which gives both the names and the development of these institutions.

15. The lay leaders of the David Wolfson School reached this decision in order to overcome the stagnation in the number of pupils which threatened the continued operation of the school. In contrast, the founding of the Ramat Shalom School was the result of extended discussions between the ZWISHO leaders and is an example of innovative understanding of the possibilities inherent in the day school given the new educational situation in Argentina.

16. The following table lists the institutions. With the exception of Beit El, supported by the conservative movement, all the other institutions belong to the Sephardic community and are Orthodox in outlook. Many of these schools are currently associated with the Central Education Committee:

Name of the Institution	Type of School or Educational Levels	Educational Level			
		Kinder-garten	Elem. School	Post High School	Total
Yesod Hadat	Day school & kinder.	64	240		304
Eliyahu Soli	Day school & kinder.	42	106		148
Sha'arei Ziyon	Supp.school & kinder.		70		70
Yeshurun	Supp.school		15		15
Yehuda Halevi	Kindergarten	35			35
Yagdil Torah	Talmud Torah		10		10
Shuva Yisrael	Talmud Torah		36		36
Shuva Yisrael (boys)	Talmud Torah		52		52
Shuva Yisrael (girls)	Beit Jacob	12	24		36
Ahava ve'ahva	Supp.school		34		34
Beit El	Kindergarten, Rabbinical seminary	32		9	41
Total		185	587	9	781

17. A comprehensive study of the economic implications of running a day school has yet to be undertaken, despite the importance of this subject. Such a study should analyze all economic aspects of operating a school, such as payment of salaries to extra educational personnel, provision of a lunch program, purchase of new educational aids and the like.

18. At the beginning of the school year, the rumor was found to be exaggerated. Many teachers who had expected to be without jobs received employment, but in other schools.

References

Aguerrondo de Rigal, I. (1970). "Sobre los diagnosticos educativos en la Argentina". *Catedra y Vida*, No. 81.

Avni, H. (1972). *Yahadut Argentina: Ma'madah hahevrati udemutah ha-irgunit*. Ministry of Education and Culture, World Zionist Organization, and the Institute of Contemporary Jewry, The Hebrew University, Jerusalem. (Hebrew).

Barylko, J. (1975). "La educacion en la Diaspora actual". *Dispersion y Unidad*, No. 15. Jerusalem.

Consejo Nacional de Educacion (1969). *La Escuela de Jornada Completa, Bases para su funcionamiento*. Buenos Aires.

Cursos Religiosos Israelitas de la Republica Argentina (1940). *Memoria y Balance al 31 de diciembre de 1939*. Buenos Aires.

Dushkin, A. (1967/68). *Jewish Education in the Diaspora – The Problems of Teachers and Teaching*. Study Circle on Diaspora Jewry in the Home of the President of Israel, Series 2, no. 5/6. Institute of Contemporary Jewry, The Hebrew University, Jerusalem. (Hebrew).

Epelbaum de Weinstein, A. and Grinspun de Luterstein, S. (1973). *Actitudes, opiniones y conductas de madres que no envian sus hijos a la escuela judia*. Comite Judio Americano, Oficina Latinoamericana, Buenos Aires.

Finkelstein, C. (1943). *Analitishn lern program, Sholem Aleichem Schul*. Buenos Aires.

Fisher, A.A. (1963). "Di idishe parteyen in Buenos Aires". *Pinkas von der Kehilla, 5717–5722*. Buenos Aires.

Hanik, Y. (1963/64). *Analizen un oysforn fun a yor tetekoyt*. Va'ad Hakhinukh, Buenos Aires.

Di Idishe Tsaytung (1970). "Tsuhilf undzer badratn shul wezen." 31 October.

La Luz (1971). "Grave crisis de la escuela judia". 2 January.

Lerner, F. (1971). "An impravizatsie mit eventuele gefarn". *Di Prese*, 1 December. Buenos Aires.

Mayrn-Lazar, M. (1948). *Das Idishe Shul in Argentine*. Buenos Aires.

Mendelzon, Y. (1953). "Der Hebreish-Yudisher Lerer Seminar, Zayn Grindung, un Itsuker Tsustand". *Yarbukh, 5714*. Der Idisher Kehilla, Buenos Aires. pp. 173–190.

Primera Convencion de la Ensenanza Privada (1964). Buenos Aires.

Reykhenberg, C. (1967). *Un discurso programatico para 1967.* Buenos Aires. (mimeograph).

Shapira, Y. (1971). "Di khinukh problematik oyen seder hayom". *Di Idishe Tsaytung.* Buenos Aires.

Shusheim, A.L. (1953). "Tsu der geshikhte fun der anshtayung fun dem idishen kibbuts in Buenos Aires". *Yarbukh, 5714.* Der Idisher Kehilla, Buenos Aires. pp. 15–84.

Va'ad Hakhinukh Hamerkazi (1960). *Baricht funem Tsvaytn land kinus far Khinukh.* Buenos Aires.

Yagupski, M. (1940). "Di idishe Dertziung in di Kalanies un Provintsn". *Yoivl Bukh fun Di Idishe Tsaytung.* Buenos Aires. pp. 445–458.

6

Jewish Education in Rio de Janeiro

David Schers

Unlike the Jewish settlement pattern in other Latin American countries, the majority of Brazilian Jews are not concentrated in the capital city – Brasilia – but in two main centers – Sao Paulo and Rio de Janeiro. On the whole, despite differences in the educational systems in the various communities, the principles, characteristics and problems of Jewish education in Rio apply to Jewish education throughout Brazil.

The Jewish community in Rio is comparatively recent, and its school system began only around sixty years ago. Almost every synagogue started its own heder, and there were also small secular schools which developed into modern day schools after World War II. Since then, the economic advancement of Jews and changes in the general society of Rio have brought about an increasing emphasis on education. With the rapid development of the private school sector, Jewish schools expanded into all-day schools. They gained prestige from the standard of studies they provided, compared to state schools and other private schools. However, the process which contributed to this rapid development also contributed to the creation of a problematic situation – the emphasis on general studies was greater than on Jewish studies. In other words, the success of Jewish schools has been greater in the secular fields than in Jewish education.

The Societal Context of Jewish Schooling

The Normativeness of Private Schooling

Education in Brazil is divided into a primary or elementary school for the first eight years extending through ages 7–14, and a secondary school, covering ages 15–18. The general curriculum includes communication, social and natural sciences, Portuguese and mathematics at the primary level, and Portuguese, literature, history, geography, politics, mathematics, physics and biology at the secondary level. As in many other Latin American countries, public or state schools are mainly 'for the poor' – a social service for those who cannot afford private education, whereas private schooling dominates among the middle and upper classes. The Brazilian government has felt that since existing education facilities and national budgets were not able to respond to the demand for schools, private schooling should be encouraged. Since 1964, the stress which the various military governments placed on economic development provided further support for the expansion of private schools and universities, since they were viewed as important agents for achieving higher educational levels without burdening scarce government resources.

Nevertheless, the government does not support private schools financially, the rationale being that they constitute a private contribution to national needs, enabling the government to deal with other national problems, including the provision of education for the enormous mass of underprivileged children. To better understand the government's approach one must take into account Brazilian ideological orientations. Brazil is a 'liberal' state in terms of its socioeconomic philosophy, as it allows many aspects of life to be decided on the individual level. At the same time, there is a 'nationalistic' philosophy which stresses national unity and views education as the most effective instrument for achieving it. These dual tendencies, liberal and nationalist, have resulted in much private initiative in education and in a strong desire to direct such education toward national goals. In practice, however, as in many developing countries, bureaucratic government controls apply mainly to administrative and formal matters and leave private schools ample latitude to develop their educational activities in their own way. Still, principals and teachers do what they believe is expected of them – that is, they stress national symbols and patriotic activities.

Historically, private schools in Brazil have derived from:
- religious-oriented private schools with traditional roots dating from the Jesuit period;
- ethnic-culture language-oriented schools supported by upper class immigrants from France, Germany, the English-speaking countries or Italy; and
- academically-elite schools with highly qualified teachers, and concentrated preparation for university entrance examinations.

The various types of private schools – including the Jewish schools - have several characteristics in common. First they are competitive in the sense that there is a free educational market and that schools compete for students and teachers. Secondly, the curriculum in private schools is oriented toward university entrance requirements and pupils are usually successful in passing these examinations. Thirdly, private schools usually provide education from kindergarten to university entrance. Finally, the vast majority of their pupils come from middle and upper-class backgrounds.

Jewish Community-Government Relations

The Jewish community of Brazil is small and does not have great political influence. However, several individual Jews have reached prominent positions. Dr. Israel Klabin, a well-known figure in business and industry, was mayor of the City of Rio; the Bloch family is highly influential in journalism and publishing; Jews also occupy important government and other positions. In local elections, the Jewish origin of a candidate is stressed in an effort to obtain the Jewish vote.

Unlike other Latin American Jewish communities, Brazilian Jews are frequently outspoken and have expressed clear attitudes on issues such as the Brazilian vote in favor of the United Nations resolution condemning Zionism. However, there is generally no need to exert influence on matters concerning Jewish education. Restrictions on the teaching of foreign languages during Vargas' rule (1930–45) applied to all 'foreign' schools, not Jewish schools alone, and are considered an unfortunate, isolated incident of the past. Should it be necessary in the future, Jews feel they would be able to recruit local and international support for their views.

The government does not interfere with the activities of Jewish schools and the Jewish schools, with little external control, do what is expected of them – they provide privately-supported quality education with a nationalist content.

Jewish-Gentile Relations as they Affect Jewish Education

The Jews in Brazil have done well economically, and the children of immigrants have advanced from petty commerce to larger businesses and professions. The dimensions of the country and the need for people with commercial, entrepreneurial and professional skills have helped Jews advance faster and reach a higher average economic status in Brazil than in other Latin American countries, where there is a larger middle-class and a higher proportion of European immigrants in the general population.

Brazilian society is multi-racial, more religiously pluralistic than other Catholic Latin American countries and socially more open and 'easy going' in style – all characteristics which seem to be conducive to assimiliation. Rates of intermarriage with the Jewish community are not known, but the general impression is that, while still low, they are increasing.

Antisemitism (perhaps more latent than overt) is low-keyed and usually marginal. A more complex problem is the feeling of uneasiness among Jews themselves (especially the young) about the 'auto-segregation' into Jewish institutions, including schools. This feeling can be attributed to the norms of Brazilian society, lack of clarity about the meaning of Jewish identity and uncertainty about the need for separate Jewish institutions.

The Jewish Community Context

The Organizational Context

Jews have lived in Rio since the early 19th century, but the first Jewish institution was established only in 1873. The present community was shaped by waves of immigrants who arrived from Eastern Europe until 1930 and from Central Europe from 1933 onward. Before World War II the governments led by President Vargas made it difficult for the Jewish community to develop cultural and educational institutions. However, since he was deposed in 1946, these institutions have developed rapidly.

The organizational structure of the Rio Jewish community is complex - there are over 70 organizations, some very small and almost inactive. Nevertheless, several organizations have substantial memberships and considerable influence. The most prominent communal organizations are:

- the Jewish Federation of Rio (Federaçao Israelita), the representative body of the community, which, unlike the Board of Deputies of Argentinian Jews (Delegacion de Asociaciones Israelitas Argentinas – DAIA), aspires to become the central comprehensive institution of the community. The Federation is linked to the Jewish Community/Welfare Fund (Fundo Comunitario), a linkage which augments its influence;
- the United Zionist Federation (The Unificada) which is the federal body of the various Zionist parties and organizations; and
- the Burial Society (*Hevrah Kadisha*), which is an independent religious and financial factor in community life.

Other communal organizations play less central roles, though a few have large memberships. Their main concern is providing services to their members. The largest social and sports organizations of this type are Hebraica in the southern parts of Rio and Monte Sinai in the north.

Educational Organizations

In several Latin American countries, the Jewish Education Committee (*Va'ad Hahinuch*) is the central organization dealing with Jewish schools.

These committees are generally connected to the central community institutions, and fulfill several coordinating and service functions.

Several years ago, influenced by younger Board members, the *Hevrah Kadisha* sought to make its role in education more effective and invited Rabbi Gershon Vainer to examine the situation of Jewish schools. His report in 1974 recommended the hiring of a professional, preferably from the United States – whose educational system he considered appropriate for Brazil – or from Israel, in order to create a bureau of education. Although Vainer's recommendations were neither published nor implemented at the time, a favorable atmosphere was created among the small group of influential leaders for the creation of a central education bureau.

Then, in 1977, the Rio Central Education Bureau was established as part of the Rio Jewish Federation (Burla, 1977). The Bureau's basic budget was provided by contributions from the Federation, the Community Fund, the *Hevrah Kadisha* and the Communal Cemetery Society. The World Zionist Organization (WZO) Department of Education and Culture provided an Israeli educator with previous Latin American experience and he led in the establishment of the Bureau which consequently gained status and influence.

The Rio Central Education Bureau was created to increase cooperation among what were autonomous Jewish schools. There were specific matters and areas on which school presidents, committees and principals were prepared to cooperate with the Bureau, but they wanted to preserve their independence. The Bureau lacked the financial resources or other means for inducing cooperation and, in 1980, research indicated that the central education bureau actually exercised very little control over the Jewish schools, which retained their independence and autonomy.

Centrifugal factors, tending toward the independence of schools, and centripetal factors, tending toward cooperation and centralization, were in conflict. Those factors leading to a centrally-controlled educational system, through a strong central education bureau, and those leading to a highly decentralized system, in which the Bureau would play a minor role and individual schools retain their autonomy, may be outlined as in Chart 1.

In 1980, the Bureau carried out some coordinating functions, although mainly in an attempt to develop its own influence. The Bureau has been seeking to maximize centralizing factors in the community and minimize decentralizing factors, thereby enhancing its prospects of becoming the central education organization it aspires to be.

Schools seek services and financial support from the Bureau, while central communal organizations, private interest groups and the WZO Department of Education seek a strong coordination and organizational role for the Bureau. These roles could become complementary should a balance between centralization and decentralization be achieved.

CHART 1.   FACTORS OF CENTRALIZATION AND DECENTRALIZATION IN
BRAZIL'S JEWISH SCHOOL SYSTEM

Centralizing Factors	*Decentralizing Factors*
Problems and interests common to the different schools.	Each school is an independent organization, preoccupied only with its own problems and interests.
The desire to avoid unbridled competition between schools.	Each school's existence depends on competition with other schools for students, teachers, and financial support.
The desire to obtain support from institutional and private donors, more willing to help a centralized school system than individual schools.	The desire to obtain support from reliable donors, linked to the school emotionally or ideologically, and to avoid the dependence which funds 'with strings attached' might engender.
Encouragement for centralization from the WZO Department of Torah Education and from the Bureau's local sources of support.	The reserved relations between the WZO Department of Torah Education and the Bureau.
Fear of enrollment decline and the need to develop schools in new areas.	Fear of decline if the individual school were to become dependent on others.

Geographic and Social Mobility

In Rio, as in Brazil as a whole, the link between the socioeconomic and the geographic mobility of the Jewish population is evident. From the downtown area of the first Jewish settlement, Jews moved to middle class areas in the northwest sections of Rio and to nearby middle class houses and apartments in densely populated city neighborhoods. From there, Jews moved to upper middle class residential areas in the south and southeastern parts of the city – such as Copacabana, Leblon, and Ipanema.

Geographic mobility was a consequence of the changing Jewish occupational structure, increased affluence and upward social mobility. As in other

Latin American Jewish communities, the proportion of professionals has risen steadily, along with the proportion of Jews in industry – especially light industry – partly due to a shift from artisanship and small industries to large manufacturing enterprises. Similarly, there has been a shift from retail to wholesale commerce (Schers and Singer, 1977b).

The effects of geographical mobility on Jewish educational development have been significant. In the first place, the fate of individual schools was decided largely by Jewish residential mobility. Thus, of the six existing Jewish schools in Rio, only two remain in the northern part of the city, struggling for survival in a steadily declining Jewish population. Several other schools in this area, such as the Perez, Bialik, and Mendele Mocher Sforim schools have closed. The Gimnasio Hebreo Brazilino merged with the Talmud Torah Herzlia school, since it could no longer carry on alone. It is noteworthy that the two schools which have survived – the Sholem Aleichem and the Talmud Torah schools – have different ideological commitments; the former has a secular Yiddishist orientation, while the latter is religious, and this difference between them probably contributed to the continuation of both.

The remaining four Jewish schools are located in or near areas where Jews currently reside. While they have larger enrollments, they must cope with difficulties of physical expansion, since the area is small and densely populated and land is extremely scarce and expensive. The possibility of moving the schools to a new development area, Barra de Tijuca, is under consideration but the smallness of the Jewish population there is a drawback. The possibility of establishing one district school as a collective effort by all, or at least, several schools, has also been proposed; however, in view of the forces encouraging decentralization, the prospect of success for this proposal is slight.

Parents frequently mention distance as a determining factor in their choice of school, along with the school's prestige, and that children of friends or relatives are attending the school. Distance between home and school is relevant, for instance for the Sunday service – a common feature of most private schools in Latin America, including Rio – which requires the bussing of smaller chidren in either school-owned or private charter busses.

Demographic Trends Affecting Jewish Education

From 1960 to 1975, the percentage of elderly (65+) Jews in Rio de Janeiro more than doubled, from 6% to an estimated 13% of the Jewish population. In the same period, there was a substantial decrease in the proportion of children in the 0–14 age group, from 28% to 24%. The proportion of children in the Jewish population is higher than in many West European Jewish communities. Nevertheless, the low fertility rate, the high proportion of older people, negligible immigration, mixed marriages and assimilation all indicate a clear trend toward a diminishing or at best a static Jewish population in the future.

It follows that the potential enrollment in Jewish schools is also diminishing. That Jewish schools have maintained a stable pupil population, therefore, means that they have been able to attract a higher proportion of the diminishing number of Jewish children. The high standard of Jewish schools, compared to other available possibilities, is the principal factor explaining this success.

Notwithstanding the lack of statistics on Jewish divorce rates, the general impression is that this rate is lower in Rio than in the United States, but rising. The number of working mothers in the Jewish population, particularly in the professions, is also increasing. Single parent families and working mothers tend to prefer private school education which provides a better child-minding service than the public schools. Thus, several of the parents interviewed referred to the longer hours of schooling and the hot lunches available to pupils as attractive features of the Bar-Ilan School.

Parental Motivation for Jewish Education

Affluence and social advancement have created the desire and the means for the establishment of Jewish schools. About half of the Jewish parents, wishing to perpetuate their socioeconomic class, send their children to private Jewish schools. While this does not explain the choice of a Jewish rather than another good private school, the character of Jewish schools and the status of Jewish studies subjects, is affected.

While there are surely some parents who are religiously motivated, and there is a religious element in the motivation of others, for the vast majority, religion is not the main reason that children are enrolled in a Jewish school, since most Jews in Latin America, including Rio, are not religious. Although two of the six Jewish schools in Rio define themselves as religious, most of the families of their students are not observant. Thus, there is tension on religious issues between the sponsors and leaders of the two schools, on the one hand, and the majority of parents, on the other hand.

Convenience is another factor in parental choice of Jewish schools. One aspect of this is geographic proximity. Another is the convenience of being able to relegate responsibility to the school for imparting Jewish knowledge. This convenience, which involves an ideological component, arises in many cases from parental inability rather than lack of desire to undertake this responsibility and task. Only 50% of parents with children at Jewish schools are estimated to have attended a Jewish school themselves, and most of these for only a brief duration: many lack any Jewish education whatsoever. Thus, many parents cannot transmit Jewish knowledge to their children, but they want them to have at least a basic knowledge of Judaism.

Furthermore, parents regard Jewish schools favorably from an educational perspective. They consider the atmosphere, staff and prestige of Jewish schools better for young children than that of non-Jewish private schools, which are their alternative; they also assume that the Jewish school will provide sound preparation for the university entrance examination and for university studies, an important consideration for older children.

Parents are also motivated by considerations concerning the Jewish identity and commitment of their children. They want their children to know that they are Jewish, and to have feelings of belonging and loyalty to the Jewish people. They believe that this is more likely to be the outcome of a Jewish education.

Only a small minority of Jewish children, those whose parents cannot afford private schools, attend state schools. However, only some 50% of Jewish parents with school-age children actually prefer Jewish to non-Jewish private schools. Preference for non-Jewish private schools seems to be mainly influenced by judgements regarding the academic standards of the particular school and its suitability to the child's social class and general Brazilian society. Children's attendance at a non-Jewish private school does not mean, however, that parents do not want their children to remain Jewish. While some are indifferent, many do care, but either believe that they can provide Jewish identity and knowledge at home and through other Jewish institutions, or that attendance at the pre-school and primary Jewish school is sufficient for maintaining Jewishness.

Trends in general education, such as the high status accorded to education and the normativeness of private education, operate in favor of attendance at Jewish schools, provided that their academic standards are high. Occupations associated with the middle class, to which most Jews belong, usually require a university education.

Adolescents generally conform and subscribe to the general patterns of society and to the expectations of their parents – that they obtain a good general education leading to university studies. They are, however, not eager to accept the additional burden of Jewish studies. Moreover, while the community – as represented by its leaders – considers a good Jewish education to be the principal means to ensure Jewish survival, they nevertheless concur that Jewish schools should also provide high standards of general education.

Thus, Jewish schools reflect the preferences of their clientele in two main areas – the stress on high academic standards in secular studies and the diminishing importance attached to Jewish studies.

Structural Characteristics of Jewish Education

Jewish Day Schools

There are six Jewish day schools in Rio de Janeiro. Quantitative data about these schools including their names, age, enrollment, size and religious orientation are summarized in Table 1.

In addition, the Jewish school system includes:
- a technical institute (ORT) enrolling both Jewish and non-Jewish pupils. Jewish students are estimated to constitute some 30% of the school population, but very few Jewish students are enrolled in the evening course;
- a remnant of the disbanded Ecole Normale Brazil-Israel, now located at the A. Liessin School. It consists of 22 pupils and two secondary level classes whose studies include a pedagogic orientation;
- a very small school, consisting of a kindergarten and the first four grades of primary school, in the Rio suburb of Niteroi;
- two religious boarding schools – a yeshiva at Petropolis and the *Michlala* School for girls in Terezopolis – located not far from Rio. Students at these two schools are drawn from all over Brazil, and their proximity to Rio is only incidental.

The six day schools constitute the core of the Jewish educational system. They offer pre-school, primary and secondary levels, and provide both secular and Jewish studies. They are full-time schools, operating five days per week. At Bar-Ilan School, the hours of instruction are 7 a.m. to 3 p.m.; the other day schools operate on a two-shift system, roughly from 7 a.m. till noon

TABLE 1.   DAY SCHOOLS IN RIO DE JANEIRO – 1978

Name	Year Founded	Religious Orientation	Area	Enrollment				
				Pre-School	Primary 1–4	Primary 5–8	Second-ary	Total
Sholem Aleichem	1928	Secular	North	180	159	116	26	481
Talmud-Torah Herzlia	1938	Religious	North	143	176	173	70	562
A. Liessin	1945	Traditional	South	297	349	366	240	1,252
Max Nordau	1950	Traditional	South	143	172	160	114	599
Eliezer Steinberg	1954	Traditional	South	185	180	201	63	629
Bar-Ilan	1955	Religious	South	156	119	193	33	501

and from 12.30 p.m. to 5.30 p.m., each shift being a full school day. The double shifts mean increased utilization of premises, an important consideration given land scarcity and costs in school locations. The morning shift is usually for older pupils (grades 5 and up), and secondary pupils may commence studies at 7 a.m. and continue till after 12.30 p.m. several days weekly; the afternoon shift is for pre-school children and the primary grades to grade 4.

The hours of classroom instruction vary from school to school. At the primary level, total hours range from 16 to 22 hours weekly for grades 1 to 4 and from 30 to 36 hours weekly for grades 5 to 8, while at the high school level the amount varies from school to school between 26 and 36 hours per week.

The number of hours devoted to Jewish studies also varies according to school and age of pupils. In the first four grades, it ranges from 7 to 14 hours weekly, amounting to some 23% to 42% of total classroom instruction time. In grades 5–8, some 6 to 15 hours weekly, or 20% to 41% of classroom teaching time is spent on Jewish studies. At the secondary level, Jewish studies occupy between 0–6 hours per week, or up to 17% of teaching time. Table 2 summarizes the proportion of time spent on secular and Jewish subjects in the day schools.

TABLE 2. HOURS OF WEEKLY STUDY IN SECULAR AND JEWISH SUBJECTS – RIO DE JANEIRO, 1978

School	Primary Level								Secondary Level			
	Grades 1–4				Grades 5–8							
	Total Hours	Hrs GS	Hrs JS	% Hrs JS	Total Hours	Hrs GS	Hrs JS	% Hrs JS	Total Hours	Hrs GS	Hrs JS	% Hrs JS
Sholem Aleichem	29	21	9	23	30	24	6	20	30	30	0	0
Talmud-Torah Herzlia	29	22	7	24	32	23	9	28	36ᵃ	31	5	14
A. Liessin	30	20	10	33	30	21	10	33	35	29	6	17
Max Nordau	30	16	14	47	30	21	9	30	30ᵇ	26	4	13
Eliezer Steinberg	30	21	9	30	34	26	8	24	38ᵇ	36	2	5
Bar Ilan	Not available				36	21	15	41	35ᶜ	29	6	17

GS = General subjects. JS = Jewish subjects.
(a) This is the median number of hours; in the 1st year of secondary schooling, there are more, and in the 3rd year, less.
(b) Does not offer Jewish subjects in the 3rd year of the secondary level.
(c) Does not have the 3rd year of the secondary level.

Number of Students

In the late 1970s, 46% of the estimated total of school-age Jewish children attended Jewish schools (Sicron, 1978). The number of students, like the number of schools, has been quite stable in recent years, though enrollments at the secondary level have been increasing. Whenever there is substantial enrollment growth in one school, there seems to be a corresponding enroll-ment decline in other schools. This suggests that the schools compete with one another for the same pool of pupils, an assumption supported by the fact that few students transfer from non-Jewish to Jewish schools.

There are some 4,000 students enrolled in the six day schools. An addi-tional 30 to 50 students attend the Yeshiva and *Michlalah* schools, a similar number of Jewish students attend the ORT secondary school, and 22 pupils attend the secondary 'normal' school attached to the A. Liessen school. In addition, bar mitzvah preparation is conducted by some congregations, but data on the number of pupils is not available. There is no marked dispropor-tion of genders among Jewish school enrollments.

While specific data are unavailable, there is some indication of drop-out trends. The fact that 1,209 pupils were enrolled in the upper primary grades (grades 5 to 8), but less than one-half of that number were enrolled at the sec-ondary level, indicates that many students leave Jewish schools at the end of their primary schooling. This is confirmed by other sources. However, in Rio children remain in the Jewish elementary schools for a longer period than they do in Argentina. Given research indicating that a minimum number of school hours is necessary to influence adult Jewish identity, it may be conjec-tured that Jewish education in Brazil is more effective than its counterpart in Argentina. But research on the relationship between the quantity of Jewish schooling and adult Jewish identification in Brazil has not been carried out.

School Sponsorship and Ideological Orientation

Many Latin American Jewish schools are not affiliated with congregations or central community institutions nor were synagogues ever the central factor for controlling and maintaining them. In Brazil, central communal and edu-cational organizations play a supporting rather than a highly influential role. The schools are primarily maintained and controlled by their parent-clientele and/or other community groups and sectarian bodies. Jewish schools in Rio may be regarded as 'independent', in the sense that they are neither spon-sored by the community at large nor by other communal institutions such as synagogues.

According to school principals and other sources, two of the six day schools in Rio have a religious orientation, one a secular orientation and three are traditional. Among the traditionally-oriented schools, the degree of 'tradition' varies considerably – one school provides optional morning prayer, while another teaches Jewish tradition with no religious connotations.

Of the two schools remaining in the north of Rio, for example, one school is avowedly religious, stresses Hebrew, is closely associated with the Torah Education Department of the WZO and employs several Israeli teachers who come for two year periods. The second school stresses its secular character, places emphasis on Yiddish, and has only very loose ties with Israel.

In the early years of the schools' establishment and development, ideological sponsorship was an important influence. However, as new generations of parents have become active and assumed leadership on school committees, these ideological influences were weakened. The general trend is to move away from emphasis on ideology and ideological differences. Competition between schools on the basis of ideological differences has diminished and is being replaced by competition based on the academic quality and standards of the schools.

Finance

Detailed information about sources of finance for schools is not readily available. However, schools report that some 90% of their financial needs are met by tuition fees, which helps explain why the role of central community institutions is not very influential and why it is difficult for such institutions to gain a greater measure of control.

The remaining 10% of the school budget is obtained primarily through fund-raising activities. These are organized by school committees, staff, parents and others. Schools rent out their premises after teaching hours for sporting, learning or social activities. Contributions are received from burial societies (the *Hevrah Kadisha* and the smaller Communal Cemetery Society), but these are sporadic and ad hoc, dependent on factors such as the school's financial situation (crisis-solving help), attitudes of the Board members towards the school, and so on.

Plans have been made to centralize the appropriation of communal funds to Jewish schools through the Central Education Bureau. However, the *Hevrah Kadisha* has appeared reluctant to give up the influential position it has achieved by distributing financial aid to the schools. The *Hevrah Kadisha*'s style in carrying out this role is very informal, reminiscent of the atmosphere of traditional Jewish communities, especially in Eastern Europe.

The financial problems of schools in northern Rio, where the number of students is declining, are more serious than those of schools in the southern areas. Mergers and school closures in the northern areas of the city are often explained by the financial problems they confront as a result of declining enrollments and reduced income from tuition fees. Moreover, the lower income level of Jews in the less affluent north has effected lower tuition fees and greater financial assistance to individual needy students.

Day School Personnel

Staffing

Principals

The central staff member of every school is the principal whose influence is significant in educational and administrative matters. He represents the school in inter-school, community and official matters. Formerly, most principals of Jewish schools had immigrated from Europe or the Middle East, and lacked higher general education, but had a strong Jewish background and identity of a traditional kind, whether religious or secular. Principals of this type are being replaced by Brazilian educated university graduates. Three of the six principals in Jewish day schools are males, even though the majority of the teaching staff is female. In the religious schools, the locally-qualified principals share their role with the *shaliah*.

Coordinators and Counselors

A noteworthy feature of the staffing structure is the proliferation of coordinators and counselors. They are in charge of educational supervision, guidance to teachers and counseling to students. They act as intermediaries between the students and members of the school staff, including teachers, and between the school staff and parents. They comprise a professional cadre above the regular teacher, providing pedagogic and psychological knowledge.

The contribution of these professionals has both positive and negative aspects. For instance, the counselors are often ill-prepared to help the regular teacher and succeed only in creating further organizational complexity and problems by restricting direct contact between teachers and parents or between pupils and principal. A positive benefit is that the positions of coordinator and counselor within the school provide an additional rank to which teachers may be promoted, which is most important in a profession with low status and few opportunities for upward mobility.

Teachers

In Rio's six Jewish day schools, there are about 400 teachers of secular subjects and some 80 teachers of Judaic subjects. The majority (over 80%) of teachers are women. Most of the men are found at the upper primary and secondary levels. One factor in the predominance of female teachers in the lower grades is that for teaching at this level, training at a 'normal' secondary school (the final three years of secondary education) is sufficient qualification.

Salaries and working conditions of teachers in general are inferior to those in other professions. In 1979, teachers went on strike, demanding a 100% increase of their very low 'minimum salaries' fixed by law, paid annual leave of five weeks, and, in case of dismissal during the school year, compensation pay of one-half their regular salary until the end of the school year.

The situation of teachers in private schools is better than in public schools because of inter-school competition for teachers. Jewish schools make an effort to engage good teachers, and so, pay salaries competitive with those of other private schools, though still lower than those obtained in other professions. The salary of each teacher is a matter of negotiation with the employer and is usually known only to the few involved in these negotiations.

In 1979/80 semi-structured interviews were conducted with 102 teachers in Rio Jewish day schools. 43 teachers of secular subjects in Jewish day schools, mostly non-Jews, indicated that:

- they feel they are not well paid but regard this as a general problem of the profession;
- they work in two or more schools and are usually paid by the hour;
- for many, teaching is a temporary occupation while completing university studies;
- very little in-service training is provided;
- they know the specific character of the Jewish school and have an understanding attitude toward its goals;
- they are generally satisfied with their work and with the support they receive from their schools;
- the fact that students and parents regard the subjects they teach as important seems to make the secular teacher's work more agreeable and less problematic.

Of the 59 teachers of Judaic subjects interviewed, most were female (85%), young (71% were between 20 and 39 years of age) and Brazilian-born (73%). Many taught more than one subject, or coordinated an educational area. Given generally accepted impressions about their low qualifications, a surprisingly high 56% possessed a university degree, while 80% had completed post-secondary courses. These teachers considered themselves badly paid. Twelve also taught in non-Jewish schools.

These teachers believed that defection was common among teachers of Jewish subjects, the main cause being, in their view, the low salaries and lack of appreciation for their work. The work load of the elementary school teacher is 15 hours per week, while secondary teachers are paid on an hourly basis, necessitating long hours to make up a livable wage. In their opinion, better salaries and status would encourage young people to consider Jewish education as a profession.

Teachers of Jewish subjects move from one Jewish school to another. Of the 59 teachers interviewed, 30% had already taught in another school – some in two or three other schools – prior to their present one. There is competition for employment in the most prestigious schools, which is regarded as upward career advancement. Downward mobility, though less common, also does occur. It appears that only teachers who really need to work and have no alternatives move to less prestigious schools.

The most common motivations for working as teachers of Judaic subjects were strong personal Jewish identification, links with Israel and attraction to the subject being taught. Religious motivations were rare. Teachers maintained that they were satisfied with their choice of profession and planned to continue as teachers of Jewish subjects although they realize that the subjects they teach and their profession do not have high status. They feel, however, that they are fulfilling an important mission which represents the will of the 'conscious' community and its leadership.

The problems most frequently mentioned by teachers of Jewish subjects were lack of student interest, classroom discipline, and lack of parental involvement. Nevertheless, the majority had established good relationships with pupils and parents. The explanation may be that teachers accept the views and values of students and parents, and do not try to change them. This should be explored in further research.

Teacher-Shlihim

The teacher-*shaliah* position began with the scarcity of local teachers, the willingness of Israeli institutions and teachers to aid Diaspora Jewish schools, and the desire of Israel and each Diaspora community to strengthen ties.

In 1979, there were 18 teacher-*shlihim* in the Jewish schools of Rio, 13 of whom were *shlihim* from the Torah Education Department of the WZO, and five were from the Education and Culture Department of the WZO. The latter Department's sixth *shaliah* was mostly involved with the Central Education Committee and general matters of education, and was not school-based. Thus, in the two religious schools, Jewish subjects were mostly taught by the 13 teacher-*shlihim*. In the other schools, the five teacher-*shlihim* were mainly occupied with coordination and guidance of Jewish subjects, and actually taught in the upper grades.

The role of the *shlihim* provokes controversial responses. The nature and impact of their activities depend on personal traits rather than well-developed educational doctrine. Their contribution to the local Jewish schools is limited by their scant knowledge of Portuguese and local culture, by their short period of service and by the lack of a systematic educational approach which would cater to and harmonize with both Israeli and local community aspirations. Nevertheless, some of the teacher-*shlihim* have had a very positive influence on students and fellow-teachers.

Goals, Curricula, Teaching Methods

Goals and Curricula

The obvious common goal of all Jewish schools is the transmission of Jewish identity and cultural values, as well as the establishment of strong links between the Jewish community, the Jewish people and their students. Moreover, each of the groups involved in Jewish education places high priority on the goal of creating good Brazilian citizens and worthy human beings.

Each school is autonomous, and within the broad framework of the Jewish school's humanist, Brazilian and Jewish goals, priorities and emphases vary from school to school. Moreover, individual leaders and teachers have their own ideas and views. The impression is that Brazilian and humanist goals take precedence over Jewish goals.

One practical goal of the schools is to enable students to enter their chosen professions. Success in achieving this goal is, by implication, an indication of the school's quality and achievements and is a matter of prestige. Hence, schools pursue academic prestige, creating tension between the declared central goal of Jewish education and the practical need to compromise with other priorities.

The main subjects of Jewish studies are Hebrew, Bible, and Jewish history. Each school uses its own curriculum, syllabus and textbooks of Israeli or Argentinian origin. The high degree of school decentralization and the lack of experienced, well-trained teachers creates problems of curriculum development. However, there are devoted and capable teachers who make use of the latitude given them to be creative and effective.

Cognitive Knowledge vs. Emotive Learning

The Brazilian public education system stresses cognitive knowledge, although memorizing and rote-learning are still common. Efforts to modernize the system are often not implemented or are limited to small-scale innovations. Nevertheless, the school system does involve emotive learning, generally revolving around patriotic content, in which national symbols, history, and national heroes play a central role. This is seen in both private and Jewish schools. Jewish teachers have been particularly successful in the lower grades at linking cognitive knowledge with emotive learning.

Teaching Methods

Teaching is usually teacher-centered, the most common form of classroom organization. At the pre-school and primary levels, the influence of pupil-centered methods used in Israel and other local private kindergartens is apparent.

Methodology in Jewish schools is influenced by the fact that classes are small, a characteristic unique to Jewish schools. The average class has 15 to 20 pupils, compared with other private schools where classes of 40 to 50 are common. In some public schools which are oriented toward university preparation, there can be even 60 to 80 students per class. Even with formal methods of teaching, the low teacher-pupil ratios in Jewish schools in Rio allows personal relationships between teachers and pupils.

Although there is great respect for new teaching media and techniques, in practice these pedagogic developments are – as in most developing countries – not frequently used. Even when they are implemented, they are often unsuccessful, due either to technical problems or lack of training in such methods. The gap between theory and practice on this and other pedagogic issues is part of the problem of modernization and development in Rio, as in all Brazil and not only in the Jewish schools.

School Climate

Atmosphere

Observation of the atmosphere of Jewish schools and the stated views of staff, students and parents, indicate that Jewish schools are active and noisy. Discipline is maintained with a certain rigor. In some schools, 'inspectors' of discipline sit in the corridors to control the movement of students, maintain order, etc.

The relations between staff and students are a strange mixture of formal distance and the easy-going friendliness which characterizes the social atmosphere of Rio de Janeiro. In most cases, students feel that their teachers are friendly and flexible. By contrast, non-Jewish private schools are more formal and less personal. Jewish schools apparently are pleasant places where students can enjoy their studies.

Student Mix

The students in some of the schools come from families with different religious backgrounds. The number of Orthodox Jews in Rio is very small, and only a few of the children are Orthodox. The majority of students, even in the two religious schools, come from non-observant homes.

Overall, the number of non-Jewish students is insignificant. In the ORT technical school, most of the students are non-Jewish, but among the 4,000 pupils in Jewish day schools, less than 2% are not Jewish. The percentage is somewhat higher at the Sholem Aleichem school, which, due to its location, must augment its Jewish enrollment with non-Jewish pupils. Furthermore, its ideology views this mix positively as a means of integration into Brazilian society.

Student Motivation and Interest

The decision to enroll in a Jewish school is made early, usually at the pre-school age, and most students remain in the schools for six or more years.

A majority of older children confirm that they are happy with their parents' decision to send them to a Jewish school, and particularly to the school they attend. These pupils expressed satisfaction with the standard of secular studies, but complained of the burden of Jewish studies. Students continued studying in a school if it prepared them well for university entrance, despite their low interest in Jewish studies.

In a sample of students who left Jewish schools, 36% sought better preparation for the university entrance examination, 30% complained about the 'closed' environment of Jewish schools, 13% thought there was an excess of Jewish studies, and 12% left for financial reasons, some transferring to state schools.

Extra-Curricular Activities

Students participate in sports and other recreational activities organized by their Jewish schools. However, because of short school hours these activities and sometimes extra-curricular academic studies (often English) are arranged privately by the students outside school hours.

There are no student committees or student representatives on committees, partly to avoid any political overtones concurrent with student involvement.

Effects of Schooling

The effectiveness of any school must be assessed according to its own goals and criteria. On this basis, Jewish schools are successful in preparing students to obtain high marks in the university entrance examinations, and for younger children, who are the majority, they provide a 'good, sound general education.'

Schools also measure their effectiveness in quantitative terms, that is, the number of pupils they reach, and the number passing external examinations. A further measure of effectiveness is the extent of influence which the schools exert both on the Jewish community as a whole and on their own students. From this perspective, Jewish schools are successful: they are centers of Jewish life. Some 4,000 children attend them five days each week during the school year. They are essentially Jewish institutions, with Jewish students, Jewish principals, Jewish school and parent committees, and they impart Jewish education. Communal leaders, activists, parents and supporters focus on recruiting funds and on helping to organize social and cultural activities. Central community organizations, including the Central Education Bureau, help the schools in various ways and also try to influence them where possible. Thus, Jewish schools are community institutions, involving the community and its activities, and playing an important role in keeping the community's formal and informal networks alive and active.

Moreover, the Jewish school is a small community within itself. There are close relations among students, and these links of friendship remain even if children transfer to non-Jewish schools for their secondary education. The overall impression is one of interaction which influences and continues into the child's life in later years.

The influence that Jewish schools have on their own students was assessed in a survey of 304 secondary students in Rio Jewish schools (50% of the total number of pupils enrolled in secondary Jewish schools), 68 former Jewish school students, and 34 Jewish students who had never attended Jewish schools. The survey embraced attitudes to Judaism, to Brazil, to the Brazilian Jewish community, to Israel and to perceptions of antisemitism. The purpose was to identify differences in attitudes between the three groups and to assess the school's influence in forming these attitudes.

The students who were currently attending Jewish schools showed more favorable attitudes toward Judaism and Israel, and saw their futures as being less linked with Brazil than did the two groups who had either attended for a short time or not at all. The main conclusion drawn from the survey was that the school strengthens positive attitudes toward Judaism and Israel. However, reinforcement of the school's influence was an important factor; Jewish school attendance, home background, and membership in Jewish organizations were always strongly linked.

The Jewish school appears to strengthen feelings of Jewish identity especially in the face of perceived external threats, e.g. antisemitism. In religious schools where there is greater stress on Judaism, Jewish identity is less related to the degree of perceived antisemitism, despite the fact that the per-

CHART 2. THE POSITION OF JEWISH SCHOOLS IN BRAZIL AND MAIN
FACTORS INFLUENCING THEM[a]

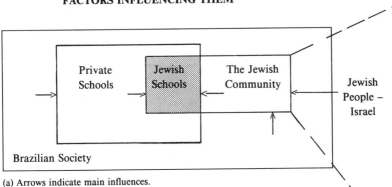

(a) Arrows indicate main influences.

ception of antisemitism is stronger. Furthermore, in the religious school context, the influence of home is less than that of the school.

In short, the Jewish school provides students with a social framework
which is Jewish. The friendships made at school, the relationship with Jewish
educators and the overt affiliation and attachment with a Jewish institution
is a foundation for pupils to maintain their identity after leaving school.

Nevertheless, the unclear status of a Jewish secular minority within a
nationalistic and predominantly Christian society creates uneasiness among
some Jews about remaining in a 'closed' and segregated milieu. Confused
attitudes about the meaning of being Jewish and the content of Judaism create problems which make the work of the Jewish school more difficult and
lessen its effectiveness.

Several external factors influence Jewish schools. Chart 2 depicts the
sources and directions of these external factors. The first factor is Brazilian
society, which has offered opportunities for rapid economic advancement
and has influenced Jewish social and cultural life. Second is the Jewish community, which regards the schools as the principal instruments for its own
survival, and imposes on them the collective values of the community. Third
is Israel, which, by its very existence and through its organizations, has
encouraged Jewish life in Rio and influenced the schools. Finally, other Jewish communities, particularly that of the United States, have encouraged religious expression of Judaism, for example, through visits of American yeshiva
students to religious schools in Rio.

Conditions in Brazilian society have fostered the development of the Jewish school system, which now reaches about half the Jewish elementary and
secondary school population. The main problems these schools must confront concern:

- educational philosophies and assumptions;
- the recruitment and training of teachers; and
- finance.

It is not clear whether the tendency will be to solve these problems with a coordinated approach, or whether the independent status and competitive relationships between schools will continue. The future of the Central Education Bureau depends on the outcome. Perhaps the Bureau will be able to increase its own independent and central role and thereby overcome the decentralizing tendencies of the schools.

Informal Jewish Education

Youth Movements

There is a rich tradition of Zionist pioneer youth movements in Latin America, and Rio is part of this tradition. In 1979, there were three youth movements in Rio – *Hashomer Hatzair, Dror Habonim,* and *Bnei Akiva.* Hundreds of the members and leaders of these movements have migrated to Israel, the largest numbers being from *Hashomer Hatzair* and *Dror Habonim.* The Brazilian *Dror* members concentrated on Kibbutz Bror Chail, while those of *Hashomer Hatzair* settled on several other kibbutzim. Those who left the kibbutz moved to various cities in Israel, although a minority returned to Brazil.

It is estimated that in 1979, *Bnei Akiva* had 40 to 60 members, *Hashomer Hatzair* had between 250 and 400, while *Dror Habonim* membership was somewhere between the two groups. Membership is difficult to assess, since members are not formally registered and participation in activities varies considerably.

The three movements are affiliated with local bodies as well as with their international movements. *Hashomer Hatzair* and *Dror Habonim* have full-time *shlihim,* while *Bnei Akiva* has a half-time *shaliah* who is employed also as a teacher in a Jewish school. These *shlihim* are sponsored in Rio by the WZO and by the international headquarters of each movement in Israel. Local individuals or groups also provide some support, either due to ideological affinity or as parents of movement members.

Bnei Akiva enjoys the direct support of the religious Jewish schools. Nevertheless, its membership remains small, probably because the majority of the Jewish community is not Orthodox. The other two youth movements have no direct relationship with the schools, but they can usually gain access to them for the purpose of announcing their activities and attracting members. *Hashomer* leaders are critical of the schools and their approach to Jewish education, but estimate about half of their members attend them.

The position of the schools vis-à-vis the youth movements is not uniform. The attitudes of a particular principal and the leaders of the school committee determine the relationship between a given school and each youth movement. Thus, the religious schools permit *Bnei Akiva* activities on school premises during hours when the schools are not functioning. Some schools permit movement activists to enter the premises to announce activities and recruit members. But at least one school forbids even this minimal support.

Youth movements organize summer camps for younger children in the vicinity of Rio, while older members participate in national camps with members from other Brazilian Jewish communities. However, the tradition of private or institutional permanent premises for summer camps has not developed in Brazil, where Jewish children usually spend their vacations with their families.

Since 1973, a summer program – *Tapuz* (Orange) – has brought several dozens of Jewish youngsters from Rio to Israel for two months of kibbutz work-experience, seminars and tours. This program was initiated by Kibbutz Bror Chail, which hoped to solve a manpower problem in the orchards after the Yom Kippur War while carrying out educational work with Brazilian Jewish youth, and has since expanded to all Latin American communities.

Student Organizations

In Rio, there are three student groups which conduct lectures and discussions, on Israel and Judaism, and organize social activities. They usually meet on the premises of a communal organization, although one of the groups meets in private homes. While members of this group are upper middle-class, most of the student groups seem to attract those with modest economic resources.

The university student groups mainly offer their members, who include non-students, a Jewish social environment, and the organizations which support them have the satisfaction that they are helping to keep Jewish young people within the community. However, the Jewish student organizations have small, varying memberships, and include only a very small proportion of that age-group. This is possibly due to the difficulty of organizing students immersed in studies and the age-group's preference for informal friendship groups. Yet this seems to be an area of Jewish education in which too few resources and efforts have been invested.

Discussions with students in post-secondary education indicated that several were critical of Jewish schools. Some mentioned that they had left Jewish schools because of the high cost to their parents – not only tuition fees, but also the cost of maintaining social standards.

University and Adult Jewish Education

In Rio, there are no post-secondary Jewish institutions of religious learning. Three local universities offer limited Judaica programs which consist of courses in Hebrew, Jewish history, and literature. Since the majority of students are not Jewish, and take these courses as second-choice options (other courses being full, etc.), there is little meaningful impact on Jewish education. Attempts to attract Jewish students to these courses by offering teaching certificates have met with little success. In one such incentive scheme, the promised accreditation was not provided, and there is serious concern that non-Jewish graduates of university Judaica courses might apply for positions teaching Jewish subjects, despite their unacceptable level of knowledge and their lack of understanding of the problems of Jewish education.

Until the 1960s, much of the teaching of Jewish subjects was carried out by teachers who had immigrated from Europe, or, in some cases, from Middle Eastern countries. In Argentina, a local teacher-training seminar was established when the stream of immigrants which brought Jewish teachers came to a halt. Today, its alumni constitute the majority of teachers in Argentina and its graduates teach in other Latin American countries as well. A few teach in Brazil, mainly in Sao Paulo. In Rio, however, various attempts to establish a stable and effective system of training Jewish studies teachers have been largely unsuccessful. The teacher-training class now located at the Liessin School attracts a very small number of students, all of whom are women.

The Departments of Education of the WZO have provided assistance in training Brazilian teachers in Israel – at the Chaim Greenberg College and the Gold College for religious teachers, established in Jerusalem as boarding institutes in 1954 and 1958, respectively. From 1955 to 1971, an average of 10 Brazilian students per year attended Greenberg College; after 1971, the number declined sharply. In the 1972–78 period, the total of 20 students from Brazil was only 10% of the number from Argentina. Gold College attracted even fewer students from Brazil than did Greenberg College. Enrollments at the two colleges are detailed in Table 3.

Although separate statistics for Rio are not available, it is estimated that one-third of the total Brazilian figures are from Rio. Of the 59 teachers of Judaic studies interviewed in 1979/80, only a handful were students at the two Israeli institutions. Sixteen had studied at the Ecole Normale Brazil-Israel (now in the Liessin School). Of this group, 56% possessed a university degree, but only a small number had followed the Judaic courses available at local universities.

A program of Jewish studies, aimed at university students and graduates 25 to 40 years old, was initiated in Argentina by the Tel Aviv University and the WZO and is being implemented successfully in Rio under the sponsorship of the Hebrew University of Jerusalem and the *Dor Hemshech* Division

TABLE 3. BRAZILIAN STUDENTS ENROLLED AT GREENBERG AND GOLD
COLLEGES – JERUSALEM, 1965–1978

Greenberg College		Gold College (girls only)	
Year	No. of Students	Year	No. of Students
Total	20	Total	39
1972	5	1965	3
1973	8	1966	3
1974	2	1967	3
1975	4	1968	12
1976	1	1969	13
1977–78	0	1970	4
		1971	1
		1972 –78	0

of the WZO. The program consists of weekly evening classes and discussions, culminating in a three-week seminar program at an Israeli university.

Personal observation, confirmed by reviewing the Jewish press, indicates that despite individual lectures and sporadic cultural events, there are no systematic adult or parent education programs provided by Jewish organizations. The importance of adult education is only minimally recognized. The Center for Jewish Studies recently established for the *Dor Hemshech* program may bring about a change in attitudes to adult education in Brazil, as it did in other Latin American countries. However, it is too soon to assess the influence of the Center or its prospects of becoming a stable and effective adult education institution.

Research and Policy Implications

There are many areas which require future research, notwithstanding scarcity of resources. First, there is a need to map out the Jewish educational situation in the other cities of Brazil, which would enable comparison with Rio. Secondly, there are many lacunae in the existing research on the Jewish education in Rio. For instance, research is needed on curricula, on the long-term influence of schools, on the school culture and descriptions of school life and on comparative analyses of schools. Mechanisms built into the administrative system could retrieve basic current data on students, teachers and other factors, which could be useful for future research and to the schools themselves. A stronger Central Education Bureau could facilitate and coordinate such data collection across schools. The present situation does not encourage schools to surrender information: researchers should be aware of this factor and take 'access' to schools into account in their methodological preparation.

In relation to policy, the following points should be considered:

- the struggle for Jewish identity and for community survival and development is too important to be left to formal education in schools alone. Complementary youth, adult and family education is essential and should be allocated a significant share of resources;
- clarification of communal and educational goals should be carried out with a high level of community participation, implemented by the central community institutions and incorporated into teacher-training and educational programs;
- commitment should be made to improve the status and prestige of the teaching profession and of educators – in terms of salaries, symbolic recognition and sabbatical periods in Israel;
- regardless of differing ideological orientations and individual autonomy, community responsibility for all schools should be acknowledged. The community should provide financial and other support to free schools from threats of bankruptcy and constant budgetary crises;
- assessments should be made on how to more efficiently utilize resources available from Israel and other countries;
- parents and teachers should be knowledgeable about, and involved in, the process of policy formation, planning and periodic school evaluation.

Acknowledgements

This chapter is based on a research project conducted at the David Horowitz Institute, Tel Aviv University, with funding from the Klabin Foundation, in 1980. The research team, led by the author as Director of the Project, included Moshe Sicron, Hadassa Singer, E. Pszcol (Brazil), R. Nathanson, Itamar Rogovsky. Hadassa Singer, whose vital contribution to the project was greatly appreciated, passed away while this chapter was being written. It is dedicated to her memory.

References

American Jewish Committee (1977). *Education and Jewish Identity*. Colloquium Papers, New York.

Burla, E. (1977). *Relatorio Resumido das Atividades do Vaad Hachinuch.* Federaçao Israelita, Rio de Janeiro.

Centro Brasileiro de Estudos Judaicos (1972). *Nos Caminhos de Diaspora.* Sao Paulo.

Chazan, B. (1978). *The Language of Jewish Education: Crisis and Hope in the Jewish School.* Hartman House, New York.

Gleizer, I., ed. (1979). "Simposio sobre Educaçao Judaica no Rio de Janeiro". *Comentario,* no. 78. Rio de Janeiro.

Gur, S. (1960). "The Jewish and Religious Education in Brazil." *Sde Hemed,* no. 4–5. pp. 291–295. (Hebrew).

Hershlag, Z.Y., Schers, D., Singer, H., eds. (1975). *The Structure of Latin American Jewry.* Final Report. David Horowitz Institute, Tel Aviv University, Tel Aviv. (Hebrew, mimeograph).

Instituto Brasileiro de Geografia e Estatistica (1977, 1978). *Anuario Estatistico do Brasil.* IBGE, Centro Editorial, Rio de Janeiro.

Jaguaribe, H. (1968). *Economic and Political Development: A Theoretical Approach and a Brazilian Case Study.* Harvard University Press, Cambridge.

Kedmi, Y. (1965). "On the Jewish Education in Brasil." *Betfutzot Hagola,* No. 1. pp. 79–82. (Hebrew).

Lipiner, E. (1962). *Breve Historia des Judeus no Brasil.* Ediçoes Ltda, Rio de Janeiro.

Lipiner, E. (1971). "The Jews of Brazil from the Time of Discovery to the Present". *Gesher,* no. 3–4. pp. 52–67. (Hebrew).

Malamud, S. (1972). *Contribuiçao Judaica ao Desenvolvimento Brasileiro nos 150 anos de Independencia.* Federaçao Israelita do Rio de Janeiro, Rio de Janeiro.

Niskier, A. (1978). *A Nova Escola.* Blach Educaçao, Rio de Janeiro.

Pinsky, J. (1973). "Educaçao Judaica no Brasil". *Shalom,* Vol. VIII, no. 97. pp. 110–116.

Rattner, H. (1977). *Tradiçao e Mudanca: a Comunidade Judaica em Sao Paulo.* Edotora Atica, Sao Paulo.

Reicher, P. (1975). *Jewish Education in Brasil.* David Horowitz Institute for the Study of Developing Countries, Tel Aviv University, Tel Aviv. (Hebrew, mimeograph).

Rogovsky, I. and Hashbi, S. (1976). *Jewish Education and Jewish Identity.* David Horowitz Institute for the Study of Developing Countries, Tel Aviv University, Tel Aviv. (Hebrew, mimeograph).

Schers, D., and Singer, H. (1977a). *Nationalism and Development in Latin America: Mexico and Brazil.* David Horowitz Institute for the Study of Developing Countries, Tel Aviv University, Tel Aviv. (Mimeograph).

Schers, D. and Singer, H. (1977b). "The Jewish Communities of Latin America: External and Internal Factors in Their Development". *Jewish Social Studies*, Vol. 39, no. 3. pp. 241–258.

Shipman, M.D. (1968). *The Sociology of the School.* Hazel Watson Viney Ltd, London.

Sicron, M. (1978). *Some Notes on the Demography of Brazilian Jewry.* David Horowitz Institute for the Study of Developing Countries, Tel Aviv University, Tel Aviv. (Hebrew, mimeograph).

Vainer, G. (1974). *Educaçao Judaica no Rio de Janeiro.* Chevra Kadisha, Rio de Janeiro. (Mimeograph).

7

Jewish Education
in Other Latin American Countries

Efraim Zadoff

The 15 Jewish communities discussed in this chapter are those in Mexico, Uruguay, Chile, Venezuela, Colombia, Peru, Puerto Rico, Panama, Guatemala, Paraguay, Ecuador, Bolivia, the Dominican Republic, Costa Rica, and Cuba. All these communities were established around the beginning of this century. The immigrants who founded them came from Eastern and Central Europe, the Balkans and Turkey, the Middle East and North Africa. They arrived in an almost continuous stream, interrupted only by the First and Second World Wars, from the early 20th century until the 1960s.

The total Jewish population in the countries examined here does not exceed 130,000, two-thirds of which are concentrated in Mexico, Uruguay, and Chile; some 20% live in Venezuela, Colombia and Peru. The remaining communities are small, varying in size between 3,500 Jews in Panama, to only a few score in the Dominican Republic.

If one assumes that school-age children (3–4 years old to 17–18 years old) constitute about 20% of the Jewish population, there would then be some 30,000 Jewish children in these countries. Of these, some 16,000 attend Jewish schools or just over half. However, this is an average for the 15 communities. In four communities over 80% attend Jewish schools; in three communities – from 50 to 70%, while in the remaining eight, the percentages are lower, varying from 25 to 50%.

The proportion of children attending Jewish schools is unrelated to the size of the community. Of the three largest communities, only Mexico has a high rate of Jewish school attendance; Uruguay and Chile are among those with the lowest Jewish school attendance rates. Among the medium size communities, Venezuela and Peru have high rates of Jewish school attendance, whereas Colombia is in the low attendance category.

For those concerned with Jewish education, the number of children attending Jewish schools is only one of the problems. The main issues of Jewish education are its quality, its power to attract pupils and the results it achieves. Furthermore, formal education is only one part of the Jewish educational network in the Latin American communities. The parallel networks of informal education are also important. Informal education is conducted in Jewish sports centers, Jewish community centers, or within independent organizations such as the Zionist youth movements. Sometimes informal education cooperates with one other elements in the community and with the Jewish schools; at other times it acts independently.

Historical Background

The Jewish communities in these Latin American countries generally concerned themselves with education only after the facilities for basic Jewish needs such as burial, marriage, circumcision, public worship, ritual slaughter, and social welfare for the needy, sick and immigrants had been provided.

The first Jewish educational facilities for children were heder or *kutab* type schools, modelled on those in the East European or Arab countries of origin. The number of children in these schools was very small, probably because their parents were preoccupied with the basic problems of establishing a home and securing a livelihood. There was a lack of Jewish consciousness, and school facilities may not have been available.

Accordingly, those who were responsible for providing religious services also provided Jewish education which they viewed as inseparable from prayer and ritual. The schools that they established were thus similar to those in their countries of origin. This is apparent in the larger communities of Uruguay and Mexico, as well as in the small community of Costa Rica, where the Ashkenazic, Sephardic and Oriental communities established traditional schools in which the emphasis was on Pentateuch, prayer, and translation from Hebrew.

Once the Jews had established themselves economically and their communal institutions were firmly based, both they and their community leaders became aware of the need for Jewish schools, and around the 1920s, they began to meet this need. In 1924, the first modern school to teach secular subjects along with Jewish studies was opened in Mexico City. Probably the last community to establish a day school was that of Ecuador, where the first one was opened in 1973. By the 1970s, all the Latin American Jewish communities had established their own schools, either supplementary or full-time. The earlier ones provided Jewish education only, outside the hours of regular state schooling, that is, supplementary Jewish education. Those that were established later provided both Jewish and secular education. Since these full-time schools introduced integration between Jewish and secular studies, they were called 'integral' schools (commonly known in other countries and also here referred to as day schools).

Eventually, in accordance with the needs of most communities, the long-established supplementary schools which operated five days per week were turned into day schools. However, a number of supplementary schools operating on Sundays and occasionally on one weekday, have continued to exist. These are connected with synagogues or with particular sectors of the community as, for instance, in Uruguay, where Talmud Torah classes are provided by the communities of Sephardic and German origin.

The type of school established in a community was determined by a number of factors. One was the ability and readiness of parents to pay for private secular education, particularly where the alternative of acceptable free state schooling was available. Another factor was whether parents wanted their children in schools with non-Jewish children (in state or non-Jewish private schools) or in segregated institutions providing a totally Jewish social environment. A third factor was whether supplementary schools alone were sufficient for Jewish education, and finally, there were considerations about the quality and conditions of state schools compared with private schools whose educational standards were generally higher and where parents had some degree of control.

The relative importance of each of these factors in the development of day schools is difficult to assess. Financial resources were of central importance, but funds could be found if awareness of the need for a school existed. The quality of secular studies was also important and was a prime concern of day school founders and directors, since unless the secular academic standards were very high, parents would send their children to, or leave them in, other private schools. Thus, a proposed or existing school's academic standards were crucial to its attracting students and hence, its viability.

The desire for a Jewish social environment, in which children would spend most of their time outside the home, was another important factor. Parents regarded the social environment and culture of the Jewish day schools as a means of ensuring the community's continued existence and preventing intermarriage.

The convenience of providing formal Jewish and secular studies in one place without extra travelling time or reduced leisure were arguments to support the establishment of new schools. Moreover, the day school lessened cultural conflict for the child, since his/her Jewish and general knowledge and experiences were acquired as an organic whole.

One community in which a constellation of factors acted to delay the establishment of a day school was that of Uruguay. The resources which the Jewish community of Uruguay was able or ready to invest in Jewish schools were meagre. The standard of the state schools was considered satisfactory, and supplementary Jewish education was regarded as sufficient. Hence, segregating Jewish children for education was deemed unnecessary. The establishment of the first Jewish day school in Uruguay was delayed until 1962. By the mid-1970s, supplementary schools, operating five days weekly, had been converted to day schools,[1] as state schools became less acceptable for educational, security and political reasons. This caused parents to look to the alternative of Jewish private schools, which would provide all the child's educational needs.[2]

Overall, the constellation of determining factors eventually resulted in the establishment of day schools and the conversion of supplementary schools into day schools in most of the Latin American communities. The first three day schools – two in Mexico[3] and one (later nationalized) in Cuba[4] – were opened as early as the 1930s. During this decade, there were also unsuccessful attempts to establish day schools in Colombia, such as in Cali in 1932 and 1934, and Barranquilla in 1935. Most of the schools in existence today (other than in Uruguay) were established or reorganized as day schools in the 1940s. These included six schools in Mexico,[5] two in Chile,[6] and one each in La Paz (Bolivia),[7] Caracas (Venezuela),[8] Lima (Peru),[9] Barranquilla,[10] Cali[11] and Medellin (Colombia).[12]

The number of schools established in a given community was also determined by its ideological and ethnic fabric. Despite their sectional interests, the small communities, such as Lima, Santiago (Chile), Monterrey (Mexico), Baranquilla, Caracas, and San Jose de Costa Rica, pooled resources and established jointly-run schools. But in communities numbering 30,000 or 40,000 Jews, a single school could simply not reflect the various ideological outlooks of their sponsors. For example, in the communities of Uruguay and Mexico, schools were supported, since the 1930s, by the Orthodox Zionists,[13] the observant Conservatives,[14] the non-Zionist Orthodox,[15] the secular Zionists, some of whom supported teaching Yiddish alone,[16] some Yiddish and Hebrew[17] and some only Hebrew;[18] by the secular non-Zionists, who favored teaching of only Yiddish;[19] and, by left-wing secular non-Zionists who wanted their schools to have a proletarian character.[20] Separate schools were also founded due to differences in ethnic backgrounds. Jewish immigrants from Arab lands and those of Sephardic origin wanted Jewish studies taught in accordance with their own traditions.[21] and were often reluctant for their children to learn Yiddish in schools established with an East European background.[22]

The dynamics of Jewish life in Latin American communities and interaction with the non-Jewish environment have blurred the essential differences in curricula, which were originally an expression of the different types of schools. Today, most Jewish educational institutions are day schools which devote much of the time to secular studies on a high level, with a certain amount of Jewish studies, including study about Israel, taught either in Hebrew or in Spanish. Only in isolated cases, such as the Ariel School in

Montevideo and the *Yiddishe Shule* in Mexico, is instruction still given also in Yiddish.

The desire to provide vocational training facilities for Jewish pupils within a Jewish framework was achieved by cooperation between local agencies and ORT. This cooperation led to the establishment of specific independent Jewish educational institutions to provide vocational training for Jewish and non-Jewish pupils. A school on these lines was founded in 1943 in Montevideo. The school provides scientific and technological education in accordance with general and vocational high school requirements,[23] and pupils study Jewish subjects in addition. The school also offers postsecondary studies in engineering and technology, commercial, secretarial and linguistic studies, computer training and modern Hebrew language programs. The agreement between ORT and local agencies also led to counselling and auxiliary services for other schools and institutions in the Jewish community in the fields of technology, commerce and the arts. For example, in 1943 ORT helped establish short-lived commercial-secretarial courses. These were unsuccessful, but in their place, vocational training courses for adults were established. The attempt by ORT to establish vocational courses at a school in Lima in the late 1960s was also unsuccessful.

However, since the mid-1970s, cooperation between ORT and existing Jewish schools has been more successful. Schools in Santiago and Lima introduced programs supplied by ORT into their curricula and obtained pedagogic assistance and materials. The school in Santiago officially joined the ORT Latin American network, changing its name to the Chaim Weizmann-ORT Hebrew Comprehensive School. The courses provided by ORT are handicrafts, arts, science and humanities at the primary level and technology and sciences at the secondary level. At the time of this writing (1983), negotiations for a similar cooperative relationship are proceeding between ORT and the Moral y Luces-Herzl Bialik School in Caracas.

Normativeness and Government Control of Private Schooling

Jewish schools in Latin America are legislatively defined as private schools. Their status is similar to that of private parochial schools, such as the Catholic schools, to that of schools with a cultural-national nature, such as English, German and other ethnic-language schools, and to those with a vocational nature, such as private commercial schools.

The only exception is the Jewish school in Havana, Cuba (Kovadloff, 1974, pp. 122–124), formerly a private institution, which was nationalized late in 1961, and has become a state school. In this school, formerly called Theodore Herzl and now the Albert Einstein, Jewish studies are taught daily for two hours from 3 to 5 p.m. and are totally government-financed, including the salary of a teacher from Israel. Until 1975, this 'Jewish' state school received special treatment. Despite zoning regulations requiring attendance at the local school, Jewish children were permitted to attend the Albert Einstein School even if they did not live in its neighborhood. The authorities even provided transportation and a gasoline allowance for pupils living far from the school. Acknowledging the long school day resulting from the additional Jewish studies, the authorities provided subsidized lunches. Finally, Jewish children were released from the school's afternoon program to attend Jewish studies classes. In 1975, much of this preferential treatment ceased with the reclassification of the school as a zoned neighborhood school which could accept only local Jewish and non-Jewish pupils.

In order to operate, private schools must earn government recognition by meeting requirements regarding the standard of studies and the condition of buildings. Recognized schools are considered 'incorporated', and offer the same secular education as in the free and compulsory state school system. In many Latin American countries, where the state schools cannot provide education for all children, private schools are seen to be filling an important role in assisting the state's educational objectives. Most private schools, including Jewish schools, receive no significant financial support from the state, which they actually free from the burden of educating some pupils, thus making room for others who are obliged or wish to enroll in state schools.

The various Latin American education ministries maintain departments responsible for supervising private schools. They mostly examine the standard of studies, though sometimes they also investigate the ideological orientation of the school and whether it is compatible with government policy or with the values held by policy-makers. This interest in ideology in the Latin American countries is due to concern with the maintenance of a national-cultural character in the face of large-scale immigration, and state-regulated education is seen to be an important agent of national and social crystallization.

Changes in government policy depend on the current regime's conceptions of the national aims of public education, and consequent attitudes toward private schools. These attitudes dictate the degree of severity with which education ministries supervise private schools, the amount of interference with programs of study and the extent of freedom or autonomy granted to private schools.

One example of the effects of such government policies relates to the Jewish school in Lima, Peru. Under the leftist military regime in the early 1970s, the Ministry of Education tried to impose on the private school system its own interpretation of Peruvian nationalism and its leftist-marxist concept of both historical and contemporary events. Government control of private schools was implemented through legal directives regarding programs of study, increased Ministry inspection and through ideologically-oriented seminars and courses for teachers of all subjects. Attempts were also made to force private schools to accept without charge needy pupils from the neighborhood, thus forcing Jewish schools to enroll needy non-Jewish pupils. This was particularly unacceptable since, due to a law requiring schools to provide religious instruction of a particular denominational character if requested by at least 40 pupils, there was danger that the Jewish school might be required to provide Catholic instruction. In response to these attempts, the private Catholic schools, together with the Jewish school, established the National Council for Parochial Education to protect their interests, with the Jewish school principal as head of this joint public body. As the regime's leftist leanings diminished in 1976, its rulings concerning private schools were implemented only gradually. With the subsequent change to a democratic government in 1978, attitudes to private schooling improved, and in 1981, a new Education Act granted considerable independence to private schools and encourged the establishment of new ones.[24] The schools were allowed to determine most of their own curricula and to formulate their guiding principles.

Chile provides another example of changing governmental attitudes toward private education. Under President Allende's socialist regime, there was a trend toward converting private schools into neighborhood schools which had to accept all pupils in the area. Jewish schools were allowed to accept only those Jewish pupils who lived in the vicinity and, in place of Jewish pupils from farther away, they were required to accept local non-Jewish pupils. Only special negotiations prevented the authorities from changing the Jewish character of the schools. Subsequently, the military coup which replaced Allende's socialist regime heralded a change in attitude toward private schools and inaugurated a process whereby far-ranging powers were granted to private educational establishments at all levels of formal education, including the university. Schools were granted increased internal autonomy, including greater freedom to determine programs of study, and there were great reductions in Ministry supervision.

A third example is Uruguay, where during the military regime, the authorities closely supervised all schools, including private ones. Inspectors from the Ministry of Education constantly checked whether the schools were teaching Uruguayan history, moral instruction, and civics in accordance with Ministry directives. Control was also exercised over the selection of teachers on the basis of political outlook, and the Ministry of Education investigated the fitness of candidates for teaching positions by virtue of their political opinions, and on this basis confirmed or rejected any appointment. In contrast, in other Latin American countries (including Uruguay since 1984) schools are free to select teachers, subject only to professional qualifications.

In Mexico during the government of President Cárdenas (1934–40), the leftist attitudes of the government were expressed in efforts to ban the Catholic Church and other religious groups from the educational sphere and all religious studies including Bible instruction were banned throughout the country. Jewish schools sometimes risked teaching Bible as Hebrew literature.

The current relationship between Jewish private schools and the education authorities in the Latin American countries is satisfactory. The schools have complete autonomy over their Jewish studies programs, which vary from year to year and from school to school. In general the authorities cooperate with the Jewish schools. For example, the Hebrew language component of the Jewish studies program is sometimes recognized as part of the secular curriculum, and a sufficient standard in Hebrew is required to obtain the secondary school diploma.

Another example of cooperation between the authorities and the Jewish schools concerns the use of symbols of the State of Israel. In Colombia, in the early 1970s the law prohibited flying the flag of a foreign nation or singing its national anthem except on its national day, and then, only if it was a nation friendly to Colombia. Nevertheless, the authorities, during that period, permitted Jewish schools to fly the flag of Israel and sing the *Hatikvah* following the raising of the Colombian flag and the singing of the Colombian national anthem at the weekly school ceremony.

The authorities often permit a large measure of freedom to Jewish schools also in regard to the secular curriculum relying on the high standards the schools set for themselves. There is evidence that educational authorities regard Jewish private schools as professionally prestigious. At times, representatives from the Jewish schools are among the few advisers who help formulate curricula and new laws (for example in Peru and Chile), and the Jewish schools are sometimes (as in Venezuela) among those selected by ministries of education for the operation and examination of experimental programs prior to their introduction into the school system.

The Financial Basis of Jewish Education

Jewish schools in the Latin American countries under discussion rarely receive direct financial assistance from governments, and then, only on a very limited scale, as in Chile or Colombia. Indirect assistance is sometimes provided by means of tax exemptions, as in Uruguay, or by allowing donations to Jewish schools to be deducted from taxable income, as in Peru.

The primary source of income for all Jewish schools in the Latin American communities is the tuition fees paid by parents. It is estimated that tuition fees cover 60 to 80% of the schools' current expenses, explaining the schools' need to maintain clientele by meeting parental expectations. Dependence on income from tuition fees is particularly evident in the small communities, where the number of Jewish pupils is insufficient to finance a day school. Accordingly Jewish schools are forced by financial necessity to accept non-Jewish pupils. At the Einstein School in Quito (Ecuador), only one third of the pupils are Jewish, while only 15% of the pupils at the day school in La Paz (Bolivia) are Jewish. One quarter of the pupils at the Weizmann School in Viña del Mar (Chile) are non-Jewish, as were, in 1970, one third of the pupils at the Union School in Barranquilla.

The main financial problem is development and building. Funding for these purposes and for deficits in running costs comes from two sources - the community itself and external sources. Local funds come from:
- fund-raising drives and activities organized by parent committees (Zadoff, 1974);
- contributions by communal institutions from their current income, sometimes given in the form of grants or scholarships; and
- a proportion of the community's United Jewish Appeal funds.

External sources of finance include the various departments and special funds of the World Zionist Organization (WZO), ORT, the Joint Distribution Committee (JDC), and the Israeli Ministry of Education and Culture. ORT provides direct finance for buildings and the purchase of equipment in the educational institutions under its patronage, and considerable indirect financial assistance by providing professional personnel to instruct and supervise ORT activities in other schools, and teaching materials for its specific programs. Financial aid from the Israel Ministry of Education to Jewish education in the Diaspora began in 1980 and is aimed at nurturing Jewish education and developing special Jewish education programs. The Latin American communities benefit from this aid.

Most external support for Jewish education in Latin America except for Argentina and Brazil comes from the Departments of Education and Torah Education of the World Zionist Organization. This aid is both direct and indirect and consists of:
- day-to-day maintenance costs, as extended, for example, to the Albert Einstein School in Quito since 1980;
- funding for new buildings as received by the Moral y Luces-Herzl Bialik School in Caracas in the late 1970s;
- provision of *shlihim* for administrative, counselling and teaching posts in the schools. The cost of *shlihim* is sometimes borne by WZO alone, sometimes shared by the WZO and the schools, and sometimes by local institutions alone;
- teacher-training courses in long-term programs of one or more years or

short refresher seminars in Israel, as well as in-service and refresher courses within the local communities;
- preparation and supply of curricular and supplementary study materials;
- organization of special programs for pupils in Latin American Jewish schools ranging from short study seminars to a year of study in an Israeli school.

Support for Jewish Education

The Education Committees that are attached to all or most schools in a given community influence the development and character of the Jewish schools there. Such committees exist in Mexico, Venezuela and Uruguay.

The Education Committee (*Va'ad Hahinuch*) in Santiago is a body of professional community leaders interested in Jewish education who determine the general guidelines of school policy. It is a committee for the school, rather than a joint education committee for a number of schools.

The Education Committee in Mexico is actually a sub-committee of the *Nidchei Yisrael* Ashkenazic community, which is concerned with the needs of the schools of the Ashkenazic community. In fact, the Education Committee's main task is maintaining a teachers' seminary, which provides a two year program in Hebrew and Yiddish for teacher-training.[25]

In Caracas, the Education Committee coordinates three schools – the Moral y Luces-Herzl Bialik School, the Hebraica School, and the Yavneh School, with joint planning and curricula, as well as construction of shared buildings. Representatives of the three school committees are members of the *Va'ad Hahinuch.*

The Education Committee is concerned with general educational policy. It also plays a financial role, since through sub-committees it grants loans and scholarships in accordance with an open-door enrollment policy, and allocates funds for construction, such as for a new joint high school.[26]

Until recently, the role of the Ashkenazic community's Education Committee in Montevideo was limited almost entirely to dealing with scholarships for needy pupils and to determining the salary and status of teachers. Since 1981, the committee has acquired a pedagogic and ideological role.

It is apparent that since not all schools in a given community are affiliated with the existing Education Committee, the Committee's influence on the country-wide development of a school system is limited. Furthermore, the affiliated schools are not always responsive to the suggestions, requests and directives of the respective Education Committees.

The Schools

The majority of educational institutions in Latin America are day schools. Most of them cater to pupils from kindergarten through matriculation, although some day schools comprise kindergarten and primary departments with two or three post-elementary (junior secondary) classes, so that students desiring to complete secondary education or matriculate must transfer to other Jewish or non-Jewish schools.

Time Allotment

The actual allotment of time to Jewish and secular studies varies from grade one to the final year of secondary school and from school to school. In some schools (e.g. Einstein School, Quito; Weizmann School, Viña del Mar; Leon Pinelo School, Lima; Weizmann School, Santiago), from 4 to 10 hours weekly are devoted to Jewish studies in the primary grades, that is, not more than one-third of the total number of formal teaching hours. Some schools (e.g. the Integral, Yavneh and Ariel schools in Montevideo and the Einstein school in San Jose de Costa Rica), devote from 13 to 18 hours weekly to formal Jewish studies, which is one-third to one-half of the hours of formal instruction. There is less difference between schools in the time devoted to Jewish studies at the junior secondary level. By the three final grades of secondary school, all schools devote from 4 to 9 hours weekly, i.e. from 10% to 20% total teaching time to Jewish subjects.

However, formal studies are not the sum of Jewish education in schools. From the educational viewpoint, informal and extra-curricular activities such as ceremonies connected with the Jewish festivals, fasts and memorial days, morning and Sabbath prayer services, and informal activities which some schools provide in cooperation with youth movements, in which pupils play an active role, may be at least as important as formal instruction.

Status of Jewish Studies

The status of formal Jewish studies can be measured not only by the number of hours devoted to Jewish subjects, but also by the esteem with which these studies are regarded by pupils and parents. To date, no comprehensive in-depth research has been undertaken to examine the attitudes of parents and pupils toward the Jewish education offered in day schools in the communities under consideration, nor has there been any investigation of the extent to which the pupils' attitudes and their Jewish identity have been influenced or molded by the education obtained (Rogovsky and Tishbi, 1976; Smith, 1972; Hodara, 1977).

Nevertheless, it is safe to say that secular studies are the most important reason for the attraction of pupils to day schools, and constant efforts are directed to improving their standard; from the outset, the initiators of day schools were greatly concerned to provide general studies of a standard at least equal to the best government and private schools, and suited to the university entry aspirations of pupils.

Furthermore, aided by ORT, day schools are continually experimenting with projects for introducing high-standard technological courses into their curricula. These attempts to make schools more attractive to a broader Jewish clientele is proving successful, indicating that parents are attracted to schools for professional and vocational preparation.

Therefore, though unresearched, there is general consensus among those educators and educational activists whose opinions were sought that it is not Jewish studies which attract pupils to Jewish day schools, and that Jewish studies are less popular than secular studies among pupils.[27] Some claim that parents themselves are not particularly interested in Jewish studies for their children, but choose a Jewish school for its proven reputation as an excellent, even elitist, secular school. Moreover, they think that in times of political upheaval, a Jewish school may be safer than government schools, and it provides the additional benefit of a Jewish social environment, reducing the risk of their children's marrying out of the faith (Smith, 1972, pp. 49–51).

In the Jewish communities of Latin America, religion and religious values, which in the past were the principal basis of Jewish identity, have been replaced by a traditionalist-nationalist orientation. However, when parents choose to educate their children in day schools, they may be less concerned with the preservation of nationalist Jewish values than with the preservation of their own socio-ethnic class status, with no special regard for Jewish nationalism in terms of behavior or action.[28]

One way to raise the low status of Jewish studies and to encourage pupil interest, particularly in Hebrew, has been to make the Jewish studies curriculum compulsory. A number of schools have succeeded (sometimes despite parental opposition) in obtaining official recognition of Hebrew as a compulsory foreign language required for matriculation by Jewish day school pupils. Hebrew is so recognized (usually second to English) in Jewish day schools in Colombia, Chile and Costa Rica. In Caracas, the Education Committee negotiated with the education authorities for Judaic studies to be recognized as an integral part of the Jewish day school curriculum and hence as compulsory; so far though approval has not yet been granted. In Lima, the authorities in the early 1970s agreed to recognize Hebrew rather than English as the first compulsory foreign language at the Jewish day school: however, the school declined this opportunity for fear that parents would transfer their children to other schools where English was the first foreign language.

Mix of Students

Jewish schools enroll a high proportion of non-Jewish pupils – in some cases, such as the Einstein School in Quito and the day school in La Paz, more than two-thirds of the pupils are non-Jewish. The main reason for this is financial: in many cases, there would be no Jewish day school at all if non-Jewish pupils were not accepted to supplement pupil numbers and tuition fees. However, there are also pedagogic, ideological and perhaps political reasons for non-Jewish enrollments in Jewish day schools.

From the pedagogic perspective, it is extremely difficult to conduct classes with less than 10 pupils, so that the addition of non-Jewish pupils often results in optimal class sizes. From the ideological viewpoint, some parents and agencies which determine school policy are interested in enrolling Catholic pupils, since they believe that contact with Catholic children is an enriching experience for the Jewish pupils, and teaches tolerance to both the Jewish and non-Jewish students. From the political viewpoint, the law in some Latin American countries categorically forbids discrimination in school registration on the basis of religious belief: Jews in these countries wish to avoid disputes with the authorities.[29]

Supplementary vs. Day Schools

The limited time spent on Jewish studies in the day schools and the low status with which they are regarded by both parents and pupils have revived the controversy (Zadoff, 1980, pp. 76–77; Smith, 1972, p. 50) between supporters of the day school principle and those who favor intensive supplementary schools.[30] In some countries such as Uruguay and Chile, since state schools operate on a long school day which leaves no time for supplementary Jewish studies, the only practical Jewish educational institution is the day school. This was discussed at great length in the Jewish communities of Argentina and Uruguay, and to some extent, also in Mexico. There the debate was largely theoretical, since in Mexico supplementary education had never achieved substantial status and the overwhelming majority of existing schools were day schools.[31] On the other hand, in Argentina and Uruguay the debate concerned the actual choice between continuing the supplementary school system or converting existing institutions to the day school format. The presentation of arguments for and against supplementary and day schools has highlighted the problems of Jewish education and has stimulated re-thinking of previous assumptions. Educators holding central positions in schools which were established as day schools have begun to wonder whether the day school is really the most desirable framework for Jewish education, what changes might improve it, and whether an alternative format or structure might not better serve Jewish educational objectives.

The opponents of day schools claim that while Jewish education is what justifies the existence of Jewish day schools, Jewish studies in these schools have not attained appropriate or satisfactory status either from the standpoint of allotted teaching time or from the standards and attainments of pupils. They maintain that in practice, the day schools are mainly concerned with general subjects, including technological studies which parents and pupils regard as important. This is particularly evident in the later stages of secondary education, when schools cater to their pupils' wishes to concentrate on general studies in order to matriculate well and enter the university of their choice, by cutting the hours allotted to Jewish studies to a minimum. The critics of day schools further claim that, at the senior secondary stage, Jewish studies, which provide no material or vocational educational benefits cannot compete for attention with general studies. The very notion of competition between Jewish and general studies is wrong, and Jewish educational objectives would be better met by intensive supplementary education in part-time schools which provide Jewish studies alone, where pupils attend for 15 to 20 hours over four to five days weekly from kindergarten through and including the secondary school years. In such supplementary schools, Jewish studies would constitute the only activity and sole focus of interest, enabling pupils to attain desired academic standards and Jewish knowledge (Vorzogger, 1970, pp. 551–555).

Day school critics also claim that the day school does not prepare pupils for the life that awaits them after graduation. It creates the illusion of some kind of autonomous Jewish existence in the Diaspora, segregates and alienates pupils from the non-Jewish environment, and prevents pupils from gaining experience in coping with that environment. It is claimed that when day school pupils enter the university, they are bedazzled by the new world they encounter and are often lost to Jewish society.

A further argument is that very heavy investments are required for the necessary infrastructure to maintain the high standard of general studies, such as spacious buildings, laboratories and other installations needed in a good modern school. Day-to-day running costs are also high. Although most of the current budget for general studies comes from tuition fees, part of that budget and a great portion of the money invested in infrastructure comes from local Jewish organizations, benefactors and national Jewish institutions. It has been said that if this money were invested in providing Jewish studies alone, the results would be impressive. Furthermore, since in several day schools a large proportion of the pupils are non-Jewish, Jewish funds intended to support Jewish education are in fact subsidizing the education of non-Jews.[32]

Supporters of day schools agree that the notion of competition for esteem between Jewish and general studies is unfair, but maintain that they do not place the two components of the curriculum in competition. According to the principal of one day school, Jewish studies deal with values and sentiments, while general studies prepare one for professional or vocational development. Hence, the two branches of the curriculum should properly be regarded as complementary rather than competitive. They further maintain that it is not the day schools which place the two components of the curriculum in competition, but their clientele. There are valid grounds for the contention that if day schools did not cater to this clientele by means of a secular education comparable to the best state or private schools, the overwhelming majority of Jewish children would not attend a Jewish school at all, since they would not attend supplementary schools providing Jewish education alone. Hence, Jewish pupils who would otherwise receive no Jewish education at all, attend Jewish day schools, attracted to a framework in which they are exposed to some kind of Jewish education, both of a formal and informal nature, instead of none at all.

Moreover, compared to the high drop-out rates from supplementary schools, day schools have high retention rates. The drop-out rate in day schools is small and in many schools, non-existent, which means that pupils are exposed to Jewish education for a longer duration.[33]

Unlike supplementary part-time schooling, day schools are credited with creating a Jewish social environment in which the child grows and develops, assuring the physical survival of the Jewish people by preventing intermarriage. This social environment keeps the child from having to compartmentalize between the alien environments of the general and the Jewish school. It enables the school to minimize the disparities between the two environments represented by the two branches of the curriculum, and create an integrated program whereby the pupil can relate harmoniously to both cultures – the local general culture and that of the Jewish people. All the data – interviews, school publications, and research studies - point to the fact that the schools see themselves as bi-cultural. They attempt to transmit to their pupils an integrated culture which will enable them to function well in both the Jewish community and the Latin American country in which they live. They grow up, it is claimed, able to function as Jews in every way, equal to other citizens, without feeling foreign to their local environment. To some extent, the existence of non-Jewish pupils reflects the local component of the bi-cultural environment. Moreover, as noted before, the enrollment of non-Jewish pupils sometimes makes it possible for a Jewish school to exist at all in places where there are too few Jewish children or insufficient numbers wishing to enroll.

The Teachers

In their daily role, teachers determine the character of a school. Teachers in day schools fall into two groups – those who teach general studies and those who teach Jewish studies. Teachers of general subjects have usually obtained their training in local institutions recognized by the relevant government authorities. Only a minority of teachers of general subjects are Jewish, and they do not always identify with the aims and principles of the schools in which they teach. Indeed, there are instances in which the declared bias of the teacher is contrary to that of the employing school. For example, in the early 1970s some Peruvian teachers at the Leon Pinelo School in Lima spoke against 'Israel's imperialist occupation of Arab lands', condemned oppression and exploitation of poor Peruvians by rich factory owners (who included the parents of their own pupils) and opposed the display of the Israeli flag and the singing of Israel's national anthem. Problems of conflicting ideologies between teacher and school are exacerbated by the inability to dismiss teachers without Ministry of Education and Teacher Union agreement, and by the difficulty involved in proving ideological incompatibility as grounds for dismissal.

Teachers of Jewish subjects may be categorized into five groups according to their country of origin and training. These are:

- those educated in their lands of origin – Eastern Europe, Western Europe, and North Africa;
- those who obtained most of their Jewish education and training locally as Jewish studies teachers. A large proportion in this category completed various special training programs in Israel;
- those who obtained their education and professional training in other Latin American countries, mainly in Argentina and Uruguay. Some of these completed their studies in Israel;
- Israelis living in Latin America for various reasons, some of whom lack professional teaching qualifications and are employed only because of their knowledge of Hebrew;
- teacher-*shlihim* from Israel, who serve as teachers, counsellors and directors for pre-determined periods of time. In 1982, some 100 teacher-*shlihim* were employed by schools in Uruguay, Chile, Paraguay, Peru, Colombia, Venezuela, Costa Rica, Panama and Mexico.

Status of Teachers

On the whole, the status of teachers is low throughout Latin America, and the status of Jewish studies teachers in particular is low. Of the teachers in the five categories, the teacher-*shlihim* from Israel are the most highly esteemed. This is because many *shlihim* are not funded by local agencies and most have a higher level of training than other Jewish studies teachers. A corollary to the higher esteem they receive is that expectations of the *shlihim* are also higher. They are expected to be not only good teachers, but also cultural leaders, strong personalities, and representatives and role models of the State of Israel, with whom parents and pupils can identify (Hodara, 1977, p. 233).

A lowering of the status of the Jewish studies teaching body has been associated with its feminization. Thus, the higher esteem of teacher-*shlihim* probably is related to the fact that most are males. The vast majority of Jewish studies teachers other than *shlihim* are female. The same trend towards femininization of the profession also exists among teachers of general subjects, but the preponderence of females is less pronounced.

At the Yavneh School in Montevideo, less than 10% of Jewish studies teachers, including *shlihim*, are men, against over 20% of general studies teachers. At the Ariel Elementary School in Montevideo, the entire Jewish studies teaching staff is female, while some 10% of general studies teachers are males. The trend is similar at the Leon Pinelo School in Lima, where females comprise only 3% of the general studies teaching staff, against 44% of the Jewish studies teaching staff.

Another reason for the low status of teachers is poor salary. While Jewish studies teachers are better paid than the teachers of general studies, their incomes are relatively low when compared with potential earnings in other professions in Latin America. Thus, most high school graduates opt to study for professions such as medicine, engineering and architecture, economics and business administration and the sciences, rather than the humanities and social sciences, which include training in education.

Yet another reason for the low status of Jewish studies teachers is the low standard of these subjects in all Latin American communities. The lack of interest in specialized, advanced Jewish studies leads to the low level of provisions for such study. Despite local initiatives[34] and WZO efforts[35] in Chile, Uruguay and Mexico, in none of the communities discussed here have institutions been established for post-secondary Jewish studies or the training of teachers in Jewish subjects. Hence, local teachers at both the elementary and secondary levels lack a suitable level of knowledge in Jewish subjects as well as in teacher training for Jewish studies. The graduates of the courses that do exist (almost all females) become kindergarten and primary school teachers, usually after taking supplementary courses in Israel or locally. Thus, the low status of the local Jewish studies teaching body is reinforced by concentration of employment in the lower grades.

Over the past decade, this situation has perhaps been changing. As alternatives to the local provision of advanced studies and teacher training in Jewish studies, special programs of Jewish studies and Jewish education at universities in Israel have been made available, along with significant financial assistance. The attitude of Jewish youth towards teaching and management positions in Jewish schools has become more positive, and there are examples of young Jewish graduates in engineering, science or law embarking on academic studies in education and Judaism at Israeli universities. An engineer from Caracas completed his Master's degree in Jewish Education in the Diaspora at the Melton Center of the Hebrew University, and is now head of the Moral y Luces-Herzl Bialik School. A science teacher at the Leon Pinelo School in Lima, who studied education and Jewish studies at the Hebrew University, returned to direct that school. Students from Santiago and Lima, presently studying at Jerusalem's Melton Center, plan on completing their studies and returning to Latin America to take up positions at local Jewish schools.

Adult Education

A number of projects for adults who have school-age children have been developed, although few of the projects are specifically aimed at parents of children in Jewish schools per se. These projects are offered by a few schools which, through courses or 'schools' for parents, provide programs in Jewish subjects and in Hebrew language, with the object of enhancing the Jewish identity of parents and enriching their knowledge of the Jewish subjects their children are being taught at school. The program for parents at the day school in Montevideo offers lecture series on subjects dealing with child-rearing, cultural themes, and Jewish topics.

Other Jewish educational programs for adults consist of more or less systematic courses whose principal subject matter is Jewish. Such courses are provided by the Sephardic community in Santiago, and the *Bet El* Conservative community in Mexico City. However, most adult education activities are initiated by the Young Leadership Division of the WZO, in collaboration with universities in Israel (Tel Aviv University, The Hebrew University of Jerusalem, Everyman's University), and with organizations in the various local communities.

In almost all the communities, the WZO has established a network of institutes for Jewish studies and for the development of young leadership. The aim is to nurture the participant's sense of Jewish and Zionist identification and to develop young leaders for community organizations by means of various types of organized educational programs.[36] The adult education network, whose graduates themselves sometimes initiate similar programs for other groups of Jewish adults,[37] has also begun to have an effect on Jewish schools. On the one hand, Jewish studies teachers enter the programs to improve their Jewish knowledge.[38] On the other hand, teachers who participate are encouraged to place more emphasis on Jewish studies in the schools[39] and promote recognition among parent participants of the necessity for formal Jewish education for their children.

Apart from collaboration with local agencies in the development of both informal and systematic adult education, the direct involvement of Israeli academic institutions in Jewish studies has been limited to teacher training and study programs. The main two projects in this area have been the joint program between The Hebrew University's Melton Center for Jewish Education in the Diaspora and the *Tarbut* school in Mexico, and the joint program between the Center and the Moral y Luces-Herzl Bialik School in Caracas. Neither project seems to have involved systematic programs for influencing parental attitudes to Judaism in general, or their children's Jewish education in particular.[40]

Conclusions

The existence of Jewish schools in Latin American countries depends on three factors – the legal, the material and the ideological dimensions of Jewish education.

The legal basis of Jewish education appears to be assured, provided that there is no change of attitude toward the Jews. The material basis of Jewish education would appear to be assured as long as Jewish parents are interested in the existence of Jewish educational institutions for their children and succeed in persuading local and national Jewish organizations of the need to continue maintaining them.

It is, however, the qualitative and ideological dimensions of Jewish education that must be evaluated and justified. It is doubtful whether Jewish education is qualitatively sound, and much needs to be done to strengthen it. Many people involved in Jewish education consider that qualitatively, Jewish education is undergoing a crisis which will cause a Jewish identity crisis for children. This crisis is expressed by the lack of interest of some parents in programs of Jewish education, by a lack of conviction of some teachers concerning the importance and validity of the subjects they teach, and in the feeling of many senior secondary pupils that Jewish education is an unnecessary burden to be avoided if possible.

This crisis situation requires a lessening of concern with the absolute or relative numbers of children attending Jewish schools – i.e., quantitative considerations – and an increased concern with the quality of Jewish education. Three aspects call for special attention:

- influencing and educating parents about their children's need for Jewish education, and encouraging them to become partners in this Jewish educational development;

- influencing and educating teachers – in both the professional and the emotional-ideological spheres – to have faith and conviction in the task entrusted to them; and
- encouraging re-examination of the formal Jewish educational structures and their modes of operation, and promoting the development of new educational structures and methods. Encouragement of educational changes and innovation should include attention to experiential teaching and learning and to critical thinking.

Research Implications

In order to best understand the existing Jewish educational system and introduce extensive improvements, in-depth and comprehensive research is required in the following areas:
- research on educational aims. This includes investigation of the actual aims of Jewish schools by studying what is done in classrooms and within the school walls, as compared with the stated aims of agencies involved in maintaining the schools;
- attitude studies, such as: attitudes of parents and pupils toward major subjects relating to existence and survival of the Jewish people; attitudes of pupils and graduates toward specific subjects which schools regard as important, in order to evaluate the school's effectiveness; and attitudes of parents and pupils to Jewish education as it is today and as they would like it to be;
- studies of the informal educational frameworks and the reciprocal relationships between the informal and formal educational system.

Acknowledgements

This chapter was drawn upon data from interviews by the author in 1981–82 with Rafi Shaniak, regarding Jewish education in Venezuela; Bracha Margolis Shilkolevsky and Juana Umansky Gaishtott, directors of Jewish studies and general studies at the Integral School in Montevideo, Uruguay; Eli Ayoun, *shaliah* and principal at the Integral School in Montevideo; Avraham Magenzo, principal of the Jewish school in Santiago, Chile; Yitzhak Bergstein, principal of the Jewish school in Viña del Mar, Chile; Arie Lovel, principal of the Jewish School in Lima, Peru; Yizhak Magnes, teacher-*shaliah* at the Jewish School in Quito, Ecuador. Margalit Bejarano has permitted use of source material on Cuba, which she obtained for her own research.

Notes

1. An influential factor was the increase in hours of instruction at state high schools, which left no time for supplementary Jewish studies (Reicher, 1973).

2. During this period, non-Jewish private schools also strengthened and expanded considerably, due to the political and security situation.

3. The *Yiddishe Shule* founded in 1924, and the Monterrey School in 1935.

4. The Autonomous School which was state-incorporated in 1939.

5. Yavneh School and *Tarbut* School (1942), Monte Sinai Community School (1943), *Tarbut Sephardi* School (1944), *Zedaka Umarpe* School (1949), *Naie Yiddische Shule* (1950).

6. One school in Santiago in 1944, and another in Valparaiso in 1948.

7. In 1941.

8. The Moral y Luces-Herzl Bialik School (1946).

9. Leon Pinelo School (1946).

10. Hebrew Union School (1946).

11. Jorge Isaacs Hebrew School (1945).

12. Theodore Herzl Hebrew School which commenced in 1947 with the opening of its Tel Aviv Kindergarten.

13. Yavneh Schools sponsored by *Mizrachi*.

14. The school conducted by the New Jewish Community (Nueva Comunidad Israelita) in Montevideo.

15. The *Machzikei Hadat* School in Montevideo, the Yeshiva de Mexico, and others.

16. Sholem Aleichem School in Montevideo, conducted by the left-wing *Poalei Zion*.

17. *Yiddishe Shule* in Mexico.

18. *Tarbut* School in Mexico. The *Yiddishe Shule* and the *Tarbut* School in Mexico are supported by *Hashomer Hatzair, Poalei Zion*, and the General Zionists.

19. *Naie Yiddishe Shule* in Mexico, supported by the Bundists.

20. The *Folk Shule* network (supported by Jewish Communists) which operated in Montevideo of which the Dr. Haim Zhitlowsky School was the most prominent.

21. For example, the supplementary school of the La Fraternidad community in Mexico, where in the 1930s, the language of instruction for religious studies was Arabic.

22. The *Tarbut Sepharadi* or Monte Sinai Schools in Mexico.

23. Education legislation enacted in the late 1970s divided the final three years of high school into scientific and humanistic streams.

24. For example, by making donations to private schools tax deductable.

25. Although this teachers' seminary is open to all graduates of Jewish schools, the requirement that candidates have a knowledge of Yiddish effectively precludes Sephardic and Oriental candidates.

26. The Rambam School in Caracas and the Jewish school in Maracaibo are not affiliated with the Education Committee.

27. Besides the evidence from the author's interviews relating to Uruguay, Chile, Peru, Ecuador and Venezuela, Dr. Haim Constantiner of Mexico has said that "at the *Tarbut* School, they discerned a deterioration in the field of Jewish studies. It is necessary to introduce changes of content and system" (Rinot, 1979, p. 2).

28. Ginzberg (1964, p. 16): "The erosion of religious values has had a great influence on Jewish education, which was always connected to and rooted in, the preservation of the faith...one cannot nurture the education of the young unless the parents are interested in preserving the traditional values. Yet many parents are more concerned for the social values of their class than for specifically Jewish values."

29. This applies particularly to the schools in Colombia (Smith, 1972, p. 125).

30. Intensive supplementary education refers to Jewish studies of 15–20 hours each week, 4 to 5 days per week, from kindergarten to the completion of secondary school.

31. During the 1930s and early 1940s, a number of supplementary education networks were maintained in Mexico City by Jewish immigrants from Damascus and Aleppo, by the *Nidchei Yisrael* Ashkenazic community which ran a religious-nationalist Talmud Torah, and the Talmud Torah of the Orthodox Ashkenazim.

32. In the case of Colombia, in accordance with the law, the day school provided Catholic education for gentile pupils until the mid–1970s.

33. Lack of verified data from many of the schools makes it difficult to obtain a clear, exact or even a picture on this issue.

34. Such as the Teachers' Seminary established in Mexico City in 1946 on the initiative of the educator Abraham Golomb.

35. As in Uruguay from the late 1950s.

36. For example, weekly or fortnightly meetings for lectures, seminars, workshops and practical exercises plus study seminars in Israel, as well as specific reading programs in the Everyman's University style.

37. As in Montevideo, where a graduate of a *Dor Hemshech* program established a study group in the Ashkenazic community, and in Chile where graduates of the Santiago program set up similar classes in Viña del Mar.

38. As in Santiago where, in cooperation with the school, a study group composed entirely of teachers was organized to study Jewish history according to the Everyman's University system.

39. As in Mexico, with a group of teachers and professional community leaders from the *Beit Hayeladim* School, which operates on the Montessori system.

40. See Rinot (1979). Also interview with Rafi Shaniak, Coordinator of joint program at Moral y Luces-Herzl Bialik School in Caracas.

References

Ginzberg, E. (1964). *Agenda for American Jews*. Columbia University, Kings Crown Press, New York.

Harel, E. (1969). "Finf Yor Shlichus in di Tfutzes". *Naie Yiddishe Shul Yorbuch*, 20.

Hodara, J. (1977). "La Estructuracion Comunitaria en Mexico: El Caso del Colegio Hebreo Tarbut" in: Kovadloff, J. (ed.). *Comunidades Judias de Latino America 1973–1975*. Comite Judio Americano, Instituto de Relaciones Humanas, Buenos Aires.

Kovadloff, J., ed. (1974). *Comunidades Judias de Latino America 1971–1972*. Comite Judio Americano, Instituto de Relaciones Humanas, Buenos Aires.

Reicher, P. (1973). *Hahinuch Hayehudi B'Uruguay (Jewish Education in Uruguay)*. David Horowitz Institute for the Study of Developing Countries, Tel Aviv University, Tel Aviv.

Rinot, H. (1979). *Beit Sefer Hoter leShinui*. Project Tarbut-Yerushalayim 1970–1977, Jerusalem.

Rinot, H. (1981). *Iyunim betahalichei Shinui Beit Sefer Yehudi*. Jerusalem.

Rogovsky, A. and Tishbi, S. (1976). *Hinuch Yehudi V'zehut Yehudit B'arzot America Halatinit*. David Horowitz Institute for the Study of Developing Countries, Tel Aviv University, Tel Aviv.

Rubinstein, M. (1953). "Eltliche iker frages fun unzere Shulvezn". *Unzer Shul Yorbuch*, 17.

Smith, J.K. (1972). *Jewish Education in Colombia: Group Survival versus Assimilation*. University of Wisconsin, Wisconsin.

Di Stime (17.2.1945). "Di Shverikaitn fun a lerer".

Vorzogger, H. (1970). "Der Yiddisher Hinuch in Uruguay – Vos s'iz geven un vos s'iz faranen". *Hessed leAvraham – Sefer hayovel leAvraham Golomb*. Los Angeles.

Zadoff, E. (1974). *Ha'Cooperativim leashrai hayehudiyim beArgentina, u'tmichatam bachinuch hayehudi'*. Unpublished manuscript, Jerusalem.

Zadoff, E. (1980). *Ideological Trends in Secular Jewish Education in Mexico and Argentina 1935–1955*. Unpublished M.A. thesis, The Hebrew University, Jerusalem. (Hebrew).

Jewish Education in Latin America: Two Comments

Haim Barylko

Education is doing. Of course, ever since the Jewish people spoke at Sinai of doing and listening, the camp has been split between doers and listeners, with the listening being interpreted in many ways – all of them referring to thought, speech, understanding, or, in the words of Rabbeinu Bahye, the obligation of the heart.

When life is lived more or less wholly and healthily, doing dominates over listening. When everyday doubts arise in daily life, the listening takes precedence over the doing, for of necessity one must reconsider where one is going. In a shattered and diverse world, one has no choice but to think, to listen, to speak up and to search for meaning – precisely because the description of accepted meaning has collapsed.

Education takes place in this world of uncertainty and searching. But education has no other alternative: doing or failure. Achieve something or else nothing. Such a situation does not rule out thought and enquiry - that is, 'speaking of education' becomes education.

Ever since we entered the Western world, starting from the Emancipation and its offshoots, Jewish education has had its thinkers, but it has no thought-out being. Moreover, ever since Jewish education has become a matter of concern, its path has been one of cessation, despair, degeneration, and getting lost in fog.

This is a fact. It is not vital to explain it or justify it. It is a fact that if, on the one hand, we review all the giant efforts which have been devoted to Jewish education and, on the other hand, the situation these efforts have created, we shall have to admit and confess that we went astray and led others astray: every one of us has gone his own way, and we haven't done anything. We've spoken, announced, argued; we've gotten bogged down in parlors over a kind of analytic philosophy of word mysteries, such as 'Jewish,' 'Zionist', 'National', 'formative', 'creative'. And we have even cried. We've cried over those not getting their education from us. We've cried over assimilation. We've spoken. We've licked our tears – over the gentile, the far-off, the wicked son. Speakers, prophets, rabbis, leaders, kabbalists and boors – they have all become experts in continuation, that is, education. Review it again.

Behind the scenes they sit, modest and shy, the educators – the only people really doing education. The forgotten ones. They will continue to do. At this point, we can reverse our calculations: if we compare the educators' doing – those doing education – with the indifference or lack of support of the Lords of Education, we have to rejoice and recite *Hallel* for despite everything, there is Jewish education, even good education, even very good. It is still active, an action and activity worthy of our hopes.

* * *

What is education? In terms of educational thought, education is innumerable psychological, anthropological, philosophical and social observations and formulations. In terms of educational doing, education is a teacher-educator-counsellor who meets a group of people and does something with them.

It is best to limit the doing to this realistic-minimalistic-materialistic description. To do something. Someone, doing something with someone else. Once a week, or five times a week. One hour or 20 hours a week. Continuously for eight to ten months per year. And if you wish, and if you succeed, continuously for a few consecutive years. Something to do. To do something.

These definitions, which grate against the delicate ear accustomed to Plato, Pestalozzi, Buber, I did not discover in books or in lectures, but rather in work. In the practice of education for 25 years, I discovered that my major problem in class, with students or members of youth groups, is what to do.

My hesitations are not philosophical, but rather extremely pragmatic. You are a teacher. You have undertaken to educate. You walk into the classroom. It is a 45 minute period. What are you going to do? How will you do it? In summary: how will you salvage 45 minutes from boredom, from loss, from existential failure, from disappointment for you and for others?

What to do? To do something. Choose principles and ideologies for yourself. One holds a Zionist leaflet, another believes in universalist secularism, and a third in traditional nationality.

Have you chosen? Are you already aware of your principles, your ideas, your ambitions? Now do, realize, raise up flesh and tendons for them, reality. There are 45 minutes before you. What are you going to do with them? We're discussing Jewish education in the Diaspora. Non-compulsory education. Education which is completely voluntary, a matter of free choice.

These students and their parents expect something special of Jewish education. They don't relate to you as they do to other teachers in other schools, in the state education systems. There, when they don't find satisfaction, they take the child out of the school and look for another school for him. There it's not the education which fails, only perhaps the educators.

With us, in all kinds of Jewish education, if we don't succeed in what we do, it's Jewish education that has failed, and the pupil will not transfer to another school, another system, but will rather transfer out and disappear, and after him many more.

Forty-five minutes. There is a lesson facing you. Do something with it – something good. Something to attract the heart of the student, and the spirit of his parents. If we do not do, we will not succeed.

* * *

The indifferent parents who do not send their children to our schools are surely worthy of condemnation. Now let's look at the education and see how attractive it is. We don't do anything. I shall not add adjectives such as 'good', 'nice', 'attractive'. I shall describe what we do not do.

Every expert in education can enter an educational book store and get a series of texts to study English, French and so on. Is this also true of the Hebrew language? No. "We don't do anything" means there is no set of books, no program, no graduated curriculum for studying Hebrew for, let's say, seven consecutive years, from six years of age until bar mitzvah age. There is none! There are books, very many books. But one planned, organized and systematic set of books for doing Jewish education does not exist. Efforts there are, even too many. Organic fruit developing from beginning to end – there is none.

We don't do anything – order, discipline, planning, research, thoughts of doing, rules of doing. Jewish pluralism can hardly explain the situation and justify it. One can argue about hundreds of matters, what should be given and what shouldn't be given the child before us. However, each ideology is capable of creating its own system to meet the needs of its doing and its rules. And yet, there is no system of doing.

Not for teaching Hebrew. Not for Jewish history. Not for a few chapters from the Bible, undisputed by anyone. We are capable and yet, apparently incapable.

Our educational doing belies the rhetorical concern of the entire Jewish people, its heads and leaders, its worriers and functionaries, for education. Jewish education is made up of doing; there is no other, it alone exists. Glorious and poor at the same time. Heroism – and sadness.

* * *

"Moses left us the Torah.

A legacy for the community of Jacob."

Text. Education = doing = text. When I enter the classroom, tell me what to do in the classroom. Didactic, psychology, general instructions are insufficient for me. Not how or in what way, but what. This comes first. The Jewish people understood the concept of 'Torah' as a fundamental text, a clear, tangible basis for content, a curriculum. This is the educational 'what'.

Text. Upon it one builds mountains. According to it, you form creative education, develop thought, or repeat it over and over again in absolute automatism. Everyone according to his own method. Text. You choose it. And you choose from it.

Rashi's first comment to the Torah hints that the stories of creation are secondary to the list of commandments beginning with "This month is for you..." Choose it and choose in it. Emphasize your line: Zionist, religious, nationalist, traditional, universal-moral, philosophical, historical.

A text. What. By means of slides, films, or old, faded books. By adding recordings, using group methods, research projects, or by reading one Biblical verse and repeating it twice in translation. A text.

"Moses left us the Torah.

A legacy for the community of Jacob." From this one should learn the nature of the desired text. It is authoritative. It has special value. The community authorizes it.

Education at the service of the values of the community – the society. But this community, that of Jacob, is defined by this Torah, this text, and views this 'what' as its substance. An authorized text.

This is what Jewish education was. A discipline of text and freedom of action around the text. Freedom of commentary, freedom of method, freedom of didactics, of choice. This is what Jewish education was when the Jewish people was the People of the Book, i.e., the owner of a basic text upon which it built its life and education, which is only a tool, a means of life.

Slogans such as "Choose yourself a rabbi, and purchase yourself a friend" alongside "set up many pupils", and all these based upon Torah-legacy, acceptance – served as a clear, strong entirety. They knew the goal, for they knew what. They had a text, and from it and after it many texts, sons and grandsons of the text – the Book.

Out of 'what' comes the goal. Out of doing. When one knows what to do, the why and wherefore of doing so converge. Education is doing. How much more is this true of Jewish education?

And this is the main point of my modest discovery made after 25 years of teaching and doing in a classroom – it is, after all, identical throughout communications theory: the means is the goal. In simple language: tell me what you teach, and I'll tell you what your goal is in teaching, in educating.

The opposite is also true. As the *Zohar* puts it: the body is the garment of the soul. For the *Zohar*, the soul is, indeed, the main thing. The kind of soul is decisive in the education of the body. In the kabbala, there are bared souls which precede the body, and which remain behind after it. In education and in life, the body/the dress/the 'what' testifies to the substance of the soul.

In short, a fixed text determines:
– the existence of education;
– that this education aims at some goal;
– that the way to realize this goal is found in this text.

Bring education! – call forth those who understand, the ideologists. Bring me a text!

* * *

The problem of this generation is not, precisely, its confusion and bitterness towards the past and the Torah we inherited. This generation lacks Torah. Any Torah. A text, a fundamental, an accepted authority, and a formulated one.

Without Torah there can be no lasting education. This Torah, this law, or another one. I repeat this definition: a basis, an authority, a formulated text, a tangible, material one, and not just a collection of ideas.

Ideas are souls fluttering in the air. "A song is not written ideas, but words" – explained the poet Mallarmé. Jewish education does not lack ideas, but rather it lacks texts. It is as simple as that.

We know, in exciting pathos, where we want to arrive, what we want to achieve. There is no real hardship in constructing texts for this purpose. Yet there is hardship: diverse, strained, one here and one there, and every one born – diverse texts, sections of sections, a maximal dispersion of searches and inventions with no roof, classrooms, or common ground. Without a curriculum.

From generalities to details. This generation demands Zionist education. Some support the idea, others oppose it. I support it, because I support all Jewish education. I ask: tell me what, how. Give me a text, that is, a program, a work-plan, 45 minutes for each lesson.

I have before me a list of many lessons. I have to do something for Zionist education, in any educational form whatever. Yet the Zionist camp has not done anything for realistic Zionist education, besides speeches, sermons, accusations, and passing on responsibility to others.

There has been, there is, and there will be Zionist education, or any other kind of education you prefer, for there have been, are, and will be educators doing something in their classrooms. And so it seems that the educational act can be Zionist in content, without being so by declaration.

Or in reverse, you can support Bundism, and to this end, introduce Peretz's stories into your classes, and then despite one's declarations, it will turn out that you teach, you educate in the spirit of Grandfather Israel, full of the spirit of the tradition and the nation, our history and the Messianic dream.

The doing determines the ideology. Alongside one's opinion of education, there is also an opinion stemming from education. The only reality is this latter.

Another example: he who claims that national, traditional, or Zionist education can be given without the Hebrew language, according to a basis he determines, is mistaken. If the text is not national, or traditional, or Zionist (and the Hebrew language serves these three possibilities), then the education will only be indirect, a kiss in a letter, discussing something but not tasting it.

On the contrary, give out Amihai in Hebrew, and a selection of commandments 'between man and his fellow man' in Hebrew, and Ephraim Kishon in Hebrew, and Ber Borochov in Hebrew , and declare your internationalist leanings, or your Marxist humanism, and so on. It won't work.

The text is decisive along with your opinions of the text. The inside and outside of the text. Amihai's heretical Hebrew contributes more to the acquisition of the Jewish tradition than any article about Maimonides in some pure, international foreign tongue.

I don't think there's any room here for argument. The means determines the goal. The beginning testifies to the end.

*   *   *

These pedagogic contemplations did not come to me out of the blue but rather from my direct, personal experience. It is the experience of a generation which, like any other generation, is interwoven into the fabric of generations, in the plural. Without extensive checks and hypotheses about how and why Jewish education developed as it did, it would be best to go straight to describing existing conditions.

Of course, it is desirable to begin with Argentina itself. When you enter *Beit Hatefutsot* in Tel Aviv, you learn a clear and decided chapter in law; our environmental context makes us and grafts its colors onto us:

– in Argentina education is free, from kindergarten to university;

– in Argentina a 'private school' is an institution which has no meaning for the existence and reality of popular awareness. In other words, it is intended for minorities with money or understanding or certain family ties;

– in Argentina, government education embraces the entire population, from the woodcutter to the leaders of the people;

- in Argentina, according to the estimate of Argentine citizens, state schooling ranges from good to very good;
- in Argentina, Jewish education, in the general set-up, is exceptional because it costs money, and a lot of money at that; and because, in addition to the economic effort, it requires spiritual efforts and even material efforts. For example, there is a government school wherever you look, whereas a Jewish school requires transport, a time loss, and a child leaving home at 7.30 a.m. and returning home at 6.00 p.m.;
- in countries like Peru, Mexico and Venezuela, one has no choice: Jewish education is almost forced on you by the public at large because there is nothing but private schooling. The choice, there, is a question of which private school. The Jew is inside the alternative. In Argentina, Jewish education must be chosen freely against the natural stream of economic, pedagogic and social conditions. It is a completely voluntary decision, and if it is not characterized by dedication, then it does entail a kind of sacrifice in certain areas;
- if the estimate is correct that in Argentina there are some 250,000 Jews, then two-thirds of the students begin in the educational system;
- this educational system provides 15 hours per week of Jewish studies;
- the studies are in Hebrew. For a time they were offered both in Yiddish and in Hebrew, and at present Yiddish is still favored in a number of schools. Texts are in Hebrew, speech is Hebrew, as are writing, conversation, commentaries, games, songs and dancing. Everything is directly from its source, whether the Torah, Rashi, H.N. Bialik, or A.B. Yehoshua;
- in Argentina the religious institutions did not become dominant and did not play a central role in community life including, therefore, education;
- secularism was expressed at the beginning of the century even as an anti-religious struggle, but this aspect of secularism gradually faded away. Placing Jewish sources and Hebrew language at the center of Jewish education worked against secularist ideology. This is the irony I have already pointed out: the educational act sometimes belies the idea which gave it birth;
- Argentina's strong point (because Argentina had and still has social strata – the proletariat and middle class – to a degree unknown in other Latin American countries) is its many teachers. Thousands of Hebrew teachers grew up in Argentina, were educated there, and many of them have already emigrated to Israel, others are still doing so, and they continue to work as teachers;
- textual education is progressing and drawing ideologies after it. It is already generally known that without knowledge of the textual sources there is no hope for any ideology desirous of being considered Jewish.

This is why it no longer seems ridiculous in a 'secular' framework to teach the siddur, and to learn Torah with Rashi's commentary, Midrash, Maimonides' 'Eight Chapters' and so on. According to the texts, the education is of a religious nature. According to the declaration, it's secular. Which is right? Naturally, the educational act.

Let me quickly say: it is not religious, it is Jewish. There is no other Jewish education than that which is Jewish, from Jewish sources. The taste of the texts is like the taste of manna. You define it. Why specifically 'religious'? Is Rashi's commentary to *Genesis I, 1* religious or Zionist?

The modern world helps us. It is already permitted to be and to live outside the borders of science. It is already known that human values have their roots 'elsewhere'.

The theory of symbols is gaining ground at present in the world of thought. This is a good thing. Suddenly we are allowed to be Jews in our Judaism without ultrarational explanations. The hour of the nightingale has come.

It is at present possible to begin the text "In the beginning..." without enlightened and cultured people shuddering at the threat of a theology of the Middle Ages. All modern philosophies allow us to provide Jewish education without apologizing.

Moreover, the example I deduced from Argentinian education testifies that:
- students tire of empty thoughts and abstract ideas;
- there is no need to be religious or to believe, in order to deeply enjoy a midrash or a page of Gemara;
- choose the correct text for the correct student in the correct way, and education will succeed.

*   *   *

After these thoughts, each reader may re-evaluate his reality, the educational reality closest to him, body and spirit.

The time has now come to strengthen all the various systems: religious-in-a-foreign-tongue, the original-Hebrew-secular, speaking about Judaism, speaking Judaism; declaration and deeds; I want, I can; speakers of education and educators. Every healthy mind viewing Jewish education abroad can adopt a Berditchev style and eulogize: "Be happy, O Israel, that you still have the *Qamatz Alef,* that there are still tens of thousands of children from the babbling of whose mouths we have drawn our life, that we can still hear half-verses here and there, a passage on philosophy, and even a few sentences in not such bad Hebrew..."

At any rate...perhaps it is possible to do more, to repair, to improve? Maybe it really is possible to build a few programs (according to ideological streams) from start to finish, using the Hebrew language, from the kindergarten level to bar mitzvah? And perhaps also in Jewish history? And maybe even in Zionism or Zionist education. Is it possible?

Moshe Nes-El

A definitive study of Jewish education in Latin America will reveal what I view as the heroic struggle of the few to prevent the disappearance of the remnants of the Jewish people on the Latin American continent.

Jewish immigration to Latin America was the result of the poverty and oppression to which Jews were subjected in Eastern Europe and other parts of the Old World. The masses who reached the New World wanted freedom, and the opportunity to radically improve their academic condition. Both goals were attainable on the new continent. Thus, it is not surprising that many of the immigrants desired to assimilate in their new homelands. The process of assimilation was slower and of smaller scope in those places where large scale immigration was organized by charitable and other Jewish institutions. On the other hand, nearly total assimilation occurred in the course of a few years in those places where Jews arrived in smaller numbers with no organizational backing.

The wave of immigration also included a number of idealists who wished to strengthen Jewish life on the Latin American continent. The ideological backgrounds of these idealists were varied. There were individuals from the religious, Socialist, Bundist, and even Communist camps, but all viewed the education of the next generation as supremely important. They were among the first to be actively involved in Jewish education – either by entering the already established educational networks of the Jewish charitable or immigration agencies, or by founding heders and independent study groups which met in the afternoon or evening after public school hours. In some of these settings, the children of the immigrants even learned to read Hebrew. In others, Jewish education was limited to the study of Bible stories or Jewish history.

Despite the development of these schools and the increased participation of the *Kehillot* and other Jewish organizations, the educational endeavor achieved only partial success. The majority of Jewish children did not attend these schools, and the schools themselves had serious shortcomings, including the lack of trained teachers, and the absence of curricula and textbooks. The entire enterprise was carried out in an amateurish fashion. Nonetheless, in spite of the difficulties, education workers continued to improve both the standards and the physical settings of the schools. Their efforts were rewarded, even if only partially, and today we have spacious functional schools in most Latin American countries. Educational methods, textbooks and the level of teaching have also improved.

Two events have strengthened Jewish education in Latin America since the beginning of the 1940s:
- the conversion of afternoon schools into day schools where secular studies are taught according to the governmental curricula; and
- the establishment of the State of Israel which brought about a Zionist orientation in the Jewish schools and closer ties with Israel, developed through the education departments of the World Zionist Organization.

Although first steps have been taken, much remains to be done. The following are my suggestions for possible ways of strengthening and broadening Jewish education on the Latin American continent.

1. The number of pupils in existing educational institutions must be increased, especially at the high school level. As an incentive for pupils to continue on to Jewish high schools, courses of study, ensuring acceptance of pupils to Israeli universities and institutions of higher learning, should be set up. At present, the criteria for acceptance at Israeli institutions of higher learning make no distinction between pupils graduating from public or Jewish schools. This situation calls for the creation of a matriculation degree for Jewish schools in the Diaspora, which will provide an incentive for Jewish pupils to study in Jewish high schools.

2. A standardized curriculum should be developed for use by *shlihim* and teachers in the Diaspora. At present, with the exception of Argentina, the situation is anarchic, and there is no continuity between the work of one *shaliah* and the next with regard to Hebrew language, Bible, or history. Confusion is created by the fact that a pupil who completes twelve years of study may change both his teacher, and the texts and methods used, up to four times.

3. Local personnel should be recruited as Jewish educators. The profession of Jewish educator exists, but working conditions are poor, and the pedagogical and Jewish knowledge of the teachers does not meet the needs of the schools. In addition, the low salaries paid to Jewish educators prevent the attraction of more qualified personnel.

4. Experienced educational personnel should be encouraged to attend in-service courses in Israel, and these programs should be expanded. The ultimate goal is that every Jewish educator attend at least one such course in Israel. The present situation is deplorable – there are principals of large Jewish schools who have never visited Israel, or whose visits took place many years ago, and were not connected with their profession. In recent years, such

in-service courses have been held for teachers from Argentina, Uruguay, Brazil, Chile, Mexico and Venezuela. The positive effects are evident in these countries. However, there are places where such programs have not yet been organized, and in the countries where programs have been held, there is still room for improvement.

5. The visitor to Jewish schools on the Latin American continent is struck by the general lack of school libraries and modern teaching aids. However, conditions vary from country to country. In some places, schools are well equipped, while in others, the schools have almost no equipment. Education centers do exist in Argentina, Uruguay, and Brazil (in Rio de Janeiro and Sao Paolo). Yet, even in those places where education centers exist, there is no guarantee that they will be fully utilized, or that schools will establish libraries for their pupils.

6. Moreover, the school must also serve as a community center where extracurricular activities for pupils and programs for parents take place. In recent years, some experiments in this direction have been carried out, but much remains to be done.

The purpose of these remarks has been to outline the past, present, and future of Jewish education in Latin America. Various other forces influence both the educational work itself, and the making of future plans. These forces of change include general legislation, the economic situation and internal communal processes.

In conclusion, we can cite the tens of thousands of Jews from Latin America who are now living in Israel as the best indication that despite the as yet unmet challenges, Jewish education there has borne fruit.

Part Four

Western Europe

The Jewish communities of Western Europe do not form one integrated unit. The countries in this region are separated by different linguistic and cultural traditions. Historical and sociological factors have created significant differences in the structure of Jewish communities, carrying implications for Jewish education and other communal institutions. Nevertheless, European Jewish communities do share some common patterns and interests and in recent years there has been increased economic and organizational cooperation.

Adrian Ziderman, Professor of Economics at Bar Ilan University, has written the chapter on Jewish education in Great Britain. The Anglo-Jewish community and educational system were comparatively less affected by World War II than most Jewish communities of the continent. The structure of Jewish education seems to be more a product of changing orientations in general British education and the relative strength of the dual and somewhat opposing goals of British Jewry to integrate fully into British society, while maintaining a distinct Jewish identity. Ziderman points out that this ideological perspective has resulted in missed opportunities for greater government support of Jewish day schools in Great Britain, where the Jewish supplementary school system still predominates, although less than in the United States.

In chapter 9 the efforts of Lucien Lazare, an experienced French Jewish educator, and Yair Auron, an Israeli educational researcher, are combined to analyze Jewish education in France. France today has the third largest Jewish community in the Diaspora after the United States and the USSR. French Jewry, perhaps the most secularized Jewish community in Western Europe in this century, has undergone dramatic change due to a great influx of more traditional Jews from North Africa during the 1950s and 1960s. It has had trouble establishing and supporting enough Jewish schools to accommodate all of those who might attend. France has the lowest overall Jewish school enrollment rate of any Western country. Yet, its current rate has substantially increased from a decade ago.

The final chapter in this part is a brief overview of Jewish education in the other Jewish communities of Western Europe. Some of these smaller communities have undergone dramatic changes since World War II, and have been rebuilding their communal structures and institutions. Many suffer from the constraints of small size. Yet, a remarkable effort of recuperation and revitalization has been deployed after the devastation of war. Stanley Abramovitch, who has worked closely with these communities as an educational consultant for the American Jewish Joint Distribution Committee, details the current status of Jewish education in these countries and the events that have affected them.

8

Jewish Education in Great Britain

Adrian Ziderman

The Jewish educational scene in Britain is a mosaic of contrasts. Currently, over 30,000 children, comprising about 55–60% of all Jewish children of compulsory school age, are enrolled within the formal Jewish educational framework, while over 2,000 more children attend Jewish nursery schools, the majority of which are attached to Jewish day schools.

The education provided in these schools varies markedly in scope, sponsorship, philosophy and, most significantly, in achievement and effectiveness. The institutions range from full-time Jewish day and boarding schools and yeshivoth (37%) to part-time Sunday morning or midweek centers usually attached to synagogues (50%), and to Jewish religious instruction 'withdrawal' classes provided by the Jewish educational authorities in non-Jewish secondary schools (13%).

All of the full-time institutions, particularly the day schools, are in varying degree religiously orthodox in orientation, though not necessarily in their organizational sponsorship. 'Withdrawal classes' are the province of the central Orthodox education institutions. The Progressive streams of Judaism are involved only in part-time Jewish educational centers. The Reform sections of the community (roughly parallel to the left-of-center Conservative Judaism in America) and the Liberal sections (equivalent to American Reform) account for some 35% of the children enrolled in the part-time sector.

The origins of this educational patchwork parallel the growth and the development of the organized Jewish community in Britain as a whole. Levin (1970) provides a lively account of the historical origins of Jewish education in Britain, while Steinberg (1965) describes more recent developments.

The Societal and Communal Context of Jewish Schooling

Anglo-Jewry is a community in numerical decline. The Research Unit of the Board of Deputies of British Jews – the central representative body of

Anglo-Jewry – recently assessed the size and structure of Anglo-Jewry during the late 1970s (Haberman, Kosmin and Levy, 1983). The Unit estimated[1] that in 1977 the Anglo-Jewish population was 354,000, plus or minus 32,000. Compared with the Unit's estimate of 410,000 for 1960–65, this represents an average annual net loss of 0.88%.

Jewish birth and fertility rates, and synagogue marriages, are both indicators and causes of the numerical decline in the Anglo-Jewish population. In recent decades, synagogue marriages have declined in absolute number, in proportion to the community's size, and in comparison with general marriage rates.[2] An increasing number of Jews marry in civil ceremonies, and the majority of these marriages presumably involve a non-Jewish partner. Since in Britain conversion to Judaism is rare intermarriage often involves a loss to the Jewish community of the Jewish partner and of potential offspring. Moreover, the low Jewish birthrate - which is lower both than that of the general population, and than the required rate for population replacement – further adds to the strong downward pressures on the size of the Anglo-Jewish population.

The population trends are highly relevant to considerations of Jewish education since, on the one hand, they imply a declining target population of Jewish school children[3] and, on the other hand, they highlight the crucial need for Jewish education to counteract some of the causes of this population decline.

Anglo-Jewry's high degree of social and geographic mobility also has important implications for Jewish education. The upward social mobility is demonstrated by the replacement – within one generation – of predominantly working class lifestyles and values by middle class ones. Although there remain substantial numbers of Jews of lower socio-economic status in such London working class districts as Hackney and Stepney, the predominantly middle class ethos of the Anglo-Jewish community today is unmistakable. To illustrate, the considerable Jewish trade union and radical working class activities during the early years of this century (Fishman, 1975) stand in marked contrast to the minimal amount of such activities at the present time.

Because of this middle class orientation, and also because of the very high (middle class) value placed on general educational attainment, even in otherwise predominantly working class families seeking upward mobility, English Jews have availed themselves of the secular educational opportunities offered by the dramatic expansion of general education since World War II. For example, Jewish representation in the high-quality academic state schools is far in excess of that expected from the number of young Jews in the relevant age-group. Similarly, studies of Jews in the 1950s indicate the proportion of Jewish students to be more than three times that expected on the basis of Jewish population figures.

This pursuit of secular educational achievement may well have been to the detriment of Jewish religious education. In aspiring to high levels of academic success and entry into choice schools on the next rung of the educational ladder, heavy inroads were made into the available leisure time of Jewish pupils attending secular schools. One effect is that part-time Jewish education centers, which compete with other activities for the limited leisure time of Jewish youngsters, show declining attendance, particularly among teenagers. It follows that many Jewish youngsters obtain only minimal Jewish education, often insufficiently robust to answer the challenges to traditional Jewish values and practice which are posed during – and which arise directly from – their secular education.

An extremely high level of geographical mobility parallels, and partly reflects, Anglo-Jewry's upward social mobility. With some three-quarters of the community residing in the five largest cities and 69% in London alone, Anglo-Jewry's high geographical mobility is evident both in the overall drift (particularly of younger families) from provincial towns to the metropolis and in the movement from the old inner-city traditional centers of Jewish concentration to the more geographically dispersed developing suburban areas. These trends have led to the need for increasing concentration of Jewish educational facilities in the London area. At the same time, this fluidity of Jewish population movement in the metropolis has rendered the efficient planning of Jewish education to meet this need an ever more difficult task.

Religious Orientation

The hegemony of the Orthodox religious trend in the life and affairs of the community is particularly marked. Whereas Orthodoxy in the United States represents a minority trend, in Britain, the various Orthodox groupings account for some 80% of the community – that is, the majority of the identifying Jewish population, whether measured in terms of synagogue affiliation, synagogue marriages or burials. The large majority of Jews are affiliated with the Orthodox community via membership in synagogues attached to one of the Orthodox synagogue groupings, such as the dominant United Synagogue or the smaller waning Federation of Synagogues.

Orthodox affiliation does not necessarily mean orthodox practices. Indeed, the majority of Jews affiliated with the Orthodox synagogues are lax about such practices as kashruth and regular Sabbath synagogue attendance. Nonetheless, the community is predominantly Orthodox in institutional orientation. Virtually all major community institutions observe kashruth and the Sabbath, and acknowledge the authority (and leadership) of the Orthodox Chief Rabbi (technically, the Chief Rabbi of the London-based United Synagogue). The central-Orthodox umbrella has proved sufficiently broad to encompass both strictly observant, religiously-educated Orthodox Jews, as well as groups who in the American context would be found within the Conservative fold. The inherently conservative and highly traditional ethos of Anglo-Jewry has actually acted as a bulwark against any threatened inroads of the American Conservative movement into the religious life of Anglo-Jewry. The dominance of Orthodoxy extends also into the Jewish educational scene where, parental religious orientation notwithstanding, virtually all Jewish day school pupils attend Orthodox schools.

In recent years the balance between the Orthodox and Progressive sectors of Anglo-Jewry has remained fairly stable, at 80% and 20% respectively. The Orthodox community itself is, however, far from homogeneous or stable in structure. One of the remarkable trends over recent years has been the increasing strength of the strictly Orthodox, the right-wing elements of Orthodoxy. For example, some 8% of all synagogue marriages take place today in right-wing Orthodox synagogues (over double the group's percentage of total male synagogue membership). This compares with only 2.5% of all synagogue marriages being performed in right-wing Orthodox synagogues two decades ago. Similarly, the average size of the right-wing Orthodox family (2.7) is not only higher than that of the rest of the Jewish community but larger than that of the general population. The move toward the right within the Anglo-Jewish Orthodox community is now clearly discernible and has many facets. The popularity of yeshiva study at the post-school level reflects this trend to the right. It has been estimated that well over 1,000 British youngsters are currently engaged in full-time courses of Jewish religious studies at strictly Orthodox seminaries and yeshivoth in England or abroad – more than double the number a decade or two ago, and comprising about 10% of the estimated total number of Jewish students attending universities.

Thus while the community as a whole is slowly declining numerically, the trends leading towards the increasing absolute size and influence of the right-wing element suggest that the Anglo-Jewry of the future will be smaller in size but more religiously committed.

The Jewish Education System

The Historical Background

The passing of the Foster Education Act of 1870, under which elementary education in Britain became compulsory, constitutes a milestone in the history of both Jewish and general education in Britain. The Act led to the establishment of the network of non-denominational 'Board' (i.e. State) Schools, supported by the public sector, which in time dominated the educational scene in Britain. Prior to this Act, formal schools were mainly in the hands of the religious denominations; formal Jewish schooling was confined to eight elementary schools in London, with some additional schools in the major provincial towns enrolling some 5,500 pupils. The *raison d'être* of these voluntary (charity) schools, attended mainly by children from the poorer sections of the community, was three-fold: philanthropic, the Anglicanization of new immigrants, and the countering of Christian missionary activity among the Jews at tuition-free missionary schools. The Jewish education of children from the more affluent sections of the community, like their secular education, was imparted by private sectors.

The 1870 Act effectively stunted the growth of the community-supported voluntary schools which could not compete with the Board Schools. For one thing, tuition at Board Schools was free. For another, the so-called 'conscience clause' of the Education Act, which forbade the teaching of any particular religious doctrine in state schools, rendered these schools acceptable for the first time to large numbers of Jewish parents. Jewish voluntary schools declined[4] and indeed no new Jewish schools were established for over half-a-century.

However, the flood of East European immigrants reaching Britain as from the 1880s did infuse new life into the existing Jewish voluntary schools. Immigrant children filled vacant places in these schools in the areas where they lived. Indeed, by the turn of the century, the roll of the famous Jews' Free School (JFS), housed in various satellite buildings, exceeded 4,500 (with a predominance of recent immigrant children), making it the largest primary school in the country. The total enrollment in all the Jewish voluntary schools reached 8,250. The influx of immigrant children overflowed into the local Board Schools, transforming them virtually into 'synthetic' Jewish schools, from the perspective that the vast majority of staff and pupils were Jewish and the internal schedule and content of the schools responded to their observance of Jewish traditions and festivals. Hence the immigrants were able to benefit from free state education.

However, coming as they did mainly from intensely traditional backgrounds, the immigrants supplemented the Jewish religious education their children attained at the day and Board Schools. Hundreds of heders sprung up all over the East End of London and other areas of Jewish immigrant settlement. Thus the heder was introduced to Britain with all its inadequacies (Fishman, 1944), including long hours of ineffective study in cramped unsanitary conditions, before and after school hours and even during the lunchtime break!

Communal opposition to unsatisfactory heder conditions and teaching led to the development of the Talmud Torah movement, which attracted immigrant children. Like the heder, the Talmud Torah maintained a strictly Orthodox orientation, but it was better housed, offered fewer (more reasonable) hours of instruction and operated on a larger scale, frequently catering to many hundreds of children. In 1906, the Talmudei Torah united together in the Talmud Torah Trust (associated with the Federation of Synagogues), becoming one of the two antecedents of the present part-time system of Jewish education. The other antecedent, which developed in parallel to the Talmudei Torah, was the religious classes organized by, and meeting at, local synagogues. The inadequacies of the private teacher in the old-established Jewish areas along with the lack of Jewish teaching facilities in the new areas of Jewish middle-class settlement, led the various United Synagogue constituent synagogues to assume the task of Jewish education at local synagogue classes. These classes, meeting for only a few hours a week, usually on Sunday mornings, were in many ways more in character with the Church of England Sunday Schools (a parallel that extended to other aspects of United Synagogue activities) than with the traditional heder (Bermant, 1969). A third type of part-time education, the forerunner of the present 'withdrawal' classes which meet in non-Jewish schools, was provided by the Association for the Diffusion of Religious Knowledge (later, and more happily, called the London Board of Jewish Education). This took the form of religious classes after school hours at Board Schools, where formal Jewish religious instruction was prohibited by the 1870 Act during regular school hours. These classes were provided mainly in areas of immigrant settlement.

Thus were laid, during the latter years of the last century, the origins of the present system of Jewish schooling in Britain. Over the years the various components of the system have thrived or waned: the after-school classes meeting in Board Schools reached their zenith in the years prior to World War I but declined subsequently, as did the Talmud Torah, as the migrant Jewish population moved from their first concentrated areas of settlement.

At the outbreak of World War II, part-time Jewish schooling was still predominant, and the synagogue classes constituted the major (and still expanding) sector, reflecting the growth of the Jewish population and United Synagogue membership in the new suburban areas. Jewish voluntary day schools had continued their long term decline; enrollment was one third of that registered at the turn of the century.

Developments since World War II

The historical orientation of Jewish education in Britain, with its emphasis on part-time education and relative neglect of Jewish day schools, was confirmed by a communal conference of the Orthodox institutions, convened in 1945 to reconstruct the Jewish education system following the upheavals of the Second World War. This Communal Conference for the Reconstruction of Jewish Education in Great Britain (at which, however, neither the right wing Orthodox nor the Reform and Liberal trends were represented) met under the cloud of the havoc wrought by war-time destruction.

Indeed, the war had also taken a heavy toll on Jewish education; for example, of the 14 Jewish day schools with some 3,600 pupils operating prior to the outbreak of the war, only seven reopened in 1945 with a total enrollment of less than 1,000. Valiant concerted communal efforts had been made to ensure the continuity of Jewish education during the war years; these ensued despite the destruction of Jewish residential areas in the inner cities (including religious school premises) and the widespread evacuation of Jewish children, frequently to areas almost totally lacking Jewish religious facilities. Thus the religious education of a whole generation of Jewish youngsters was seriously impeded.

The early post-war period posed daunting challenges to those responsible for Jewish education in Britain: yet, it also offered unparalleled opportunities in the form of those provisions of the 1944 Butler Education Act which related to denominational education.

If the Butler Act essentially changed the face of education in Britain in the years following the Second World War, its provisions relating to denominational (including Jewish) schools were potentially no less far-reaching. Aimed largely at (and in response to pressures from) the Catholic establishment in Britain, the introduction of the concept of 'voluntary-aided' status offered the possibility of incorporating existing (and new) denominational schools in the state system, while allowing the denominational bodies to essentially retain full autonomy. The state would assume financial responsibility for virtually all current operating expenditures and for half the capital cost of building improvements and new projects. These same provisions still apply today; subsequent changes have been in the direction of considerably raising the state's share of capital expenditures.

Accordingly, conditions were extremely promising for the rapid development of Jewish day schools within the state sector. Indeed, it might be supposed that an examination of the post-war Jewish educational scene would reveal an Anglo-Jewish community eagerly grasping the opportunities offered by the Butler Act to build a comprehensive network of modern Jewish state day schools. Yet, in spite of considerable progress and some marked achievements in this direction over the intervening years, the fact remains that forty years after the passing of the Butler Act, only some 15% of Jewish children are enrolled in Jewish state voluntary-aided schools; (the inclusion of Jewish private day schools raises the percentage, but only to little under 23%). This contrasts with the gains secured by Britain's Catholic community, with over three-quarters of its children so enrolled. Why has the Jewish community fallen short? It will be argued later that answers to this question are to be sought both in Anglo-Jewish communal attitudes and the community's failure to rise to the challenge of the time. But it also stems from the official

Government stance which, despite the formal provisions and subsequent minor amendments of the Butler Act, has made it increasingly difficult for the Jewish community in practice to take advantage of the Act's provisions.

Thus, religious instruction at part-time educational institutions continued to be the linchpin of the Jewish educational system, as it had been for the past three-quarters of a century. However, it was restructured, modernized and given a far greater degree of unity and comprehensiveness. While the dominance of part-time Jewish schooling has diminished over the years, it still characterizes Jewish education in Britain. The question is, with what effect?

Although the general order of magnitude of numbers and proportions of children receiving Jewish education in the various Jewish schools is well known, we remain ignorant of the amount and quality of instruction that each child receives. This gap in our knowledge has been partially repaired by a survey of Jewish children's Jewish education (Prais, 1974). This survey yielded some alarming information about the amount of formal religious instruction Jewish children had received from all sources since the age of five. Although the survey (summarized in Table 1) relates specifically to 15 year-old Jewish children in London, the overall picture that emerged was thought to be fairly typical of Jewish school children generally. For the sample as a whole, Prais found that each child had received on average over his school life a quantity of religious instruction equivalent to some four school-

TABLE 1.   WEEKLY HOURS OF RELIGIOUS INSTRUCTION RECEIVED BY JEWISH 15 YEAR-OLDS THROUGHOUT THEIR SCHOOL CAREERS – LONDON, EARLY 1970S

Type of School		Percentage of Children	Average Equivalent Number of Weekly School Periods		
Primary	Secondary		Boys	Girls	Total
Total		100	4.6	3.2	4.0
Non-Jewish	Non-Jewish[a]	75	3	2	2.5
Jewish	Jewish	9	16	10	13
Jewish	Non-Jewish[a]	9	9	6	8
Non-Jewish	Jewish	7	5	5	5

(a) Includes those schools operating the London Board withdrawal classes scheme.

Source: Prais (1974).

periods a week (taking a 'school period' as being of 45 minutes, for forty weeks in the year). This overall average figure, which may appear surprisingly high, in fact hides some very considerable variation in the amount of instruction received by particular groups of pupils. Thus, half of all pupils received only 2.9 periods or less a week, and, on average, boys received about 50% more instruction than girls (respectively, 4.6 and 3.2 periods). A quarter of all boy pupils received only 1.5 periods a week, or less; for girls, the corresponding figure is 0.9. The average number of school periods of religious instruction increases each year up to the age of ten, but by the early teens, there is a sharp decline; children aged 14 receive only 2.4 periods on average, and very many receive considerably less. The largest and most alarming disparities, however, come from a comparison of those school children who have attended both Jewish primary and Jewish secondary day schools with those who had attended only non-Jewish schools. The former received an average of 13 periods per week of Jewish instruction while the latter received an average of only 2.5 periods a week (Table 1). As would be expected, children whose schooling was only partly Jewish received amounts of schooling somewhere between these two figures.

There is a clear dichotomy between the amount of Jewish education obtained, on the one hand, by the minority of Jewish children who have attended Jewish day schools, and, on the other hand, by the vast majority of Jewish children who received minimal part-time or no religious education.

Part-Time Schooling

In the following discussion, detailed attention is given to institutions operating under the auspices of the central-Orthodox London Board of Jewish Religious Education, the dominant body in the field. Availability of detailed London Board Annual Reports and comprehensive published statistics covering most of the post-war period up to 1978, facilitates this discussion.[5] However, in addition to various very much smaller groupings of Orthodox part-time centers in London, some 6,800 pupils attend Orthodox part-time centers and withdrawal classes in the provinces, while the part-time centers of the Reform and Liberal movements, throughout the country, account for a further 4,000 and 1,500–2,000 pupils respectively. However, much of the discussion relating to London Board centers is appropriate also to centers conducted under other auspices.

The present structure of part-time religious education in Britain derives from the 1945 Communal Conference, as described above, which essentially restructured the organizational framework of part-time religious education for the mainstream central-Orthodox community. Of the two new organizations established, the London Board of Jewish Religious Education was by far the more dominant, charged with the task of operating part-time education for the majority of Orthodox children in the metropolis. The Central Council for Jewish Religious Education, responsible for education in the provinces, was given little more than a coordinating national and inspectoral role. Attempts were made to establish sound financial arrangements at least for London, though not very successfully.

The main responsibility of the London Board today, as then, relates to the part-time sector, including both part-time religious classes and the 'withdrawal' classes in non-Jewish secondary schools. The Board was charged with responsibility for the development of syllabi, national examinations relating to various levels of attainment, the provision of textbooks and other teaching aids and, not least important, the employment of teachers for the part-time sector, particularly synagogue classes and Talmudei Torah. The various synagogues attached to the United Synagogue and the Federation provide the premises for part-time centers, assume formal responsibility for all the purely organizational functioning of the centers and meet all the non-teacher expenses.

Part-time Classes and Centers

The early post-war years saw a substantial growth in the number of part-time centers and part-time enrollments. The number of pupils in London Board synagogue and Talmud Torah classes rose from 7,500 in the early 1950s to a peak enrollment of nearly 13,000 in 1957. Since then, steady and marked decline has set in, with current registration only half that of the peak period. These enrollment trends are due, inter-alia, to the diminishing number of Jewish children and parental apathy, but also to the growth of Jewish day schools.[6]

The London Board statistics do, however, reveal some constructive trends over the post-war decades, in terms of average class size, attendance, and the percentage of girl pupils enrolled. The declining total enrollment which has been accompanied by a reduction in the number of centers from a peak of 100 to only 50, did produce the beneficial result of a fall in average class size from 25 on Sunday mornings in the 1950s to only 18 in the late 1970s.

Unlike day schools or withdrawal classes, enrollment statistics may give a misleading picture of actual attendance at part-time centers. Indeed, a considerable gap does exist between actual attendance and the enrollment figures. Sunday attendance at part-time centers displays a clear upward movement in the post-war period, from 70% enrollment in the 1950s to a stable 82% over the past decade. However, weekday attendance has fallen from approximately 50% of enrolled pupils at the start of the post-war period to only one-quarter now. This reflects the demise of the more intensive Talmud

FIGURE 1. NUMBER OF CHILDREN ATTENDING PART-TIME CENTERS IN SELECTED PROVINCIAL TOWNS – GREAT BRITAIN, MARCH 1958

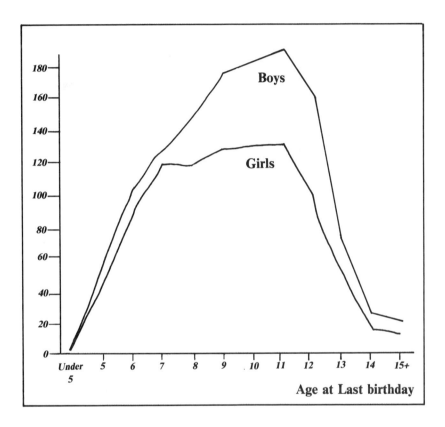

Torah and the increasing tendency for part-time classes to assume the characteristics of 'Sunday School', a far cry indeed from the intense study of the traditional heder or Talmud Torah. Finally, the religious education of girls in Britain suffers from relative neglect. Yet here a positive trend is observable: whereas in the 1950s one-third of all pupils were girls, the percentage now is well over 40%.

Notwithstanding any progress which has been achieved over the years, any system of Jewish education rooted in part-time instruction outside the day school framework has never seemed likely to prove satisfactory. This is no less true for the part-time central-Orthodox centers in the provincial towns than it is for those conducted by the London Board. In practice, the system continues to be plagued by a shortage of qualified teachers, less than satisfactory facilities, and low educational standards concomitant with, and partially causing, a considerable degree of parental and pupil apathy. This is evidenced most clearly in the pattern of enrollment and attendance which decline with age. At London Board centers, for example, pupils aged 15 years and over have seldom constituted more than 7% of total enrollment. In 1978 no less than 81% of all pupils were under 12 years of age, and the 14+ group constituted merely a small percentage of the total,[7] despite considerable and imaginative efforts by the London Board to avoid the massive drop-out of teenagers. The establishment of regional teenage centers, now catering to some 450 youngsters, with facilities for the continuation of formal and informal education (such as drama, crafts, and cookery groups) in parallel with courses of Jewish instruction, constitutes the leading example of these efforts. Detailed data relating to pupil enrollment in relation to age, provided by a survey of enrollments in part-time centers in the major provincial towns (see Figure 1), clearly illustrate this well-known, yet persistent problem. Many first enrollments are made at quite late ages, only to fall off dramatically in the early teens due to lack of motivation, interest and the competing pressures of secular schooling. Thus, at the very time that the child is embarking upon a serious program of studies at his secondary school, he is shedding all formal education in Jewish matters.

In principle, this should provide a clear role for 'withdrawal' classes of the type provided by the London Board in non-Jewish secondary schools.

'Withdrawal' Classes

'Withdrawal' classes are so called because of the right, established under the 1944 Education Act, of parents to withdraw their children from the premises of State schools to another building in order to give them denominational instruction during periods of religious instruction within the school. Such an arrangement is unlikely to prove practical in the short 40 minutes of a typical religious instruction period, even in the rare cases where synagogue buildings are in very close proximity to the school. In practice, the Jewish educational authorities have utilized the opportunities afforded by a specific provision of the Act relating to secondary schools, which allows that, if withdrawal is physically impracticable, and satisfactory arrangements can be made by the religious authorities to provide denominational education on the school premises (including the provision of teachers), then the local authority should be expected to provide these facilities.

The London Board and the various provincial education authorities have availed themselves of this right to operate withdrawal classes for Jewish children on school premises in various secondary schools with sufficiently large numbers of Jewish pupils. In the early 1950s, some 3,000 pupils attended withdrawal classes operated by the London Board at some 25 schools. Subsequently the numbers declined steadily, reaching a low of only 680 pupils at 8 schools in 1975, after which the trend reversed. In 1983 some 1,600 pupils were enrolled at London Board withdrawal classes, while the total enrollment in all withdrawal classes probably approached double this figure.[8]

Although withdrawal classes offer fewer weekly periods of instruction per pupil than part-time centers, they compare favorably in a number of ways, notably attendance, proportion of female pupils, average age, and quality of teachers. At withdrawal classes run by the London Board the attendance is seldom less than 95% of enrollment (the shortfall being due to normal school absence), and on average, 50% of the pupils are girls. Moreover, being restricted to secondary schools, they cater to the older age groups. In recent years only some 10% of pupils were below 11 years of age, while over 50% were aged 14 and over. The teachers, who are experienced and highly trained, contribute to various aspects of Jewish life in the schools, and interact with pupils in various ways, such as individual counselling, that are broader than regular teaching.

Although the long-term decline in the number of pupils has recently been stemmed, many factors mitigate against any dramatic increase in the future. These include the increasing number of children attending Jewish day schools, the continued dispersal of the Jewish population, and the particular difficulties involved in setting up withdrawal classes in those schools which now contain larger numbers of Jewish children. Indeed, not only is the good will and cooperation of the headmaster necessary, but many local educational authorities (including some in the outer London area where many Jewish children attend school) have insisted on the letter of the law, granting withdrawal on an individual basis only rather than collectively, in response to parental requests to withdraw children to nearby synagogue buildings for religious instruction.

Jewish Day Schools

Enrollment Trends

A glance at the post-war statistics of children enrolled in Jewish day schools (Table 2) suggests impressive growth in the number of places available. The number of Jewish children attending Jewish day schools has risen by 200% over the last 25 years, or by over 3% on average every year for the past two decades. As a result of the war-time destruction of school buildings and the changing location of the main centers of Jewish population, as well as the general decline in Jewish day schools, at the end of the war there were

TABLE 2. JEWISH PUPILS ATTENDING JEWISH SCHOOLS, BY SCHOOL TYPE AND LOCATION – NUMBER AND RATES OF INCREASE, UNITED KINGDOM, 1952–1981

School Type and Location	Number of Pupils					Average Annual Rate of Increase (per cent)			
	1952	1954	1961	1971	1981	1952–61	1961–71	1971–81	1961–81
Total pupils	–	–	7,499[a]	12,478	13,959	–	5.2	1.1	3.0
London	2,203	2,706	4,730	7,691	8,569	9.0	5.0	1.1	3.0
Provinces	n.a.	n.a.	2,769[a]	4,787	5,490	–	5.6	1.4	3.0
Total pupils (excluding nurseries)	–	4,400	6,726	10,293	11,590	6.3[b]	4.4	1.0	2.7
Nurseries, total	–	–	773[a]	2,185	2,369	–	11.0	0.8	5.8
London	n.a.	n.a.	543	1,591	1,312	–	11.4	-1.9	4.5
Provinces	n.a.	n.a.	230[a]	594	1,057	–	10.0	5.9	7.9
Primary schools, total	–	3,607	4,474	6,708	6,639	3.1[b]	4.1	-0.1	2.0
London	1,735	2,073	2,636	3,752	4,184	4.8	3.6	1.1	2.3
Provinces	n.a.	1,534	1,838	2,956	2,455	2.6[b]	4.9	-1.8	1.5
Secondary schools, total	–	793	2,252	3,248	4,561[c]	16.8[b]	3.7	2.9	3.3
London	468	633	1,551	2,348	3,073	14.2	4.2	2.7	3.5
Provinces	n.a.	160	701	900	1,488[c]	23.5[b]	2.5	3.3	2.9
Special schools	n.a.	n.a.	n.a.	n.a.	60				
Boarding schools	n.a.	n.a.	n.a.	337	330				

n.a. = not available.
(a) Excludes children in nurseries not attached to primary schools.
(b) 1954–1961 only.
(c) Includes a small proportion of non-Jewish pupils.

Sources: Davis (1971), Taylor (1981), Worms (1981).

only 1,000 pupils in the seven Jewish schools in Britain. By 1954, this figure had risen to 4,400, reaching 6,726 by 1961, and a decade later well exceeded 10,000. The estimate for 1981 shows 11,350 Jewish pupils enrolled (or some 13,500, if nursery education is included). If this appears to have been an extraordinary success story, the impression needs to be tempered by the fact that a century ago, when the Jewish population was half its present size (though more geographically concentrated), over 8,250 children attended Jewish day schools, a number not surpassed until about 1965. More important, the rapid growth in the early post-war years was not sustained in later years, particularly in secondary day schools.

Information on the average annual rate of increase in the number of Jewish pupils enrolled in day schools for each of the latter three decades is provided also in Table 2. In the 1950s, extremely high rates of growth in enrollment were recorded for pupils attending secondary schools: an overall annual growth rate of 16.8% with even higher growth in the provinces; for primary schools the rate was over 3% and somewhat lower in the provinces. The 1960s saw a dramatic slowdown in secondary school enrollment growth: 3.7% per annum, or roughly equal to the rate of growth of primary schools. For the period 1971–1981 secondary schools grew at an even slightly lower rate and primary schools remained stagnant.

These trends indicate an improvement in the ratio of primary to secondary school pupils. In London, for example, the ratio fell from 3.7 in 1951, to 1.7 in 1961 and in 1981 it stood at 1.4. Whereas in the 1950s there were about 3.5 primary school places for each place at a secondary school, the numbers are now more evenly matched. Of course not all Jewish pupils enrolled at secondary schools have attended a Jewish primary school. However, in terms of the provision of a comprehensive system of Jewish schooling, there are now sufficient Jewish secondary school places to provide for some two-thirds of the pupils currently at primary schools, thus in principle allowing for the continuity of full-time Jewish education for the large majority of children attending Jewish primary school.

The overall picture emerging from Table 2, that of rapid expansion in the early post-war years followed by subsequent decline, might suggest that the initial enthusiasm for Jewish day schools evidenced earlier has waned. In reality, however, the opposite has been the case.

In the early post-war years little more than perfunctory attention was given by the community to the task of opening new Jewish day schools. Much of the post-war expansion may be seen more as a response to the task of making good the war-time erosion than as an expression of any great community desire to extend the numbers or coverge of Jewish day schools. Indeed, the attitudes of communal leaders toward the comprehensive development of Jewish day schools in Britain in the early post-war period was, at best, lukewarm. Whether this should be interpreted as a case of dereliction of duty on the part of the communal leadership or as a dutiful, and realistic, reflection of contemporary negative parental attitudes, is a matter on which opinions may differ. Nonetheless, it is clear that Anglo-Jewish priorities did not then lie in the direction of any massive, sustained expansion of the Jewish day school system. Subsequently, both leadership and parental attitudes have become more favorably disposed toward Jewish day school development.

Types of Day Schools

Much of the growth that did take place was initiated and undertaken by various institutions other than the central-Orthodox communal bodies. This partly accounts for the large diversity among the Jewish day schools in terms of ethos, religious orientation and attitudes toward secular studies in Britain today. In general, it is possible to classify the schools into three main groups, all within the Orthodox fold (Davis, 1971).

Group A schools are associated with the local representative Jewish educational authorities (particularly the London Board), the Zionist Federation and synagogues. In Group A schools, some 7 hours a week are devoted to Jewish studies, with increasing stress on *Ivrit b'Ivrit*. Group B schools are more intensively religious in orientation, are members of the Jewish Secondary Schools Movement (JSSM), and they allocate at least 8–12 hours weekly to Jewish studies, including Mishnah and Talmud at the higher levels. Frequently, additional voluntary hours of Jewish studies are provided. Finally, Group C includes schools attached to the more right-wing elements of the Orthodox community. These schools offer a more intensively religious, yeshiva-oriented education, with Jewish studies comprising at least 50% of total school hours, including compulsory Sunday attendance.[9]

In the early post-war period, the schools of the Jewish Secondary Schools Movements (Group B) which are not represented in the provinces, were dominant in London and accounted for half of all Jewish day school pupils there. The principle of *Torah 'im derekh eretz* brought to England from Germany by the movement's founder, Rabbi Victor Schonfeld, has governed the Movement's approach to the question of integration of Jewish with secular studies since its formation in the late 1920s. The aim was to increase both the number of hours and the intensity of Jewish studies to a level higher than the norm at the time, while maintaining high secular academic standards. Then perceived as being to the right of main-stream Orthodox Anglo-Judaism, the Movement's orientation is now far closer to the center, due to both the increasingly observant ethos of Orthodox Jewry in recent years, and to the rise and rapid growth of the more right-wing Group C which includes Lubavitch, *Yesodei HaTorah* and Satmarer schools, all of which are termed ultra-Orthodox as are the relatively closed communities from which their pupils are drawn. These schools pay only perfunctory attention to secular studies and usually oppose subsequent university education.

Group B and Group C schools are mostly attached to particular local communities or to various sections of right-wing Jewry. Group A, however, today forms the backbone of the day school system. Schools in this group resemble main-stream central Orthodoxy in practice and orientation. They are for the most part associated with a major communal organization, such as the London Board or a local provincial representative educational board, or the Zionist Federation through the Zionist Federation Educational Trust. Indeed, the pivotal role played by the Zionist Movement in Britain in fostering the concept of day schools, both in popularizing the idea among Jewish parents and rendering it more acceptable to communal leaders, must be acknowledged. As early as the 1950s, at a time when the future of Jewish education was still seen to lie mainly in the direction of part-time centers and withdrawal classes, the Zionist Federation (which does not include the religious-Zionist *Mizrachi* Organization) moved decisively into the day school field and, envisaging a nation-wide structure, established the foundation for a network of schools mainly in the provinces, but also in London. The role of the Zionist Federation in pioneering the concept of a Jewish day school network, nation-wide in coverage (a clear change from earlier attitudes), has been explained as a realistic reaction to the narrowed scope for political Zionist activity following the establishment of the State of Israel. In the view of Chaim Bermant, the Zionists, "faced with the prospect of a Jewish state without a Jewish world...turned to the oldest panacea of all, education" (Bermant, 1969).

The notable (and unexpected) absence of the *Mizrachi* Organization as a participant in the development of Jewish day schooling in Britain helped avoid the dichotomy between secular and religious Zionist schools that characterizes the State educational sector in Israel. Given the traditional orientation of Anglo-Jewry and the lack of religious Zionist activity in the day school field, it was not unexpected for the Zionist Federation to veer towards the middle ground. Its schools accept the authority of the Chief Rabbi and are conducted on generally Orthodox religious lines, though with rather a greater emphasis on Hebrew and Zionist education and somewhat less attention to Jewish religious knowledge than is the case in other Group A schools. Purely secular Zionist schools are unknown in Britain today.

Zionist Federation schools today account for some 40% of Group A Jewish primary school pupils in London and the Federation gives financial support for Jewish and Hebrew studies to a number of Jewish secondary schools.

Most of the remaining Group A schools are attached to various Jewish educational bodies in the major local communities – particularly the London Board – which have followed the Zionist Federation's example in Jewish day school sponsorship and provision. The London Board, through the JFS

TABLE 3. DISTRIBUTION OF PUPILS BY SCHOOL GROUP AND
PERCENTAGE OF PUPILS IN STATE-AIDED SCHOOLS –
LONDON, 1952–1981

School Level and Group[a]	1952	1961	1971	1981
Number of Pupils Enrolled				
Total Pupils	2,203	4,187	6,100	7,257
Primary schools, total	1,735	2,636	3,752	4,184
Group A	763	1,076	1,681	1,815
” B	772	916	1,086	1,055
” C	200	644	985	1,314
Secondary schools, total	468	1,551	2,348	3,073
Group A	0	514	1,316	1,500
” B	368	724	673	886
” C	100	313	359	638
Percent Distribution of Pupils by School Group				
Primary schools, total	100	100	100	100
Group A	44	41	45	44
” B	44	35	29	25
” C	12	24	26	31
Secondary schools, total	100	100	100	100
Group A	0	33	56	50
” B	82	47	29	30
” C	18	20	12	21
Percentage of Pupils in State-Aided Schools				
Total pupils	22	40	56	56
Primary schools, total	23	29	43	50
Group A	89	47	46	72
” B	0	28	78	74
” C	0	0	0	0
Secondary schools, total	20	58	77	67
Group A	0	100	100	100
” B	25	52	74	64
” C	0	0	0	0

(a) For definition of school groups, see text.

Sources: Davis (1971), Taylor (1981), Worms (1981).

school, accounts for all the secondary school places and also for over 40% of primary school places in Group A schools in London. The considerable increase in the number of pupils in London schools over the past three decades has been accompanied by substantial changes in the relative importance of the various groupings. Table 3 shows the absolute numbers and changing relative importance of the three school groupings in London for selected years during the period 1952–1981. The main changes have been the considerable relative decline in the Jewish Secondary Schools Movement (Group B) schools at both the primary level (parallel with the growth of the more right-wing Group C schools) and particularly at the secondary level (with the opening of the JFS school and, over the last decade, the resurgence of Group C schools).

The picture is somewhat different for the provinces as a whole. Group A schools are dominant, with Group C schools constituting roughly only half the London percentage (i.e., some 15% of primary school pupils and 10% of secondary). Group B schools are not represented at all. Finally, the Orthodox monopoly on Jewish day schooling in Britain was brought to an end with the opening of the first Progressive (Reform) Jewish day school in the 1981–82 school year in the London area. This is a further indication of the increasing acceptability of, and potential parental demand for, places in Jewish day schools in Britain.

Private vs. State (Voluntary-Aided) Day Schools

The distinctive and possibly unique feature of the Jewish day school system in Britain is the large number of schools – accounting for the majority of pupils attending Jewish schools – which are for all intents and purposes an integral part of the state school system.

The relative importance of state-aided and independent (private) Jewish day schools is shown in Table 4. Of the 53 Jewish schools in the United Kingdom in 1981 – including two Jewish boarding schools but excluding nursery schools – 20 (or 38%) come within the state sector, and these 20 schools account for the majority (64%) of pupils enrolled in Jewish schools. State schools are predominant in the provinces, with well over half of all Jewish day schools in the state sector, and no less than 85% of all pupils enrolled in Jewish day schools. The London percentages are considerably lower (28% and 56% respectively) due mainly to the greater number in London of right-wing Group C schools, which have remained outside the state system. Table 4, indicates that in London, no state schools are to be found among Group C schools. Table 4 also shows that overall, the percentage of Jewish day school pupils attached to state day schools has failed to grow over the last decade, in contrast to the enrollment expansion of earlier years.

TABLE 4. INDEPENDENT AND STATE-AIDED JEWISH SCHOOLS, BY SCHOOL TYPE AND LOCATION – UNITED KINGDOM, 1981

School Type and Location	No. of Jewish Schools			State-Aided Schools as % Total Schools	% of Pupils Enrolled in State-Aided Schools
	Total	Independent	State-Aided		
Total	53	33	20	38	64
Day schools, London					
Total	32	23	9	28	56
Primary	20	13	7	35	50
Secondary	12	10	2	17	67
Day schools, Provinces					
Total	17	8	11	53	85
Primary	13	5	8	62	87
Secondary	6	3	3	50	83
Boarding schools	2	2	0	0	0

Sources: Taylor (1981), Worms (1981).

The 1944 Education Act established the procedure whereby denominational schools could be taken over and maintained by local authorities. The denominational sponsors of such so-called 'voluntary-aided' schools retain full autonomy regarding the appointment of teachers and religious instruction as well as a majority of members in the managing body. The levying of compulsory fees is forbidden in state schools. Costs of religious instruction are met mainly by the Jewish educational authorities, supplemented by a (usually) small voluntary parental contribution. However, the burden of virtually all running expenses, including teachers' salaries and internal maintenance, falls on the local authorities. Thus, for existing denominational schools, the financial advantages stemming from 'voluntary-aided' status are extensive indeed. Moreover, a newly planned denominational school could, under the 1944 Act, receive a grant of 50% of the building costs if it replaced a defunct denominational school. The subsequent Education Act of 1967 both raised the grant to 80% and extended it to any new denominational school which was included in the official school building program (rather than limiting it only to new schools that replaced former schools). Finally, under the Act of 1974, building grants were increased to 85%.

   The financial support available to aided denominational schools is very high and furthermore, successive Education Acts have both broadened the criteria for receiving support and substantially increased its level. How has the community reacted to these opportunities? At least for the earlier part of the post-war period, the official community response could, at best, be described as lukewarm. It has been noted above that the community failed to designate any central role for day schools in the post-war system. Moreover, recognition of new schools had to be negotiated through protracted procedures, undertaken largely by the London Board, before the schools could qualify for the sizable state building grants which involved great savings for the community. The more pragmatic, but costly, approach of the Zionist Federation was largely that of setting up schools, which involved meeting all capital costs, and subsequently seeking aided status, whereby annual operating costs would be covered by the state. In this way the Zionist Federation was able to build up a network of 13 schools, more than half of which are now state-aided. Their approach then, though far more costly, yielded quicker results. However, for Anglo-Jewry as a whole, communal priorities did not lie in the direction of a massive or hurried expansion of the day school system, since although communal funds were available for other uses, they were not sufficient for this purpose.

In recent years, community attitudes have swung nearly full circle, as Jewish day schools have increasingly come to be regarded as the general panacea for many of the community's major ills, including the increasing drift of youth away from the community, outmarriage, and so on. Indeed, the imaginative proposals for the future development of Jewish education in Britain, published by the Office of the Chief Rabbi, included the provision over a 15-year period of more than 20 new state-aided day schools in London and the provinces, with the intention of doubling the number of pupils attending Jewish day schools. Moreover, via a newly established Jewish Educational Development Trust, financed largely by individual charity donations, the total capital cost of these developments was to be met by the community rather than relying on negotiations with the educational authorities and the uncertainty that these plans would be included within official building programs, to attract what was an 80% capital grant. However, a hardening of official attitudes toward the granting of voluntary-aided status has retarded the progress of these plans and has placed them in jeopardy.[10] It is perhaps ironic that as the community's interest in extending the network of Jewish day schools has awakened, in concert with the increased advantages available to denominational aided schools, the general climate has deteriorated so as to make it increasingly difficult to achieve this desired voluntary-aided status within the state sector.

To understand how this came about requires a careful reading of the relevant but tantalizingly vague Section 76 of the 1944 Act, which constitutes the legal basis for the granting of voluntary-aided status by the educational authorities to denominational schools. Section 76 established the principle that "pupils are to be educated in accordance with the wishes of parents" with the proviso that this is "compatible with the provision of efficient instruction and training and the avoidance of unreasonable public expenditure". While it has been argued (Jacobs and Prais, 1977) that the sole object of these caveats was to prevent the authorities from being obliged to set up a denominational school in areas where the number of children of that denomination was insufficient to justify an entire school, in more recent years the caveats have been interpreted so as to severely curtail the possibility of gaining aided status. Formerly, Section 76 was interpreted so that parents and the Church – and most notably the Roman Catholic schools – were able to take full advantage of its provisions, to the extent that some 80% of Catholic children studied in 'voluntary-aided' schools. Now, however, any existing or proposed new school applying for aided status must demonstrate not only a real denominational need for the school in that location ("in accordance with the wishes of parents") but also, the existence of an overall shortage of state school places in the area (the recent more stringent, official interpretation of an "avoidance of unreasonable public expenditures"). That this latter condition has become extremely difficult to satisfy may be deliberate, considering that this has been a period of much under-utilization of existing school buildings and facilities as a result of the severe decline in number of primary school pupils since the mid-1970s and in the number of secondary school pupils since the beginning of the 1980s. Even when an acceptable argument in principle could be presented for a proposed new school to gain voluntary-aided status, the school would still need to gain inclusion into the scheduled building program of the local authority – no easy task during a period of general educational retrenchment and curtailed building of new schools.

At the same time, the adverse general economic climate has jeopardized the finances of the 60% of Jewish schools which remain in the private sector; yet, applying for aided-status is unlikely to provide a solution to these financial difficulties since the authorities increasingly hesitate to assume extra burdens at a time of expenditure curbs and budgeting in education.[11]

Thus, as the heady days of high educational expansion enjoyed over most of the post-war period recede, Jewish day schools, in common with other educational institutions, have entered a period of slowdown rather than rapid expansion. From this perspective one may pass an overall judgement on the earlier post-war period as one of ungrasped oppportunity. Since growth on any large scale must be ruled out for the next few years, the most that can be hoped for is a period of consolidation and a rise in the standards of existing Jewish day schools. This in itself is a worthwhile goal since, by comparison with many day schools elsewhere, the quality of Jewish education in many British Jewish day schools – particularly in Group A – is unacceptably low.

The Financing of Jewish Education

In Britain, as in many Diaspora communities, Jewish education is perennially short of funds. How is Jewish education in Britain financed? The answer, in a nutshell, is: mainly – and inadequately – by the community as a whole, in large part by the State, and hardly at all by the parents! Although the present financial arrangements, which evolved during the era of communal reconstruction after World War II, still leaves the education system perilously short of funds, there remains strong community resistance to the concept of any serious parental financial responsibility for Jewish education.

The 1945 Communal Conference agreed upon the principle of communal taxation as the means of financing the part-time centers and withdrawal classes which were to be the predominant modes of post-war Jewish education.

In his history of the United Synagogue, Aubrey Newman (1976) maintains that the decision that part-time Jewish education be financed communally from contributions from the major synagogue bodies was one of the crucial post-war decisions made by the United Synagogue. Yet, despite the avowed intention that Jewish education become a primary charge on community resources, designated synagogue funds have in practice not been adequate for the needs of the educational institutions. The education levy is equal to a third of membership contributions by the United Synagogue and other synagogue bodies was subsequently eroded to one-quarter in 1951 and by 1959 (because of the exemption of deficit synagogues and those with heavy building programs) was effectively equal to only 17%. Attempts were made to tap other communal sources of funds. In 1959, a scheme for an educational levy on functions supervised by the Kashruth Commission did not result in much income – by the early 1970s less than 1% of the London Board income came from this source.

The community hesitated to commit sizeable sums for the provision of Jewish day schools, evidently giving higher priority to other community needs. Indeed, Prais (1972) notes that even in the face of an imminent demand for day school places, the community spent some £6.5 million on the construction of new synagogues during the 1960s – that is, between five to ten times more than the amount spent on day schools during the same decade.

The question then arises: why have school fees not been levied more extensively as a means of providing additional soures of funds? Although the possibility of charging fees at part-time centers has been raised from time to time,[12] it has generally been rejected, partly because of administrative difficulties but mainly because of the fear that it would result in children being deprived of education. Yet, the impression remains that the main source of opposition to fees is essentially ideological. Thus, even the suggestion of a scheme of voluntary parental contributions failed to find support (until recently) because it "cut at the root of the principle of free education" (Rubin, 1975) which reflects paternalistic attitudes parallel, and concurrent, with those underlying the early post-war development of the Welfare State. More recently, in 1975, a voluntary parental level was introduced at London Board centers. Nevertheless, the most recently published financial statements of the London Board show the scheme to have produced a mere 4% extra to London Board income (about £2.50 on average for each child on the roll at London Board centers). The smallness of the sums raised, however, should be seen as a sign of parental willingness and not inability to contribute voluntarily toward the Jewish education of their children. The substantial sums spent on private bar mitzvah lessons for the many children dropping out of the part-time system before age 12 attests to this.

The attitude that a realistic policy of fee charging in Jewish education should be avoided is felt also in the day school sector. The parents of the minority of pupils studying in independent, non-state schools obviously do pay significant fees (though these vary greatly from school to school). These fees, however, are seldom high enough to cover costs and, as in other Diaspora communities, the finances of independent day schools must be buttressed by support from other sources – fund-raising drives, charity donations and grants from communal institutions. Although general schooling is free for the two-thirds of day school pupils who attend the voluntary-aided schools, these schools must finance the larger part of the Jewish studies program, notably teacher salaries, for which state support is not available. Yet not all schools in the sector are prepared to call upon parents to pay a realistic fee even for this small part of total educational costs. In some schools, a significant fee is charged, but in others the fee is either purely nominal, takes the form of voluntary donations (as at the JFS secondary school), or does not exist at all. Thus, for example, in 1978 as much as 20% of the gross expenditure of the London Board supported Jewish studies departments in its day schools. At the JFS secondary school, the voluntary parental contribution offsets only 8% of the London Board's payments to support the school's Jewish studies department. A more realistic policy has been introduced at the London Board's new multi-entry, Sinai primary school in North West London, where fees are planned to finance half of the department's costs (the rest to be borne by the London Board). Yet again the question arises: Why the subsidy here?

A system of communal taxation may be acceptable if it produces sufficient sums to meet the multifarious needs of Jewish education. The evidence however is that Jewish educational institutions in Britain operate on a shoestring. Though making a valid contribution to the amelioration of the problem charitable donations to education probably account for only about 10% of the total funds raised for Jewish causes. Thus, the financial crisis in Jewish education continues.

An inevitable casualty of the parsimony in Jewish education has been the teaching profession. Since teachers' salaries absorb the bulk of educational budgets, the resulting low levels of salaries have over the years had an effect on the quality and supply of teachers. Teacher training has also suffered. For example, the London Board spent only £2,500 on teacher training in 1978, out of a total expenditure of £380,000! This is clearly false economy viewed over the longer term.

Teachers in Jewish Education

Today in Britain over 2,000 teachers are attached to the Jewish education system, roughly 1,100 in Jewish day and boarding schools (about a third of them on a part-time basis) and a further 1,000 in the part-time system (including some 400 at London Board Centers). Yet so widely heterogeneous is this body of teachers that it is difficult to think of them as constituting a 'Jewish teaching profession'.

A high but unknown proportion of secular subject teachers at day schools are non-Jewish, while the teaching of Jewish studies is greatly dependent upon Israeli teachers on short-term (generally biennial) contracts. While some of the Jewish day school teachers also teach within the part-time supplementary sector, some of the staff at part-time centers are themselves pupils at either secondary schools or colleges who lack formal teaching qualifications and experience though they do not necessarily lack motivation.

A great deal of lip service, but also real effort, has been devoted to the perennial problem of teacher supply in the Jewish education system in Britain. Yet as Levin puts it: "The shores of Anglo-Jewish education are strewn with the wrecks of teacher training schemes proposed for over one hundred years" (Levin, 1970). Teacher availability and quality remains an issue that has eluded a lasting solution over the years. More recently, however, some ameliorations have given rise to mild optimism concerning the future.

Teachers in the Part-time Sector

Teachers attached to the part-time centers have traditionally been drawn from a wide range of backgrounds. A high percentage are synagogue functionaries and students, all differing markedly in Jewish religious knowledge and observance and in general educational background. One trait common to all has been the very low level of pedagogic skills. This, combined with high staff turnover, often inadequate multi-purpose classrooms, and unimaginative teaching materials has resulted in an educational experience which, over the longer term, may well have been counter-productive for many thousands of youngsters. It is fair to suggest, as does one leading Anglo-Jewish educationalist (Conway, 1981), that conceivably as many Jews have been alienated from their religion by poor quality teaching as by ignorance due to lack of any Jewish education.

Some years ago, the development of the day school network was seen as the basis of a solution to the problem of teacher supply for the part-time sector (Fishman and Levy, 1964). It was envisaged that the increased numbers of full-time qualified teachers attached to the Jewish day school network would provide a significant and much needed infusion of strength to the part-time sector as these teachers sought to supplement their relatively modest incomes. In practice, however, most teachers in Jewish day schools, as well as Jewish teachers at non-Jewish schools, have preferred to moonlight in activities more personally rewarding psychologically as well as financially than supplementary teaching, and have not responded positively to calls that they strengthen the part-time sector.

Thus in practice, unable to rely on qualified day school teachers, the part-time sector has had to develop its own teacher training. While in the past such schemes failed, new elements in the situation are contributing to a more successful outcome, albeit as yet on a limited scale. One positive result of the high rate of staff turnover (for example, nearly 20% of the teachers at London Board part-time centers leave each summer) is the opportunity this provides for requiring numbers of new inexperienced teachers to undergo part-time induction courses. A new and successful venture is the course sponsored by the London Board for all new applicants for teaching vacancies at its centers. This course also includes a period of teacher practice under the guidance of experienced tutors (Jewish Educational Development Trust, 1978).

Also noteworthy are the teacher certification courses provided by the Education Department of the Leo Baeck College, the major seminary servicing the Reform and Liberal communities in Britain. The program includes both general educational and Jewish studies, and is based on a combination of tutor-directed individual study, attendance at short residential courses, and the use of an audio-visual workshop and resource center.

In addition to these steps taken by the educational authorities to offer courses to inexperienced teachers coming to their centers, the Orthodox (London Board) teacher supply situation has improved as a result of two other factors. The Orthodox community's move to the religious right has resulted in an infusion into the teacher ranks of the London Board of a large group of religious youngsters (often with yeshiva backgrounds) who are both highly motivated as well as Jewishly knowledgeable. This new positive element is now predominant in centers in the major North-West London area of Jewish residential concentration. The long-term decline in the numbers of pupils enrolled at London Board centers, which has been the result both of a smaller 'attached' Jewish population and the growth of Jewish day schools, has in itself also ameliorated the teacher-pupil balance.

Teachers in Jewish Day Schools

The expansion of Jewish day schools since the war has been too slow in terms of both the available opportunities and pupil need at the time. In a sense, however, the growth was too rapid, in that the expansion continued apace in the face of a persistent and chronic shortage of suitable teachers. Notwithstanding some cooperative valid efforts by Jews College and the London Board, the Anglo-Jewish community was simply unable to supply the required number of qualified teachers to service the growing day school sector. This lacuna, particularly evident at the secondary-school level, exists in the teaching of secular as well as Jewish subjects. Yet the current methods of filling the teacher gap – the widespread employment of Israeli teachers on short-term contracts for Jewish studies and non-Jewish teachers for secular subjects – must be viewed at best as palliatives rather than as a lasting solution to the problem of teacher supply.

The use of qualified Israeli teachers on a limited scale is no doubt highly beneficial in adding a positive dimension to the Jewish life of the school. Yet, Israeli teachers frequently suffer from a lack of knowledge of the English language, from a lack of familiarity with the local educational system and the socio-communal background of Jewish life in Britain. The effectiveness of using Israeli teachers is further reduced by the often lengthy acclimatization period at the beginning, and preparation (both material and psychological) for return at the end of their tour of duty. For the teaching of secular subjects, the system relies heavily on non-Jewish teachers or Jewish teachers lacking in a strong Jewish educational or cultural background. Many of these teachers are highly qualified professionally. But while the perfunctory use of such teachers may be very satisfactory in purely pedagogic terms, the wider contribution that they can make to the Jewish life and atmosphere of the school is minimal.

The question remains: What are the domestic sources of Jewish teacher-supply in Britain? The major community effort to train teachers in Jewish studies for the day schools is the program for Jewish, secular and educational studies conducted jointly by the Orthodox Jewish seminary, Jews College and one of the leading London polytechnics, complemented by an extended period of study at a teacher-training college in Israel. The course is unique in Europe, leading teachers of Jewish subjects to a first degree qualification that is fully recognized by the general educational authorities. Unfortunately, the handful of students who qualify annually can make only a marginal contribution to solving the teacher supply gap. Larger numbers study at the strictly

Orthodox Jewish Teachers Training College at Gateshead in North-East England. Attended by some 250 young women from all over the world, the seminary offers a thorough grounding in Jewish and professional educational studies. Yet while its standards are high, as is the case with the smaller teacher training institutes in London, the non-recognition of its graduates by the educational authorities precludes their employment in the voluntary-aided schools, which the majority of Jewish day school pupils attend. A significant number of these graduates, however, do make a valid contribution to the independent Jewish day school sector.

Yet, whatever the adequacy of present Jewish teacher training, even a marked increase in the provision of facilities will not have any dramatic impact on the problem since a supply of teacher training college places does not create a corresponding demand. The very low status of teaching in relation to alternative professions – particularly in the eyes of the dominantly middle-class Jewish population – acts against any easy solution to the problem of teacher supply. The relevant and far-reaching recommendations of the Committee on Teacher Training and Career Structure (Jewish Educational Development Trust, 1978), relating to the introduction of an attractive career structure in Jewish day schools (some of which have since been implemented), are unlikely to lead to any basic change in the relative attractiveness of the Jewish teacher profession. Unfortunately, like the Rabbinate, the Jewish teaching profession is simply not regarded as suitable for a 'nice Jewish boy'.

The intractability of the problem of augmenting the supply with new teachers has led to an emphasis on raising the quality of existing teachers. Such efforts have taken two major directions. The first is in-service training programs, whether in the form of short-term training courses and individual counselling, in which a significant role is played by selected Israeli experts, who are familiar with the Jewish educational scene in Britain and were brought over specially for this purpose or in the form of various summer teacher training courses in Israel. In the three years since the latter program has been in operation, over 100 Jewish teachers have attended these summer in-service courses provided by various Israeli universities. The second major direction has been the development and dissemination of teaching-aids, audio-visual materials, mobile resource centers and so on, both within the Orthodox and Progressive networks in the provinces as well as in London. Directed more toward teachers in the part-time centers than to day schools, these efforts represent a dramatic improvement over the pedestrian pedagogic norms existing only a decade ago in Britain. Even if it is unlikely that these measures will inaugurate a 'revolution' in Jewish education in Britain (Conway, 1981) they will certainly exert a positive impact in the long term in raising the quality of teaching within the Jewish day schools and part-time centers in Britain.

Jewish Educational Provision:
The Overall Picture

Having dealt with the salient aspects of the Jewish educational system in Britain, some account is needed of the overall statistical picture.

Data on Jewish education in Britain are extremely varied both in availability and quality. For detailed, usually biennial, statistics relating to the Jewish day school sector, we are indebted to the late Dr. Jacob Braude for the regular statistical surveys which were published at regular intervals in the *Jewish Chronicle* and have been conveniently brought together in the booklet *Let My People Know* (Davis, 1971), for the period 1952–71. Surveys relating to 1973 and 1975 were published in the *Jewish Chronicle* in July of those years. More recent estimates, based on information appearing in the yearbook of the Jewish Educational Development Trust, *Jewish Education 1981/82* (Taylor, 1981), have been compiled by F. Worms (1981). Another set of available comprehensive educational statistics derives from the detailed annual, later biennial, reports of the London Board (published regularly until 1978), which embraces its multifarious activities in the part-time sector. Apart from these sources, information is spotty and ad hoc. However, from time to time, overall estimates of Jewish educational provisions for the

TABLE 5. NUMBER OF PUPILS OF COMPULSORY SCHOOL AGE ENROLLED IN JEWISH EDUCATIONAL INSTITUTIONS, BY SCHOOL TYPE – UNITED KINGDOM, 1976/77

School Type	London	Provinces	Total[a]
Total pupils	21,380	11,010	32,390
Day schools[b]	7,200	4,070	11,270
Yeshivoth	120	140	260
Boarding schools	–	320	320
Withdrawal classes	1,450	1,740	3,190
Part-time centers			
London Board	6,610	–	6,610
Other Orthodox	1,460	3,690	5,150
Reform and Liberal	4,540	1,050	5,590

(a) Includes pupils in Eire.

(b) In addition, 450 non-Jewish pupils attended Jewish day schools, predominantly in the provinces. Also, 1,520 additional children attended kindergartens attached to day schools.

Source: Braude (1977).

country as a whole have been prepared, relating inter alia to 1962 (Fishman and Levy, 1964), and 1976/77 (Braude, 1977). Details of the 1977 overall count are given in Table 5. This shows a total enrollment for children of compulsory school age (5–16 years) at Jewish educational institutions of over 32,000[13], of which 5% attended part-time centers and 35% attended Jewish day schools (nearly 37% if boarding schools and yeshivoth are included).

Partial information relating to 1981 suggests that the overall picture will have changed only marginally during the intervening five years. Enrollments at day schools and part-time centers attached to the Progressive trends have been more or less stable, though some decline in the number of pupils attending orthodox part-time centers has been recorded.

The year 1977 is a convenient vantage point from which to analyze the overall picture, since the recent authoritative reassessment of the size and structure of Anglo-Jewry conducted by the Research Unit of the Board of Deputies of British Jews relates to that year (Haberman, Kosmin and Levy, 1982). The Unit's population estimates enable us to measure, with a greater degree of accuracy than had been possible, the proportion of Jewish children attending Jewish educational institutions. Since the estimated Jewish population per cohort for ages below 10 is set at some 4,510, and for ages 10–19 at some 5,120, the total Jewish child population aged 5–16 may be estimated to be 53,200, of which some 32,400, or 61% received institutionally-provided Jewish education in 1977.[14] This figure is deceptively low, however. The numbers who receive Jewish education for some period during their school years will not yet have enrolled in, while others will have already left, the institution providing it. Although it is customary to add a factor of 25% to take account of the limited period that many children are in attendance (as in Braude, 1977), there is no statistical basis for this arbitrary adjustment.

The Effectiveness of Jewish Education

Discussion of past trends and present problems of Jewish education in Britain raises questions concerning the effectiveness of the overall educational effort. How can the outcomes of these educational programs be evaluated? The literature on social evaluation points to the use of two contrasting, but complementary approaches: the evaluation of educational processes, and of educational impacts (Borus, 1979).

Process evaluation focuses on the educational process itself and is concerned with the general efficiency of the program as a whole. Statistical information on such issues as the percentage of children reached by the facilities provided, attendance and drop-out rates, cost-effectiveness and the standards of Jewish religious knowledge achieved in relation to proclaimed objectives (such as in the official syllabi) all shed light on the efficiency of the Jewish educational process. Available statistical information of the type used here, although seriously deficient in quality and coverage, does indicate the overall efficacy of the educational process, from which general (partially positive) conclusions may be drawn.

However, as opposed to the narrower, internally-directed process evaluations, impact evaluation takes a broader, longer-term perspective: it focuses on outcomes, relating particularly to the after-effects of the education on both the lasting Jewish thought orientations of pupils, and particularly, on behavioral patterns in relation to Jewish community norms and expectations. Here the emphasis is on such questions as: has the educational process inculcated enduring Jewish values, producing a generation of knowledgeable committed Jews, has it given sufficient and lasting reinforcement to Jewish youngsters, promoting positive approaches to such issues as Jewish religious observance, the State of Israel, communal loyalty and participation and, ultimately, to adherence to the Jewish community including marriage within the fold; has it played any role in stemming the tide of increased apathy towards Jewish values and tradition, and towards outmarriage? Given the neglect of adequate research into these issues, we are woefully ignorant about these educational impacts.

The booklet, *Let My People Know*, issued by the Office of the Chief Rabbi (Davis, 1971), which contained challenging proposals for the far-reaching development of Jewish education in Britain, pointed to the grim prospect facing Anglo-Jewry in the concluding decades of this century. The authors foresaw in the defection of the young, in the growing rate of outmarriage and in the drop-out rate of the uncommitted, the roots of an impending unprecedented crisis for Anglo-Jewry, avertable only by a sufficiently forceful Jewish educational effort. They claimed that "inadequate Jewish education clearly lies at the root of the problem" and saw the solution as being in a greatly improved educational effort. Yet, the view that Jewish education does indeed provide a panacea remains little more than an act of faith. It will remain so until the evidence of research can cast some more decisive light on the issue of Jewish educational impacts in Britain over a longer term. The task of devising such a research program and its implementation remains a challenge still to be taken up by researchers in the field of Jewish education.

Acknowledgements

This paper was completed Pesach 1983. Assistance in its preparation, afforded by the Memorial Foundation for Jewish Culture, New York, is gratefully acknowledged. Moshe Davis, Executive Director of the Office of the Chief Rabbi, London, provided helpful comments on a first draft. The author's thanks are extended to all those institutions and individuals in the

U.K., and in particular to Michael Cohen, Director of Education of the London Board of Jewish Religious Education, who supplied relevant information and statistics.

Notes

1. In the absence of any communal census or question on ethnic origin or religion in the Census of Population in Britain, the traditional method of estimating the size of the Jewish population, since the beginning of the century, is to apply an age and sex specific mortality rate to the annual number of Jewish deaths (as measured by the number of burials and cremations recorded by the various synagogal organizations in Britain).

2. For the first half of the present century, the number of synagogue marriages per 1,000 Jewish population was roughly equal to that of the general population in Britain (about 8.0 per 1,000); since then a rapid decline has ensued. For the quinquenium 1975–80, there were on average only 1,320 synagogue marriages a year (only 70% of the average number registered for the previous 15 years), representing a rate of only 3.0 per 1,000.

3. The Board of Deputies Research Unit estimates that during the 1970s, only 4,500 Jewish children were born each year, compared with 5,100 a year in the previous decade.

4. Standards of Jewish education at the Jewish voluntary schools steadily fell, as a result of the so-called 'pass' system, whereby the size of state grants to voluntary schools was related to pupil achievement in a specified range of subjects, not including Jewish ones. This led (not surprisingly) to the neglect of Jewish subjects. For example, The Jews' Free School, which prior to the 1870 Act offered 12 hours of Jewish and 18 hours of secular studies, subsequently taught an average of 7.5 and 22 hours of Jewish and secular studies, respectively.

5. Unfortunately, publication of annual reports ceased after 1978.

6. Part of the registered decline in London Board enrollment is more apparent than real. Following the conflict which arose from the election of a new Chief Rabbi, the Federation terminated its various cooperative activities with the United Synagogue, including education. From June 1966, The Federation ceded from the London Board (with its 17 centers and 1,000 pupils). Today the Federation runs 8 centers which contain 525 children.

7. Private communication (11.4.83), Michael Cohen, Director of Education, London Board of Jewish Religious Education.

8. Results from the International Census of Jewish Schools in the Diasopra (Project for Jewish Educational Statistics) relating to Great Britain indicate that in 1982, withdrawal classes were operating in 19 schools.

9. In addition to these school groupings, there are two small schools for children with special educational needs and also two secondary-level boarding schools, including the prestigious (and expensive) Carmel College.

10. A revised prospectus, issued in 1977 by the Jewish Educational Development Trust, set lower, more realistic objectives.

11. For example, except in the provinces, the right-wing Group C schools have traditionally remained aloof from the state system. However, recent applications from three existing Lubavitch and *Yesodei HaTorah* schools for aided status were refused on the grounds of unacceptability of premises and the schools were also informed that no general need for additional maintained places existed in the area.

12. It was also argued that payment of fees would foster positive parental attitudes on the grounds that one values only what one pays for.

13. This figure includes some double-counting of children attending more than one Jewish educational institution, but does not include the unknown number of children receiving private tuition.

14. 22% of all Jewish children attended full-time Jewish educational institutions (mainly day schools), and 39% attended part-time centers and withdrawal classes.

References

Bermant, C. (1969). *Troubled Eden: An Anatomy of British Jewry.* Vallentine, Mitchell, London.

Borus, M.E. (1979). *Measuring the Impact of Employment-Related Social Programs.* The Upjohn Institute, Kalamazoo, Michigan.

Braude, J. (1977). "Jewish Education in Britain Today". Paper presented to the Second Conference on Jewish Life in Modern Britain, London.

Conway, E.S. (1981). "The Contemporary State of Jewish Education". *L'eylah*, Spring.

Davis, M., ed. (1971). *Let My People Know.* Office of the Chief Rabbi, London.

Fishman, I. (1944). *The History of Jewish Education in Central Europe.* Edward Goldston, London.

Fishman, I. and Levy, H. (1964). "Jewish Education in Great Britain"/in: Gould, J. and Esh, S., (eds.). *Jewish Life in Modern Britain.* Routledge and Kegan Paul, London.

Fishman, W.J. (1975). *East End Jewish Radicals, 1875–1914.* Duckworth, London.

Haberman, S., Kosmin, B.A. and Levy, C. (1983). "Mortality Patterns of British Jews 1975–79: Insights and Applications for the Size and Structure of British Jewry". *Journal of the Royal Statistical Society*, Series A, No. 146, Part 3. pp. 294–310.

Himmelfarb, H.S. and DellaPergola, S. (1982). *Enrollment in Jewish Schools in the Diaspora Late 1970s*. Institute of Contemporary Jewry, The Hebrew University, Jerusalem. (Project for Jewish Educational Statistics, Research Report No. 1). 97 pp.

Jacobs, S. and Prais, V. (1977). "Developments in the Law on State-aided Schools for Religious Minorities". Paper presented to the Second Conference on Jewish Life in Modern Britain, London.

Jakobovits, I. (1977). "An Analysis of Religious vs. Secularist Trends on Anglo-Jewry Especially During the Past Fifteen Years". Paper presented to the Second Conference on Jewish Life in Modern Britain, London.

Jewish Educational Development Trust (1978). *Report on the Findings of the Committee on Teacher-Training and Career Structure*. London.

Levin, S.S. (1970). "The Changing Pattern of Jewish Education" in: Levin, S.S., (ed.). *A Century of Anglo-Jewish Life, 1870-1970*. The United Synagogue, London.

Lipman, V.D. and Lipman, S.L., eds. (1979). *Jewish Life in Britain, 1962-77*. K.G. Sauer, New York.

Newman, A. (1976). *The United Synagogue*. Routledge and Kegan Paul, London.

Prais, S.J. (1972). "Synagogue Statistics and the Jewish Population of Great Britain, 1900-70". *The Jewish Journal of Sociology*, Vol. 14, no. 2.

Prais, S.J. (1974). "A Sample Survey on Jewish Education in London, 1972-73". *The Jewish Journal of Sociology*, Vol. 16, no. 2.

Prais, S.J. (1977). "Polarization or Decline". Paper presented to the Second Conference on Jewish Life in Modern Britain, London.

Rubin, N. (1975). *Voluntary (Denominational) Schools Within the State Educational System*. London Board of Jewish Religious Education, London.

Steinberg, B. (1964). "Jewish Schooling in Great Britain", *The Jewish Journal of Sociology*, Vol. 6, no. 1.

Steinberg, B. (1965). "Jewish Education in Great Britain – Some Aspects of its Post-War Development". *Jewish Education*, Vol. 36, no. 1.

Taylor, D. (1981). *Jewish Education 1981/1982*. Jewish Educational Development Trust, London.

Worms, F.S. (June 1981). *Memorandum*. London. (Mimeograph).

Ziderman, A. (1966). "Leisure Activities of Jewish Teenagers in London". *The Jewish Journal of Sociology*, Vol. 8, no. 2.

9

Jewish Education in France

Yair Auron and Lucien Lazare

Prior to World War II, Jewish education in France was mostly part-time, either as religious instruction in the state schools or in a heder or Talmud Torah. In the primary and secondary public schools, class schedules included a weekly hour of religion. Students were grouped according to denomination (Catholic, Protestant or Jewish) and the lessons were taught by a priest, pastor or rabbi, respectively. Religious instruction classes in state schools were obligatory in the three border *départements* (counties) near Germany (Moselle, Bas-Rhin and Haut-Rhin)[1] and voluntary in the rest of France. Jewish religious instruction included Biblical history and Jewish living (Shabbat and holidays, kashruth, home and synagogue ritual), but not Hebrew or liturgy. The principal of the public school could excuse a child from obligatory religious instruction on presentation of a written request from his parents, and this was usually the case when a child reached bar mitzvah age.

The heder or Talmud Torah operated from four to six hours per week, on Sundays and Thursdays, when regular schools were closed throughout the country. Its syllabus included the Hebrew of the siddur and Torah (reading, writing, grammar), liturgy, translation of the most important prayers and texts, and, occasionally, also the Mishnah. Precise information about attendance rates, levels and achievement is not available. Some religious Jews registered their children in the heder at the age of six, with the start of their formal general schooling, but most children were enrolled at a later stage. Heder attendance usually ceased with the collective bat mitzvah ceremony for girls and the individual bar mitzvah ceremony for boys.

During the 19th century, France had only two full-time Jewish schools. One was the Jewish Seminary of France, founded in Metz in 1830 and transferred to Paris in 1859, which specialized in the training of rabbis. The other was the Eastern Jewish Normal School (Ecole Normale) of Paris, opened in the 1860s, where the Alliance Israélite Universelle trained teachers for its schools in North Africa, the Near East and the Balkans.

302   Yair Auron and Lucien Lazare

From the end of the 19th century, an influx of Jewish immigrants from Central and Eastern Europe to France necessitated the founding of charitable institutions which, in turn, opened Jewish elementary schools in Paris. Most of these 'charitable' schools were established through the generosity of the Barons Hirsch and Rothschild. During the German occupation of Paris in 1940 they were closed.

The purpose of the schools for immigrant children was to ease their transition from their former culture to that of France. Jewish studies were only marginal in the education program, which emphasized the 'Frenchification' of the pupils. This was characteristic of the French Jewish community's faith in the values of the bourgeois parliamentary democracy and French culture; whereas Jewishness was to be retained, it was adapted to the norms of French liberal, moderate society.

Most French Jews considered themselves immune to the antisemitic discrimination and violence spreading across Europe, but the more farsighted developed their own means of self-defence during the 1930s. Others, aiming to reinforce Jewish consciousness and provide the spiritual basis for resistance, turned to Jewish education. In 1936, the Ecole Maimonide for secondary pupils was established in Paris, and in 1938, a fledgeling yeshiva was opened in a suburb of Strasbourg. The German occupation of France in June 1940 caused the suspension of these schools. However, they were reopened when the war ended – the Ecole Maimonide in an inner suburb of Paris and the yeshiva in the Alps at Aix-les-Bains.

The French Jewish community was influenced by several developments during and after World War II. These included the loss of between 85,000 and 90,000 Jews, which was about one third of French Jewry, and the emergence of new groups of leaders from among the Holocaust survivors; the resettling in France of groups of survivors from Eastern and Central Europe; as well as the establishment of the State of Israel and the subsequent wars with the Arabs. Moreover, the settlement in France of several hundred thousand North African Jews during the 20 years after World War II changed the French community's character, ethnically and demographically.

These changes were expressed in Jewish education by the development of the Jewish day school movement, which took place in two stages – the first, from 1948 and throughout the 1950s; the second, since 1975.

The first phase in the establishment of day schools was limited almost entirely to two geographic locations – Paris and its surrounding region, and Strasbourg. Kindergartens, primary schools, secondary schools and yeshivoth were opened. In all cases, the initiative was taken by small groups of educational activists. The established local organizations, such as community bodies, consistories and the Fonds Social Juif Unifié (FSJU - United Jewish Community Fund) did not participate even when approached. In a few cases, however, the founders of the schools did obtain the cooperation and help of the Education Departments of the World Zionist Organization, while some of the yeshivoth were associated with movements in Israel and the United States, such as the Lubavitch Hasidim.

In the late 1950s and early 1960s, attempts were made to open Jewish day schools at Lyons and Marseilles, which were the main points of entry for Jewish immigrants from North Africa. However, it was many years before these schools were firmly established.

During the second, more intensive phase, day schools were established in centers other than Paris – in Toulouse, Marseilles, Metz, Nancy, Mulhouse, and elsewhere. Sometimes the initiative came from the community itself, but the main impetus came from two major organizations: *Otzar HaTorah*, which had conducted kindergartens and day schools in Morocco and Iran, and *Or Yosef*, which had established a modest yeshiva in the 1950s and which, since 1975, has become one of the most dynamic promotors of Jewish education in France. The latter established various educational institutions and (by agreement between the World Zionist Organization and the FSJU) received support from the Fonds d'Investissements Pour l'Education (FIPE – Investment Fund for Education). This fund has allowed for the establishment of new schools and the modernization and enlargement of others. In addition, the Lubavitch movement is deeply involved in establishing kindergartens and primary schools.

The Societal Context of Jewish Education

Normativeness of Private Schools and Government Support and Control

In France, parents may choose between the state school system and private schools. All state education, including the secondary and university stages, is free, whereas private schools usually charge tuition fees.

Jewish schools are part of the private educational system. Jewish day schools in France are all defined as private religious schools, disregarding differences in religious orientation, emphasis and the status accorded to Jewish studies.

Private schools in France, which are also called 'free', that is, independent schools , enroll some 2 million pupils from a total student body of 13 million. Private schools are a response to certain economic factors, or represent different educational or ideological approaches (Dreyfus, 1981). There are Catholic, Protestant, Jewish and secular private schools in France, altogether numbering around 11,000.

Whereas the expansion of the Jewish educational network has been associated with specifically Jewish factors, it has also been influenced by the growth of the private school sector as a whole. The growth of the private system in general, including Jewish schools, can be explained partly by increasing government aid to private education prior to and until May 1981, and partly by the perceived deterioration in the state school system. Enrollment growth in the private school sector reflects a decline since 1968 in the quality and standards of public education.

Despite the separation of Church and State in France since 1905, a private school can obtain government recognition by meeting the general educational requirements stipulated by the French Ministry of Education. Schools which receive government recognition obtain government aid, whether the government pays the salaries of teachers of general subjects or gives grants directly to the school or to pupils.[2]

Most Jewish day schools have obtained government recognition and are therefore government-aided. An example is ORT-France, about 80% of whose budget in France is covered by the government and by donations from industrialists, although it is part of the private education sector.[3]

During the period of Socialist government in the 1980s, French Jewry was worried about the possibility that the government might change its relationship with the private school sector. On the one hand, the government declared its intention to reform private education; on the other, it stated its recognition of the special religious-cultural nature of Jewish education, with which it did not wish to interfere.

At the end of 1981, the parents of the 4,500 children attending the eleven Jewish schools in Paris established a central parents' committee for all the Jewish schools – the Fédération des Associations de Parents d'Elèves des Ecoles Juives (FAPEEJ). The purpose of this organization is to preserve and protect the status and autonomy of Jewish schools, in light of the possibility that the French Government might strike a blow against the status of private schools. The committee also tried to find a place for itself among the Jewish organizations.

Community-Government Relations

External factors play a major role in unifying the Jewish community and determining community-government relations. Thus, Israel and governmental attitudes to it, as well as antisemitism, in France and elsewhere, have been instrumental in the shaping of Jewish identity and identification in France.

Both before and immediately following establishment of the State, the French public opinion supported Israel both in principle and in practice. France was regarded as Israel's ally. However, relations between the two countries changed, and since the Six-Day War in 1967, French government attitudes towards the Middle East conflict have been perceived as increasingly pro-Arab.

This contrasted markedly with the impact of that war on French Jewry, an effect which was due mainly to two factors – the demographic changes resulting from Jewish immigration from North Africa in the late 1950s and early 1960s, and reaction to France's reserved relations with the State of Israel. The result has been that since 1967, Israel has occupied a more central role in Jewish identity and existence, even among those Jews not formerly concerned with Jewish national identity. Hence, 1967 marked a change in the relationship of French Jewry, on the one hand with the State of Israel, and, on the other hand, with the French government.

General de Gaulle's description in 1967 of the Jewish people as "proud, self-confident and over-bearing" provoked reaction even from Jews who had previously not openly identified as such (Auron, 1979). The organized community – including the President of the Representative Council of French Jewish Institutions (CRIF – Conseil Représentatif des Institutions Juives de France) and the Chief Rabbi of France – protested the statement. This organized protest represented a milestone in relations between the French government and the organized Jewish community (Kaplan, 1976). Some Jews accused the Jewish establishment of being insufficiently outspoken in its protests, while others claimed that de Gaulle's statement encouraged antisemitic sectors in society to resume overt activity.

During the 1970s, the French government was accused by French Jews of not taking a firm enough stand against antisemitic organizations or at least against those committing antisemitic acts in France. Indeed, some Jews accused the government of aiding anti-Zionist groups, and indirectly fostering antisemitic elements by its reserved and even hostile attitude toward Israel.

The foreign policies of Presidents de Gaulle (1958–69), Pompidou (1969–74) and Giscard d'Estaing (1974–81) tended to be pro-Arab, and this attitude was instrumental in the shaping of French public opinion. French Jewry responded with mass protest demonstrations in 1970 against the sale of planes to Libya, and, in 1973 with pro-Israel demonstrations during the Yom Kippur War. The 'twelve hours for Israel' gatherings held since 1976 have also served as an avenue for criticizing government policy. Only after the 1981 election of President Mitterrand, did France's policy toward Israel and the Middle East became more balanced.

Antisemitism

French attitudes and actions regarding Jews were embodied in the French Revolution which gave equal civil rights to Jews. But French attitudes also encompass modern antisemitic ideas, such as the racism of Gobineau in the 1850s, Drumont in the late 19th Century, the Dreyfus Affair (1894–1906), and the pre-war and World War II discrimination and persecution of French Jews. There has been a resultant tension in French attitudes toward Jews which, in turn, influences Jewish attitudes. Alongside a sense of belonging to the French nation, there are also fears of being alien, as well as anxieties about the situation of Jews in France.

The government headed by Giscard d'Estaing was accused, by the left and by some Jews, of not taking a sufficiently strong stand against extreme right-wing organizations which were allegedly cooperating with Arab terrorist organizations and discouraging the distinction between antisemitism and anti-Zionism. Simultaneously, these leftist sectors, again including some Jews, expressed political and emotional opposition to Israel, often in harsh terms, and even questioned Israel's right to exist. This latter tendency had weakened somewhat by the late 1970s.

Against this background of ambivalence, antisemitic acts continued – including the drawing of swastikas on Jewish buildings, violation of Jewish cemeteries, and damage to Jewish buildings – climaxing in the explosion near the rue Copernic synagogue in 1980 and the terrorist attack on the Goldenberg restaurant in 1982.

In post-war France, issues involving the conduct of the French government, French institutions and the French people toward Jews during World War II have been avoided.[4] There have been no programs in government schools to combat antisemitism and racism, to include French Jewry in the history of World War II or to study the Holocaust. Indeed, apart from memorial ceremonies, little has been done in this respect even in Jewish schools.

The Community Context of Jewish Education

Community Support and Control of Jewish Schooling

After World War II, French Jewry needed external assistance to re-establish itself and absorb the large post-war immigration of Jews to France. Faced with urgent reconstruction tasks, the community regarded Jewish education as a minor item on the agenda until the 1960s. The importance of Jewish education was recognized, but no serious steps for its development were taken. Only through the initiative of individuals or organizations that assigned high priority to education were any schools established. However, since the 1960s, there has been a continuous and significant increase in the importance attached to education by French Jewish communal organizations.

The central communal organization of French Jewry[5] is the FSJU. When founded in 1950, its main goals were:

- to coordinate the activities of the community's welfare and charity organizations; and
- to coordinate collection and distribution of funds for the various organizations which until then had competed for contributions.

The Joint Distribution Committee played a central role in organizing and financing the FSJU in its early years, and without the Joint's help, the FSJU could not have become the central organization of French Jewry. However, the Joint's influence and financial assistance have declined: in 1960, the Joint covered 50% of the FSJU budget, 41% in 1965, but by the late 1970s, over 80% of the FSJU budget was borne by French Jewry. From 1954 to 1964, the FSJU also received some 1.8 million francs per year from German group reparations funds. This money was earmarked by the FSJU for the construction of new community centers and cultural projects.

The main fund raising organization is the Appel Unifié Juif de France, (AUJF – United French Jewish Appeal), founded in 1968 in the aftermath of the Six-Day War. According to an agreement between the FSJU and the Jewish Agency (on Israel's behalf), the AUJF collects money both for French Jewry and Israel. The agreement stipulates how the funds are to be allocated. The FSJU actually assigned some 25% of the funding received from the AUJF to educational and cultural activities in each year from 1974 to 1977.[6]

The increasing importance attached to Jewish education is reflected in the establishment of FIPE. This fund, whose establishment was part of the agreement between the FSJU and the Jewish Agency, was created to establish an overall educational policy for formal and informal Jewish education in France. A committee, representing the two parent organizations, produced a Five-Year Plan in which 54 programs were to be established between 1977 and 1982. These included 17 formal educational programs, designed to create 3,400 additional places for students in day schools, 25 programs in community centers, four programs related to vocational training, and four programs for the development of Hebrew language studies. The total budget for the 54 programs was 66 million francs for the five-year period, two-thirds to be financed by the FSJU and one-third by the Jewish Agency. Of this sum, 80% was allocated to the development of formal Jewish education.

To receive FIPE aid, a school is required to:
- observe Jewish traditions and customs in its everyday program;
- promote aliyah through the study of Israel and Zionism;
- integrate students and teachers into the French Jewish community; and
- create bonds of identification with Jewish communities throughout the world.

Accordingly, the curriculum in FIPE-aided schools must include:
- Bible studies with traditional commentaries;
- modern Hebrew as a compulsory subject at primary and secondary levels;

- Jewish history – students must study the complete history of the Jewish people, including modern Jewish history, at least once by the completion of schooling;
- Jewish Law and Customs, with the study of Mishnah and Gemara at least in secondary school.

Each school seeking FIPE aid is expected to develop its own curriculum and syllabus in accordance with these requirements. Every teacher of a Jewish subject must be trained in both pedagogic and Jewish studies. In reality, these requirements are not always met.

Geographic, Social and Occupational Mobility

Mass immigration to France from North Africa – mainly from Tunisia and Morocco in the late 1950s, and Algeria in the early 1960s – radically altered the character and size of French Jewry. After Israel, France now has the largest number of North African Jews in the world. The number of Jewish immigrants to France between 1950 and 1970 has been estimated at about 250,000, giving it the largest Jewish community in Western Europe, and the third largest in the Diaspora, after the United States and the Soviet Union (DellaPergola and Bensimon, 1978).

Jewish migration from North Africa to France had significant demographic consequences such as the formation of new Jewish communities and the expansion of existing ones. The greatest change was the increased Jewish population in and around Paris which today contains more than half (55–60%) of the French Jewish population. The next largest concentration of Jews is in Southern France, along the Mediterranean coast.

It is estimated that less than 10% of French Jews live in the Alsace-Lorraine region, a similar percentage in the Lyons area, and another 10% around Toulouse. It follows that the Jewish population in the North, the West and the broad Paris basin is small – altogether less than 10% of French Jewry.

Some 55 towns in France contain Jewish communities of over 1,000 – the largest being Paris, Marseilles, Lyons, Toulouse, Nice, Strasbourg, Grenoble and Bordeaux. Most of the rest of these have less than 5,000 Jews. In these small communities, the limited Jewish population and the corresponding number of school-aged children is a crucial factor in determining the existence and nature of Jewish educational facilities.

French Jewry is a predominantly lower-middle to middle class group which has been economically integrated into the general society and tends toward upward social and occupational mobility (Bensimon and Della Pergola, 1984). The socioeconomic integration of Jewish immigrants from North Africa has been rapid, largely because of their adaptation via the Jewish educational system. Salaried, mostly medium-income earners comprise over 60% of the Jewish labor force in Paris and over 80% in the suburbs; many are employed in the public sector. The proportion of Jewish laborers is low, and that of independent craftsmen and merchants is declining, but there has been a significant increase of Jews in the liberal professions and in managerial positions. The occupational profile and socioeconomic status of French Jewry have important implications in terms of participation in the development of Jewish education.

Trends in Family Life

French Jewry is generally an aging population, but there are regional differences between Paris and its suburbs in the average age of the Jewish community and the percentages of children. The Jewish population in the suburbs tends to be younger with a higher proportion of children, than the Paris Jewish population with its higher percentage of old people. Moreover, the age-breakdown of European-origin Jews, due to the Holocaust and low wartime birth rates, shows the highest percentage of elderly. This trend toward an elderly Jewish population is likely to continue and will require some reorganization of Jewish institutions. Provisions for the aged will require an increasingly larger share of the community's financial resources, whereas the educational system may have to cater to a shrinking student body.

The Jewish birth rate in Paris and its suburbs was estimated in the 1970s at about 10–11 births per 1,000. Since this figure approximates the mortality rate, there is no natural increase. Data on the current fertility of Jewish women in Paris in the early 1970s indicate an average of 1.5 children which is too low for generational replacement. The rate is particularly low among women born in France and other European countries. Women born in North Africa still have a slightly higher rate, but compared to the 4–5 children among older (60+) women of this origin, a strong downward trend among the younger women is evident. It appears that most children of large families were born either while the family was still in North Africa or else during their early years in France, whereas the younger generation has quickly adapted to the low birth rate of the French Jews (Bensimon and DellaPergola, 1984).

The Jewish population, which increased dramatically with post-war immigration, can no longer rely on this source of growth, and in the future, Jewish educational development will be affected by the community's trends towards aging and declining birth rates. The number of school-aged children will decrease correspondingly, exacerbating the problems of Jewish education, particularly in the smaller communities.

Intermarriage

The rate of intermarriage in France has been rising since the late 1950s. Of all marriages involving at least one Jew before 1955, less than one-sixth were mixed marriages. By 1956–65, the proportion had risen to one-third, and it reached one-half in the years 1966–75. This means that about one-third of all Jewish brides and bridegrooms intermarried in the late 1960s and early 1970s (DellaPergola, 1986). Recently, a significant increase has been noted in out-marriages by Jewish women.

There are significant differences in the frequency of mixed marriages among the various ethnic groups within French Jewry. Among European Jews (including those born in France) intermarriage accounted for over 60% of marriages between 1966 and 1975. In the same period, the rate was about 25% among Jews from North Africa, which represented a significant though smaller rise. Among North African Jews, there were significant sub-group differences according to country of origin. In the period under consideration, there were less than 5% mixed marriages among Moroccan and Tunisian Jews who married in France, compared to 49% among Algerian Jews, among whom intermarriage was relatively common as early as the 1950s (Bensimon and DellaPergola, 1984).

Intermarriage rates also seem to be age-related, and late marriages are more often mixed marriages. Furthermore, mixed couples appear to have fewer children.

Intermarriage is likely to remain one of the major problems confronting French Jewry; indeed, it will probably become more acute. Most of the present Jewish population still originates from Eastern Europe or North Africa, with strong traditions of opposition to intermarriage, whereas the younger generation – the future marriage partners – lives and is being educated in an open society together with non-Jews, and possesses fewer such inhibitions regarding out-marriage. Moreover, French society and culture have probably been more assimilative than other open Western societies with large Jewish communities, such as the United States and Britain.

The Jewish educational system does not provide a solution for the children of intermarriage, and very few of them are educated in Jewish schools. Formal Jewish schools, with their religious character, hardly offer a suitable framework for such children, and are unlikely to accept them particularly since in most cases, it is the mother who is not Jewish. Occasionally, a mixed family desires some Jewish education for its child, but such a child will find difficulty in entering the Jewish educational institutions of France.

There are also very few children of mixed marriages in Jewish youth movements. A survey conducted among senior members of youth movements in France found that only 4% of the children in these groups were the offspring of mixed marriages (Auron, 1979). Accordingly, the claim that youth movements serve as a 'shelter' for children of mixed marriages cannot be supported by evidence. Indeed, such children are rarely found even in the left-wing non-Zionist youth movements, in the socialist-Zionist youth movements, or in the Jewish scouting movement.

Parental Motivation and Support

In spite of the erosive trends just noted, the French Jewish family is a positive force in the development of Jewish education. In a number of cases, it has been the parents who initiated the establishment of Jewish schools. Moreover, parental demand for Jewish education is demonstrated by the fact that, despite the significant increase in Jewish day schools, hundreds of applicants are refused annually due to lack of places.[7]

The motivation of parents to provide a Jewish education for their children can be explained by a number of factors, one of which is the desire for a child's upward social mobility. The *Baccalauréat* (matriculation) examinations are therefore an important criterion for a school and the success rate in these examinations is higher. For the 1979–80 school year it was 76% in Jewish schools compared to 64% in the general schools in the Paris region.

Another factor which has increased the attraction of Jewish schools is the apparent lowering, in the state schools, of the standards of schooling which is required for further education and occupational advancement. Furthermore, the complex problems which confront government schools in the large cities, towns and suburbs, such as discipline and heterogeneous student populations, are less acute in fee-paying private schools, which tend to be more selective in pupil-intake.

Demographic factors are also reflected in parental motivation. The large section of French Jewry originating from North Africa had aspirations of upward socioeconomic mobility, and, having achieved that quite swiftly and easily, they concerned themselves with the preservation of their Jewishness. Evidently these Jews on occasion suffer feelings of alienation and fear for the future, which reinforces their feelings of Jewishness and their demand for Jewish education.

At the same time, feelings of Jewish belonging and identification have been revived among many French Jews, encouraging many parents to provide Jewish education for their children. While such parents are still a minority, the number of children receiving Jewish education on a daily basis has increased.

Furthermore, increasing acknowledgement of the multi-cultural composition of the general French population has encouraged recognition of ethnic, regional and religious sub-groups. This has created an atmosphere which reinforces the maintenance of Jewish identity through Jewish education.

All the existing Jewish schools are religious, and there are those who feel that this fact may have limited parental support and participation, and that the expansion of the Jewish educational system has been slowed because parents who want to provide Jewish education not of a religious, but of a nationalist or cultural character are deterred. It follows that while religious schools serve the needs of the Orthodox and even 'traditional' Jewish sectors, they do not satisfy the educational needs and motivations of those who are not religious in orientation or practice.

Given the increasing parental motivation toward Jewish education perhaps this need for non-religious Jewish day schools may be realized in the future despite the attendant difficulties.

The Structural Characteristics of Jewish Education

Full-time Schools

Available information indicates that in the school year 1980/81, some 50 Jewish day schools (full-time schools) were operating in France. These included kindergartens, primary and secondary schools. They were distributed as follows: 10 schools in Paris (20% of the total), 16 (32%) in the Paris suburbs, and 24 (48%) in other cities and towns. Of the latter, six were in Marseilles and five in Strasbourg.

Enrollment distribution indicates that the largest concentration of Jewish school pupils is in and around Paris. In 1980/81 there were some 8,352 students from kindergarten to the secondary school level in Jewish day schools throughout France. Of these, 69% were in the Greater Paris area – 2,568 (31%) in the city itself and another 3,184 (38%) in the Paris suburbs. Of the remaining 31% (2,600 pupils), 10% were in Marseilles and 9% in Strasbourg.

The overall picture is of a concentration of Jewish day schools in Paris and its suburbs, small concentrations in Marseilles and Strasbourg, Aix-les-Bains (5% of all pupils), Lyons (3%) and Nice (2%) and very small educational projects in other places, amounting in any one place to not more than 1% of the total day school enrollment in France.

Precise information regarding 36 of the 50 Jewish day schools was supplied to the FSJU. These 36 schools accounted for 6,412 of the 8,352 students attending Jewish day schools in France in 1980/81. Twenty-five of them, attended by 4,446 pupils, were supported by the FSJU. Two yeshivoth – Yeshiva d'Aix-les-Bain founded in 1945 and Yeshiva *Etz Haim*, Elizabethville, founded in 1979, which together enrolled 246 pupils – also received FSJU support.

The ORT system, which enrolled 2,993 pupils in vocational schools for youth and another 1,631 students in vocational training courses for adults in

TABLE 1. DISTRIBUTION OF 36 EDUCATIONAL INSTITUTIONS, BY LEVEL – FRANCE, 1980/81

School Level[a]	Institutions				No. of Pupils	Institutions sponsored by the FSJU	
	Total	Paris City	Paris Suburbs	Other Cities		Schools	Pupils
Total	36	7	12	17	6,412	25	4,446
M.	11	2	2	7	339	8	258
M.E.	3	1	1	1	158	3	158
M.E.C.	5	1	2	2	1,429	3	1,178
M.E.C.L.	3	0	2	1	1,297	1	338
E.	2	0	0	2	123	2	123
E.C.	1	1	0	0	58	0	–
E.C.L	3	0	2	1	1,293	2	880
C.L.	5	1	3	1	1,202	4	1,083
L.	3	1	0	2	513	2	428

(a) M. = Kindergarten (Maternelle); E. = Elementary School (Ecole); C. = Junior High School (College); L. = High School (Lycée).

TABLE 2. DISTRIBUTION OF 36 EDUCATIONAL INSTITUTIONS, BY SCHOOL LEVEL – FRANCE, 1980/81

School Level	Divisions	Classes	Pupils
	Absolute Numbers		
Total	70	330	6,412
Kindergartens	22	50	892
Primary Schools	17	101	1,962
Junior High Schools	17	100	1,971
High Schools	14	79	1,587
	Percentages		
Total	100.0	100.0	100.0
Kindergartens	31.4	15.2	13.9
Primary Schools	24.3	30.6	30.6
Junior High Schools	24.3	30.3	30.7
High Schools	20.0	23.9	24.8

1980/81 is not included in the 36 schools mentioned above. Included however are the schools of the three organizations whose independent educational activities are funded from other sources – *Chabad, Or Yosef,* and *Otzar HaTorah.* The educational activities of these three organizations are of an intensively religious nature, and have increased significantly in recent years, being particularly successful among immigrant families from North Africa.

The number of hours per week devoted to Jewish studies[8] varies according to the nature, educational level and aims of each school. In the primary schools and departments, the time allotted ranges from seven to eight hours (e.g. Ecole Lucien de Hirsch, Ecole Aquiba Strasbourg) to 13 hours or more in more intensely religious schools, such as *Merkaz HaTorah,* Ecole Ariel and Ecole Moriah. In the secondary schools and departments, the allotment is similar, though it sometimes decreases in the final years, and particularly in the final year. Still more hours are spent on Jewish studies in the yeshivoth

TABLE 3.   NUMBER OF PUPILS IN JEWISH DAY SCHOOLS SUBSIDIZED BY THE FSJU AND/OR FIPE – FRANCE, 1978/79–1981/82

School Level	1978/79	1979/80		1980/81		1981/82	
	Pupils	Pupils	% Change since 1978/79	Pupils	% Change since 1979/80	Pupils	% Change since 1980/81

Absolute Numbers

Total	3,859	4,007	+3.8	4,446	+11.0	4,470	+ 5.4
Kindergarten	496	531	+7.0	615	+15.8	674	+9.6
Primary School	988	1,067	+8.0	1,250	+17.2	1,388	+11.0
Junior High School	1,245	1,187	–4.7	1,225	+3.2	1,345	+9.8
High School	1,130	1,222	+8.1	1,356	+11.0	1,333	–1.2

Percentages

Total	100.0	100.0		100.0		100.0	
Kindergarten	12.8	13.3		13.8		15.1	
Primary School	25.6	26.6		28.1		31.0	
Junior High School	32.3	29.6		27.6		30.1	
High School	29.3	30.5		30.5		29.8	

and in Yeshiva d'Aix, for example, more than 20 hours per week are devoted to studying Judaism.

It is evident from Tables 1 and 2 that some full-time schools concentrate on one specific age group or stage of schooling, such as kindergarten or secondary school, while in others more grades are taught. Some institutions, especially kindergartens, are small, with only 30 to 50 pupils, while others have large enrollments. Several schools have enrollments of over 500, such as the Ecole Lucien de Hirsch in Paris, which in 1980/81 enrolled some 775 pupils in its kindergarten, primary, and secondary departments, and the Ecole Yavne in Paris, with 698 students.

The percentage of kindergarten and first grade pupils in the day school student population has risen in recent years, which is not to imply any decrease of older pupils, but rather, that early childhood Jewish education has become more attractive to parents. Table 3 shows this increase for the school years 1978/79–1981/82.

The considerable enlargement of the day schools has not been equal to the growing demand, and in each year between 1977 and 1982, some 950 pupils were not accepted for enrollment.[9] This problem has been most acute in Paris and its suburbs. In 1979/80, for example, 200 applicants reportedly could not be accepted by the Ecole Lucien de Hirsch, another 200 were turned down by the Ecole Yavne, and 50 applicants were unable to enroll in the Ecole de Pavillons-sous-Bois.

Hebrew in State Schools

In 1981, Hebrew was taught in 60 state secondary schools, and some 1,552 pupils studied Hebrew through this provision.

Talmud Torah Schools

Formal part-time Jewish education is provided by Talmud Torah schools. Almost every synagogue in France has its own school, serving pupils between the ages of 6–7 years and 12–13. The number of boys far exceeds the number of girls. Talmud Torah classes, which at most involve 6 hours of Jewish studies per week, are held on Wednesdays and/or Sundays. It is possible that up to 10,500 pupils are enrolled in Talmudei Torah, some 50% in Greater Paris.

Talmudei Torah suffer from several basic difficulties, such as shortage of suitable teachers, irregular pupil attendance, and lack of structured curricula. Attempts have been made in recent years to introduce a uniform curriculum for three years of study, including Hebrew reading, basic rules of Jewish conduct, the prayer book, and Biblical history, but this has yet to be implemented. A pedagogic service for Talmudei Torah was established in 1973/74 by the Consistoire Central.

Talmud Torah teachers in small towns are usually local rabbis with no pedagogic qualifications. In the larger towns teachers are senior day school and tertiary Jewish students who lack the necessary Jewish learning and pedagogic qualifications as well. Teacher training provisions are minimal, but the few Talmudei Torah conducted by the Reform movement and those in the Strasbourg region appear to be more effective in attracting trained teachers and in providing teacher-training programs.

Formal Tertiary Jewish Education

In general, French Jewry has regarded higher education and scientific research as the responsibility of secular universities, and tertiary or advanced religious education has been limited to the training of religious leaders, that is, the rabbinate.

Rabbinical Training

The oldest institution of Jewish higher education is the Israelite Seminary of France, presently attended by 30 students seeking ordination as rabbis. The Seminary is under the auspices of the Consistoire Central, which is responsible for its budget.

Conventional Yeshivoth Gedoloth

The first *yeshiva gedola* was opened in the late 1930s at Strasbourg, where some refugees from yeshivoth in Eastern Europe had settled. After World War II, other *yeshivoth gedoloth* were opened, also mostly by immigrants. These were sometimes supported by individual leaders of large French Jewish organizations: however, neither the Consistoire nor the FSJU were involved on an organizational basis.

Today there are ten *yeshivoth gedoloth* in France, of which six are in the Paris region. Most are affiliated with an organization which provides funding from donations collected mainly abroad; occasionally they receive funds from international organizations such as the Lubavitch, *Otzar HaTorah* and *Or Yosef* movements, or from the Jewish Agency.

Several of the *yeshivoth gedoloth* consist of a *kollel* integrated with a secondary school. The total number of adult students in such a yeshiva or *kollel* is probably about 125.

Yeshivoth Gedoloth for Tertiary Students

In the 1960s, a yeshiva for university students was opened at Strasbourg by Rav Abitbol from Morocco. Similar institutions were subsequently established in the four university towns of Lyons, Toulouse, Marseilles and Nice. Courses were developed at different levels for both male and female students in various university faculties, and the students themselves were allowed to decide on the duration and frequency of their yeshiva courses. Several university students were admitted to the Yeshiva's *kollel*, either during or after their university studies. The optional and informal character of this type of institution creates problems in program evaluation or data collection, but probably about 100 Jewish university students presently take courses within this framework.

The university yeshivoth are the only yeshiva-type institutions frequented by young assimilated Jewish adults, and many of these continue in the process of intensive Jewish re-identification. Some train as teachers with the goal of establishing and teaching in university yeshivoth in other university towns. Rav Abitbol, the head of the network, who has been sympathetic to Jewish student activities, works outside the organized community structures, and is not beyond criticizing the politics and actions of the French Jewish establishment – features which appeal to Jewish university students.

University Judaic Studies

The number of students enrolled in Judaic studies at French universities has increased dramatically. For example, 1,200 students registered in the Hebrew department of the Institut National des Langues et Civilisations Orientales – (INALCO – National Institute for Oriental Languages and Civilizations) of Paris-III University during the academic year 1981, compared with 113 students in 1965. Even if the increase was not as dramatic in other universities which offer Jewish studies, the general trend is evident. The number of students in other Hebrew departments throughout France is estimated to have increased from 80 in 1965 to 900 in 1981.

About 20 French universities offer courses in Jewish studies, including some which lead to second and third degrees; the smaller ones offer only Hebrew language courses. Some 12 university lecturers offer Hebrew courses under the aegis of a scientific and cultural agreement between the governments of France and Israel.

There has also been a dramatic increase in post-graduate research on Jewish themes. The *Catalogue des Doctorats Hebraica-Judaica* in 1986 recorded 1,002 doctoral theses on Jewish themes either in preparation, or completed in France between 1974 and 1984.

Besides formal degree and post-graduate Jewish studies courses at universities, in Paris, the Centre Universitaire d'Etudes Juives (CUEJ - University Institute of Jewish Studies), provides university extension courses which attract a large Jewish public, of which many are tertiary students.

On the one hand, the dramatically increased popularity of Jewish studies at universities contrasts with the formal Jewish school system which, notwithstanding its significant expansion, still reaches only a small proportion of Jewish children and youth, with the corollary that the university framework provides the earliest opportunity for many Jewish students to acquire Jewish knowledge. On the other hand, the main issues concerned with Jewish studies at universities in France are:

– how to provide more intensive Jewish studies course-content and broaden the range of studies beyond the narrow requirements for a bachelor's degree, particularly in the small university departments outside Paris; and

– how to overcome the lack of textbooks and other resource materials in French required for the teaching of Jewish studies at French universities.

Personnel in Jewish Education

Who Teaches Jewish Studies

Teachers of Jewish studies in France come from a wide variety of backgrounds. These include:

– Hebrew teachers who have completed their university training with at least a first degree equivalent to a B.A. in Hebrew and teaching;

– qualified kindergarten teachers whose Jewish studies qualifications are not known;

– Israeli *shlihim* who are professionally qualified and experienced Jewish studies teachers;

– former pupils of yeshivoth or *Beth Jacob* in France, Morocco, Great Britain or Israel, qualified in Jewish studies, and possessing professional teacher training, though this may not be on a generally recognized tertiary level;

– rabbis qualified in the subject matter they teach, but with no qualifications or experience in teaching;

– community workers and university students, with Jewish background from school and/or tertiary education, but lacking formal teaching qualifications.

While teachers from all these backgrounds may be found in the part-time Jewish schools – the Talmudei Torah and ORT vocational centers – full-time Jewish schools tend to engage those in the first four categories.

Number and Sex

It would be difficult to estimate the total number of Jewish teachers in France from the fragmented information available. The situation is further complicated by the fact that many teachers of Jewish subjects in full-time schools also teach in part-time schools. However, data for the full-time schools are available for the school years 1979–1981 (see Table 4).

The professional stability of the teaching personnel in the full-time schools – notwithstanding disadvantages of poor salaries, part-time conditions, and low status – is evident from Table 4. However, in the part-time schools, the teacher holds a post between one and three years, this high turnover probably being related in part to the marginal nature of this type of Jewish education, which affects both job satisfaction and remuneration. In the rare well-structured Talmud Torah, for instance, a teacher may teach 10 to 12 hours weekly, but in most cases, the weekly teaching load is only four hours. Similarly, Jewish education in ORT schools comprises only 5% of scheduled activities. Moreover, few teachers in part-time schools are totally dependent on this teaching and many have full-time employment or studies of greater importance.

Most kindergarten teachers are women, but Jewish studies teaching at the primary and secondary day school levels is male-dominated. In eleven full-time schools and kindergartens, with a total of 3,460 pupils, there are 138 teachers of whom only 48 (34%) are female. It may be assumed that most of these 48 teach in the kindergartens or at the younger primary levels, and it follows that there is virtually a monopoly of male Jewish studies teachers in the secondary schools. Thus, while some of the Hebrew teachers may be women, teachers of Gemara in the secondary schools, and all Jewish studies teachers in yeshiva secondary schools and departments, are males.

TABLE 4. JEWISH AND HEBREW TEACHING PERSONNEL, BY SCHOOL TYPE – FRANCE, 1979/80–1980/81

School Type	Total Teachers 1979/80	Teachers Dismissed or Resigned Summer 1980	Teachers Hired Fall 1980	Total Teachers 1980/81
Total	177	48	58	187
Kindergartens	30	8	17	39
Full-time schools	147	40	41	148

Teacher Supply, Demand, Recruitment and Training

It is evident from the fact that many full-time teachers have either been trained overseas or are *shlihim* from Israel, and from the high turnover of part-time teachers, that the supply of local teachers of Jewish studies is an urgent consideration.

Despite the accepted perception of Jewish studies teachers as a disfavored low-earning group, some enter the profession for idealistic reasons, but many do because of the general employment situation in France, or as a second-choice.

The recruitment of local teachers tends to be regarded as a problem of teacher training rather than teaching conditions. Attempts have been made to provide this training for those motivated to a career in Jewish teaching, and a teacher training seminary has been established at Yerres, in the Paris outskirts, by the Lubavitch movement, while another seminary at Marseilles was founded by the *kollel* and is affiliated with *Otzar HaTorah*. Some 20 students attend these two seminaries. In 1975, a training institute was opened near the *Etz Haim* Yeshiva at Montreux, Switzerland. In 1980, the FSJU established a teacher training seminary for kindergarten and primary teachers – the Centre de Formation de Jardinières d'Enfants et d'Enseignants – which in its initial phase has enrolled five students per year. Furthermore, grants for training in Israeli institutions which specialize in Diaspora Jewish education were made available by the Department of Torah Education of the World Zionist Organization. The Central Consistoire provides for pedagogic support to provincial Talmudei Torah.

Altogether the number who take advantage of these teacher training programs is small and insufficient. Accordingly, facilities for part-time, refresher and in-service training have been developed in the hope of improving the quality and lowering the turnover of existing teachers. Some 40 participants each year attend a training course in the teaching of Talmud Torah classes, organized annually by the Education Department of the Jewish Agency in cooperation with the Consistoires of Paris and of provincial localities which culminates in a month's intensive internship in Israel during the summer vacation. In addition, the Department of Torah Education offers continuous training courses of various types and levels – in-service courses, summer and winter courses of one to several weeks' duration in Israel or Europe, and year-long courses for teachers likely to assume responsibility beyond classroom teaching. The FSJU Department for Schools also organizes in-service pedagogical seminars and provides guidance alongside its inspection of Hebrew teachers.

Participation in such training programs is voluntary and dependent on the personal initiative of each teacher. Despite the undoubted benefits in terms of staff recruitment, stability and quality, school principals and directors are rarely concerned with the continued professional development of their staff.

Salaries

Salaries paid to teachers in Jewish schools differ according to the subject-matter taught, the type of school, the teacher's qualifications, and whether teaching is part- or full-time.

Almost all full-time schools and kindergartens have opted for contracts with the French Ministry of National Education, which pays either partial or complete salaries to teachers of secular subjects, provided that the school satisfies three conditions:

- it must submit to inspection of its implementation of programs and schedules prescribed by the Ministry;
- proof must be available of minimum class sizes; and
- teachers must hold state-recognized qualifications.

The only Jewish schools which do not participate in this contract system are those with less than the prescribed minimum number of pupils or those which, for ideological reasons, provide fewer hours of secular instruction than the minimum stipulated by the Ministry.

If the day school meets Ministry conditions, Hebrew teachers receive salaries based on the contract, since, at the secondary level, Hebrew is a recognized foreign language, i.e. a secular subject. Teachers of Hebrew at the secondary level must therefore have a French university degree (or its recognized equivalent); they have the status of state teachers, and their salaries are paid either in full or in part by the state.

Teachers of other Jewish studies do not receive state-paid salaries, and for them, a salary scale based on qualifications and seniority was established by a commission of Jewish school directors. Teachers who work in schools which accept this scale receive their salaries accordingly: but this applies only to a small minority of schools. The scale provides a salary level about 80–90% of that in the state system, where promotion and pension conditions are also superior.

Salaries of the vast majority of paid Jewish studies teachers in both full and part-time schools, including ORT schools, are determined by school directors who tend to be influenced by budgetary considerations and, therefore, provide salaries at the lowest possible levels. Thus teachers must often work at more than one job – in a full-time school, a part-time Talmud Torah and possibly also private tutoring.

The poorest paid Jewish studies teachers are those employed on an hourly basis in ORT schools and in Talmudei Torah. Whereas rabbis and community workers who teach in Talmudei Torah do so as part of their regular work, the paid teachers in Talmud Torah schools receive the lowest salary, since most of them are students, and therefore not yet qualified; furthermore, the maximum possible number of hours of paid teaching is small and these schools have the most limited budgets.

There have been attempts to organize a union of Jewish teachers to improve these inferior conditions, but they failed, either because most teachers were apathetic and lacked union consciousness, or because disparities between the different categories of teachers prevented cooperation on a common interest basis.

The Functioning and Impact of Jewish Education

Goals, Curricula, Teaching Methods and Strategies

In the perception of many Jewish parents, the reputation of a full-time Jewish school depends mainly on the standard of secular studies. School directors are aware of this, and accordingly seek to engage secular staff of high quality. This is reflected in the results of Jewish schools in the final matriculation examinations, which are generally superior to the French national average.

The schools aim to inspire commitment to the local Jewish community, the Jewish people, and to the development and practice of individual and collective responsibility. This goal of personal and collective responsibility is reflected in the curriculum of Jewish studies, which includes Bible, Jewish history, Jewish law and customs, modern Hebrew, with emphasis on the study of the mitzvoth, the Sabbath and Jewish festivals. In addition, some selected contemporary Jewish topics have been introduced, such as Israel, the Holocaust and Jews in the Soviet Union.

Teaching methods in all French schools, including the Jewish ones, reflect the conservative nature of the French educational system. In general, pedagogic methods are directed only toward the development of intellectual potential. In Jewish schools, this is aggravated by the facts of:

- financial disadvantages as compared to the state schools, whose budgets stretch to cover special activities and resource materials such as audiovisual equipment; and
- Jewish teachers' lack of the pedagogic training and experience needed to avoid conservative teaching methods.

The exception to this atmosphere of pedagogic conservatism is the Jewish kindergarten, which almost always stimulates creativity, personalizes activities and integrates intellectual, manual and emotional development.

Social-recreational activities in Jewish schools, as in most French schools, are generally not part of the formal program for which qualified staff members are responsible. In any case, the potential for Jewish social, recreational and extra-curricular activities is limited by the time needed to provide both Jewish and secular studies, and by the geographic distances between pupils' homes.

Many day schools have adopted 'streaming' at the secondary stage of schooling. Because they enroll pupils at different stages and with different backgrounds in Jewish knowledge, Jewish studies pupils are divided into groups based on their level of Jewish knowledge rather than age. The advanced 'streams', which are usually allotted the best Jewish studies teachers, usually attain high achievement in Jewish studies, but the middle and lower streams barely reach elementary levels. Pupils who enter the secondary school at later stages, particularly if they lack prior Jewish education, achieve the least.

Social Climate of the Jewish School

In a small number of schools, the student population is drawn almost entirely from Orthodox homes, and the religious orientation is homogeneous. Conversely, children from Orthodox families rarely attend Talmud Torah schools, so that these schools also present an unmixed religious orientation. However, in most schools, the population is mixed, and Orthodox pupils are in the minority. On occasion, regrouping occurs within the Jewish studies program, so that some classes contain a majority of Orthodox pupils. In general, the relative proportion of Orthodox pupils is declining, since the Sephardic families, who are becoming the dominant element of the French Jewish population, are increasingly reluctant to define themselves as Orthodox.

In general, Jewish day schools do not attract non-Jews despite their high level of secular studies, because of the time devoted to Jewish studies – on average, eight hours weekly. However, a significant number of non-Jewish pupils do attend the ORT schools. More than 50% of the pupils at the ORT school of Coulomiers, Toulouse are not Jewish. This high proportion is due to the high quality of technological and vocational education. Moreover, under a Ministry of Labor plan aimed at avoiding duplication of technological options within any region, the ORT technological and vocational centers may be the only institutions in the region offering particular courses and ORT schools must therefore accept non-Jewish pupils. However, the mix of non-Jewish and Jewish pupils in ORT schools is less problematic than would be the case in other Jewish day schools because of the small amount of time devoted to Jewish studies – at most, two hours per week, from which non-

Jewish students can easily be exempted without affecting the conduct of the school, or jeopardizing the students' progress.

Effects of Jewish Schooling

A study by Doris Bensimon (1971), indicated a low rate of assimilation among adults who had been full-time pupils in Jewish schools, and a great majority of these enroll their own children in Jewish schools. A more recent study (Bensimon and DellaPergola, 1984) confirms the existence of a significant relationship between past Jewish schooling (either full-time or part-time) and current Jewishness of attitudes and behavior.

The proportion of Jewish community leaders and politicians among former Jewish day school pupils is greater than in the general community. Moreover, it may be observed that among pupils currently in Jewish day schools, there is a high degree of participation and activism in Jewish youth movements, self-defence groups, and organizations and activities to support Jewish dissidents in the Soviet Union. Senior pupils participate in the guard system established by schools following recent attacks on synagogues and schools.

It has been noted that a significant proportion of graduates from Jewish day schools – varying with the school and the particular group of students – emigrate to Israel. Moreover, it appears to be rare for former day school pupils to marry outside the Jewish community.

In short, it would seem that the Jewish day school succeeds in promoting the student's identification with his school, and in providing an education which fosters a commitment to Judaism. Schools create an atmosphere favorable to the expression of emotional attachment to Judaism and the community, and develop a social climate of cooperation between students and teachers which encourages community-mindedness both in school and in later life. Of course, this identification can neither be measured nor compared with that in state schools.

Informal Jewish Education

Besides the formal Jewish school system, vacation centers, community centers, Jewish student groups and youth movements provide informal Jewish education of varying influence and intensity. Vacation centers are part of the general French tradition of encouraging vacation and leisure time programs and have been established by government and public bodies, as well as political and ideological groups.

Vacation centers for Jewish children have been sponsored by Jewish community organizations such as the FSJU and the Centres Culturels de Vacances et de Loisirs (CCVL), as well as by political and ideological organizations to impart Jewish education together with a particular political or ideological orientation. However, this type of informal education is limited to vacation periods, and while participants may gain an awareness of issues, there is no continuity and no systematically imparted knowledge.

Jewish community centers were founded during the late 1950s and 1960s under the auspices of the FSJU or, on occasion, the Consistoire. The centers provide activities for all age groups, including adults. In general, community centers reflect the fact that the FSJU caters to all sections of the community and hence, to the common ˙denominator. Accordingly, community centers bring together Jewish youth and strengthen their sense of belonging to the Jewish community through assorted activities focussed on Israel and Judaism, but lack any defined educational programs.

The Union des Etudiants Juifs de France (UEJF – French Union of Jewish Students) was founded in 1944, and was the main Jewish student organization. While it is an ideologically independent and neutral body, it is pluralistic in nature, including students of Zionist, communist, religious, secular or other orientations. In the past, the UEJF was an influential body with several thousand Jewish students, and a number of important community figures began their public activities in this organization, but it has considerably weakened since the French student revolt of 1968. Other Jewish student organizations are special interest groups, affiliated with particular political parties or organizations. However, their size and influence is limited.

The first Jewish youth movements in France were founded in the early 1920s. The most important at the time were Les Eclaireurs Israélites de France (EIF – the Jewish Scouts) and the Union Universelle de la Jeunesse Juive (UUJJ – World Union of Jewish Youths), both founded in 1923. The youth movements of the Bund, the Jewish Communists, and the Zionist groups were also active between the two World Wars. Other youth organizations included one sponsored by the Consistoire, and another, the Ligue Internationale Contre l'Antisemitisme (LICA – International League against Antisemitism), which was almost entirely a youth group in membership. It is noteworthy that while the EIF and the UUJJ may be seen as indigenous French organizations, the other youth movements were offshoots of organizations founded in Eastern and Central Europe.

In Western and Central Europe 'youth movements for Jews' were transformed into distinctively Jewish youth organizations, but this did not happen in France, perhaps because France had no revolutionary youth groups such as the radical German youth movements. Also, French Jewry has by nature been less affected than other European Jewries by radical Jewish national movements and Zionist concepts. Despite the rapid impact of the secularization process on Jews in the 19th century, French Jewry continued to define its identity in purely religious terms, that is, French by nationality and 'Israelite' by religion. This was consistent with the emancipation ideology which maintained the legitimacy of social and cultural assimilation and viewed religion as the expression of Jewish identity and continuity.

This ideology of emanciption was first openly opposed after World War I mainly by young people and immigrants (Hyman, 1976). Although the UUJJ was not a Zionist organization, it was pro-Zionist, and it propounded Hebrew language teaching, and believed that Jewish education should be used to combat assimilation. Similarly the EIF, which originated as a Jewish branch of the French Scouts, developed into a youth movement with significantly Jewish (and later pro-Zionist) context and values, as reflected in the establishment of the Ecole des Cadres Gilbert Bloch, which was founded by the Jewish Scouts. This school, established in 1947 at Orsay near Paris and subsidized by the FSJU, was attended by young men and women who spent one year studying introductory courses to Jewish subjects. Each class numbered about 20 students.

During World War II, Jewish youth movements were very active in fighting against the Nazis, from underground activities to armed combat, and suffered heavy losses. The strongest movements in the post-war years were the EIF and the socialist-Zionist youth movements. The Jewish communist youth movement which had formerly been quite influential disbanded in the early 1950s. On the other hand, although there had been fears for the future of Jewish youth in the post-war period (Pougatch, 1955) new youth organizations emerged in response to changing circumstances. A Departement Educatif de la Jeunesse Juive (DEJJ – Jewish Youth Educational Organization) was established in 1962 within the FSJU framework, its goal being the absorption of Jewish youth from North Africa into French Jewish and general society. This function contributed to its growth in the 1960s, but the need declined during the 1970s. The DEJJ continues to exist as a youth organization.

The resurgence of religious Orthodoxy in the 1960s was associated with the North African immigration, and two religious movements – *Tikvatenu* and Lubavitch Youth, both founded in the late 1960s – consist mostly of youth from North Africa. Since the 1970s, Zionist youth movements such as *Betar* and *Bnei Akiva*, as well as religious organizations like *Tikvatenu* and Lubavitch Youth, have increased in popularity and influence. At the same time, the EIF has declined, and has encountered difficulties in attracting new members aged 16 years and over, a fact which resulted in the closing of the Ecole des Cadres Gilbert Bloch in 1972. The DEJJ is virtually redundant and the radical movements founded in the aftermath of the Six-Day War have disappeared.

Adult Jewish Education

Jewish cultural activities for adults have proliferated in the past decade. Hundreds of courses and study circles have been established and are attended by several thousand adults, though women are in the minority. Research into the programs of study, their type and quality, and numerical data on participants has not been undertaken. However, it seems that while some courses are ephemeral, in general, adult Jewish education is a successful endeavour.

There was no community concern for adult Jewish education in pre-World War II years, and it consisted mainly of several Yiddish cultural circles established by immigrant associations, and some study circles established by Jewish youth movements. Some of these developed secretly during the Nazi occupation and were continued in the concentration camps.

After World War II, cultural aspects were incorporated into some communal programs, with the aim of forming new avenues of Jewish identification among Jews who had cut off their synagogue attachments. Initially, occasional conferences and then series of thematic conferences were organized. Small Judaica libraries were established, some of which were subsequently expanded. The first cultural programs for adults were artistic and recreational, and these developed into courses which imparted information. Gradually, these activities became focussed in the community centers which were modelled both on Jewish community centers in the United States and on the youth and cultural centers then being established in France by the public authorities. Today, most Jewish communities in France contain a community center for both youth and adults.

Attendance at adult educational activities in community centers is largely dependent on the initiative of the volunteer and professional promoters. Several courses have been conducted to create a corps of professionals to direct and promote community centers. Thus we may reasonably estimate adult participation at several tens of thousands, with varying intensity and frequency of attendance.

Since the 1970s, there has been great progress in the range and number of courses offered. This may be attributed to:

- renewed adult interest in the cultural dimensions of Judaism;
- stimulus provided by the annual session of the Colloquium of Jewish Intellectuals of France, held under the auspices of the World Jewish Congress;
- persistent efforts by community leaders to promote adult Jewish education;
- the improved quality and level of the programs offered;
- the involvement of Jews in the current popular search for roots and culture; and

–   the general interest in personal self-development.

Adult education programs almost always include courses for the study of traditional source-literature (Bible, Commentaries, Mishnah, Gemara, *Zohar, Shulhan Arukh,* Jewish philosophy) and Hebrew language. Courses dealing with Jewish history, festivals, art and culture are offered less frequently. Usually, a course attracts between 10 to 25 participants. Of course there are particular courses which attract more, such as the Weekly Torah Portion Explanatory Course conducted on Shabbat by Professor Levinas on the premises of the Ecole Normale Israélite Orientale at Paris-Auteuil, and the Shabbat course offered by Chief Rabbi Sitruk at the Marseilles synagogue. Most Hebrew courses are provided in conjunction with the Jewish Agency, which is responsible for 120 *ulpanim* in community centers, attended by some 4,000 adults.

The major institutions, offering at least 12 courses each, are the University Institute of Jewish Studies (Rashi Center) in Paris' left bank; the community center (*Merkaz*) in Montmartre; the Community Center Poissonnière at Strasbourg; the community center and the *Beth Hamidrash* at Marseilles, and the *kollel* of the Chief Rabbinate at Nice. The *Beth Hamidrash* at Marseilles is privately initiated, and its program includes courses for the elderly and the physically handicapped.

In addition to institutions whose major function is adult education, various Jewish organizations provide courses, study circles and conferences for their members. These include the Women's International Zionist Organization (WIZO); B'nai B'rith; the *Mizrachi* Women's organization, *Emunah*; the Socialist organizations Tabenkin and Bernard Lazare in Paris; the Lubavitch and the *Or Yosef* movements. There are also privately initiated programs which are impossible to itemize, such as the group of Paris Jews which meets for prayer and study on Sabbath and festivals usually in at Deauville in Normandy.

Teachers in adult Jewish education programs are drawn from among the rabbis, rabbinical students, Israeli teachers in Jewish schools, *kollel* members, former students of Jewish schools and yeshivoth, Jewish academics and professionals, and occasionally the self-taught. Hebrew *ulpan* courses are usually designed and taught by Israelis living in France.

Adult Jewish education on a larger scale is provided by high quality weekly radio and television broadcasts which enjoy great popularity. Although the size of the audience is difficult to estimate, the popularity of radio as a mode of adult Jewish education is indicated by the fact that since the summer of 1982, several private Jewish radio stations have begun broadcasting.

The expansion of Jewish adult education has been paralleled by an increase in Jewish publications. Major publishers have created Jewish collections, but whether it is an exclusively Jewish clientele that is responsible for this resurgence of the Jewish book is unknown. However, the publishing of the Hebrew Pentateuch with an accompanying French translation, and an anthology of traditional commentaries selected and edited in French by Elie Munk, has been an outstanding commercial success, and despite the cumbersome and difficult content of these publications, several successive editions have been published in less than 10 years. Thus, we see a new-found demand for Jewish studies.

This demand has also created a need for audio-visual resource materials. The educational book publishers, *Keren Hasefer Vehahinukh*, have moved into the production of Jewish educational programs on cassettes, and plan to produce similar programs on videotape. They also provide radio teaching aids and learning materials for adult Jewish groups located far from the major Jewish centers.

Although various private and semi-public organizations conduct education programs, organized school-based adult education is rare in France. Provisions or proposals for systematic school-based Jewish adult education do not exist. However, one Talmud Torah school (in the Latin quarter of Paris) does assemble the parents of its pupils five times yearly for courses and conferences on themes related to their children's studies and domestic Jewish life. Also two women's organizations – WIZO and the FSJU-promoted Coopération Feminine – have established training and discussion programs for parents which are utilized by activist groups.

Conclusions

For a long time, Jewish day schools were conducted by a small activist elite, and virtually ignored by the community's official organizations. Their growth has been due to the increase in the Jewish population following large-scale immigration after World War II, and to a heightened sense of Jewish identity which has promoted participation in all modes of Jewish identification. Thus, in the past decade an increasing number of parents have chosen to educate their children in Jewish day schools and this increasing popularity has, in turn, encouraged the involvement of community organizations.

While the demand exists for intensive education of the yeshiva type, most of the French Jewish population favors an education which combines Jewish and secular studies and conforms to official programs prescribed by the French Ministry of Education. This general preference is encouraged by the financial aid provided by the state to schools which teach prescribed Ministry programs.

Jewish studies are seriously handicapped by the absence of structured courses, the dearth of textbooks, the heterogeneity of pupils, and particularly, the scarcity of teachers. The gap in quality between secular and Jewish studies is a matter for serious concern, yet there are no plans for cooperation on the issue of teacher-training in Jewish studies, excluding Hebrew – where training has been assumed by universities.

Despite the considerable increase in day school education and in the number of day schools, the Talmud Torah remains a most important framework for Jewish education. The number of Talmud Torah schools has increased with the number of synagogues, *oratoires* and community centers. The proliferation of Talmudei Torah reflects the new distribution of Jewish communities in France, including places where North African Jewish immigrants have settled.

Considerable efforts have been made to rationalize the network of Talmud Torah schools and to improve the quality of education they provide. But the lack of adequate premises and the scarcity of qualified teachers remain acute problems. Moreover, the potential of the Talmudei Torah to provide a Jewish education is hardly ever fulfilled, since the average duration of studies rarely exceeds three years.

Notwithstanding the growing day school movement and the increased numbers of Talmudei Torah, there remains a large number of Jewish youth in France who are not involved in any organized Jewish framework. While estimates of the total Jewish population, the number of Jewish youth and the membership of Jewish organizations tend to vary, it is likely that only some 10%-15% of Jewish youth[10] join or are attached, at any one time, to Jewish youth organizations. This suggests that the holding power of Jewish youth movements and student organizations may have weakened.

The percentage of children receiving either formal or informal Jewish education is relatively low. By the mid-1970s, about 22% of the 6–17 age group was enrolled in a Jewish school (full- or part-time); another 19% of the same age group had been previously enrolled, but dropped out (Himmelfarb and DellaPergola, 1982; DellaPergola and Genuth, 1983). Nevertheless, developments in both formal and informal education indicate the existence of a public demand which has not been met. Indeed, the multiple, non-institutionalized initiatives, characteristic of French Jewish education, contrast markedly with the general French tradition of institutional centralization.

In fact, little attention has been paid to planning the Jewish educational infrastructure – neither to the training and in-service training of teachers for schools, and *madrichim* for informal education, nor to data-collection and research. Moreover, much of the preparation of curricula and textbooks reflects improvisation rather than professional planning.

Many of the present problems and deficiencies of Jewish education in France could perhaps be resolved by the creation of a centralized umbrella organization for Jewish education and culture. The first priorities of such an organization would be teacher-training, the preparation of curricula, and educational research. Hopefully, the quantitative and qualitative improvement of the Jewish educational enterprise in France would follow.

Acknowledgements

Information, statistical data, and considerable assistance have been provided by Prosper Elkouby, Director of the Educational Division of the FSJU, and by the Department of Torah Education and Culture of the Jewish Agency and its Director, Jacob Hadani.

Notes

1. These three border counties were part of the German Empire in 1901 when the Law of Separation of Church and State, which provided for voluntary religious instruction, was enacted in France. The Law of Separation became applicable only after these counties were re-unified with France.

2. Government recognition may be in the form of a *Contrat simple* or a *Contrat d'association avec l'Etat.*

3. Donations by industrial organizations to vocational training schools such as ORT, which is a recognized *Organization d'Utilité Publique*, are tax-deductible. Despite the Jewish importance of ORT, only 1% of its budget in France comes from the educational fund of the French Jewish community, while another 20% is provided by the world ORT organization.

4. For example, the film *Le Chagrin et la Pitié* was approved for screening on television only in 1981, and France was among the last European countries to screen the television series Holocaust.

5. Other central organizations include the Consistoire, the Representative Council of French Jewry (CRIF), and the Jewish Agency.

6. Other budget items in the years 1974–1977 included social activities and vocational training.

7. It is estimated that there are several thousand potential pupils for Jewish day schools that neither enroll nor apply for acceptance.

8. Not including the teaching of Hebrew as either a first or second foreign language.

9. Some 482 applicants could not be accepted in the school year 1977/78, 412 in 1978/80 and some 450 in 1981/82.

10. This assumes that of the estimated Jewish population of 530,000, there are some 130,000 in the 10 to 25 age group.

References

Aron, R. (1968). *De Gaulle, Israel et les Juifs.* Plon, Paris.

Auron, Y. (1979). *Les mouvements de jeunesse Juifs en France; le Judaisme contemporain à travers le miroir de sa jeunesse.* Doctoral dissertation, University of the Sorbonne, Paris.

Bensimon, D. (1971). *Follow-up des anciens élèves des écoles juives a plein temps. Rapport d'enquête.* Paris.

Bensimon, D. and DellaPergola, S. (1984). *La population juive de France: socio-démographie et identité.* Institute of Contemporary Jewry, The Hebrew University, Jerusalem and Central National de la Recherche Scientifique, Paris.

Catalogue des Doctorats Hebraica-Judaica 1970–1979 (1980). Centre de Documentation et de Recherche Etudes Hébraiques et Juives Modernes et Contemporaines, Clichy.

DellaPergola, S. (1982). "A New Estimate of Greater Paris Jewish Population Size". *Studies in Jewish Demography, 1972–1980.* The Institute of Contemporary Jewry, The Hebrew University, Jerusalem and The Institute of Jewish Affairs, London, pp. 19–32.

DellaPergola, S. (1986). "Contemporary Jewish Family Patterns in France: A Comparative Perspective" in: Cohen, S.M. and Hyman, P., eds. *The Contemporary Jewish Family: Myths and Reality.* Holmes and Meier, New York, pp. 148–171.

DellaPergola, S. and Bensimon, D. (1978). "Enquêtes socio-démographiques sur les Juifs en France". *Dispersion et Unité,* No. 18, pp. 190–212.

DellaPergola, S. and Genuth, N. (1983). *Jewish Education Attained in Diaspora Communities. Data for 1970's.* Institute of Contemporary Jewry, The Hebrew University, Jerusalem. (Project for Jewish Educational Statistics, Research Report No. 2). 74 pp.

Dreyfus, E. (1981). *Libres écoles, enquête sur l'enseignement privé.* Le Centurion.

Himmelfarb, H.S. and DellaPergola, S. (1982). *Enrollment in Jewish Schools in the Diaspora, Late 1970's.* Institute of Contemporary Jewry, The Hebrew University, Jerusalem. (Project for Jewish Education Statistics, Research Report No. 1). 97 pp.

Hyman, P. (1976). "Challenge to Assimilation: French Jewish Youth Movements Between the Wars". *The Jewish Journal of Sociology,* Vol. 18, no. 2. pp. 105–114.

Kaplan, Y. (1976). *Judaïsme français et Sionisme.* Albin Michel, Paris.

Pougatch, I. (1955). *Se ressaisir ou disparaître.* Les Editions de Minuit, Paris.

10

Jewish Education in Other Western European Countries

Stanley Abramovitch

The Jews in Western Europe are dispersed over some twenty countries, the largest Jewish communities being those of France and Great Britain.[1] The other communities range in size from 600 Jews in Gibraltar and 700 in Luxembourg, to 32,500 Jews in Belgium and 33,500 in West Germany. The size of a community is a determining factor in its education program. However, not only size, but also the composition, background, traditions and history of the Jewish population are reflected in each community's institutions and, in particular, its school system.

The backbone of Jewish education in continental Western Europe is the full-time day school, which provides an intensive Jewish education. The number of day schools and their enrollments have grown, although Talmudei Torah, Sunday and weekday supplementary schools also provide Jewish education for thousands of Jewish children. Government regulations in many European countries make religious or ethical instruction compulsory and permit release-time Jewish studies classes for Jewish students in state schools, as in Belgium and Austria. Youth movements, summer and winter camps, and visits to Israel also play a significant role in Jewish education.

Historical Overview

During the first years following World War II, the Jews of Europe endeavored to reestablish themselves, rebuild their economic life and reconstruct their institutions. The Displaced Persons (DP) camps in Germany, Austria and Italy were emptied after the establishment of the State of Israel. Some of the former inmates decided to remain in Europe, primarily in Germany and Austria, thus creating the core of the Jewish communities now in those two

TABLE 1.   JEWISH POPULATION IN WESTERN EUROPE[a] – 1949–1980

Country	1949	1980
Total	248,150	193,750
Austria	21,500	7,500
Belgium	42,000	32,500
Denmark	5,500	6,900
Finland	1,800	1,000
Germany	55,000	33,500
Gibraltar	650	600
Greece	8,000	5,000
Italy	38,500	32,000
Luxembourg	1,000	700
Netherlands	28,000	26,500
Norway	1,200	950
Portugal	4,000	600
Spain	3,000	12,000
Sweden	15,000	15,000
Switzerland	23,000	19,000

(a) Excluding France and British Isles.

Source: *The American Jewish Year Book* (1950; 1984).

countries. Jews also migrated seeking homes and livelihood, the main areas of attraction being Antwerp, Paris and, outside Europe, the United States.

By 1950, Jewish communities with institutional infrastructures had been established throughout Western Europe but the size of most of these communities has decreased over the past thirty years. Substantial changes, wherever they occurred, resulted from political upheavals causing shifts in population. These disturbances and their impact on Jewish life generally and on the education scene in particular will be discussed in this chapter.

The total Jewish population of Western Europe (except Britain and France) decreased by about 15% over a span of thirty years (see Table 1). It is important to note this trend toward numerical decline and to recognize that there have also been significant changes in the ethnic composition of the Jewish population in some countries that did not necessarily affect the total size of the Jewish community.

The development of Jewish education in post-war Europe was influenced by a number of factors:

– community reconstruction, which allowed high priority to Jewish education;

- individuals or small groups committed to the establishment of a particular school, such as the Jewish day school in Milan and that in Madrid;
- the support of the American Joint Distribution Committee (AJDC), which recognized education as an integral aspect of Jewish communal reconstruction and rehabilitation in Europe. A high proportion of the AJDC's budget was channelled to education, and it assisted in the provision of resources such as books, teachers and buildings;
- the crucial role of the Jewish Conference on Material Claims against Germany, which from the mid-1950s through the mid-1960s annually spent over one million dollars on Jewish education, apart from the massive sums spent on welfare and rehabilitation. In addition to capital grants, the Claims Conference assisted in the maintenance budget during a project's initial years, thereby laying the foundations for Jewish education in post-war Europe. During this period, the schools in Athens, Milan, Rome and Antwerp and the first Jewish day school in Brussels received substantial funds for their development from the Claims Conference, which also supported community and youth centers, summer and winter camps, and other forms of formal and informal education; and
- the heightened dimension and deeper significance which the existence of the State of Israel gave to local Jewish education. Moreover, the State itself promoted Jewish education, insofar as various Israeli education authorities and the Jewish Agency provided substantial financial grants, teachers, textbooks, and organized visits to Israel for European Jewish children and youth.

The Structure of Jewish Education

Growth in Number of Schools

A comparison between the author's last triennial survey of Jewish education in Western Europe (Abramovitch, 1970), and statistics published eleven years later (Himmelfarb and DellaPergola, 1982) indicates a definite increase in Jewish school enrollment in Western Europe which may be attributed to the increased number of Jewish day schools. There are some 32 Jewish day schools in Western Europe, outside Britain and France, of which eight – or 25% of the total number – have opened since 1970. These eight include one in Holland, two in Belgium, two in Switzerland, two in Spain and one in Italy. The former Jewish day school in Vienna closed down some years ago, but a new school was opened in recent years, so the number of day schools in Austria remains unaltered.

Typical of the circumstances under which day schools have increased is the establishment of a new school in Zurich. In 1969 it was proposed that the mainstream Jewish community in Zurich establish a day school in addition to the school of the more Orthodox section of the community. One argument against the proposal was that such a day school might create friction between the non-religious home and the school, and it was furthermore suggested that the non-Jewish population might query the loyalty of those supporting and establishing a Jewish parochial school. The majority were opposed to educating Jewish children in a school which separated them from the non-Jewish environment, and the proposal was defeated. However, less than ten years later, the same community did open a day school – with the approval of the more Orthodox sector – catering to the large less-observant sections of the community.

A similar struggle occurred before the establishment of the day school in Stockholm. While those who had arrived more recently in Sweden supported the project, the more established Jews opposed the school and the debate extended outside the Jewish community to become a national issue. The school finally opened under the auspices not of the community but of an independent committee. Since then, differences of opinion and opposition in Stockholm to full-time Jewish schooling have been reduced by time and experience.

In addition to new schools being opened, existing schools have expanded. This is true of schools which were already large, such as the *Yesodei HaTorah* and *Tachkemoni* schools in Antwerp, as it is of smaller schools such as those in Zurich.

Growth in Enrollments

Not only the number of day schools, but also their total enrollments have increased. This trend is indicated in Table 2.

While enrollment statistics outlined in this table are approximations, they indicate the proportion of children in Jewish day schools out of the total receiving any Jewish education in 1980 – overall, almost 60% but in some countries much higher, such as 90% in Italy, 80% in Gibraltar, 83% in Denmark, and 77% in Belgium.

A dramatic example of the trend toward increased day school enrollments is provided by the Jewish school in Denmark, which was founded over 175 years ago and is the oldest Jewish day school in Europe. This school's enrollments have doubled in the past decade. It is a primary day school, and it enrolls some 70% of all Jewish children of primary school age in Copenhagen. Similarly, some 65% of all Jewish children in Brussels attend day schools,

TABLE 2. JEWISH EDUCATION ENROLLMENT TRENDS – WESTERN
EUROPE,[a] 1970–1980

Country	Pupils Receiving Jewish Education		% Increase/ Decrease 1970–80	Day School Enrollment 1980	Day School as Percentage of Total Enrollment 1980
	1970	1980			
Total	12,091	13,475	+11	7,760	57
Austria	450	480	+66	50	10
Belgium	2,866	3,850	+34	2,800	77
Denmark	275	420	+11	350	83
Finland	150	175	+17	70	40
Germany	1,625	1,500	– 8	200	13
Gibraltar	85	100	+18	80	80
Greece	472	250	–47	150	60
Italy	2,218	3,000	+35	2,700	90
Netherlands	1,288	1,200	– 7	550	46
Spain	375	500	+33	160	32
Sweden	1,108	500	–55	150	30
Switzerland	1,179	1,500	+27	500	33

(a) Excluding France and British Isles.

with some 70 to 75% of Jewish children enrolled in the junior primary levels
of the three day schools.

Positive Factors in Jewish Educational Growth

Besides the post-war situation which generally encouraged the development of Jewish education in Western Europe, various factors in the late
1960s and 1970s contributed to the growth of Jewish day schools in particular.

Change and Deterioration in General Education

The 1968 student revolution in France, and similar events on a minor
scale in Germany, Italy and elsewhere in Europe changed the atmosphere in
public schools. Even in staid Switzerland, state schools have come to be associated with laxity of discipline, increased permissiveness and problems of
drug and alcohol abuse, to the detriment of serious learning and academic

standards. Although they are not regarded as immune, Jewish schools have been less affected by these negative changes in education, and thus have become more attractive. Whereas Jews formerly regarded the state school as the stepping-stone to social advancement and integration into the non-Jewish society, they now prefer the 'healthier' social atmosphere of the Jewish school, and no longer fear its parochialism.

Revived Interest in Jewish Identity and Education

Growth in the number of day schools and in their enrollments reflects, on the one hand, a greater interest in Jewish education generally, and, on the other hand, a preference for day over supplementary Jewish schooling. Postwar reconstruction reflected the community's desire to live as Jews and to ensure the Jewishness of their children. This desire has been reinforced by latent antisemitism, blatant anti-Zionism, and a decline in the fear of being different. Thus, the Jewish school is preferred to state schools, because it transmits Jewish values and promotes Jewish identification, while also providing for the child's general educational needs.

Immigration

Migration to Western Europe has also resulted in a changed climate for Jewish education. Sweden accepted Polish Jewish refugees soon after World War II; Denmark absorbed 1,500 Jews from Poland after the Six-Day War; Belgium has attracted Jews from Romania and Russia, as has Germany. Tripolitanian Jews settled in Rome and Iranian Jews in Milan, Spanish-speaking Jews from Morocco and Latin America have migrated to Spain, while Jews from Israel have settled in all those Western European countries which granted them residence.

These Jewish immigrants tend to enroll their children in both full-time and part-time Jewish schools. Schools in all of the receiving communities contain immigrant Jewish children. This is especially evident in Rome, in Milan – whose Jewish school population around 1985 comprised 37 different nationalities – and to a lesser extent in Copenhagen and Antwerp.

Negative Factors Impeding Growth

Two contradictory forces are evident in Jewish communal life. On the one hand, there is movement toward positive Jewish identity, a re-awakened interest in Jewish education, and increased enrollment in Jewish day schools. On the other hand, European Jewish communities are more than ever exposed to the ravages of assimilation in an open society. The main weakening factors include the very smallness of many Jewish communities, their wide dispersion, and the isolation of one community from another.

Small communities cannot and do not survive Jewishly. Sooner or later, they succumb to the integrating pressures of the society around them. There are many dozens of such small communities scattered throughout Europe: the small and shrinking communities of Finland and Norway; the small groups living in Boras, Norrkoping and other places outside Stockholm, Goteborg and Malmo. The same applies to Danish Jews living outside Copenhagen, and to individual families living in small Dutch towns.

In such small communities, there is little or no Jewish education. Even in the Netherlands, with its commendable program of itinerant teachers who visit the small communities, individual children there have little opportunity to grow up as knowledgeable Jews. Of the more than sixty locations where Jews are living in Germany, only the larger ones have established Jewish schools. The situation is similar in Switzerland and Italy. In Belgium, small schools which were a combination of Talmud Torah and Zionist schools, existed at one time in Charleroi and Liege, but these closed as the communities shrank and assimilated. Casale Monferrato, near Turin, has only five Jews, while Mantua has a hundred – too few for a Jewish school. At one time in Greece there were schools not only in Athens and Salonica, but also in Janina, Trikala and Larissa; however assimilation, deaths and departures resulted in the closing of some of these schools. There seems to be no way to stem the decline of Jewish education in small communities, or, for that matter, to avert the disappearance of these communities altogether.

But even in larger communities, not all Jews can avail themselves of Jewish education. Jewish communities are no longer concentrated in a single area of any large city, such as the Jewish section of Antwerp, the Ghetto of Rome, or the Jewish quarter in the northeastern part of Amsterdam, but rather the cost and shortage of housing encouraged residential dispersion. The Jewish school can serve only those living within a reasonable distance, or within the areas reached by school transportation. Jews who live in areas too distant from the school and the main Jewish centers – such as the farther suburbs of Rome, Madrid, Stockholm and Milan – are left without access to Jewish schooling. They are thinly scattererd over a wide area, making it nearly impossible to organize formal Jewish educational facilities for them.

Paradoxically, therefore, while Jewish education is reaching more children, becoming more intensive, more coordinated, and more central to Jewish communal life, those Jews who are not integrated into the community are rapidly assimilating and disappearing as Jews. On the one hand, there is more Jewish education available to, and obtained by, the identified sections of European Jewry; on the other hand, there is less education among those on the periphery of communal life.

Full-time and Part-time Provisions

Government regulations make religious or ethical instruction compulsory for all children attending state schools in most European countries, allowing for Jewish pupils to attend release-time Jewish studies. Each community has developed its own part-time and release-time Jewish education.

In Stockholm, where there is a primary day school, a part-time school and part-time courses for children of secondary school age are conducted in the Jewish community building. In Copenhagen, where some 70% of primary school age children attend the day school, the community Talmud Torah caters to the remainder and to secondary school age children interested in continuing their Jewish education. In Amsterdam, in addition to the three day schools, Rosh Pina Primary School with 250 pupils, Maimonides Lyceum with 190, and the Heder Day School with 100 – there is a Talmud Torah. Part-time education is also provided for some 175 children living in 25 small communities at least once every other week by a team of 15 itinerant teachers sent by the central community of Amsterdam.

The larger communities in Germany have established comprehensive structured educational systems. In addition to small primary schools, the communities of Frankfurt and Munich have established supplementary Sunday schools. The Berlin Jewish community has a large Talmud Torah. Other communities, such as Hanover, Dusseldorf, Hamburg, as well as smaller Jewish centers provide part-time education in the form of Sunday school.

Day schools have been established in the larger Swiss communities of Zurich, Basle, Lucerne and Geneva, a yeshiva day school and a girls' school have been opened in Lucerne, and Montreux and Lugano have established yeshivoth. Smaller communities, like Lausanne, Berne, La Chaux-de-Fonds and Biel provide only part-time Sunday schools. But even in the larger communtiies where day schools exist, the part-time Talmud Torah remains the main channel for Jewish education. About 500 children attend day schools, whereas some 1000 attend Talmudei Torah.

For historical reasons, there are more Jewish day schools in Italy than in other European countries. Anti-Jewish laws enforced in 1938 excluded Jewish children from state education, obliging the Jewish communities to establish full-time Jewish schools. Thus, Jewish day schools were established in Rome, Milan, Genoa, Turin, Leghorn and Florence. In spite of discriminating laws being repealed after World War II, the number of day schools today would be even higher had some not been forced to close as the Jewish population declined. Accordingly, no comprehensive system of supplementary Jewish schooling developed in Italy. However, in recent years, Talmudei Torah and Sunday schools have been started in Milan by the Lubavitch movement, in Rome by the Libyan immigrants, as well as in Venice, Trieste, Bologna and Naples.

Although in Spain day schools exist in Madrid and Barcelona, there are also Talmudei Torah in these cities and in Malaga. Any discussion of Jewish education in Spain is incomplete without mentioning the Melilla community, where there is a day school, and Ceuta, where there is a supplementary school. Although both these communities are located in North Africa, they are part of metropolitan Spain.

Finally, in Greece both Athens and Salonica have supplementary schools.

Informal Jewish Education

The total picture of Jewish education in Western Europe includes youth movements, community and youth centers, summer and winter camps, and other forms of informal Jewish education.

Youth movements are an important component of Jewish education in Europe. They are usually Zionist-oriented, and encourage visits to Israel. *Bnei Akiva*, which has active chapters in Italy, Switzerland, Belgium, and the Scandinavian countries, includes study of the weekly Bible portion or other religious topics as a component of its weekly meetings. Other youth groups, such as *Habonim*, stress Jewish history and contemporary events in the Jewish world.

Youth camps also provide education. Some communities such as those of Sweden, Holland, and Italy, organize study camps for children in isolated communities. Furthermore, the geographic proximity of Western Europe to Israel encourages visits, vacations and bar mitzvah celebration ceremonies in Israel, all exposing the child to the Hebrew language and to Israeli Jewish life.

Enrollment Rates: Trends and Prospects

In the absence of reliable statistics, it is impossible to know exactly how many Jewish children will receive some Jewish education during their lives.

A survey (Abramovitch, 1970) showed that in 1970, for every 100 children of school age, about 12 to 15 attended Jewish day schools, 28 to 35 attended Jewish part-time schools, and 50 to 60 received no Jewish education. These statistics included the large French community, whose educational program was then in its initial stages of development. Since then, there has been impressive growth in the number of day schools, even when France is excluded.

There are about 200,000 Jews in Western Europe, excluding France, Great Britain and the Iron Curtain countries. It is often assumed that the school-age population represents 20% of the total population, but this is certainly not true of the Jewish communities in Europe, which have a disproportionate number of aged and a lower birthrate than the rest of the population. It may be estimated that there are about 30,000 to 35,000 children of school age in the communities discussed here.

It seems likely that of these, 40 to 45% receive some Jewish education at any given time, an increasing proportion in full-time day schools. Virtually one of every two children receiving Jewish education attends a full-time day school. If the estimates are correct, then some 7,760 children attend day schools, about 5,700 attend part-time schools, while about 2,000 receive their only Jewish education from informal sources such as youth movements, summer camps and visits to Israel. In other words, out of every 100 children of school age, 25 attend a day school, 18 or 19 attend a part-time school, and 6 or 7 receive only informal education. These estimates apply only to Jewish education at a given time; the percentage naturally increases when we consider the numbers of pupils who receive Jewish education at any time over the entire span of school life extending eleven, twelve or thirteen years, according to country.

Statistics and proportions vary from country to country. For example, Austrian law provides for compulsory education till 14 years of age. Of a total estimated 7,500 Jews, only 480 children obtain some Jewish education, about 50% in the various Talmudei Torah and small day schools and the other 50% from release-time instruction in the French, English and other non-Jewish high schools. These 480 children are probably 70 to 75% of the school-age Jewish population, indicating the small percentage of children and the predominance of older age groups in the community, and also the tendency for young people to settle in other parts of the world after marriage.

Another example is Belgium, where government regulations provide for compulsory religious instruction within the school program, usually for one or two hours weekly. This release-time instruction is provided by 72 Jewish studies teachers in 187 schools reaching 1,050 pupils, most of whom (920) are in the French-speaking region. The remainder reside in the Flemish area around Antwerp.

In Antwerp, the increased day school enrollment has reduced the number of Jewish pupils in government schools. The total 1982 enrollment of 900 pupils in the three Brussels day schools, including kindergarten level, represented a large increase from 1972. While the Jewish population of Brussels is estimated at about 18,000 to 20,000, reliable information on the total actual size of the school age population is unavailable, so that the percentage of enrollment cannot be calculated.

Day school enrollments in Europe have probably peaked, although additional small day schools may be opened by special-interest groups such as the Liberal community in Amsterdam or the younger section of *B'nai B'rith* in Germany. Enrollment trends in part-time schools already indicate a decline which will continue in the foreseeable future, since the Jewish population in European communities – especially the smaller ones – is decreasing.

The enrollment increase in day schools has reflected both greater community interest in Jewish education and recognition that supplementary part-time education makes little impact on the child. It has also been an outcome of the polarization in Jewish religious life.

For example, a new day school was started in Antwerp by the *Mizrachi* supporters in the community which could accept neither the religious education provided by one existing school, nor the trend to the right of the second school. Similarly, the *Agudah* school in Antwerp has lost pupils to the more extreme Orthodox schools opened by the various Hasidic groups.

Another example is the *kollel* started in Amsterdam by teachers of the Maimonides Lyceum. The *kollel* opened its own day school to provide an intensive religious program and attracts those families within the *kollel* community whose children would otherwise be in the community day school. Similarly, a new school was started in Milan by the Lubavitch community, who regarded the existing day school's Hebrew program as an insufficient Jewish education.

Religious polarization has involved the Liberal as well as the Orthodox sections of the communities. For instance, the non-religious schools in Brussels were opened by parents who found the strictly Orthodox policy of the Ecole Israélite unacceptable. The Liberal community in Amsterdam may in time open its own school, since Liberal parents feel that they cannot accept the Orthodox orientation of the community day school for their own children.

In short, religious polarization has resulted in increased day school enrollments and in more schools fighting for the same children. It has not however affected decreasing enrollments in part-time Jewish education.

Demographic Trends

The Rome Jewish community exhibits typical trends in births, intermarriage and assimilation.[2] In 1979, 100 children were born in the community, compared to 200 in 1973, a drastic decline which is strongly felt by the community day school. There used to be five parallel first grades in the school, then there were four, and this drop merely presaged further decline. The school enrolls some 70% of the Jewish primary school-age population in Rome. Even if this percentage were to increase, enrollments in fact would decrease because of the reduced birthrate. The middle school (junior secondary grades) enrolls about 60% of the age group, while 15 to 25% of Jewish children continue into the community high school (Lyceum). The only potential for real enrollment expansion is at the secondary level, but this would involve providing more subjects which need costly equipment and would thus require increases in the total Jewish educational budget.

Rome Jewish community statistics indicate that in 1978 there were 150 marriages in the community, compared with about 80 marriages in 1980. Some 40% of all the 1978 marriages involved a non-Jewish partner. The community consists of some 6,000 couples, of whom perhaps 15% are mixed. About three-quarters of the children of mixed marriages attend the Jewish day school, while the others are lost to the Jewish community. These statistics spell out some possible decline in Rome's future Jewish population and, correspondingly, in Jewish school enrollments.

The situation in other Italian Jewish communities is much worse, particularly in Northern Italy. Mantua has 120 Jews, almost all couples being mixed; Venice has 70 to 80% mixed couples. The outlook for the future is that the smaller communities will in time disappear. Rome and Milan will have much smaller communities, and the present middle-size Jewish communities in Italy, today with populations of 1,000 or over, will survive with only small remnants. This pessimistic prognosis portends a decrease in school enrollments in Rome and other Jewish centers in Italy.

Similar scenarios apply, with local variations, to other European Jewish communities. The large enrollment increase at the three day schools in Brussels during the past decade or so, for instance, occurred during a period of shrinking potential enrollments. The birthrate there has been declining and there were only 120 Jewish births in 1981. At that rate, the Jewish community of Brussels could be substantially reduced in the next 12 to 15 years.

School Orientation and Goals

An increasing polarization within the Jewish community, arising from the resurgence of the more extreme expressions of Orthodoxy, is reflected in the orientation and goals of schools.

Practically all Jewish schools, with rare exception, declare themselves Orthodox, a term with a broad connotation. Actually, these schools embrace the entire range of Jewish religious approach, from the ultra-Orthodox Lubavitch and *Yesodei HaTorah* schools in Antwerp to those which emphasize a nationalistic approach, altogether avoiding religious indoctrination. Only the *Ganenu* and the *Beth-Aviv* schools in Brussels were initially established as non-religious schools, but even they have gradually introduced various Jewish observances.

The goal of all Jewish schools, perhaps excepting only the two in Brussels, is to teach religious customs and prepare the child for participation in synagogue services. However, few go to the extent of the Athens Jewish community, which regarded the learning of the Sephardic synagogue liturgy so important that they arranged for children to be bussed to and from the synagogue on the Shabbat to hear the ancient music of Salonica as it is still sung in the Athens synagogue. Beyond this basic goal, there are wide variations.

The tendency in recent years has been for the Jewish schools to emphasize religion rather than Hebrew language despite parents' wishes to stress language. For example, the Scandinavian schools formerly catered to parents' religious practice. Hebrew used to be stressed in the Copenhagen day school as well. Because of its mixed pupil population, ranging from the very Orthodox to the more assimilated, the school provided intensive religious studies for those children who were interested, but the feeling was that the school could not successfully achieve its goals in Hebrew language during the primary school years, after which children transferred to state schools; accordingly, the orientation was changed with the conviction that primary school children should be taught Jewish observance and practice.

Most school principals in Western Europe set the goals for their own schools. Thus, the religious orientation of the schools does not necessarily indicate a community's religiosity. In fact, the schools rarely reflect the religious life of the families. Despite parental involvement, the schools are usually more Orthodox than is the norm in the community since the school principal, as the final arbiter of school goals, is usually influenced by the more cohesive, structured and articulate sections of the community, and these are usually the more Orthodox.

This tendency toward increasing religiosity applies even in schools which accept children from mixed marriages, such as in Finland, Stockholm, and Athens. The schools in Amsterdam and Antwerp, and the Ecole Israélite in Brussels, do not accept such children, while the Jewish school in Milan does, but only on the condition that the non-Jewish parent promises to convert to Judaism within one year.

Thus the schools are becoming more attractive to those sections of the community which are committed, active and identified with Judaism and less so to those with more secular or nationalist Jewish goals as well as those who have become more assimilated into the general society. The gap between home and school for less observant Jews is a major factor underlying the paradox of increased Jewish education among identified Jews, and less Jewish education among those near the peripheries.

Responsibility for Jewish Education

Sponsorship

The responsibility for schools, both part-time and full-time, is vested either in a committee elected by the community, or in a special committee independent from, but often supported by, the community. If a school is managed as a communal responsibility, the community supplies the funds to cover all expenses. Independent school committees have greater financial difficulties.

The day schools of Helsinki, Copenhagen, Amsterdam, Germany and Italy are the sole responsibility of elected communal committees, whereas those in Sweden, Belgium, Spain and Switzerland are the creations of independent committees. These committees provide either for a like-minded constituency within the community, as is the case in Belgium or Switzerland, or open their schools to the entire community, as in Stockholm or Spain.

While the community or the school committee may set the general parameters of educational policy, as stated above, the school principal usually has the final say in all educational matters. It is he who sets the program, chooses textbooks, appoints teachers, and thereby controls the tools for policy implementation.

Occasionally, a struggle for control may arise between different interest-groups in the community, as occurred in Zurich. Generally, however, school life proceeds peacefully, the final authority resting with the lay body and effective policy execution depending on the principal. Responsibility for the general program also lies with government educational authorities who normally supervise the general education provided in order to ensure adequate standards.

The part-time schools and Talmudei Torah are appendages of the Consistoire or synagogues. In this case, the Rabbi has the educational responsibility while the synagogue movement assumes the financial responsibility. Informal education, such as youth movements and community centers, is independent, autonomous and responsible for itself, albeit supported by the community.

Finances

In examining the economics of Jewish schooling, a distinction must be made between day and part-time education. Day schools depend on four main sources of financial support: government allocations, tuition fees, the Jewish community and donations. The percentage from each source varies from country to country, depending on local laws and the level of government support for minority schools. The Copenhagen school receives 85% of its income from the government; the Dutch schools and the school in Helsinki are heavily dependent on government grants; and so, to a lesser extent, are those in Belgium, Germany and Italy. The Swiss Jewish schools receive government authorization and recognition but not financial support. The same applies to day schools in Spain and Greece. Generally, where schools do not receive government support, such as in Switzerland or Spain, the schools struggle with deficits and debts, and are often on the verge of bankruptcy.

School fees are the second source of day school income. The policy of all communities is to accept all children who apply, despite inability to pay school fees or transportation costs. The Milan and Rome schools charge only an annual subscription fee. Other schools ask a small monthly fee. Where there is no government support, school fees are of necessity higher.

The remainder of the budget is covered by grants from the community and from donations. Schools sponsored by separate committees, even though they receive some communal support, have difficulty covering their expenses. This is particularly true of the schools in Brussels and in Spain. In the Jewish communities today, there is a better understanding of the need for modern facilities and educational aids. Parents also demand that academic standards in the Jewish schools be comparable to, and often better than, those in government schools. Those schools that do not receive government support find it increasingly difficult to maintain these standards and to offer a full, rich program financed only by the community and school fees. Variety in program, in educational aids, and experimentation are accordingly rare in Jewish schools.

Because reliable information is not available, per capita costs for education cannot be compared from country to country. In 1970, there were big differences between costs per child in primary and secondary schools, and between countries like Italy and Spain compared to Switzerland and the Scandinavian countries. Standards and costs of Jewish schooling are always influenced by the general standards and costs of education in the particular country. Day school fees in Continental Europe have been generally low, compared to those in England or the United States.

Despite the fact that governments do not support Talmud Torah education, school fees are minimal and the communities cover virtually the entire cost. However, governments do finance release-time Jewish studies in state schools. Youth movements and summer and winter camps are primarily financed by the participants, with occasional grants for camps from the community.

School Effectiveness

School Programs

The programs of Jewish schools are textbook-centered. Hebrew reading is taught both in the part-time and day schools so that the child can participate in synagogue services and as preparation for study of the Bible and other texts. The prayer book and the Bible, sometimes with commentaries, comprise the basics of the school program. The Jewish calendar, with emphasis on festivals, provides the second major component of the Jewish studies curriculum.

Many precious school hours are devoted to Hebrew language study without satisfactory results. Based on experience and observation that a few months' stay in Israel provides a better foundation in Hebrew than several years of school study, an increasing number of schools are devoting less time to language instruction. The Copenhagen school, for instance, decided to send pupils of its top class (Grade 9) to Israel for one month on the premise that pupils would learn more Hebrew in this way than in the school over a much longer period of time. In general, schools interested in teaching *Ivrit b'Ivrit* devote more time to Hebrew language in the early school years, hoping thereby to make more progress in the traditional subjects from the third year onwards.

Jewish history is rarely taught in Jewish schools, the main reason being the limited time for Jewish studies which schools prefer to use for core subjects. There is little experimentation and little attention is given to immediate interests or effectiveness. The program is usually preset and the modes of teaching rarely change. Now and then, a day of study will be devoted to teaching about the Holocaust or Soviet Jewry, but for the most part Jewish studies content and teaching methods are conservative.

Quantity and Duration

Studies conducted in the United States suggest that there is a positive correlation between time spent in Jewish classrooms during childhood and youth, and adult involvement in informal Jewish social networks, knowledge of Jewish culture, and identification with Israel. Jewish schooling is as important a factor as Jewish home background in shaping Jewish identity.

The years spent in the school and the intensity of the Jewish studies program are decisive in their impact on the individual. According to Bock (1976), 1,000 hours of instruction were necessary before Jewish schooling had any significant effect. Himmelfarb (1977) found that a minimum of about 3,000 hours of school attendance were necessary to make any real impact on adult religious behavior.

These findings from Bock's and Himmelfarb's studies are also valid for Europe, and raise painful questions about the effectiveness of Jewish schooling there. One or two day schools provide less than five hours of Jewish studies per week; about one-quarter provide five, about one-half provide 6 to 10, and only one-quarter provide more than 10 hours. A number of day schools are really yeshivoth with a program of general studies in the afternoon.

The part-time schools present a completely different picture. Some 50% of them conduct two sessions weekly with 5 to 6 hours of Jewish studies, while the remainder provide only one session of three hours a week. The amount of hours thus attained assumes regular attendance; but for a more accurate picture, allowance should be made for absenteeism, from which supplementary schools suffer more than day schools.

Not only is the number of weekly hours insufficient according to the studies on effectiveness; the same is true of the total number of years that pupils study in Jewish schools. The growth of the day school movement and the increased number of Jewish day schools in the past decade has been emphasized above. One must point out, however, that this increase is at the primary and not at the secondary level. In fact, of all pupils attending Jewish day schools in the countries examined here, less than 20% are at the high school level.

Few communities have secondary schools. The Copenhagen school offers nine years of education – providing the beginning of secondary education but not its completion. The Maimonides secondary school in Amsterdam has 190 pupils, 220 attend the Brussels high schools, Antwerp has 550 pupils enrolled at the secondary, and Milan and Rome have high schools with a total enrollment of 450 pupils. The school in Zurich does not prepare students for university entrance. In Stockholm and Copenhagen, provisions are made for children to be accepted to high schools near the Jewish primary day school so that they can continue to attend part-time classes on the Jewish school premises.

This does not mean that there is no Jewish education for secondary school pupils. The youth movements are active among teenagers, and study visits to Israel cater to this age group. A few Talmudei Torah have post-bar mitzvah classes.

European Jewish communities are plagued by the fact that formal Jewish education ends in the early teenage years. While growth in the number of Jewish day schools in Europe is certainly welcome, cessation of Jewish schooling at the primary level to a large extent nullifies the efforts invested in the early years of education. Without effective Jewish secondary schools Jewish education cannot achieve its goals. Nor is part-time Jewish education for secondary school pupils a viable option, since heroic efforts to keep children in Talmudei Torah beyond the bar mitzvah age have failed to compete with leisure activities for the child's spare time.

The most successful solutions to extending the duration of Jewish schooling have been study programs in Israel. Most of these are in the summer, but some schools have experimented with a semester's study in Israel during the school year. This is possible because the education authorities in Denmark, Sweden, Holland, and other countries, permit a class to move to another country for a period of study during the school year. The results have been very encouraging. In Israel the pupils receive intensive Jewish studies while pursuing their regular courses, often with teachers from their own school. This is certainly one of the more promising innovations of recent years, which ought to be extended to additional schools. It seems that study in Israel, in one form or another, even when combined with touring, can partially meet the challenge of Jewish education for teenagers. Additional Jewish secondary day schools and increased youth activities are other channels for reaching this group.

Personnel: Supply and Training

The pivotal point of the educational process comes when the teacher communicates with his pupil. Many factors contribute to the success or failure of this decisive moment. The manner in which the teacher carries out his role will determine what and how his pupil will learn.

Teachers of Jewish studies in Europe include graduates of yeshivoth, of *Machon* Gold, *Beth Midrash LeTorah* and *Machon* Greenberg, Israeli universities, immigrants from Israel, and a large number of *shlihim* from the Jewish Agency. The Teachers' Training College in Gateshead, England, prepares about half a dozen teachers annually for Continental Europe, mainly for France.

A number of local teacher-training institutions serve local needs. The Almagià College in Rome offers courses in Jewish studies for future day school teachers. A general lack of job openings for teachers in Italy permits the community to oblige all prospective Jewish secular studies teachers to take courses in Jewish studies at Almagià College. These teachers are then certified to teach both secular and Jewish studies in the Rome Jewish primary day schools. However, their knowledge is far from adequate, a fact which led the Rome community to inaugurate an intensive weekly, 14–hour in-service training program aimed at up-grading the level of Hebrew teachers. The upper grades of the Rome school are taught by teachers who have studied in Israel or are *shlihim*.

A two-year teacher-training program, for girls only, is conducted at the *Yesodei HaTorah* school in Antwerp for graduates of its high school. The course is recognized by the government and graduates teach in the school or in other schools in Belgium. They rarely leave the country and generally stop teaching after marriage.

The yeshiva *Etz Haim* in Montreux, Switzerland some years ago started a teacher-training course for yeshiva graduates. This is a three-year course, one year of which is spent in Israel at the Teachers' School in Har Etzion. The course follows the teacher-training requirements of the Israel Ministry of Education. Some of the graduates now teach in France and at the yeshiva in

Montreux. This school could provide qualified teachers for schools in Europe if enough suitable students could be attracted to the teaching profession.

Gateshead College in England, the Antwerp *Yesodei HaTorah*, the Montreux Teacher Training College, and the Almagià College in Rome, all together produce between 12 to 18 teachers a year, mainly women, except for two or three young men from the Montreux College. Marriage, residential mobility, emigration and other causes often shorten the careers of these young teachers.

Israel, through its representatives and the various training programs of the Jewish Agency and the Pincus Foundation, is the most active promoter of Jewish teacher-training in Europe. The Jewish Agency, through its two Departments of Education, has been the main source of Jewish studies teachers in Europe. There are over 27 *shlihim* in the European region, the largest group being in Belgium. The second largest group of teachers is the Israelis who have settled in Europe either temporarily or permanently.

There have been repeated efforts to train teachers in Europe, the Montreux College program and a teacher-training project initiated by the former Chief Rabbi of France René Sirat being the most recent. In the past all similar efforts failed because it was impossible to attract suitable candidates. This was largely due to the poor employment conditions of teachers, which have never been, and are still not competitive with other professions. Nevertheless, they have gradually improved, although the communities themselves are still unable to offer adequate salaries and attractive fringe benefits to obtain the right teachers. A central Jewish authority, similar to a Ministry of Education, is needed to guarantee Jewish teachers normal and permanent conditions of employment, to supplement the salaries provided by the local communities and to add the fringe benefits customary in modern times. Since Jewish education is a national, not a local, enterprise and problem, the solution must come from the central Jewish bodies rather than from the individual communities.

Until a permanent solution is found to teacher training and supply, the schools will continue to depend on graduates from yeshivoth and on *Beth Jacob* female graduates who, despite their dedication, lack suitable training, on *shlihim* whose time in the community is too short to learn local problems and understand local needs, and on *yordim* who present an educational dilemma. The supply of school principals is an even more complex problem. The Brussels school searched the world for a replacement for its retiring school principal, and found one only with great difficulty. The *Tachkemoni* school in Antwerp and the Zurich school import principals from Israel. The day schools in Stockholm, Copenhagen and Athens appointed non-Jewish principals. The school principal in Rome retired without a replacement. This saga is repeated from country to country, from school to school.

Two praiseworthy initiatives have been undertaken by Israel. One is a scholarship fund provided by the Pincus Foundation for promising teachers to spend a year in Israel to improve their skills and knowledge. The second is a fund aimed at training educational leadership for Jewish communities throughout the world, set up by the Jewish Agency. This fund provides very generous scholarships for a three-year period, usually for a doctorate in education.

Two projects of the Education Department of the AJDC in 1969 have also contributed to the upgrading of educational personnel in Europe. The first project is the establishment of the Association of School Principals of Jewish Day Schools. This Association limits its concern to professional problems, such as teaching methods, teachers' and principals' functions and educational materials.

The second project is the pedagogical quarterly, *Hamoreh*, which is published in Paris by the AJDC in cooperation with the Fonds Social Juif Unifié (FSJU) and the European Council of Jewish Community Services. *Hamoreh*, the only Jewish pedagogical journal in Europe, celebrated 25 years of existence with the appearance of its 100th issue in 1982.

Conclusions

Jewish education in Western European countries other than Great Britain and France, has improved and expanded in the past 10 to 15 years. The expansion and growth of the day school movement has been especially impressive. Recent statistics, personal acquaintance with the situation in various communities and information from lay leaders and educators there have provided a basis for evaluating trends and noting developments.

About 40% of all school age children receive Jewish education at any given time. Over half of these children study in day schools and the remainder in part-time schools.

The impressive growth of day schools reflects social developments in Europe, especially the consequences of changes in government schools which resulted from the 1968 student revolution in France and elsewhere. The growth in enrollment is also due to immigration of Jews from countries of oppression and unrest, as well as from Israel. Finally, it reflects a change in thinking as evidenced by the new schools in Zurich and Geneva. Latent antisemitism, blatant anti-Zionism, coupled with the disappearance of the fear of being different and a desire to reassert one's Jewishness, have influenced attitudes regarding Jewish education.

The part-time schools have not grown during this period, and may even have declined. Dispersion of urban Jewish communities to outlying suburbs has reduced the possibility for steady attendance at central schools or for organizing Jewish studies in each neighborhood. Europe is sprinkled with many dozens of small communities of less than 500 Jews, and very often less than 100. Even the efforts of central communities to help these isolated small groups of Jews cannot prevent the process of their final disappearance.

The shift to the religious right evident in some communities is paralleled by an ever faster movement towards the periphery of Jewish life by the majority who tend to integrate and assimilate into the non-Jewish surroundings. The Jewish community is polarizing, creating one section of the community which demands more intensive Jewish education, and another - the majority – that receives and wants little or no Jewish education.

Altogether, there is a low level of continuation of Jewish education beyond the primary level in Western Europe. For example, only 15 to 25% continue in the Jewish high school in Rome, and 120 children attended the Jewish high school in Brussels while four times as many were in the primary school. There are no Jewish high schools in Scandinavia, Spain or Greece. Estimates indicate that 80% of all children in day schools attend Jewish primary schools and that less than 20% proceed to Jewish high schools.

Since part-time schools rarely attract secondary school pupils, most teenagers receive little or no Jewish education. Study tours in Israel and youth movements provide only a partial solution.

The problem of teachers has not been resolved. There are improvisations and patch work measures, but no basic solutions. The communities are either unwilling or unable to make Jewish education an attractive and honorable career.

A concentrated coordinated effort must be made to extend, expand and widen the scope of Jewish education in Western Europe. Jewish communities must see Jewish education as the single highest communal priority; they must make Jewish education the central concern of Jewish leadership; they must create conditions which attract candidates to the teaching profession, and encourage schools to improve and renovate the school program. Only then can the Jewish heritage be passed on to ever wider circles of the Jewish community.

Notes

1. Jewish education in France and Great Britain is dealt with in other chapters in this volume.

2. Based on information supplied by Tullio Perlmutter, former Director of the Rome Jewish Community.

References

Abramovitch, S. (1970). *Survey of Jewish Day and Supplementary Schools in Western Continental Europe.* AJDC, Geneva.

Bock, G.E. (1976). *The Jewish Schooling of American Jews: A Study of Non-Cognitive Educational Effects.* Unpublished doctoral dissertation, Harvard University, Cambridge.

Himmelfarb, H.S. (1977) "The Non-Linear Impact of Jewish Schooling: Comparing Different Types and Amounts of Jewish Education". *Sociology of Education*, Vol. 50, no. 2. pp. 114–129.

Himmelfarb, H.S. and DellaPergola, S. (1982). *Enrollment in Jewish Schools in the Diaspora; Late 1970s.* The Institute of Contemporary Jewry, The Hebrew University, Jerusalem. (Project for Jewish Educational Statistics, Research Report No. 1.) 97 pp.

Part Five

South Africa and Australia

In this part of the book we complete the analysis of major Diaspora Jewish educational systems. Although on separate continents and having little direct interaction, the Jewish educational systems of South Africa and Australia have much in common. The structures of their educational systems are quite similar, both having been based on the British model. Both countries attained political independence only after World War II. Both Jewish communities are about the same size, are heavily Zionist in orientation, like Latin American communities, but both are more religiously traditional than the Latin American. Of course, there are differences too.

The internal politics of South Africa has had major international repercussions and the reaction of Israel to those issues has been concerned with any consequences for South African Jewry. Whether changes in the balance of power between blacks and whites will affect the Jewish community of South Africa and its strong Jewish educational system remains to be seen. Obviously, it could affect Jewish emigration from the country. In his analysis of South African Jewish education, Bernard Steinberg, Professor of Education at the University of Cape Town, discusses the concerns of the Jewish community with the main issues affecting South African society and the place of the Jewish community within it. Steinberg has written extensively on the need for the comparative study of Jewish education, including his own analyses of Jewish education in the United States and Great Britain.

Geulah Solomon, when she wrote her chapter on Australia was a Professor of Education at Victoria College in Melbourne. Her doctoral dissertation was on the history of Jewish education in Australia. Here she extends that analysis to deal with contemporary issues and trends.

11

South Africa: Jewish Education in a Divided Society

Bernard Steinberg

The very nature of contemporary South African society, with its political institutions and its economy, provides a unique setting for Jewish life. However South African Jewry itself is in many respects a unique entity in terms of its historical background, its present-day structure and its place within this multi-racial and multi-cultural host society. The Republic of South Africa has a total population of about 24 million, comprising some 16.5 million members of the various black African peoples, 2.5 million 'Coloureds' of mixed racial descent, 750,000 Indians whose forebears came to the country as indentured laborers during the last century and a white European population of about 4.5 million. The white population is itself divided into two distinct linguistic and cultural groups – about 60% being the Afrikaners, whose language, Afrikaans, is derived from Dutch, and the other group being the English speakers. The Jewish community is almost exclusively English-speaking, although many Jews are also fluent in Afrikaans (Republic of South Africa, 1980).

Since the arrival of the first European inhabitants in 1652, whites have played the dominant role in the unfolding of South Africa's destiny. Notwithstanding their numerical status as a minority they have effectively always had political power, as well as economic control over the vast agricultural, mining, industrial and commercial wealth of the country. The present regime, in power since 1948, instituted the policy of separate development or apartheid, which, through legal processes, has institutionalized the segregation of the various racial groups. Among other things, this policy sets aside exclusive residential areas for each group, forbids sexual relations and marriage across racial lines and provides for separate self-contained educational systems for each of the four racial groups.

South African Jewry

South African Jewry, an integral part of the politically and economically dominant white minority, numbered 118,120 according to the 1970 census. The report of a demographic survey in the mid-1970s calculated the number of Jews in the six largest communities as 97,789.[1]

The Jewish community has always played an important part in the development of the country as a whole, while at the same time retaining its own distinct identity as a religious national group.

According to some historians, Jews first arrived in South Africa in the 17th century. However, the first authenticated records of Jewish settlement date from the 1820s when some European Jews were among the pioneers who made their way through the vast territories of the Cape of Good Hope. The first Hebrew congregation was established in Cape Town in 1841, followed by a few in different parts of the country. Today, there are virtually no Jewish descendants of these early settlers.

In the 1870s diamonds were discovered at Kimberley and rich gold deposits were found on the Witwatersrand. The resultant influx of immigrants and fortune seekers, particularly to the Transvaal, included a substantial number of Jews. At the turn of the century, from 1899 to 1902, the Anglo-Boer War was fought between the British and the descendants of the original white settlers. When the Boers were defeated, South Africa became part of the British Empire. By this time, there were about 38,000 Jews in the country and a number of established Jewish congregations (Herrman, 1935; Saron and Hotz, 1955).

The Jewish newcomers came mainly from Germany, the Netherlands and Britain. They set themselves up as storekeepers, merchants and farmers throughout the country. The congregations which they established formed the foundations of today's communities and the structure of the communal institutions. These foundations were strongly Anglo-Jewish by inspiration, due both to the influence of immigrants from Britain and to South Africa's new place within the British Empire.

At the start of this century, Jewish immigration from Eastern Europe began to make itself felt. This was notably from Lithuania, and these Jews superimposed a solid 'Litvak' ethos on the Anglo-Jewish traditions and standards established by the earlier Jewish immigrants. Today, the vast majority of South Africa's Jews are Lithuanian in origin. The process and its consequences have been described as "pouring Lithuanian wine into Anglo-Jewish bottles" (Saron, 1967). It is reflected today in such things as the structure of South African Jewry's communal and synagogal institutions, and especially in the influence of Zionism within the community.

Zionism has indeed been the most distinctive feature of South African Jewish life.[2] Many of its distinguished and influential communal leaders, past and present, have been active in the Zionist movement and a number of them eventually left South Africa and went to Israel. One reason for this strong Zionist influence is the fact that Zionist ideals were integral to the Jewish consciousness of the East European immigrants. Another reason lies in the nature of South African society as a whole, with its distinctive groupings and their historical backgrounds of independent development. Thus, "South Africa's peculiar inter-colour pluralism and intra-white dualism was conducive to the cultivation of a national mode of identification for Jews" (Shimoni, 1980).

Significantly, of the two most important national Jewish organizations, the South African Zionist Federation was founded in 1898, five years earlier than the South African Jewish Board of Deputies. These two bodies co-exist today reflecting not only South African Jewry's concern for its own affairs, but also its close bonds with the State of Israel (Aschheim, 1970).

The Board of Deputies is a representative body which holds biennial congresses of representatives from each of the four provinces, and can thus speak with one voice for South African Jewry. The various departments of the Board deal comprehensively with public relations, welfare and cultural activities.

The Zionist Federation finds itself in the remarkable situation of enjoying a status equal to that of the Board of Deputies. It disseminates information, organizes special activities, concerns itself with Hebrew education and aliyah, and has affiliated societies and groups throughout the country. Furthermore, the Federation publishes a weekly newspaper, the *Zionist Record and South African Jewish Chronicle*.

Two women's organizations occupy an important position in the communal structure. The first, the Union of Jewish Women has branches in all the main Jewish centers. Its stated objective is to serve the Jewish community as a whole, the peoples of South Africa and the State of Israel. The second is the Women's Zionist Council made up of over 100 affiliated groups which are occupied with educational, welfare and fundraising activities, with a special focus on Israel. Both these organizations have always been involved in various educational activities, ranging from seminars and courses for their membership to the establishment, maintenance and support of nursery schools.

A number of studies and surveys from the mid-1970s provide the basis for a profile of the contemporary South African Jewish community and its salient characteristics (Dubb and DellaPergola, 1977–1978).

Congregational membership is mainly Orthodox, although it is generally acknowledged that the present generation is not as observant as its forebears. A survey in the mid-1970s concluded that an estimated 77% of South African Jewry expressed preference for Orthodox synagogues, 17% for Reform congregations, 1% for both Orthodox and Reform, while 5% had no affiliation. Furthermore, 20% of Jewish males and 13% of females reported once-a-week synagogue attendance while 15% of males and 20% of females stated that they never attended. In terms of actual synagogue membership, 79% were paying members of Orthodox or Reform congregations, 8% non-paying members and 7% sympathizers (Dubb and DellaPergola, 1978(11)).

The Orthodox congregations are affiliated either with the Federation of Synagogues of South Africa, based in Johannesburg, or with the Union of Orthodox Hebrew Congregations Board in Cape Town. Reform congregations function under the aegis of the South African Union for Progressive Judaism. Both the Orthodox and Reform movements directly provide Jewish education both for adults and children, and most afternoon schools are located on premises belonging to the congregations.

In comparison with other groups in South Africa, the Jewish community is an aging group, with a high proportion of men and women over 65 years of age and a comparatively low and declining fertility rate. When we add to this fact the numbers who do not marry and the phenomenon of Jewish emigration, we arrive at demographic projections for a future drop in numbers or, at most, a static population (Dubb and DellaPergola, 1978(3)).

South African Jewry is almost entirely urban. Before World War II, there were some small but active communities in the villages and rural areas. Over the past few decades, these have been drastically depleted and most have disappeared (Clouts, 1982). By the mid-1970s, somewhat over 80% of the Jewish population lived in the cities of Johannesburg (59,051), Cape Town (25,192), Durban (6,244), Pretoria (3,842), Port Elizabeth (2,319) and Bloemfontein (1,141) (Dubb and DellaPergola, 1978(9)).

In the mid-1970s, Jews formed 12% of the white population of Johannesburg and 7% in Cape Town. Jews tended to concentrate in certain residential districts and suburbs in the main cities. In a number of Johannesburg and Cape Town suburbs, over half the population is Jewish (Dubb and DellaPergola, 1978(9)).

Synagogues, day schools and other communal institutions are generally situated near the centers of Jewish population, although these centers have moved due to intra-city residential changes as Jewish families left the city centers for the suburbs. Conversely, in a number of instances the siting of day schools has influenced residence patterns, as young families move to homes within easy travelling or walking distance from the school, in most cases in newly developed suburbs.

Compared to the general population, the occupational structure of South African Jewry reveals a high representation of employment based on higher educational qualifications, that is, professionals and holders of managerial and administrative posts, particularly in the commercial sector. Indeed, the upward economic and social mobility of South African Jews has been great in a land where opportunities have long existed, particularly in the entrepreneurial field. By dint of hard work and initiative, many immigrants established themselves economically, enabling successive generations to advance in occupations associated with higher status as well as income. While in 1936 professionals and administrative personnel together accounted for 12% of economically active Jews, by 1970 this figure had increased to 38%. Between 1964 and 1974, the percentage of Jewish heads of households who were professionals or administrative personnel had risen from 60 to 70%. By 1974, 36% of economically active Jews were employers (Dubb and DellaPergola, 1978(10)).

Kashruth is observed in 59% of Jewish households, although full observance is the case in only 27%. In practice, there is an element of duality in the religious observance of South African Jewry, as illustrated by the staunch adherence to certain religious observances concurrent with complete laxity in others.

> The emerging image is one of a community deeply affected by certain characteristic patterns of traditional Jewish culture, though the selective choice of observed traditions suggests the latter are not the expression of an orthodox-religious way of thinking but rather the interplay of secular and traditional elements in the overall pattern of Jewish identity in South Africa (Dubb and DellaPergola, 1978(11)).

On the basis of this profile, South African Jewry is in certain respects an anomalous community. It benefits from the attendant advantages and privileges of being an integral part of the politically and economically dominant white minority in an environment where for the past few years there has been little sustained overt antisemitism or anti-Zionism. While in other Diaspora countries such conditions might be conducive to assimilation, it is possible that in South Africa there are characteristics inherent in the host society which foster group identity among the separate ethnic groups. 'Jewishness', therefore, emerges under unusual conditions.

The Afrikaner-English dichotomy has a background of political conflict, largely concerned with the preservation of Afrikaner cultural identity. It follows that the exclusivity of each group was important and this was expressed by differences in language, occupational structure and residential patterns. Until the end of World War II, the Afrikaners were a largely rural farming population in contrast to the English-speakers who were generally concentrated in the industrial areas (Davenport, 1977). In the midst of these settings, Jews encountered social and cultural conditions that tended to discourage acceptance by the host society. Since 1948 when Afrikaner nationalism emerged as the dominant political ideology, these conditions have persisted.[3]

Today, Jewish identity is expressed in a national-ethnic rather than a religious-cultural form. It is based on spontaneous sentiment rather than a deep involvement in religious practice or culture and learning. At the organizational level, this is manifested in its wide network of synagogues, communal and welfare institutions, Zionist societies, sports and social clubs, the Jewish press, and most characteristically in the form and structure of its education system (Dubb, 1977).

Events and development within the host society inevitably effect the Jewish community. The South African Jewish Board of Deputies reacts in the name of the community by way of resolutions and pronouncements relating to the general situation. Moreover, the Board and a number of other communal organizations, such as the Union of Jewish Women, are active in welfare work and other activities directed at alleviating the problems of the underprivileged and promoting the creation of a harmonious and just society from the disparate groups that make up South Africa's population. Furthermore, many individual members of the Jewish community take full part in civic, political and social affairs, as well as in other aspects of public life. Jewish representation in so many fields, from the professions to the arts, has always been distinguished and far out of proportion to the actual size of the community ("South Africa's Jewish Community...", 1979).

In the past South African Jewry has benefitted from its status within the white minority, but it has also produced outspoken and active opponents to the policies of apartheid. Still, the Board of Deputies has felt impelled as a representative body to avoid a hard and fast line that would commit Jewry as a whole. At the Board's 1980 Congress, the following resolution was passed:

> While welcoming recent reforms Congress believes that unless more meaningful and more significant changes in our social, economic and political structure are initiated, the ever-mounting external and internal pressures may well erupt into violence and bloodshed. Congress accordingly urges all concerned, in particular all members of our own community to co-operate in securing the immediate amelioration and ultimate removal of all unjust discriminatory laws and practices based on race, creed or colour. Only in this way can we hope to stem the widening gulf and dangerous polarization between our different population groups and establish that common bond of trust and loyalty essential for a peaceful, united and just society (SAJBD, 1980a).

One current phenomenon within South African Jewry, particularly since 1976, is its comparatively high rate of emigration. While many have chosen aliyah to Israel, considerable numbers of Jews, and these mostly younger people, have chosen Canada, the United States, Australia and Great Britain as their destinations. Emigration has been specifically cited as one reason for the drop in enrollment of Jewish children in nursery schools (SABJE, 1978). Alumni of Jewish day schools are now living in many other parts of the world. Many have become active members of their new Jewish communites, and, interestingly, many retain links with their old schools, often acknowledging the benefits they derived from their Jewish education (*Herzlia Headlines*, 1981).

Since 1945 Jewish immigration has been minimal – with one exception. Over recent decades, an increasing number of Israeli families and individuals have come to live and work in South Africa. Their precise number is difficult to ascertain, but according to some estimates, it is today as high as 20,000 or about one-fifth or one-sixth of the total Jewish community (Diamond, 1981). An estimate of half as many would probably be more realistic. While these newcomers prefer to be considered sojourners rather than immigrants, their presence must be acknowledged. An important responsibility for integrating them and their children into the community rests with the Jewish education systems and to this end, special arrangements were made in a number of day schools to accommodate Israeli children.

Jewish Education: Historical Background

From the earliest stages of organized communal life, efforts were made to provide Jewish education for children. In Cape Town, religion classes were held in the 1840s, and in 1878, a Sunday school was established. In 1895, the Cape Town Hebrew Congregational School became the first Jewish day school in the country where Jewish as well as secular subjects were taught (Katz, 1980). This school was subsidized by the Cape of Good Hope Crown Colony as well as the Cape Town Jewish Congregation. Similar schools opened in Johannesburg in 1902, in Pretoria and in the small town of Oudtshoorn in 1905. None of these schools achieved wide acceptance within the Jewish community. Immigrants from Eastern Europe in particular preferred to send their children to government schools and even to Catholic schools for their general education, and to the Talmud Torah or heder after school hours for Jewish learning in the East European tradition. By 1899, the first Talmud Torah in South Africa was already functioning in Cape Town. In due course, the Talmud Torah became the characteristic educational institution in the main urban centers as well as in the smaller communities. At first, each educational institution had operated independently under congregational aegis. Organization of Jewish education on the national level was begun in 1928 with the establishment of the Johannesburg-based South African Board of Jewish Education. Then, in 1932, the Cape Board of Jewish Education was established as the administrative and supervisory body for the Cape Town area.

By the end of World War II, Jewish education consisted predominantly of congregation-sponsored part-time institutions of the Talmud Torah type, with classes held after school hours and on Sunday mornings. At the national level, the Johannesburg and Cape Town-based Boards made an attempt at overall coordination and tried to solve endemic problems. The few day schools, with their stress on secular subjects at the expense of Jewish studies, had more or less faded out of existence.

The curriculum of the Talmud Torah was generally based on a synthesis of the traditional *Yiddishkeit* and Zionism that characterized the *heder metukan* – Bible, religion and ritual, Hebrew language and literature. Most of the teachers were themselves immigrants from Eastern Europe, and among them were the 'reverends' who, as spiritual leaders of the smaller congregations, also provided Jewish education for the children. By the 1930s, there were also a number of teachers who had attended seminaries in Lithuania or Poland. Other than these, there was no established Jewish teaching profession.

The Holocaust and the establishment of the State of Israel marked the formation of new patterns of Jewish education in South Africa (United Herzlia Schools, 1973). The Jewish day school has become the most important institution of education, concurrent with the decline of organized part-time schooling of a supplementary nature. The South African Board of Jewish Education has emerged as the most important administrative body, with which the vast majority of day schools and afternoon schools are affiliated.

The post-war years have also seen the emergence of a 'traditional-national' ideology of Jewish education, an expression of the unique character and composition of South African Jewry given the wider socio-political setting in which it exists (Katz, 1980; Adar, 1965). At conferences of the South African Board of Jewish Education during the 1950s and 1960s, this ideology evolved in the wake of debates by two separate and often conflicting groups – those communal leaders who wanted to stress the centrality of religious content, and those who maintained, on the other hand, that Jewish schooling should be based on Zionist ideology (Saron, 1980). Traditional-national Jewish education is a synthesis of the religious foundations of Jewish life and the influence of Zionism upon Jewish identity in South Africa. As such, it is a form of compromise that attempts to comply with the outlook of the average South African Jew who cannot be described as thoroughly Orthodox, and yet for whom continued Jewish existence and group identity are vital considerations.[4] Mainstream Jewish education in South Africa has been criticized in certain Orthodox circles for being too secular in orientation and not placing enough stress upon the teaching of the Jewish religion as such. Still, the Reform movement continues to maintain its own education network, with the South African Board of Jewish Education remaining, at least nominally or by implication, an Orthodox-oriented body.

A further significant development concerns the post-war evolution of the national education system in South Africa. Successive National Party governments since 1948 have effected a policy of applying the ideology of Christian national education to the very ethos of all government schools. The National Education Policy Act of 1967 officially confirmed the Christian character of education in South African schools "through the spirit and manner in which all teaching and education, as well as Administrative and organization, are conducted." (Republic of South Africa, 1974; Saron, 1973). This took full effect in 1972, and although Jewish pupils were exempt from participation in the Christo-centric religious instruction by means of a "conscience clause", the wider implications of the Act remain.[5] Regular morning assemblies, of which the central features are Christian prayers and hymns, are important to the daily routine of government schools. Similarly, religious instruction and 'Scripture' based upon Christian doctrine are an integral part of the classroom time-table.

The recent history of Jewish education in South Africa is thus influenced by a number of complex factors – some inherent in the nature of completely spontaneous inner resurgence of Jewishness. Isaac Goss, a distinguished Jewish educationalist and rabbi, who was director of the South African Board of Jewish Education for twenty years until his retirement in 1979, summed up all these prevailing circumstances as follows:

> Can you expect the Jew in South Africa to be at home in three cultures – English, Afrikaans and Jewish? The implications of Jewish education and the fact that the Jew here must also be a South African, require him to be at home in three cultures. Can he be? (Goss, 1961).

The Jewish School System

Administrative Structure and General Profile

As the largest and most important Jewish education agency, the South African Board of Jewish Education (SABJE) administrates, supervises and makes general policy for a network of day, supplementary and nursery schools, a teachers seminary and a pedagogic center. Under the direct supervision of the Board are most of the education institutions in the greater Johannesburg area, and nearly all the remaining education institutions in the rest of the country are affiliated with it. In a separate context, the Cape Board of Jewish Education directly supervises a group of supplementary schools within its metropolitan area and in nearby suburbs and towns. The United Herzlia Schools of Cape Town, with nearly 2,500 pupils, comprise a separate regional system which until recently was completely independent of SABJE. These schools are now affiliated with SABJE, but nevertheless remain an autonomous administrative and supervisory body.

Given the above outline, the bulk of the Jewish education system is, in effect, unified and coordinated under one umbrella organization. It is, however, by no means a monolithic entity. While SABJE directly administers and supervises the Jewish education network in Johannesburg itself, the schools in the rest of the country, notwithstanding their affiliation, retain their autonomy while benefitting from the services of the Board. Such services include inspection, inter-school liaison, financial assistance and general consultation.

Only the following organizations and institutions are not connected with SABJE: the South African Council for Progressive Jewish Education (part of the Reform movement); the schools of the Lubavitch movement; and the *Sha'arei Torah* schools, which function under the aegis of the Johannesburg *kollel*.

Since government policy in South Africa does not provide for substantial aid to denominational schools, the day schools of Jewish as well as the various Christian denominations must look to their own resources for financial and other support. This applies to the construction and maintenance of school buildings, the provision of books and equipment, the salaries of teachers and every other facet of the system. The main sources of income are the United Communal Fund, pupils' fees, bequests and legacies, and ad hoc and other grants from such bodies as the South African Zionist Federation and the Union of Jewish Women. In the province of Natal, a special annual grant has been provided by the authorities for Carmel College, the Jewish day school in Durban, while negotiations have been concluded for a similar grant from the Cape Province authorities for the Jewish day schools in Cape Town and Port Elizabeth (Behr and Macmillan, 1971).[6]

The afternoon supplementary schools, under the aegis of SABJE and the Cape Board, are almost all congregational schools. Since many of these schools serve the Jewish communities in the smaller towns throughout South Africa, the functions of the two regional Boards are primarily to provide syllabi and pedagogic materials as well as regular inspections. The United Hebrew Schools of Johannesburg is the SABJE agency which supervises a group of 25 supplementary schools in that city. Apart from Johannesburg and the Cape Town area, there were 29 congregational supplementary schools in the rest of the country in 1981 (SABJE, 1981a; CBJE, 1980a). The Reform movement's South African Council for Progressive Jewish Education administers its own afternoon schools in Johannesburg, Cape Town, Pretoria, Durban, Port Elizabeth and Springs.

South Africa's 82 Jewish nursery schools function under the aegis of a number of communal organizations, including SABJE, various Orthodox and Reform congregations, the Union of Jewish Women and the Cape Town Hebrew Pre-Primary Association. In contrast to the official status of Jewish day schools, the nursery schools receive financial aid from the provincial authorities in return for partial control. In the Cape and in Natal, nursery school teachers are paid by the provincial authorities, while in the Transvaal, grants are provided on the basis of enrollment.

Jewish nursery schools have always accepted a significant proportion of non-Jewish children. In 1981, these nursery schools contained a total of 4,606 pupils and 281 teachers, Jewish as well as non-Jewish. While proportions vary from school to school, approximately 75% of the total number of pupils in Jewish nursery schools are actually Jewish (SABJE, 1975, pp. 18–19; 1978, pp. 30–32; 1981a, pp. 25–26; 1981b).

Available figures show that in 1983 Jewish day school enrollment in South Africa was 4,869 primary school pupils aged 6 to 13 years, and 3,768 high school pupils between 14 and 17 years old, making a total of 8,637. These students were enrolled in a total of 13 primary and 13 high schools, indicating that most of these schools are substantial units in terms of enrollment. Indeed, only four of them have fewer than 100 pupils, while the largest, King David Primary and High Schools, Linksfield, Johannesburg, have 1,037 and 1,171 pupils respectively (SABJE, 1981a, p. 48).

In 1981, the proportion of boys enrolled was slightly over 52% and indications are that this percentage has remained much the same. The day schools in 1981 employed 111 full-time teachers for Judaic studies, 88 for secular studies, and the adminstrative staff totalled 53 and maintenance and domestic workers, 182.

With the diminishing Jewish population in the smaller towns and country areas, the number of supplementary schools outside the Johannesburg and Cape Town areas decreased from 31 in 1978 to 29 in 1981, with a corresponding reduction in enrollment from 829 to 699 pupils. In the entire country, there were only five part-time centers with enrollments exceeding 100 pupils, and of these four were situated in Johannesburg and one in Cape Town. In Johannesburg, where the part-time centers function under the direct supervision of the United Hebrew Schools of Johannesburg, there was a slight rise in numbers between 1978 and 1981, from 1,020 to 1,094 pupils (718 boys and 376 girls) and from 64 to 68 teachers. However, during the same years, the number of supplementary centers in Johannesburg was reduced from 28 to 25, and the number of classes from 109 to 106. Comparatively few pupils stay on after bar mitzvah or bat mitzvah age. In Johannesburg supplementary schools in 1981, only eight boys and nine girls were over the age of 13.

An additional 400 pupils receive supplementary education in Johannesburg in early morning classes on government school premises before the commencement of the school day proper. And in 1980 there were 505 pupils (including 30 pupils who met early in the morning) at 15 supplementary centers under the supervision of the Cape Board of Jewish Education (SABJE, 1980a; 1981a, pp. 14, 17–18, 48; 1981c; CBJE, 1980b, pp. 1–38).

In 1981, about 5,800 pupils from Johannesburg and other centers in the Transvaal, as well as from the provinces of Natal and the Orange Free State, participated in correspondence courses. In Cape Town and the surrounding region, special classes in Jewish religious instruction provided 995 pupils in 26 government schools with 60 visiting teachers (SABJE, 1981a; SAJBD, 1982, p. 2). The Pedagogic Resource Center of the SABJE employs a director and staff of seven to prepare the correspondence course material and correct the work of the pupils. In the Cape and Orange Free State provinces, the visiting teachers in most cases hold no formal qualifications in Jewish studies.

The afternoon supplementary schools organized by the South African Council for Progressive Jewish Education comprise classes for some 500 pupils with 30 teachers (SACPJE, 1981).

From the above description and the available statistical data on which it is based, three overriding characteristics of Jewish education in South Africa can be adduced:

- first, the system is highly organized and coordinated, with the South African Board of Jewish Education as the umbrella body with which most full and part-time Jewish schools are affiliated;
- second, the scope of the entire network of full-time and part-time schooling, under the aegis of SABJE and other agencies, is such that Jewish education reaches the clear majority of Jewish children of school age;
- third, the Jewish day schools are the center of the system and the majority of children receiving any form of Jewish education in South Africa are pupils of these schools.

It is estimated that about half the Jewish children of school-age attend Jewish day schools, about 15% attend supplementary schools and participate in correspondence courses or withdrawal classes in government or private non-Jewish schools. This conclusion is based on the estimated child and adolescent population in 1980 of 4,100 between the ages of 3 and 5 years, 11,300 between 6 and 13 years and 6,000 between 14 and 17 years.

Jewish Day School Education: Curricula and Content

The spectacular development and growth of Jewish day schools in South Africa since the late 1940s is a phenomenon that needs elaboration and explanation. These schools are the products of communal initiative endeavour and self-sacrifice, since they were all established and are to this day maintained without any significant material assistance besides South African Jewry. From time to time they have experienced crises, particularly in the financial sphere, but at no time have they suffered from lack of communal support (King David Schools, 1968). Their achievements in the field of Jewish education were recognized in 1972 when the President Shazar prize was awarded in Jerusalem to the Cape Town Herzlia Schools. In addition to their coordinated administrations, other policies and activities help to maintain their cohesiveness. For example, every year organized groups of pupils exchange visits between Johannesburg, Cape Town, Durban and Port Elizabeth for sporting, cultural and social activities.

The emergence of the day school as the normative agency of Jewish education may be ascribed to a number of factors. Above all, it relates to the inherent character and situation of South African Jewry. South Africa has been classified as one of those countries in which there are special conditions which make it desirable for Jews to set up their own day schools, "even without the financial support of the State" (Dushkin, 1963). Thus, the structure of South African society as a whole, with its segmentation into racial and ethnic groups has encouraged Jews to revitalize their own cultural heritage, including Zionism, as a prominent component thereof.

It should also be noted that public education in South Africa is subdivided administratively into four self-contained systems for Blacks, Whites, Coloureds and Indians respectively. Above all, the post-war development of the public education system, particularly with its emphasis on the Afrikaner Christian-National ideology, has deterred many Jews from sending their children to government schools. Indeed, a significant group of non-Jewish independent schools has also emerged, mainly under the aegis of Christian denominations, for the same reasons. While many of these fee-paying schools were established long before World War II, today they have no shortage of pupils, most of whom are drawn from the English-speaking sector of South Africa's white population (Malherbe, 1977; The Association of Private Schools, 1981).

It can therefore be postulated that in addition to the usually cited causes of reaction to the Holocaust and the inspiration of the State of Israel there are also clearly-defined local incentives to the comparatively high Jewish day school enrollments. Besides those already mentioned, a few other factors are noteworthy. Uncertainty about the future prompts many South African Jews to think of aliyah, hence the importance attached to a sound Hebrew-based education for their children. In addition, a number of parents who have recently transferred their children to Jewish day schools cite antisemitism in government schools as the cause. Finally, many Jewish parents, particularly in the Transvaal, have expressed dissatisfaction with the educational standards in government schools, many of which are at present experiencing critial teacher shortages in such key subjects as science and mathematics.[7]

The Jewish day schools have striven to attain high standards in secular as well as Jewish studies, since it is known that many Jewish parents send their children to Jewish schools precisely because of their high standards in secular subjects. The Chairman of SABJE has acknowledged the problem of lack of harmony between home and school in the field of Jewish knowledge and observance.[8] The reputation of the day schools is often justified on the basis of success in the annual final school Senior Certificate and Matriculation Examinations. In terms of the national average, pupils from Jewish schools have for the past decade consistently achieved higher academic success than pupils from other schools in South Africa. Similarly, sports, which are so much a part of the South African way of life, are an important activity in all Jewish day schools, where high national standards at all competitive levels are regularly attained (*Herzlia Headlines*, 1980).

Within the schools themselves, stress is given to the secular subjects, while Hebrew language and Jewish studies fit into the general time-table without occupying a specified portion of the day. As a typical example, in a school week averaging 25 classroom hours for primary pupils and 30 hours at the secondary level, eight hours are devoted to Jewish subjects. This means that out of an average of 40 teaching periods per week, each of 35 to 40 minutes duration, between 10 to 15 periods are devoted to Jewish subjects. In addition, there are five periods for what is termed 'practical *tefillah*'. The notable exceptions to this general picture are the Yeshiva College schools, the Torah Academy and the *Sha'arei Torah* schools, where considerably more time is spent on Jewish studies, particularly of the more traditional kind – Torah, Mishnah, Gemara and *dinim*. In these schools, Orthodox Jewish education is stressed. At Yeshiva College, for example, Jewish subjects occupy 1.5 hours daily in the primary school, 2 hours in the girls' high school, and between 2.5 and 3 hours in the boys' high school.

The Jewish studies curriculum in most day schools is divided into Hebrew and Jewish studies, the latter comprising mainly religious laws and customs but also including Jewish history. A typical week's schedule for a high school class is seven lessons for Hebrew and four for Jewish studies, in addition to the daily prayer sessions.[9] One reason for the priority given to Hebrew is the fact that it is officially included in the Matriculation Examination, whereas other Jewish subjects are not.

Jewish day schools have stressed Hebrew language and Israeli-oriented subject matter to the detriment of more traditional studies, thus eliciting criticism that the Jewish studies curriculum is too secular in its approach and that pupils remain comparatively ignorant of the religious aspects of Jewish life. During the 1960s and 1970s, this criticism was voiced regularly at conferences of SABJE (Saron, 1980). In the course of his opening address at a conference on education organized by the Jewish Agency in Johannesburg in October 1982, the then Chief Rabbi of the Federation of Synagogues of South Africa, B.M. Casper, stated: "I am making a plea for the strengthening, in plain terms, of the religious element in all our education work." The opposing – and prevailing – viewpoint has been that since day school pupils come from a variety of home backgrounds, in terms of Jewish religious observance, and only a minority are Orthodox, it would not be sound policy to place greater stress upon religious content.

The debate is an ongoing one. For schools such as the three Orthodox institutions mentioned above, there is no compromise in presenting and maintaining the Orthodox viewpoint or in requiring an appropriate response from the pupils not only in school but also outside it.[10] At the remaining institutions, which comprise the vast majority of day schools, the attitude is more flexible, despite the fact that officially the prevailing religious ethos is that of Orthodox Judaism.

On the question of prayers and religious observance, each school adopts its own policy. In some high schools, attendance for all pupils is compulsory, since the morning service is an integral part of the assembly which starts the school day. At the King David High School in Linksfield, Johannesburg, attendance at prayers is optional for pupils in Form V, the highest class, but compulsory for all others. At Herzlia High School in Cape Town, the usual daily minyan is voluntary, but the monthly *Rosh Hodesh* morning service is attended by the entire school. At the junior schools, where most pupils are below bar mitzvah or bat mitzvah age, prayers at daily morning assembly are extracts from the prayer book. The only schools where there is no compromise over attendance at daily prayers in their complete form are Yeshiva College, Torah Academy and *Sha'arei Torah.*

An important feature of the religious education of the Jewish day schools since the mid-1970s has been the Counterpoint Program, based on similar projects in the United States, Australia and other countries. In its setting and atmosphere of a retreat, the Counterpoint experience takes place away from school and home as a residential seminar. The emphasis is on the affective experience of Judaism, observance of mitzvoth and *dinim,* especially Shabbat, and the programs are supervised by young Orthodox youth workers from America supplemented by local helpers. Well over 1,000 day school pupils have so far participated in Counterpoint programs, and the SABJE has for some time given its official support and financial assistance to the project (SABJE, 1981a, pp. 22–23).

Every year since 1963 groups of day school pupils with their teachers have participated at a special ulpan in Israel. The duration of this course is about fourteen to fifteen weeks. In addition to continuing with their normal secular curriculum, ulpan pupils undergo intensive courses in Hebrew and in Israel-based subjects taught by local teachers, culminating in an extensive tour of the country. A further dimension is added to this experience by the full observance of Jewish halacha. Between 1963 and 1981, 1,185 boys and 793 girls participated in the day schools' ulpan, which in recent years has been located at Kiryat Moriah in Jerusalem. As an established facet of day school education in South Africa, the ulpan program is fully accepted in terms of the financial outlay by parents as well as the Board of Education (SABJE, 1981a, pp. 24–25, 53).

A number of day school pupils come from rural areas, and some from as far afield as Zimbabwe. While a few of these pupils board with local families, accommodation for the majority is provided in hostels. The King David Schools' hostel in Johannesburg accommodates over 80 children, and that of Yeshiva College between 20 and 30 (SABJE, 1981a, p. 39). At the Herzlia Schools in Cape Town, a hostel functioned until 1978 for about 40 pupils. Despite the shrinking rural communities, there will be a continued need for hostel accommodation for several years to come.

Supplementary Jewish Education

Part-time Jewish education, notably the afternoon school, has declined in almost inverse proportion to the growth of the day schools. Between 1978 and 1981, the number of part-time centers in Johannesburg diminished from 28 to 25, while in Cape Town the number of pupils dropped from 624 to 505 (SABJE, 1978, pp. 26–27; 1981a, pp. 18–19; CBJE, 1980a, p. 1). While many of the pupils concerned transferred to Jewish day schools, it is a reality that there will always be a substantial number of Jewish children who receive their education at government schools. For this reason, SABJE and the Cape Board of Jewish Education continue to give urgent consideration to the various forms of supplementary Jewish education.

The supplementary Jewish school has problems inherent to its very nature, mainly concerned with regular attendance, adequate standards, the recruitment of suitable teaching personnel and the bar- or bat mitzvah age as the termination of studies. Nevertheless the past record of these part-time centers is impressive.

The decline in Jewish population outside the four main communities has brought about a decrease in supplementary schools in South Africa's smaller communities. Scattered over a wide area, in some cases several hundred souls have steadfastly maintained Jewish communal functions. Those groups too small to employ their own rabbi or minister have the benefit of regular visits from the South African Jewish Board of Deputies' Rabbi to the country communities (SAJBD, 1980c). The Board of Deputies also regularly distributes a special magazine edited by this rabbi, *Chayenu*, for children in small isolated country communities. There are a number of such small communities that manage to hold regular synagogue services and provide some kind of Jewish education for their few children. In many respects, this is an admirable achievement. One of the most inspiring themes in the history of Jewish education in South Africa is that of the Litvak 'reverend' of the old school, who among his multifarious duties taught the children and instilled in them high standards of *Yiddishkeit*.

In those country communities where part-time schools function, education is the responsibility of the local spiritual leader. If there is no rabbi, one of the members of the community, usually a mother, acts as teacher, or there is a visiting teacher from the nearest larger Jewish community. One of the important functions of the South African Board and the Cape Board is to maintain contact with these remote Jewish families by means of regular visits by the deputy director or inspector for consultations, advice and encouragement. Both Boards also compile core syllabi and provide teaching aids and materials in accordance with the special circumstances prevailing. From time to time, senior day school pupils travel to outlying country areas to spend a Shabbat or Festival with the local community, in order to arrange an appropriate program for the children, and officiate at religious services. Pupils at Johannesburg's Yeshiva College have an excellent record in this respect, having over the past decade officiated at High Holyday services in small isolated communities where otherwise no religious service would have been held (*The Yeshivite*, 1980).

Of the supplementary schools in rural areas supervised by SABJE, over half have fewer than 15 pupils. In the 15 part-time centers of the Cape Board of Jewish Education enrollment has dropped severely in recent years: seven of these are located far from the Greater Cape Town area (CBJE, 1980b). The 1980 report from the community of Upington, some 500 miles from Cape Town, illustrates the problems as well as the sense of dedication.

> Although I am not a qualified Hebrew teacher, I hold Hebrew classes which are attended by a few girls from 9–10 years of age... Over the years the Cape Board of Jewish Education has always tried to assist us with books and material when required. Unfortunately three years have now elapsed since the visit of the Director of the Cape Board of Jewish Education to Upington to give assistance and advice (CBJE, 1980b, p. 37).

In a similar vein, part of the 1982 report from the country town of Worcester, some 50 miles from Cape Town, where 11 children were receiving their Jewish education from a visiting teacher, reads as follows:

> There are problems in small communities where only a few Jewish families live. Only occasionally is there a minyan, but the few Jewish families who still live in Worcester want to uphold our religion and traditions and it is most rewarding to see the pupils progress and learn through activities (CBJE, 1982, p. 40).

Despite the difficult conditions under which education is provided for all these isolated groups of Jews, official policy is to maintain standards at all costs and not deprive Jewish children, wherever they happen to be, of their spiritual heritage.

As for part-time Jewish education in the larger centers of Johannesburg, Cape Town, Pretoria, Durban and Port Elizabeth, it must be reiterated that the supplementary schools have declined, largely as a direct consequence of the growth of the day schools. Furthermore, within the context of an urbanized larger community there is not the same incentive to adhere tenaciously to one's Jewishness as there is in a remote country area. A Jew in Johannesburg, for example, is always near to some Jewish influence, even if he himself makes little effort at observance or at providing appropriate Jewish education for his children. With the inherent problems of part-time education in mind, policy-makers have over recent years begun to concentrate on reaching pupils in the government schools during school hours. In a sense, the implementation of the Christo-centric scripture syllabi in the government schools, together with the option for Jewish pupils to be excused from these lessons, has provided an important opportunity. This applies particularly to high school pupils who, had they been attending supplementary schools, would in most cases have terminated their studies at bar/bat mitzvah age. Efforts are also being made to preserve the afternoon classes in cities such as Johannesburg and Cape Town, notwithstanding the steady drop in enrollments.

The United Hebrew Schools of Johannesburg has also been trying to reach children not enrolled in any of its centers. To this effect they have offered special instruction to prepare girls for their bat mitzvah. These pupils write a special proficiency test and participate in an essay competition. These arrangements involve an average of sixty girls per year. As part of these efforts to attract high school pupils, facilities have been offered to prepare candidates for the university entrance Matriculation Examination. However, between 1978 and 1981, only one pupil took advantage of this opportunity (SABJE, 1981a, p. 18). In addition, the United Hebrew Schools arrange special joint assemblies and functions for their pupils on such occasions as Purim and Lag B'Omer. In recent years, an annual *zimriya* (groups' song contest) was also held.

Both in Cape Town and Johannesburg, an important variant of supplementary Jewish education takes place before the start of the school day. At a number of government schools permission has been given for Jewish pupils to receive daily Jewish instruction early in the morning, generally between 7.30 a.m. and 8.30 a.m. It is noteworthy that apart from the cooperation of the authorities, in some cases, the initiative for holding such classes has come from the non-Jewish school principals concerned. The only problem has been to find sufficient teachers for these early morning classes (CBJE, 1980b, pp. 29–30).

The most important recent development in the sphere of part-time Jewish education has been access to pupils in government schools during school hours. In the past, during the statutory Christo-centric religious instruction periods, Jewish pupils either participated or were allowed to withdraw and carry on with other activities. During the 1970s, when the four provincial education departments published their new scripture syllabi, the South African Jewish Board of Deputies in Johannesburg and Cape Town negotiated with the authorities for Jewish pupils to receive Jewish religious instruction during these periods. This was at a time when unofficial arrangements of this kind were in effect at a few schools.

As a result, since 1975, Jewish pupils at government schools in the Transvaal province have been receiving correspondence course material as part of a Jewish education syllabus on which they work during the official scripture lessons. The material is provided by the Office of the Chief Rabbi and the Pedagogic Resource Centre of the SABJE, an arrangement which was reached after the authorities did not give permission for Jewish religious instruction teachers to enter the schools. In the Transvaal, the correspondence programs in high schools was launched in 1975, and in primary schools a year later. In effect, this constitutes a totally new sector of Jewish education. Lesson material must be prepared in an attractive form, then delivered and distributed to the pupils at the various schools. The completed exercises must be collected, marked and returned to the pupils. By 1981 several thousand pupils were participating in the scheme (SABJE, n.d.; 1980b).

In the Cape Town area, where visiting teachers are allowed to give religious instruction to Jewish pupils during the normal scripture lesson, the challenge of inaugurating another new sector of Jewish education has been just as important. In this case, permission first had to be sought from junior and high school principals by the Board of Deputies, which administers the scheme. An appropriate set of syllabi had to be drawn up, taking into consideration the fact that for most pupils, this would be their only exposure to Jewish education, while for others, it would augment attendance at supplementary schools. The main problem was to find enough suitably qualified teachers, a mission which proved to be impossible. As a result, a number of Jewish mothers of suitable background, but not necessarily with formal teaching qualifications, were recruited. These women participate in regular in-service courses in Jewish studies and teaching methods, and receive nominal remuneration for their services. They have become a highly motivated and effective teaching force of over 50 teachers. By 1981, they were teaching in 27 schools and one teachers' college, and nearly 1,200 pupils in 171 classes participated in an average total of 180 lessons per week.

Finally, the Hebrew Nursery School movement in South Africa is also a sector of the part-time system. In the immediate post-war years, various Jewish organizations were prominent in pioneering the development of nursery schools in South Africa. Since the 1960s nearly half of all the nursery schools in Johannesburg have been Jewish. This is in spite of the fact that there has been a drop in enrollment, resulting from the low Jewish birthrate and the increasing Jewish emigration of recent years (SABJE, 1981a, pp. 26–27, 51–52; CBJE, 1980b, pp. 42–44).

Notwithstanding the official status of the Hebrew Nursery Schools, and the fact that they receive financial aid from the provincial authorities, there is no interference in their day-to-day activities which are rich in Jewish content. Material on aspects of Jewish heritage such as Bible stories, festivals, Israel and Hebrew songs is distributed regularly by the two supervisory bodies. Parents are encouraged to become involved and relevant material is sent to them in the form of regular bulletins.[11] In the past few years there have also been sponsored consultants' visits to South Africa by distinguished Israeli pre-primary educators. While precise figures are not available, it is estimated that the majority of Jewish nursery school pupils eventually proceed to Jewish day schools.

Some Characteristics of the Teaching Profession

Although most of the personnel for both day and part-time schools can be drawn from the communities themselves, the number of South African Jewish teachers is inadequate and additional sources had to be found. The first comprises Israelis, either teacher-*shlihim* on limited contract, or Israelis who for various reasons are temporarily or indefinitely resident in South Africa. These Israelis have become indispensable to the teaching of Hebrew and other Jewish subjects. Furthermore, the day schools have always had a significant number of non-Jewish teachers for secular subjects, many of whom occupy posts of high responsibility; one of them is a day school principal.

The important local source for trained and qualified teaching personnel is the Rabbi Zlotnik-Avida Hebrew Teachers' Training College in Johannesburg. Since its establishment in 1944, this College has trained over 200 Hebrew teachers, most of them women. Between 1978 and 1981, there were 21 graduates (SABJE, 1981a, pp. 12–14). In addition to their Jewish studies at the College, the majority of students also work toward their B.A. degrees through correspondence courses from the University of South Africa. Many fulfill part of their requirements in Israeli educational institutions, including the Hebrew University. The College also organizes refresher courses for qualified teachers. Over the past decade, a small number of rabbinical students have studied at the College toward rabbinical degrees (*Smicha*).

In addition to its important function of producing teachers of Hebrew and Jewish studies, the Zlotnik-Avida College provides a Jewish Students' University program. This program enables students at local universities and other centers of tertiary education to pursue their studies while taking part-time courses in various Jewish subjects at the College. Students accepted to this program are also given financial assistance toward the completion of their secular studies.

Other local sources of Jewish teachers are the South African universities and colleges of education. Most Jewish graduates of these institutions who are employed in the Jewish day schools teach only secular subjects, but there is also a not insignificant number who teach Hebrew and Jewish studies.

Also in the part-time schools, in both the urban and rural communities, teachers are recruited from a number of sources. In the large cities, many of these teachers also work in Jewish day schools. However, particularly in the smaller communities much of the teaching is done by rabbis and 'reverends'. In the majority of these communities, the function of the spiritual leader as teacher of the children is crucial, and in certain respects takes priority over all his other duties.

In South Africa as a whole there is a shortage of qualified teachers, and in certain subjects this also applies to Jewish day schools. One-quarter of the teaching staff in the day schools specializes in Judaic studies (SABJE, 1981a, p. 54). It is noteworthy that at the moment, there is no serious shortage of Hebrew language teachers due to the availability of qualified Israelis. On the other hand, there is a dearth of teachers in other branches of Jewish studies.

In addition to teachers from Israel and non-Jewish teachers, the personnel is further characterized by a preponderance of women, particularly in the primary schools, and by the presence of part-time staff in all subjects of the curriculum. In aggregate, part-time teachers comprise nearly 20% of the teaching force.

In 1962, the first conference of Jewish day school principals and heads of Hebrew departments was held. In 1970, an Association of Headmasters of Jewish Schools was formed, which has since then arranged annual meetings of its members.

Every attempt is made to attract suitably qualified teachers of the highest caliber to the day schools. Accordingly, employment conditions include salaries and increments equivalent to those of teachers in government schools, medical aid facilities and pension schemes. Fringe benefits include one month's leave of absence from duties after each two and one-half years of service and an annual bonus equal to an additional month's salary. A full time day school teacher has a weekly teaching load of between 35 and 40 lessons, each of about 40 minutes. In the nursery schools, however, qualified teachers receive the equivalent of only 85% of the salary paid by the Transvaal Education Department (SABJE, 1980c; 1981d).

Higher Education and Adult Education

With its two distinct programs of Jewish studies, the Zlotnik-Avida College is the main institution of South African Jewry devoted exclusively to formal advanced Jewish studies and with a full-time student body. In addition, Johannesburg has three yeshivoth gedoloth, all established within the past decade. One is under the aegis of the Yeshiva College group of schools, and the others are attached to the Johannesburg Orthodox congregations which are unaffiliated with SABJE. In all, between 50 and 60 young men study at these three traditional yeshivoth, about eight learn at the Johannesburg *kollel*, and an indeterminate number of former day school pupils attend yeshivoth in Israel or the United States before returning to complete their secular education at a South African university.

A total of nine South African universities provide courses in Hebrew or Judaic studies, either as independent departments or within the framework of Semitic or Religious studies. At the Afrikaans universities such as Pretoria, Stellenbosch and Potchefstroom, courses are given in classical Hebrew and Old Testament in the Faculties of Divinity for students preparing to enter the Christian Ministry. The University of South Africa, which conducts its courses by correspondence, includes a comprehensive Hebrew and Judaica course in its Department of Semitics, as well as facilities for higher degrees, all of which attract a number of Jewish students. At the three English language universities of the Witwatersrand (Johannesburg), Cape Town and Natal (Durban), there are departments of Hebrew.[12] In 1980, at the University of Cape Town, the endowed Isaac and Jessie Kaplan Centre for higher Jewish studies and research was established as the first of its kind in South Africa. Of the approximately 4,000 Jewish university students in the Republic, it would be difficult to ascertain the precise numbers who enrolled in Hebrew or Judaica-related subjects but these numbers do not appear to be large.

There are as yet no university courses of modern orientation in subjects such as Jewish thought or Jewish history, philosophy or civilization, of the type that emerged in a number of American universities during the 1970s. Only one such course was given in South Africa in the early and mid-1970s but this has unfortunately been withdrawn. A real need for this type of course is felt within the Jewish community as there are many Jewish students who would wish to pursue Jewish studies in a broad, modern context, as distinct from the more traditional Hebrew language and Bible studies (Arkin, 1975, pp. 41–42).

Adult education has always been important to Jewish life in South Africa. The Board of Deputies, the Zionist Federation, the Union of Jewish Women and other communal bodies as well as local congregations, organize regular programs of lectures, *ulpanim*, symposia, exhibitions, film festivals and seminar courses. Speakers from Israel, the United States and other countries are regular visitors to South African Jewry, and their itineraries include country communities as well as the large cities. All cultural activities have the widespread support of the community and are well attended (South African Zionist Federation, 1980). There are probably several reasons for the success of adult education and cultural programs:

- first, the strong ethnic-national ties of the community are particularly evident among the older generation;
- second, the establishment of regular television service as late as 1975;
- third, the availability of adequate leisure time for many South African Jews.

There were more than 180 cultural functions recorded in the report of the director of the Cape Town-based Department of Culture and Education of the Western Province Zionist Council for the two years preceding August 1980. Attendance usually numbered between 100 and 400, and the functions were held in association with 12 organizations, including B'nai B'rith, the Reform congregation, the Lubavitch movement, and the Extra-Mural Department of the University of Cape Town. Titles of lecture series ranged from "The Philosophy and Teachings of Modern Jewish Thinkers" to "Famous Trials in Jewish History" (Western Province Zionist Council, 1980).

Ambitious plans are afoot for inaugurating set courses at a higher level similar to those of the Open University or University Without Walls in other countries.

On the threshold of an era of lifelong education, South Africa's Jewish community is faced with an excellent opportunity to develop its already well-established tradition in this field. There is an awareness of the potential of Parent-Teacher Associations and the various day schools to become agents in the development of a coordinated pupil-parent Jewish education system in which the basic teaching unit is the family.[13]

Youth Movements and Related Activities

The uniformed aliyah and *halutziut*-oriented movements were already well-established in South Africa by the late 1930s and, at a time when overt antisemitism was a reality, they provided Jewish youth with a powerful sense of pride and purpose. There has been a steady stream of *olim* from these movements, and many ex-South Africans have distinguished themselves in all walks of life in Israel and seem to be especially well-represented within the kibbutz population. At the time of the Six-Day War in 1967, the number of volunteers from South African Jewry was higher pro rata than from many other Diaspora communities.

The success of the youth movements may be attributed to a number of factors. First, there is the Zionist ethos itself, which is an integral part of Jewish education; secondly, these movements with their pioneering ideals can be seen as a reaction against the bourgeois values characteristic of so many South African Jewish families.

Today, the Zionist youth movements continue to provide an important dimension to Jewish education that complements the work of the day schools. Their ranks include a substantial proportion of children and adolescents who do not attend day schools, and for whom membership and experience within a youth movement is the only contact with Jewish education. Almost 40% of the total 6 to 17 year old age group are members of the four movements affiliated with the South African Zionist Federation, with their approximate membership numbers as follows: *Habonim*, 2,500; *Betar*, 1,800; *Bnei Akiva*, 1,600; *Maginim*, 750 (Katz, 1980, pp. 644–648). *Maginim* is the youth wing of the South African Union for Progressive Judaism which until 1975 was known as 'Temple Youth'. In its new form, it has adopted Israel-oriented goals similar to those of the other three movements. In the four largest cities, there are Zionist youth councils which strive to coordinate and develop youth activities. On the executive level, each of the four movements has its own Israeli *shlihim*.

In addition to the regular meetings of the youth groups, volunteer schemes and education-work tours in Israel are organized annually. Between 1978 and 1981, some 450 young people visited Israel through programs arranged by the Central Youth Council of the Zionist Federation (South African Zionist Federation, 1980, p. 47). Without a doubt, however, the climax of the annual activities is in the summer camp held at the end of the year by each movement.

The educational value of these camps is stressed by *shlihim* and local movement leaders who cite the positive feedback received. Furthermore, these camps regularly attract an inordinately large number of children and adolescents, including many non-members of the movements and many children from the small country communties. The camps held at the end of 1980, for example, had nearly three thousand participants (South African Zionist Federation, 1980, pp. 42–51).

The predominance of the Zionist ethos in informal educational activities is reflected in the supportive functions of other groups similarly involved with the younger generation. For example, regular study tours to Israel have been organized. The *Maccabi* movement is actively concerned with sports activities and maintains close links with its sister movement in Israel.

A number of clubs sponsored by communal organizations for adolescents and young singles do have some cultural activities, but most of their functions are of a social and recreational nature. The South African Jewish Board of Deputies has for many years been concerned with the number of young people in the community without Jewish social or cultural affiliations. Until a few years ago, the Board had its own Israeli youth *shlihim* and, until 1979, its own Youth Department.

Similarly, in its services to young Jewish conscripts in South Africa's armed forces, the Board, through its Chaplaincy Department, strives to provide educational material and experiences in addition to religious and welfare services and facilities. For example, *shabbatonim* for servicemen have been held in the military operational area of Namibia in South West Africa (SAJBD, 1980c, pp. 26–29). The Chaplaincy Department also issues a regular newsletter for Jewish national servicemen, entitled *Shma Koleinu* – Hear our Voice.

Since only a small number of Jewish students continue their formal Jewish education within the framework of an official university degree or through the Zlotnik-Avida College, the activities of Jewish student organizations are an important alternative. The estimated five to six thousand Jewish university students in South Africa represent a significantly high proportion of the 17 to 21 year old age group within the community. Jewish student numbers are particularly high at the Universities of the Witwatersrand and Cape Town.

Despite the prominence of the day schools, there is still an important part to be played by informal education, particularly the Zionist youth movements. There is awareness of the potential dangers arising from the political and social ferment characterizing South Africa today. The university campus, where the average Jewish student is for the first time exposed to new ideologies that often conflict with his or her background and identity is an especially problematic area in this respect.

Most South African universities have Jewish student groups which are affiliated with the South African Federation of Jewish Student Associations. The actual number of students who are members of these associations is, however, relatively small. In 1981, at the University of the Witwatersrand, of approximately 4,000 Jewish students, only about 450 belonged to the SJA. In Cape Town, the corresponding figures were, respectively, approximately 1,500 and 200. Jewish educational activities include inter-university summer and winter schools, weekend seminars and work-study visits to Israel (*Zionist Record and S.A. Jewish Chronicle*, 1980, p. 11).

The system of *B'nai B'rith*-sponsored Hillel Foundations has not been established at South African universities. Instead, the Board of Deputies and the Zionist Federation jointly support the South African Federation of Jewish Student Associations activities, the appointment of *shlihim* and student advisors, the engagement of visiting lecturers, and they provide maintenance budgets for the individual associations. These communal bodies together maintain a Hillel House in Grahamstown for Jewish students at Rhodes University, which is a predominently residential institution, but also serves as a meeting place for social and cultural activities.

A Commission of Enquiry into the Jewish students' movements was sponsored and carried out by the South African Zionist Federation in 1981. Its terms of reference covered an investigation of JSA activities at the various campuses, with notable regard to such aspects as Zionist activities, involvement of day school alumni in JSA activities and unaffiliated Jewish students. The report of the Commission, concentrating somewhat heavily on the University of the Witwatersrand, presented a rather mixed impression of achievements and shortcomings. However, its conclusion is noteworthy for its recommendation "for the implementation of a meaningful and practical Zionist and Jewish program on the campuses", with the admonition, "Unless this is attended to expeditiously, there is the probability that the Zionist movement, and indeed the Jewish community, will find itself with a lost generation" (Friedman, n.d.).

Conclusions: Outcome and Prospects

Jewish education in South Africa has been described here as the composite product of Anglo-Jewish communal organization and Zionist ideology superimposed on East European traditions, each of which today remain a crucial factor. Just as important has been the socio-political context. Since any consideration of contemporary Jewry must subsume a concern for its future existence in addition to its present well-being, this dimension must complement the above substantive account.

As a unique socio-political entity, beset by its own specific problems and issues, South Africa as a whole has in recent years been undergoing a process of upheaval and change that points to an uncertain and undefinable future. Inevitably this setting has affected the Jewish community. Recent and current developments in South Africa have found their focal point in the country's education system itself. Attention was focused on education in June 1976 when black pupils in the African townships of Soweto, near Johannesburg, rioted to protest against the inferior educational facilities and opportunities provided them (Kane-Berman, 1978).

Many question the very existence of a future for South African Jewry. At the 1981 Conference of the South African Jewish Board of Deputies Cape Council, the outgoing chairman in his farewell address predicted that by the year 2000 there would be no Jews left in South Africa (*Sunday Times*, 1981, p. 5). The spectre of antisemitism, of which the community has bitter memories from the 1930s, accentuated by the loss of relatives in Europe during the Holocaust, has again become a preoccupation. This time, however, in addition to the 'traditional' sources among the white population, there have been manifestations from the black community, by whom the Jews are associated with their privileged white oppressors. Similarly, within the Coloured community, with its high proportion of Muslims, anti-Israel sentiments are inevitably felt by local Jewry (Smith, 1980).

In August 1982 a number of ugly confrontations took place between Jewish students and Muslim and black students, following meetings held by the respective groups in connection with Israel's Lebanon campaign. At the University of the Witwatersrand where several hundred students were involved, insults were exchanged and scuffles took place. At Rhodes University, after a meeting called by black students, Hillel House was daubed with anti-Zionist graffiti (SAJBD, 1983, pp. 2, 25).

The implications of these recent developments reach far beyond the university campus. They illustrate the painful reality that the more influential and organized of the underprivileged groups are becoming increasingly linked to the PLO ideologically and are comparing that struggle to their own. Furthermore, these same groups openly link Israel, and by association South African Jewry, with the present apartheid regime. This situation is all the more ironical in the light of past Jewish involvement on behalf of South Africa's blacks. The sad reality was succintly defined in an address to Jewish students by Philip Tobias, a distinguished Jewish academic and professor:

> How do we reconcile traditional Jewish sympathy for the underprivileged and the persecuted with the current rejection of Jewish friendship and support by many of your fellow-students who belong to the underprivileged sections of South Africa's populace (Tobias, 1983).

As part of the process of change inaugurated and regulated by the regime, a commission was delegated in 1980 by the Prime Minister to investigate, report and make appropriate recommendations on education in South Africa. The report of this commission, published in October 1981, and known as the *de Lange Report* calls for some significant changes with a view to greater equality and integration (Human Sciences Research Council, 1981). The implications for Jewish day schools in South Africa are interesting. What would be their attitudes, policies or status in the event of legislation permitting desegregation? Recently, the private schools of various Christian denominations have sought and been granted permission to admit pupils of other race groups into hitherto exclusively white schools. In addition, the example of the neighboring state of Zimbabwe with its new regime can be cited: both Jewish day schools in that country now have a high proportion of non-Jewish pupils, black as well as white (SABJE, 1981a, pp. 44–49).

Until now in South Africa only very occasional enquiries have been received from 'non-white' non-Jewish pupils for places in Jewish day schools, and after appropriate explanations these were not pursued further. It should be added that at the moment, one or two Jewish day schools do have a small number of Christian pupils, black as well as white. With the *de Lange Report* in mind, one option cited for the future of the Jewish day school is the community school, within the framework of an emergent national system of centralized structures representing religious denominations, communities and cultural interests (Kessel, 1983).

Against this general background, two trends in South African Jewish education are discernable. The first confirms the dominance of Jewish day schools as the main educational agency. This refers both to the support these schools now receive from parents within the community and to official commitment toward the expansion of existing facilities, in spite of uncertainty regarding the future and the falling birth rate.

In particular, over the past decade, increasing numbers of applications for enrollment have begun to cause problems of over-crowding at schools in Johannesburg and Cape Town. As a result, the construction of new buildings has become important. In Johannesburg, a new King David Primary School has been opened in the outer suburb of Sandton, while at the Herzlia High School in Cape Town, a new one million rand building complex has been constructed to accommodate the middle school and thus relieve present congestion. Most day schools project increased enrollments for the next few years, in spite of South Africa's dwindling Jewish population (*Zionist Record and S.A. Jewish Chronicle*, 1981; *Herzlia Headlines*, 1982). On the other hand some think that in Cape Town enrollments are already reaching their peak, and a subsequent decline is expected (Peisach and Schach, 1980).

Perhaps the most ambitious and interesting development in this respect is the acquisition of a large site in Johannesburg by the Lubavitch movement for the development of a campus-type education complex for its Torah Academy. Existing nursery and primary school buildings on this site provide amenities for about 300 children. The entire project, when completed, will provide comprehensive nursery, primary and secondary facilities as well as informal adult and *yeshiva gedola* institutions.

The work of the Lubavitch movement also illustrates the second discernable trend, the growing influence of Orthodoxy on the education system. Despite the modest beginnings in the 1970s, the Torah Academy and the *kollel*-affiliated schools (excluding the nurseries) in 1983 accommodated 488 pupils, compared with 304 in the previous year (SABJE, 1983). In the past, while South African Jewry as a whole had strong religious sentiments, neither it nor its institutions were extremely Orthodox. The religious leaders of the community almost invariably had to be brought in from other countries. Similarly, until the 1960s there were no traditional yeshiva-type institutions for Jewish learning. Today the situation has changed, so that while the traditional-national ideology in Jewish education remains dominant, it is no longer the only approach. The Yeshiva College group of schools marked the first move toward a greater emphasis upon the Orthodox approach to education, and for a time it remained separate from the mainstreams of South African Jewish education. When the Lubavitch movement subsequently began its work in South Africa in the early 1970s, the process was intensified. Finally, the Johannesburg *kollel* with its attached school units has introduced a degree of uncompromising Orthodoxy hitherto not widely represented within South African Jewry.

In numerical terms, the influence of these three groups has reached only a minority within the community. However, this influence has grown considerably in a short time. Apart from this, it is evident that within the mainstream day school movement, the concern for the Orthodox component within the Jewish studies programs has increased. This tendency is illustrated by the stress now placed upon Counterpoint activities and regular *shabbatonim*. While it would be rash at this stage to conclude that South African Jewry, and in particular its educational system, is veering toward a more intensively religious ethos, the next few years will provide an answer.

The basic criterion of effectiveness in any Jewish educational system is the attitude of the new generation of adults entering the community to Judaism per se, but especially to Jewish education for their own children. Despite the lack of empirical data, there are clear indications that alumni of all types of Jewish schools, but particularly day schools, on the whole remain committed to their Jewish identity. Supporting this view is the overwhelming majority of young parents, themselves 'first generation' alumni of Jewish day schools who now enroll their children in the same type of schools. Furthermore, the continuing trend of increasing enrollments, especially at the high school level, concurrent with the continuing decline in the supplementary schools, indicates that the day schools are becoming the dominant medium. But ultimately perhaps most noteworthy is the current paradoxical situation of an expanding day school system within a diminishing community.

Concrete evidence as to the effectiveness of Jewish education is more difficult to assess. In the early 1970s, two studies attempted to compare the effectiveness of day school and supplementary school education in South Africa. It was pointed out that the crucial determinant in preserving Jewish identity is the home rather than the school (Kark, 1972; Dubb, 1972).

An interesting indication of the consequences of day school education lies in the backgrounds of the active leadership within the Zionist youth movements, the Jewish student associations and the *B'nai B'rith* youth organization. Responses to enquiries by this writer gave the clear impression that a substantial proportion of young people who did not attend Jewish day schools were nevertheless interested in and, in some cases, active in communal affairs. This was particularly evident in the leadership of the Jewish student associations at the Universities of the Witwatersrand and Cape Town. A number of Jewish educators, when questioned about this phenomenon, attributed it to the prevailing attitude among many day school alumni that their Jewish education had been completed. This view was supported by the comparatively small number of students at the Universities of the Witwatersrand and Cape Town who took Hebrew as a degree course, but particularly by the even smaller number of day school alumni who did so. The need for a department of Jewish studies, as distinct from Hebrew, at the University of the Witwatersrand and other universities has been frequently stressed in recent years, and the South African Jewish Board of Deputies has been taking steps toward the creation of such an entity (SAJBD, 1983, p. 53).

Despite all its achievements, the fact remains that the educational system of South African Jewry can, to a significant extent, be regarded as the product of its host society. In other words, if the unique social structure and social institutions did not exist, then the problems of assimilation would arise. For this reason, it is vital to submit South African Jewry's educational system to constant scrutiny, lest its very existence be accepted as an unqualified success story.

Research on Jewish education in South Africa should concentrate not so much on the proportion of children receiving either inadequate Jewish schooling or none at all, as on the quality, content and standards of Jewish education within the cognitive and affective realms. One criticsm levelled against the local educational institutions has been that they tend, in the words of the *cliché*, to become schools for Jewish children rather than Jewish schools. A comparison between the local Jewish studies syllabi and those of equivalent institutions in other countries lends support to this opinion. Therefore future research should ideally concentrate on curriculum planning and development. In short, is Jewish identity in South Africa predominantly a reaction to external influences, or is it based upon the conviction and knowledge derived from a sound Jewish education? (Sarzin, Wolf, Osrin, Goss, Arkin, 1982).

A second area of research related to content, curriculum and goals, should concern the place of the Jew within South African society. The question here is: to what extent does Jewish education prepare children and youth to adopt specifically Jewish attitudes toward South Africa's daunting problems and controversies? The issue of local and contemporary relevance is one that faces Jewish educationalists throughout the Diaspora, and even in Israel. In South Africa, there are alumni of Jewish day and supplementary schools who assert that in terms of Jewish ethics, they are inadequately equipped to face the problems of the country. Such a viewpoint is frequently expressed by Jewish students. Moreover, while accurate statistics are not available, it appears that only a minority of young Jews who leave the country actually settle in Israel.[14] Is Jewish education, therefore, escapist and inward looking, parochial and not sufficiently concerned with the place of the Jew within South African society? Is the traditional overriding stress on Zionism and

Israel tantamount to an avoidance of facing up to local issues? And despite this stress, why does only a minority of the Jews who leave the country actually settle in Israel?

South African Jewry today is a community with its own distinct ethos - remarkably homogeneous in its origins and structure, imbued with strong Zionist loyalties, traditionally religious in sentiment but not in observance, materialistically successful and prosperous within a unique pluralistic host society, characterized by ongoing political controversy, acute social problems and an uncertain future. The overriding theme in any present-day assessment of this community remains that of uncertainty for its own future. It is all the more noteworthy that of all its present-day priorities, that of maintaining its Jewish education institutions remains the most important in terms of action, dedication and achievement.

Acknowledgements

This writer is grateful to Shlomo Mayer, General Director, South African Board of Jewish Education, for his kindness in placing relevant source material at his disposal in the course of the preparation of this paper.

Notes

1. This report is part of the South African Jewish Population Study conducted in the mid-1970s by the Social Research Unit of the South African Jewish Board of Deputies, with the participation of the Division of Jewish Demography and Statistics of the Institute of Contemporary Jewry, The Hebrew University of Jerusalem (Dubb and DellaPergola, 1978(3)).

2. Marcus Arkin describes Zionism in South Africa as "an anchor for Jewish identity", and the Zionist movement as the "backbone of Jewish life" in South Africa (Arkin, 1980).

3. Simon Herman writes: "In the case of South Africa, the concept of 'South Africanism' has been slow in developing, and in viewing the white sector of the population the emphasis is on three distinct ethnic elements, Afrikaans-speaking, English-speaking and Jews" (Herman, 1977).

4. Isaac Goss expresses this ideology in a wider context as follows: "I must emphasize that equal stress must be laid on Zionism and Judaism. For me the two are synonomous. For without the creative healthy people the values of Judaism would be superfluous, and yet without the values of Judaism I do not believe that we could live a worthwhile and dignified life anywhere in the world" (Goss, 1961).

5. For example, the official Scripture Syllabus for Primary and Secondary Standards of the Cape of Good Hope Province Education Department states as its aim, "to prepare the pupil through his knowledge of the bible, to accept Jesus Christ as his personal Saviour..." and adds, "Scripture teaching must be Christo-centric."

6. For a number of years, the Province of Natal Education Department has granted aid to private schools, corresponding to 75% of teachers' salaries. Carmel College, the Jewish day school in Durban, has since its inception benefitted accordingly. In 1979, government legislation permitted all four provinces to grant financial aid to day schools. While the provinces of Transvaal (in which most Jewish day schools are situated) and the Orange Free State have so far refused to implement this policy, the Cape of Good Hope has from the beginning of 1980 granted private schools an amount of 140 Rands per pupil per annum. The Jewish schools benefitting from this new legislation are the Herzlia group of schools in Cape Town and the Theodor Herzl School in Port Elizabeth (Cape Education Department, 1980).

7. These views are set out in an SABJE memorandum dated 13.03.80, by the Director of General Studies, King David School, Linksfield, on projected enrollment, 1981–85 (mimeographed).

8. "It is no secret that a large number of our children attend the (day) school for the wrong reasons. We constantly remind parents that the school was founded to provide our children with the understanding and knowledge which will enable them to understand and love Judaism, Hebrew and Zionism. The fact that most of our schools provide an outstanding secular education is a valuable bonus" (Katz, 1983, p. 6).

9. See note 7.

10. An information sheet for parents of prospective pupils at the newly-established Lubavitch Primary School in Johannesburg makes the following point: "On the other hand, in the case of children who come from homes that are on the most minimal level of Jewish knowledge and observance, and who come to our school and who end up following a Lubavitch custom, is that to be lamented? If you take people who aren't *Davening* at all, and because of their child at our school they are soon inspired to start *Davening* and they say an extra verse in the *Bensching* (Grace after Meals) *à la* hasidic custom – is that something calamitous?" (S.A. Lubavitch Foundation, 1978).

11. For example, Parents Bulletin, Purim, Adar 5741, March 1981 Nursery School Department, SABJE.

12. Details from the prospectuses of South African universities.

13. The Herzlia Schools in Cape Town, through the medium of their parent-teacher associations, have during the past few years organized a number of successful adult education projects.

14. In the course of a survey of the Jewish community in Great Britain in 1981, Chaim Bermant has written: "...there has been a considerable influx of South

Africans, and although their number is not yet large and they are usually areligious, they have immeasurably enriched the social and cultural life of the Community" (Bermant, 1981, p. 27.)

References

Adar, Z. (1965). *Jewish Education in South Africa – A Report.* The Hebrew University, Jerusalem.

Arkin, M. (1975). "Wither our Jewish Students?" *Jewish Affairs*, Vol. 30. n.

Arkin, M. (1980). "South Africa" in: Davis, M. (ed.) *Zionism in Transition.* Arno Press, New York, pp. 133–139.

Arkin, M. (1982). "Jewish Studies in South Africa". *Jewish Affairs*, Vol. 37, no. 1.

Aschheim, S.E. (1970). "The Communal Organization of South African Jewry". *The Jewish Journal of Sociology*, Vol. 12, no. 2, pp. 201–231.

Association of Private Schools (1981). *Private Schools of South Africa.* Johannesburg.

Behr, A.L. and Macmillan, R.G. (1971). *Education in South Africa.* Van Schaik, Pretoria.

Bermant, C. (1981). Article in the *Jewish Chronicle.* 13 November. London.

CBJE (Cape Board of Jewish Education), (1980a). *Report by the Director to the 20th Biennial Conference,* (1978–1980). Cape Town.

CBJE (Cape Board of Jewish Education), (1980b). *Reports of the Hebrew Schools to the 20th Biennial Conference.* Cape Town.

CBJE (Cape Board of Jewish Education), (1982). *Reports of the Hebrew Schools to the 21st Biennial Conference.* Cape Town.

Cape Education Department (1980). *Private Schools – Granting of Aid.* (Circular No. 27, Ref. No. L15/101/2).

Clouts, L. (1982). "The Slow Exodus of S.A. Country Communities". *The Jewish Herald.* p. 25.

Davenport, T.R.H. (1977). *South Africa – A Modern History.* Macmillan, Johannesburg.

Diamond, D. (1981). "South Africa". *American Jewish Year Book*, Vol. 81. pp. 275–283.

Dubb, A.A. (1972). *Report on a Study of Jewish Day School Matriculants in the Republic of South Africa.* Social Research Unit, South Africa Jewish Board of Deputies, Johannesburg.

Dubb, A.A. (1977). *Jewish South Africans – A Sociologial View of the Johannesburg Community.* Rhodes University, Grahamstown.

Dubb, A.A., DellaPergola, S. and others (1977–1978). *The South African Jewish Population Study.* South African Jewish Board of Deputies, Social Research Unit; Division of Jewish Demography and Statistics. Institute of Contemporary Jewry, The Hebrew University, Jerusalem, Advance Reports:
No. 1 (1977) – Methodology of the Study.
No. 2 (1977) – Emigration.
No. 3 (1978) – Demographic Characteristics.
No. 4 (1978) – Country of Birth and Period of Immigration.
No. 5 (1978) – Mortality.
No. 6 (1978) – Educational Attainment and Languages.
No. 7 (1978) – First Data on Fertility.
No. 8 – Not published.
No. 9 (1978) – Geographical Distribution and Mobility.
No. 10 (1978) – Occupational Characteristics.
No. 11 (1978) – Religion and Religious Observance.
No. 12 (1978) – Jewish Community Activities.
No. 13 (1978) – Marriage and Mixed Marriage.

Dushkin, A.M. (1963). "Analysis of Some Recent Developments of Jewish Education in the Diaspora." *Scripta Hierosolymitana*, Vol. XIII. Magnes Press, The Hebrew University, Jerusalem.

Friedman, M.W. (n.d.). *Report of the Commission of Enquiry into Students' Jewish and Zionist Movements.* (Mimeographed).

Goss, I. (1961). "Some Reflections on Zionism and Judaism." *Adventure of Jewish Education – Essays in Survival and Salvation.* South African Board of Jewish Education, Johannesburg.

Goss, I. (1982). "The Judah Leib Zlotnik Seminary". *Jewish Affairs*, Vol. 37, no. 1.

Herrman, L. (1935). *A History of the Jews in South Africa.* South African Jewish Board of Deputies, Johannesburg.

Herman, S. (1977). *Jewish Identity: A Social Psychological Perspective.* Sage Publishers, Beverly Hills.

Herzlia Headlines (1980). 40th Anniversary issue, No. 28, Cape Town.

Herzlia Headlines (1981). No. 29. Cape Town.

Herzlia Headlines (1982). "Herzlia Opens 'New Middle School'". No. 32.

Human Sciences Research Council (1981). Education Provision in the RSA – Report of the Main Committee of the HSRC Investigation into Education. Pretoria.

Kane-Berman, J. (1978). *Soweto: Black Revolt, White Reaction.* Ravan Press, Johannesburg.

Kark, G. (1972). *The Jewish Day School Matriculate*. University of the Witwatersrand, Johannesburg (Unpublished M.Ed. thesis).

Katz, K. (1983). "Jewish Day School Education – A Perspective". *The Pedagogic Centre Newsletter*, Vol. 1, no. 2.

Katz, M.E. (1980). *The History of Jewish Education in South Africa*, 1841–1980. University of Cape Town (Unpublished Ph.D. dissertation).

Kessel, M. (1983). "The Jewish Day School as a Community School" in: Ashley, M.J. and Philcox, S.E., eds. *My Kind of School*. University of Cape Town.

King David Schools (1968). *King David Schools 20th Anniversary Celebration, 1948–1968*. Johannesburg.

Malherbe, E.G. (1977). *Education in South Africa*, Vol. 2, 1923–1975. Juta, Cape Town.

Osrin, E. (1982). "The Greatest Mission". *Jewish Affairs*, Vol. 37, no. 1.

Peisach, M. and Schach, S. (1980). *Forecast of Herzlia Enrollments from 1980 to 1996*. (Mimeographed).

Republic of South Africa (1974). *National Education Policy Amendment Bill*. Government Printer, Pretoria.

Republic of South Africa (1980). *South African Statistics 1980*. Government Printer, Pretoria.

Saron, G. (1967). "The Making of South African Jewry – An Essay in Historical Interpretation". *South African Jewry 1965–1966*. Johannesburg. pp. 9–49.

Saron, G. (1973). "Christian Education: The Position of Jewish Pupils and Teachers". *Jewish Affairs*, Vol. 28, no. 11. pp. 8–13.

Saron, G. (1980). "The Struggle over 'Religion' in South African Jewish Education". *The Federation Chronicle*, Rosh Hashanah 5741. pp. 14–15, 27–29.

Saron, G. and Hotz, L. eds. (1955). *The Jews in South Africa: A History*. Oxford University Press, Cape Town.

Sarzin, A.L. (1982). "Herzlia Values". *Jewish Affairs*, Vol. 37, no. 1.

Shimoni, G. (1980). *Jews and Zionism – The South African Experience*. Oxford University Press, Cape Town.

Smith, M. (1980). *Is There Anti-Semitism in South Africa Today?* SAJBD, Cape Town.

SABJE (South African Board of Jewish Education), (1975; 1978) *Report to 17th; 18th National Education Conference*. Johannesburg.

SABJE (South African Board of Jewish Education), (1980a). *United Hebrew Schools of Johannesburg: Statistics as at end of the Third Term 1980*. Johannesburg. (Mimeographed).

SABJE (South African Board of Jewish Education), (1980b). *Report for the period ending June 1980.* Pedagogic Resource Centre, Johannesburg.

SABJE (South African Board of Jewish Education), (1980c). *Salary Scales for Nursery School Teachers, 1980.* Johannesburg. (Mimeographed; memorandum no. 54/6/80).

SABJE (South African Board of Jewish Education), (1981a). *Report to the 19th National Education Conference.* Johannesburg.

SABJE (South African Board of Jewish Education), (1981b). Statistics - South African Hebrew Nursery Schools. Johannesburg. (Mimeographed).

SABJE (South African Board of Jewish Education), (1981c). Chadarim. Johannesburg (Mimeographed; Document no. 45/5/81).

SABJE (South African Board of Jewish Education), (1981d). Regulations applicable to Personnel. Johannesburg. (Mimeographed; memorandum no. 40/5/81).

SABJE (South African Board of Jewish Education), (1983). SABJE – Jewish Day Schools in South Africa: Enrollment figures – 1982/3. Johannesburg (Mimeographed).

SABJE (South African Board of Jewish Education), (n.d.). *Handbook of the Pedagogic Resource Centre.* Johannesburg.

SACPJE (South African Council for Progressive Jewish Education), (1981). *Report to the 31st Biennial National Conference.* Johannesburg.

SAJBD (South African Jewish Board of Deputies), (1980a). "List of Resolutions Adopted". 31st National Congress (Mimeographed).

SAJBD (South African Jewish Board of Deputies), (1980b). *1980 Annual Reports for Primary and High Schools in the Western Cape.* Religious Instruction Department, Cape Council, Cape Town.

SAJBD (South African Jewish Board of Deputies), (1980c). *Report to South African Jewry, 1978–1980.* Johannesburg.

SAJBD (South African Jewish Board of Deputies), (1982). *1982 Annual Reports for Primary and High Schools in the Western Cape.* Religious Instruction Department, Cape Council, Cape Town.

SAJBD (South African Jewish Board of Deputies), (1983). *Report to South African Jewry, 1980–1983.* Johannesburg.

South African Lubavitch Foundation (1978). The New Primary School under the Aegis of the S.A. Lubavitch Foundation – Questions and Answers. Johannesburg. (Mimeographed).

South African Zionist Federation (1980). *Operation Rethink.* Report to 36th Conference, Johannesburg.

"South Africa's Jewish Community – Profile of a People" (1979). *To the Point*, November 9. pp. 8–11.

Sunday Times (1981). "Jews warned of New Exodus". 30 August. Johannesburg.

Tobias, P. (1983). "Anatomy of the South African Jewish Student". *Jewish Affairs*, Vol. 38, no. 5.

United Herzlia Schools (1968). *King David Schools 20th Anniversary Celebration – 1948-1968*. Cape Town.

United Herzlia Schools (1973). *This is Not a Fable*. Brochure published on the opening of the Herzlia Primary School, Southern Suburbs, Cape Town.

Western Province Zionist Council (1980). Reports of Activities, 1978–1980. Department of Culture and Education. (Mimeographed).

Wolf, E.M. (1982). "Education in a Changing Society". *Jewish Affairs*, Vol. 37, no. 1.

The Yeshivite (1980). Yeshiva College, Johannesburg.

Zionist Record and South African Jewish Chronicle (1980). "SAUJS Looks at Student Problems", 28 March.

Zionist Record and South African Jewish Chronicle (1981). "New King David to be built", 28 August.

12

Jewish Education in Australia

Geulah Solomon

Jewish education in Australia developed in four stages. The first stage spanned the penal settlement and the early decades of organized Jewish life, from 1788 to about 1850. The consequence of various attempts to provide education in a new, religiously-pluralistic society was the establishment of government-assisted schools associated with specific denominations, which later became the private school system. During this period, when Jewish life had to be established 'from scratch', the children of Jewish free settlers, convicts and emancipists acquired their general education in denominational and rare non-sectarian schools, and Jewish education was supplemented by parents, private teachers, and later by synagogue officials.

The second stage spanned the second half of the 19th century as the number of Australian-born and immigrant school-age children increased. The establishment of facilities for a Jewish way of life heightened awareness of the need to overcome religious apathy and ignorance, which had been aggravated by pioneering conditions. Moreover, during this period, the existing system of government-aided denominational schools continued and expanded, while a system of government elementary schools gradually became the basis of the state school system. In this colonial era, Jews saw education as a means for fulfilling their aspirations to full political, religious and educational equality. They regarded Jewish denominational (day) schools as the vehicle for both the maintenance of Jewish identity in a pluralistic society and for the recognition of the rights of Jews to participate in government-aided denominational education; however, they also insisted, through Jewish politicians and non-Jewish sympathizers, that any secular government school system must permit the attendance of Jewish children without infringement of conscience or special treatment.

Thus, while tuition by parents, private teachers, and congregational officials continued, the Melbourne and Sydney communities established the three main streams of Jewish education which have continued in Australia to the present day. These were Jewish denominational or day schools providing both Jewish and general education, afternoon schools for supplementary education, and community-provided Jewish instruction in state and some non-Jewish private schools.

A few of the colonial Jewish day schools were private profit-making ventures. Most prominent, however, were the Sydney Hebrew School, which opened in 1859 and closed in 1880, and the Melbourne Hebrew school, which opened in 1859 and closed in 1894. These schools were communal in clientele and function, under congregational or community control, and as schools belonging to the Jewish 'denomination', they received aid based on a similar, though not identical, formula as other denominational schools.

For Jewish children general education was of great importance and this was reflected in the literacy rate of Jews as compared with other denominations. Jewish day schools provided general education to attract pupils to Jewish education. The philosophy underlying these schools was that Jewish education was integral to Jewish identity and a prerequisite to Jewish survival; that secular knowledge was necessary for an emancipated, modern Jewish life, to integration into Australian society, socio-economic advancement and political equality; and that secular education needs the moral foundation of religious education.

Similar considerations were the basis for part-time Jewish education. It was recognized that Jews would inevitably attend private middle-class non-Jewish schools as well as free state schools. Hence, each Jewish community established two forms of part-time Jewish education to supplement general education. One form was the right-of-entry or release-time classes in government and some non-Jewish denominational schools, set up by those who established, or taught in, the Jewish day schools. Even when the various Education Acts in the 19th century established non-denominational, and later through considerable Jewish pressure, purely state education, right-of-entry religious instruction was continued by all the major denominations on school premises outside the regular school day.

The other form consisted of part-time Jewish schools, where classes were conducted on one or two weekday afternoons after school hours, on Shabbat mornings or afternoons, and on Sunday mornings – usually on synagogue or day school premises or in the teacher's own home. If attendance was sufficiently frequent and regular, it was theoretically possible for the part-time school to provide education comparable to that of the day school. Furthermore, supplementary Jewish instruction allowed the community to argue strongly in favor of secular state education, contending that parents and denominations who desired anything in addition could furnish it for themselves, as did the Jewish community.

The third stage in the development of Jewish education was the era of rationalization, from the closing of the community day schools in Sydney and Melbourne until the emergence of the contemporary day schools after World War II. This era, spanning over half a century, was characterized by dependence on part-time Jewish education taught in a rationalized and centralized system. Each community established a State Board of Jewish Education, which assumed responsibility for the right-of-entry Jewish instruction in state schools, and gradually also acquired control over teachers, pupils and curricula in part-time Jewish schools. Jewish education was available solely on a part-time basis. But while the Education Boards were corporate bodies of the communities, they never gained a monopoly on Jewish education. Sometimes because of dissatisfaction with the content, quality and orientation of education provided by the Boards, part-time education was also provided by individual congregations, by groups with specific cultural or Zionist orientations, Yiddish language emphases or more Orthodox requirements, and by private teachers.

The rationalization of Jewish education during this period helped to develop Jewish corporate structures and a collective Jewish identity. However, reliance on part-time schooling alone also reflected colonial assumptions about the limited importance of Jewishness in an open society and the inability of the Jewish community, unlike the Catholics, to maintain anything else during these years. The part-time monopoly was at least partially responsible for the compartmentalization of education into two separate and unrelated branches of Jewish and general knowledge; the relegation of Jewish knowledge to the private domain, related only to minority identity and marginal or ancillary areas of life; the lower status, esteem and standards of Jewish compared with general education; and the tendency for loss of interest in Jewish studies in the contemporary day schools at the secondary level.

The fourth stage of Jewish educational development in Australia is the current one. Since the opening of the first day school, Mt. Scopus College, in Melbourne in 1948, other day schools have been opened in Melbourne, Sydney, Perth and Adelaide, and still others are being established. In the remaining communities, Jewish education is still provided only on a part-time basis. Moreover, part-time education by state Education Boards, by sectional-interest groups and by private teachers has continued also in the communities where day schools exist.

The philosophical rationale for modern day schools includes the colonial denominational theory of education, reinforced by recognition of Jewish education in group-strengthening and survival and in the maintenance of organized Jewish life. Today's Jewish day schools are not simply a revival of the colonial schools which reflected and were a response to voluntarism and religious pluralism in a monoculture or Anglo-conformist society; they aim to impart familiarity with the Bible, knowledge of Jewish religion and observance, and the synagogue service, and are more a response to the multicultural ideology which has developed from religious pluralism. Moreover, while the majority of day schools regard themselves as orthodox or traditional in religious orientation, the Jewish education they provide is conceived in terms of multi-faceted Jewish identity, based on Judaism as not only a religion but also an ethnicity, a culture and a super-national entity.

Jewish day schools in Australia are essentially a post-World War II phenomenon. In the aftermath of the Holocaust, the need to preserve surviving Jewish communities and to create future Jewish leadership strengthened Jewish activity and increased the priority given to Jewish education in Australia as elsewhere. This was reinforced by the establishment of the State of Israel, which heightened pride in Jewish identity, revived identification with the Jewish community and culture and stimulated interest in Jewish knowledge and the Hebrew language. World War II also brought an increase in the Australian Jewish population – not only larger numbers of children required Jewish education, but there were more adults from Central and Eastern Europe committed to the philosophy, establishment and support of Jewish day schools.

The deterioration of the part-time system also contributed to the strengthening of the Australian day school movement. The supplementary schools have failed to attract pupils in significant numbers or retain them on a regular basis throughout their years of general education; they offer a shallow and repetitive curriculum with low expectations and standards, and they suffer from organizational and pedagogic difficulties. Also, dissatisfaction with teachers, standards, facilities and conditions in the state school sector, contributed to the growth of private schools in general.

Changing economic circumstances of the Jewish communities have also affected day school growth. Difficulty in financing the colonial day schools on a voluntary basis was a major factor in their eventual closure; financial adversity, due to periodic economic recessions and the Great Depression played a major role in the subsequent centralization of part-time Jewish education and inhibited its development. In contrast, while not all Australian Jews are affluent today, the prosperity of the post-war years provided an economic climate in which the establishment of day schools was feasible. Since the 1960s significant state aid for capital development, special projects (libraries, science laboratories) and per capita expenditure to individual schools has been a major source of financial support.

The day school movement has been self-perpetuating, the first schools acting as models and stimuli for additional schools, catering to different ideological orientations and educational approaches. The period from 1948 to the present has been an era of development and expansion, as existing schools have grown and new schools have been established.

The Societal Context of Jewish Schooling

Normativeness of Private Schooling

Australian education is divided into two broad sectors – public and private. Government (public) education comprises a state school system in each state or territory of Australia. Non-government (private) schools either belong to a system such as the Catholic schools or operate as autonomous units. Non-government schools include all the denominational schools, non-sectarian Christian 'grammar' schools, alternative, free and community schools in the progressive education tradition and the very recently established 'ethno-specific' schools, opened by migrant and ethnic communities.

Private schooling in Australia became normative with the help of the various State Education Acts legislated in the late 19th century. These Acts established compulsory education and free, secular state elementary school systems. State aid to private schools was abolished, but the right of parents to provide private schooling at their own expense was recognized. The legitimacy of private schooling has also been acknowledged in public policy statements by both the Australian Labour and Liberal Governments. Both parties have reiterated the right of parents to choose between state and private schools, and both have provided Commonwealth and state funding to non-government schools.

The normativeness of private schooling is also demonstrated by enrollments, which exceed half-a-million children – that is, between one-quarter and one-third of Australian children. While the majority of these were enrolled in the Catholic school system, the non-Catholic schools have also undergone institutional and enrollment expansion.

The relationship between the public and private sectors has been largely determined by assumptions that the public schools could not accommodate all Australia's school population if private schooling were abolished. Such assumptions have resulted in renewed government aid to private schools, cooperation in areas such as curriculum, facilities and pedagogic resources, and teacher-training. The public sector has also gained by this cooperation by duplication of educational materials developed for the private school sector.

In 1978, the Jewish day schools accounted for 0.6% of non-government schools. They are non-systemic autonomous units, commonly perceived as religious, rather than ethnic or community schools. With the development of multicultural public policy and the opening of day schools by ethnic communities such as the Greek and Turkish communities in Melbourne, there is some current ambivalence, even within the Jewish community, as to whether Jewish day schools, the Jewish community, or Judaism should be defined as religious or ethnic. This dilemma is accentuated by perceptions of benefits to be acquired or withheld on the basis of the categorization.

Jewish part-time schools form part of the non-formal part-time private sector. Part-time schools were historically religious schools, which incidentally taught basic general subjects as well. In the past two decades, there has been a growth of 'ethnic' part-time schools, such as the Saturday schools conducted by the Greek dioceses and by the Turkish community. These teach the community language, religion and history, and provide assistance with the child's regular studies. Such ethnic schools receive some government support, unlike Jewish part-time schools.

Government Support and Control

Government financial support to the private school sector was resumed on an ad hoc basis following its abolishment in principle in the late 19th century. In recent years, most private schools, including Jewish day schools, have depended heavily on government funds for their existence or for maintaining fees at a payable level.

Since World War I, the greater part of government funding has come from federal funds to the states for education or directly to schools for specific purposes and from state treasuries. The federal government has invested heavily in private schools through a variety of educational expenditures – grants for science laboratories and secondary school library subsidies, per capita grants and scholarships and grants for buildings. Nevertheless, this has been insufficient to meet the costs of private schooling, which have risen together with the standards of the education provided; enrollments have expanded, education has become more labor-intensive, teaching conditions and salaries have improved and inflation has increased.

Consequently, since the establishment of the Schools Commission in 1973, federal aid to private schools has been rationalized and systematized and aid has been directed towards equalizing educational opportunities, facilities and conditions within and between the private and state sectors. Private schools have since then been funded on the basis of need which is determined by grading private and state schools on a scale of items such as teaching salaries, operating costs, other staffing and equipment items, and enrollments. The rating scale favors schools with high pupil/teacher ratios and low expenditure on auxiliary staff and equipment.

Jewish day schools throughout Australia in 1978 received grants which made up approximately 35% of income per student, of which slightly less than half were state grants and slightly more than half were federal grants. The main thrust of government aid was to support the disadvantaged Catholic school system. The 'need basis' has benefitted Jewish schools very little, since they are not assessed as being highly needy.

Since 1980, there has been mounting public opposition to government aid for all but the Catholic system, and the intended policy is now to withdraw state aid from private schools deemed 'not in need' and to define disadvantaged private schools and the extent of aid they receive more rigorously. According to this policy of discrimination in favor of the state and Catholic systems, Jewish private schools will receive vastly reduced aid although support is still available for the introduction of programs and projects which it is government policy to promote.

Governments indirectly support private schools by virtue of the fact that they bear the cost of teacher-education in Australia. Tuition at all levels in tertiary colleges and universities is free and fully government-funded. That all private schools, including Catholic schools (which increasingly utilize lay teachers), draw at least their general staff from this government education pool means that they obtain these teachers at no cost to the schools or their sponsors. This has been a significant factor inhibiting the development of Jewish teacher-training institutions, nor have concerted efforts been made by Jewish schools to encourage the development of appropriate courses for the local training of Jewish studies teachers within the existing colleges and universities.

Government controls the content and standards of the 'secular' curriculum, insuring that basic general studies in private schools are equivalent to those provided by state schools. Whereas government funding tends to be mainly federal, government control of the education imparted is a state responsibility. Teachers of secular subjects are required to register with the relevant state authority in order to ensure that they are qualified, and to maintain parity of teaching methods and standards between the state and private sectors. Such registration is not required of Jewish studies teachers.

The public examinations act as a controlling device. Jewish schools have gained increasing responsibility for public examinations in Modern Hebrew and Biblical Studies, and have developed appropriate new subjects for public examinations, such as Modern Jewish History.

The legal rights, responsibilities and liabilities of teachers and schools apply to both the state and private sectors, e.g. hours of attendance, truancy, corporal punishment, accident liability and workers' compensation. Similarly, social legislation such as Anti-Discrimination and Equal Opportunity Laws apply to students and staff in all schools, without distinction.

Finally, strict government control is applied to the physical environment of all schools, which includes health, sanitation and space.

Community-Government Relations

In general, the relationship between the various Jewish communities and their respective state and Commonwealth governments has been harmonious, influenced at times by Jewish perceptions of mainstream discrimination and prejudice, by antisemitic and anti-foreign attitudes and statements and by Jewish interests.

The community, it its relations with the government, tends to speak through representative organizations – either the Executive Council of Australian Jewry, the State Boards of Jewish Deputies, the Australian Jewish Welfare Society, or the Zionist Federation of Australia and its state components, depending on the occasion. In addition, specific organizations, such as *B'nai B'rith*, Jewish academic 'experts' and Jewish politicians have represented the Jewish community when necessary.

While the political salience of religion and denominational affiliation has declined, ethnic origin has gained in importance. In community-government relations, Jews now appear as both a religious denomination and an ethnic interest group. Current concerns involve public policy and practice on issues such as immigration, mainstream-minority group relations, anti-Jewish discrimination and defamation, and Middle East foreign policy.

Jewish-Gentile Relationships in Education

In the past, Jewish-Gentile cooperation in the field of education was mainly with other minority denominations, in particular the Catholics, and was dictated by common interests in establishing an educational system designed to ensure the education, equality and survival of the minority communities in Australian society.

Jewish-Gentile relationships affecting education may be categorized as follows:

–   minority Jewish – mainstream Gentile relationships. These largely comprise Jewish-government relationships already discussed, but also include participation in School Cadet programs, inter-school sports, social service activities and Jewish staff membership in teacher organizations, unions and professional associations;

–   Jewish school – other private school relationships. Jewish day schools cooperate with other private schools, particularly the smaller ones, in areas such as secular education and extra-curricular activities. Formal inter-school relations are less frequent. Most Church schools tend to relate to one another through their own state, national or international Church and educational bodies. Some Jewish schools have been involved with organizations established by the non-Catholic sector;

–   minority Jewish – minority Gentile ethnic relations. Since the late 1970s, there have been direct relations between Jewish individuals, organizations and schools with their counterparts in other ethnic minority groups. Such relationships have led to modelling on Jewish day schools and resulted in the establishment of the first Greek day school in Melbourne.

The Community Context of Jewish Schooling

Major Socio-Demographic Patterns

Today there are some 80,000 Jews in Australia, comprising just under 0.5% of the total population. The Jews are highly urbanized, concentrating almost entirely in the capital cities of each state. The bulk (90%) of Australian Jewry is divided almost equally between the two largest cities of Sydney (New South Wales) and Melbourne (Victoria): the remaining communities vary in numbers from 3,000 Jews in Perth (Western Australia), 2,000 in Brisbane (Queensland), 1,000 in Adelaide (South Australia), 300–400 in Canberra (the national capital) and a mere handful in Hobart (Tasmania) and Darwin (Northern Territory).

Australian Jewry is largely of immigrant origin, contributing to the immigrant and multicultural nature of Australian society. Between the major waves of migrants, on whom the community's numerical viability has heavily depended, the proportion of Australian-born and third generation Jews has risen. Each major group of Jewish immigrants, in attempting to transplant and maintain its own customs, attitudes and institutions has affected the pattern of Jewish education.

The result has been ethno-cultural pluralism within each Jewish community, and this is seen in educational pluralism. However, differences in ethnic origin have declined in relevance. Communal leadership today is not dominated by any single Jewish ethnic group, and ethnically-derived differences no longer cause rivalry and conflict, though they have not entirely disappeared.

Socio-Economic Integration

Despite their high visibility, Jews in Australia have been a highly-integrated and acculturated immigrant group. Virtually all Jewish immigrants become naturalized Australian citizens, and the vast majority remain in Australia. Jewish education must, then, prepare children to live both as citizens of Australia and as Jews.

Culture and cultural identity are inseparable from language. In Australian society, English is the major agent of cultural assimilation, while for Jews, Hebrew and, to a lesser extent, Yiddish are the major languages of Jewish culture and identity. The extent of cultural assimilation is demonstrated by the fact that English is the sole language of the vast majority of Australian Jews today (the use of another language, either alone or in conjunction with English, is acknowledged in only some 20% of Jewish homes).

Australian Jewry is also well-integrated into Australian economic life. While Jews are not represented in the full range of Australian occupations (e.g. they are not involved in banking), and they are over-represented in certain sectors such as medicine and law, they are not occupationally segregated.

There are no social or legal restrictions regarding place of residence, and even in Melbourne – where Jewish residential patterns show voluntary ghettoization – Jews live among non-Jews in middle class suburbs where private schooling is the educational norm. Hence, even segregated Jewish day schooling conforms to middle-class educational patterns; only its content and the social effects of an exclusively Jewish school population prevent the day school from being part of the actual process of cultural assimilation.

Most Australian Jews have friends who are all or mostly Jewish. Non-Jewish friends are often made through business contacts, and these tend not to be intimate friendships. However, those Jews with higher levels of general education, in higher status occupations, or with a secularist identification, have both more and closer social relationships with non-Jews. Similarly, younger age-groups – those below 40 years – and Australian and British-born Jews have the most non-Jewish friends, while those living in areas of dense Jewish residential concentration appear to have fewer or none.

These trends do not necessarily confirm the widespread assumption of a positive correlation between having intimate or close non-Jewish friends and assimilation and intermarriage. It is likely, however, that those groups with the highest percentages of non-Jewish friends are also the most vulnerable to assimilation. Thus, one purpose of the day school is to be an agent of social control, by constituting a Jewish social world which promotes Jewish peer groups and friendships among the young, the Australian-born and the non-Orthodox.

Secular education in the Jewish day schools is acknowledged to have higher standards than many state and private schools, and Jewish education may provide better higher education and life chances and choices on leaving school. Certainly the importance attached to secular studies suggests that one major role of the school as seen by the parents is the preservation if not the improvement of the family's socio-economic class. But Jewish schools promote upward social status only, if at all, within the Jewish community. They are viewed in Australian society as academically, rather than socially, elite.

Family Life

The numerical stability of Australian Jewry no longer depends mostly on migration, but rather fertility has become the main factor. Birth rates have been low, largely related to the unbalanced age profile, with hollowness in the middle age groups and heavy weighting in older age groups following World War II.

Marriage patterns – intermarriage, delayed age of marriage and a social climate in which there is less pressure to marry – have been the basis for predictions of further lowering in fertility rates. However, there is some evidence that fertility rates have risen for women in the 20–45 age groups, that the numbers of women in the peak child-bearing years is higher than it was in the directly preceding years, and that the proportion of married Jewish women in this relevant age-group has significantly increased.

Moreover, in response to crises involving Israel in the 1970s there has in the past 10 to 15 years been a distinct heightening of Jewish consciousness and group attachment, possibly as a result of improved and more intensive Jewish education. Economic, socio-cultural, and educational considerations, may be more significant than fertility rates in affecting family support for Jewish education.

Despite the growing relevance of divorce, re-marriage patterns, and single-parent family trends, these have received far less attention in studies of Australian Jewry and Australian Jewish education than have intermarriage and reproductive trends. Despite acute social change, the ideal of marriage and the extended nuclear family are still regarded as the Australian Jewish norm on which expectations concerning the relationship between school and home are based. Jewish schools have failed to deal systematically with the implications of the changing family unit – for example in terms of appropriate new roles for schools, from counselling and pastoral care to curricular innovations in Jewish parent education.

Schools need to cope with the children of single parents, who are victims of the social stigma attached to divorce as compared with widowhood in the Jewish community, and they must deal accordingly with the subject of marital breakdown and divorce in Jewish law, custom, and the contemporary community. Moreover, there are implications for schools in the consequent teacher-parent relationships where single-parent or two-family situations are concerned.

Jewish schools implicitly assume that their clientele are conventional two-parent families where the husband is the income-earner and the wife is occupied with home duties and child-rearing. This stereotypical family is expected to take an active interest in the children's schooling, participate in parent organizations, and provide financial support.

Most studies of Jewish occupational distribution in Australia have focused on male heads of households. However, the economic recession, since the late 1970s, has adversely affected the financial circumstances of many Jewish families, whether two-parent families with a sole male bread-winner or single-parent families, where the sole income-earner is often a woman. Accordingly, the incidence of mothers with school-age children who work out of necessity (as well as those who work by choice) is more frequent than commonly supposed.

Schools can probably assume the two-income family's continued ability to pay school fees, but will be less able to rely on school participation and involvement in the child's studies or participation in parent-teacher organizations. The consequence of increasing numbers of double-income families, however, is not only the reduced involvement in the child's school and schooling: more of such families are likely to apply for a reduction, or partial or even total abolition of fees, or even to transfer their children to state schools where tuition is free.

Antisemitism

Assimilation and intermarriage in Australia have not been motivated by the desire to escape antisemitism. Nevertheless, despite their high identifica-tion as Australians and the minimal discrimination most Jews encounter on a personal level, Australian Jews have been concerned about both overt and latent antisemitism.

Antisemitism in Australia tends to draw on Australian social values rather than religious beliefs. Australia is not an egalitarian or homogeneous society; yet, Australian culture stresses conformity and mainstream solidarity against outsiders and strangers. Much of Australian antisemitism is really anti-foreignism, expressed as hostility towards those who dress or behave differ-ently or are not native English-speakers.

The main Jewish response has been to attempt to forestall and to contain the growth of antisemitism by opposing immigration which might be antisemitic in nature. More recently, Jewish organizations have utilized Anti-Discrimination Laws to deal with acts of antisemitic prejudice, and state Boards of Jewish Deputies have established watchdog anti-defamation com-mittees.

Since 1973, latent antisemitism has taken the form of anti-Zionism and anti-Israelism. Since Jews equate anti-Zionism with antisemitism and since Israel is a major focal point for Australian Jewish existence and identity, anti-Israel actions and sentiment are perceived as threats to Jewish existence and identity. This new variety of antisemitism, espoused by both the extreme Right and the extreme Left, is more alarming to the mainstream Jewish community for it helps the emergence of Israel critics or 'Jewish antisemites' within the Jewish community. On the whole, however, overt acts of antisemitism and isolated terrorist activities in Australia receive little support.

Jewish schools are, nevertheless, expected to equip their pupils to understand, cope with, and combat antisemitism and anti-Zionism. The successful cultivation of active Jewish religiosity or ethnicity by Jewish schools is regarded as the best defence against antisemitism in Australia.

Patterns of Jewish Identity

Minority Jewish identity in Australia has always included religious, cultural, community and nationalist dimensions. For much of Australian Jewish history, Jewish identity was perceived by both Jews and non-Jews mainly in terms of religion. On the one hand, religion's major role in Jewish identification has gained from the strengthened influence of both the Reform and the Lubavitch and *Mizrachi* movements. On the other hand, the declining importance of religion in Australian life in general is reflected within the Jewish community by the fact that the vast majority of Jews are non-observant, and they identify increasingly with their historical culture, with the Jewish people, with the community and with Israel.

Community Support for and Control of Jewish Education

Jewish education in general, and day schools in particular, receive practical and emotional support from the various Jewish communities. All schools are regarded as community institutions, open to all the community's children, irrespective of the school's sponsorship or control.

The Jewish communities must support Jewish education financially, since, unlike the endowed private schools, Jewish schools have no alternative resource base. Of the average per pupil expenditure, some 79% consists of recurrent costs and about 20% of capital expenditure. While existing data do not provide estimates as to the proportion of expenditures which is devoted to Jewish studies teaching salaries, it is known that the salaries of secular teachers make up around 63% of recurrent and 50% of total per pupil expenditure.

The basic sources of Jewish day school income are tuition fees, government funding and long term loans, and communal support. For several years even the rising tuition fees have failed to keep pace with the per pupil cost of Jewish day schools. In 1977, about 50% of per pupil income came from fees which parents paid. Another 29% came from federal and state funding, and some 7% from long term loans. The shortfall of about 14% came from the community, which made up the balance of the per capita income to meet the increased real costs of Jewish schooling.

Communal support is provided in a variety of ways – congregational, organizational, and individual grants, bequests, endowed scholarships and specific purpose and general benefactions. Fundraising by parent and school organizations is a major source.

Part-time schools derive most of their income from their sponsoring organizations, modest tuition fees, minor fundraising activities, and from communal and congregational allocations and appeals. The State Education Boards (rather than the individual affiliated schools) participate in communal revenue according to the method which applies to day schools and other organizations in that community.

Indirect support has come mainly from Israel – through the Education Departments of the World Zionist Organization and the Jewish Agency, the Ministry of Education, and the Melton Center for Jewish Education in the Diaspora at the Hebrew University; and from the United States. For example, the Reform schools and the Lubavitch schools receive educational support respectively from the Union of Progressive Judaism and the Lubavitch movement, while traditionally Orthodox schools receive from Yeshiva University.

Most of this indirect support has been directed toward curriculum, textbooks and teaching resource materials, teacher education programs and supply of teacher-*shlihim*. In the past decade, support has been extended to pupils in such programs as Yeshiva University's Counterpoint program in Australia and the Mt. Scopus program which is an arrangement for a class to spend part of the school year in Israel.

Parental Motivation for Jewish Education

Since World War II, the vast majority of Jewish children obtain some Jewish education, whether from day schools, part-time schools, right-of-entry classes, or private teachers. Jewish education is the major agent for transmitting Jewish knowledge and for promoting Jewish identity and identification. The degree of importance attached to Jewish education and differing perceptions of Jewishness are reflected in the type and orientation of Jewish schooling which parents choose. The choice depends also on the variety of Jewish education available in a given community; where options include day schools, the parental decision is based on educational and ethnic background, Jewish orientation and feelings about being Jewish in Australia.

The vast majority of part-time and day schools in Australia are religious in orientation, and most Jews see themselves as sharing a common religious basis, despite a generally low level of adult religious observance. An increasing minority of parents are motivated by the desire for their children to become religiously-observant Jews. For the majority, however, the religious content and orientation of Jewish education serves to develop understanding and knowledge of the religious component of Jewishness rather than personal religious commitment or observance.

Parents with low cultural attachments to Jewishness are less motivated toward Jewish education. In general, parents who identify as Jews but are not commmitted to a specific Jewish orientation are the most fearful of assimilation and intermarriage. They want the socialization of a full-time school and prefer the larger 'community' day schools whose pupils reflect the community's entire range of Jewish ideological orientations. Overall, however, parental levels of secular education seem more significant than their achievements in Jewish education. University-educated Jews appear to have lower Jewish identification. However, the younger the parents, the greater the preference for day schools and the higher the proportion of university educated adults.

Geographic convenience of a neighborhood Jewish school and the lower tuition fees and transport costs of smaller neighborhood schools are factors in parental motivation. The convenience of not having to attend two schools, of leisure time outside regular school hours and of relegating all the child's education to one school has also motivated parents to prefer day schools. Convenience is also a factor in the choice of a particular day school, often outweighing ideological considerations. The growing popularity of small neighborhood day schools is partly due to their proximity to home, to the easy access by and to parents, and to the fact that many such schools are associated with, or the core of, after-school and holiday programs and provide Jewish congregational and cultural facilities for the whole family.

Convenience is especially significant for kindergarten and young school-age children, particularly among young parents in newer suburbs who are reluctant for their children to travel long distances to school. Accordingly, many day schools have established kindergartens and elementary feeder schools from which pupils transfer to the larger, more distant main campuses at a later stage.

The improved level and duration of secular education among Australian-educated parents has increased their awareness of the psychological and pedagogic needs of their children. For many parents, small classes, individualized attention, qualified and experienced staff, modern equipment and facilities, and efficient administration are significant. Indeed, the importance attached by these parents to pedagogic considerations has resulted in the opening of day schools which offer progressive and innovative education. Moreover, there is increasing general parental demand that Jewish schools apply the same pedagogic standards to Jewish studies as to general education.

The Structural Characteristics of the Jewish Educational System

Number of Schools

Day Schools

In 1984, there were 16 day schools in Australia – 8 in Melbourne, 5 in Sydney, and one each in Adelaide, Perth and Canberra. Of these, two single-sex schools are treated in government statistics as one mixed-sex school.

Part-time Schools

Many congregations associated with day schools also conduct part-time schools. For instance, the Victorian Union for Progressive Judaism sponsors both the King David Day School and three congregational Sunday Schools in Melbourne, and the *Mizrachi* Organization sponsors both Yavneh College and the *Mizrachi* Talmud Torah. Occasionally, a day school will itself conduct a part-time school, e.g. Shalom Aleichem School sponsors the Shalom Aleichem Sunday School.

School Organization

Day Schools

All full-time schools in Australia are organized on the basis of five-days a week and, with some flexibility, hours from 9 a.m. to 4.p.m. The majority of Jewish day schools follow this pattern, though the Yeshiva College in Melbourne requires senior secondary students to attend classes for an additional hour each weekday and some for 2–4 hours on Sunday mornings for Jewish studies. In general, however, most day school pupils are in attendance for 40 hours per week.

All full-time schools in Australia are conducted on the basis of three terms per year, commencing in February and concluding in mid-December.

Part-time Schools

Since part-time schools are not required to meet compulsory minimum attendance requirements, their organization varies according to availability of teachers and pupils. Most part-time institutions parallel the full-time school year, with similar term vacations and an extended summer vacation. Some part-time schools operate for 3–4 hours on Sunday mornings alone, while others conduct afternoon classes 1–4 times a week.

Curriculum Structure

Day Schools

All Jewish day schools divide pupils into homogeneous classes or grades based on chronological age and scholastic achievement, and most schools are organizationally divided at both the elementary and secondary levels into departments of secular studies and Jewish studies.

In some schools pupils remain in the same class and grade level for both secular and Jewish subjects; in other schools, the child may be at one level for secular subjects and at another for his Jewish studies. Some schools stream pupils into classes based on scholastic performance in key or all secular subjects (mainly English and mathematics), and some stream pupils on the same basis in Jewish studies.

In most day schools, modern Hebrew is treated as part of the Jewish studies program, but in a few, it is regarded as a secular subject. In a very few innovative schools, moves toward an integrated curriculum have been implemented.

Part-time Schools

Part-time schools organize their pupils into classes based on roughly-equivalent levels of Jewish knowledge. Class groups, therefore, tend to be heterogeneous in ability and age, unless the number of pupils permits viable class sizes based on both Jewish knowledge and age. Few schools have enough pupils to provide the full range of levels of elementary and secondary Jewish instruction; most provide a curriculum for primary age children up to bar mitzvah age. While part-time schools describe their Jewish studies curriculum in terms of specific subjects, in many schools there is no clear demarcation in practice between the various Jewish subject areas.

Time Spent on Jewish Studies

Day Schools

The time spent on Jewish studies varies from school to school, with certain subjects like modern Hebrew located in the time allotments of secular studies departments in some schools, and sometimes with a degree of integration of Jewish and secular subjects. Moreover, many schools increase the time devoted to Jewish studies as pupils move from elementary through secondary schooling; many include time spent on informal and extra-curricular Jewish activities such as daily prayer services, participation in communal functions, attendance at Counterpoint and similar programs, and some vacation activities such as the Mt. Scopus *ulpan* program in Israel as elements of the Jewish education they provide.

The minimum time devoted to Jewish studies in the formal classroom is two periods per day, or 10 periods ranging from 35–60 minutes, each week. Some schools spend considerably more hours on formal Jewish instruction. The Yeshiva College in Melbourne for instance devotes up to four hours daily (mornings), five hours daily for senior students and two to four hours on some Sunday mornings.

Part-time schools

Irregular attendance, ad hoc dropout, and crossover and overlap between schools, make it difficult to estimate the average hours attended by individual pupils or the average time spent on Jewish education in part-time schools. A child in a part-time school receives a minimum of one two-hour session per week or a maximum of two hours for one afternoon per week and another two hours on Sunday morning. Few children attend more frequently. However, the time is in some cases limited to the half-hour per week of the right-of-entry class; few part-time schools offer class time equivalent to the minimum given by the day schools, although the potential theoretically exists.

School Level and Size

Day Schools

The Australian education system begins with a 1–2 year period of non-compulsory pre-school, followed by six years of primary/elementary school and six years of secondary school. In almost all states, schooling is compulsory from 6 to 15 years of age, encompassing primary and junior secondary schooling; in practice, most secondary schools provide education from grades 7–12, i.e. both compulsory junior secondary and non-compulsory senior secondary. For all practical purposes, promotion is automatic until the end of compulsory schooling.

There are Australian schools which provide only primary education (primary schools), only secondary education (secondary schools), or both primary and secondary education (mixed or composite schools). Only 5% of state schools, but 17% of private schools are mixed or composite schools. The incidence of large schools varies widely, but they are a minority in both the government and the non-government sector.

The usual pattern in establishing day schools in Australia has been to begin with kindergarten and add a grade level and often parallel classes with each new school year. In some cases, the original intention was to progressively develop a composite school with complete primary and secondary departments. In other cases, only a primary school was planned, but this has rarely remained so; most primary day schools have proceeded into grades 7 and 8 or grades 7 to 10 of secondary education, and the dream of all day school principals and their sponsors is to develop grades 7–12 as well. For this reason, federal statistics which distinguish between primary and composite Jewish day schools are somewhat misleading. It is significant to note that the trend toward expansion at the secondary level reflects low drop-out from primary Jewish day schools.

The vast majority of day schools are co-educational, with varying degrees of internal sex-segregation. *Beth Rivka* college, a composite school for girls only, is a sister school of the single-sex boys' Yeshiva College, but they share a co-educational kindergarten, facilities and teachers when necessary.

Jewish day schools tend to be small, particularly when kindergarten pupils are not counted. The smallest schools tend to be the most recently-established ones. Most had between 100 and 400 students – 3 schools had 100–200 pupils, 3 had 200–300, and another 3 had 300–400 students. Only two schools were larger – Moriah College (Sydney) with over 800 pupils, and Mt. Scopus College (Melbourne) with over 1,000 pupils. These two schools are among the larger private schools in Australia, with Mt. Scopus being one of the four largest private schools in Victoria and one of the six largest in Australia.

Part-time Schools

Part-time schools tend to fluctuate in size, but most have only between 25 to 50 pupils and few have more than 100. They provide elementary, i.e. pre-bar mitzvah education, to pupils in grades 3–8, although a very few conduct post-bar mitzvah classes for secondary age pupils who have not necessarily reached a post-elementary standard of Jewish knowledge. The more Orthodox the orientation of the part-time school, the more likely it is to have sex-segregated classes, but the majority of part-time schools and classes are co-educational.

Ideological Sponsorship

Day schools

Despite their comparatively small number, Jewish day schools in Australia represent the entire spectrum of ideological orientations. They include schools sponsored by the Jewish community at large, by parent-groups, by all the religious sectors from the *Adass Israel* and Lubavitch to the *Mizrachi* movement as well as the Reform movement, by the Zionist movement, and by the secular Yiddishist sector of the community. The majority of schools, irrespective of sponsorship, regard themselves as Orthodox/traditional and are conducted as autonomous and virtually independent units.

TABLE 1.   JEWISH DAY-SCHOOL ENROLLMENT, BY CITY, AND SCHOOL –
AUSTRALIA, 1979

City and State	School	Pupils	% of Jewish Day-School Enrollments	
			State	Australia
Total		5,051	–	100.0
Melbourne, Victoria	Total	3,548	100.0	70.3
	Adass Israel School	123	3.5	2.4
	Bialik College	238	6.7	4.7
	King David College	124	3.5	2.5
	Mt. Scopus College	1,930	54.4	38.2
	Shalom Aleichem School	85	2.4	1.7
	Yavneh College	348	9.8	6.9
	Yeshivah College (Boys)	321	9.0	6.4
	Beth Rivkah Girls School	379	10.7	7.5
Sydney, New South Wales	Total	1,226	100.0	24.2
	Massada College	244	19.9	4.8
	Moriah College	809	66.0	16.0
Perth, Western Australia	G. Korsunski-Carmel School	254	100.0	5.0
Adelaide,South Australia	Massada College	23	100.0	0.5

Part-time Schools

Part-time schools can similarly be classified by ideological sponsorship and affiliation into:
- schools having denominational or congregational sponsorship of either Orthodox or Reform orientation;
- schools administered by central State Boards of Jewish Education, by an entire community (e.g. Canberra), or by a neighborhood Jewish community center or group;
- schools with ethnic group sponsorship, this being mainly Yiddishist.

Enrollment

The most revealing feature of the Jewish school system and the day school movement in particular is its enrollment profile. For the purposes of this analysis, enrollments are limited to primary ages, usually 5 to 11, and secon-

TABLE 2. JEWISH DAY-SCHOOL ENROLLMENT, BY CITY, SCHOOL AND LEVEL – AUSTRALIA, 1979

City and School	Primary	Secondary	Total
Total	3,323	1,728	5,051
Melbourne, total	2,276	1,272	3,548
Adass Israel School	104	19	123
Bialik College	217	21	238
King David College	124	–	124
Mt. Scopus College	958	972	1,930
Shalom Aleichem School	85	–	85
Yavneh College	322	26	348
Yeshivah College (Boys)	220	101	321
Beth Rivkah Girls School	246	133	379
Sydney, total	847	379	1,226
Massada College	244	–	244
Moriah College	430	379	809
G. Korsunski-Carmel School	177	77	254
Massada College	23	–	23

dary age groups, usually 12 to 17, though a few students complete secondary education at age 18.

Day Schools

A picture of 1979 day school enrollments in Australia is shown in Table 1. It is evident that those communities with the largest number of day schools (which also have the longest established schools) enroll the largest numbers of pupils. Despite the similarity in potential enrollment, the eight day schools in Melbourne enroll some three times more pupils than the three day schools in Sydney.

The distribution of day school students according to primary and secondary levels is indicated in Table 2. Where primary enrollments are high, secondary enrollments are also high, though less so. In Melbourne, for every two children in primary day school departments, one child is in a secondary department. However, the number of secondary enrollments is influenced both by educational factors and by day school rates of level expansion.

Day schools tend to maintain their enrollments, with little drop-out occurring in the transition from primary to secondary departments, at the minimal school leaving age, or during the two years of non-compulsory senior secondary schooling. The enrollment decline from primary to secondary departments is due largely to the many newer schools which have not yet matured into secondary levels, as well as to a tendency for schools not to encourage, and parents not to consider, enrollment directly into senior departments. Most Jewish parents seem to prefer their children to continue in the type of schools they commenced in, whether Jewish or non-Jewish.

There is, however, some movement between day schools. Transfer from one school to another is usually due to secular and Jewish educational considerations, to social factors and to the primary school having only a partial or no secondary department rather than to geographic mobility.

Senior secondary school retention rates in non-government schools are generally high, and grade 12 retention rates reached 90% in non-Catholic schools in 1974. The percentage of day school students remaining through grades 10, 11, and 12 probably exceeds that, since the majority of students intend to continue to tertiary education, and the vast majority of parents and pupils regard the grade 12 certificate as the completion of secondary education. The few students who leave the day schools at the end of grades 10 or 11 are mostly those who seem unsuited to the academic standards required by the particular school, or who are entering training or work for which senior secondary schooling is not required. A very small minority of students transfer at grade 11 or 12 to non-Jewish secondary schools for a variety of individual reasons.

During the 1970s, the day school movement was continuously expanding, and it grew from an estimated 2,700 pupils in 1971 to 5,051 in 1979. Existing schools expanded to accommodate this growth which occurred in each state. While enrollment expansion will probably continue, a higher rate of increase is likely to occur in those communities in which there is still a substantial gap between actual and potential enrollments.

In order to provide a meaningful comparison between potential and actual enrollments, 1976 census population data have been used in conjunction with actual enrollment in 1977 (see Table 3). It is apparent that Melbourne day schools reflect a consistently higher proportional enrollment than day schools in other states. In general, just over 50% of Jewish children in Australia attended a Jewish day school in 1977: 8 out of 10 children in Melbourne, 3 out of 10 in Sydney, and almost 5 out of 10 in Perth.

Proportionate enrollments in primary and secondary levels of day schools are shown in Table 3. It is apparent that:
– the proportion of primary age children enrolled in day schools is considerably higher than the proportion of secondary age children;
    However, conclusions about dropout from primary to secondary day school should be treated cautiously. The main explanation for the higher primary enrollments is that expansion is first felt at the primary level

TABLE 3. POTENTIAL AND ACTUAL ENROLLMENT, BY SCHOOL LEVEL AND CITY – AUSTRALIA, 1976–1977

School Level	Melbourne	Sydney	Perth	Adelaide	Total 4 Cities	Total Australia
Total age group 5–17						
Jewish population (1976)	4,259	3,338	442	313	8,352	8,624
Enrollments (1977)	3,386	990	229	14	4,619	4,619
Enrollment rate, %	79.5	29.7	51.8	4.5	55.3	53.6
Primary level, age 5–11						
Jewish population (1976)	2,232	1,743	288	233	4,496	4,635
Enrollments (1977)	2,032	705	174	14	2,925	2,925
Enrollment rate, %	91.0	40.4	60.4	6.0	65.1	63.1
Secondary level, age 12–17						
Jewish population (1976)	2,027	1,595	154	80	3,856	3,989
Enrollments (1977)	1,354	285	55	–	1,694	1,694
Enrollment rate, %	66.8	17.9	35.7	–	43.9	42.5

and takes time to move into the secondary level, and that many new day schools have not yet established secondary departments;

– the proportion of Jewish children in Melbourne enrolled in primary departments of day schools is quite startling;

– despite the decline between proportionate primary and secondary enrollments, 2 out of 5 Jewish secondary pupils in Australia are in day schools;

– the success of the day school movement is especially obvious at the primary level, where 3 out of every 5 Jewish children in Australia attend day schools – almost all in Melbourne, 2 out of 5 in Sydney, and 3 out of 5 in Perth. Enrollment expansion in day schools has continued since 1977. This may be a response to the potential enrollment pool.

Despite differing attitudes toward the value of Jewish education for girls, day schools enroll almost equal numbers of boys and girls. On a country-wide basis, enrollment of girls is not significantly lower in day schools, either at the primary or at the secondary level. Enrollments in Victoria suggest that even in day schools with Orthodox orientations there is no longer a significant bias against enrolling girls.

Despite the diversity of ideological orientations and choices between schools offering different brands of Judaism, current patterns indicate a trend toward enrollment in schools with denominational or communal sponsorship. The largest number of students attend day schools sponsored by the community, followed by denomination-sponsored schools. The two community-sponsored schools enroll almost twice as many students as the six schools with denominational sponsors, and more than the combined enrollments of all the other schools. One explanation is that the communal schools are the longest-established ones. But it seems likely that their high enrollments are due to a preference for Jewish education with a broad, general nature, as well as approval of their secular scholastic standards.

Part-time Schools

Day school enrollment expansion, together with other factors already mentioned, has resulted in some decline in part-time enrollment. Right-of-entry classes, which formerly added to the higher enrollment figures in Melbourne and Sydney, for instance, have declined as Jewish enrollments in state schools have decreased. The addition by the G. Korsunski-Carmel College in Perth of a secondary department, and the establishment of Massada College in Adelaide, have reduced part-time enrollments in those cities at both the primary and secondary level.

Kindergartens

Enrollment age in kindergarten is not standardized – it is usually from 3 to the age of school entry which is between 5 and 6, but it is not uncommon for kindergartens to accept children below 3, or to retain them in their fifth year. There are also various types, some which emphasize social contact and play, and others which place greater stress on providing skills and knowledge required at school.

Some idea of potential kindergarten enrollments is provided by census statistics regarding Jewish population age-groups. The kindergarten age-group, according to the 1981 census, is significantly smaller than older age groups. Hence, assuming no change in attitudes of parents, kindergarten enrollments will decline.

While kindergartens are sponsored primarily either by day schools or congregations, there appear to be no gender differences regarding enrollments. Impressions are that parental attitudes toward Jewish kindergartens reflect virtually no sex discrimination. Moreover, irrespective of the degree of Orthodoxy of sponsors, Jewish kindergartens are all co-educational and internally non-segregated.

Personnel

Teachers in Day Schools

The use of part-time teachers for Jewish studies on the one hand and, on the other hand, the emerging tendency in some primary day schools to use one teacher for both Jewish and secular studies, have complicated the statistics on teaching personnel. Almost all Jewish schools still employ separate staff for Jewish and secular studies. In 1979, Mt. Scopus College employed some 172 teachers, of whom 126 (73%) taught general subjects and 46 (27%) were in the Jewish studies department. The proportion of Jewish to secular staff was about 1:2 in the primary level and 1:4 at the secondary level. In some schools, however, such as the Yeshiva College in Melbourne, the proportion of Jewish studies staff was higher, reflecting a larger proportion of rabbis teaching full- or part-time.

Secular studies staff are often not Jewish. The practice of employing non-Jewish teachers for general subjects arose in the past due to the lack of trained Jewish teachers, and has since acquired legitimacy. However, this situation is slowly changing, due to vastly improved conditions generally in the teaching profession and the readiness of Australian-born and Australian-educated Jews to work in a non-Jewish educational context with favorable career prospects. Moreover, many day school graduates have chosen the teaching profession. Accordingly, there is a trend toward employing Jewish day school graduates as teachers in secondary secular studies departments, and in some schools, to employ such teachers to teach in both branches of the curriculum in the primary grades. Jewish studies teachers are regarded as role models. Since the majority of schools transmit an Orthodox or traditional religious Jewish world-view, Jewish studies teachers in most schools are expected themselves to be Orthodox or at least to present an Orthodox stance.

Besides teaching staff, day schools employ professional support staff, ancillary instructional staff, and administrative, clerical and general workers. Some idea of the personnel involved in Jewish day schools is provided by the student-staff ratio (Table 4).

Teacher Training

The general studies staff of Jewish day schools – whether Jewish or non-Jewish – has always been trained in government universities, teachers' colleges or colleges of advanced education. Teacher-registration and certification today, which reflect the upgrading of teaching into a profession, require that all general studies teachers possess a first academic degree plus post-

TABLE   4.   STUDENT-STAFF   RATIOS   IN   JEWISH   DAY-SCHOOLS   –
AUSTRALIA, 1977

Ratios	Primary Schools Only	All-through Schools	
		Primary	Secondary
Student/Teacher	16	25	14
Student/Professional Support Staff	875	686	332
Student/Ancillary Instructional Staff	146	387	229
Student/Administrative Clerical and General Staff	169	114	56

graduate teaching qualifications or else a four year education degree which is
equivalent to an academic degree.

Nevertheless, there has never been an accredited Jewish teacher-training
institution in Australia for either academic Jewish studies or teacher-
training, so that all teachers of Jewish studies were trained overseas. It is possible to obtain a BA degree in Hebrew and/or Jewish History at Sydney University, Melbourne University, or Victoria College of Advanced Education,
followed by a regular teacher-training course. However, most schools expect
their Jewish studies teachers to be capable of teaching the entire Jewish studies curriculum and do not employ teachers solely for Hebrew language teaching; they consider existing tertiary Judaic studies courses insufficient or inadequate for their needs.

There have been obstacles in the way of establishment of a local Jewish
training institution other than cost:
–   the Jewish academic content involves not only knowledge but also a cer-
    tain personal relationship with the subject matter which is consistent
    with the ideology and sponsorship of the employing school;
–   there is no career path for teachers trained only for work in Jewish
    schools;
–   there are problems in coordinating the diverse requirements of the vari-
    ous day schools, let alone catering to the training needs of both day and
    part-time schools; and
–   uncertainty as to whether such training should focus only on Jewish
    subject-matter or should include teacher-training of a general type.

In the past, assessments of the number of teachers required and of small
local staff turnover were used to suggest that it was cheaper to import or use
overseas-trained staff than to set up a local community-financed training

institution. However, the increased number of teachers required by day schools has revived interest in local training.

In the meantime, schools continue to rely significantly on teachers with overseas qualifications and/or experience who have settled in Australia, and teacher-*shlihim* from Israel. Mt. Scopus College is the largest single employer of teacher-*shlihim*, who comprise some 50% of the Jewish studies staff there. Local Jewish studies staff at Mt. Scopus and other schools include a high proportion trained in Israel, South Africa and the United States. Indeed, the temporary and transient character of teacher-*shlihim* together with the fact that most of the other Israel-trained teachers are *yordim* teaching children in aliyah and Zionist oriented schools has reinforced current interest in local training.

Some schools have attempted to resolve their teacher-training needs on their own. Thus, *Ohel Chana* in Melbourne, which provides post-secondary Jewish studies for girls, includes a teacher-training program for Jewish studies which, while not leading to an accredited degree, provides introductory training for Jewish studies teachers at *Beth Rivka* College. Mt. Scopus College has in recent years entered an arrangement for the training of teacher-*shlihim* at the Melton Center for Jewish Education in the Diaspora, at the Hebrew University of Jerusalem, which also provides short (3 month) courses at the Center for 'local' Jewish studies teachers at Mt. Scopus College.

In addition, the two Education Departments of the World Zionist Organization have provided in-service training courses and personnel in Australia which have been used by both day and part-time schools. It is also becoming more common for day school graduates to study in Israeli yeshivoth, universities, and teacher training institutions like the Greenberg and Gold institutes in Jerusalem.

Conditions

Salaries of teachers in day schools are based on rates for teachers in state schools, which vary according to experience and level of responsibility. While salaries of secular teachers are usually the same as in the state system, each school negotiates salaries and conditions with teachers individually, so there is some variation. It is more difficult to generalize about salaries of the Jewish studies staff which generally conform to the rates for secular teachers: the larger schools tend to classify teachers for salary purposes, so there is scope for greater salary variations in the smaller schools.

Salaries and conditions have generally improved for teachers as they have gained professional status. These conditions include a theoretical four week annual leave which, in practice, is virtually all school vacations; holiday leave, annual cumulative sick leave entitlements, long service leave, and employer-employee contributory super-annuation – conditions generally applicable to the state public services sector. In addition to the advantage of teaching smaller classes, children of teachers in the school are enrolled on a sliding scale of reduced fees, which, for a family with two children attending an expensive private school, can represent a saving after taxation of some $6,000 per year. For teacher-*shlihim*, fringe benefits include the opportunity, to visit another country and community and gain knowledge and experience of a Diaspora school system, but only rarely do the *shlihim* visit non-Jewish schools or learn about the Australian schools.

Profile of Teachers

In 1974, 44% of Jewish studies teachers were below 30 years old, 40% and of these, were aged 26–30. It is likely that the preponderance of young teachers has continued, reflecting national trends, the growing attraction of teaching in the Jewish world, and employment of the day schools' own graduates.

In the past, the average day school secular teacher was more experienced than his state school counterpart. Little information is available about the work experience of Jewish studies teachers, but there have occasionally been queries regarding the teacher-*shlihim* who were trained in Israel to teach subjects other than those they teach in Australia, for which they may be relatively inexperienced if not unqualified.

The large majority of teachers in the primary grades (both secular and Jewish studies) are women, reflecting the global situation, but the proportion of men is higher among secondary teachers. Teaching has long been considered a female Jewish profession, though this is slowly changing: the recruitment of teacher-*shlihim* is often based on both husband and wife teaching, which affects the sex-distribution.

Teaching conditions of secular and Jewish studies staff are similar and, despite variations from school to school, reflect general teaching conditions. Teachers are required to be at school for the whole school day, and, in secondary schools, to teach 18 periods per week. Staffrooms are usually used for assignment corrections and lesson preparation during free periods, for eating and relaxation, and for staff discussions. Most teachers enjoy virtual autonomy in their classrooms, although what and how they teach is influenced by pre-determined syllabi, and by staff consultation with senior subject teachers and heads of curriculum areas.

Senior teaching staff are usually teachers with more experience and proven teaching ability. Women are rarely appointed to the most senior positions in Jewish day schools, and it has been rare for a woman to be appointed principal. All day school principals are Jewish, most have been recruited overseas, and virtually all have overseas experience. Their salaries are negotiated with the school's sponsors or governing bodies, and reflect the scarcity of available personnel with both personal stature and appropriate Jewish and secular reputations in education.

Teachers in Part-time Schools

The majority of teachers in part-time schools are employed and paid on an hourly or sessional basis and few are fully employed in the part-time sector. Most part-time teachers today also function as *madrichim* in youth movements, regular teachers in state or day schools, tertiary students, rabbis and communal employees. In the large communities, a few full-time administrators are employed by the local Education Boards to provide coordination and support. Teaching conditions reflect the disadvantages of a supplementary, ancillary, voluntary and less esteemed area of education, though facilities and conditions are improving.

Evaluation of the Jewish School System

Goals, Curricula, Teaching Methods

Jewish school goals, curricula and teaching methods in Australia are influenced by traditional Jewish education, modern developments in Jewish education in Israel and in the major English-speaking Jewish communities, contemporary Australian Jewish perceptions of Jewish educational needs and priorities and the general Australian education system of which Jewish schools are a part.

Contemporary Jewish day schools were established for the purpose of increasing the proportion of time spent on Jewish studies and enhancing the relevance, status and esteem of Jewish knowledge, placing it on par with general education. The goal of the founders of these schools was to ensure Jewish identification and survival on both a personal and communal basis. However, the tension and conflict between the secular and Jewish goals of day schools has persisted.

Jewish schools in Australia have always given priority to secular education in terms of importance, status and value, and time allocation. The pragmatic compartmentalization of Jewish and secular instruction was reinforced by the general Australian attitude which places high priority on utilitarian knowledge and on education as professional or vocational preparation. The practical considerations and educational climate which had originally led Australian Jews to give such esteem to secular education was reinforced by each wave of Jewish immigrants, who saw secular education as the means to acculturation, socio-economic advancement, acceptance and equality. Irrespective of the Jewish education provided, enrollments depend on the level of secular education as measured by student pass rates and grades in the final secondary school examinations which rank students for entry to tertiary education.

The schools' concession to parental motivations and demands is the relaxation of emphasis on Jewish studies at the secondary level, allowing students to drop modern Hebrew should their secular results be jeopardised or making Hebrew non-compulsory in the final school year. Moreover, unlike secular studies, Jewish studies do not reflect the innovative curricular developments and progressive teaching methodology prevalent in many non-Jewish schools, partly because Jewish studies teachers are often not aware of the modern educational developments in Australia.

Cognitive Knowledge vs. Emotive Learning

In principle, Jewish education in Australia aims at all three areas of educational objectives – cognitive, affective and behavioral, i.e. knowledge, attitudes and behavior.

Little research has been done as to the influence of day schools in the affective and behavioral domains. Existing studies suggest that while day school students learn more facts regarding Judaism than students attending non-Jewish schools, differences in Jewish identification between the two groups may not be as great as commonly supposed. Moreover, the teaching of Jewish attitudes and values is largely incidental to the transmission of knowledge; Judaic values such as the responsibility of one Jew for another, are rarely taught specifically.

Indeed, the bulk of Australian Jewish education – apart from modern Hebrew – emphasizes Jewish classical knowledge of the distant and immediate past. This often leads to students who regard the attitudes and values associated with this historic knowledge as irrelevant to their own social reality.

Most day schools use extra-curricular experiential learning to promote behavioral objectives. Thus, Orthodox schools require boys to wear *kipot*, attendance at daily school prayers is encouraged, pupils participate in the school seder and *Kabbalat Shabbat*, eat in the school *succah* and so on. Nevertheless, it appears that the majority of students do not become religiously observant. Schools usually attribute this to family and home environment, contending that the school can only achieve behavioral objectives if they are reinforced at home.

Emphasis on Particular Subjects

Hebrew is the basis of Jewish education, yet for most pupils, Hebrew is neither a vernacular nor a second language, but a foreign one. This has implications for the teaching of Hebrew. While Australian educators have been in the forefront of developing Teaching English as a Second Language (TESL) and Teaching English as a Foreign Language (TEFL) programs and in creating sophisticated and innovatory programs for the teaching of minority community languages, Jewish schools rarely take advantage of these developments. They continue to teach Hebrew by traditional heder methods or use programs developed for teaching Hebrew as a second language in Israel. Moreover, few Hebrew teachers are qualified to teach Hebrew as a second or foreign language. Attempts have been made to obtain recognition of Hebrew as a community language and to thereby receive the government funding and pedagogic support available through the community languages policy and programs.

The teaching of Hebrew serves three main purposes: a modern functioning language, preparation for understanding the Bible and Hebraic literature, and preparation for reading prayers and liturgy. The Bible is taught in all the schools, though the more Orthodox the orientation, the more attention is given to Talmud. In Australian day schools, Talmud generally consists of teaching rabbbinic doctrine, ethics and philosophy and serves as a means of maintaining classical Orthodox Judaism in a non-Orthodox environment. Its role as a mental discipline involving logic and legalistic dialectics is less common outside the yeshiva-type schools. The teaching of Jewish history emphasizes identification with the past, development of a sense of cultural continuity, enhanced understanding of Jewish life and promotion of a commitment to Jewish survival. However, a historical perspective is not developed – Jewish history is presented with no relationship to the present, or to general history. In recent years, this approach has changed with the employment of teachers having tertiary academic qualifications in history and qualifications in both general and Jewish history.

Modern Israel has only recently been introduced in some schools as a separate subject. In most schools, Israel was introduced mainly in conjunction with other subjects and through extra-curricular activities.

Teaching Methods

In most day schools, Jewish studies are characterized by structured teaching methods which include formal classroom layout, frontal teaching, teacher-initiated activities, teacher-directed learning, authoritarian teaching styles and textbook-dominated instruction. This is partly due to the structured nature of the textbooks and the prevalence of textbook-centered teaching. Other explanations are the revival of traditional methods (chanting, rote-learning, repetition); the fact that many Jewish studies teachers are accustomed from their own schooling and professional training to traditional structured methods; and the lack of in-service education for Jewish studies teachers who are, therefore, unaware of, or uncomfortable with, alternative teaching strategies. However, in many schools, more open teaching approaches – including student-initiated activities, group projects and individualized learning – are being used.

Use of New Media

Media which have long been accepted in secular education have gradually come to be used in many day schools for teaching Jewish studies. These include audio-visual equipment such as records, radio, open and closed circuit television, cassettes, slides and films. However, even where such media facilities are available and commonly used in secular subjects, their use in Jewish studies tends to be restricted by the ingenuity and imagination of individual Jewish studies teachers. Furthermore, appropriate media materials and resources are scarce in the Jewish studies area. In general, the more Orthodox the school, the greater the tendency to rely on textbooks as the medium of instruction.

School Climate

Mix of Students

Since the overwhelming majority of Australian Jews are non-Orthodox, the overwhelming majority of students in Jewish schools are also non-Orthodox. This is true even for the student population in Orthodox-oriented Jewish schools, although the proportion of Orthodox pupils increases dramatically the more ultra-Orthodox the school.

One condition for receiving government aid is non-exclusivity, i.e. that the school accept children of any religious persuasion. However, the proportion of time spent on Jewish studies, and the religious image which non-Jews associate with Jewish day schools markedly restricts the attraction of non-Jewish clientele, despite the excellent secular reputation of the schools. Children of non-Jewish teaching staff, like those of the Jewish staff, can attend the school with significantly reduced fees. However, the Jewish studies requirements effectively preclude all but one or two such children from enrolling in day schools.

A small proportion of non-Jewish pupils is found from time to time in non-Orthodox Jewish day schools. These pupils appear to be attracted to Jewish schools by a number of factors, including:
- Jewish friends who attend the school;
- the parental associations with Jews whose children attend the school;
- the compensating benefits of the school's secular standards for the additional burden of Jewish studies;
- a parental desire to expose children to a multi-cultural or ecumenical educational environment or experience, or to teach them the Judaic basis of Christianity and humanism; and
- geographic convenience.

In the past even Orthodox-oriented schools, such as Mt. Scopus, have enrolled a small proportion of non-Jewish, usually South-East Asian students in the final two years of secondary schooling. However, there have rarely been more than 4 or 5 such students at any one time, amounting to some 0.2% at most of the Mt. Scopus pupil population.

While the mix of Orthodox and non-Orthodox Jewish and non-Jewish pupils has little impact on the Jewish school climate, the enrollment of children from mixed marriages creates a potential problem. Children with non-Jewish mothers whose two parents are socially integrated into the Jewish family circle and society and who wish their children to be brought up as Jews despite the absence of formal conversion, not infrequently attend the larger communal or non-Orthodox day schools. While there are only a few pupils who are non-Jewish by halachic criteria, the number is likely to be higher when one includes recent Soviet Jewish immigrant children of admitted or concealed mixed parentage.

In schools with Orthodox orientations, such as the larger community-sponsored schools, the awareness of an incipient problem is causing concern: in adult life, a Jewish day school graduate may wish to marry a fellow graduate, unaware of the mixed marriage background. An obvious extension to this problem is marriage in Reform synagogues. To date, only the Orthodox rabbinate of Australia has, for purposes of marriage, required evidence of the Jewishness of the partners and their parents. It is conceivable, however, that difficulties could arise for a couple desiring an Orthodox marriage, if one partner's parents were married in a Reform synagogue which does not require such evidence.

Children of members of Reform congregations rarely attend ultra-Orthodox schools, but they do attend the larger community Orthodox-oriented schools and the non-Orthodox schools. Bar mitzvah preparations are the earliest problems caused by the Orthodox-Reform mix, since preparation for an Orthodox bar mitzvah is an accepted function of the day schools, but is unsuited to the Reform ceremony. Moreover, friendships between Orthodox and Reform children are affected by the fact that the Orthodox peers will usually not attend the Reform ceremony or social festivities since the problem of the observance of kashruth can arise. These factors were major catalysts in the establishment of day schools in Melbourne and Sydney sponsored by Reform congregations.

That Orthodox-Reform intermarriage is regarded as a day school, rather than an adult community, problem indicates the extent to which Jews in Australia perceive Jewish socialization to be one of the main roles of the school, and prevention of intermarriage and conservation of Orthodox Judaism to be one of the school's main responsibilities.

As the day schools have become more successful in attracting pupils, they have enrolled more pupils born outside Australia, although the vast majority studying in day schools throughout Australia today were born there. Of those born elsewhere, two groups stand out – those born in Israel and those recently arrived from the Soviet Union. The mix of Australian-born and Israeli/Soviet students affects the climate of the school to a varying extent.

While pupils from Israel apparently integrate well with their peers, there is some prejudice from locally-born pupils and staff against children of *yordim* and children of Soviet Jewish immigrants. This is further accentuated by the competitive climate of Jewish schools – the Israeli pupils' fluency in Hebrew, and the Russian pupils' abilities in mathematics are sometimes seen as unfair advantages. In subjects such as these, the heterogeneous levels of achievement among pupils may create difficulties in classroom grouping for teachers accustomed to relatively homogeneous ability and achievement groups.

The school climate is also affected by cultural differences between Australian and Soviet Jewish children. In the early years of the day school movement, the majority of pupils were of immigrant origin and the school climate reflected the diversity of pupil backgrounds. While ethnic prejudices persisted in the adult community, the day school constituted a melting pot where ethnic and cultural traits were accepted and modified. In contrast, Soviet Jews represent a major, highly visible and distinct minority group in the contemporary community, and it is they, rather than the mainstream community, who are expected to conform and adapt.

Student Motivation and Interest

It is often claimed that student interest and motivation in Jewish studies is related to parental attitudes toward these subjects. The act of enrolling one's child in a Jewish school is insufficient evidence in itself of the value parents place on Jewish education. Schools often attribute poor performance and classroom misbehavior in Jewish studies to lack of parental involvement and concern; they ascribe the child's attendance at a day school to the perceived quality of the secular education and the Jewish socialization provided.

However, observation of a number of day schools suggests that motivation and interest in the Jewish studies curriculum is high in the kindergarten and early primary grades, progressively lower in the senior primary and junior secondary grades, and revives again in the final year of secondary school among some pupils.

This fluctuation in student motivation may be related to duration of Jewish studies learning. Jewish studies deal with aspects of minority rather than mainstream Jewish life (the major difference between education in Australia and Israel), and twelve years is a long time to sustain interest in any one subject, particularly if the curriculum design and content is repetitious rather than progressive in the development of knowledge and cognitive skills.

Student motivation also appears to be related to teaching methods and organization. One reason that children are motivated in the early years of schooling is probably that at this stage, teachers emphasize learning through play and activity, such as Hebrew singing and dancing. The schools which do best at sustaining pupils interest in Jewish studies are those which integrate Jewish and secular studies and use progressive teaching methods.

Motivation also appears to be related to the student's performance and the teacher's expectations of the child in the particular Jewish studies subject. It is a truism in education generally that the teacher's expectations of the child's performance are self-fulfilling prophecies and that poor and failing results in the subject engender loss of student motivation and further failure.

Finally, motivation and interest in Jewish studies subjects at the senior secondary level is affected by professional/vocational considerations. Since entry to tertiary institutions and faculties is dependent on the scores obtained in competitive grade 12 final examinations, students are reluctant to jeopardize these scores by taking examinations in any subject in which their performance is poor or to spend time studying subjects not required by the faculty of their choice.

Effects of Jewish School

On Providing Good Secular Education

That Jewish schools succeed in providing a good secular education is evidenced by students' results in state examinations and by the high proportion of day school graduates who proceed to the faculties of their choice at tertiary institutions. However, good secular education may be defined not only as preparation for tertiary study. For instance, few Jewish schools provide secular education that is not academically-oriented. The notions that technical, vocational and leisure education can also be termed 'good secular education', and that Jewish schools should provide for children with non-academic aspirations receive little consideration. Similarly, few schools provide for disabled, handicapped or retarded children.

On Continuing Jewish Education

The vast majority of day school graduates feel that their school has provided a 'sufficient' Jewish education. Any further education they receive is largely incidental to their subsequent organizational and communal involvement. A small proportion involve themselves in one or more of the many Jewish adult education facilities available for personal or (in the case of students and teachers) professional development.

Whether graduates decide to further their Jewish education appears to be related to:
- their level of Jewish consciousness and orientation;
- the suitability of available education facilities in terms of time demands and location; and
- the content of further education programs.

One important reason that the majority of students do not continue their Jewish schooling may well be that after 12 years of day school, the content of higher education seems to be merely an extension, continuation or repetition. For the majority of students, the effect of school on continuing Jewish education is either neutral (makes no difference) or negative (discourages further study).

On Jewish Identification

Undoubtedly, Jewish schools effect Jewish identification by fostering social networks which promote future social identification and cohesion, thereby inhibiting intermarriage. Moreover, since lack of Jewish knowledge is a major reason for non-identification (e.g. with synagogue and festival rituals and customs), the cognitive education imparted by Jewish schools remove many of the intellectual obstacles to Jewish identification.

At the same time, it seems that there is a tendency for the school's 'ghetto' environment and stress on Jewish identity and cohesion to create a backlash effect among some students. In other words, one effect of Jewish schools is to develop in some students a sense of cultural claustrophobia, curiosity about non-Jews and other cultures, and experimentation with non-Jewish values and lifestyles.

Usually, however, the effect of the Jewish school appears to be to reinforce and consolidate the Jewish identification which the student has developed at home and, where relevant, in his youth organization. The school alone does not seem to make the difference; it acts in concert with other institutions in the community.

On Providing Leadership for the Community

Overall, Jewish schools have significantly improved the level of Jewish knowledge throughout Australian Jewry and among its leadership, and have helped alleviate Jewish illiteracy and ignorance, which was widespread prior to the establishment of day schools. Corresponding to the increase in Jewish school enrollments and graduates, there has been a demand for more Jewishly-educated leadership.

However, the day school movement in Australia has not yet existed long enough to provide a significant proportion of the community's leaders. The first generation of day school graduates in Melbourne, for instance, is now only in its early 40s, which is usually the age to first take on leadership roles in communal organizations. Given the limited demand for leaders in comparatively small communities such as Australia, and the tendency for individuals to assume leadership activities when they are personally and professionally settled in their mid-life years and to retain that leadership for a long time, then it may be claimed that a surprising number of day school graduates do become community leaders. The proportion of communal leaders who are day school graduates will likely increase as day schooling becomes the norm for educating young Jews.

It is a subjective impression that the school has the most effect on active adult participation and leadership among those graduates who developed leadership aspirations and skills while they were in school. Those graduates who become leaders in the adult community are mostly drawn from those who were also leaders at school. There is a kind of leadership path, wherein pupils who are leaders in the school community tend also to be leaders in youth organizations, Jewish tertiary student organizations and later (or at the same time) in adult organizations.

It is a corollary of a Jewish school system with a non-selective open enrollment policy which educates the majority of the community's children that the function of day schools is not perceived as the elitist one of creating future leaders. Despite the democratic nature of Australian Jewish schools, they succeed in producing not only the future leaders of the community, but also the community's proletariat.

On Zionist Commitment

Most of the members of Zionist youth movements are pupils of Jewish schools and the majority of movement leaders are day school graduates. The tertiary student organizations reflect the orientation of their leaders who are also the products of day school education, as are high proportions of young Australian *olim* and students in Israeli yeshivoth. It may be assumed, therefore, that overall, Australian day schools provide an effective Zionist education and successfully develop a commitment to Israel.

Extra-Curricular Jewish Education

Youth Groups

Youth groups in Australia have four major functions – promoting a specific focus of Jewish identity; encouraging community involvement; providing a Jewish social reference group; and increasing Jewish knowledge and consciousness.

The number of youth groups increased considerably in the 1980s. In 1974, there were 53 separate youth groups in Sydney and more than that in Melbourne, with some 30% of the 15–25 age group involved in these organizations. Since then both the number of groups and the proportions of youths involved have substantially increased. The major groups are:

- Zionist youth groups: *Bnei Akiva, Betar, Habonim* and *Hashomer Hatzair*;
- non-political Zionist youth groups such as *Netzer*, which emerged in the 1970s and is associated with the Union of Progressive Judaism, i.e. the Reform Movement;
- synagogue youth groups of the various denominations. Some of these groups emphasize their educational roles, but others see their function as primarily social;
- Yiddishist organizations such as SKIF (Sotsialistisher Kinder Farband) in Melbourne, whose main educational role is to foster Yiddish language and culture and which caters mainly to children of Yiddishist and secular non-Zionist backgrounds;
- non-ideological youth organizations such as AZA, the youth branch of the *B'nai B'rith* in Australia;
- miscellaneous clubs and societies with Jewish memberships such as sporting and social clubs, whose purpose is recreational and not educational;
- Jewish branches of general youth organizations, such as the Jewish Scouts and Girl Guides which are really 'cells' of Jewish members within an international organization.

There is a correlation between day school attendance and youth group membership. Until the mid-1970s, day schools maintained only minimal formal association with Zionist youth groups: since then, the various Zionist youth movements have been permitted to publicize their activities and attract members on the campus of Mt. Scopus College (though problems still exist with *Hashomer Hatzair*).

Tertiary Student Organizations

Jewish student societies exist on almost all Australian university and college campuses. Individual student societies cater to the educational and social needs of their members, during the week both on and off campus. Their educational aim is to attract identified and non-identified Jewish students, proliferate knowledge about Judaism and Israel among Jewish and non-Jewish students, identify Jewish student leaders and develop a local Jewish intelligentsia.

The Australian Union of Jewish Students (AUJS) is the roof body of all the Jewish student societies throughout Australia and New Zealand, a counterpart and affiliate of the Australian Union of Students (AUS), and a member organization of the World Union of Jewish Students (WUJS). In 1981, some 2,000 of the estimated 5,000 Jewish students in 20 campuses in Australia and New Zealand were members of AUJS. Like the AUS, AUJS activities on campus in recent years have been heavily concerned with student politics related to the Middle East and Israel, their main task being active opposition to the anti-Israel stance of AUS and pro-PLO sentiment on campus. AUJS provides a wide range of educational activities for the various Jewish student societies and their members.

While not strictly a student organization, Hillel serves the Australian Jewish student body. Both the Melbourne and Sydney communities have a Hillel Director. Hillel encourages Jewish student activities, and its functions include continuing Jewish education, counselling services for Jewish students, strengthening Jewish consciousness and the establishment of a visible Jewish presence complementary to that of other denominational chaplaincies on campus.

Due largely to common aims and membership overlap, the demarcation between the educational activities of the Zionist youth groups at their senior level, AUJS and Hillel are often blurred.

Summer Camps and Weekend Retreats

Almost every youth organization conducts its own summer camps, term vacation camps and weekend seminars for each age-group of its membership. In addition, the Zionist youth movements, AUJS and sometimes AZA conduct separate joint leadership training programs, often in the form of camps. AUJS in conjunction with Hillel also conducts an annual national summer conference camp in a different state each year prior to the annual AUJS assembly. The day schools themselves also utilize the idea of camping for informal and extracurricular enrichment.

Apart from camps, some Jewish schools and youth groups provide day-long urban school holiday programs which combine extra curricular Jewish education with social and recreational activities.

Trips to Israel

Programs in Israel are an integral part of informal education. The Zionist youth movements promote one-year programs centered on kibbutz, and are also involved in the short and long term programs organized by AUJS in conjunction with Hillel. A few thousand participants have come to Israel in recent years as participants in these programs. In addition, AUJS is associated with *Sherut La'am*, programs of one year or less, one-year study/work programs based at the WUJS Institute in Arad, one year programs at Israeli universities, and a semester program at the Hebrew University.

The main program for school-age pupils is an *ulpan* during the regular school year, arranged by Mt. Scopus College in conjunction with the Hebrew University, which was initiated in 1982.

In addition to trips to Israel specifically designed for Jewish participants, from 1975 to 1979 an Education Study Tour which combined touring with intensive study of Israel was organized on a national basis for tertiary students, graduates, teachers and other professionals, both Jewish and non-Jewish. Organized trips to Israel for adults and families are also organized by other communal groups, such as the Jewish National Fund, *T'nuat Aliyah* and the Australian Academics for Peace in the Middle East. Furthermore, many Australian Jews have visited Israel privately.

Adult Jewish Education

Adult Jewish education is provided by Jewish and non-Jewish tertiary institutions, by synagogues, by Jewish communal organizations, by the Jewish press and media and by adult education organizations and study circles. Jewish schools and non-Jewish adult education organizations provide courses on subjects of interest and relevance to Jews.

Yeshivoth Gedoloth

In Melbourne and on a smaller scale in Sydney, Jewish education for men is provided by *yeshivoth gedoloth* affiliated with the Lubavitch movement. These are residential institutions providing intensive advanced Judaic studies as well as non-residential programs and courses. They attract some 30–40 students annually to full-time programs. The counterpart for girls is *Ohel Chana* in Melbourne, which provides post-secondary education on both a residential and non-residential basis.

Universities and Colleges

Judaic studies are offered at undergraduate and post-graduate levels in the Semitic Studies department of Sydney University, in the Middle East Studies department of Melbourne University and in the Jewish Studies department at Victoria College of Advanced Education in Melbourne. Of the three, only the Victoria College department is devoted exclusively to Judaic studies.

Several tertiary institutions offer units, components of units and elective courses with Jewish content or relevance. Examples are the one-year course on contemporary Jewry in the Sociology department at the University of New South Wales, the 10–week elective unit on Israeli society, culture and education conducted jointly by the Rusden campus (secondary teacher education) of Victoria College and the Education faculty of Monash University, in Melbourne and 10–week units on the Holocaust in the History departments of both Sydney and Melbourne universities. Within politics, history, sociology, religious studies, multicultural studies, education courses and inter-disciplinary centers, there is also teaching about Judaism, the Jews and Israel, including case studies and assignments.

The community's concern and involvement in these courses has been motivated by the desire to provide opportunities for Jewish study for the large number of tertiary Jewish students and to provide the next stage in the educational ladder for pupils completing secondary education in day schools. A large proportion of tertiary students have attended day schools, and the majority of Mt. Scopus graduates, for instance, have passed the final public examinations required for university entrance in the subject of Hebrew (which includes history). Nevertheless, while some 55–70% of Jews in the 18–22 age group attend higher educational institutions, very few enroll in Jewish studies and even fewer obtain their BA in this field. At Melbourne University, of an estimated 600 Jewish students, only some 2% take double majors in Jewish studies and only 3% take a Jewish studies major such as Hebrew, with a second major in another department or faculty. However, some 5–6% do enroll in single subjects or minor sequences, and numbers are significantly augmented by part-time enrollments and by older students in single subjects or post-graduate research.

One explanation is the perception of university education as career preparation, and most Jewish students gravitate toward careers in the independent professions, e.g. medicine, law, economics, dentistry and engineering. If communal or Jewish teaching career is the objective, many students prefer to study overseas, in Israel or the United States, and they receive encouragement from communal and overseas institutions. Many of those who do study in Australia do not want to be dependent solely on employment by the Jewish community and so prefer an education which will prepare for another career as well. Another explanation is that many day school graduates, after ten or twelve years of schooling, regard the content of the tertiary Judaic courses as too close to the school curriculum they have completed.

Within the framework of continuing education programs those departments which teach Jewish studies also offer short courses in Jewish history. Beginners' and Intermediate Hebrew, Jewish Literature, and single lectures or short courses on, for example, the Old Testament, Ancient Israel, and the Jewish religion are offered by staff or visiting overseas lecturers. These are open to the community at large, and form a basic component of informal Jewish education for adults.

Adult and informal education is provided in Sydney also by Shalom College, located at the University of New South Wales, which is the only Jewish residential college in Australian universities. It is not a teaching college, but it does provide informal Jewish educational programs as well as religious and cultural activities for its resident students, the overall Jewish student body and the adult Sydney community. As the location and often sponsor of national academic and communal conferences, the college functions as a country-wide Jewish institution for adult education.

Dor Hemshech

Zionist education for the 25–40 age group is mainly dealt with by the Young Leadership Group of the United Israel Appeal. Although primarily concerned with fundraising, the group is also involved in non-party Young Leadership education with the support of a *shaliach* in Australia specifically for that purpose.

Zionist and communal leadership courses are conducted by the various state Zionist Councils and their member organizations, by State Boards of Deputies and by Zionist youth movements and tertiary student organizations. Most of these courses are directed at the 18–25 age group: the 25–40 age group learns from experience in communal organizations and information-gathering visits to Israel rather than formal local adult education programs.

Jewish Organizations

Almost every Jewish religious, cultural, service, and even social and sporting organization includes in its activities cultural programs and functions which may be termed Jewish adult education. Some of these activities are restricted to the organization's members; many are open to the whole Jewish community.

The main organizational sponsors of adult education are:

- religious organizations, which include synagogues, and in Melbourne, the *kollel* which, in conjunction with the Yeshiva Center, was established specifically as an adult Torah education center. Activities range from synagogue sermons and lectures to study courses on contemporary religious issues, the Jewish household and childrearing laws;
- women's organizations, of which the major ones are the Women's International Zionist Organization (WIZO), the National Council of Jewish Women (NCJW), *Mizrachi-Emunah, Na'amat* and their component bodies. Synagogue ladies' auxiliaries and school mothers' clubs also have a cultural and informal role in adult education;
- Zionist organizations, which range from state Zionist Councils and their constituent bodies to Hebrew language clubs such as *Brit Ivrit Olamit*. Activities include lectures, forums and debates, *Yom Yerushalayim* and *Yom Ha'atzmaut* commemorations; Hebrew language classes and the maintenance of a resource center with materials about Israel, Jews, Judaism and Zionism;
- service organizations such as *B'nai B'rith*, the various state Jewish Welfare Societies, Jewish veteran service men's organizations and the Young Men's Hebrew Association (YMHA);
- community centers, which include social clubs like the *Hakoah* Club in Sydney and the Northeastern Jewish Center in Melbourne. Yiddish cultural and adult education activities in Melbourne are mainly centered around *Kadimah* and its facilities, which include a Yiddish library, a Yiddish theatre and a cinema specializing in Israeli and Yiddish films;
- the Jewish Museum of Australia, located in Melbourne, which arranges exhibitions of Judaica and Jewish life, sponsors lectures, and produces audio-visual programs; and the Holocaust Museum, also recently established in Melbourne; and
- the Jewish press: the *Sydney Jewish Times* and the *Australian Jewish News* in Melbourne both devote a significant proportion of their space to

syndicated news of Jewish importance and to reprinting of articles from the Israeli, American and English press;

– government-sponsored ethnic radio and multicultural television stations have also made possible the development of systematic Jewish adult education via the media. The Jewish community radio programs in English, Yiddish and Hebrew in Melbourne and Sydney cover Jewish cultural and artistic activities as well as the main government and three commercial stations; they broadcast contemporary Israeli films and documentaries dealing with topics of Jewish interest such as Judaism, the Holocaust, Israel and contemporary Jewish life;

– the considerable number of organizations established locally to support institutions in Israel, such as the various Friends of Israeli universities, conduct functions for the wider Jewish community with local and overseas guest speakers, film evenings, etc.;

– parent education courses, conducted by school mothers' clubs, parent and teacher associations, former student associations and women's organizations, usually take the form of single lectures or discussions on topics like childrearing, and awareness-raising about educational issues. They rarely include Jewish education.

The Melbourne Jewish Survey of 1968 found that most adults expect Jewish adult education to teach either about contemporary events related to Jewish life and Israel, or Hebrew language skills. There was a tendency for younger adults to prefer Hebrew language classes and older adults to prefer topics of Jewish historical, current and Zionist interest. Almost one-half of those interviewed did not regard adult education as a necessity, and very few at that time actually attended classes. Since then, however, heightened Jewish consciousness after 1967 have increased interest in adult education. While statistics are not available, the proliferation of facilities suggests a corresponding increase in participants. The Jewish press, for instance, has a reading audience of some 50% to 75% of Jewish families in Melbourne and Sydney, and Jewish ethnic radio reaches a wide and increasing listening audience.

Jewish adults also participate in programs offered for the general Australian public by groups such as the Council of Adult Education in Melbourne. The courses offered include some with specific Jewish relevance – Jewish history, literature, and the Arab-Israel conflict – which attract both Jews and non-Jews.

The development of adult education has accompanied the emergence of day schools, but there is unlikely to be a causal connection – it is more probable that both the day school and the adult education movements are responses to national trends as well as to factors such as increased Jewish consciousness. Still, the proportion of day school graduates participating in adult education, at both the development and the recipient levels is increasing.

Adult education as part of the total Jewish education system has received little serious consideration. Its role at least in part is the development of an informed Jewish public, capable of understanding their Jewishness, withstanding anti-Jewish attacks and presenting the case for Israel and Jews to the general public and specific interest groups.

Implications

Research Implications

Jewish education in Australia has attracted some research interest. Much of this research falls into the following categories:
- historical studies of Jewish education in Australia;
- education as a sub-topic of Jewish community surveys;
- studies of individual schools – historical, sociological, anthropological;
- studies of the contemporary day school movement in Australia;
- comparative studies of Jewish and other non-government schools;
- studies of immigrant Jewish children, such as Soviet adolescents, including their education;
- studies of the effectiveness of Jewish schooling on Jewish identification;
- curriculum studies, including research on specific subjects of Jewish studies;
- studies of the Jewish school culture, including cross-cultural research;
- linguistic studies, e.g. of Hebrew second language competence among secondary students.

Nevertheless, broader and more systematic research is necessary. There is a basic need for data collection, dealing with statistics in all areas of Jewish education, curriculum, school organization and administration, and pedagogy, including teaching methods and styles. While considerable information is available about some schools, little is known about others.

Achievements and effectiveness evaluations of Jewish education are also areas for future research. The vast majority of parents claim, despite their complaints, that they are satisfied with their children's Jewish education in terms of achievement level of factual knowledge and the development of Jewish identification. Conversely, among the minority of dissatisfied parents the main complaint has been the poor level of Jewish knowledge acquired, poor teaching and poor organization. However, many parents have no clear criteria by which to assess Jewish education other than subjective impressions and hearsay. The day school movement as a whole has usually been evaluated quantitatively in terms of enrollment, number of schools, and the number of day school graduates who enroll their own children in day schools. Such quantitative data alone do not provide the basis for valid qualitative judgements about the achievements and effectiveness of schools. Researchers should also clarify the philosophy of Australian-Jewish education. Educational planning, development and reform involve clearly formulated interpretations of the nature, function and objectives of Jewish education in this country.

There is not enough research on curriculum and pedagogic issues such as teaching methods and styles, classroom interaction, and integrated vs. concurrent studies. Sociological and psychological studies, such as the school as a social organization, the class as a social system, and the school as a Jewish socialization agent, would be useful areas for research.

Most of the existing projects on Jewish education are individual, isolated studies motivated by the personal interest of the researcher. Neither the community nor the Jewish schools, individually or collectively, have been much involved in the encouragement, initiation, support or coordination of this research, nor has it been utilized by them.

Policy Implications

Affluent societies can afford *laissez-faire* growth. However, if Jewish schools are threatened – in particular by possible declining potential and by economic recessions – then a policy based on rationalized and articulated approach to Jewish educational development may be indicated for the future. At present, within the day school movement, there is considerable rivalry, individualism and self-interest. As a reflection of communal pluralism, the *ad hoc* development of schools has fostered educational diversity but practical circumstances may compel the Jewish schools to develop, cooperate and coordinate on an institutional, state and national basis.

In establishing Jewish education facilities, the Australian Jewish communities have thus far accepted traditional views of education as an intellectual activity, and have catered only to the academic Jewish and secular education of 'normal' children. However, increasing numbers of pupils in academically-oriented day schools are seeking education with options other than university studies, and increasing numbers of parents are demanding concurrent Jewish and secular education for their disabled, handicapped or mildly retarded children.

Accordingly, future policy developments may well involve different types of Jewish education for different types of Jewish pupils. Whether such policy developments will involve integrated or segregated institutions, modification of existing schools or the establishment of new, small, special type schools remains to be seen. That such developments will require consideration however, is clear from the fact that Jewish children requiring technical, vocational or special education today are obliged to attend non-Jewish schools.

Finally, Jewish education is not limited to the education of children; it is an activity and a community enterprise which, ideally, involves all Jews from the cradle to the grave. The educational enterprise should develop and encourage Jewish education at all stages and levels of formal and informal education, so that the Jewish school and adult Jewish education will strengthen and complement each other to promote a knowledgeable, committed and creative Jewish community.

Acknowledgements

I am indebted to Mr. W. Lippmann for supplying information about the 1976 and 1981 Censuses, and to Mr. P. Symons, President of Mt. Scopus College, for details on enrollments in existing Australian Jewish day schools.

References

"Analysis of 1976 Census" (1981). *Victorian Jewish Board of Deputies Annual Report 1981.* Melbourne, pp. 58–69.

Bergman, G.F.J. and Levi, J.S. (1974). *Australian Genesis: Jewish Convicts and Settlers, 1788–1850.* Rigby, Sydney.

Bullivant, B.M. (1975). *Competing Values and Traditions in an Orthodox Jewish Day School: a Study of Enculturation Dissonance.* Unpublished Ph.D. dissertation, Monash University, Melbourne.

Bullivant, B.M. (1978). *The Way of Tradition.* ACER Research Series No. 113, Melbourne.

Caplan, S. (1974). *The Jewish Day School in New South Wales.* Unpublished M.Ed. thesis, University of Sydney.

Chazan, B. (1970). *Jewish Schooling and Jewish Identification in Melbourne.* The Institute of Contemporary Jewry, The Hebrew University of Jerusalem, Israel.

Encel, S., and Buckley, B. (1978). *The New South Wales Jewish Community: A Survey.* New South Wales University Press, Sydney.

Getzler, T. (1970). *Neither Toleration nor Favour: The Australian Chapter of Jewish Emancipation.* Melbourne University Press, Melbourne.

Lippmann, W. (1966). "The Demography of Australian Jewry", *The Jewish Journal of Sociology,* Vol. VIII, no. 2, pp. 213–239.

Lippmann, W. (1969). "Australian Jewry in 1966", *The Jewish Journal of Sociology*, Vol. XI, no. 1, pp. 67–73.

Lippmann, W. (n.d.). *Australian Jewry Five Years Later*. Federation of Australian Jewish Welfare Societies, Melbourne.

Medding, P.Y. (1968). *From Assimilation to Group Survival: A Political and Sociological Study of an Australian Jewish Community*. Cheshire, Melbourne.

Medding, P.Y., ed. (1973). *Jews in Australian Society*. Macmillan and Monash University, Melbourne.

Patkin, B. (1972). *Heritage and Tradition, The Emergence of Mount Scopus College*. Hawthorne Press, Melbourne.

Schools Commission in association with The Australian Bureau of Statistics (1979). *Australian Students and their Schooling*. Commonwealth of Australia, Canberra.

Solomon, G. (1970). *Report on Teacher-Training for Jewish Education in Australia*. Melbourne. (Typescript).

Solomon, G. (1972). *Minority Education in a Free Society: A Community History of Jewish Education in New South Wales and Victoria 1788–1920*. Monash University, Melbourne.

Solomon, G. (1973). "Jewish Education in Australia", in: Medding, P.Y., ed., *Jews in Australian Society*. Macmillan and Monash University, Melbourne.

Solomon, G. (1978;1979). "Jewish Schools in Australia", in: *Half a Million Children: Studies in Non-Government Education in Australia*. Longman, Australia; republished in Medding, P.Y. and Solomon, G., *The Jews in Australia: Tefutsot Israel*, Vol. 17, no. 2, Jerusalem (Hebrew).

Solomon, G. (1980). "Jewish Identity in Australia", *Forum*, no. 37.

Solomon, G. (1982a). "Teaching about Israel in Australia". Paper presented to International Workshop on Contemporary Jewish Civilization, International Center for University Teaching of Jewish Civilization, Jerusalem.

Solomon, G. (1982b). "Whither Tertiary Jewish Education". Lecture to Young Men's Hebrew Association, Melbourne.

Solomon, G. and Overberg, H. (1982). "Inter-ethnic Modelling and Group Relations in Australia". Paper presented to National Conference on Ethnic Politics, Australian National University, Canberra.

Steinkalk, E. (1982). *The Adaptation of Soviet Jews in Victoria: A Study of Adolescent Immigrants and Their Parents*. Unpublished Ph.D. dissertation, Monash University, Melbourne.

Taft, R. (1965). *From Stranger to Citizen*. University of Western Australian Press, Perth.

Taft, R. (1972). "Ethnic Groups", in: F.J. Hunt, Angus Robertson, eds. Socialization in Australia.

Taft, R. and Solomon, G. (1974). "The Melbourne Jewish Community and the Middle East War of 1973". *The Jewish Journal of Sociology*, Vol. 16, no. 1, pp. 57–73.

Waller, L. (1976). "In the Tents of Japheth: Jews in Australian Universities". Report of Symposium on Australian Jewry in the Next Twenty-Five Years. Executive Council of Australian Jewry, Melbourne.

Part Six

Muslim Countries

This part of the book discusses two formerly prominent and large Jewish communities in Muslim countries – Iran and Morocco. These communities lost most of their Jewish populations over the last four decades through extensive emigration. The relatively small communities remaining are influenced by the vicissitudes of Israeli-Arab relations, and by trends in local nationalism. International Jewish educational organizations, like the Alliance Israélite Universelle and ORT have played a large role in building and staffing Jewish schools in these countries.

The chapters in this part are much less comprehensive and detailed than in the previous ones. Moreover, we do not have coverage of all of the relevant countries. Turkey, for example, today has a larger Jewish population than Morocco, but historically was not as prominent.

Amnon Netzer, Professor of Iranian Studies at the Hebrew University of Jerusalem, presents here a historical outline of the development of Jewish education in Iran. Shlomo Philipson, an educational consultant for one of the major international Jewish educational organizations, presents a brief up-to-date account of Jewish education in Morocco.

13

Jewish Education in Iran

Amnon Netzer

Jewish and general education among the Jews of Iran has never been thoroughly researched. It is a complicated subject, part of whose importance lies in the interest in uncovering an educational-cultural portrait of this ancient and little-known community. We would like, for example, to learn the background to the brief statement of Rabbi Petachia of Ratisbon (12th century), that: "There is no one so ignorant in the whole of Babylon, Assyria, Media and Persia, but he knows the twenty-four books, the punctuation, the grammar, the superfluous and omitted letters; for the precentor does not read the Law, but he that is called up to the scroll of the Law reads himself" (Benisch, 1856, p. 15). And we would like to know the educational and cultural background of a community from whose ranks rose such intriguing and controversial personalities as Abu 'Isa al-Isfahani (8th century?), Hiwi of Balkh (second half of the 10th century), Binyamini ben Moshe Nehavandi (mid-9th century), Daniyal ben Moshe al-Qumisi (end of the 9th and early 10th century); outstanding poets such as Shahin (died after 1359), 'Imrani (died after 1536); and mystics such as Sarmad of Kashan (died 1661)[1] and Siman-Tov Melammed of Meshed (died 1828?).

An in-depth investigation of Jewish and general education among the Jews of Iran would require the study of manuscripts bequeathed to us by the Jews of that land. This article makes no claim to assume so weighty a mission, but will deal, in brief, with a few aspects of the history, significance and role of education among the Jews of Iran.

Nineteenth Century to World War I

Since the Jewish population was scattered over wide areas of the Kingdom of Iran and very loose connections existed between one Jewish community and another, there was no united Jewish community in terms of educational organization. It is possible, however, to discern trends in traditional Jewish education which were common to the various communities throughout Iran. Jewish education was, first and foremost, religious in character, based on the reading and study of sacred texts, the repetition of prayers and the obser- vance of Jewish festivals. The special character of the Jewish religion, with its ordered calendar cycle binding the individual to the Jewish people and its history, was inextricably interwoven with the Jew's own life-cycle, from birth to the day he died, making it necessary for the Jewish boy, at least, to acquire a Jewish religious education.

From reports of the impressions of 19th century travellers and emissaries to Iran, it seems that apart from a handful of rabbis and doctors, the commu- nity was not well-endowed with intellectuals in the Jewish sphere. In all of Iran, there was not one yeshiva capable of training a generation of rabbis on a fitting level. All the Jewish communities in Iran suffered from a serious shortage of properly-educated teachers and educational material. In most cases, sacred texts were supplied by travellers and *shadarim* (emissaries from the Holy Land sent to collect charitable donations), by merchants or by returning pilgrims (members of the local community returning from the Land of Israel), and travellers returning from Turkey, Iraq or other countries.

Pupils generally began their studies at the age of four and ceased Jewish education at bar mitzvah. In most cases, their education lacked real content and was endured rather than enjoyed. Lessons were given at the teacher's home or in the synagogue, where pupils of all ages and levels congregated in the same classroom, or *maktab*, where they learned to read and write. Often, the local rabbi served as teacher, assisted by older pupils who taught the beginners.

In general, there was no pre-determined program of studies, but appar- ently in many communities there was an accepted order according to which children were taught. The pupils first learned the letters and their formation into words; they learned to read the weekly Torah portion with its accompa- nying translation and commentary (*tafsir*).[2] In the higher classes, pupils learned to read the Books of the Prophets and the Writings, with the appro- priate *tafsir* for each, and they listened to sermons seasoned with tales from the Agada and Midrash. At first, pupils learned prayers by rote but over the years they delved deeper into their meaning.

The study of Talmud was not an important part of the curriculum, other than a few tractates of the Mishnah, such as *Pirkei Avoth*. For the most part, the *maktab* allowed no intellectual discussion, and the pupils chanted their lessons, repeating in chorus the words of their teachers. Pupils who misbe- haved or who lagged behind in their lessons suffered corporal punishment, while outstanding pupils were encouraged by their teacher and the commu- nity. A student who sought to continue his studies had to rely mainly on his own resources. There were dictionaries available for Biblical words, which contained the Judeo-Persian[3] translation of the difficult words in the Bible and Mishnah, in order of their appearance in the Bible and the various tractates. Some of the scholars who rose from the ranks of the various communities were self-taught, apart from the sons of rabbis who studied for the rabbinate with their fathers. Some of these took an interest in aspects of the human experience, that is, they not only studied the works of the religious philosophers, but also secular philosophy. In the 1860s, the French ambassador to Iran, Gobineau, met such scholars, of whom he writes: "The Jews have doctors, some of whom, in the course of their studies in Talmud and philsophy, have become very knowledgeable. I was astonished when one of these scholars spoke to me with admiration of Spinoza and asked me to enlighten him on the doctrine of Kant" (Gobineau, 1928, p. 52).

The teacher received his salary both in money and in goods, according to the parents' ability to pay. Poor pupils were educated free of charge. A few pupils, mainly the sons or other relatives of the teacher, continued their studies after reaching bar mitzvah age. Most children discontinued their studies, either because of learning difficulties or their family's economic situation and entered the work force in order to contribute to the family's livelihood.

At first glance, the educational-cultural world of Iranian Jewy seems to lack content and depth. This was also the impression received by travellers and Jewish emissaries (*shadarim*) who visited the Jewish communities in Iran during the 19th century. The reality, however, was different. Although far from the mainstream of intensive Torah and Talmudic study, Jewish cultural life in Iran was rich and varied. Beside sacred texts, the Iranian Jews had a magnificent literary tradition, peculiar to their community. This principally comprised poetic works in Judeo-Persian and covered a wide range of sacred and secular subjects. The Jew who had learned only to distinguish the characters of the Hebrew alphabet was able to read these works which were written in a language he understood. It was difficult to find a Jewish house in Iran which did not possess manuscripts containing the monumental works of the community's poets (Netzer, 1982). They wrote Biblical stories and homiletical commentary in Judeo-Persian and even attempted enthralling secular tales. In addition, the works of the great Iranian poets, such as 'Attar, Sa'di, Rumi, Hafez and others, which were transliterated from Persian to Hebrew characters, enriched the cultural world of the Jews of Iran. This aspect of Iranian Jewry was neither known to, nor understood by, the travellers and emissaries of the 19th century, nor even by those, including emissaries of the Alliance Israélite Universelle, who came into contact with the Jewish communities of Iran during the 20th century.

The 19th century was without doubt one of the most difficult and traumatic periods in the history of Iranian Jewry, a period in which the community reached its lowest ebb in almost all aspects of life. Continuous persecution over many generations caused psychological traumas to members of the community. In certain communities, principally those of Teheran, Hamadan,

Kashan and the surrounding regions, thousands of Jews were unable to stand up to their persecutors and abandoned the faith of their fathers. Throughout the Islamic countries, there is no parallel to the rate of apostasy among the Jews of Iran during this period.

Nevertheless, it was rare to find Jewish children who did not know how to read and write Hebrew or who did not know the basics of Judaism, although many of them were not very proficient. Inability to read the weekly portion of the Law and ignorance of the prayers were considered a shame to one's family; according to one of the community elders, families refused to give their daughters in marriage to boys who could not read and write Hebrew (Levi, 1960, p. 667). It was against this socio-educational background, with the Jews of Iran struggling desperately for both their physical and cultural survival, that the Alliance representatives became involved in the community's education.

As soon as the Alliance schools were opened in Baghdad early in 1865, the Alliance institutions in Paris began discussing the possibility of opening schools in Teheran and other towns throughout Iran (Leven, 1911). From 1865 there was correspondence between Iranian Jewry and the central committee of the Alliance in Paris, often via the Alliance institutions in Baghdad (Cohen, 1981). These letters dealt with the political, legal and economic position of the Jews and from time to time succeeded in bringing about the diplomatic involvement of European agencies, especially those of France and England, to save the Jews from their oppressors. This intervention included financial assistance, especially in times of plague and famine. However, the principal and oft-repeated demand of the Iranian Jews, for the establishment of Alliance schools in Iran, failed to bring about any positive results.

An important turning point in the relations between the Alliance and the Jews of Iran occurred around the summer of 1873, when the ruler of Iran, Nasser al-Din Shah (ruled 1848–96) made his historic journey to Europe. Representatives of the local Jewish communities in the capital cities of those countries visited by the Shah – Amsterdam, Berlin, London, Paris, Istanbul and Rome – approached him with requests that he do all in his power to improve the miserable lot of the Jews of Iran. The most important of these historic meetings took place in Paris on 12 July 1873, between the King, his Prime Minister and Foreign Minister on the one hand, and the Alliance delegation headed by Crémieux, on the other (Alliance Israélite Universelle, 1873).

Nor were the Jews of Iran idle. As soon as they learned of the negotiations between the Shah and the Alliance central committee in Paris concerning the establishment of schools in Iran, a few Jews from Teheran organized themselves and, on their own initiative, founded a school in Teheran. The French Ambassador to Iran reported on this initiative early in 1875 to the Alliance central committee, essentially in the following terms: there is a Jewish population numbering 1,800 in Teheran; they need someone capable not only of teaching their children but also of protecting their interests before the Shah and the government; some 150 children now attend the school where they study Torah, Talmud and the English, French, Turkish and Arabic tongues, as well as reading and writing in Persian; two or three Jewish teachers in Teheran know Torah and reading and writing in Persian; two teachers give instruction in French at the government school;[4] construction of a school will cost 30,000 Francs and the Jews of Teheran are all poor (Alliance Israélite Universelle, 1875).

We do not know what prevented the Central Committee in Paris from responding to the initiative of the Jews of Teheran in the matter of establishing a school. Alliance claims of budgetary difficulties do not seem serious in the light of the effort they invested in other countries in the Middle East, North Africa and Eastern Europe.[5] On Shah Nasser al-Din's third visit to Europe (1889), the Alliance central committee did not display the same enthusiasm it had shown in 1873 with regard to the establishment of schools in Iran. At a meeting in London between the leaders of the Jewish Community in England and the Shah in 1889, the subject of opening Alliance schools in Iran did not receive proper attention; this time, the Shah was asked to permit his Jewish subjects to attend state schools (Anglo-Jewish Association, 1889/90). Such a request could not, of course, be granted, as no Muslim school could admit Jews, who were 'impure' in the eyes of the Shiite Muslim population.

In the light of increasing missionary activity in the 1870s, especially in Teheran, Hamadan and Isfahan, it was felt that the establishment of schools should not be neglected. On the initiative of the young Jews and with funds donated by local Jews, a school was established in Teheran in 1897, and served as the basis for the establishment, a year later, of the first Alliance school (Confino, c. 1946, p. 60).

In establishing and running schools in the cities of Iran, the Alliance emissaries met with a certain amount of opposition on the part of teacher-rabbis, who feared for the loss of their livelihood and spiritual authority. There was also some opposition from those parents who did not want their daughters to study modern subjects. For the most part however, the public was enthusiastic and within a few years, the Alliance had established schools in Teheran, Hamadan, Isfahan, Shiraz, Sanandaj and Kermanshah, and was supporting community schools in other towns as well (Confino, ibid.). The Alliance schools were established by permission of the Shah, the government and other authorities, and in a few cases, there was even active participation on the part of official Iranian agencies. On the establishment of the Alliance school in Teheran, the Shah donated 200 Tuman (1,000 French Francs) in order to express his satisfaction with the educational enterprise being undertaken in his country (Alliance Israélite Universelle, 1898, p. 65).

TABLE 1.   THE STATUS OF ALLIANCE SCHOOLS IN SIX COMMUNITIES IN
THE YEAR EACH WAS ESTABLISHED – IRAN, 1898–1904

City	Jewish Population	Year of Establishment	Pupils		Teachers[a]
			Male	Female	
Teheran[b]	5,100	1898	350	200	6
Hamadan[c]	5,000	1900	346	215	9
Isfahan[d]	6,000	1901	345	125	12
Shiraz[e]	5,000	1903	350	85	9
Sanandaj[f]	3,000	1903	225	100	6
Kermanshah[g]	1,400	1904	205	45	7

(a)   The number of teachers for both boys and girls, including teachers of handicraft.
(b)   BAIU, 1er et 2e semestre, 1898, pp. 129ff.
(c)   BAIU, 1900, pp. 143–149.
(d)   BAIU, 1901, PP. 115–140.
(e)   BAIU, 1904, pp. 99–113.
(f)   See under "Seneh" in BAIU, 1903, pp. 185, 198–213.
(g)   BAIU, 1904, pp. 99–133; also BAIU, 1911, pp. 85,99–112. The girls school in Kermanshah was founded in 1911.

The language of instruction in the Alliance schools was French and the program of studies was designed to produce an enlightened, secular and modern-thinking person who would be a loyal and useful citizen of his country. Little attention was paid to Jewish studies, the Hebrew language and the study of Jewish history; these were presented from a secular point of view, as in the Alliance schools in France. In almost every school there were vocational classes in which very small groups of boys and girls learned such trades as carpentry, shoemaking, printing and sewing. Besides the teachers recruited by the Alliance from its own ranks, there were also local Jewish teachers, and the school principals usually taught as well. Apart from these teachers, the staff included 'instructors', whose subject was not specifically defined. All the Alliance schools went only as far as the sixth grade.

Table 1 shows the initial enrollment of Alliance schools in Iran's six major communities encompassing a population of 25,500 people, that is, about half the country's Jewish population (Netzer, 1976). The 2,591 pupils of both sexes who were studying in these schools represented about 10% of the total Jewish population of these towns. However, in 1911, when the Jewish population of the six towns rose to 27,400, the number of pupils dropped to 1,515, that is, to 5.5% of the population (Netzer, 1981). The position of the Alliance schools deteriorated still further during World War I, when communications with the Alliance center in Paris were disrupted, thereby weakening financial support and making recruitment of teachers more difficult.

The Inter-War Period

After the first World War several important changes which took place in the Jewish community and in Iranian society which influenced the state's educational system (Elwell-Sutton, 1941, pp. 119–153; Sadiq, 1957; Banani, 1961, pp. 85–111; Arasteh, 1969). Between 1918 and 1919, Zionist organizations were founded in Teheran and other towns on the initiative of young Jews, most of whom were graduates of Alliance schools (Netzer, 1980b). The Zionist activity prodded the Zionist and community leaders into demanding changes in the curriculum of the Alliance schools, especially for more time devoted to Persian, Hebrew and the history of the Iranian and Jewish peoples and less emphasis on French culture. In 1921, there was a military coup which left a deep impression not only on Iranian society in general but also on Iranian Jewry. Reza Khan, the leader of the coup was an officer in the Iranian army. His chief concerns were the preservation of Iran's political independence and territorial integrity, the unification of the people, 'Iranization' and the secularization of Iranian society as well as its westernization, utilizing a maximum of western technology, combined with the values and symbols of pre-Islamic Iran.

In 1921, after the coup, the High Council of Education was established which laid the foundations for educational reforms in government and private schools throughout the state. The years of study were henceforth divided into six years of elementary school and six years of high school. High school studies, as in France, were divided into two parts, each of three years. In the final year, one could study in one of three trends: humanities, natural science or pure science. Likewise, unified nation-wide final examinations were established for pupils of the 6th, 9th and 12th grades.

In the Alliance schools of Iran pupils still studied only up to 6th grade, so these reforms did not produce any significant change. However, subsequently the Alliance began to lose its status as a superior educational institution, and in some respects its standards actually fell in comparison with government and other private schools throughout the country.[6] There were several reasons for these developments, the principal ones being:

1. As early as 1911, the State had begun to organize teacher-training and about 15 students and teachers were sent each year to educational establishments in Europe and the United States. The first Teachers' Seminary was founded in Teheran in 1918 on the model of the French Ecole Normale, and each year from 1928 onwards, 100 students were sent abroad to teacher-training courses. By 1941, 36 teacher-training colleges had been founded throughout Iran. Teacher-training was always the weak point of the Alliance schools in Iran. Apart from the school principal and his deputy, many teachers – and in some towns, all of them – did not have suitable qualifications. Teachers' salaries at the Alliance schools were considerably lower than those

of their colleagues in non-Jewish schools. This trend accelerated with the ascent to the throne of Reza Khan (1926).

2. From 1928 on, edicts and ordinances were issued whose effect was the Iranization and secularization of the country's educational system together with the weakening and discrediting of foreign schools. The edicts and ordinances issued in 1928, 1932 and 1939 may be summarized as follows:

- pupils in foreign schools must study according to the curriculum proposed by the Ministry of Education in all classes from 1st to 12th grade;
- these schools must cease instructing Muslim pupils in Bible studies;
- these schools may not accept 'Persian pupils' in grades 1 through 6;
- the government would close foreign schools which failed to abide by these edicts and pay compensation.

The first victims of these edicts were the mission schools which were already under Ministry of Education supervision at the beginning of the 1928/29 scholastic year (Arasteh, 1969, pp. 155–171). The Ba'hai schools were closed in October 1934, due to their insistence on observing Ba'hai religious festivals which were not recognized by the state. In 1939 the Armenian schools were closed in order to assimilate this minority group into the Iranian population. The Alliance schools did not suffer in the same way as those mentioned above, but they lost their independence and freedom of action. As early as 1940, with the growth of nationalistic feelings, all foreign teachers were ordered to leave the country – an order of great significance for the Alliance school principals, almost all of whom were French citizens.

3. Because of the reforms in the educational system and Reza Shah's earnest desire to pull down barriers, erase distinctions between the tribes, sects and minority groups and unite them into one nation, members of the religious minorities, including Jews, were permitted to attend government schools. Many Jews, mainly those from well-to-do families, preferred to send their children to government or private schools and even to schools run by the Americans and the British in Teheran, Isfahan[7] and other cities, because they considered the educational level of Alliance schools and their pupils to be of a low standard.

4. An additional factor which increased the Jews' desire to study in non-Jewish schools was the prevailing spirit of nationalism in Iran at the time. Despite differences in the history of the Jewish and Iranian peoples, many Jews saw in Iran's distant past an integral part of the history of the Jewish people, especially since the historic image of Iran (Media and Persia) appears in a positive light in the Bible and Talmud, as compared with other nations. The Jews earnestly desired to appear Iranian and to be identified with the values and symbols of Iranian nationalism while remaining within the Jewish faith. They loved Persian poetry and literature, enjoyed Persian music, celebrated Iran's national festivals with enthusiasm, changed their Jewish names to Iranian names and gloried in Iran's pre-Islamic past. The Jews of Iran were

not faced with nationalistic Zionist challenge, as Zionist activity had been declared illegal and remained insignificant throughout the period of Reza Shah until his overthrow in August 1941 (Netzer, 1979).

5. During World War II, France suffered serious military setbacks, dealing the Alliance educational network a severe blow in Iran and other countries. Financial assistance from France came to an end and the Jews of Iran, the vast majority of whom were poor, could not finance their children's education on their own. Welcome assistance of the Joint Distribution Committee prevented the total collapse of the Alliance, which had been a symbol of Jewish grandeur and pride in Iran. Nevertheless, the Alliance schools had difficulty attracting Jews who wished to receive an adequate education; throughout Iran, not one of these schools offered an education up to 12th grade. The first school in which it was possible to study from elementary through high school was not opened in Teheran until 1950/51.

In 1948, when Israel gained independence and most of Iran's 90,000 Jews prepared to emigrate and settle there, 20 Alliance schools were functioning in Iran, with an enrollment of 6,612 pupils (*Les Cahiers*, 1948, p. 3). It is estimated that over 10,000 Jewish pupils attended Jewish community schools and non-Jewish schools.

Jewish Education Since World War II

After World War II three important changes took place in Jewish education in Iran:

1. In 1946/47, the *Otzar HaTorah* schools were opened in Teheran and other Iranian cities. These were well-funded, well-staffed and highly motivated. But *Otzar HaTorah* made its appearance at an inauspicious time. From the fall of Reza Shah until 1946, the Jewish youth of Iran had had 5 years of Zionist activity. Moreover, most of the emissaries from Israel belonged to the secular-socialist movement which saw the activities of the anti-Zionist *Agudat Yisrael* as sabotaging Zionism and aliyah to the Land of Israel.[8] On the other hand, the more traditional parents saw in the emissaries and *halutzim* elements which were detrimental to the values of the traditional-patriarchal society of Iran, with its ethnic groups and communities. These emissaries sought to bring girls out of the ghettoes to mingle with boys, conducted mixed hora dancing sessions, lessons and seminars, and displayed a certain disdain for the customs of the community, even going so far as to strike at the religious and moral values sacred to most of its members.[9] Against this background, by means of a struggle and by utilizing the rifts between the two groups, Rabbi Yitzhak Meir Levi,[10] of *Agudat Yisrael*, succeeded in founding a broad network of *Otzar HaTorah* schools, known in Persian as *Ganj-e Danesh*.

2. Given the great wave of emigration to Israel which swept the Jews of Iran in the 1950s, most of the emigrants being poor and unskilled; the economic prosperity which Iran enjoyed in the 1960s and 1970s; and the rise to wealth of a large segment of the remaining Jewish community, more attention was devoted to education. This was expressed mainly in the establishment of new community schools and more active participation in the budgeting of the Alliance schools. However, the educational level of the Jewish schools still remained questionable, due to the lack of trained and qualified teachers.[11] Many teachers were forced to manage on salaries considerably lower than the national average of their colleagues, which was also not particularly high.

3. The proportion of Jewish pupils who graduated from high schools and universities rose in comparison to Muslim pupils. In particular, a larger number of Jewish girls finished high school and university. It is estimated that about 4,000 Jewish students attended universities in Iran and abroad during the 1976/77 scholastic year, constituting 5% of the entire Jewish population and 4% of the student population of Iran,[12] even though the Jewish community in that year constituted less than 0.25% of the country's total population.

TABLE 2.   JEWISH EDUCATION STATISTICS – IRAN, 1977/78

Location	Jewish Population	No. of Schools	No. of Pupils
	Otzar HaTorah[a]		
Teheran	60,000	11	2,000
Shiraz	10,000	3	1,150
Rezaiyeh	250	1	170
Abadan	1,000	1	150
Kerman	500	1	110
	Alliance Israélite Universelle		
Teheran	60,000	7	1,800 (Jews?)
Hamadan	300	1	650 (45 Jews)
Isfahan	3,000	1	450 (all Jews)
Kermanshah	1,500	1	350 (180 Jews)
Yezd	400	1	160 (all Jews)
Borojard	500	1	145 (100 Jews)
Sanandaj	500	1	140 (40 Jews)

(a)   Most of the *Otzar HaTorah* schools contain 6 grades, although some contain 9, and the school in Shiraz teaches through grade 12.

In 1977/78, one year before the upsurge of demonstrations against the Shah in Iran, 11,000 pupils, out of an estimated total Jewish population of 80,000, studied in 38 Jewish schools in Teheran and the smaller towns. In addition to schools associated with *Otzar HaTorah* and the Alliance (Table 2), other schools in Teheran and Shiraz included:[13]

- the Ettefaq School founded in Teheran in 1946 by Jewish immigrants from Iraq.[14] Until 1955, the language of tuition in this school was English. In 1977/78, it had an enrollment of 1,160 in 12 grades;

- the Koresh School established in 1931 on the initiative of the Jewish community in Teheran. In 1977/78, about 700 Jewish and 50 non-Jewish pupils attended its 12 grades. In the past, there were Koresh community schools in other cities as well, but they closed when the Jews emigrated to Israel;

- the Abrishami School founded in Teheran in 1966 by the philanthropist Abrishami. In 1977/78, 300 pupils attended its 6 grades. A kindergarten was attached to the school.

- the Ruhi-Shad School founded in 1965 by a neighborhood committee in the center of Teheran. Its 6 grades were attended by 160 pupils in 1977/78;

TABLE 3.   JEWISH EDUCATION STATISTICS – TEHERAN, 1979/80–1981/82

Name of School	No. of Schools		No. of Jewish Pupils		No. of non-Jewish Pupils
	1979/80	1981/82	1979/80	1981/82	1981/82
Total	16	15	4,274	2,174	3,222
Otzar HaTorah	7	9	1,700	1,122	1,070
Alliance	4	3	721	457	812
Ettefaq	1	1	400	535	665
ORT	1	1	490	25	600
Koresh (girls)	1	35	75		
Koresh (boys)[a]	1	?	450	?	?
Abrishami	1	350			
Ruhi-Shad	1	163			

(a)   *Shofar*, the monthly journal of the Los Angeles Iranian Jewish Federation, refers to 18 schools; information about the Koresh Boys' Schools, the Abrishami and Ruhi-Shad schools is not clear. The third issue of *Shofar* includes a news item (p.2) according to which the name of the Koresh School was changed to Tabataba'i School, in honor of a Shiite religious leader (Iranian Jewish Federation, 1982).

- an ORT school established in 1950 with 2 branches, one each in Isfahan and Shiraz. This was a vocational school attended in 1977/78 by about 1,000 pupils, 20% of whom were non-Jews; ,
- the Sheybani School established in the Shiraz ghetto with 5 grades attended by about 250 pupils.

With the overthrow of the monarchy and the establishment of the Islamic Republic in Iran, about half of the Jewish population left the country, most for the United States and some for Israel. The greatest exodus was from Teheran. The status of education during the 1979/80 scholastic year in this city, whose Jewish population fell to an estimated 25,000, is illustrated in Table 3.

According to sources within the Jewish community (Iranian Jewish Federation, 1982, p. 2), in the 1980/81 scholastic year, 2,914 Jewish pupils and a total 3,643 non-Jewish pupils attended 18 Jewish schools in Teheran. The breakdown of pupils for the 1981/82 scholastic year appears in Table 3.

The following schools are forced to conduct classes on Jewish Sabbaths and holidays: the Suleiman Haim School, with 50 Jewish and 220 non-Jewish pupils, affiliated to *Otzar HaTorah*; one of the three Alliance schools, with 90 Jewish and 410 non-Jewish pupils; the Koresh girls' school and the ORT school (Iranian Jewish Federation, 1982).

Conclusion

These statistics tell us nothing about the quality of education, the level of instruction, pedagogic methods, textbooks or the problem of overcrowding in the classrooms. Under the present regime of the Islamic Republic, it is impossible to conduct a comprehensive and thorough investigation of all the questions connected with the education system of the Jewish community. What seems apparent is that *Otzar HaTorah* is gradually replacing the Alliance. It is possible that this suits the general atmosphere in the country, that of a search for redemption through religion.

Whatever criticism one may level at the Alliance and its treatment of education for the Jewish community for over 80 years, one must admit that at least during the first two decades of this century, Iranian Jewry owes its intellectual development to the Alliance schools. The Alliance also did much toward the physical salvation of the Jews from the hands of their persecutors and their spiritual salvation from Christian and Ba'hai missionaries.

Notes

Note: This article is partly based on Netzer (1981).

1. At some stage in his life he converted to Islam, became a Sufi and wandered as far as India.

2. Tafsir, in its limited sense, means a translation to Juedo-Persian of holy texts. However, many *tafsirim* were not merely translations, but included commentary and explanations of the Hebrew or Aramaic source.

3. Works written by Iranian Jews in classical Persian with Hebrew characters. This literature has its own special linguistic characteristics.

4. In 1873, a government school for the study of foreign languages was established in Teheran (Elwell-Sutton, 1941, p. 132).

5. Most of these schools were founded in the 1860s and 1870s.

6. A not inconsiderable number of scholars and high-ranking army officers and government officials in Iran attended the Alliance schools; i.e. the outstanding scholar Mohammed Qazwini (died in 1949) and the Chief of Staff who, toward the end of his life, served as Prime Minister, Razmara (assassinated in 1951).

7. Alborz High School in Teheran and Adab High School in Isfahan.

8. The *Otzar HaTorah* emissaries did not adopt a unified position *vis-à-vis* Zionism. The local emissaries reflected positive attitudes toward Zionist activities for the establishment of a state, but opposed *Hehalutz* activities in Iran (*Otzar HaTorah*, 1959).

9. See interviews with the leaders of *Hehalutz* and emissaries of the Jewish Agency in Iran – Nathan Shadi, Shimon Hanasab, Aharon Kohen and Siyon Rokni. These interviews, conducted by Esther Kanka, may be found in the Oral History Division of the Institute of Contemporary Jewry, Hebrew University of Jerusalem.

10. Yitzhak Meir Levi was a Polish Jew who arrived in Iran in 1941 to organize the dispatch of parcels to rabbis and synagogues in Russia. Controversy surrounds his personality and scholarship.

11. There are also the opposite opinions of persons who regarded the Alliance schools as excellent institutions (Rosen, 1959). Some even claimed that the graduates of Alliance high schools in Hamadan were the most brilliant students in Iran (Vreeland, 1957, p. 273).

12. The statistics presented here are mostly estimates based on meetings with representatives and heads of Jewish institutions in Iran, and on personal field-work surveys during these years. See also the *Statistical Yearbook of Iran* (*Salnameh-e Amari-ye Keshvari*) for 1976, according to which 140,000 students attended Iran's institutes of higher education during 1976, of which about one-third attended post-secondary institutions.

13. These data are derived from persons connected with the educational system in Iran and from Rabbi David Shofet, then the rabbi of the community, now living in Los Angeles as the rabbi of the Iranian Jews in Los Angeles.

14. Most of these were wealthy people who had settled in Iran, mainly in Teheran, in several waves of migration which commenced in 1941. The number of Iraqi Jews in Teheran in 1978 was estimated at about 3,000.

References

Alliance Israélite Universelle (various years). *Bulletin de l'Alliance Israélite Universelle (BAIU)*. Paris.

Anglo-Jewish Association (1889/90). *Report of the Anglo-Jewish Association*. London.

Arasteh, A. (1969). *Education and Social Awakening in Iran 1850–1968*. Leiden.

BAIU. See: Alliance Israélite Universelle.

Banani, A. (1961). *The Modernization of Iran 1921–1941*. Stanford University Press, California.

Benisch, A., translator (1856). *Travels of Rabbi Petachia of Ratisbon*. London.

Les Cahiers (1948). No. 24–25.

Cohen, A. (1981). "Yahasam shel Yehudai Iran le'Haskala Modernit". *Pa'amim*, Vol. 9.

Confino, A. (c.1946). *L'action de l'Alliance Israélite en Perse*. Algiers.

Elwell-Sutton, L.P. (1941). *Modern Iran*. London.

Engelman, U.Z. (1962). *Jewish Education in the Diaspora*. The Hebrew University, Jerusalem. pp. 115–127. (Stencil).

Glanz, J. (1972). *A Study on Jewish Education in Iran*. Teheran. (Stencil).

Gobineau, Comte de (1928). *Les religions et philosophies dans l'Asie Centrale*. Paris.

Iran (1976). *Salnameh-e Amari-ye Keshvari (Statistical Yearbook of Iran)*. Teheran.

Iranian Jewish Federation (1982). *Shofar*, nos. 3, 4. Los Angeles.

Leven, N. (1911). *Cinquante ans d'Histoire d'Alliance Israélite Universelle (1860–1910)*, Tome 1. Paris.

Levi, H. (1960). *Tarikh-e Yahud-e Iran (History of the Jews of Iran)* Vol. 3. Teheran.

Netzer, A. (1974). "The Jews of Persia and Alliance in the late nineteenth century: Some aspects". *International Conference on Jewish Communities in Muslim Lands*. Jerusalem. (Stencil).

Netzer, A. (1976). "Godla shel ha'okhlossiya ha'yehudit be'faras bemeah ha-19". *Divrei HaKongress Ha'olami Lemada'ei Hayahadut*, Vol. 2. Jerusalem. pp. 127–133.

Netzer, A. (1979). "Be'ayot ha'integrazia hatarbutit ha'hevratit ve'hapolitit shel Yehudei Iran". *Gesher*, No. 1/2. pp. 69–83.

Netzer, A. (1980a). "Yehudei Iran, Yisrael ve'harepublika ha'islamit shel Iran". *Gesher*, No. 1–2 (100–101), p. 54.

Netzer, A. (1980b). "Zionism in Iran", in: Davis, M., ed. *Zionism in Transition*. Arno Press, New York. pp. 225–232.

Netzer, A. (1981). "Kavim u'magamot bema'arekhet hahinukh ve'hahora'a be'Iran al reka pe'ilut Kol Yisrael Haverim bashanim 1865–1911", in: Zohari, M., et. al. *Hagut Ivrit be'Arzot Ha'Islam*. Jerusalem. pp. 448–460.

Netzer, A. (1982). "Sifrut Yehudei Paras". *Pa'amim*, Vol. 13.

Otzar HaTorah (1959). *Otzar HaTorah in the Middle East and North Africa: Facts and Figures*. New York.

Rosen, L. (1959). "Les écoles de l'Alliance en Iran". *Les Cahiers de l'Alliance Israélite Universelle*, No. 125. pp. 16–33.

Rosenfeld, L. (1961). "Jewish Education in Iran". *Jewish Education*, Vol. 31, no. 2. pp. 18–33.

Saddiq, I. (1957). *Tarikh-e Farhang-e Iran (History of Education in Iran)*.

Vreeland, H.H., ed. (1957). *Iran*. New Haven.

14

The Present State of
Jewish Education in Morocco

Shlomo Philipson

In the mid-1980s there were approximately 2,350 Jewish children in the Jewish schools of Morocco. The transition from the small study rooms (heders) of the past to today's relatively modern schools where both Jewish and general studies are taught is an important chapter in the history of the Moroccan Jewish community. All of the significant events in both the general and Jewish history of Morocco such as French colonial control, mass emigration, disappearance of rural and village Jews and Moroccan independence had an effect on the schools.

In modern Morocco private schooling is the norm for Jewish children. Most families send their children to Jewish schools, while a significant minority utilize the French Cultural Mission schools. There are virtually no Jewish children in the state-run Muslim schools.

There is some government support for the Alliance schools, but the other three systems (Lubavitch, ORT, and *Otzar HaTorah*) are funded completely by private sources. Any control that the government asserts is implicit and not overt. Obviously, Arabic must be taught and Israel-related topics are avoided.

The official policy of the kingdom is that Jews are citizens with full and equal rights. At one time, the Jews were a major economic, cultural, and social force in Morocco, and many Moroccans of both religions remember that period with warm nostalgia. With the rise of pan-Arab nationalism and under the influence of the Israel-Arab conflict, the foreign policy of the Moroccan government became anti-Zionist while maintaining an internal policy of philosemitism. The relationship of the Jews to the government is as healthy as that of any minority to the ruling authority in an absolute monarchy. On a number of occasions, King Hassan II has invited all the Moroccan Jews who emigrated to return to Morocco.[1] They would be welcomed by a broad spectrum of Moroccan society, but not by all.

The relationship of the man in the street to the Jews is much more complex. Many Moroccans are Berbers and see themselves as distant from the Arab world (as implied in the Arabic name of the country – *Maghreb* = West). They know that as Berbers they share a great heritage with the original Jewish population (pre-15th century). Others, however, have been more influenced by current trends in the Arab world and do not distinguish between Jews and Zionists. Violent anti-Israel propaganda in all the official media led to justifiable fear within the Jewish community during the 1967 and 1973 Israel-Arab wars.

Even during the 1982 fighting in Lebanon, although the Arab world had virtually abandoned the Palestinians, the Jews were more careful than usual. The leaders of the Jewish community speak of Arab-Jewish co-existence, but the goal has never been integration. Businesses are run side by side, sometimes even jointly, and among the very affluent, there is some social contact. However, there is almost no intermarriage. One senses great fear and mistrust on the street level. The general uneasiness with the majority culture has been one contributing factor to the almost total enrollment of the community's children in Jewish schools.

It must be remembered that Moroccan Jews were not directly subjected to the two major forces that disrupted the continuity of European Jewry. The enlightenment of Western Europe affected Moroccan Jewry only indirectly through the Alliance schools, and the last major immigration from Europe to Morocco was at the end of the fifteenth century. That immigration from Spain was a source of strength, both in quantity and quality. Unlike many of the Jewish immigrants to America, Spanish Jews saw no reason to leave their tradition behind them. Nor did the Holocaust produce catastrophic consequences for Moroccan Jewry – even if the community was not entirely spared by the German occupation of North Africa during World War II. Moroccan Jewry remained relatively intact and at peace with its ancient heritage until the mass emigration of the 1950s after the establishment of the State of Israel. Through this emigration, Morocco lost its Jewish population to Israel, France, Canada, Venezuela, and other countries. What is left is a skeleton community that lives on nostalgia, antiquated forms and external assistance.

All the schools hire Moroccan teachers and teach Moroccan Jewish children, yet all are influenced by foreign sources and funded by Jews abroad. No schools are funded by the local organized Jewish community. A detailed description of each school is given below. The community itself maintains no teacher-training facilities. Although two of the schools run a joint *kollel* for male teachers, and the Lubavitch movement has a *michlalah* for female teachers, the effect they have on teacher training is negligible. The only coordinating body is the Casablanca office of the American Jewish Joint Distribution Committee which partially funds *Otzar HaTorah* and Lubavitch locally and directly, and the Alliance Israélite Universelle and ORT globally and indirectly. The local office of the JDC is therefore actively involved in educational work and in coordinating school activities. Each school system, however, maintains its own autonomy and administers its own programs.

Since most of the Jews who wanted to leave Morocco have already done so, a major concern of the community is the maintenance of the status quo. However, even those who have remained realize that the future of their children lies elsewhere. Therefore, they want the best Jewish and general education for their children both so that the tradition will be carried on and so that their youngsters will be able to make a new life in Israel, France or Canada. Only a very few families value Jewish studies so little that they opt for the French Mission schools.

The Schools

Alliance Israélite Universelle.

The Alliance Israélite Universelle (AIU) was established in Morocco in 1862. It is the only Jewish school which receives government support. The ideological commitment is similar to Alliance schools elsewhere with complementary loyalty to Jewish Moroccan tradition. In 1984 there were four AIU schools in Casablanca, two primary and two secondary. There are also four provincial schools in Fez, Marrakesh, Meknes, and Tangier where the AIU takes responsibility for secular studies and *Otzar HaTorah* teaches Jewish subjects. There are small AIU secondary schools in Meknes and Fez. The AIU is responsible for the Jewish studies program at ORT. Including the students shared with *Otzar HaTorah* (185) and those taught at ORT (224), the total Jewish enrollment at AIU schools in 1983/84 was 1,247.

Lubavitch

The Lubavitch movement sent its first emissary to Morocco in 1950. Its present school activities center around a primary and secondary girls' school in Casablanca with 316 students. Lubavitch also runs an American yeshiva with 8 students in Casablanca. A *kollel* with approximately 40 men is jointly sponsored by Lubavitch and *Otzar HaTorah*, and a *michlalah* for women has about fifteen students. The girls' schools (*Beth Rivka* and Séminaire Lubavitch) and the men's yeshiva are the only full-day schools in the Lubavitch system. Though the schools are committed to their own Hasidic master, in Morocco they teach Sephardic customs and rites.

ORT

ORT maintains one vocational school in Casablanca with 224 Jewish students. This school, established in 1947, is administered locally but is under the direction of World ORT in London.

Otzar HaTorah

Otzar HaTorah was established in Morocco in 1947. It is the most Moroccan of all the systems, but is also influenced by its leadership which was trained in France, and its external offices in Paris and New York. There are five schools in Casablanca, two primary and three secondary. The 185 students in Fez, Marrakesh, Meknes, and Tangier are shared with AIU as noted above. Counting these students and eighty more in supplementary settings, the *Otzar HaTorah* schools taught 1,057 pupils in 1983/84.

All of the systems maintain some dormitories in Casablanca for high school children from the provinces. The gender breakdown in all of Morocco is about even. There is a constant decline in enrollment as a consequence of rising emigration and a declining birthrate. In 1983/84 enrollment was 12.5% lower than in 1982/83.

Informal Jewish Education

There are three active youth organizations in Morocco: the Département Educatif de la Jeunesse Juive (DEJJ), Eclaireurs Israélites (Scouts), and Jeunesse Lubavitch. All three have their headquarters and center in Casablanca, with some minimal activity in the provinces. In recent years, each of the movements has expanded its Casablanca services with the encouragement and financial support of the JDC. Statistics for membership and active participation are not accurate, but it is evident that several hundred children use the three different facilities on a regular basis. The activities during the week, on Shabbat, or on Sundays consist of sports, arts and crafts, communal singing, celebration of Jewish holidays, video screenings, Jewish study, drama, etc. There are 2–3 week summer camps sponsored by each youth organization as well as others sponsored by a school and a child welfare society. DEJJ runs a winter leadership seminar, while Lubavitch and the Scouts each run winter camps. There is, obviously, no Zionist youth organization, but youth groups are sent to Israel on an organized basis.

There is very little adult Jewish education. Besides the *kollel* and the *michlalah* described above, two of the local clubs sponsor occasional lectures but this kind of activity has limited appeal.

Personnel

As in other communities, the lack of qualified personnel is a critical problem for the schools. In Morocco, this issue is further aggravated by continuing emigration and lack of training. Most of the primary schools hire Jewish studies teachers on a full-time basis whereas the secondary schools hire part-time staff for specific areas. The teachers generally have very little secular education, and even their Jewish education is limited to Moroccan yeshivoth, the *kollel* and summer seminars abroad. There is little awareness of pedagogics and no knowledge of complementary disciplines, such as psychology or the media. The one major advantage is that all the teachers are Moroccan and can easily identify with the children and their socio-cultural milieu. The Alliance teachers are usually better trained than the others.

Salaries and fringe benefits are very low by Western standards, but compare favorably with available alternative occupations (unskilled labor). The schools make a sincere effort to adjust salaries to rates of inflation.

The approximate numbers of teachers are as follows:

School	Full-time	Part-time
Alliance	11	4
Lubavitch	5	4
ORT	1	1
Otzar HaTorah	24	11

Administrators earn considerably higher salaries than teachers, but still much less than their Western counterparts. Their training is generally not much more advanced than that of the teachers under their supervision.

Curricular Goals and Teaching Methods

Some planning was done many years ago, and the present systems still operate on the basis of decisions made then. ORT sees itself primarily as a vocational school, and Jewish studies has a low priority in their curriculum. The Alliance is devoted to the French system but sees itself as a Jewish school with a serious commitment to Jewish learning. *Otzar HaTorah* and

Lubavitch see their basic *raison d'être* to be Jewish study and practice, but both maintain reasonable standards of general education. Most teaching and learning in Morocco is highly structured, frontal, and based on rote memorization. Attempts to introduce new media, non-frontal models and a basic awareness of child development have met with limited success.

School Climate

Most Moroccan families are traditional in that they observe Shabbat to some extent and keep a kosher home. Synagogue attendance is also quite frequent. The most observant usually send their children to Lubavitch or *Otzar HaTorah*, with others using the Alliance and ORT. There are, however, many exceptions. ORT and the Alliance admit Arab students, but there are few overt problems with the mix. The limits of social contact are clear to all parties, and the Arab students feel privileged to study in a quality school. Student interest seems to be directly related to family background. Children from poor homes with illiterate parents are less motivated. The classic problem of understimulation in poor settings has a disastrous effect on certain classrooms. It is important to note that most of the teachers received as limited an education as they are now giving their students.

Despite all their faults, the Jewish schools in Morocco provide general and Jewish instruction of a relatively high calibre to over two thousand children. Most students leave Morocco with the ability to read and understand classical textual Hebrew and even speak modern Hebrew. Their general knowledge is usually sufficient to permit entrance into higher education abroad. In the Jewish sphere, the impact of the school is complemented by active observance of Jewish life in the home and the synagogue. The need for a sound general education is underscored by the fact that emigration continues apace. Moroccan Jewish communities abroad (in Israel, France, Canada, Venezuela, etc.) have suffered a great spiritual loss. The native community is attempting to maintain the grand tradition and to ensure its continuation after emigration.

Note

1.   Since the writing of this chapter, a number of significant developments have taken place in the relations between Morocco and Israel. The major one was the visit to Morocco and meeting with King Hassan II of the then Israeli Prime Minister Shimon Peres in July, 1986.

Part Seven

Eastern Europe

No survey of Jewish education worldwide should omit large Jewish populations. This justifies the inclusion in this volume of three brief chapters on the forms of Jewish education that are available in a geographical region where the prevailing conditions have made formal Jewish education practically non-existent. Eastern Europe, primarily the Soviet Union, contains the second largest Jewish population in the Diaspora. However, Jewish life is barely surviving there. The general political context of Eastern Europe is strongly anti-religious, but religious freedom outside of the Soviet Union has been considerably greater than within it.

William Orbach, who is Professor of Religious Studies at Louisville University, Louisville, Kentucky, in his chapter on Jewish education in the Soviet Union discusses the various legal restrictions and anti-semitic discriminatory practices that have developed over time to severely restrict religious, educational, and cultural activities for Jews there. Formal Jewish education is virtually non-existent; what does exist is primarily concentrated in underground circles for studying Hebrew language and occasionally religious texts.

The situation in Hungary and Romania is better. Both countries enjoy some formal Jewish education although the numbers of children in attendance is quite low. Both communities are aging quite rapidly and declining in number. The late Rabbi Alexander Scheiber, noted scholar and former head of the Rabbinical Seminary of Budapest, describes the activities of the seminary and the overall Jewish educational scene in a brief chapter on Jewish education in Hungary. The Chief Rabbi of Romania, Dr.Moses Rosen, describes the Jewish educational activities in Romania which are commendable and uniquely extensive for a communist country. In Romania an emphasis on Jewish choral and music groups is helping keep Jewish culture and tradition alive.

15

Soviet Jewish Education

William W. Orbach

Although often thought of as a homogeneous mass, Soviet Jews are actually made up of three separate groups. Heartland Soviet Jews, those who live within the central cities of pre-World War II Russia, have been the most exposed to Soviet influence and this, for the longest period of time. Southern Soviet Jews, those living in Georgia, for example, have been both less subjected to Soviet influence, at least in the religious sphere, because of the regime's tendency to permit the 'backward' peoples of these areas to continue in their antiquated ways. Finally, 'Western' Soviet Jews, those Jews who fell under Soviet control during and since World War II, have been under Soviet control for only the past forty years. Generally, our analysis will concentrate on heartland Soviet Jews because the trends affecting them now will in the longer run also affect 'Western' Soviet Jews, and because a substantial proportion of the southern Soviet Jews have emigrated to Israel.

Sociologists and professors of religious studies have long struggled with the anomaly of the Jews, not only who they are, but what they are. Are they a religion, a people, a nation, or do they belong to some other category? The founders of the Soviet regime also struggled with this issue; Stalin, in his famous essay *Marxism and the National Question*, argued that the Jews lack the prerequisites of nationhood which include "language, territory, economic life, and psychological make-up as manifested in a community of culture" (Stalin, 1913, p. 8; Miller, 1978, p. 50). Lacking a national territory but possessing a common religion in the officially atheist but actually anti-religious Soviet Union, the Jews were bound to suffer on all counts. While in its early years the regime permitted the development of Jewish national culture, which it defined as Yiddish-oriented, it ruthlessly attempted to destroy any religious manifestations as well as any Hebrew-oriented works.

The "Declaration of the Rights of the People of Russia" which abolished all "national-religious privileges and restrictions" (Rothenberg, 1978, p. 170) was the first act which affected the Jews as a group. The first act affecting the

Jewish religion, however, struck against Jewish education. On January 23, 1918 the Council of People's Commissars published a decree entitled "On Separation of Church from State, and School from Church" which inter alia decreed the confiscation of religious property and funds, and prohibited religious instruction in schools. This prohibition was to prove particularly devastating to Soviet Jewry. The first conference of the Yevsektsia, the Jewish section of the Communist Party, decreed the dissolution of the *Kehillot*, the local Jewish communal religious bodies. By 1919 then, the Jews had lost both their religious communal bodies and their schools. The Yevsektsia and local government authorities embarked on a campaign to quickly eradicate the Jewish religion by utilizing anti-religious show trials, by closing synagogues ostensibly for pressing community needs, and by shutting down all Jewish schools, even in areas which lacked public schools. Often some of these methods were combined, as in the show trials against the heder in Vitebsk and the yeshiva in Rostov in 1921. Furthermore, Jewish clergymen were increasingly persecuted in the 1920s, arrested, deported, and deprived of the most basic necessities. Anti-religious demonstrations, parades, and spectacles became commonplace, especially around Jewish religious holidays; Jewish religious objects were ruthlessly confiscated. And, finally, Hebrew itself was labeled reactionary and was ruthlessly suppressed by all means available. In 1930, the Yevsektsia, which had officially led this campaign, with, of course, considerable support from the Soviet authorities, was itself dissolved (Rothenberg, 1978, pp. 171–177).

By the 1930s only remnants of Jewish culture and religion remained, and these were also eventually to be stifled over the next two decades. Not only had the vast majority of religious institutions been abolished, but a psychological climate was created which attempted to destroy any Jewish, especially religious, identification among the vast majority of Soviet Jews. Religious Jews were regarded with suspicion and could hardly hope to advance in their professions.

Yet Jewish education did not totally disappear. There were groups, especially among the traditional Hasidim, which continued to maintain Jewish religious education, although clandestinely. Groups of religious Jews continued to function despite Soviet harassments. The Bratslav and Lubavitch Hasidim continued to maintain illegal yeshivoth to teach their children (Rothenberg, 1978, p. 178–181).

The outbreak of World War II and the Nazi invasion of the Soviet Union precipitated several changes. The regime, in an attempt to unify the country against the Nazi invasion, became more permissive toward religious practice in general, and this applied also, at least to a degree, to Judaism. The murder of over one million Jews by the *einsatzgruppen* blurred the distinction between assimilated and religious Jews; the Nazis wanted to murder them all. A substantial proportion of the surviving Jewish population was uprooted from their homes and some resettled in the Asian portion of the Soviet Union where the Hasidic groups again set up illegal yeshivoth. Finally, the end of the war saw the Soviet absorption of surrounding states which contained significant numbers of the 'Western' Jews mentioned above who had not yet encountered Soviet anti-religious restrictions.

The year 1948 represented the turning point for any secular Jewish culture which had managed to survive, albeit with difficulty, up to that point. The regime turned on it furiously, shutting down nearly all Jewish organizations and Yiddish publications, and imprisoning or killing Yiddish intellectuals. Although the "Black Years of Soviet Jewry" affected Jewish culture more than religion, Soviet Jewry was deeply shaken (Gilboa, 1971). The Doctors' Plot with its overtones of Jewish disloyalty could not fail to touch the lives of all Soviet Jews. Five years later, in 1957, the government closed a large number of the remaining synagogues, although as a concession to the West, 3,000 prayerbooks were printed and a yeshiva was opened in Moscow. However, this school was harrassed in every possible way by the authorities and virtually disappeared; students were not granted the right to live in Moscow and the regime created immense hardships for those who dared to teach there (Rothenberg, 1978, pp. 186–192).

Paradoxically, the creation of Israel probably engendered the post–1948 wave of persecution by the regime while it created a new spirit of defiance among Soviet Jews. The wave of enthusiasm with which they received Golda Meir, the first Israeli ambassador to the Soviet Union, probably unnerved some of the authorities. The specter of dual loyalty reared its ugly head, and the Soviet leaders apparently decided to thwart all the remaining possibilities for Jewish identification. Since religion already had a relatively weak hold on Russian Jews, the government concentrated on Yiddish culture, which was, from their paranoic perspective, far more dangerous. They quickly crushed it and hoped that with the withering away of Jewish religion and the destruction of Jewish culture, Jews would lose all their motivation to remain Jews. Yet the very existence of Israel presented Soviet Jews with a new rallying point, and the government, despite its attempts to the contrary, also strengthened Jewish identification. By having Jews identified as a nationality on their internal identity card and by discriminating against them in economic and educational areas, the regime forced Soviet Jews to maintain an awareness of their Jewishness and fueled the desire for emigration, not so much out of love for Jewish culture, but because of their desire for better economic opportunities. In many respects, Soviet policy regarding Jews has been self-defeating because the regime always seemed unable to decide what it actually wanted of its Jewish population. This ambivalence continues to the present day.

Officially, then, there is no Jewish education in the Soviet Union. Whether by decree or by harrassment, the regime has all but eliminated any vestiges of formal Jewish education in the Soviet Union, with the exception of the southern areas. However, thanks to the very existence of Israel as well as to the increasing international outcry about the fate of Soviet Jewry, a significant group of Soviet Jews has experienced a revival of Jewish consciousness which has, in turn, created a desire for Jewish education. Jewish consciousness has been further reinforced by the emigration of approximately a quarter-million Soviet Jews in the 1970s which established strong personal ties between Soviet Jews and their relatives in the West. Lacking official possibilities for Jewish education in the Soviet Union (with the exception of the almost nonexistent Moscow Yeshiva and Hebrew classes for KGB agents heading toward the Middle East), Soviet Jews have turned increasingly to informal channels. They have been aided only by a trickle of Jewish books that come through the mails or with the few Jewish tourists from the West.

Interested Soviet Jews have begun to teach themselves as well as others in a variety of ways. With the increase in Jewish materials filtering in from abroad, Soviet Jews have been given at least a marginally greater access to Jewish literature. Soviet Jews in various cities have learned Hebrew and Jewish culture and religion. Some have become Orthodox Jews (not an easy decision in the Soviet Union) and have even managed to follow Jewish precepts within Soviet jails or labor camps. Others, having taught themselves Hebrew, have now organized classes or private lessons. The emigration of the 1970s contributed to this phenomena because it raised Soviet Jewish consciousness, engendered hope for emigration (with the consequent need to learn a new language), and created links between Soviet Jews who are still in the Soviet Union and those who have already emigrated. The constant flow of letters, telephone calls, etc. sparked an interest in World Jewry and in its culture and religion. Thus Hebrew teaching has begun to develop within the major centers of Jewish population in the Soviet Union. Individual and group classes have been organized. Never officially sanctioned, these take place within private apartments with only a handful of people involved. Since Soviet citizens often get together with friends for an evening, these social gatherings can often be combined with study sessions.

Since 1983, however, the Soviet regime, with increasing ferocity, has begun to arrest and jail these Jewish studies and Hebrew teachers with a variety of excuses. The KGB has raided their apartments on various pretexts; Yuli Edelshtein was arrested and his home searched on September 4, 1984. His teenage Hebrew students were forced to sign statements that Edelshtein had required that they purchase Hebrew kits for 15 rubles each – hence he was charged with illegal profiteering. At his trial, however, he was accused of using drugs (which, the KGB insisted, are necessary for religious observances) and sentenced to three years in a labor camp (NCSJ, 1984). Alexander Kholmiansky was charged with "mailbox tampering" and attempting to establish a nationwide Hebrew study program. Kholmiansky is also a *hozer bet'shuvah* (a Jew who has become Orthodox) (NCSJ, 1984). The regime cut off the telephones of Hebrew teachers in Leningrad (NCSJ, 1982) and harassed them in every manner possible. Between July 1984 and November 1985, the KGB arrested at least ten Hebrew teachers, a record which the U.S. State Department called a "major sustained crackdown on Hebrew teachers and other Jewish cultural activists" (NCSJ, 1985). Soviet Jewish teachers have been summoned to OVIR (the Soviet office in charge of emigration) only to be told that they would never be given permission to emigrate because of their activities on behalf of Hebrew teaching and general Jewish learning. On October 23, 1982, *Izvestia* published an article by A. Kostrov, entitled "Uninvited Guests" which attacked the Hebrew seminars in the Soviet Union for having ulterior motives, i.e. covering up for Zionist illegal activities (NCSJ, 1982, pp. 5–6).

There have also been attempts to create seminars on Jewish subjects with colleagues from outside the Soviet Union, but these were prevented by the Soviet authorities. Samizdat (clandestine unofficial publications) on Jewish subjects such as *Morashtenu*, a collection of articles about Jewish history, literature, and religion (NCSJ, 1983, p. 2) circulate within various groups in the Soviet Union. Furthermore, in addition to books sent in from the West, Radio Free Europe and the Voice of America have expanded their programming to include broadcasts aimed at Soviet Jews (NCSJ, 1983, p. 3).

Particularly tragic was the case of Iosif Begun who was tried and punished three times for his Hebrew teaching activities (NCSJ, 1983, p. 1). *Leningradskaya Pravda* described him as a "cunning and impudent wheeler-dealer selling the interests of his motherland wholesale and retail" (NCSJ, 1984, p. 2). Even in labor camps, the Jewish prisoners underwent unusual cruelties, especially if they were Hebrew teachers. Iosif Berenshtein was attacked and nearly totally blinded in a prison camp, while Yuli Edelshtein who was repeatedly attacked at Vydrino labor camp, was prevented from resting after work and was forced to begin work earlier than the others in an effort to "exorcise his religious fanaticism" (NCSJ, 1985, p. 1).[1]

Perhaps *Svetskaya Moldavia* expressed the regime's motivations and fears best when it published an article entitled "Always on the Alert" stating that "Zionist centers and organizations...try to impose on our people the Hebrew language...try to draw them closer to Judaism...and use them as a background for forming organizational links in the fight against the Soviet regime" (NCSJ, 1985, p. 1).

In summary, then, we see that the Soviet regime prohibits any Jewish or Hebrew learning in an organized way for heartland or 'Western' Soviet Jews. Even informal Hebrew lessons were quashed under numerous pretexts and their teachers were persecuted. Nevertheless, there are Hebrew teachers and Hebrew lessons in the Soviet Union, though these exist only on an unofficial, quasi-secretive basis.

But not only are Jews prohibited from learning their own tradition, they are also often denied access to higher general education. Jewish students are not admitted to universities, especially the more prestigious ones. Thus, on January 21, 1983, Boris Kanevsky was sentenced to five years internal exile for documenting discrimination against Jewish students by university mathematics departments, a process he termed "intellectual genocide." These universities utilized special admissions examinations with particularly difficult questions for any prospective Jewish students (NCSJ, 1983, p. 2). The Soviet regime has hereby engendered a vicious circle. Because it distrusts Soviet Jews and believes that they will emigrate to the West at their first opportunity, Soviet leadership has apparently decided not to provide them with a higher education. As a consequence, Soviet Jewry's desire for emigration has grown, less due to religious motivations than economic ones. Hence, the phenomenon of *neshirah*, drop-outs who immigrate to the United States rather than Israel.

In the final analysis, under current conditions, the Soviet Jewish plight seems more grim than ever. Denied access to their own spiritual sources, harassed at every turn if they attempt to acquire some Jewish learning, they are also excluded from higher secular education and culture. With large scale emigration, at present, not a viable possibility, Soviet Jews face a discouraging future.

Note

1   Since this article was completed Iosif Begun, Iosif Berenshtein and Yuli Edelshtein were allowed to emigrate to Israel.

References

Gilboa, Y. (1971). *The Black Years of Soviet Jewry*. Little, Brown and Co., Boston.

Miller, J. (1978). "Soviet Theory on the Jews", in: Kochan, L., ed., *The Jews in Soviet Russia*. Oxford University Press, Oxford.

NCSJ (National Conference on Soviet Jewry) (1983; 1984; 1985). *Newsbreak*.

NCSJ (National Conference on Soviet Jewry) (1982; 1983). *Press Service*.

Rothenberg, J. (1978). "Jewish Religion in the Soviet Union", in: Kochan, L., ed., *The Jews in Soviet Russia*. Oxford University Press, Oxford.

Stalin, J. (1913). *Marxism and the National and Colonial Question*. Martin Lawrence, London.

16

Jewish Education in Hungary

Alexander Scheiber

Jewish education in Hungary is provided mainly by the part-time Talmudei Torah in and around Budapest and in the rural communities. The Budapest community operates an orphanage in which girls and boys are cared for separately. The Orthodox section of the Budapest community maintains a kindergarten in addition to its Talmudei Torah.

The only full-time Jewish educational institutions are the Jewish Theological Seminary and the co-educational Jewish Grammar School conducted on the premises of the Seminary. The same building also houses a school for *hazanut* (cantors).

The Jewish Grammar School

The idea of founding a Jewish Grammar School was put forward in 1886 by Mór Kármán, who obtained funds for this purpose from Antal Freystadter von Kövesgyüri in 1892, Sandor Wahrmann in 1893, and Salamon Taub in 1895. In 1909, Kármán formulated the syllabus for the proposed school, and in 1912, construction of a building, designed by Béla Lajta, began on a building site purchased in 1910. However, this construction was suspended during World War I and only slowly resumed after the war.

In 1919, the Jewish Grammar School, under the direction of Bernard Heller, opened for both boys and girls, on separate campuses. The entire school moved into its own premises only in 1931 when that project was completed. At present, the Grammar School is located on the Jewish Theological Seminary premises, and is attended by some 50 students.

The staff consists of teachers, rabbis, and members of the community. While statistics on past enrollments are unavailable, the school's graduates include world-wide celebrities, and its teaching staff has included such outstanding scholars as Odön Beke, Mihály Fekete, Raphael D. Fuchs, Bernard Heller, Joseph Turóczi-Trostler and Jeno Zsoldos.

The Rabbinical Seminary

Various historical and social factors led to the founding of modern rabbinical seminaries throughout Europe – in Padova, Metz, Breslau, London and Berlin. As early as 1806, David Friesenhausen, a Jewish scholar of Bavarian origin, submitted a memorandum to Josephus, Palatine of Hungary, concerning the establishment of a modern seminary for rabbinical studies.

In 1850, Franz Joseph I established a school-fund from the million forints which Hungarian Jewry had paid into a war indemnity tax levied for the War of Independence in 1848–49. In 1856, Franz Joseph decided that this fund should be used to build a Jewish Rabbinical Seminary. The Seminary was opened in 1877 in the presence of the Prime Minister, Kálmán Tisza, and the Minister of Religion and Public Education, Agoston Trefort. The historian Heinreich Graetz gave an address on behalf of the mother seminary in Breslau.

The professors and graduates of the Budapest Seminary laid the foundations of Jewish scholarship in Hungary. There were three generations of notable professors. The first generation included teachers such as Moses Bloch, noted for research into Talmud Law; William Bacher, who systematized the Haggada and rediscovered Persian Jewish literature; David Kaufmann, historian and philosopher of religion; and Ignacz Goldziher, professor of religious philosophy.

The second generation of professors were themselves Seminary graduates. They included Ludwig Blau, who wrote monographs on ancient Hebrew books, on Jewish magic, and on divorce in Judaism; Michael Guttmann, compiler of a Talmudic encyclopedia; Bernard Heller, folklorist; Simon Hevesi, philsopher; and Ludwig Venetiáner, historian and scholar of religious history.

In 1944, when the Germans invaded Hungary, the Seminary was the transit station for 20,000 Jews on their way to death and thus became the first concentration camp in Hungary. Among these 90 ordained rabbis, 39 undergraduates, and 24 secondary school students suffered martyrdom.

After World War II and the liberation of Hungary, the Budapest Seminary was re-opened by the Hungarian government, while the two institutes in Berlin and Breslau had ceased to function. It was directed by Samuel Löwinger, a scholar of Hebrew manuscripts. The third generation of professors included István Hahn, historian; E. Roth, Talmud scholar; and Alexander Scheiber, cultural historian. Today, the Seminary in Budapest is the only rabbinical seminary in Eastern Europe. At present, the Seminary has 20 students of whom 10 are from Hungary itself and 10 from abroad – the Soviet Union, Czechoslovakia and Eastern Germany.

The Seminary trains rabbis as well as cantors. There is also a seminary choir which performs concerts, accompanied by lectures, in Budapest and the provincial towns. Since 1983, the Seminary has also provided extension courses for adults. An important undertaking has been the publication of major works dealing with Hungarian Jewry, with the financial assistance of the Claims Conference and the Memorial Foundation for Jewish Culture (see References below).

Conclusion

Some 50% of Jewish school age children in Hungary receive a Jewish education. They are taught by teachers, rabbis, and members – mostly women – of the community. A major problem in educating these children is the lack of suitable texts and materials, such as illustrated children's Bibles and Hebrew-Hungarian or Hungarian-Hebrew dictionaries.

It may be assumed that the remaining 50% of children who do not obtain Jewish education include those who live in remote areas, and children of assimilated and intermarried families.

The Rabbinical Seminary represents a major achievement for Hungarian and Eastern European Jewry. Its contribution to Jewish life is demonstrated by the outstanding staff it has consistently attracted, by the number and caliber of its students and by its role in producing graduates for the maintenance of Jewish life throughout Eastern Europe.

References

Geyer, A. (1958). *Bibliography of Jewish Persecution under Fascism in Hungary.*

Indictment against Nazism. 3 volumes of documents dealing with the persecution of Hungarian Jews under Nazism in Hungary. Two volumes are still to be written.

Karsai, E. (1962). *They Stood Unarmed on the Minefields.*

MIOK Yearbook (1970–   ).

Monographs of the Hungarian Jewish Communities, 11 vols. To date dealing with the history of Jews in the counties of Pécs, Szentes, Hajdu, Köszeg, and Tolna, among others.

Monumenta Hungariae Judaica (1903–   ). 19 vols. Original documents relating to the history of Hungarian Jewry since the early 18th century.

Scheiber, A. (1969). *Héber kodexmaradványok magyar-országi kötéstáblákban* (Hebrew codex remnants in binding-boards in Hungary).

Scheiber, A. (1974; 2nd ed. 1977). *Folklór és Tárgytörténet* (*Folklore and Comparative Literature*). 3 vols.

Scheiber, A. (1983). *Jewish Inscriptions in Hungary.* Academy of Sciences Publishing House, Budapest and Brill, Leiden. (1st ed. in Hungarian, 1960).

17

Jewish Education in Romania

Moses Rosen

The Federation of Jewish Communities is the officially recognized agent of about 68 local communities and over 130 synagogues in Romania. It has organized 28 Talmudei Torah which are attended by some 600 students aged between 6 and 25; some classes have as few as 2–3 students, but others have 15–30. Rudiments of Hebrew language and religious tradition are taught using Hebrew textbooks with religious themes or other supplements obtained from Israel. The *History of the Jews* by Dubnov, translated to Romanian by a team of teachers, is used as the text for teaching Jewish history. The classes are held in synagogues or, where possible, in community houses. There are no tuition fees, and the staff is paid by the Federation, which supplies all teaching materials as well, and coordinates all teaching activities.

Eighteen choirs, some with instrumentalists, have also been organized by the Federation, as have two independent orchestras in Bucharest. The choirs have approximately 800 members, most of whom are children and young adults below the age of 30. Their repertoire is made up of traditional religious music and Jewish folk songs in both Hebrew and Yiddish. Translations and vocabulary lists are appended to the songs to help the singers understand and render them appropriately. The choirs perform on the Jewish holidays (Simhat Torah, Hanukkah, *Tu b'Shvat*, Purim, Passover, Lag b'Omer, Shavuot), in honor of visitors from abroad and often following lectures organized by the Federation of the individual communities themselves.

Each year, the Chief Rabbi, together with the hundreds of boys and girls who are members of the youth choirs, tour between 30–40 communities all over Romania in the Talmud Torah Hanukkah tour. This 'Hanukkiada' marathon of 10–15 days has become a tradition since the 1960s, and missions come from all over the Jewish world each year to participate in Romania's unique spectacle of Jewish identification.

In the past few years, country-wide competitions were organized in the areas of Hebrew knowledge and Jewish music. The most knowledgeable become contestants in the central competition held in Bucharest where the winners are awarded prizes by the Chief Rabbi.

Also for Passover, collective Seders are organized in kosher restaurants, community houses and synagogues. Talmud Torah students and choirs read and sing texts from the Haggadah together with their elders.

The choirs have also performed outside Romania: the choirs of Bucharest and Iasi jointly gave about 10 concerts in Israel in August 1980 and July 1984, and, in April 1984, the Iasi choir gave 10 concerts in Switzerland. The foreign press reported the success of all these concerts.

Of the 400,000 Jews who remained in Romania after World War II, almost all emigrated to Israel; only about 27,000 lived in Romania in 1985. One consequence of this mass aliyah was the age structure of today's Jewish community: 60% are over 60 years of age, and only 7% are under 20.

Most of the Jewish households within the community are quite assimilated, and the children receive anti-religious and anti-Zionist education from the State. Nevertheless, the large majority receive some Jewish education at least up to bar mitzvah and their Jewish identity is stronger than would be expected under such circumstances.

There are also weekly lectures given in Bucharest and other Romanian towns. The lecturers are selected from among distinguished Jewish personalities in the country. In 1983–84, for example, more than 30 lectures were delivered in the Federation of Jewish Communities Hall in Bucharest and over 60 in other towns, many of which were followed by musical-artistic performances or films. The large audiences which attend these lectures attest to the interest in Jewish culture. The lecturers are usually introduced by the Chief Rabbi, or, in his absence, by other leaders of the Federation who draw conclusions and make comments. The lecture series is planned every year from shortly after Simchat Torah through late summer, and has been referred to as "the real Jewish open university, a forum of Judaism in Romania."

Despite the small size of the contemporary Romanian Jewish community, participation in the activities of the Federation has been lively, and has actually increased.

Part Eight

Israel

The goals and challenges of Jewish education in Israel are obviously different from those met by Jewish communities in the Diaspora. The context is that of a sovereign state with a majority of Jews, rather than that of a minority group. The financial means and operational tools are, at least in the majority of cases, those of a governmental Ministry of Education, rather than those of private voluntaristic organizations. Yet, some of the problems which are encountered in the Israeli Jewish educational system do belong to the wider theme of Jewish education in the contemporary world. Keeping this in mind, the two chapters on Jewish education in Israel presented in this volume introduce, on the one hand, a sociological perspective, and, on the other, a historical-philosophical focus on ideological issues and trends.

Chaim Adler, Professor of Education at the Hebrew University of Jerusalem, discusses what he sees as the three major challenges faced by Israeli society in the educational field since the establishment of the State: developing a vast and egalitarian educational system with which to bridge the social gaps between the various population groups brought together by mass immigration; meeting the manpower needs of a developed industrial nation that made it necessary to educate and cultivate a skilled elite; and promoting the emergence of a relevant, modern Jewish identity, especially for the large majority whose background is secular. Adler suggests that the Israeli educational system has been highly successful in arriving at a modus vivendi reconciling the first two conflicting challenges. The Israeli educational system has been less successful in meeting the third challenge which, the author feels, is the most crucial to the future of Israel.

Michael Rosenak, Professor at the Melton Center for Jewish Education in the Diaspora of the Hebrew University of Jerusalem, discusses the ideological contents of Jewish education in Israel. Jewish education in a Jewish society is never an adjunct; it is always, in some sense, synonymous with education as such. This explains the intensity and seriousness of the controversy that has existed since the beginning of modern Jewish education in Palestine. Rosenak reviews the roots and orientations of the major educational alternatives – religious and secular – that have been proposed and implemented before and since Statehood. After the Six-Day War, as new approaches emerged concerning the role of the religious dimension in education, the competing positions have tended to polarize. The debate on Jewish education in Israel is bound to continue, as it reflects the deeper confrontation concerning the practices and meanings of Jewishness when faced with the challenges of modernity.

18

Jewish Education in Israel:
A Sociological Perspective

Chaim Adler

Unlike several other new nations, Israel has had a fully-operative education system since its emergence. When Israel was established in 1948, a full-fledged education system from kindergarten through university had already existed for about 45 years. This included teacher-training institutions, a curriculum – albeit from the 1920s –, a school inspectorate and an elaborate examination system. Perhaps most important, as of the early twenties there was a language – Hebrew – which was universally used in the schools as the vehicle of instruction and which symbolized the emergence of a revived culture for which schools constituted the major arena.

This heritage, however, presented some dilemmas which have remained unresolved to the present day. Three prominent features characterized the pre-Independence educational system.

Uniformity

The education system of the *Yishuv* (the pre-state Jewish community of Palestine) – was essentially uniform both in structure and in content. This uniformity reflected the social, cultural and demographic homogeneity of the Jewish population during the 1930s and 1940s, when a basically non-differentiated education system could still meet the educational needs of most children. However, with the foundation of the State in 1948 and the tremendous growth of its population due to mass immigration from four continents, the almost perfect fit between students' needs and the educational opportunities offered, diminished.

Loose Linkage to the Labor Market

Before 1948, the education system was not expected to be responsible for preparation of the sophisticated manpower needed by industry, scientific endeavors or a complex bureaucracy. Most of the positions which required such training were occupied by people who had been educated in Europe. Since independence, however, Israel's education system has been increasingly called upon to develop its own sophisticated manpower. It remains to be seen whether the system inherited from the *Yishuv* was sufficiently equipped to fulfill this function.

Partisan Affiliation

The education system, as it developed in the *Yishuv*, was subdivided along partisan lines. In the absence of centralized state institutions, including public schooling, the school system was owned, conducted and supervised by the main political parties. This resulted in three major trends of schooling – socialist, religious (or essentially Orthodox) and general (Rieger, 1940, pp. 1–95; Bentwich, 1965; Elboim-Dror, 1982, pp. 55–74). This political subdivision, which was essentially ideological, did not contradict the curricular and structural uniformity already mentioned. Although schools were run by one of three different political movements, they did not differ dramatically in their curricular emphases and certainly not in their general structure, educational emphases or academic standards. In 1953, the political 'trends' in education were abolished, and a bipartite state school system was introduced, which included general and religious (Orthodox) state schools. The 'segregatedness' of two distinct educational institutions within one public-state education system (Elboim-Dror, 1982, pp. 74–81) has been problematic, as has been the very nature, contents and flavor of the Jewish identity to be nurtured in the general non-religious sector which caters to about 75% of the school population.

Against this background three basic challenges have crystallized, affecting Israel's education to this day:

1. The need for a democratic and egalitarian education system to give equal educational opportunities to all despite serious social and economic gaps has been responsible for extensive policy and curriculum adaptations, contrary to the essential uniformity of the original system. The dilemma is thus the distinction between uniformity and equality (Elboim-Dror, 1982).

2. Even while attempting to bridge these serious gaps Israel had to mobilize all its existing potential for human and intellectual excellence, so as to secure its survival and sustained growth. Equalizing opportunities and nurturing excellence are, however, usually responsible for conflicting and even opposing policies.

3. Israel's education system must address itself to the fact that between two-thirds and three-quarters of the nation's children grow up in secular homes and attend the non-religious public schools. They thus need motivations and sources of legitimation for their Jewishness which differ from tradi-

tional religiously-based teachings. The general school is being torn between a non-Orthodox though traditional and a modern-scientific non-Judaic orientation (Kahane, 1968).

The First Challenge: Bridging the Social Gaps

From the late 19th Century until 1948, the Jewish settlers in Palestine were predominantly of European origin. In 1948 more than 90% of Israel's Jewish inhabitants were of European background. At that time the mass immigrations began, doubling the population in the first three years of statehood, and trebling it over the first twelve years. It is the combination of the origin of the immigrants and their numbers which is of interest here. Since Independence, just over 50% of the new immigrants have been of European or American origin, and the rest have come from Near and Middle Eastern Jewish communities – mainly Iran, Iraq, Yemen, and North Africa. The chief ethnic division in Israel, therefore, is between citizens of European background (including those born in America, South Africa and Australia), and those of Asian or African origin (Central Bureau of Statistics, 1981, p. 134).

Because European cultural styles and institutional patterns prevail in modern Israel, immigration for many Asian-African Jews meant an encounter with an unfamiliar social system, basically different from what they knew previously. Some characteristics of the Asian-African immigrant groups constituted a-priori existing obstacles to immediate social integration. For example, many Asian-African adults had little or no formal schooling, and very few had technological training congruent with the needs of a modern economy. In addition, many arrived with very large families and often were either ignorant of, or opposed to, family planning. These characteristics served to place these immigrants in the lower socio-economic strata of Israeli society. In consequence, a high correlation between socio-economic status and ethnic origin emerged, a correlation manifested in school performance as well as in other institutional spheres (Adler, 1969).

At the same time, the school system has been one of the main agents of social integration ever since the early 1950s (Frankenstein, 1976). The main strategies applied by the schools to accelerate the bridging of the gap between the ethnic groups may be summed up in the following five categorie

Administrative Measures

In the first years mass failure showed up even in the low grades, where schools were overwhelmed by the growth in student numbers on the one hand, and by the wide gaps in achievement on the other. All that the education system could do was administrative in nature. For instance, class repetition was abolished. This measure removed the obstacles faced by students of disadvantaged backgrounds from promotion to the following grade, but it did not – like most other administrative measures – have any impact on the roots of the problem.

Pedagogical Measures

Toward the end of the 1950s, pedagogical interventions were initiated. Some of the measures introduced were:

- early intervention, mainly through kindergartens and nurseries. Home intervention programs were introduced at a later state;
- experimentation with didactic measures, remedial teaching methods and curricular innovations;
- enrichment programs of different kinds aimed especially at the upper achievers among the disadvantaged.

Structural Differentiation Measures

These and other similar enrichment and compensatory programs were aimed at the removal, or at least limitation, of the causes for school failure. It is very difficult to accurately measure the impact of such programs, since this is not immediate, and at times may be felt only over the long range. It is thus not surprising that along with the numerous compensatory measures mentioned above, around the late 1960s additional strategies were introduced to promote solutions to the problems with which the schools were trying to cope. More specifically, as in other countries, schools which faced mounting numbers of 'under-achievers' instituted patterns of ability groupings. Even though such measures helped schools to overcome the problems incurred by great gaps in student achievement, they concurrently contributed to the segregation of students by ethnic background without having any impact on their actual achievement levels (Dar and Resh, 1981).

Since the mid-1960s more and more students were Israeli-born and even those born abroad had been raised in Israel, these measures were felt to be insufficient. Although the gap between students of European-American (EA) origin and those of Asian-African (AA) origin had not widened, the fact that it persisted at all contradicted the proclaimed goals of social policies. This gap opposed the very ethos of Israeli society, which was committed to egalitarian principles and to the ideal of the formation of a united modern Jewish nation, and was dependent on strong internal solidarity capable of withstanding external military pressures. It could thus not tolerate the persistence of an ascriptive social and economic gap based on ethnic origin. More powerful measures to complement the already existing ones were therefore sought.

Structural Integration Measures

Against this background, the introduction of integrated education should be examined. A school reform, the core of which was the formation of integrated junior high schools, was introduced in 1968 as a result of a resolution by the Knesset (Chaim, 1980; Peled, 1982). This policy was conceived as a further measure of enrichment, aimed at raising scholastic achievement and school retention rates among students of disadvantaged origin. At the same time, however, it carried a symbolic message, even if no dramatic changes in scholastic achievements were to emerge. It offered all students in the integrated system, irrespective of origin, a shared school environment – the building, teachers, and curriculum – thus symbolizing structurally the commitment to national unity, social solidarity and equality (Klein and Eshel, 1980; Chen, Adler and Klein, 1977). In fact, research shows the quality of educational input in integrated schools is considerably better than that of the segregated ones (Davis, Sprinzak, Osizon, 1982).

Intensive Focusing on Hard Core Disadvantaged Communities

In the early 1970s, the newest policy in this area was introduced, namely the Educational Welfare Program. The most depressed and disadvantaged communities were singled out, and through special budgets were made the targets of intensive, concerted, compensatory efforts which had been specifically decided upon by local steering committees. School integration and the Welfare Program indeed complemented each other: secluded and mostly homogeneous towns or neighborhoods, with hardly a chance for integration without massive busing, became the target for this program (Adler and Melzer-Druker, n.d.).

It would be impossible to give an overall evaluation of the impact of the diversified and essentially different measures that have been tried for more than three decades. We might suggest, however, the following data as indicators of their possible effects.

Perhaps the most impressive indicator is the expansion of the educational system (Central Bureau of Statistics, 1981, p. 586). Not only has the school-leaving age been raised twice since the establishment of the State so that compulsory schooling today embraces ages 5 to 16, but all 4–year-olds and almost all 3–year-olds are in kindergartens and nurseries (Bilezki and Turki, 1982, p. 7). Near-universal school attendance for over 13 years cannot but leave its imprint on the students, even though differential school achievements persist, and ability grouping (from seventh grade on) and tracking (subject matter specialization, from tenth or eleventh grade on), effect the school paths of students of both AA and EA origins, rendering them less than identical. As from the early 1980s, almost 2/3 of the 17–year olds in Israel complete twelfth grade, given the abolishment of school fees through age 18 in 1978, and the success of many of the compensatory measures applied over more than a generation. It should be added, however, that about 2/3 of the AA students complete vocational, non-university directed programs, whereas 2/3 of the EA students complete academic university-directed programs (Central Bureau of Statistics, 1981, Table XXII/12). An additional 6% combine study and work during their adolescent years (Bilezki and Turki, 1982, p. 17).

This expansion of the education system may be viewed as a policy directed at the opening up and equalizing of educational opportunities for all children. Yet, at the same time, the dramatic reduction of drop-out rates from secondary schools during the 1970s is, at least partially, a result of these policies and measures (see Tables 1 and 2). Furthermore, a very impressive body of evidence exists to the effect that additional years of schooling are positively related to social mobility (Musgrove, 1979).

Success rates in the government-administered matriculation examinations may be another gauge of policy impact. These examinations, taken mostly by the about-to-graduate students of academic high schools, are a requirement for university acceptance. In the late 1960s, only about 6% of all AA 17–year-olds successfully passed these examinations (as compared with about 33% of all EA 17–year-olds), but this rate rose to about 15% in the early 1980s, while the EA rate stayed the same.[1]

Therefore, although the achievement gaps have not disappeared and opportunities for secondary and university education are not yet equal, nor have the differences deepened or grown; in fact, in some respects they have considerably decreased. Whether the change is socially significant (considering the very short time in which these developments took place, and the circumstances under which they occurred), or whether they are too meager and

TABLE 1.   TRANSITION RATES FROM FIRST THROUGH TWELFTH GRADE – ISRAEL, COHORTS COMMENCING 1ST GRADE IN 1957/58 AND 1967/68

Grade	First Cohort Commenced 1st Grade in 1957/8		Second Cohort Commenced 1st Grade in 1967/8	
	Year They Reached Grade	% of Cohort Reaching Grade	Year They Reached Grade	% of Cohort Reaching Grade
8th	1964/65	82.7	1974/75	95.5
9th	1965/66	64.8	1975/76	91.2
10th	1966/67	55.7	1976/77	77.9
11th	1967/68	44.7	1977/78	64.6
12th	1968/69	32.2	1978/79	55.9

Source: Egozi and Bilezki (1980, Table 11).

TABLE 2. TRANSITION RATES FROM TENTH THROUGH TWELFTH GRADE – ISRAEL, 1970–1972 AND 1975–1977

Year	Grade	Total	Israel and European- American Origin	Asian-African Origin
	First Cohort: 1970–72 *Secondary Education – Total*			
1970	10th	100.0	100.0	100.0
1971	11th	78.5	84.8	72.8
1972	12th	59.6	68.4	48.2
	Second Cohort: 1975–77 *Secondary Education – Total*			
1975	10th	100.0	100.0	100.0
1976	11th	78.9	84.1	74.4
1977	12th	67.8	75.0	61.5
	Vocational and Agricultural			
1975	10th	100.0	100.0	100.0
1976	11th	71.4	75.9	69.2
1977	12th	67.8	75.0	52.7
	Academic Education			
1975	10th	100.0	100.0	100.0
1976	11th	88.7	89.4	87.4
1977	12th	83.1	83.0	83.3

Source: Egozi and Bilezki (1979, Table 16).

thus insignificant, is a matter of value judgement. I lean strongly toward the former opinion.

As Table 3 indicates, the rate of under-representation of AA adolescents (aged 14–17) in all secondary schools went down 8.9%, from 14.3% in 1966/67 to only 5.4% in 1979/80. However, over the same period of time, under-representation in academic schools decreased only 7.1%, from 24.5% to 17.4%. Table 4 shows that in academic schools, the rate of under-representation shrank – in the 12th grade – from 33.5% to 25%. And, indeed,

TABLE 3. PERCENT OF ASIAN-AFRICAN ORIGIN AMONG ALL 14 TO 17-YEAR OLDS AND AMONG ALL STUDENTS IN SECONDARY EDUCATION – ISRAEL, 1966/67–1979/80

Year	Among all 14–17 Year Olds	Total % in Secondary Education	9th Grades	12th Grades	Academic Schools	Vocat. Schools	Agricultural Schools
1966/67	49.9	35.6	45.3	18.9	25.4	47.0	52.4
1976/77	58.7	50.6	54.6	46.6	37.5	63.7	65.9
1977/78	58.4	51.3	55.0	47.5	38.4	64.1	65.3
1978/79	57.7	51.5	53.5	48.3	38.7	64.3	64.7
1979/80	57.3	51.9	54.9	49.6	39.9	64.4	64.6

Source: Egozi and Bilezki (1980, Table 25); Bilezki and Turki (1980, Table 26).

TABLE 4. PARTICIPATION OF 14–17–YEAR OLD ADOLESCENTS OF ASIAN-AFRICAN ORIGIN IN ACADEMIC SECONDARY SCHOOLS – ISRAEL, 1966/67–1976/77

Year	1966/67	1973/74	1976/77
Rate of adolescents of Asian-African origin among total 14–17–year olds	49.9	57.7	58.7
Rate of Asian-African adolescents:			
Secondary schools, total	35.6	46.6	50.6
Academic schools, total	26.7	32.1	36.1
thereof: 9th grade	33.9	37.2	39.7
12th grade	16.4	27.7	33.7

Source: Egozi and Bilezki (1978, Table 13).

Table 5 shows that the participation of young adults of AA origin in higher education expanded between the years 1966/65 and 1974/75 much more than did the participation of the same age group of EA origin. The rate of growth approached 100% for Israeli-born young adults. This quite considerable growth in AA participation in secondary and higher education may be related to the emergence of an AA middle-class in Israel, as well as to the beginning of the group's penetration into elite positions – mainly in the political, military, business, managerial and, to a lesser degree, professional spheres.

TABLE 5. RATES OF UNIVERSITY ATTENDANCE OF 20–29–YEAR-OLDS PER 10,000 IN RESPECTIVE GROUPS OF THE POPULATION[a] – ISRAEL, 1964/65–1974/75

Continent of Birth and Origin	1964/65	1974/75
Total	413	716
Israeli Born, total	893	951
Father Israeli born	524	297
Father Asia-African born	158	299
Father Europe-American born	1,074	1,405
Asian-African born	79	211
Europe-American born	535	842

(a)   Due to the mandatory military service in Israel, freshmen at Israeli universities are 20 to 21 years old.

Source: Egozi and Bilezki (1979, Table 33).

Despite this progress, essentially all of Israel's lower class is composed of people of AA origin. Policies enacted in the last decade such as Project Renewal are to be welcomed, since they are directed at ecological pockets of lower-income and lower-class groups in Israel's population, which exhibit signs of a self-perpetuating 'culture of poverty', rather than at entire ethnic groups. This statement does not contradict the fact that in recent years 'ethnic consciousness' among the AA origin group has risen and has been partially translated into political power. The analysis thereof, however, is beyond the scope of this paper.

The Second Challenge: Israel's Education Policies and the Manpower Needs of an Industrialized Nation

Every nation must decide on the policy of education best suited to its ideology and needs: either a democratic system offering mass education and equal opportunities – in which case the standards of achievement are often compromised – or, alternatively, a system designed to maintain high academic standards which would thus be selective or even elitist. Given the second alternative, fewer students would complete a full-fledged academic course of studies and consequently fewer would be prepared for employment requiring academic certification. Israel has been forced in its short history to try to achieve the benefits of both policies at the same time. Whereas it was faced with serious social and economic gaps between groups of different ethnic origins, with the establishment of the State, a rapid process of industrialization was initiated. This industrialization based itself on a generation of skilled manpower which had been trained in Europe and America prior to immigration, and would eventually have to be replaced with locally educated personnel. It is as yet very hard to judge whether the results were merely a compromise between essentially conflicting goals, or whether they succeeded in complementing each other. As the following analysis will indicate, I tend to lean toward the latter conclusion.

The following dual trend has been salient throughout the entire period: on the one hand, the expansion of education led both to the inclusion of the very young (3–to 4–year-olds) in the system as well as to the opening up of secondary education to all adolescents – clear strategies of democratization. Table 6 shows an annual growth rate which exceeded the population growth rates in the respective age groups between 1970 and 1981, and particularly in the post-secondary and higher academic education institutions. At the same time, however, the education system did not give up its selective track of senior academic high-schools, whose curricula are largely determined by faculty members of Israel's institutions of higher learning. Indeed, only some 25% of each year's age cohort successfully complete the course in these schools and thus become the main pool of candidates for the universities. Since the abolishment of school fees in 1977, this track has accepted students almost exclusively according to their academic performance. If we assume (as in Table 7) that some 85% of the graduating academic class successfully pass the matriculation examination, then in 1975/76 this included about 12,700 students (24% of 17–year-olds in that year). By 1980/81 this number had risen to about 16,800 (30.5% of 17–year olds in that year). Recently vocational edu-

TABLE 6. TOTAL NUMBER OF STUDENTS BY SCHOOL LEVEL (IN THOUSANDS) – ISRAEL, 1970/71–1981/82

School Level	1970/71	1975/76	1980/81	1981/82	Annual Average Growth Rates 1970–81
Total	730.9	883.0	1,009.3	1,026.2	3.1
Kindergartens	107.6	180.6	211.9	208.8	6.2
Elementary schools	409.8	441.7	509.6	523.0	2.2
Secondary schools	155.7	177.8	195.9	199.8	2.3
Post-Secondary schools	18.3	31.6	34.9	36.7	6.5
College, Universities	39.5	51.3	57.0	57.9	3.5

Source: Bilezki and Turki (1982, Table 2).

TABLE 7. THE NUMBER OF 17-YEAR-OLDS IN THE TOTAL POPULATION
AND IN THE GRADUATING CLASS (12TH GRADE) OF ACADEMIC
HIGH SCHOOLS - ISRAEL, 1975/76-1981/82

	1975/76	1981/82
Number in population	52,000	55,000[a]
Number in graduating class of academic high schools	14,900	19,800[b]
Number of matriculated graduates	12,690	16,800[c]
Percent of total	24	30

(a)   The number of 14-17-year-olds in those years was 209,000 and 215,000 respectively. We assumed that each age cohort comprised about 25% of the four-year group.

(b)   The number of students in 12th grade in 1975 was about 27,500 and that about 55% of those studied in academic high schools; similarly in 1981/82 about 36,000 studied in 12th grades and 53% were in academic high schools.

(c)   Based on the assumption that about 85% of the graduating class successfully passes the matriculation examination.

Source: Bilezki and Turki (1982, Tables 12, 23).

cation has also been contributing graduates who pass the matriculation examination, thereby increasing the pool of university candidates.

Although this policy may be judged by some as being too selective, and even in contradiction to the ideals of open and democratic opportunities for all, it has allowed the dramatic expansion of Israel's system of higher education over the past thirty years; indeed, having begun with one university (The Hebrew University of Jerusalem) and one technological institute (the Technion in Haifa), Israel now has several additional universities (Tel Aviv, Bar Ilan, Haifa, Ben Gurion in Beer Sheva, The Weizmann Institute in Rehovot, Everyman's University). More important perhaps is the fact that many of the academic positions in these institutions of higher learning are today occupied by scholars and researchers whose education was received mostly in Israel. A growing number among the faculty acquired even their Ph.D.s here. Furthermore, the rate of publications by Israeli academicians and participation in international research teams, symposia or conferences by Israeli scholars is steadily rising. Thus, for instance, there was a total of about 450 publications by Israeli scholars before 1959, but in 1967 alone there were about 2,000 publication in the field of natural science (Kahane, 1979). The number of students in Israeli institutions of higher learning rose from about 200 in 1929 and 1,700 in 1949 to more than 63,000 in 1982/83 (see Table 8). This high rate of growth (almost 35 times) far transcends that

TABLE 8. NUMBERS OF STUDENTS IN INSTITUTIONS OF HIGHER LEARNING, BY DEGREE – ISRAEL, 1948/49–1982/83

Degree	1948/49	1959/60	1969/70	1978/9	1980/81	1982/83
Total	1,635	9,275	36,239	48,790	61,920	63,365
First degree (B.A.)	1,549	8,348	28,053	39,010	40,910	43,380
Second degree (M.A.)	(a)	(a)	5,156	2,370	13,550	11,555
Third degree (Ph.D.)	86	927	1,346	2,970	3,070	3,000
Diploma	–	–	819	1,390	4,390	4,830
Special programs	–	–	865	3,050		

(a)   Students working toward a second degree are included in the number of those studying for the first degree.

Source: Central Bureau of Statistics, (1980, Table XXII/26; 1983, Table XXII/36); Bilezki and Turki (1982, Table 21).

of the population growth over the same years (about 6 times). The growth rate of degree recipients is even more dramatic (more than 50 times – see Table 9). The number of Israeli applications for patent registrations rose from 638 in 1949 to 2,917 in 1982 (Central Bureau of Statistics, 1983).

Paralleling this development has been the 'explosion' of technological and vocational training. This has already been mentioned mainly because this training has become the main avenue of educational mobility for adolescents of AA origin. About two-thirds of the technological and vocational student body today comes from AA backgrounds, a fact which gives the appearance of a discriminatory selection procedure. However, an ever-growing rate of skilled blue-collar workers are of AA origin, as are a majority of foremen in industry, and an ever-growing number of technicians. Even if top management and most senior staff of Israel's industry is still of EA origin, the fact that there has been successful integration into modern industry cannot be explained without citing the massive expansion of vocational training and technological education, which has included many young men and women whose families originated in the Near and Middle East. It is interesting to note that between 1970/71 and 1981/82 the rate of vocational school students rose from 29% to almost 47% of the total 12th grade student population (Bilezki and Turki, 1982, Table 12). Moreover, in 1981/82 about 25% of the 12th grade vocational students studied in the vocational academic track, and of these, about 65% (some 6,000) took a full matriculation examination (Central Bureau of Statistics, 1983, Table XXII/28). That is, of the 16,000 students who took the matriculation exam in 1981/82 the vocational track contributed about 38% (Central Bureau of Statistics, 1983, Table XXII/27).

TABLE 9. RECIPIENTS OF UNIVERSITY DEGREES, BY DEGREE – ISRAEL,1948/49–1980/81

Degree	1948/49	1959/60	1969/70	1978/79	1980/81
Total	193	1,197	5,566	9,556	10,088
First degree (B.A.)	135	779	4,064	6,602	7,396
Second degree (M.A)	48	337	807	1,767	1,754
Third degree (Ph.D)	10	81	238	401	353
Diploma	–	–	457	786	585

Source: Central Bureau of Statistics, (1980, Table XXII/32; 1983, Table XXII/42).

Israel's success, even as measured by international criteria in medicine, advanced technology and agriculture, not to mention the military – is consequently in many respects the result of a secondary school system which kept emphasizing quality of education and standards of achievement, in spite of understandable and perhaps legitimate efforts in the opposite direction.

We may thus conclude that Israel's massive investment in the expansion of public education and in the means for making it accessible to all – and the deep commitment to education and willingness to share in the burden of its maintenance and growth through taxes or fees by ever growing parts of the population – may to an extent explain the co-existence of a relative openness and democratization of the educational system alongside its relatively high educational standards.

The Third Challenge: The Role of Israel's Education System in Addressing the Emergence of a Relevant, Modern Jewish Identity

It may well be that this issue is ultimately more crucial for the future of Israel than the two mentioned previously. However, there are unfortunately only very few data upon which to base our argument. My personal view, which I shall try to substantiate, is that while Israel has been relatively – or maybe even very – successful in coping with the two challenges mentioned above, this is not true of the issue we address now.

To its founders, it was quite obvious that the educational system of Israel had to help give Jewish meaning to the emerging and struggling movement for a modern, Jewish creative and politically independent entity. It was at the same time acknowledged that this Jewish meaning had to be relevant to a modern, free and democratic society. E. Rieger in his two-volume analysis of education in the new society, devotes a whole chapter to the strengthening of the religious authority in the schools; then, in a section called "The Encouragement of Pioneering Elements", he discusses kibbutz education, the role of the school in nurturing relations with Arab neighbors, the need to deepen the concern of students for the Diaspora, the Jewish National Fund as an educational inspiration, etc. (Rieger, 1940). These are all Jewish values which the school should emphasize and nurture as one of its main tasks – tasks which of course are uniquely relevant to the Jewish society in Israel.

In the fifty years of the *Yishuv*, the division of the education system into three political-ideological trends brought about three different interpretations of the issues at hand – all of which, however, drew on Jewish sources as the basis for their new identity. For example, the need to justify the return to *Eretz Israel* and to this end they emphasized the struggle for Jewish independence in other historical eras – whether Joshua's original conquest and settlement of the land, the Hasmonean war, or Bar Kochba's uprising. The negative aspect of this emphasis was the critique and repudiation of the Diaspora, mainly of the shtetl. But above all was the commitment to the revival of Hebrew as a modern language and its adaptation to current needs. The revived language of the Bible certainly represents important elements of Israel's cultural heritage and national identity even though it was not in daily use during the centuries of dispersion (Kleinberger, 1969, pp. 1–37).

After the foundation of the State and the abolishment in 1953 of the political-ideological trends in education, the issue under discussion became much more complicated. First and foremost, the establishment of Israel as an independent Jewish democratic state was conceived by many as the realization of the Zionist dream, even though it can be argued that in certain important ways, this is far from the case.[2] Yet the widespread acceptance of such a notion is perhaps responsible for the fact that large segments of the younger secular population, sons and grandsons of the founding fathers of Israel, tend to take Israel's statehood for granted and do not feel the need to keep searching for sources of collective identity. It is thus foreseeable that for this majority of youth there is a real danger of blurring and even loss of what is Jewish in their culture and lifestyle. The existence of the state religious school subsystem probably prevents the non-Orthodox state schools – which enroll about three-quarters of the student population – from contributing constructively to the formation of a meaningful Jewish identity for their students. The existence of a state religious school casts a shadow over the Jewishness of the other – apparently 'less Jewish' – school system, and only if the non-religious schools can offer genuine non-Orthodox based Jewish elements through their curriculum can such a shadow be dispersed. However, lacking such modern Jewish elements, it is not surprising that in a number of empirical studies concerning the identity of Israeli youth, Orthodox religious elements were found to play a central role among students of the non-religious state school (Guttman and Levy, 1974, 1976), possibly due to the absence of other meaningful sources of Jewish identification.

It should, of course, be stated that all schools, as indeed the society at large, live by a 'Jewish rhythm' i.e. the calendar is the Jewish calendar; the week starts when the Sabbath ends, and Sunday is the first school day of the week; the Jewish holidays are important in school life; the language spoken, studied and very much stressed by the school is Hebrew; the study of the Bible is the one subject to which all schools allot a major portion of time from second through twelfth grade; Jewish history and Hebrew literature are taught in all schools (in addition, of course, to general history and literature). In other words, all Israeli schools certainly place a heavy emphasis on Jewish curricula. Yet, it is often asked whether this is the best possible strategy for shaping a coherent Jewish identity which will both continue Jewish history, and also be meaningful to the generation which was born into modern Jewish statehood (Eisenstadt et al., 1972).

Perhaps the very serious challenges faced by the society in the military, economic and social spheres have preempted the search for modern Jewish meanings to their national existence. Nor are schools any longer the arena for such a search (Adar and Adler, 1965). One might find parallels between these developments in Israel and similar difficulties in the Jewish education of many non-Orthodox children in the free-world Diaspora.

While other issues may be assessed in terms of the success or failure of education, there are hardly any indicators to similarly assess the 'educational product' in the area of identity formation. We witness many expressions of popular Israeli culture in song, dance, humor and slang. However, these are inspired mainly by current events, by Eastern Jewish folklore and by the styles of speech and behavior evolving in the Israel Defense Forces. It is doubtful whether this popular culture draws much on authentic Jewish traditions. Many claim, indeed, that it is rather a sign of our growing 'Americanization' with an essentially non-Jewish basis (Eisenstadt, 1985). A rich Hebrew poetry, drama and literature, as well as different types of high quality journalism, have also been emerging, but they too seem to draw more on the 'Israeli way of life' and on universally-faced problems, pressures and experiences than on Jewish tradition. This varied cultural creativity can hardly be seen as a basis for a modern Jewish image or identity for the young generation if that identity is to be part of the continuum of Jewish history.

Recently there has been a trend emphasizing the need to base such a modern Israeli identity on earlier Jewish sources. As a result of the 1977 elections, the leading political party changed, accelerating a process begun about a decade earlier, namely the ideological retreat of the Israel Labor movement. This movement served in many respects as the backbone and spearhead of the social and cultural framework that ultimately led to independence and statehood. As a political movement, it was driven by a futuristic orientation, with an image of an innovative, just, egalitarian and creative modern Jewish society. Even though the founding fathers and later the political leaders of this movement were not observant Jews, they were familiar with Jewish tradition and therefore sought and accorded it an authentic basis for their orientation. Israel's legitimation was rooted mostly in the needs of the present, and this constituted the initial setback to the futuristic orientation of the Labor movement, which had been searching in Jewish tradition and history for the bases of such legitimation.

The growing religious polarization since Independence (or alternatively, the trend of lending religious meaning to political strife) created ambivalence among many secular youth toward the values or ideals of Jewish tradition. The peak of this development was reflected in the tendency for the new political forces at the helm of society to search for inspiration and legitimation for their actions in the mythological past rather than in an ideal future of a just, creative and modern Jewish society. It is no surprise, therefore that some new images of the future Israeli society evolve around the notion of 'greater Israel,' a vision stemming from King Solomon's Kingdom, completely detached from the current demographic and political realities of the region.

Since all schools reflect general social trends and developments, these phenomena do effect Israeli schools. An example is the increase in emphasis on and the time allotted to, the study of traditional Jewish texts at the expense of other facets of the curriculum, and the sustained effort to deal with modern Jewish cultural expressions (Firer, 1980). It may well be that the search for a modern Jewish identity is a problem commonly faced by the 'secular' majority of Israel's population and greater parts of the Jewish people in the Diaspora. While Israel seems to be able to meet the first two challenges discussed in this chapter out of its own social resources, this third challenge may call for a joint effort on the part of both Israel and the Jewish communities of the free world.

In this respect the 'secular' majority of Israel's population (and certainly that segment of it which is deeply concerned about our future as a modern Jewish society) and greater parts of the Jewish people in their respective communities share a similar challenge. Could it be, that in this respect, not only "from Zion will come forth the Torah"?

Acknowledgements

I wish to express thanks to my colleagues, Lorrain Gastwirt, Assistant Director of the National Council of Jewish Women, U.S.A., Research Institute for Innovation in Education and Reuven Kahane of the Department of Sociology and the School of Education for suggesting changes in the manuscript; to my colleague Ilana Felsenthal of the NCJW Research Institute and the School of Education for her careful reading of the manuscript and valuable suggestions for changes and additions; to Geulah Solomon of the Institute of Contemporary Jewry, The Hebrew University, and to Chaya Buckwold for her kind help and patience in typing and retyping the manuscript.

Notes

1. The relevant statistics have never been officially published. This statement is thus my own approximated calculation, based on unpublished reports, as well as on growth rates in university attendance. (See for instance: Central Bureau of Statistics, 1983).

2. This statement is based mostly on the fact that unlike the earliest Zionist vision, most Jews do not live in Israel. Judging from the immense difficulty of encouraging aliyah even from suppressed Jewish communities (such as that of the USSR), it is doubtful whether that vision will ever materialize.

References

Adar, L. and Adler, C. (1965). *Education for Values in New Immigrant Schools in Israel.* The School of Education, The Hebrew University, Jerusalem.

Adler, C. (1969). "The Place of Education in the Integration of Ethnic Communities in Israel" in: Eisenstadt, S.N. and Zloczower, A., *Ingathering of Exiles.* Magnes Press, Jerusalem. (Hebrew).

Adler, C. and Melzer-Druker, P. (n.d.). *A Survey of Evaluations of Educational Intervention Programs Sponsored by Project Renewal.* National Council for Jewish Welfare, Research Institute for Innovation in Education, The School of Education, The Hebrew University, Jerusalem. (Mimeograph).

Bentwich, V. (1965). *Education in Israel.* Routledge and Kegan Paul, London.

Bilezki, P. and Turki, Ch. (1982). *The Educational System as Mirrored by Numbers, 1982.* Jerusalem. (Mimeograph, Hebrew).

Central Bureau of Statistics (1981, 1983). *Statistical Abstract of Israel*, Vols. 32, 34.

Chaim, A. (1980). "The Evaluation of the Israeli School Reform" in: Goldstein, S. (ed.) *Law and Equality in Education.* The Van Leer Foundation, Jerusalem.

Chen, M., Adler, C. and Klein, Z, eds. (1977). *Megamot: Behavioral Science Quarterly*, Vol. 23, no. 3/4. Jerusalem. (Hebrew with English abstracts).

Dar, Y. and Resh, N. (1981). *Homogeneity and Heterogeneity in Education.* The National Council of Jewish Women Research Institute for Innovation in Education, The School of Education, The Hebrew University, Jerusalem. (Mimeograph).

Davis, D., Sprinzak, D. and Osizon, R. (1982). *Who Benefits from Educational Resources: Allocation of Resources in Years 1973, 1978, 1981.* Israel, Ministry of Education and Culture, Jerusalem. (Hebrew).

Egozi, M. and Bilezki, P. (1978; 1979; 1980). *The Educational System as Mirrored by Numbers.* Jerusalem. (Mimeograph, Hebrew).

Eisenstadt, S.N. (1985). *Transformation of Israeli Society.* Weidenfeld and Nicolson, London.

Eisenstadt, S.N., Adler, C., Bar Yosef, R. and Kahane, R., eds. (1972). *Israel – A Society in the Making, A Sociological Analysis of Sources.* Magnes Press, Jerusalem.

Elboim-Dror, R. (1982). "Israel's Educational Policies" in: Ackerman, W., Carmon A. and Zucker, D. (eds.). *Education in Israel.* Klett-Cotta, Stuttgart. (German).

Firer, R. (1980). *Formation and Information: The Influence of Zionist Values on the History Textbooks of the Jewish People Written in Hebrew and Used in Israel Between the Years 1900–1980.* Ph.D. dissertation, The Hebrew University, Jerusalem. (Hebrew, English Abstract).

Frankenstein, C. ed. (1976). *Teaching as a Social Challenge.* School of Education, The Hebrew University and the Ministry of Education and Culture, Jerusalem.

Guttman, L. and Levy, S. (1974; 1976). *Values and Attitudes of School Students in Israel.* The Institute of Applied Social Research, Jerusalem. 2 vols. (Hebrew).

Kahane, R. (1968). *Patterns of National Identity in Israel.* Academon, Jerusalem. (Hebrew).

Kahane, R. (1979). "Preliminary Reflections on the University in Israel: A Sociological Perspective". Paper presented at the Symposium on the International Issues in University Administration, Ankara University, Ankara.

Kahane, R. (1980). "Patterns of National Identity in Israel" in: Kahane, R. et al. (eds.) *Problems of Collective Identity and Legitimation in the Israel Society, A Reader.* Academon, Jerusalem.

Kahane, R. and Starr, L. (1984). *Education and Work: Vocational Socialization Processes in Israel.* Magnes Press, Jerusalem. (Hebrew).

Klein, Z. and Eshel, Y. (1980). *Integrating Jerusalem Schools.* Academic Press, Jerusalem.

Kleinberger, A.F. (1969). *Society, School and Progress in Israel.* Pergamon Press, London.

Musgrove, F. (1979). *School and the Social Order.* John Wiley and Sons, New York.

Peled, E. (1982). "The Educational Reform in Israel – the Political Aspect" in: Ben Baruch, E. and Neumann Y. *Educational Policy and Policy Making.* Vinpress, Herzlia.

Rieger, E. (1940). *Hebrew Education in Palestine.* Dvir, Tel Aviv. (Hebrew).

19

Jewish Education in Israel: The Ideological Factor

Michael Rosenak

Speaking at the Home of Israel's President on the state of Jewish identity, ideology and education in Israel, Moshe Davis noted that "somewhat more than eighty percent of the Jewish children in the world who receive satisfactory Jewish education...are in the State of Israel, as against less than twenty percent in the Diaspora. This....is actually the reverse of the Jewish demographic situation in the world" (Davis, 1978).

One may argue about the criteria to be used for determining what 'satisfactory Jewish education' is and, indeed, this argument is the subject of our paper. But if some 80% of the hours and institutional efforts devoted to the transmission of Jewish culture and heritage throughout the world are located in *Eretz Israel*, then a decision not to deal with the meanings assigned to the term 'Jewish education' in Israel could be justified only on such stipulative grounds that, for example, Jewish education is 'by definition,' non-Israeli, or that any education which does not correspond to a specific conception of Jewish tradition is not 'really Jewish'. According to the first assumption, Israel would be seen as an alternative to Jewish existence rather than a form of it; according to the second stipulation, only the education given in, say, pockets of ultra-traditional Jewry, whether in Brooklyn or in Bnei Brak, 'count'. But such stipulative definitions would ignore both the complexity of the Jewish tradition and the social and ideological realities governing the attitudes and ideals of contemporary Jewry. It is our contention that both the tradition and the realities should be taken seriously in Jewish education.

The discussion of Jewish educational thought in Israel is especially pertinent because the on-going discussion about desirable responses and accommodations to modernity on the part of those who wish to retain a meaningful Jewish identity and commitment is most concentrated (territorially), most comprehensive (socially) and perhaps most revolutionary (politically) in the framework of Zionism and the State of Israel. As Rotenstreich has pointed out, Israel embodies the decision to restore the Jews as a collective political entity to the arena of world history (Rotenstreich, 1958; 1977). Tal has also described how Israel signifies, for its ideological and educational thinkers, an attempt to translate aspects of the Jewish normative and Messianic tradition into social reality (Tal, 1971). As Tal portrays it, Israel represents the aspiration to achieve a new and 'relevant' Jewish authenticity which utilizes halachic and traditional mystic resources, but which also endeavors to incorporate other cultural sources and influences to achieve a new Jewish-human ideal in a historically continuous, yet truly contemporary society.

The 'eighty percent' of Jewish education located in Israel is thus not simply a source of pride or vindication; the ideological writings which have fostered and recorded its growth testify also to perplexity, polemic and occasional despair. Together with satisfaction at the fact that "never in Jewish history has the Bible been studied so seriously," there is recognition of the sore neglect of the Oral Tradition in 'general' (non-Orthodox) schools.[1] Pride at the restoration of Hebrew as a spoken language, revived from the dead by zealots and idealists (among whom teachers were heavily and articulately represented), has been qualified by educational onslaughts on "Hebrew-speaking-goyim" (Kurzweil, 1965, Ch. 12; Urbach, 1967, pp. 62–71). Educational methods designed to cultivate a close tie to the land and a love for its landscapes have been developed and have largely succeeded; yet some have insisted that Jewish identification limited to "love of *Eretz Israel*" is not necessarily or even centrally related to the historical culture of Judaism (Kurzweil, 1953; Gelber, 1976). Already in the 1940s and 1950s writers representing diverse ideological and educational orientations complained about the 'un-Jewish' character of many Israeli youngsters and of the society being created in *Eretz Israel*; the opponents of these critics insisted that such strictures were based on arbitrary and monolithic definitions of Jewishness or resulted from lack of historical or sociological perspective.[2] In recent years, Katz has commented on the diversity of viewpoints within (even) contemporary religious communities and has noted the role of religion as a divisive (as well as historically unifying) feature of modern Jewish life, and Eisenstadt has argued that traditional patterns of Jewishness persist to a large extent despite changes in overt ideology and allegiance to specified cultural symbols (Katz, 1975; 1977; Eisenstadt, 1977). Thus, there is constant change and 'movement' within situations of stability, and, conversely, one may perceive perennial patterns even within upheaval and revolution.

The question of Jewish education in Israel must therefore be seen against the backdrop of discontinuity and the search for legitimate (i.e., rooted in cultural tradition) change which mark the modern era in Jewish history, thought and education, and which is reflected in a singularly intensive manner within Zionism and its institutions. Zionism has been both a reflection and an outcome of the discontinuities and of the search. The entire spectrum of Jewish self-understanding *vis-à-vis* modern thought and society are to be found within Zionism, and the seminal figures of the Zionist movement run the gamut from Jews who grew up in traditional environments and 'strayed' to those who saw themselves as pristinely 'European' and 'returned'. Ahad Ha'am was a prominent representative of the former – those who sought in Zionism a solution to the problem of Judaism in the modern age (after having experienced the traditional beliefs and practices as untenable and assimilation as inauthentic). As for the latter category, it was classically represented by Theodore Herzl, who wished to solve the problem of the Jew whose assimilation was thwarted by antisemitism; Herzl spoke for a group of 'Europeans' whose disinterest in the concrete Jewish tradition was commensurate with their ignorance of it, but who learned to recognize that they were Jews. There were Zionists like the Orthodox Kalisher who anticipated the consummation of Jewish historical yearnings through the return to *Eretz Israel* (including the restoration of the sacrificial service in the Temple); others, like the Marxist Borochov, saw in Zionism a framework for economic normality which would enable Jews to engage in a 'healthy' class struggle. For secularists like Klatzkin, Zionism meant the survival of the Jewish group beyond the demise of the (formerly) nation-sustaining religious legal regimen, on the foundation of the 'normal' attributes of language and territory; for theologically-minded thinkers like Buber, it meant the rehabilitation of the covenant, which required for its human-divine encounter a comprehensive and responsible society (Hertzberg, 1959).

Intellectually and ideologically, Zionism was a stock-exchange of options and theories concerning Jewish existence, which included the religious mysticism of Rabbi Kook as well as the bitter antagonism to religious tradition of Brenner (ibid.). All Zionists could agree that their movement incorporated a desire to continue Jewish existence and to rebel against features of Jewish history or tradition which were 'unhealthy' or 'distorting', but there was little agreement as to what constituted continuity and what had to be rejected. The General Zionist found central European bourgeois values (such as liberal democracy) admirable and sometimes liked Jewish piety even when he did not adhere to it, but he had no tolerance for Gentile condescension or Jewish religious 'fanaticism'. The *Mizrachist* (religious Zionist) continued to see the traditional codes as normative for Jewish practice but rejected the traditional pattern of passivity which left Jewish physical safety and survival to God and benign temporal princes. The cultural Zionist insisted on maintaining the terminology of 'sacred' Jewish tradition, but declared that such terms as 'mitzvah' and 'redemption' should be seen in a valuative perspective nourished by secular learning and ideology. And while the spiritual Zionist wished to create a new collective ethos of cultural Jewishness, the political Zionist, who sought to restore ancient glories and consciousness, preferred to leave the salvation (religious or 'spiritual') of the soul to the individual – an attitude which was characteristic of Western contemporary religion but a radical departure from, or reinterpretation of, the Jewish tradition.

Writers such as Avineri and Samuel have shown (Avineri, 1980; Samuel, 1948) that on the emotional level, Zionism was a complex network of associations, shaped by nostalgia and utopian yearnings, romance and realism. The 'shtetl' and other communities in exile, the newly encountered hues and contours of the landscape of *Eretz Israel* and the memories of biblical epics intertwined with medieval imaginings – all these clashed and blended, and the result was sometimes astonished happiness and sometimes bitter disappointment. For example, the attitude towards the Arab was ambivalent; it was both romantic and realistic. Similarly, there was an urge to throw off the trappings of *galut* (from jackets to the conventions of courtesy) and to live simply, yet also to revive ancient symbols and ceremony. The Zionist wished to be 'normal' and, at the same time, expected no less of himself than to be "a light unto the nations".

All of the above entered into deliberations on education and were expressed as dilemmas. Could there be Jewish education that was not religious? Could there be religious education which would give a respected status to secular studies? How was an educational ideal to be devised in which Judaism and humanity would be indivisible, in which the tendentious distinction between Jewish and general studies would be overcome? Such questions had already been raised in modern national educational frameworks in Europe, but in *Eretz Israel* they became more pressing, since the ideal Jewish society and not only the ideal Jewish soul was at stake. Therefore, education was burdened with the ideological tension occasioned by the demand to socialize and revolutionize, to transmit culture and transform it.

Debating the 'New Jewish Education' in Eretz Israel: Consensus and Confrontation

The debate about what should comprise the 'new Jewish education' in *Eretz Israel* can be viewed via three competing conceptions of Judaism and Jewish education which may be termed the theological, metaphysical and naturalistic conceptions.[3]

In the theological view, Judaism is 'traditionally' seen as inseparable from religious obligations and meanings, and the Jewish people is to be understood within the context of revealed teaching. *Eretz Israel* and the national movement are viewed as important because Judaism requires land and society for its total application and scope. While not all representatives of the theological view have been Orthodox, theological education is always related to the cultivation of a religious sensibility, a religious view of Jewish peoplehood and a 'covenantal' conception of *Eretz Israel*. And the 'return' to the land is to be seen in the perspective of divine promise and Jewish commitment to God's will.

The metaphysical view constitutes an attempt to maintain an 'objective' conception of Judaism while divorcing its normative standards from religious moorings. Judaism becomes a philosophy of life, a system of values representing the cumulative experience of the Jewish people with moral and cultural issues. It establishes the consciousness and cultural 'language' in which Jews, optimally in their own society, may embody and develop their model of human existence. As in the theological approach, Judaism is a historically specific spiritual view and reality. Through its texts and heroes, its memories and events, it transmits this 'culture' to the young and shapes them in its image.

The naturalistic view denies that education is concerned primarily with the transmission of systems or traditions per se. Rather, it brings the young, through vital experience, into the life of a group which shapes identity and permits individual self-realization. The group has its own distinct history and environment, but it is primarily concerned with challenges to its meaningful and secure existence, with 'actual' problems. The Jewish naturalistic or 'realistic' educator desires to teach the young how to recognize such problems and how to gain competence in resolving them. Thus Jewish Zionist education conveys an understanding of what is problematic in contemporary Jewish life and fosters the ideal and the ability to deal with it. Among the ideals proposed by Mahler, a proponent of this view, are pioneering (*halutziut*), ingathering of the exiles and the construction of a viable and dynamic Jewish society (Mahler, 1961).

These three views of Jewish identity and education may be seen as roughly corresponding to ideological foundations for the three Jewish school systems which developed during the mandate period in *Eretz Israel*: the General Zionist, the *Mizrachi* (religious) and the Labor systems though there was much ideological overlapping and some diversity within the systems or 'trends' themselves. The development of these diverse educational orientations, at a time of great financial stress within the Zionist movement and with a total Jewish population of only several hundred thousand, bears eloquent testimony both to the seriousness with which educational-ideological questions were treated and to the diversity of outlooks.

Historians of Jewish education in *Eretz Israel*, (Rieger, 1940; Lamm, 1973; Bentwich, 1965), have described the ideological tensions behind the emergence of the three Zionist systems. The General Zionist system, initiated in 1913 with the establishment of six schools, represented the ideological orientation of 'general Zionists' in the main; but it saw itself as the national-educational framework for all, and its educational philosophy the blueprint for the new national education as such. In the 'general' school, civic and classically liberal virtues were stressed, its social philosophy was broadly 'cultural', and it cultivated, by and large, a positive attitude and reverence for the religious tradition, without, however, fostering religious beliefs or practice. The 'general' school prided itself on its affinity to the best insights and methods of modern European pedagogy, and on its ideological breadth which would make possible a national-cultural concensus that would steer clear of religious and 'class' (i.e., socialist) separatism.

Yet, despite the flexibility and the wide range of opinion reflected in the writings of educators who wished, through the curriculum of the general school, to make Jewish tradition significant and congenial to all, the 'general' approaches clearly could not satisfy the Orthodox religious Zionist. For the general school did have an ideology concerning tradition, and that ideology was, in the eyes of the Orthodox, at odds with religious teaching. In the General Zionist school, the Talmud was reduced to 2% of the curriculum of the primary school; the Bible, though accorded 16% of instructional hours, was taught according to 'national' or 'humanistic' conceptions which did violence to traditional axioms concerning its normative and revealed character. Thus, in 1920, the *Mizrachi* system was established.

The population drawn to this network of schools was the (then) minority among Orthodox Jews who shared the vision of national revival and Hebrew culture but believed that religious Orthodoxy was not only compatible with, but the authentic blueprint for, this renaissance. Thus, while instruction in sacred texts (not including Hebrew, history and post-Talmudic and modern Jewish literature) were allotted some 18% of instructional hours in the general school, these texts were given about 49% in the *Mizrachi* schools. While, as noted, only 2% of the 'General-Zionist' curriculum dealt with the Oral Tradition and there was no instruction in prayer and halacha, the *Mizrachi* school devoted more time to Talmud (Mishnah and Gemara) than to any other subject (19%), followed closely by Torah and commentaries (14%). It distinguished between the Torah and other biblical books (to the latter it devoted only 10%) and alloted 6% of the curriculum to prayer and halacha. Hebrew (and literature) were less emphasized in the *Mizrachi* school, as were studies concerning *Eretz Israel*, nature and art.[4] The *Mizrachi* schools had their own educational policy-making and supervisory personnel, and teachers were expected to be strictly observant. The ideal was an educated Jew who would be loyal to the Orthodox Jewish tradition, open to the world of modern science and a full partner in the Zionist enterprise.

As the General Zionist trend could not achieve unity or consensus on national-religious issues, neither could it satisfy the socialist (especially kibbutz) public, which insisted that the national homeland be erected on 'realistic' and pioneering principles of Jewish identity and socialist conviction. In 1922, the Labor schools were recognized as a separate system under the auspices of the Histadrut. Just as with the General Zionist and the *Mizrachi* schools, Labor educators considered their institutions to be a model for all

Zionist education in the envisioned future. In these schools, social studies, nature studies and vocational training were heavily stressed, and the study of classical Jewish sources was almost exclusively limited to the Bible, which was taught in one of three ways:

- the secular-scientific mode first proposed by Mossinson (Mossinson, 1910);
- a 'national-moral' approach; and
- a tradition-oriented approach.[5]

In the secular-scientific school of thought, the Bible was taught as a rich literature depicting the fullness of ancient 'Hebrew' life in *Eretz Israel*, regrettably edited by puritan religious censors who had made a national literature into a priestly one. The teacher was charged with the task of rediscovering with his pupils the 'pristine' Bible which could serve as a model for the new Hebrew life being built. The 'national-moral' approach sought pioneering ideals or the battle for social justice in the stories and teachings of patriarchs and prophets, while the traditional approach – inspired by the quasi-secular piety of such mentors as Aaron David Gordon – looked to the Bible as a model of authentic experience and "encounter with the Absolute" (Simon, 1952; Schoneveld, 1976, pp. 102–103). In the Labor system of schools, the Oral Tradition was virtually ignored; conversely, such Jewish subjects as social studies and Jewish history received more emphasis than in either the General Zionist or the *Mizrachi* systems.

After the establishment of the State of Israel the close identification of the various school systems with political parties became a source of tension and conflict. With the influx of hundreds of thousands of new immigrants, mainly from Islamic countries, political forces behind the different types of schools were accused of pressuring the new immigrants into sending their children to one or another of the systems for reasons ostensibly ideological but often, in fact, partisan. The situation that resulted led to the adoption of the State Education Law of 1953 which abolished the 'systems' and established State education. 'State Education' made provision for both 'state schools' and 'state religious schools', and kibbutz schools continued to enjoy relatively autonomous status. Thus, it can be argued that the systems were not really or effectively abolished by the law. Certainly, it did not resolve the ideological issue of "what Jewish education really is" (Bentwich, 1965, pp. 43–44).

Indeed, Clause 2 of the State Education Law formulated 'ideological aims' for the Israeli school; it was to be based on "the values of Jewish culture and the achievements of science, on love of the homeland and loyalty to the state and the Jewish people, on practice in agriculture and manual work, on *halutzic* (pioneering) training, and on striving for a society built on freedom, equality, tolerance, mutual assistance and love of mankind" (Bentwich, 1965, p. 42). But these 'ideals' were clearly attempts to bridge differences semantically. They were sometimes so formally defined as to be of little practical use-fulness (e.g., what is 'Jewish culture'?), and/or evasive. For example, the clause carefully refrained from clarifying the relationship between Jewish tra-dition and modern science; it spoke of the 'values' of the former and the 'achievements' of the latter (Yadlin, 1978). Indeed, it could be claimed that this ideology contained blatant contradictions, such as the concomitant ide-als of inculcating loyalty "to the State and the Jewish people". The legitima-tion of Diaspora Jewish life, it was argued, implied a renunciation of the Zionist vision of 'ingathering' while firm civic (Israeli) loyalty seemed to at least imply condescension toward the Diaspora and its *'galut* mentality' and life-styles (Dinur, 1959; Halpern and Kolatt, 1971).

The more specific ideological questions within the 'state schools' focussed on such issues as:

- making the Bible meaningful and accessible to the modern non-religious child;
- creating familiarity and empathy with the Oral Tradition and later Jew-ish culture as it developed in the Diaspora; and
- inculcating consciousness in the pupil that the State of Israel is a part of Jewish history and of Jewry throughout the world, and, at the same time, avoiding a normative relativism about trends in contemporary Jewish life.

Within the state religious schools, central ideological questions included:

- the negotiation of diverse religious traditions (Ashkenazic and Sephar-dic) in the school;
- the degree of insulation from 'general' social tendencies required to fos-ter pious personalities and the related question of 'general' studies and their status in the religious school; and
- the desirable relationship with religious non-Zionists who claim greater authenticity of religion, specifically the 'world of the yeshivoth' and the adherents of *Agudat Yisrael* (Schoneveld, 1976, Ch. 5; Ormiyan, 1973. pp. 87–102; 106–117).

Here it becomes essential and pertinent to note that the disputes among Zionists about educational principles and ideals never exhausted the ideolog-ical complexity of Jewish education in modern *Eretz Israel*, since Zionism has had to cope with ideological and educational opponents both on the reli-gious right and on the radically 'anti-traditional' left.

To begin with, there were the traditional heders and yeshivoth of the non-Zionist ultra-Orthodox Jews which preceded the Zionists and their 'systems' or 'trends'. While the more moderate of these ultra-Orthodox Jews eventually created their own 'trend' (*Agudat Yisrael*) which made room for secular stud-ies and survived into the post-1953 period as an 'independent' (though almost totally subsidized) school system, these Jews rejected the principle of reconciliation with modernity that characterized all Zionist parties and movements. Among these radical groups, there was total rejection of Zionist interpretations of Judaism and contemporary Jewish life. Ultra-Orthodox moderates wished for co-existence and some tactical cooperation with the Zionist *yishuv*, but even they considered Zionist education as heretical (in the secular schools) or spiritually corrupted (in the religious Zionist ones). For those on the extreme right, total rejection included spurning even the 'independent' school system; for the more moderate, it became a (theological) national alternative to Zionism, accepting Zionism's political-civic framework for what was declared to be a more authentic, classic and universal Jewish allegiance (Friedman, 1975; Selzer, 1970, pp. 1–47).

On the opposite side of the ideological spectrum, one must mention the 'Canaanite' group, which was never more than a tiny and marginal circle, but which, as an orientation enjoyed covert influence in larger circles. Members of this group argued that the return of some Jews to *Eretz Israel* must inevitably and fortunately bring about the real – and therefore un-Jewish – normalization of the Hebrew nation. Their claim has been that a 'Jewish state' is a contradiction in terms; such a 'Jewish' commonwealth can never be more than one of many Jewish communities in the world. It will be as abnormal and neurotic as the Jewish life Zionism wished to transcend. Their ideology and historical prognosis is that the State of Israel lays the foundations for a return to the web of cultural origins that precede the Bible and its stultifying moral and historiosophical conceptions (Kurzweil, 1953).

In confrontation with both of these non-Zionist conceptions, the Zionist disputants discovered and learned to articulate their common assumptions. These assumptions underlie and facilitate diverse educational ventures in which a shared ideology plays a central role but in which controversy is acknowledged and consensus is broadly (sometimes vaguely) conceived. Thus, the army provides extensive courses on Judaism and Zionism, and the Ministry of Education conducts in-service training seminars on Jewish subject-matter which attract teachers of diverse convictions. Such semi-formal educational projects as the Institutes for Zionist-Jewish education, associated with the Ministry of Education, place clarification of Jewish identity and values at the center of their curricular activity (see below). For it is generally agreed that all Zionists, whether religious (Orthodox) or secular (i.e. non-Orthodox religious or non-religious in conviction), whether left-wing or right-wing, share three value axioms:

- the aspiration to reconstitute a national, all-encompassing Jewish life in *Eretz Israel* in which there will be the greatest possible 'ingathering of the exiles' which is a crucial national ideal and task;
- the determination to maintain or restore a spiritual link to Jewish culture in all its epochs and expressions (no matter how diversely interpreted) and to insist not only on historical continuity but cultural continuation; and

- the consciousness of responsibility for the physical survival and well-being of the Jewish people as a collective entity endowed with its own polity and occupying, therefore, its own 'existential space' alongside the nations of the world (Rosenak, 1979).

The first of these value-axioms means that *Eretz Israel* and the rehabilitation of the Jewish people are normative features in education. In practical terms, such 'ideological' activities as hiking and camping are never considered frills and the ideal of integration in society and education (between the well-established and the newcomers, between East and West) is given at least formal allegiance. The educational ideals that flow from the second of these value-axioms is that the tradition of Judaism should be known (however selectively chosen from) even by those who do not consider it binding and that cultural assets and activities of the present deserve attention and respect (even if carefully screened and critically appraised). And the third value-axiom, translated into education, demands the fostering of a national disposition that sees self-defense (i.e. army service) as a moral obligation, and critical loyalty to the State of Israel as a Jewish imperative. These commitments of Zionism are grounded in diverse ideologies and metaphysical assumptions, and they evoke differently graded enthusiasms and priorities but they are shared by all Zionists.

In rounding out the social context in which the ideological questions of education are debated, we must recall that Zionists strive for a common ground not only because they must confront the worlds of the ultra-Orthodox and the totally iconoclastic. There is also the non-European Jewish world which came prominently upon the scene with the mass aliyah of Jews from Islamic countries, particularly in the first years after the achievement of statehood. Generalizations in this area are particularly risky and questionable given the different cultural biographies of Jews from, for example, Morocco and Iraq. But one may note that Jews from these communities, who today constitute more than half of the Jewish population of Israel, were not drawn to the country by the classic dilemmas of the European Jew. Their concern was not usually with the conflict between Western philosophy and tradition; they were little influenced by European conceptions of nationality and religion, and they generally enjoyed a more traditional (though not always ideologically rigorous) relationship to *Eretz Israel* and to Jewish tradition. Both those who came to Israel before the establishment of the State and those who were later brought to the country, were usually Zionists in a religiously Messianic sense.[6] Their view of modern secular culture, especially in the intense and self-confident form it took in Israel, was eclectic and ambivalent. They were often enamored of technology and Western freedom from traditional arbitrary restraints, yet deeply offended by Western-Jewish condescension and by secular disruptions of family and community ties. The choice between religious (Western Orthodox) and secular schools was not, it was increasingly pointed out, broad enough or representative of their view-points. Articulate non-Ashkenazic Jews declared that they neither liked to pray with Polish melodies nor did they want their own history ignored and traditions ignored or dismissed as primitive (Nini, 1971).

For the dominant social groups of the pre-State community (i.e. Zionists of all stripes and non-Zionists in the 'independent' and yeshiva systems), the Jews of the Oriental communities became the objects of educational sociali-zation – though there were fierce debates about how this was to be done (Frankenstein, 1953). But what appeared to the Ashkenazic leadership as an issue of socialization and cognitive rehabilitation was increasingly perceived by the partially socialized non-Western Jews as a valuative issue, involving the retention or abandonment of their attitudes, life-styles and heritage. The intensity of the resentments and the enduring nature of the ambivalences most clearly surfaced with the emergence of young leadership among Sephar-dic Jewry, who expressed dissatisfaction with both the secular and Orthodox models of European Jewishness, and who began to give this dissatisfaction political expression.

Deepening 'Jewish Consciousness'

Doubts and soul-searching about the Jewish education given to the Israeli youngster first became a public issue – beyond the confines of the school, the youth movements and professional journals – in 1955. At that time, the Knesset authorized the government to make innovations in the curriculum of state schools which would lead to the "deepening of Jewish consciousness among Israeli youth...to root them in the past of the Jewish people and its historic heritage and to imbue them with the feeling of belonging to world Jewry, springing from an awareness of their commmon destiny and historic continuity, which unites the Jews throughout the world in all countries and throughout all generations" (Israel, State of, 1959; Kleinberger, 1969, pp. 323–329).

The directives and syllabi concerning "the deepening of Jewish conscious-ness in the State School" (1959) were designed to achieve these aims by mak-ing several changes in units of instruction and in orientation:

– the aim of "rootedness in the spiritual heritage" was to be furthered by intensified study of the weekly portion of the Torah read in the syna-gogue, systematic study of Agada and Mishnah, study of the holiday prayerbook before holidays, and the use of the Hebrew calendar;

– Israeli youth were to be helped to become more "rooted in the past of the Jewish people" by changing emphases in the teaching of Jewish history. Essentially this involved fostering appreciation of Jewish creativity and heroism in the Diaspora rather than the previously more common depre-cation of Jewish existence outside of *Eretz Israel*;

– the aim "to acquire a feeling of belonging to...the Jewish people as a whole" was to be furthered by more instruction and educational activity related to Jewish communities in the Diaspora and familiarity with their problems and achievements (Kurzweil, 1965, pp. 272–283).

The law and program of 'Jewish Consciousness' was heatedly debated. In the Knesset, Orthodox members argued that it was superfluous, since the state religious school was accessible to all, and it alone gave 'real' Jewish con-sciousness; left-wing secular members declared that the law undermined Zionist ideology and that its real and hidden purpose was to re-introduce reli-gion "through the back door" into general education (The Knesset Debate..., 1959).

Among educators, the argument was perhaps more professional but equally passionate. Proponents of the program, like Bentwich, insisted that Jewish national life and education which was not nourished by the ideal ani-mating the Jewish tradition ("to be a holy people") was not worthy of the name of Jewish education; 'general' education should not fall prey to the error that spiritual and religious sensitivity was pre-empted by Orthodoxy. Similar arguments were put forward by Aryeh Simon, Ernest A. Simon and Eliezer Schweid. Though they were not all in agreement with the 'Jewish Consciousness' program, they developed philosophic rationales and didactic proposals for restoring Israeli youth to its sources and argued for an encoun-ter with the existential insights and options available within the Jewish tradi-tion (Bentwich, 1958; Simon, 1960; Schweid, 1972). On the other hand, edu-cators such as Adar, arguing from a humanistic perspective, and Bloch, basing his position on a militantly secular one, spoke out against the pro-gram. Adar insisted that the program was an attempt at indoctrination, that subjects such as history would be taught for ideological reasons extrinsic to them, that such subjects as the Torah portion of the week were unconnected to the lives of the children and that the message being conveyed to pupils in the general schools was that they were Jewishly inferior to their fellows in the state religious system (Adar, 1977; Association of Secondary Schools in Israel, 1956).

The program itself ran into manifold difficulties. This was due, in part, to the ambiguity of its aims; it was also the result of the inability and often the unwillingness of teachers to teach what they felt conveyed a normative mes-sage that ran counter to their beliefs. Yet the program occasioned stimulating and original thinking (and writing) on the problem of Jewish education in Israel. And, in the wake of the discussion, research into 'Jewish identity' and frank articulation of the 'Jewish problematic' became widespread and respectable (Ayali, 1973, pp. 102–106; Goldman, 1964, pp. 84–106).

The Post-1967 Era

The problems encountered in the 'Jewish Consciousness' program may have helped non-Orthodox educators to clarify their positions and to distinguish between their real and their simply verbalized commitments to Jewish tradition. These clarifications were reflected in the new curricula for Bible instruction in the post-1967 era. And as we shall see, the Six-Day War itself created a new curricular emphasis in the religious school, unrelated to the 'Jewish Consciousness' program.

Schoneveld has studied these curricular changes in Bible study, so central in gauging ideological objectives and tendencies in Israeli education. He notes that the non-religious (general) curriculum differs from the religious one on a clear-cut educational plane, as well as in content.

> The syllabus for the religious schools displays great certainty and articulateness with regard to the purpose of Bible teaching, characteristics which are absent in the list of objectives for the general school. Considering the various categories of educational objectives according to Bloom and Krathwohl's taxonomy, we note that the affective domain and the area of intellectual abilities and skills of the cognitive domain are dominant in the list of objectives for the religious school, whereas for the general school the emphasis is strongly on the cognitive domain's area of knowledge...The new syllabus is...very sober and low-key in defining the educational objectives of Bible teaching, as if a realization had come about that the lofty tone of the old curriculum somehow had a hollow ring to it (Schoneveld, 1976, pp. 128–129).

Thus, in the general school, the new (1971) curriculum stresses knowledge of biblical history, culture, geography and the religious-moral concepts which characterize the Bible. It then moves to the location of universal values and experiences in the Bible, and only thereafter to intellectual abilities and skills. Though the moral and valuative aspects of the Bible are to be 'acknowledged' by the pupil, only the eighth and last objective is in the affective realm, but it too is cautious. "The pupil should appreciate the values and figures of the Bible and develop an attachment to them" (Schoneveld, 1976, pp. 129–130).

As for the religious school, its objectives remain strongly affective, inculcating belief in God "Who has chosen the people of Israel and given it His Torah (and) Who has chosen the Land of Israel and bequeathed it to His people." Schoneveld observes that while this course of study continues to feature observance of the commandments, study of Torah and the competences associated with these, it has a significant new emphasis: the centrality of the Land of Israel. The new curriculum for the state-religious school (1969) views the

State of Israel as "the beginning of the realization of the words of the Torah and the prophetic vision concerning the redemption of Israel."

> It is likely that the conquest of additional parts of the historic homeland of the Jewish people in the Six-Day War and the subsequent emergence of the Land of Israel Movement which opposes withdrawal from the territories acquired during this war have left their mark on the formulation of the aims...then the view of the State of Israel as *hathalta dig'ula* (the beginning of the redemption) won wide acceptance in religious circles (Schoneveld, 1976, p. 131).

In retrospect, the period since the Six-Day War may be considered a new chapter in the story of Jewish self-understanding and ideology of Jewish education in Israel. During the Six-Day War, many non-observant and 'non-believing' young Israelis discovered previously unsuspected residues and resources of inner 'Jewishness', however defined (Ben Ezer, 1974; Shapira, 1970). And those sectors of religious youth with a strong national-Zionist orientation found their theological understanding of Israel, and the Messianic process it represented to them, apparently vindicated. Moreover, public appreciation was expressed for the national-religious youth, the 'generation of the knitted kipot' and the educational institutions which were shaping them, specifically, the Yeshiva high schools generally associated with the ideology of the *Bnei Akiva* youth movement. This created new self-confidence among religious youth, who had previously often felt somewhat less pioneering and Zionist than secular movements and 'not as religious' as *Agudat Yisrael*. The public esteem, voiced by senior army officers and journalists among others, for the 'real' Zionist idealism of the religious youth and of the yeshiva high schools reflected self-doubt among secular writers and educators and their suspicion that they had failed to impart 'Zionist ideals'; it also intimated an admission on the part of the older educational establishment of the *Mizrachi* orientation that their schools had not succeeded in transmitting loyalty to Orthodox observance. The new Torah-Talmud oriented schools became centers of the *Gush Emunim* ideology which viewed the Six-Day War as a redemptive event and opposed the return of conquered territories to non-Jewish sovereignty on both theological and halachic grounds (Tal, 1976; "Siach Lohamim...", 1968).

Those sympathetic to this development may argue that the new religious consciousness and even extremism, nourished by these new educational institutions, constitutes an original synthesis between the national-patriotic elements of political Zionism, the ethos of settlement and 'redemption of the land' of Labor Zionism and the ultra-Orthodox religiosity of the traditional yeshiva. Both enthusiasts and antagonists have traced this synthesis to the teaching of Rabbi Zvi Yehudah Kook and his disciples at Jerusalem's Yeshivat *Mercaz HaRav*. In any case, the *Gush Emunim* ideology created a new image of the Israeli Orthodox young person and, as noted, re-focussed educational emphases even within the Orthodox community, particularly in the *Bnei Akiva* movement. Though there continued to be a minority of religious Zionist educators who were ambivalent about this development and even unhappy with it, the tendency in religious education was to move away from the halachic dialectic of discovering God's will in every moral dilemma and toward the historic dialectic of finding His Providence in current historical events. At the same time, there was a strenghtening of the non-Zionist religious educational enterprise; here, the visible successes of sectarian withdrawal from a Zionist society "no longer sure of itself" created self-confidence. This new strength and self-esteem was perhaps most clearly reflected in the growth of a movement of *T'shuvah* (return to Judaism), stimulated and served by charismatic educators and yeshivoth especially established for those wishing to 'return' to Judaism. The phenomenon has been described by Aviad; she argues that a disenchantment with modern culture and with the non-Orthodox State of Israel seen as an embodiment of the 'soul-less' culture of modernity has led several thousands (including famous army and show business personalities) to the environment of the ultra-Orthodox community (Aviad, 1983).

Non-Orthodox educational writers have responded in two ways. On the one hand, especially among kibbutz members and the leadership of the Labor movement, there is evidence of a renewed dedication to secular-humanistic values. Though, in most cases, the 'religious dimension' of this spiritual secularity is not denied and sometimes even stressed, it is sharply and polemically distinguished from 'formalistic' and empty orthodoxies which are now also readily charged with romantic and 'Messianic' chauvinism (Whartman, 1965). Journals with an ideological-educational orientation like *Shdemot* (associated with the kibbutz movements), teacher-training seminaries like *Kerem* and *Oranim*, and those Institutes for Jewish-Zionist education serving youngsters in non-religious schools have proposed theses and suggested curricula designed to spur a Jewish renewal in Israeli education. This type of Jewish education would stimulate the asking of existential questions; it would seek authenticity for the pupil within the Jewish tradition (with a renewed emphasis on post-biblical texts) and yet the tradition would be approached on the basis of criteria organized and located through a comprehensive encounter with humanistic culture).

The 'Institutes for Jewish-Zionist Education' (*Machonim l'chinuch Yehudi-Tzioni*) under the auspices of, though organizationally separate from, the Ministry of Education, are of particular interest in this regard. The large number of participants in the Institutes' seminars, the intensive curricular work done on structuring clarification of values around questions of Israeli-Jewish identity and culture, and the accessibility of both religious and 'general' school populations to this program makes it worthy of study. By 1985 close to two hundred thousand youngsters of high school age had been exposed to the 2–4 day seminars, since the Institute was established in 1973. There were thirteen institutes throughout the country, staffed by educators who underwent frequent courses in matters related to Judaism, Zionism and the didactics of informal education. In the *machonim*, much material, including audio-visual presentations, has been produced to stimulate the discussion and study of such topics as the nature of Jewish identity, the Israel-Arab conflict, Israel society and Israel-Diaspora relationships. The emphasis in both the general and religious *machonim* is on deliberation, the location of problems and enhanced self-understanding (Sherlo, 1981; Beckerman, 1981).

But this approach is not limited to the education of youth. In educational frameworks like *Shorashim*, designed to restore Jewish learning to cultural respectability among wide circles of adults without demanding a priori convictions, teachers and lecturers, both 'religious' and 'secular', have been urging an honest confrontation with the sources through a Zionist, Jewishly informed, yet 'open' orientation. Conversely, this orientation has also been translated into school curricula. This has been done in a secular vein by educators in the kibbutz movement like Ben Aharon; others, influenced by the Zionist religiously-oriented thought of Schweid, have suggested programs which both "take the text seriously" and insist on the existential significance of the community as an inherently religious fellowship (Ben Aharon, 1974; Schweid, 1974).

The second approach has been to reconsider ways of rehabilitating and strengthening traditional values and practices which have become residual among Israeli youth, especially those of 'Oriental' origin. One school principal in a northern development town, an Ashkenazi and former kibbutz member, several years ago made the 'revolutionary' suggestion to his non-religious student body that those who wished to conduct a daily service at school would be welcome to do so. To his surprise, some eighty youngsters, equipped with prayer books and tefillin showed up the following morning for the service.[7] There has been a statistically significant movement of children from non-Ashkenazic backgrounds from state-religious schools to state schools where, as noted, they are often confronted with a Western secular ethos that does not reflect the Jewish culture of their homes. The decision of the Ministry of Education to establish a new 'traditional' type of school, a framework which may be expected to more closely correspond to Jewish cultural-religious spirituality as it is found in the 'Oriental' community, is undoubtedly related to the growing recognition of the importance of diverse strands in the emerging patterns of Israeli Jewishness. (Paradoxically, the first 'traditional schools' were initiated in Jerusalem at the demand of American *olim* who came from predominantly Conservative backgrounds.) Also, organizations like *Gesher* and its branches working closely with the Ministry of Education, have been developing new curricular units designed to make the bar mitzvah year more meaningful to the Israeli school child, devising pilot television productions that present traditional Judaism in a contemporary idiom, and conducting weekend seminars for those seeking not only contact with the sources, but a framework of traditional intepretation and conviction.

Concluding Remarks

The discussion of what Jewish education in the Jewish State should be and what the models are for the ideal and truly educated Israeli Jew is still going on and is not likely to abate. The intensity of the controversy and its seriousness is a consequence of the fact that Jewish education in a Jewish society is never an adjunct. It is always, in some sense, synonomous with education as such. Thus, paradoxically, it may sometimes appear to be 'less Jewish' than that which is differentiated from general education in the Diaspora. The Zionist thesis – echoing classic Jewish conviction – has been that comprehensive education must be more Jewish, because nothing of human value can be foreign to it.[8]

Israeli Jewish educators are not always certain that this can be done and they are certainly not in agreement about how it is to be done. But to the extent that their controversies testify to the determination to settle for nothing less, they may be credited with a large achievement and a significant consensus.

Notes

1. On the prominence of Bible study, see Goitein (1957). For a thorough English discussion of Goitein and all approaches to biblical teaching in modern Palestine-Israel, see Schoneveld (1976). On the problem of teaching the Oral Tradition in the 'general' (non-Orthodox) school, see Adar (1977).

2. See, for example, Simon (1953); Katzenelson (1949). But it has also been argued that such criticisms are too oriented to religion. Yaron (1975, p. 6) cites Bar Nir, D. (*Al Hamishmar*, November 7, 1965) who urges people to study anti-religious thought. Many examples of both trends could be cited.

3. This division is similar to that suggested by Mahler, who speaks of the religious, the idealistic-metaphysical and the realistic-national conceptions.

4. The percentages refer to primary schools, grades 3 to 8, as found in Rieger (1940, p. 39). On secondary schools, see Bentwich (1965, Ch. IX).

5. For a description of these approaches, see Schoneveld (1976, Ch. Six), "Bible Teaching in the Labour Trend". The terms we use in discussing the three approaches are Schoneveld's.

6. The religious and Messianic motivation of Sephardic Jewish ties to Israel have been increasingly noted in recent years. See, for example Abitbol (1981).

7. As related to me by the principal. My experience is that many Israeli youngsters of non-European or American background who study in non-religious schools are in a position diametrically opposite to that of, say, Conservative youngsters in the United States. Many of the former feel comfortable with religious (ritual) observance only at home; many of the latter consider such observances 'normative' only when away from home, in the Jewish institutional framework (e.g. Camp Ramah, seminars, etc.).

8. Ahad Ha'am in his essay "National Education" insisted that Jewish education should be seen as universal education through the prism of the national culture. This conception has won wide acceptance in Israeli education (Ahad Ha'am, 1947, 1965, pp. 410–414).

References

Abitbol, M. (1981). *North African Jewry Today.* Study Circle on Diaspora Jewry in the Home of the President of Israel, Series 11, no. 5. Institute of Contemporary Jewry, The Hebrew University, Jerusalem. (Hebrew).

Adar, Z. (1977). *Jewish Education in Israel and in the United States.* Samuel Mendel Melton Center for Jewish Education in the Diaspora, The Hebrew University, Jerusalem.

Ahad Ha'am (1947, 1965). "National Education". *Kol Kitwai Ahad Ha'am.* Tel Aviv-Jerusalem. (Hebrew).

Association of Secondary Schools in Israel (1956). *Jewish Values in Secondary Education.* Tel Aviv. (Hebrew).

Aviad, J. (1983). *Return to Judaism; Religious Renewal in Jerusalem.* University of Chicago Press, Chicago.

Avineri, S. (1980). *Hara'ayon Hatzioni L'gevannav (The Varieties of Zionist Thought).* Am Oved Publishers Ltd., Tel Aviv.

Ayali, M. (1973). "Zionist Education and Jewish Education" in: Ormiyan, H., (ed). *Hachinuch B'Yisrael.* Ministry of Education and Culture, Jerusalem. (Hebrew).

Beckerman, Z. (1981). *An attempt to Characterize and Define the Jew in the State of Israel – Some Hints for a Possible Solution to his Identity Problem.* Jewish Zionist Institutes, Jerusalem. (Mimeograph, Hebrew).

Ben Aharon, Y. (1974). "Tikhun Hachevrah K'Ma'ase Shel Tshuvah". *Shdemot*, No. 68.

Ben Ezer, E. (1974). "Zionism: Dialectic of Continuity and Rebellion; an interview with Gershom G. Scholem" in: Ben Ezer, E. *Unease in Zion.* Jerusalem Academic Press, Jerusalem

Bentwich, J.S. (1958). "Concerning Israeli-Jewish Consciousness". *Urim* no. 15. pp. 17–21. (Hebrew).

Bentwich, J.S. (1965). *Education in Israel.* Routledge and Kegan Paul, London.

Davis, M. (1978). "Introductory Remarks" in: Yadlin, A. *The Jewish Component in Israeli Education.* Study Circle on Diaspora Jewry in the Home of the President of Israel, Series 9, no. 4. Institute of Contemporary Jewry, The Hebrew University, Jerusalem. (Hebrew).

Dinur, B.Z. (1959). "The Revolt Against the *Galut*". *Forum*, IV, Proceedings of the Jerusalem Ideological Conference, August 1957. World Zionist Organization, Jerusalem.

Eisentstadt, S.N. (1977). *Comments on the Continuity of Some Jewish Historical Forms in Israeli Society.* Study Circle on Diaspora Jewry in the Home of the President of Israel, Series 9, no. 2. The Institute of Contemporary Jewry, The Hebrew University, Jerusalem.

Frankenstein, C. (1953). "The Problem of Ethnic Differences in the Absorption of Immigrants" in: Frankenstein, C., (ed.). *Between Past and Future.* The Henrietta Szold Foundation for Child and Youth Walfare, Jerusalem.

Friedman, M. (1975). *Society and Religion.* Yad Ben Zvi, Jerusalem (Hebrew).

Gelber, Y. (1976). "Hirhurim B'ikvot Hasefer *Hayisraeli K'Yehudi*". (Reflections on the book The Israeli as Jew). *Petachim*, No. 36.

Goitein, S.D. (1957). *Hora'at HaTanakh; Ba'ayoteha 'Drach'eha (Bible Instruction; problems and paths).* Yavne, Tel Aviv.

Goldman, E. (1964). *Religious Issues in Israel's Political Life.* World Zionist Organization, Jerusalem.

Halpern, B. and Kolatt, I. (1971). *Changing Relations Between Israel and the Diaspora.* Study Circle on Diaspora Jewry in the Home of the President of Israel, Series 3, no. 6/7. Institute of Contemporary Jewry, The Hebrew University, Jerusalem.

Hertzberg, A., ed. (1959). *The Zionist Idea*. Doubleday Co. and Herzl Press, New York.

Israel, State of (1959). *Deepening of Jewish Consciousness in the State School; Directives and Syllabi*. Ministry of Education and Culture, Jerusalem. (Hebrew).

Katz, J. (1975). "Religion as a Uniting and Dividing Force in Modern Jewish History" in: Katz, J. (ed.). *The Role of Religion in Modern Jewish History*. Association for Jewish Studies, Cambridge, Mass.

Katz, J. (1977). *The Jewish Nature of Israeli Society*. Study Circle on Diaspora Jewry in the Home of the President of Israel, Series 9, no. 1. Institute of Contemporary Jewry, The Hebrew University, Jerusalem.

Katzenelson, B. (1949). "Shutfut Hagoral Hayehudi V'hanoar Ba'aretz" (The Common Jewish Destiny and the Youth in the Land of Israel). *Molad*, January.

Kleinberger, A.F. (1969). *Society, Schools and Progress in Israel*. Pergamon Press, Oxford.

"The Knesset Debate on the Issue of Jewish Consciousness" (1959). *Bachinuch U'Batarbut*, No. 9–10 (21–22). (Hebrew).

Kurzweil, B. (1953). "The New 'Canaanites' in Israel; an Analysis". *Judaism*, Vol. 2, no. 1.

Kurzweil, Z.E. (1964). *Modern Trends in Jewish Education*. Yoseloff, New York.

Lamm, Z. (1973). "Ideological Tensions; Conflicts concerning Educational Aims" in: Ormiyan, H., (ed.). *Hachinuch B'Yisrael (Education in Israel)*. Ministry of Education and Culture, Jerusalem. (Hebrew).

Mahler, R. (1961). "Chinuch Yehudi B'Ruach Realistit Leumit" (Jewish Education in a Realistic-National Spirit). *Encyclopedia Chinuchit (Encyclopedia of Education)*, Vol. 1, col. 372–381. Ministry of Education and Culture and Bialik Institute, Jerusalem.

Mossinson, B.Z. (1910). "The Bible in the School". *Hachinuch*, No. 1. (Hebrew).

Nini, Y. (1971). "Reflections on the Third Destruction". *Shdemot*, No. 41 Responses to this article may be found in *Shdemot*, No. 42. pp. 96–98. (Hebrew).

Ormiyan, H., ed. (1973). *Hachinuch B'Yisrael* (Education in Israel). Ministry of Education and Culture, Jerusalem.

Rieger, E. (1940). *Hebrew Education in Palestine*, Part I. Dvir, Tel Aviv. (Hebrew).

Rosenak, M. (1979). "Three Zionist Revolutions". *Forum*, No. 34.

Rotenstreich, N. (1958). "Trends in Modern Jewish Nationalism". *Judaism*, Vol. 7, no. 2.

Rotenstreich, N. (1977). "Israel within World Jewry" in: Davis, M., ed. *World Jewry and the State of Israel*. Arno Press and Herzl Press, New York.

Samuel, M. (1948). *Harvest in the Desert*. Jewish Publication Society, Philadelphia.

Schoneveld, J. (1976). *The Bible in Israeli Education*. Van Gorcum, Assen, Amsterdam.

Schweid, E. (1972). "Teaching Jewish Subjects in the Israeli High School". *Petachim*, No. 21. pp. 6–18. (Hebrew).

Schweid, E. (1974). *Judaism and the Solitary Jew*. Am Oved Publishers, Tel Aviv. (Hebrew).

Selzer, M., ed. (1970). *Zionism Reconsidered*. Macmillan, London.

Shapira, A., ed. (1970). *The Seventh Day*. Charles Scribner's Sons, New York.

Sherlo, Y. (1981). *The Religious Institutes System "Blue Book"*. Jerusalem. (Mimeograph, Hebrew).

"Siach Lohamim B'Yeshivat Mercaz HaRav" (1968). *Shdemot*, No. 29.

Simon, E.A. (1952). "Some Remarks on the Bible in our Education". *Urim*, Nos. 4–5. (Hebrew).

Simon, E.A. (1953). "Are We Israelis Still Jews?" *Commentary*, Vol. 15, no. 4.

Simon, E.A. (1960). "The Common and the Particular". *Da'at U'ma'as Bachinuch; Memorial Volume for Avraham Arnon*. Tel Aviv. (Hebrew).

Tal, U. (1971). "Jewish Self-Understanding and the Land and State of Israel". *Union Theological Quarterly*, Vol. 26, no. 4.

Tal, U. (1976). "The Land and the State of Israel in Israeli Religious Life". *Proceedings of the Rabbinical Assembly*, Vol. 38. New York, pp. 1–40.

Urbach, E.E. (1967). *Al Yahadut V'hinuch (On Judaism and Education)*. School of Education, The Hebrew University and the Ministry of Education, Jerusalem.

Whartman, E. (1965). "Mevakshai Derekh; Seeking a Path". *Conservative Judaism*, Vol. 19, no. 2. pp. 40–48.

Yadlin, A. (1978). *The Jewish Component in Israeli Education*. Study Circle on Diaspora Jewry in the Home of the President of Israel, Series 9, no. 4. Institute of Contemporary Jewry, The Hebrew University, Jerusalem.

Yaron, Z. (1975). "Religion in Israel". *American Jewish Year Book*, Vol. 76. American Jewish Committee and Jewish Publication Society, New York and Philadelphia.

Part Nine

International Jewish Educational Activities

In this final part of the book two chapters deal with the international scope of activities in Jewish education.

Ernest Stock, a political scientist associated with the Jerusalem Center for Public Affairs and former director of the European Council of Jewish Community Services in Paris, describes in detail the numerous organizations which have developed to aid Jewish education around the world and the nature of their activities. It is clear from Stock's analysis that Jewish education has developed extensive international links and more than a few countries have become dependent on Israeli institutions for curricular, supervisory, teaching, and even financial aid. By inference Stock's work gives us for the first time an outline of the structure of the worldwide Jewish education system.

In the last chapter in this volume Uziel Schmelz and Sergio DellaPergola, of the Institute of Contemporary Jewry at the Hebrew University of Jerusalem, outline the research activities that need to be undertaken to further our understanding of Jewish education worldwide. While their focus is mainly on quantitative research, the needs outlined reflect the complex interplay of qualitative and quantitative aspects in the Jewish educational enterprise.

20

Multi-Country Agencies in Jewish Education

Ernest Stock

In examining the role of multi-country agencies active in the field of formal Jewish education, it is useful to distinguish between two types of such organizations:

– those directly engaged in maintaining educational facilities across national boundaries; and

– those groups indirectly involved – through planning, promoting, financing educational programs, or furnishing supporting services to educational institutions maintained by others.

It becomes apparent that the direct activity – maintenance of schools, enrollment of pupils, hiring of teachers, etc. – has remained essentially a field for local initiative and control. This is true especially in the developed countries of the West, where the necessary resources can be mobilized locally. The high cost of modern schooling is financed by tuition payments, and by community and public bodies. All of these are normally linked to a specific locale, and are not easily available 'for export' elsewhere. Agencies which are engaged in direct activity on a multi-country basis have traditionally been active in areas devoid of such local initiative and resources; their programs fit into the rubric of mutual assistance – intervention by the stronger on behalf of the weaker communities. *Kol Yisrael 'arevim ze ba-ze* is a motto which has been applied in the area of education as it has in other fields.

The prototypical agency in this category is the Alliance Israélite Universelle (*Kol Yisrael Haverim* in the Hebrew translation) which as early as the 1860s undertook the task of sponsoring Jewish instruction on a then modern basis in the Oriental communities which were then under Ottoman rule.

A second major body in this category is the American-based *Otzar HaTorah*, which was founded shortly after World War II to set up Jewish schools in countries where burgeoning Islamic nationalism was giving new impetus to sectarian religious schooling.

A third network is that of the Lubavitch Movement, also founded after World War II. In concentrating mainly on kindergartens and instruction in the lower grades, the Lubavitcher made up in religious fervor what they were lacking in structure and methodology.

A fourth organization directly engaged in education on a multi-country basis is ORT (Organization for Rehabilitation through Training). Although ORT operates by far the most widely ramified network among these groups, its main purpose is to impart occupational skills, and instruction in Jewish subject matter occupies a minor place in the curriculum.[1]

While the reasons for the absence of any truly multi-country operational network of schools are quite obvious, the paucity of organizations functioning across borders on the indirect level is more difficult to explain. There is at present no structure which embodies either educational institutions or personnel the world over, with a program designed to serve the common interests of its membership. This is the case even though the principles underlying Jewish education are universal, the subject matter taught is nearly identical and the goals the same everywhere.

Attempts at a global approach were undertaken as far back as 1947, when a first postwar conference on worldwide Jewish education was convened to face the fact that the war had "destroyed the entire Jewish educational apparatus and the educational resources, human and material, built up during many centuries." Another attempt was made in August 1962, when a second World Conference was called in Jerusalem under the auspices of COJO (Conference of Jewish Organizations). In the introduction to the report submitted to that Conference, *Jewish Education in the Diaspora*, the late Uriah Z. Engelman declared

> Notwithstanding the important differences among Jewish communities in social setting and outlook, in organizational forms and programs, in communal institutions and needs, there are sufficient common elements and common problems to warrant thinking and working together in regard to the education of their children (Engelman, 1962, p. 1).

Consequently, the gathering envisaged the establishment of a permanent World Council on Jewish Education, with a secretariat which would work through existing institutions and serve as a clearing house for educational materials; it would assist in devising curricula, maintain a central library and be a source of information on and for Jewish schools worldwide.

But in spite of a wide consensus on the need for such an agency, intensive efforts to set it up proved abortive. This is not the place to analyze the reasons for the failure of this initiative. But the long drawn-out negotiations provide an object lesson in the almost general disinclination to subordinate parochial interests to larger considerations and in the difficulties of securing financing for purposes that do not entail a clear cost-benefit advantage to the disbursing body. In this instance, there also surfaced the latent anxiety of the Diaspora groups over disproportionate Israeli influence in the structure to be established, and in the process it was to initiate. This expressed itself in the form of opposition to having the seat of the new worldwide body located in Jerusalem. Although the Diaspora (read, American) group eventually conceded this point, the elan for setting up the new body seemed to have spent itself by that time. While the preeminence of Israel as a source of inspiration for Jewish education was readily acknowledged, the translation of this hierarchy into structural terms was doggedly resisted.

As formulated by Rabbi Alexander Schindler, representing the Reform Movement, the objection of the North American group to establishing the new body's offices in Jerusalem was the fear "that the concerns of Israel would completely swallow up the valid concerns of Diaspora Jewry" (World Conference of Jewish Organizations, 1970, p. 125).

In light of the abortive efforts to set up a new worldwide forum, the World Zionist Organization remains the major multi-country body operating on the indirect level in the field of formal Jewish education in the Diaspora, mainly through its Departments of Education and Culture in the Diaspora and Torah Education in the Diaspora. The other important agency in this category is the American Jewish Joint Distribution Committee (JDC).

In the absence of an all-encompassing organism, this article will examine the programs and structures of the existing organizations active on the world Jewish educational scene. They will be discussed in alphabetical order, as follows:

- Alliance Israélite Universelle
- American Jewish Joint Distribution Committee
- European Council of Jewish Community Services
- Lubavitch Movement
- ORT
- *Otzar HaTorah*
- Universities in Israel
- World Zionist Organization (including the Pincus Fund).

Alliance Israélite Universelle

The Alliance Israélite Universelle was not originally founded with education as its primary aim; nor is the organization as it functions today concerned exclusively with education. The impetus for the establishment of this first Jewish 'defense organization' came from the anti-Jewish developments in Syria in the mid-1860s. Its first priority was to defend Jews who were being persecuted in Europe (including the Balkans and Czarist Russia) as well as in the Orient, and its second was to raise the level of the downtrodden Jewish population in the Muslim world. It was to this end that the Alliance entered the field of education; from the beginning, its program called for modern schools to replace the heders, which were the prevalent mode of education for the Jews of the *mellahs* on the southern and eastern shores of the Mediterranean. But the means to bring the Jews of these backward areas into the modern world was not Jewish education primarily, but education in the modern idiom in general. Thus, the Alliance network became an effective instrument for Westernization among the Jewish communities of the Levant, and the specific Western cultural orbit into which its pupils were drawn was French culture. The language of instruction in the Alliance schools was French; the curriculum was strongly influenced by the policies of the French Ministry of Education; and much of the teaching staff was French-trained and educated. In the period before World War I, the Alliance's role was greatly facilitated by the prestige enjoyed by French civilization: most parents were pleased to have their children brought up in a French-language environment (Israel, 1960). The Alliance Israélite Universelle curriculum has always included a generous portion of Jewish lore and tradition, but the Alliance schools have never been identified with Orthodoxy. To this day, the schools include far more secular studies in their curriculum than those of *Otzar HaTorah* or the Lubavitch movement.[2] In certain communities, the emphasis on French culture triggered opposition which viewed its propagation as a threat to the traditional framework of Jewish life.

In its heydey in the 19th century, the Alliance network expanded rapidly with the help of Baron Maurice de Hirsch, who donated the munificent sum of ten million gold francs "to improve the position of the Jews in the Turkish Empire by instruction and education." Ten schools were opened in Greece, most of these in Salonica; some in Romania, later together with the Jewish Colonization Association (JCA); ten in Bulgaria between 1870 and 1885, and in the Ottoman Empire itself the Alliance operated 71 boys' schools and 44 girls' schools by 1912, of which 52 were in the European and 63 in the Asian part of the Empire. In Morocco, 5,500 pupils attended 14 schools in the same year. Tunisia, Syria, Iraq and Iran also became fertile ground for Alliance educational activities.

World War I put a virtual end to the Alliance's role in Eastern Europe, except for an attempt, in the early 1920s, to function in the Ukraine in conjunction with the JDC program there. The interwar period, then, saw a concentration of educational efforts in the Muslim world, with special emphasis on Syria and Lebanon as well as on Palestine, where the famous *Mikve Israel* Agricultural School trained several generations of expert agriculturalists.

During World War II, the Alliance Israélite Universelle's schools functioned more or less autonomously as the head office in Paris was forced to close down. After the liberation, the Alliance resumed its normal activities in Paris, with substantial assistance from American Jewry through JDC. The upsurge of nationalism in the Arab countries posed delicate problems, at first in Syria and Iraq and eventually also in the new states of formerly French North Africa.

Moreover, the Israel War of Independence in 1947–48 resulted in the persecution of Jews living in some Arab countries and in their mass exodus from others. Thus, in Iraq, the schools of the Alliance closed down, as did almost all of the schools in Syria and Egypt. In Morocco and Tunisia, Israel's independence resulted in aliyah and an exodus to France, and shook the foundations of the Alliance's educational projects. In Morocco, where there had been as many as 10,000 pupils in the system in 1959, the government decided to integrate part of the Alliance schools into its own system. The Alliance retained its remaining schools under the name of Ittihad-Maroc, with a local committee put in charge, but they gradually lost their specific character. The same process took place in Tunisia and in Iran. In Algeria, whose Jews had been French citizens who attended the state schools, the Alliance has operated only Talmudei Torah (with the support of the Rothschild Foundation); indeed the name Alliance in that country has been synonymous with Talmud Torah. In Israel itself, the Alliance Israélite Universelle's elementary schools were integrated into the education system, and the Alliance concentrated on development of secondary schools in Tel Aviv, Jerusalem and Haifa.

The Situation in the 1980s

In 1980–81, The Alliance Israélite Universelle's network comprised 38 schools in eight countries attended by 13,627 pupils. There were three institutions in France, seven in Iran, one in Syria, seven in Israel and 11 in Morocco. In addition, there were associated schools in Spain (2), Canada (6) and Belgium (1). The number of pupils attending the Alliance and associated schools was virtually the same as ten years earlier (see Table 1).

In Israel, in addition to the secondary schools, the Alliance Israélite Universelle maintains a school for children with impaired hearing in Jerusalem enrolling 98 pupils, both Jewish and Arab. Furthermore, it sponsors *Kerem*, an Institute for Humanistic and Jewish Studies, where secondary school teachers are trained in both the humanities and Jewish studies. Founded in 1974, the Institute enrolls a class of about 290 carefully chosen students each year.

TABLE 1. THE SCHOOLS OF THE ALLIANCE ISRAELITE UNIVERSELLE –
1981

	No. of Students	No. of Schools
Total	13,627	38

The AIU Network

	No. of Students	No. of Schools
Total	10,635	29
France		
Paris: Secondary school of ENIO	227	1
Pavillons-sous-Bois:		
Secondary school	160	1
Primary school	142	1
Iran (Ettehad Schools of the AIU)		
Teheran, Isfahan, Kermanshah, Yezd	2,014	7
Israel		
Jerusalem, Tel Aviv, Haifa, Holon	5,532	7
Morocco (Ittihad Schools of the AIU)		
Casablanca, Fez, Meknes, Marrakech,		
Agadir, Tangier	2,002	11
Syria Damascus	558	1

Affiliated Schools

	No. of Students	No. of Schools
Total	2,992	9
Belgium		
Brussels: Athénée Maimonide	562	1
Canada		
Montreal:		
Maimonides schools	671	3
Folk schools and Peretz School	1,500	3
Spain		
Madrid: Colegio Toledano	145	1
Barcelona: Liceo Sefardi	114	1

Source: *Les Cahiers de l'Alliance* (1981).

The *Mikveh Israel* Agricultural School, symbol of Alliance's contribution to the *Yishuv*, now functions under government auspices.

In Iran, non-Jewish pupils are admitted to the schools under government edict; some of the schools in the outlying areas have lost their Jewish character and are maintained only in order to retain the valuable property. At the same time, the Iranian authorities favor religious education for Jewish children.

Structure and Finances

It is clear that the Alliance Israélite Universelle, in spite of its name, was never really universal in the full sense, but rather a French organization whose purpose was to assist Jews in other lands.

The statutes of the Alliance stipulated a typically French centralization; the organization was to be administered by a Central Committee, located in Paris and two-thirds of its members had to be Paris residents. Regional and local committees everywhere had to transfer their funds to the Central Committee, or to use part of them locally with the Central Committee permission. All Alliance presidents have been French, with the exception of the German S.H. Goldschmidt (1881–98).

At present, the governing body is a Board of Directors, whose 12 members are all French; the Central Committee has been transformed into an Advisory Board. Traditionally, educational activity in France itself was limited to the training of teachers and principals (at the Ecole Normale Israélite Orientale, founded in 1867). However, since the recent influx of North African Jews, the former teacher-training college functions as a regular secondary school and another secondary school has been opened in the Paris suburb of Pavillons-sous-Bois.

The budget of the Alliance Israélite Universelle amounted to 22.7 million French francs in 1981 (about $5.5 million). Of this, Fr. 14 million was budgeted for schools outside of France and Fr. 3.5 million for institutions in France. The balance went for headquarters and administrative expenses. On the income side, some Fr. 5 million ($1 million) came from the American Friends of the Alliance. Financial support was also forthcoming from the Jewish Agency, the FSJU, JCA, Memorial Foundation for Jewish Culture, Canadian Jewish Congress, the Central British Fund for World Jewish Relief and the South African Jewish Appeal. Governments in the countries where schools are maintained, the French government among them, generally contribute to the cost of the secular education. As a rule, no tuition is charged, but where boarding arrangements exist, parents are charged for part of the cost.

The American Jewish Joint Distribution Committee

American Jewry's premier welfare organization in the field of overseas relief is rarely referred to by its full name. In America itself it is known as the JDC; in Europe, the Middle East and wherever else it has left its mark, simply as 'the Joint.'

The JDC's involvement in Jewish education dates back to its role in Eastern Europe in the interwar period, when its reconstruction program included support for Jewish schools "so as to help build a generation of Jewish people who would be well adapted to the world around them, without foregoing the kind of Jewish education their elders wanted for them" (Bauer, 1974, p. 35). In Poland in particular, the JDC enabled fully one-third of the more than half a million Jewish children of school age (1935 figure) to study at Jewish institutions of different kinds, ranging from the religious primary schools (heders) where Jewish law and religious observances were the main studies, and yeshivoth to the Zionist-oriented *Tarbut* schools, where most subjects were taught in Hebrew, through the modern religious schools of the *Yavneh* group (also Zionist) and the network of left-wing, anti-Zionist Yiddish schools organized by circles close to the Bund, with 16,000 children.

> JDC had the choice of supporting all the different trends in Jewish education or none.... Subsidies therefore went to all types of schools; but the principle of supporting only capital investments, not current budgets, was carefully observed. From 1933 to 1939, JDC school expenditures trebled (from $44,000 to $121,000) and while the total sums were quite small, a great deal was done with them. As in other cases, JDC made its support conditional on the raising of local funds. Without JDC contributions these funds would never have materialized. With them, many schools either were built or were salvaged for the use of thousands of pupils (Bauer, 1974, pp. 207–209).

JDC similarly supported Jewish education in the Baltic states, Lithuania and Latvia, which embraced some 190 elementary schools as well as a number of Hebrew and Yiddish high schools.

After World War II, a considerable share of JDC funds spent in Europe were designated for cultural, religious and educational institutions. While the JDC did not set up schools itself, it helped the specialized agencies active in this area (Alliance Israélite Universelle, *Otzar HaTorah*, Lubavitch and ORT) to do so. In addition, the JDC involved itself in informal education, helping set up over one hundred community and youth centers, as well as summer camps and youth programs throughout Europe.

Morocco

In March 1982, the JDC Executive Committee reconfirmed that Jewish education continues to be an integral part of the Joint's program – a commitment which was reflected in a budget allocation of over $10 million in the 1982–83 budget (out of a total of $45 million). Of this amount, $1.5 million was budgeted for Morocco where, of a remaining Jewish population of about 15,000, 3,500 Jewish children attend schools of the Alliance, *Otzar HaTorah*, Lubavitch and ORT, all of which benefit from JDC subventions. (Another 800 children attend non-Jewish French-language schools.) Part of the JDC budget is spent locally and part through grants to Alliance Israélite Universelle and ORT centrally for their programs in Morocco.

The Alliance has an enrollment of 1,400 children (including about 300 non-Jews). *Otzar HaTorah* about 1,350, Lubavitch 400, and ORT about 300. In all these systems, the general program follows the French curriculum, but Hebrew studies vary from one system to another. Thus *Otzar HaTorah* and Lubavitch teach Hebrew 10–15 hours per week; the Alliance 5–8 hours, and ORT, 2–4 hours. In *Otzar HaTorah*, the lessons in the upper grades are conducted in Hebrew.

In addition to supporting the schools, JDC sponsors a number of programs to upgrade the quality of teaching. These include:

- bringing specialists to Morocco to conduct summer seminars for teaching personnel;
- weekly study meetings with teachers in Casablanca;
- a two-year program of certification in cooperation with the Torah Education Department of the WZO, consisting of intensive studies during the school year plus two summers of seminars; and
- maintenance of a resident educational consultant in Morocco who works on a regular basis with the teachers.

As the local community had no tradition of pre-school education, the JDC opened kindergartens and trained young women as teachers. The schools have since integrated pre-school education into their systems, but the JDC continues to train kindergarten teachers and to supervise their work. The JDC also helped develop informal youth programs through groups such as the scout movement, which serve young people the year round, along with summer and winter camps. Scout counselors are sent for training in Israel.

Tunisia

The 5,000 Jews of Tunisia are concentrated in two main centers – Tunis (4,000), and Djerba together with adjacent smaller communities (1,000). The JDC has helped these communities develop part-time schools for the Jewish education of their children, who attend Muslim schools for general studies. The Lubavitch movement is active in the country, sponsoring a school for boys and one for girls starting from kindergarten and leading up to the *Baccalauréat*. There is also a small community primary school in Tunis under the jurisdiction of the Chief Rabbi, and 200 Jewish children attend the French Lycée (high school).

Iran

There are still more than 4,000 Jewish children in full-time day schools in Iran, as compared to 7–8,000 before the revolution. The government insists that every child receive a religious education, and Jewish children who attend government schools must study in Talmudei Torah in the afternoon. The government supports Jewish schools and pays the salaries of teachers; as a result, the Jewish schools operated by the *Otzar HaTorah* and the Alliance Israélite Universelle have large non-Jewish enrollments (see also sections on these organizations).

Eastern Europe

The bulk of JDC activity in Eastern Europe now consists of aid in the field of welfare, as there is little Jewish educational activity left there. However, the JDC has helped the Orthodox community in Budapest to maintain a kindergarten and has sent books and religious supplies to other countries. In Yugoslavia, an informal education program is being supported through a summer camp.

Israel

JDC began its educational activities in 1914 with a grant for the needy of the Old *Yishuv* in Palestine and has been supporting religious and cultural programs in Israel ever since. While other organizations also help finance yeshivoth, the JDC prides itself for working with them selectively and intensively. It does this on three levels:
- through direct support of the yeshiva, its programs and facilities, the size of the grant being based on size of enrollment;
- through ensuring a healthy and esthetic environment for the students, and providing guidance for them; and
- by helping to locate yeshivoth in development towns and border areas,

so as to maximize the benefits derived by communities from the presence of the yeshiva and its students.

JDC provides ORT with financial assistance for its schools in Israel. In the field of informal education, JDC supports the *Matnassim* (Israel Community Centers' Association) and works with the centers on projects to help socially deprived communities. It established the Joseph Schwartz program within the Paul Baerwald School of Social Work at the Hebrew University to help train manpower for these centers. A program of Jewish education was devised to cater primarily to the non-Orthodox population attending the centers. JDC also pioneered in developing early childhood education (age group 0–3) programs at the community centers.

Western Europe

Having helped rebuild the educational infrastructure of European Jewish communities after the war, JDC turned over direct responsibility for their educational institutions to the communities themselves. The one West European country in which the JDC still operates today is France. It supports the main organizations active in that country (Alliance Israélite Universelle, *Otzar HaTorah*, Lubavitch and ORT) and also gives subventions to the Fonds Social Juif Unifié which is deeply committed to the promotion of Jewish education.

JDC has been encouraging more effective cooperation and coordination among those responsible for educational programs in France, and has initiated discussions for setting up a central coordinating body.

The JDC maintains a consultant in its Paris office who has assisted communities in France, Italy, Belgium, Luxembourg and other countries to set up new kindergartens and improve existing ones.

The JDC's educational consultant, Stanley Abramovitch, was the moving spirit in the establishment, in 1969, of the European Association of Jewish School Principals, with which virtually all day schools in Europe are affiliated. The Association has since come under the auspices of the European Council of Jewish Community Services. *Hamoreh*, a pedagogical quarterly in French, was also started by (and is still being supported by) JDC and later turned over to the European Council. Over the years, the JDC has developed a number of principles guiding its involvement in the field of education which reflect its overall philosophy. As cited by Abramovitch, these are:
– the starting point for an education program must be the local community. Programs are never imposed from the outside, but developed from grass roots initiative;
– while the JDC provides help on several levels, including financial aid to launch new projects, its aim has always been to disengage itself from

financial responsibility and transfer funding to local bodies as soon as feasible;

- the JDC cooperates with other agencies specializing in the area of its concern, such as the Jewish Agency, the *Matnassim* and the European Council of Jewish Community Services;
- the JDC strives to be a catalyst for coordination, centralization and cooperation among different segments of the community.

The European Council of Jewish Community Services

In the postwar period, leaders of European Jewish communities in various countries felt a growing need to come into contact with one another and they conceived the idea of an inter-European forum where they could meet to exchange experiences and discuss their common problems.

This idea led to the creation, with the help of JDC, of the European Council of Jewish Community Services (known at first, in the early sixties, as the Standing Conference of European Jewish Communities). The European Council now has 19 members, including three in Eastern Europe.

The Council works through commissions and affiliated bodies which deal with areas of common concern to the member communities. One of these is formal education. The Association of Jewish School Principals (see above) seeks to improve methods of teaching, curriculum planning and school administration through exchange of experience among the principals of 82 affiliated day schools throughout Europe. The Association provides a forum for discussion of pedagogical issues while avoiding interference in the religious or educational aims of the member schools. It does examine programs, methods of teaching, teachers' and principals' functions and educational material.

In the area of informal education, an Association of Jewish Community Centers fosters cooperation among professional center personnel in the area of programming, sponsors European-wide encounters among its membership and arranges training seminars for both professionals and volunteers, frequently in close collaboration with the Youth Department of the WZO.

In addition to the Principals' Association, the Council also seeks to activate lay leadership in the field of formal education (chairmen and members of school boards, etc.) who meet at the Council's annual assemblies. Security arrangements for Jewish schools have risen on the agenda.

The pedagogical quarterly, *Hamoreh*, has been published for 25 years in Paris by the European Council in cooperation with the Fonds Social Juif Unifié and the JDC. It provides a link among French-language educators and plays an important role in upgrading their work.

In an article on "Jewish Education in Continental Europe", Stanley Abramovitch discusses some of the successes as well as major problems of Jewish schools in Europe:

> No basic answer has been found to the shortage of adequately trained and truly qualified teachers for Jewish Studies, and no solution has been found to the economic, social and psychological forces which dissuade suitable candidates from choosing Jewish education as their life career (Abramovitch, 1981).

Concerning the problem of textbooks, Abramovitch recalls that there was a time when each community, almost each school, printed its own textbooks, with inadequate and sometimes disastrous results. The schools now choose from what is available in Israel and the US or from what is printed in Europe. More and more schools introduce audio-visual aids into their teaching, often with excellent results. However, attempts made from time to time to create a common minimum program of Jewish studies have been doomed to failure "since each school is autonomous and decides its own educational goals."

On an optimistic note, Abramovitch cites the existence of day schools in communities where no such schools existed before the war as evidence of a revived and serious interest in Jewish education. Day schools are no longer opposed on religious, philosophical, social or political grounds; "that battle has been won." The schools' problems are material: lack of funds and qualified teachers, unsuitable buildings, transportation problems and, most recently, security risks.

The Lubavitch Movement

The educational activities of the Lubavitch movement in Europe and North Africa began in the postwar era with the arrival in France of a group of Lubavitch Hasidim who had managed to make their way from Russia to Germany as Polish citizens. Some of them had been exiled in Siberia for engaging in illegal education in Soviet Russia. Shortly after arriving in Paris in the late 1940s, the group at first set up Talmudei Torah for their own children, and subsequently opened these to outside pupils. Eventually a primary school for girls was added, with boarding arrangements for pupils from Morocco. After initially concentrating in the Paris area, the movement later also sent *shlihim* to provincial cities to set up Talmudei Torah and kindergartens, generally in conjunction with existing synagogue congregations, but in some cases independently. In Toulouse, the movement also sponsors a primary school. Evening courses for adults are offered in various provincial towns.

JDC, having supported the underground educational activities of Lubavitch in Soviet Russia, agreed to grant financial help to the movement's efforts in Europe. It also subsidizes the Lubavitch day schools in Morocco and Tunisia, a girls' primary and high-school in Morocco, and a primary school for boys and girls in Tunisia. In both countries, the Lubavitch schools are recognized by the state, and offer the required secular curriculum. More recently, Lubavitch has expanded into Italy, having opened a day school in Milan with 100 pupils.

A report in the *Jerusalem Post* (September 23, 1982), describes the Lubavitch program in Milan as follows:

> The religious scene has been stirred by the entry of Lubavitcher (*Chabad*) Hasidim, who came into the city with a bang. They do not recognize the authority of the Chief Rabbi and have formed a flourishing congregation with their own school of 100 pupils. Recently they established Milan's first yeshiva to train *Chabad*-style rabbis. It has 12 students, some from Milan and others from outside Italy. A few years ago, as part of their soul-winning campaign, *Chabad* brought four or five rabbis to Milan to work among the city's smaller congregations, including Sephardic ones, which lacked spiritual leaders. They succeeded in attracting adherents from many different backgrounds. The sizeable *Chabad* congregation is highly concentrated, all its members living within 10 blocks of the synagogue.

In Israel, Lubavitch maintains an education center at Kfar Chabad; its curriculum is recognized by the Education Ministry as a separate 'trend' and receives government aid.

While world headquarters of the Lubavitch movement are in Brooklyn (seat of the Rebbe), the above educational programs are directed from Paris with the highly respected Rav Benjamin Gorodetzki in charge of operations. A yeshiva is located in the Paris suburb of Brunoy.

JDC finances half of the French program, whose total costs amount to some $500,000 annually, and 70% of the Moroccan and Tunisian programs. Total Lubavitch outlay in each of these countries is about $250,000 per annum.

Independent of the Paris-based operation, an English-based Lubavitch Foundation maintains nursery, primary and secondary schools in London. These schools, in rigorous competition with the full range of day schools in the London area, offer both Jewish and secular studies at a high level. Thus, the prospectus of a girls' secondary school declares that

> The school aims to produce educated and well-adjusted observant Jew-

esses who will become an integral part of modern society... The school achieves its ends by providing a high standard of secular education integrated with religious study to a high intellectual standard... The school building is very modern and purpose-built, with a Science Laboratory, Music Room, Domestic Science Room, Art Room, Library and Typing Room.

The prospectus for the boys' school points out that the school has a gymnasium, playing fields and a swimming pool. For both boys and girls, Jewish studies occupy a full 50% of the curriculum.

ORT (Organization for Rehabilitation Through Training)

ORT describes itself as the largest private vocational and technical training organization in the world, with schools, training programs and technical assistance projects in 36 countries; its network of vocational schools and courses enrolls more than 100,000 students and employs 4,000 teachers, with an annual budget of over $80 million. However, the technical assistance aspects of ORT's worldwide program relate mainly to Third World countries in Africa, Asia and Latin America, where ORT's experience and personnel serve local (non-Jewish) populations under contracts from governments or international organizations.

If we consider only the programs aimed at Jewish student populations, we find that on January 1, 1982, ORT maintained schools in 16 countries with a student body totalling 66,679 (see Table 2). Instructional and supervisory staff numbered 3,950, supplemented by 1,350 administrative personnel. By far the largest operation was being conducted in Israel, which accounted for nearly three-fourths of the students (45,426) and instructional staff (2,903). Of the remaining 21,253 students in 15 countries, the largest number were in Argentina (6,656) and France (5,047) and the smallest in Paraguay (62) and Switzerland, where 100 students attended the ORT Central Teacher Training Institute at Anières.

Disregarding Israel (since our major concern is Jewish education in the Diaspora), it is evident that the size of the student body and the farflung nature of its operations make ORT the most extensive network by far among those considered here. But the question arises whether ORT should be counted as a factor in the field of Jewish education, since its primary mission is not education in or for Judaism, but rather toward a trade or profession. Certainly, the ORT school cannot be considered, from a Jewish pedagogic point of view, the equivalent of the classic Jewish day school. The statistics of Jewish children receiving a full-time Jewish education in France do not usually include those attending ORT schools.

TABLE 2.   THE ORT STUDENT BODY – JAN. 1, 1982

Country	Male	Female	Total
Total	43,636	23,043	66,679
Argentina	3,739	2,917	6,656
Brazil	321	174	495
Chile	513	558	1,071
Colombia	60	79	139
France	3,833	1,214	5,047
India	293	157	450
Israel	30,558	14,868	45,426
Italy	985	847	1,832
Mexico	624	426	1,050
Morocco	424	314	738
Paraguay	32	30	62
Peru	356	380	736
Switzerland[a]	99	1	100
Uruguay	879	486	1,365
USA	443	104	547
Venezuela	477	488	965

(a) Central ORT Institute.

However, the ORT curriculum does include a certain amount of Jewish subject matter, especially Hebrew language instruction. In recent years, increasing emphasis has been given to the Jewish component in the curriculum, although the quantity and type of such instruction is generally left to the educational management in each country. The following excerpt from the annual report of ORT in Argentina is characteristic of the new emphasis on Jewish content:

> The year 1980 was marked by a significant rise in the number of Jewish Education teachers following an increase in the scope and importance given to this subject at the Technical School. Teaching methods have not undergone any substantial change, with the same structure in application as in the past where the number of hours are concerned, that is, six hours a week in the junior high school (three for Jewish History and three for Hebrew) and five in the senior high school (three for history and two for Hebrew.)... There are two levels for the teaching of Hebrew, and various kinds of teaching material prepared by the Hebrew teachers at the school have been used, including texts according to the Israeli method *Gesher* (easy Hebrew), Israeli newspapers and other texts. At the elementary level we continue to use the *Habet*

U'Shma system, but the texts have been somewhat modified by the Institute teachers. During 1980 main efforts have been concentrated on the preparation of teaching material. Extra-curricular activities have consisted of the celebration of holidays and remembrance days, such as the Warsaw Ghetto Uprising and *Yom Ha'atzmaut.* The students participated, as they always do, in the Hebrew Song Festival....A group of students went to some provincial towns where they participated in the cultural activities and learned about the history of the local Jewish community (World ORT Union, 1980, p. 8).

It should be recalled that it was not ORT's original purpose to serve as a medium for the transmission of Jewish values. The organization was founded in Russia in 1880 to transform the Jewish condition there by changing the nature of Jewish economic activity. As the American historian Oscar Handlin put it, "There was a demand for vocational education that would prepare youth for the modern world more adequately than the heder or the yeshiva" (Rader, 1970, p. 10).

The acronym ORT stood for "Society for the Promotion of Handicrafts, Industry and Agriculture Among Jews" (in Russian), and only much later were these initials Anglicized and updated into "Organization for Rehabilitation through Training."

ORT's century of existence (as of 1980) can serve as a metaphor for the Jewish history of that period, at least as far as Eastern Europe is concerned. Soon after ORT's founding, the relatively benign regime of Czar Alexander II ended with his assassination, and with the accession of Alexander III to the throne state policy toward the Jews altered drastically. The bloody pogroms of 1881 gave rise to the vast migration from Eastern Europe to America, Britain, Israel and elsewhere. Within the limits allowed, ORT assisted individual craftsmen to move out of the Pale, made loans to artisans for the purchase of equipment, granted subsidies to trade schools, established vocational courses and granted scholarships for attendance at technical and agricultural institutes. But it was only after the Revolution of 1905, with the liberalized political climate, that ORT received a charter from the government which enabled it to cope more effectively with the rush of Jews from the shtetl into the cities. There the beginnings of industrialization were producing a Jewish proletariat and a mass artisan class whose methods were usually as inefficient as their incomes were meager. Steps were taken to modernize and improve the quality of Jewish labor through vocational courses for apprentices, refresher courses for craftsmen and trade schools which introduced new occupations to broaden job prospects. ORT also formed work cooperatives along modern lines and by 1913 such groups were functioning in 20 cities.

With the outbreak of World War I, Galicia and the Pale of Settlement became a vast battlefront and hundreds of thousands of Jews were forced onto the road as refugees. ORT sponsored a program of 'relief through work,' including cooperative workshops with adjacent soup kitchens and credit offices which gave loans to destitute craftsmen. For refugee children, ORT established trade schools with dormitory facilities. As one of the primary relief organizations of the period, ORT's budget grew from 68,000 rubles in 1913 to 541,000 in 1916.

The wartime experience marked a turn to constructive work, with ORT initiating its own programs rather than stimulating and assisting others. The collapse of the Czarist Empire converted ORT into a multi-national organization, as the six million Jews of Eastern Europe were now distributed among Russia, Latvia, Lithuania, Poland, Estonia, Romania and the other entities on Russia's western flank. But the economic foundation of these communities was shattered and ORT, hitherto sustained by Russian Jewry, found itself without means. In 1919, the Central Committee of Russian ORT sent a delegation to Western Europe and America to establish ties with Western Jewry so they might help relieve the plight of their East European brethren. The delegation's mission led to a conference in Berlin in August 1921, at which the World ORT Union was established. A year later, 54 groups in Eastern Europe and 10 in Western Europe and the United States had joined the central body, the primary task of which was to obtain funds for an expanding program. At the same time, the World ORT Union adopted the principle of community responsibility and self-help, which still governs ORT policy; while seeking aid from Jewish organizations in the West, a substantial part of local budgets should come from local resources.

In 1922, an American ORT organization was established, and a regular financial relationship was agreed upon with JDC, which was renewed in 1947, and has prevailed to this day. As a result, ORT receives its major American support through the Joint. Following the agreement, ORT assumed a major role in the JDC's 'Agro-Joint' program designed to agrarianize Jews in the Soviet Union in the 1920s. In 1938, ORT, along with all other international Jewish agencies, was forced to cease operations in Russia. By that time it had developed into an international agency for the economic rehabilitation of Jews throughout Eastern Europe. Poland and Lithuania were focal points of ORT activities between the wars, but programs were also carried out in Romania, Latvia, Bulgaria and Hungary. As late as 1937, ORT established a vocational high school in Germany to provide emigrants with usable skills. Refugee programs were also established in France, including an agricultural farming colony for German refugees and workshops for those interned in camps as 'enemy aliens.' With the outbreak of war in 1939, ORT Union headquarters, which had moved from Berlin to Paris in 1933, were transferred to Vichy, then to Marseilles and finally to Geneva. There they remained until the main office was moved to London in 1978.

With the dispersion of Hitler's victims overseas, ORT established programs in North and South America in the early 1940s, specifically for the purpose of refugee retraining. Two centers in New York City trained 22,000 immigrants (including the 1956 refugees from Hungary) over a period of two decades.

The postwar period saw ORT briefly return to Eastern Europe, as well as opening vocational training facilities in the DP camps of Germany, Austria and Italy and setting up local committees to adminster the work in such countries as Holland, Belgium and Greece where ORT had no prior history. Support groups were also developed in Canada, Great Britain, Latin America and elsewhere. Above all, ORT began to shift a major part of its activities to the new State of Israel, where today most of its operations are concentrated.

Elsewhere, while the basic unit in most areas remained the ORT vocational and technical high school, a radical shift has occurred during the past decade "from skills of the hand to skills of the mind" (American ORT Federation, 1981, p. 2). Advanced educational technology, utilizing sophisticated electronic equipment, has become the norm, and the computer has been thoroughly integrated into the educational process. Some salient developments on the ORT map were the cessation of programs in Iran as a result of the political revolution there and the cessation of operations in Tunis some years earlier. On the other hand, there was expansion in France as a result of the large-scale influx of North African Jews. In Latin America, schools in Argentina, Brazil and Uruguay saw substantial growth in structures and enrollment; elsewhere on the continent, Chile, Colombia, Mexico, Paraguay, Peru and Venezuela were added to the roster of countries where ORT now operates. ORT's program for Soviet transmigrants in Italy was on the decline, due to the diminishing number of Jews coming out of Russia. In Israel, where there had been 353 educational units and 1,400 teachers in 1970, there were 424 units with a faculty numbering 2,757 in 1980. ORT's program in Ethiopia had to be virtually suspended in 1981 when the government ordered the closing of 22 schools in the Gondar province, with their 78 teachers and 2,612 pupils. ORT maintains a school in Bombay, serving India's Jewish population of about 5,000.

Finances

ORT had a budget of almost $70 million in 1981 (see Table 2). Nearly three-quarters of this amount (73%) was met by the communities served. Of the balance, JDC granted ORT $4.1 million and Women's American ORT contributed $4.2 million. Men's chapters of the American ORT Federation were expected to contribute slightly over $1 million. It was anticipated that $6.2 million would come from ORT groups in Australia, Britain, Canada, Germany, The Netherlands, Mexico, Scandinavia, South Africa, South

America and Switzerland, as well as from various charitable groups and foundations (including the Jewish Colonization Association) and governments. The 1981 program budget, by countries, is shown in Table 3.

TABLE 3.   ORT PROGRAM BUDGET – 1981

Country	US $	Country	US $
Argentina	6,105,300	Paraguay	5,000
Brazil	417,300	Peru	100,000
Chile	125,000	South American Office	165,000
Colombia	10,000	Switzerland	
Ethiopia	1,185,000	(Central Institute)	1,128,000
France	23,959,800	United States	909,100
India	268,200	Uruguay	999,900
Iran (staff severance		Venezuela	15,000
obligations)	130,000		
Ireland	5,000	Operational	1,522,000
Israel	26,147,000	Technical Assistance	1,998,000
Italy	2,124,100	Administrative and Other	1,427,000
Mexico	150,000		
Morocco	716,600	Total	69,612,300

Otzar HaTorah

The *Otzar HaTorah* Organization grew out of an effort on the part of a group of well-to-do Syrian Jews (mostly resident in the United States) to improve the situation of Jews in the Muslim world (especially in Syria) immediately after World War II. They formed a "Committee for the Forgotten Million" in 1945–46, at first to undertake pure relief work, but then decided that the best way to raise the standards of their co-religionists was through education (not unlike what the Alliance Israélite Universelle had done 80 years earlier). The new organization, based in New York with Isaac Shalom as its patron and president, declared as its purpose the "religious education of Jewish youth in the Middle East and North Africa" and proceeded to found schools in Syria, Tripoli, Teheran and Casablanca. While both religious and secular subjects were taught, the emphasis was on strict observance. The funds obtained through private contributions soon proved inadequate for the task, and the JDC was persuaded to support the schools. Subvention of the network by the JDC continues to this day.

As late as 1970, *Otzar HaTorah* operated 23 schools and a summer camp in Morocco, 41 schools and a camp in Iran and two schools in Syria. Ten thousand pupils were enrolled in its classes in Morocco and 12,000 in Iran (though in the latter country not all of them in its own schools, as *Otzar HaTorah* also took charge of teaching Jewish subjects in the schools of the Alliance).

With the attrition of Jewish life in the Muslim world, the center of gravity of the *Otzar*'s work has shifted to metropolitan France. Less than 3,000 students are left in Morocco (where schools are still maintained in Casablanca, Marrakesh, Meknes and Rabat). In Iran, 2,600 pupils continue to study in *Otzar* schools, which now operate under the aegis of the Teheran government's policy for encouraging religious education.

The *Otzar HaTorah* has constructed new school buildings in Sarcelles and Créteil, two Paris suburbs with large concentrations of formerly North African Jews. The Créteil school has some 500 pupils, of whom nearly half are in the secondary classes. Altogether, enrollment in *Otzar HaTorah* day schools is about 2,000. Boys and girls study separately. Secular subjects are taught in compliance with the syllabus of the French Education Ministry, which is responsible for the cost of secular instruction. The French *Otzar HaTorah* leadership would like to open more schools in provincial cities with concentrations of North African Jews where a demand exists, but lack of funds has so far prevented this.

The *Otzar HaTorah*'s central administration is located in New York where Steven Shalom serves as Chairman of the organization. An office in Paris is responsible for France and Iran. Educational policy is set by local committees, in line with norms prevailing in the respective countries. The total annual budget is close to $4 million.

Although the *Otzar HaTorah* at one time assisted in developing part-time schools in conjunction with local synagogues, it is committed to the idea of full-time Jewish schooling as the means to Jewish survival. The *Otzar HaTorah* leadership is convinced that its schools have made an important contribution to the training of future Jewish leadership and to combatting assimilation in the countries where they have operated.

Universities in Israel

Since 1968, when the Hebrew University of Jerusalem established the Center for Jewish Education in the Diaspora (since renamed the Samuel Mendel Melton Center for Jewish Education in the Diaspora), Israel universities have entered the field of Diaspora Jewish education. Subsequently, Bar Ilan University established its own Institute for Jewish Education in the

Diaspora, and Tel Aviv University also has a unit for Diaspora Jewish Education in its School of Education.

Taking account of the staff of the Jewish Agency Departments already cited, and of some other institutions (such as *Beit Hatefutsot*), Barry Chazan points to the emergence of a substantive profession of educators in Israel whose work is in Diaspora Jewish education (Barry Chazan, May 1987, an interview).

The Melton Center for Jewish Education in the Diaspora

The Melton Center constitutes by far the most extensive of these efforts on the academic level, and its program will therefore be described in some detail below (Samuel Mendel Melton Center for Jewish Education in the Diaspora, 1982; Barry Chazan, ibid.). The Center's activities encompass the following areas:

- training of teachers, supervisors, and administrators for Jewish educational institutions in the Diaspora;
- research into the problems of Jewish education;
- development of curricular and teaching materials for Jewish education in the Diaspora; and
- in-service training of educational personnel for the Diaspora.

The faculty of the Center includes academics in the history, philosophy and sociology of Jewish education, curriculum development, didactics and related academic areas. In addition, the Center staff also includes Jewish educators who write curriculum units, and develop in-service training programs and informal educational activities. The staff of the Center numbers over fifty people and constitutes the largest university department of Jewish Education in the Jewish world.

The Center offers courses of study in Jewish education leading to BA, MA and Ph.D degrees and a teacher-training diploma. Over thirty courses in Jewish education are offered yearly in addition to other university courses in Jewish studies, Contemporary Jewry and Education. Students at the Center come from a broad range of Diaspora communities and from Israel. There are over 120 full-time students mostly from English-speaking countries. In addition to the regular academic programs, students come to the Center within several other frameworks.

Educational Leadership Training Program

This program is co-sponsored by the Departments of Jewish Education of the World Zionist Organization and the Melton Center, with joint funding of the Pincus Foundation, the Melton Foundation and local communities. Students in this program are sent from their respective communities for one to three years of study, which include invididually tailored tutorials to meet specific local needs. The program has included students from Argentina, Australia, Brazil, Canada, Chile, England, France, Peru, Sweden, the United States and Venezuela.

One-Year Study Program (OYP Junior Year Abroad Program)
The Center, together with the Rothberg School for Overseas Students, offers a special program in Jewish education and Jewish studies for overseas students considering careers in Jewish education. Many of these students continue their graduate studies in Jewish education at the Center.

Mount Scopus Fellows – Australia
A new academic program was initiated for the year 1982–83 whereby ten to fifteen potential teacher emissaries of the Torah Education Department of the World Zionist Organization pursued a year's studies at the Center prior to their departure for teaching positions in the Mount Scopus Jewish School in Melbourne. These studies are aimed at preparing Israeli educators to effectively serve in the Diaspora and include language studies, sociology of the local community, background and structure of the school and pedagogy.

A similar program is being developed for the Herzl-Bialik school in Caracas, Venezuela.

Informal Jewish Education
An agreement has been reached with the *Gesher* Educational Programs and the Youth and *Hehalutz* Department of the World Zionist Organization whereby staff of the Zionist Institutes in Israel and of the Youth and *Hehalutz* Department will embark on an MA program in Jewish Education at the Center which will prepare them for eventual *shlihut* abroad followed by return to careers in Jewish education in Israel. In this way a professional cadre of informal Jewish educators will be developed with rich field experience in Israel and in the Diaspora, combined with an advanced academic program in Jewish studies and education.

The Pedagogic Institute for Curriculum and In-Service Training of Teachers
This Institute was formally established at the Melton Center in 1980, in partnership with the Department of Education and Culture in the Diaspora of the World Zionist Organization. The first activity of the Institute was a major curricular project in 'Jewish Values', funded by the Joint Program for Jewish Education of the Israeli Ministry of Education and Culture and the Jewish Agency. Curriculum work which was formerly organized as specific projects (such as the *Tarbut-Yerushalayim* Mexico project or with schools and Jewish Education Committees in Venezuela and Argentina) is now being channeled through this new Institute.

The core of curriculum development in the pedagogic Institute has been a weekly curriculum workshop in which curricular units are planned, written and analyzed. They are then tested in schools abroad and in in-service training in Israel before final revision by the staff of the Institute. Guest specialists on subject matter are invited to comment and participate.

During the 1980/81 year, units in the following major topics were produced: The Book of Jonah and Yom Kippur; the Book of Esther and Purim; Value Issues in the Midrash; *Pirkei Avoth*; Introduction to Oral Law; Issues in the Teachings of Maimonides; To Be a Jew in a Non-Jewish World; Between Man and Fellow Man; and Hasidic Tales.

In-Service Training Activities

One of the major aspects of the Melton Center's work is in-service and enrichment training of existing Jewish teachers and educators. The Center is committed to the continued professional growth of the teacher and conducts a wide range of programs for that purpose, which falls into two main categories:

– courses and guidance conducted in the Diaspora; and
– courses and guidance conducted in Israel.

Among the agencies with which in-service training programs have been conducted are: the Hornstein Program for Jewish Communal Service of Brandeis University; the Board of Jewish Education of Metropolitan Chicago; the Youth Worker's Program of the Fonds Social Juif Unifié, France; Mount Scopus College, Melbourne; *Tarbut* School, Mexico City; Moral Y Luces School, Caracas; London Board of Jewish Religious Education; The Spiro Institute for the Study of Jewish History and Culture, London; and Sinai School, London.

In 1982, it was decided to establish an annual Summer Institute for Jewish Teachers and Educators at the Center which would offer a regular program of summer in-service courses. The program encompassed in-service seminars in: Teaching Hebrew, Teaching Jewish Values, the Role of Israel in Contemporary Jewish Life and Education; and the Jew in the Modern World, The Teaching of Modern Jewish History; and Media in Jewish Education.

Projects of the Melton Center in the Diaspora

The Center has engaged in projects in a broad range of Diaspora countries of which Mexico is an outstanding example. The Center has concluded more than ten years of intensive association with the *Tarbut* School in Mexico City, which is an integrated day school of 1,400 students ranging in age from 2 to 18. The result of the Center's intervention in this school has been a total reconstruction of the Jewish studies curriculum, including the development of three entirely new fields of study: Contemporary Jewry, the Teaching about Israel, and the Teaching of Jewish Values. Yet another innovative experiment was the creation of a model kindergarten.

These innovations were developed in the context of an intensive in-service training program, with curriculum workshops conducted simultaneously in Jerusalem and Mexico. The next stage of the Melton Center's association with the Jewish educational community in Mexico City moved the center of activities from the *Tarbut* school to a Jewish educational in-service training center for all day schools in Mexico. This venture was sponsored by the local Jewish Community, the World Zionist Organization and a consortium of all Israeli universities, under the leadership of the Melton Center at the Hebrew University. Seven Jewish day schools, ranging from religious to non-religious, Zionist, Yiddishist and Sephardic, with enrollments of 7,500 students and over 200 teachers and a teachers' seminary of 30 students, were encompassed by this project.

Pedagogic Center

The Melton Center includes the largest Pedagogic Center of Jewish educational materials in the world. It enables students and visitors to study and use all existing Jewish educational material (including media) and conducts workshops for teachers and educators interested in specific subject areas.

New Projects

Among planned projects for the next few years, the following two areas deserve special mention:

– adult Jewish education. One can no longer discuss Jewish education without including the education of parents and adults. The Center has committed itself to a serious study of and contribution to this field;

– informal Jewish education. The Center is currently engaged in plans with the Youth and *Hehalutz* Department of the World Zionist Organization, the World Federation of Jewish Community Centers, Jewish summer camping movements, *Gesher* Educational Services, and the Fonds Social Juif Unifié to develop joint programs for staff training and program development in informal education.

The Academic Board of the Center is the overall forum concerned with policy deliberation and formulation for the Center.

The World Zionist Organization

The major body operating in the field of Diaspora Jewish education on a worldwide basis, and to a significant degree, is the (World) Zionist Organization, operating through the Departments of Education and

Culture in the Diaspora and Torah Education and Culture in the Diaspora (Engelman, 1962, p. 12).

This statement is as true today as it was when it was written. The activities of the WZO in the field of education are not confined to these two departments. However, these are the ones that deal primarily with formal Jewish education and will be the only ones discussed here. Of the remaining departments and subdivisions concerned, among their other activities, with education in the wider sense, or informal education, the Youth and *Hehalutz* Department is the most important.

There is also a division of labor according to age, at least theoretically, between the two education departments and the Youth and *Hehalutz* Department; the former dealing with the elementary and high-school age groups (and with adult education, especially in Hebrew language teaching), while 'youth' in Youth Department refers to adolescents beyond secondary school age. In practice, this division is not always adhered to; the (secular) Education Department's Hayim Greenberg Institute caters in part to college-age youth and the Youth Department includes high-school age youngsters in its summer programs.

As for the division of labor between the two education departments, the one 'religious' (Torah Education) and the other 'secular', this is more related to the political constellation in the Zionist movement than to any reality 'in the field'. The implication of this separation, that there are schools whose religious orientation makes them seek contact with the Torah Department, while others with a more secular orientation turn to the Department of Education and Culture for non-religious teachers and programming, is only partially justified.

In Europe, in any event, the division is more territorial than ideological; some countries are preempted by one department or the other regardless of the degree of Orthodoxy of the schools. Thus in Belgium, the Department of Education and Culture is in exclusive charge, servicing, among others, the Orthodox Maimonides School in Brussels. Sweden, on the other hand, is the domain of the Torah Education Department, even though Stockholm's Hillelskoolen is anything but Orthodox. There is a tradition of 'non-interference' in these territorial arrangements. The department's local clients may sometimes be puzzled by them but they acquiesce unquestioningly.

At times the division of labor is by function rather than territory. Thus in France the secular Department works with the day schools affiliated with the Fonds Social Juif Unifié, while the Torah Department is associated with the Talmudei Torah through the Consistoire. The secular Department was the first to develop programs for establishing kindergartens and training of preschool teachers in France, and thereby assured its preeminence in that field. Both Departments are represented on the committee controlling FIPE, the

Investment Program for Jewish Education in which local and Israeli funds are committed in equal parts.

The two Departments receive identical budgetary allocations ($3.6 million in 1981/82 – a reduction from the previous year, when each Department received $3.8 million). These figures are net of departmental income for seminars, which in 1981/82 was $2.1 million (Education) and $2.9 (Torah Education) respectively, a fact which does not satisfy the Education and Culture Department which claims to deal with 90% of Jewish population in the Diaspora.

The WZO, by virtue of the composition of its three-layered governing structure (Zionist Congress, Zionist Action Committee and Zionist Executive), surely qualifies as a 'multi-country' association (Stock, 1975). But this can hardly be said of the two education departments which, though functioning under the supervision of the above-named governing bodies, are in effect Israeli mechanisms operating on a world-wide basis while also maintaining programs in Israel designed for school-age youngsters from abroad. Inasmuch as the Departments directly operate programs in Israel, one might question the designation of the WZO as one of the indirectly active groups. However, the intention is to distinguish these from groups directly engaged in formal education in the Diaspora.

The Department of Education and Culture in the Diaspora

There is no doubt that the Department sees as part of its mission the strengthening of the Israeli component in Diaspora Jewish education. To that end, it is able to mobilize some of the excellent educational resources found in Israel's educational institutions, including those of higher learning. If there is occasional resistance on the part of Diaspora communities, it indicates the degree of concern felt in these quarters about possible Israeli hegemony over local institutions. The Department's emphasis on aliyah as an ultimate goal is also sometimes contrary to the local educational philosophy.

A characteristic episode occurred when the Department insisted that the Director of its North American office be an Israeli, rather than an American educator, as had previously been the case. This decision was fought vigorously by the Department's American constituency. In the end, an agreement was reached which brought Aviv Edroni, of the Tel Aviv Municipality's Education Department, to the post held by Dr. A.P. Gannes until the latter's retirement in 1980.

The Department's plans to set up 'Israeli Studies Centers' in a number of cities also ran into American opposition, again on the issue of having educational resources for the American Jewish public directed from Jerusalem.

Nevertheless, the first such Center was eventually opened in Los Angeles with the close cooperation of the local Bureau of Education.

There is a tendency in Jerusalem to see this Diaspora concern as a challenge to Israel's status of preeminence. The Chairman of the Department, Eli Tavin, wrote in June 1980 in his introduction to a Report on the Department's activities:

> In its endeavour to achieve some of its aims, the Department had to face the tendency to regard 'Babylon' to be of equal, if not of higher spiritual standing with Jerusalem and the consequent weakening of links with the State of Israel...(Tavin, 1979/80).

As stated by Tavin, the Department sees as its goal "the educating of young Jews imbued with Jewish values, proud of their Jewish identity and striving for strong bonds with *Eretz Israel* as preparation for eventual aliyah to their homeland." At the same time, he continues, "the vital continuity of the Jewish people still in the Diaspora must be preserved, and the hovering threat of rapid assimilation must be combatted through the creative programs suitable for the concluding decades of the 20th Century." It is Tavin's purpose to "transform our Department into a catalyst of Jewish education in the Diaspora, and to reach over to the ... Jewish youth who receive no Jewish education and to the children of former Israelis who, for circumstances beyond their control have been cut off from the Israeli educational system." In the same context, Tavin also promises to "persevere in our determination to extricate Jewish educational activity in the Diaspora from the deadening routine in which it now finds itself" (Tavin, ibid.).

In the pursuit of these ambitious objectives, the Department operates through central institutions in the Diaspora, including organized local communities, Boards of Education and Zionist Federations, as well as its own branches and representatives in various countries. It assists Jewish schools by supplying teachers, textbooks and teaching materials, organizing extension courses for teachers as well as seminars and conferences. Teachers from the Diaspora are trained in Israel, in cooperation with the institutions of higher learning.

Division for Elementary and High Schools

Through the Division for Elementary and High Schools, the Department maintains contact with 1,875 primary and secondary day schools and Talmudei Torah and Sunday schools throughout the world. In the United States, these contacts are maintained through the educational networks of the Conservative and Reform movements; in Canada, the Division also deals directly with six independent schools. In Latin America, the Department works with 68 schools in Argentina, 23 in Brazil, 6 in Mexico, 4 in Uruguay,

2 each in Chile, Colombia and Venezuela, and 1 each in Bolivia, Ecuador, Paraguay and Peru; in Europe, with 16 in England, 3 in France, 4 in Belgium, 3 in Germany, 2 each in Greece, Holland and Italy, and 1 each in Denmark, Finland and Spain.

The traditional day schools in South Africa are affiliated, as are four day schools and four supplementary schools in Australia.

The Division is also in contact with 11 pedagogical (resource) centers and with a number of local education bureaus and community education committees.

Division for Early Childhood Education

In the 1979/80 school year, the Department added a Division for Early Childhood Education which concentrated initially on France and Belgium, helping to establish new kindergartens and arrange seminars and training courses for teachers. Activities were subsequently extended to Latin America, and according to the latest reports, contacts have been established with 185 kindergartens in 12 countries.

Departmental Emissaries (Shlihim)

In 1980/81, 177 emissaries were active in 22 countries. Of these, 121 were financed by the local communities and 56 by the Department. The largest contingents were in Mexico (35), Canada and the United Kingdom (20 in each country), the United States (14), Brazil (13), and South Africa (12). The total includes both departmental representatives, some of whom act as educational consultants to communities, and Israeli teachers assigned to specific schools.

Teachers' Training

Israeli candidates are trained for service abroad and form a pool from which the emissaries are selected. Some 100 teachers participate in the course each year, of whom about half are eventually sent abroad.

A Pedagogical Institute for the Diaspora was set up jointly by the Department and the Melton Center for Jewish Education in the Diaspora at the Hebrew University. It prepares curricular and teaching aids for instruction in Judaic and *Eretz Israel* studies in non-Orthodox schools. The Institute has its separate Board of Directors and Academic Committee.

Training courses for teachers in the Diaspora are held in North and South America, Europe and South Africa by Israeli educators and university lecturers.

A Seminar Division arranges in-service training and seminars in Israel for teachers from the Diaspora as well as seminars and summer programs for pupils, including bar mitzvah programs and summer camps.

The Division for Publication of Textbooks and Periodicals publishes a series of teaching aids and textbooks which are sold to schools, community centers and cultural institutions.

Residential High Schools Division

This division supervises boarding schools in Israel (Kfar Blum, Kfar Silver, Givat Washington, among others) for high school students from abroad. In 1979/80 these schools were attended by 548 pupils for periods ranging from two months to one year.

The Hayyim Greenberg Hebrew College

The Greenberg College is designed to prepare young people from the Diaspora for teaching careers and to provide in-service training to teachers from abroad. The college was attended by 180 students in the 1979/80 academic year, mostly from Latin America but also from the United States, Canada, and Europe. It operates in a modern campus in the Talpiot Quarter of Jerusalem.

Division for the Dissemination of Bible Studies

This Division coordinates the World Jewish Bible Society and the Israeli Society for Biblical research, and is responsible for the World Bible Contest for Jewish youth. It also publishes a quarterly on Bible studies in three languages.

The Hebrew Language Division

This Division is responsible for running *ulpanim* in 26 countries. Nine hundred seventeen classes were attended by 11,820 students in 1979/80. This, in addition to other activities, was designed to promote the study of Hebrew, including publications, preparation for the Jerusalem Examination and participation in the training of Hebrew language teachers.

Division for Latin America and Cultural Activities

This Division engages in adult education projects in Latin America, especially in remote communities throughout that continent. In Buenos Aires, the Department, together with Tel Aviv University, sponsors the Shazar Teachers' College.

Education for Children of Former Israelis

The Department organizes classes for children of *yordim* in North American cities which offer instruction according to the Israeli syllabus. In some European cities, such children are integrated into classes for children of emissaries.

Conferences

In May 1982, the Department organized a European Conference on Jewish Education in London, which was attended by 180 lay and professional educators from all over the continent. A featured speaker was the Chief of Staff of the Israeli army who lectured on education in the Israel Defense Forces. A similar conference was held in Rio de Janeiro in November 1981, with educators from all Latin American countries attending.

Shazar Prize

The Department grants an annual prize for the advancement of Jewish education in the Diaspora in memory of the late President of Israel, Zalman Shazar.

Administration

The head of the Department is a member of the Zionist Executive and, as such, is a political appointee. Administrative matters are handled by the Director-General, who is appointed by the Department Head. For decisions in educational matters, the Department maintains a Pedagogical Secretariat, which is headed by a Pedagogical Adviser.

The Department for Torah Education and Culture in the Diaspora

The Department for Torah Education and Culture in the Diaspora operates along the same general lines as the (secular) Department for Education and Culture, except that it sees as its main task a strong emphasis on the religious aspects of education. According to Moshe Krone, a former head of this Department, it views itself as the "central address within the Jewish world for all matters relating to the strengthening and advancement of Torah education and culture" (Jewish Agency, 1982, p. 4).

Like its secular counterpart, the Torah Department maintains educator-emissaries in the Diaspora, who constitute its principal line of contact with Jewish communities and their educational institutions. In 1981/82, 221 such *shlihim* were abroad. The largest number (56) were active in Canada, followed by Australia (31), Brazil (23), the United States (22) and Great Britain (20). About 70% were maintained by the host community. Of the balance, expenses were divided between the Department and the community in most cases; only in the remaining 7% was the Department solely responsible for the cost.

Through its *shlihim*, as well as other means of cooperation, the Department maintains contact with 292 kindergartens, 1,089 elementary schools and 169 high schools throughout the world, as well as 203 Hebrew *ulpanim*,

13 yeshivoth and 19 teachers' colleges. The total number of pupils in these institutions is estimated at 211,000.

In Israel, the Department maintains the Gold College for Women, which offers a broad range of Judaic study courses including teacher-training, to graduates of day high schools from the Diaspora. About 100 women are enrolled annually, two-thirds of them from the United States. For young men, the Department operates the Jerusalem Torah College, which combines a yeshiva curriculum with Judaic, Hebrew and Zionist studies. Annual enrollment is about 175, mostly from the US. Duration of study ranges from six months to two years.

The Department also enables young men from abroad to enroll in yeshivoth and rabbinical seminaries, and young women in Torah institutes. Under this program, which receives support from the Ministry of Absorption's Student Authority, some 2,300 young people study each year in Israel.

The so-called *Yod-Gimmel* (13) program enables high school seniors from the United States to complete their last semester of secondary education in Israeli high schools or yeshivoth. Current enrollment is around 85.

The Department holds short-term seminars for teachers from abroad, and entire high school classes have been brought to Israel with their teachers for two-month periods of study. This program has been aided financially by the Joint Fund for Diaspora Jewish Education (see below).

The Torah Department operates a Center for Pedagogic Guidance which provides educational materials, library services and pedagogic consultation to the institutions with which the Department works.

In addition, an Institute for Jewish Studies Curricula in Diaspora Schools has been established. Both units enjoy the assistance of the Pincus Fund.

The Department takes credit for assisting in the funding of a number of new schools in Europe during the past several years: new elementary schools in London, Vienna, Geneva and Zurich, and a Yeshiva High School in the Parisian suburb of Elizabethville. Two elementary schools founded in France by *Otzar HaTorah* also were assisted by the Torah Department.

The Department produces and distributes texts in Hebrew and Jewish studies for Diaspora educational institutions, teaching aids in pedagogy and methodology for the teaching of Jewish subjects, books on Jewish tradition, history and philosophy for adult and continuing education. This material is published in Hebrew, English, French and Spanish. The Department operates resource centers for the dissemination of educational materials in England, France, the United States and in its offices in other countries.

The L.A. Pincus Jewish Education Fund for the Diaspora

While the Pincus Fund, as it is known in Jewish educational circles the world over, is not actually an organ of the World Zionist Organization, it operates essentially within the same orbit and will therefore be subsumed under the WZO heading in this survey. Named after the late Jewish Agency Chairman to whom the cause of Jewish education was especially dear, the Fund was established in 1974 by the Jewish Agency for Israel, the World Zionist Organization,[3] the American Jewish Joint Distribution Committee, and the Government of Israel to "encourage new and innovative projects of significant value to Diaspora Jewish education." Its initial capital was $5,000,000 but in 1978 the partners decided to increase it to $25 million over a four-year period. Grants are made from the income of the Fund. As of March 31, 1981, $4,530,000 had been allocated to 59 projects (L.A. Pincus Jewish Education Fund for the Diaspora, July 1981; Chazan, 1982).

Since that date, the number of projects approved by the Fund has more than doubled. By geographical areas, 24% of the funds were allocated to projects in France, 19% were spent in Israel for projects serving Diaspora education; England received 14%, the United States 12%; Europe (for projects serving the continent as a whole) 9%; Italy, 6%; and Switzerland, 4% with nine other countries sharing the rest.

The main subject areas were as follows: training of professional manpower (teachers, youth and community workers, rabbis), 31%; establishment of educational institutions (21%); informal education (community and resource centers, adult education (12%); curricular and pedagogic material, 17%; provision of personnel, 12.3%; and in-service training, 5%.

The Fund does not participate in the financing of building projects, nor will it support regular budgets of already existing programs. Local participation of not less than 25% of the cost of a project is a condition for support by the Fund.

The Joint Program for Jewish Education of the State of Israel, the Jewish Agency and the World Zionist Organization

This program, founded in 1979, constitutes an extension of the concept underlying the Pincus Fund in the direction of committing substantial Israeli resources to the cause of Diaspora Jewish education. While the Pincus Fund supports projects in the Diaspora, the Joint Fund makes grants for activities within Israel (on behalf of the Diaspora). In its Statement of Intent, the Joint Program enunciates the principle of the centrality of Israel:

> Israel will be utilized as the Jewish world's central Jewish education resource and staging area. This means transforming Israel into a study center for the Jewish people, one which provides a center for Jewish

experience as well as programmatic resources for Jewish education in the Diaspora. The resources are to be found in the accomplishments of Israel's educational system and the academic and intellectual contributions of its institutions of higher learning (Joint Program for Jewish Education, 1982).

In his introduction to a recent report of the Program, Leon Dulzin stressed the role of the Government of Israel in the Joint Fund, through the Ministry of Education "which shares our concern for Jewish education in the Diaspora." Dulzin also pointed out that the Joint Program has "successfully involved the Jewish Agency for Israel in education, and it is likely to become one of its preferential areas of activity." While the WZO already allocates a considerable part of its budget to Jewish education, Dulzin explains, its means are limited while the needs of Jewish education are great.

It is thus clear that the Jewish Agency, which hitherto has directed all of its resources (derived from appeals in the Diaspora) toward programs in Israel, will henceforth also devote a major effort toward education in the Diaspora.

The composition of the Fund's Directorate reflects its sponsorship. The Chairman of the World Zionist Executive and the Minister of Education are co-chairmen. The first Executive Director was Daniel Tropper, an Adviser to the Minister. The Diaspora viewpoint is represented by two members of the Jewish Agency Board of Governors: Morton L. Mandel, former President of the Council of Jewish Federations; and Michel Topiol, from France. Seymour Fox, of the Hebrew University's School of Education, is the only member of the Directorate who does not represent one of the sponsors.

Expectations for the Joint Fund are high. The Director foresees it ushering in a "new day in Jewish education throughout the world." Acting as a "catalyst of change," the Program is to "identify especially successful programs and encourage their duplication, to initiate projects which represent potential breakthrough concepts...to help develop new methodologies for reaching the unaffiliated." Morton Mandel wishes the Program to sponsor projects that are "both universal and at the same time relevant to the particular needs of a given community."

In concrete terms, the founders of the Joint Program defined its purposes as follows:
–   to bring youth and students to Israel for intensive educational programs;
–   to train and provide in-service education in Israel for Diaspora teachers and educators;
–   to develop, in Israel, curricula and other materials for Jewish education in the Diaspora.

To carry out these objectives, the Government of Israel and the Jewish Agency were to each allocate $5 million annually. Of this, $5 million were to be spent in Israel for Diaspora Jewish education and $5 million were to be added annually to the Pincus Fund (whose expenditures are mainly outside of Israel).

Projects approved during the initial years of the Program break down as follows:

	Percent	$
Development of Curricula and Educational Materials	37.4	3,308,000
Study Programs in Israel for Diaspora Youth and Students	33.7	2,979,000
Training and In-Service Training for Diaspora Teachers and Other Educators	22.8	2,018,000
Research and Development	6.1	545,000

The category of Research and Development includes the Project for Jewish Educational Statistics designed to produce basic data worldwide on enrollment trends, teaching staff, etc., and to establish a framework for continual data collection. The goal is the availability of solid quantitative knowledge of Jewish education in the Diaspora as a tool for Jewish educators and planners.

Both the Pincus Fund and the Joint Program make extensive use of existing communal and educational frameworks, in Israel and the Diaspora, for the implementation of projects. As an example, the ten projects in the area of curricula development and educational materials, approved by the Joint Fund, are listed here together with the originating (and implementing) institutions:

- teaching Jewish Values in Diaspora Schools – Hebrew University and WZO Department of Education – development of new materials and training of teachers;
- educational television – *Gesher* Educational Affiliates – development of television series on Jewish education;
- leadership training – WZO Young Leadership and Everyman's University – production of educational units in Spanish for the training of young leadership;
- university teaching of Jewish civilization – International Center for the University Teaching of Jewish Civilization – project for the implementation and expansion of Judaica courses in Diaspora universities;
- translation and adaptation of curriculum materials from Hebrew – David Schoen Institute;
- preparation of Jewish texts – Shalom Hartman Institute – preparation of texts for curricula and teacher training;

- family study units – WZO Young Leadership;
- basic Jewish bookshelf – WZO Department of Torah Education – preparation of basic Jewish books in various foreign languages;
- Jewish publications in Russian – publishing and translation of material on Judaism and Israel into Russian;
- publication of booklets in easy Hebrew for Jewish day schools – WZO Department of Education.

The Jerusalem Fellows

In July 1981, the Chairman of the WZO announced the establishment of a new program under the auspices of the WZO designed to develop leadership for Jewish education in the Diaspora by training outstanding young Jewish educators from the Diaspora in Israel. Upon completion of three years of intensive training (entirely in Hebrew), each Fellow undertakes to serve for at least five years in a central educational position in the Diaspora.

During the selection process, an attempt is made to promote a relationship between the candidate and a community with the hope that the candidate will later return to a suitable position in that same community.

In the course of the program, the Fellows are required to spend a summer in a Diaspora community and to take an active role in local educational programs. Fellows have a budget at their disposal for collection of material for their own use and for their communities upon completion of the Fellowship. They are also provided with funds for conducting an experimental project in these communities.

Of the ten Fellows studying in Jerusalem in 1982/83, six were from the United States, two from England, one from France and one from Argentina. A second group of ten began their studies in September 1983, and a third group in September 1984. Qualified Israeli citizens were included among the second and third groups of Jerusalem Fellows.

The Program is guided by an Academic Committee, of which Professor Natan Rotenstreich is the chairman. The Academic Director of the program is Professor Seymour Fox.

Summary and Conclusions

In endeavoring to draw some conclusions from the foregoing material, the following three dimensions call for comment:
- the programs of the Diaspora-based organizations;
- the programs of the WZO Departments;
- the need for a new multi-country body.

It would be presumptuous to attempt an evaluation of the Diaspora-based organizations on the basis of the material presented here, which is derived mainly from their own written reports supplemented by interviews. It is apparent that the field of activity open to the organizations involved in Jewish education in the Muslim countries has been contracting radically (except among the North African immigrant population in France) due to the necessity to stay within the scope permitted by the local authorities. Under these conditions, it is unrealistic to expect the organizations to promulgate an educational policy across borders or to expand or modernize course content; at best, theirs is a holding operation. The one truly multi-country educational network under Jewish auspices, ORT, is not engaged in Jewish education primarily, but in training technicians and craftsmen.

Nor are there common criteria by which to assess the quality of the educational work being done in these circumstances. In their absence, success or failure can best be measured on a quantitative basis. Probably the continuing allocation by the JDC of substantial funds to these agencies should be seen as authoritative endorsement from the qualitative aspect as well.

The JDC is also committed to continuing support of the same agencies' programs in France, along with its allocation to the Fonds Social Juif Unifié, which plays a major role in Jewish education there. This should put the JDC in an excellent position to pursue its efforts to set up a coordinating body, similar to the Bureaus of Jewish Education in American communities.

With the JDC's active backing, such a body could gain access to the best experience in the United States. Given France's potential for leadership in Jewish Europe, it might eventually be in a position to make its resources available to other communities on the continent.

Admittedly, such a project would have to contend with deeply rooted ideological and structural constraints in the local setting.[4] One must hope that the JDC will have sufficient influence and authority to overcome these. The record of the Association of School Principals (which was founded by the JDC and is now a part of the European Council of Jewish Community Services) has been encouraging in this direction; it indicates that multi-country organizations are capable of transcending local rivalries and differences.

The Role of the WZO and of Israel

In spite of his death, Louis Pincus' intense interest in promoting the cause of Jewish education left its mark on subsequent developments. The funds he had earmarked to finance a Commission on Jewish Education of the (World) Conference of Jewish Organizations (COJO) became the financial nucleus of the Pincus Fund which, together with the Joint Program for Jewish Education of the Jewish Agency-WZO and the Government of Israel, now constitutes a substantial resource for the improvement of Jewish education the world over.

Israel is thus no longer represented only by the WZO-Jewish Agency complex, in which it plays the leading part, but, as Barry Chazan put it, "Jewish education has become one of the concerns of the Jewish state." Moreover, "this development has taken place in a rather low-keyed fashion, and almost unknowingly, has overtaken the Jewish world" (Chazan, 1982).

Dr. Chazan acknowledges, at the same time, that "the new Israeli dynamic will bring with it its own set of problems in the realm of Israel-Diaspora relationships. It is a development which is welcomed by many, but not by all. Some in the Diaspora have regarded the significantly increased involvement of Israel in Jewish education as a cover for an effort to 'Zionize' Diaspora Jewish education; others have cast doubts on the professional competence of Israel to contribute to Diaspora Jewish education." But Chazan goes on to dispel such notions:

> Even if there is such a Machiavellian plot...the decentralized, regional or locally controlled nature of Jewish education is not readily suscepti- ble to top-down manipulation.... However, the more important point seems to be that Israelis concerned with Diaspora Jewish education have increasingly come to realize that there is a question of priorities, and the major issue is the Jewishness of the young...that the issue con- fronting contemporary Jewish education is not the question of the young person's relationship to Israel, but of his/her relationship to Judaism. Any possibility of engaging in education in the Diaspora, is likely to occur only within the context of Jewish education. (Chazan, 1982).

It will require a considerable amount of tact as well as an attitude of prag- matic realism on the part of the Israelis to overcome these apprehensions and create the optimum climate of confidence for what Chazan calls the "new constellation of forces and influences emerging in the Jewish educational world." Since the two WZO Education Departments will take an active part in the new efforts, it is important that any malevolence toward Diaspora leaders and institutions that can be detected in some of the pronouncements from Jerusalem will disappear, lest it lead to conflict over issues that are only tangentially relevant.

The continued existence of the two Departments of the WZO with very similar goals and programs appears to have the immutability of a phenome- non of nature, and there is little purpose in pointing once again to the fre- quent waste and duplication of efforts resulting from it. Although some of the individuals involved have expressed readiness to rationalize the structure, there is little likelihood of a merger under the present political configuration. Fortunately, there have been recent instances of effective cooperation on specific projects. The supervision of FIPE, the fund for investment of education in France, is an example. Such cooperation should be extended, and grants by the Pincus Fund should contribute toward that direction. For next to the rare episodes of effective cooperation, other projects perpetuate the aura of competition and duplication. An example is the setting up of new resource centers by the Torah Department, in communities where such centers already exist (mostly under the aegis of the Youth and *Hehalutz* Department). Another is the refusal of the Torah Department to participate in the setting up of a single National Advisory Committee for both Departments in the United States, or to have the same mechanism deal with the Teachers Exchange program between America and Israel (Gannes, 1979). A master plan dealing with all educational programs in Israel for Diaspora youth (including the Youth and *Hechalutz* Department) is also long overdue.

Is There A Need for a New Multi-Country Body?

What was said earlier in relation to the direct educational agencies based in the Diaspora, to a large extent, holds true for the WZO programs as well: much more is known about their quantitative aspect than about their effectiveness in relation to cost and needs. The efforts in the 1960s and 1970s to establish a supra-national, or multi-country body were made in full awareness that the WZO Departments could not be a substitute for such a body. But perhaps its sponsors did not aim high enough at that time; rather than serving as a mere clearing house, its main function should be in the area of evaluation of existing programs and planning of new ones, of developing strategies for implementation and problem solving in specific local situations. Such a body should be independent of any particular constituency, and should attract the highest professional competence.

In seeking to analyze the earlier failure, Louis Pincus concluded that an independent international professional body could not function under the conditions of Jewish life (Eisenstadt, 1967). Since then, much has changed in the world of Jewish education. Perhaps the time has come to test that harsh judgement against a new reality.

Notes

1. It is painful to note that there exists no equivalent to the network of the *Tarbut* (Jewish Culture) schools that functioned with great effectiveness in Eastern Europe during the interwar period, educating tens of thousands of pupils in schools in Poland, Romania and the Baltic states. The *Horev* and *Beth Jacob* Schools of the *Agudat Yisrael*, which made available more Orthodox forms of

education in pre-World War II Eastern Europe, are now mainly concentrated in Israel where they became the nucleus of the *Aguda*'s 'Independent' (*Chinuch Atzmai*) school system. The *Mizrachi*'s *Yavneh* schools also disappeared from the European scene but furnished inspiration for Israel's State Religious School system.

2. Whereas the Alliance schools included four hours of Jewish subjects in their elementary schools and five in the secondary schools, the *Otzar HaTorah* and Lubavitcher schools devoted 10–15 hours to these studies (Engelman, 1962, p. 108).

3. While the Jewish Agency has been responsible for practical work in Israel in the areas of immigrant absorption, agricultural settlement, housing, education and welfare, the WZO is primarily Diaspora-oriented and is charged with implementing the Jerusalem Program of 1968, which defines among the aims of Zionism, "The Unity of the Jewish People and the Centrality of Israel in Jewish Life; ... the Preservation of the Identity of the Jewish People through the Fostering of Jewish and Hebrew Education and of Jewish Spiritual and Cultural Values...." The WZO retains 50% representation on the Jewish Agency's governing bodies, but the offices of Chairman of the Jewish Agency and of the World Zionist Executive have been held by one and the same person.

4. The refusal of Orthodox bodies to cooperate with Liberal ones; opposition to co-education among certain Orthodox groups; reluctance to teach Jewish history except in its religious context – these are just a few of the ideological issues which are often compounded by organizational rivalries.

References

Abramovitch, Stanley (1981). "Jewish Education in Continental Europe", in Taylor, D., ed. *Jewish Education 1981/1982*. Jewish Educational Development Trust, London.

American ORT Federation (1981). *ORT Yearbook 1981*. New York.

Bauer, Y. (1974). *My Brother's Keeper: A History of the American Jewish Joint Distribution Committee, 1929–1939*. Jewish Publication Society of America, Philadelphia.

Chazan, B. (1982). "On Jewish Education: The Little Blue Book". *Forum*, No. 45.

Eisenstadt, A., ed. (1967). *The Early History of the World Council on Jewish Education, 1960–66: A Story of Groping and Exploration*. New York. (Mimeograph).

Engelman, U.Z. (1962). *Jewish Education in the Diaspora*. Report prepared for the World Conference on Jewish Education, Jerusalem.

Gannes, A.P. (1979). "The Centrality of Israel and the Decentrality of Jewish Education". *Forum*, No. 36.

Israel, G. (1960). "L'Alliance Israélite Universelle 1860–1960". *Cahiers de l'Alliance Israélite Universelle*, No. 127. February.

Jewish Agency (1982). *Torah Education Today*. Department for Torah Education and Culture in the Diaspora, Jerusalem.

Joint Program for Jewish Education (1982). *Report*. The State of Israel, The Jewish Agency and the World Zionist Organization, Jerusalem.

L.A. Pincus Jewish Education Fund for the Diaspora (1981). *Report*. Jerusalem.

Rader, J. (1970). *By the Skill of their Hands: The Story of ORT*. World ORT Union, Geneva.

Samuel Mendel Melton Center for Jewish Education in the Diaspora (1982). *Report on Activities*. The Hebrew University, Jerusalem.

Stock, E. (1975). "Jewish Multi-Country Associations". *American Jewish Year Book*, Vol. 75.

Tavin, E. (1979/80). *Of the Department and its Activities in the Years 1978/79, 1979/80*. WZO Department for Education and Culture in the Diaspora, Jerusalem.

World Conference of Jewish Organizations (1970). *Annual Report of COJO*.

World ORT Union (1980). *Annual Report 1980*. Geneva.

21

Statistics of Jewish Education in the Diaspora: Objectives, Topics and Procedures

Uziel O. Schmelz and Sergio DellaPergola

Statistics of Jewish education in the Diaspora are intended to supply quantitative data for management, planning and policy, as well as for researchers and other interested persons. In this respect they are like other statistics of public services, which measure and describe the respective institutions, activities and personnel, and the particular sector of the population which is being served.

Researchers of Jewish education in the Diaspora ought to be aware of the potential benefits of statistics. These can provide an overall quantitative picture, assist in making generalizations and furnish yardsticks to essentially qualitative studies. Educational research in depth can, by its very nature, investigate only selected instances of the respective phenomena. Hence statistical data and analyses can facilitate generalization from particular findings by providing information on the overall frequency of the phenomena under study. Moreover, techniques of quantitatively assessing qualitative phenomena – e.g., methods of tuition, or teachers' views – have been developed.

This chapter, however, will mainly confine itself to a consideration of the basic statistical data recommended for the rational functioning of a Jewish – or any other – educational system. In addition, studies of Jewish-educational attainment and its effects during adult life will be included here; these topics can be investigated through representative sample surveys of Jewish populations, such as demographers conduct.

The compilation of statistics of Diaspora Jewish education comprises the usual stages of statistical work: planning, collection, processing, evaluation, analysis and publication of the data. Statistics of Jewish education can be used for purposes of description, comparison or prediction. They can be local, national or international in keeping with the geographical dispersion of the Jews. They will primarily deal with basic topics for which regular updates are needed. In addition, one-time or periodic in-depth studies can be conducted on subtopics or special areas of interest.

The multi-phase process of producing statistics – from the initial conception to eventual publication – is time-consuming, particularly so if carried out on an international scale. Therefore planning for statistics should take place in time for the data to be available when needed.

Planning for statistics must obviously take into account practical considerations of feasibility, such as the availability of professional personnel, funding and its limitations, and the likelihood of satisfactory response by the institutions or persons from whom the information is to be collected. Good response will depend not only on the nature, number and detail of the questions to be asked, but also on the standing and practical influence of the body under whose auspices the information is collected from the Jewish institutions or public. A precondition for successful planning of any statistics is clarification and definition – in advance of collecting or processing the data – of the relevant concepts, terms, categories, etc. Pretesting is an indispensable step in the course of producing statistics whose topic or procedure is new. These and many other well-known features in the orderly production of statistics apply equally to the study of Jewish education in the Diaspora.

Data collection may extend to all educational institutions or to a statistically representative sample. Population studies of Diaspora Jewries usually consist of sample surveys. Data collection should be multi-purpose when possible, especially if it involves population surveys. However, the methodological aspects of gathering statistical information, processing and presentation of data are not discussed here.

In the planning for international statistics of Jewish education much importance is to be attached to comparability of the basic information for the various Diaspora communities. This should produce an overview of the main features and trends in Jewish education from the information collected locally and nationally. The creation of a body of international statistics on Jewish education requires not only data collection in a great many countries but also standardization in order to achieve comparability. The need for standardization derives from the differences between educational regimes in different countries and even within certain countries. It should be feasible to compare Jewish education in a country to general education in the same country and to Jewish education in other countries. Targets for standardization are the topics of investigation, concepts and definitions, methods of data collection, processing and presentation of data.

However, even given standardization, limitations of international comparisons may exist and should be recognized. Problems of comparison also occur within the general educational systems of most countries, and even with regard to the same type of institution – for instance, because of different quality of tuition in various institutions, which may be the result of their location in a higher- or lower-class neighborhood. In the case of international comparisons of educational information and statistics, such problems are virtually inevitable. Sources of particular difficulties with regard to international comparisons of Jewish education are the prominence of supplementary education, which is less regular than day school education, as well as qualitative and quantitative differences with regard to the Jewish content of the education provided.

The second part of this chapter contains a list of selected topics that are suitable for inclusion in a comprehensive statistical system for Jewish education in the Diaspora. The list is divided into seven main groups of topics as follows:

I. The Jewish education system
   A. General characteristics (such as type, level and Jewish ideological orientation)
   B. Institutions
   C. Teaching posts and teachers
   D. Classes
   E. Pupils
II. Informal Jewish education
III. Enrollment rates of Jewish children in Jewish education
IV. Projections of the future number of pupils in Jewish education
V. Family background of pupils receiving Jewish education
VI. Level of Jewish-educational attainment among the Jewish population
VII. Influence of Jewish education received in childhood on the behavior and attitudes of adults regarding Jewish matters.

The topics in the list that are not of a specifically Jewish character are analogous to those familiar from educational statistics in general or from data on educational attainment of general populations, such as can be found in appropriate national or international publications. Despite its apparent length, the list indicates only selected topics. This length results, on the one hand, from the separate itemization – for analytical reasons – of many subtopics for which the information can be gathered jointly (e.g., by one and the same school census). On the other hand, this list is intended as a long-range framework of targets for Jewish educational statistics in the Diaspora. For a good many items, the chances of implementation will vary according to place and time, depending on the resources available and on the particular order of priorities adopted.

Group I contains the basic information concerning the educational system, which requires the most frequent updating. However, the other groups also are of profound importance for an assessment of the actual role and efficacy of Jewish education within the Jewish community, and they – especially group VII – represent intellectually rewarding research challenges.

The list summarily indicates each topic, without entering into the formulation of questions or categorization of answers (except for a few instances of the latter kind that were inserted in order to clarify the substance of the respective topic). The potential sources of the various statistics will be briefly stated.

List of Topics for Jewish Educational Statistics in the Diaspora

I. The Jewish Education System

Sources: Educational institutions (but see the notes to sections C and E).

A.   *General Characteristics*

1. Type of education: day school, supplementary school (i.e. part-time education).
2. Educational level: kindergarten, elementary school, junior high school (where applicable), high school.
3. Jewish-ideological orientation: the situation and terminology differ as between countries. In the United States, the main denominations are Orthodox, Conservative, Reform.
4. Body in charge of the educational institution: educational network, Jewish community, synagogue, Zionist organization, association maintaining the particular school, etc.
5. Size of institution according to number of pupils.
6. Size of Jewish and general populations in locality.
7. Data for a particular year, especially the current one; data on changes over a period of time. Data on changes can be obtained by comparison of statistics from different years, or through direct inquiry using retrospective questions.

B. *Institutions*

Notes: a. An institution may encompass several educational levels (the maximum being from kindergarten through high school). Therefore the sum of institutions functioning at the specified levels is greater than the number of institutions considered integrally as administrative units.

b. Topics 3–9 should be studied according to class grades. Therefore, these topics will also appear in the section on classes.

1. Basic data: numbers of pupils, classes and teaching posts.

2. Grades existing in the institution; range of pupils' ages (standard ages for the existing grades).
3. Number of boys/girls among the pupils.
4. Number of non-Jewish pupils.
5. Number of days of instruction per week (and which days?); number of weekly hours of instruction (at what time of the day?).
6. Courses of study and specializations.
7. Number of weekly hours devoted to Jewish studies.
8. Curricula: especially for Jewish studies and Hebrew.
9. Textbooks, audio-visual and other educational aides (especially for Jewish studies).
10. Location: community center, synagogue building, separate location, etc.
11. Housing of the institution; other functions of building (if any), classrooms, etc.
12. Informal education provided by the institution (see section II).
13. Budget: sources and amount of income, expenditures by type and amount.
14. History of the institution, especially: time of foundation, mergers, splits, changes in enrollment.

C. Teaching Posts and Teachers

Notes: a. A teacher may be simultaneously employed in several teaching posts at different schools (and even at several levels of the same school). Therefore the sum of occupied teaching posts is greater than the number of individual teachers involved.

b. Detailed information regarding characteristics of the teachers must be collected directly from them. The data can be collected either by the school itself or with the help of a list of names and addresses supplied by the school, and either from all teachers or from a representative sample.

1. Teacher's current employment in the educational institution:
   - Number of teaching hours and/or hours of employment in general.
   - Subjects taught.
   - Grades in which the teacher gives instruction (with or without information on the subjects taught).
   - Additional functions (other than instruction) carried out by the teacher in the school.
2. Other current employment:
   - Instruction in other Jewish schools.
   - Instruction in general schools.
   - Jewish religious functions.
   - Other Jewish communal services.
   - Other.

3. Number of years of teaching or detailed job history of the teacher:
   - In particular institution.
   - In any Jewish educational institutions.
   - In educational institutions in general.
4. Demographic characteristics: sex, age, marital status, country of birth (if born abroad – year of immigration to country of residence).
5. General education (highest level or all levels):
   - Level of study.
   - Duration of study.
   - Place of study.
   - Degrees or diplomas.
6. Jewish education: particulars as in 5.
7. Pedagogical training: General or Jewish – particulars as in 5.
8. Conditions of employment:
   - Tenured or untenured.
   - Salary.
   - Pension rights.
9. Teachers from Israel: *shlihim*, ex-Israelis, etc.
10. Non-Jewish teachers.
11. Teacher turnover and its causes.
12. Demand for teachers and vacancies, according to subjects and special requirements.
13. Sources and procedures for recruitment of teachers.
14. Opinions, assessments, and suggestions of principals and teachers (current or past) in Jewish educational matters.

D. Classes

Note: Several classes may operate in the same grade.

1. Grade.
2. Parallel classes.
3. Size of class (according to number of pupils).
4. Distribution of pupils' ages in the class.
5. Number of boys/girls in the class.
6. Number of non-Jews in the class.
7. Number of days of instruction per week (and which?), number of weekly hours of instruction (at what time?)
8. Courses of study and specializations.
9. Number of weekly hours devoted to Jewish studies.
10. Curricula, especially for Jewish studies and Hebrew.
11. Textbooks, audio-visual and other educational aids (especially for Jewish studies).

E. *Pupils*

Note: Detailed information regarding characteristics of the pupils must be collected directly from them (or their parents). The data can be collected either by the school itself or with the help of a list of names and addresses supplied by the school, and either from all pupils or from a representative sample.

1. Demographic characteristics of pupils: sex, age, Jews or non-Jews, etc.
2. In supplementary Jewish education: general education of the pupils (level, schools attended).
3. Educational attainments.
4. Flow of pupils, especially between school years: promotion to higher grade, transfer to another Jewish school of the same type, transfer from day to supplementary education or vice versa; entry to Jewish education (initial or after a break), or drop-out from Jewish education.

II. Informal Jewish Education

Sources: Data can be obtained from the bodies organizing the activities, from surveys among participants (current or past), or from general surveys of Jewish populations.

1. Types of activities: religious activities, study groups (which?), optional subjects (which?) at school, social activities (which?), sports and excursions, summer camps (programs?), visits to Israel, etc.
2. Organizing body: school or educational network to which it belongs, the Jewish community, synagogue, Zionist organization, youth group, etc.
3. Framework and location: school, youth club, meeting place of youth organization, sports club, etc.
4. Frequency and duration of activity.
5. Instructors:
   - Total number.
   - Status: teachers, adult instructors, senior students, etc.
   - Demographic characteristics: sex, age, etc.
   - General education.
   - Jewish education.
   - Pedagogical training.
   - Special training or experience in the specific kind of instruction.
   - Number of years as instructor.
   - Additional jobs: teacher, religious or other Jewish functionary, other work, student, etc.
   - Instructors from Israel; *shlihim*, ex-Israelis, etc.
   - Non-Jewish instructors.

6. Participants:
   - Number.
   - Demographic characteristics: sex, age, etc.
   - General education.
   - Jewish education: level, type (day school or supplementary), number of years of study, currently studying or discontinued, etc.
   - Duration of participation in the specific activity.
   - Concurrent participation in various activities.
7. Opinions, assessments and suggestions on informal Jewish education from:
   - Directors and instructors.
   - Participants.
   - Parents of participants.

III. Enrollment Rates of Jewish Children in Jewish Education

Sources: Data on the number of pupils receiving Jewish education (see I above) and data on Jewish children of school-age.

Note: Enrollment rates reflect not only the demand for Jewish studies but also the availability of institutions and appropriate grades, their proximity, quality of tuition, etc.

1. General enrollment rates – for example, the number of pupils receiving Jewish education per 1,000 Jewish children between the ages of 3 and 17.
2. Specific enrollment rates, according to detailed age groups and sex.
3. General or specific enrollment rates over a period of years for study of trends.

IV. Projections of the Future Number of Pupils in Jewish Education

Sources: Projections for the number of pupils will be based on demographic projections and empirical enrollment rates. Recent trends in enrollment rates should be taken into consideration as well as factors that might affect future enrollment rates, such as: the availability of Jewish institutions on the various levels from kindergarten through high school, and practical plans for expansion of the Jewish education system; attitudes toward Jewish education and parents' readiness to send their children to Jewish schools in the future. (The latter information can be obtained from general or specific surveys of the Jewish population, see Section V.5).

Note: Despite their conjectural nature, such projections are necessary for rational medium- and long-term planning of the Jewish education system and of informal Jewish education. Preferably, the projections should be age-specific (see Section III.2).

V. Family Background of Pupils Receiving Jewish Education

Sources: Data collected by Jewish educational institutions (or at least, with the help of lists of names and addresses supplied by them), or data from surveys of Jewish populations that show whether a family has children who receive Jewish education.

1. Demographic and socioeconomic characteristics of parents, including the Jewish education they themselves received.
2. Characteristics of brothers/sisters (if any) of the pupil, and what Jewish education they received.
3. Behavior and attitudes of parents with regard to various Jewish matters (see Section VII).
4. Opinions of parents about the existing Jewish education, and suggestions for changes.
5. Parents' plans for continuation of the child's Jewish education, and for attendance of younger and future children in institutions of Jewish education.

VI. Level of Jewish-Educational Attainment Among the Jewish Population

Source: Surveys of Jewish populations.

Note: The listed items of information may relate either to the highest level or to all levels of Jewish education received in the past, or being currently received, by the individuals in the Jewish population.

1. Level of Jewish education.
2. Type of Jewish education (day school, supplementary).
3. Number of years of study.
4. Age at time of study.
5. Number of weekly hours devoted to Jewish studies.
6. Country of study.

VII. Influence of Jewish Education Received in Childhood on Adults' Behavior and Attitudes regarding Jewish Matters.

Source: Surveys of Jewish populations.

Note: The influence of Jewish education received (see Section VI) on many Jewish matters can be studied (in this context, religious observance in the parental home should also be taken into account). These matters include, among others, those listed below.

1. Preference for a specific branch of Judaism (such as the Orthodox, the Conservative, or the Reform movements).
2. Synagogue membership.
3. Frequency of synagogue attendance.
4. Sabbath observance.
5. Observance of specified holidays.
6. Kashruth.
7. Other ritual observances (specify).
8. Out-marriage of those surveyed or of specified family members.
9. Giving a Jewish education to one's children.
10. Membership and activity in Jewish organizations and institutions.
11. Donations to Jewish causes (in the country of residence and/or Israel).
12. Attitudes and opinions with regard to specified Jewish problems in the locality or country of residence.
13. Knowledge of Hebrew, Yiddish or Ladino.
14. Reading of Jewish literature and press.
15. Interest in current Jewish problems (outside Israel).
16. Attitude toward Israel.
17. Family ties with Israelis.
18. Visits to Israel.
19. Intent of those surveyed or of specified family members to go on aliyah.

Appendix

Working Outline of Chapters for Country Analyses

I. Historical Overview

A. Brief review of the most important historical trends leading to the current situation (historical facts can be provided throughout the article as needed)

II. The Societal Context of Jewish Schooling

A. The normativeness of private schooling

B. Government support and control of religious schools

C. Relationship of the Jewish community to the government (influence)

D. Jewish-Gentile relationships as they affect interest in Jewish Education

   1. Social and economic assimilation
   2. Intermarriage
   3. Antisemitism

E. Jewish community support for and control of Jewish education

   1. Community vs. congregational schools
   2. Financing
   3. Teacher-training facilities
   4. Supervisory and coordinating institutions and personnel, e.g., central bureaus

F. Geographic and social mobility of the Jewish population and its effect on the availability of, and desire for, Jewish schooling

G. Family support for Jewish education

   1. Trends in family life as they affect Jewish education
     a. fertility
     b. divorce
     c. working spouses
   2. Parents' motivations in sending children to a Jewish school
     a. religious
     b. cultural
     c. convenience
     d. relative attraction of Jewish day schools versus local public schools

H. Other societal or Jewish community factors facilitating or hindering the use of Jewish schools

III. The Structural Characteristics of the Jewish Educational System

A. Number of schools

   1. Full or part-time
     a. days/week
     b. hours/day in school
     c. hours/day on Jewish studies
   2. School level (pre-school, elementary, secondary, college)
   3. Ideological sponsorship
   4. Trends: growth or decline of various types of schools and levels in recent years

B. Number of students

   1. Enrollment rates – proportion of eligible children in school
   2. Proportion in various types of schools
     a. levels
     b. full or part-time
     c. sponsorship
   3. Gender differences in attendance at Jewish schools
   4. Drop-out rates by age

5. Trends: growth or decline in numbers, proportions and types of students attending Jewish schools

C. Informal Jewish education

1. Youth movements
2. Summer camps
3. Weekend retreats
4. Trips to Israel
5. Other

For all types of informal Jewish education:
a. availability
b. sponsorship
c. size – what proportion of school and non-school children attracted?
d. interaction with schools

D. Adult Jewish education (most important aspects)

1. *Yeshivoth gedolot* and Seminaries
2. University Judaica Studies (formal and informal, e.g., *B'nai Brith* Hillel)
3. *Dor Hemshech* (continuing education programs)
4. Courses offered by Jewish religious and cultural organizations
5. Parent education courses

For all types of adult education:
a. availability
b. sponsorship
c. size
d. what proportion of adults participate?
e. what proportion of participants are former Jewish school students and what proportion never had any previous Jewish schooling?
f. role of adult education in the total Jewish educational system

IV. Personnel Characteristics and Issues

A. Number in various types of schools

1. Full or part-time

2. Level
3. Ideological sponsorship

B. Training

C. Cultural background, e.g., native, Yeshiva student, Israeli, other

D. Rewards

1. Salary in comparison to available alternative occupations
2. Fringe benefits
3. Working conditions – facilities, autonomy, student interest, etc.

E. Supply and Demand

F. Differences between teachers and administrators on the above

V. Goals, Curricula, Teaching Methods

A. Secular vs. Jewish studies

B. Emphasis on cognitive knowledge vs. emotive learning

C. Emphasis on particular subjects

D. Structured vs. open teaching methods

E. Use of new media

VI. School Climate

A. Mix of students

1. Orthodox – non-Orthodox
2. Jewish – non-Jewish

B. Student motivation and interest

VII. School Effects

A. On continuing Jewish education

B. On Jewish identification

C. On providing leadership for the Jewish community

D. On providing good secular education

E. Other

VIII. Other Issues and Trends

IX. Implications

A. Research implications

B. Policy implications

X. Conclusions

Index

Ecole Maïmonide, Paris, France 302
Ecole Moriah, Paris, France 314
Ecole Normale Brazil-Israel, Rio de Janeiro, Brazil 210, 224
Ecole Normale Israélite Orientale (ENIO), Paris, France 301, 328, 534, 535
Ecole Yavne, Paris, France 315
Ecuador 52, 229, 230, 237, 250, 557
Edelshtein, Yuli 474, 475, 476
Edmonton, Canada 138, 141, 153, 156
Edmonton Talmud Torah 141, 153
Edroni, Aviv 555
Education Acts (1944, 1967, 1974), Britain 273–274, 278, 286, 287
Education Committee, Caracas, Venezuela 238, 240
Education Committee, Montevideo, Uruguay 238
Education Committee, Santiago, Chile 238
Education Committees in Latin America 204
Educational Leadership Training Program, Israel 550–551
Educational Resources Information Center (ERIC) 165
Egypt 533
Eisenstadt, S.N. 506
Elazar, Daniel 147
elementary schools 14, 31, 32, 33, 61, 78, 79, 83, 85, 102, 104, 106, 108, 109, 120, 121, 123, 125, 133, 143, 145, 146, 175, 176, 177, 178, 179, 180, 181, 182, 184, 186, 188–189, 190, 191, 192, 194–195, 197, 198, 210, 211, 212, 214, 218, 221, 239, 245, 270, 271, 274, 275, 280, 281, 283, 284, 285, 286, 288, 301, 302, 303, 307, 312, 313, 314, 315, 319, 323, 336, 340, 343, 345, 347, 349, 350, 353, 367, 370, 375, 377, 384, 395, 399, 409, 411, 412, 413, 414, 415, 416, 417, 418, 419, 420, 422,

429, 453, 455, 465, 467, 494, 510, 521, 533, 534, 536, 538, 541, 542, 544, 554, 556, 559, 560, 568
Eliezer Steinberg School, Rio de Janeiro, Brazil 210, 211
Eliyahu Soli School, Argentina 198
Elizabethville, France 312, 560
emancipation 5, 36, 253
emissaries – see *shlihim*; *shadarim*
Emunah 328
Engelman, Uriah Z. 530
England – see Britain
Enlightenment 5, 20, 36, 464
enrollment rates (see also attendance) 17, 18, 21, 22, 31, 32, 33, 37, 44–64, 79, 83–88, 96, 101, 104, 106, 108, 121, 124, 125, 127, 131, 141, 143, 144, 145, 146, 147, 148, 157, 163, 165, 167, 176, 178, 183, 184, 185, 187, 188, 189, 190, 194, 197, 207, 208, 210, 212, 224, 234, 235, 238, 241, 243, 271, 272, 273, 276, 278, 279–282, 285, 286, 295, 296, 298, 304, 312, 315, 330, 331, 335, 336–337, 338, 341–344, 349, 352, 362, 367, 369, 373, 374, 376, 378, 384, 385, 388, 399, 400, 414–418, 424, 426, 427, 428, 431, 436, 440, 452, 455, 457, 464, 465, 466, 477, 498, 529, 533, 537, 538, 543, 549, 560, 563, 573
Entre Rios, Argentina 175
Erikson, Erik 77
Esalen Institute, Santa Barbara, United States 90
Estonia 546
Ethiopia 547, 548
Ettefaq School, Teheran, Iran 457
Ettehad Schools, Iran (see also Alliance Israélite Universelle) 534
Etz Haim Yeshiva, Montreux, Switzerland 320, 350
Europe 214, 486, 487, 494, 507, 508, 510, 514, 515, 532, 536, 539–541, 542, 554, 557, 558, 560, 561, 565
European-American Jews 488, 489,